OUR LÁTIN
HERITÁGE

THIRD EDITION

BOOK

II

LILLIAN M. HINES, Author

EDWARD J. WELCH, Consultant

HBJ

HARCOURT BRACE JOVANOVICH, PUBLISHERS

Orlando New York Chicago San Diego Atlanta Dallas

LILLIAN M. HINES, widely known as a Latin teacher, has taught in schools in Massachusetts, Ohio, Maryland, Connecticut, and California. Prior to the Chinese-Japanese War, she taught in China and studied Chinese. She obtained her A.B. at Xavier University, Ohio, and received her master's degree in Latin from Stanford University. She has studied the classics on the graduate level in various universities in the United States. In preparation for the revision of *Our Latin Heritage,* she spent some time in Rome doing archaeological research.

Among her writings are numerous articles on Latin, on the art of teaching Latin, and on related subjects. She is also author of the book *Vocabulary Building by the Cluster Method.*

We gratefully acknowledge the assistance of the following scholars in the preparation of this revision: Professor Rita M. Fleischer, Brooklyn College of the City University of New York; Professor Robert J. Penella, Fordham University; Ms. Stephanie Russell, New York University; Professor Robert Stieglitz, Rutgers University — Newark.

PHOTO CREDITS — KEY: top (t); bottom (b); left (l); right (r)

COVER: Ray Manley/Shostal

Insert A-1: Walter S. Clark; A-2: Herschel Levit; A-3: Ray Manley/Shostal; A-4: (t) Phedon Salou/Shostal; (b) Scala/EPA; A-5: (t) C. L. Schmitt/Shostal; (b) Eric Carle/Shostal; A-6: The Granger Collection; A-7: (t,b) The Granger Collection; A-8: Kurt Scholz/Shostal; B-1: Alinari-Scala/EPA; B-2: The Metropolitan Museum of Art, Fletcher Fund, 1940; B-3: (t) Alinari/EPA; (b) courtesy, Museum of Fine Arts, Boston; B-4: (t) Alinari/EPA; (b) Giraudon; B-5: (t) The Bettmann Archive; (b) Alinari-Scala/EPA; B-6: (t) Hirmer Foto Archive; (b) Anderson/EPA; B-7: (t) The Metropolitan Museum of Art, Fletcher Fund, 1925; (b) Giraudon; B-8: Alinari-Scala/EPA; C-1: EPA; C-2: (t,b) Herschel Levit; C-3: (t) copyright © Beth Bergman; (b) The Metropolitan Museum of Art, Rogers Fund, 1906; C-4: (t,b) Herschel Levit; C-5: (t) The Granger Collection; (b) The Corning Museum of Glass; C-6: all photos, Scala/EPA; C-7: all photos, EPA; C-8: Scala/EPA; D-1: Alinari-Scala/EPA; D-2: (t) Alinari-Scala/EPA; (b) Alinari/EPA; D-3: Alinari/EPA; D-4: The Metropolitan Museum of Art, Harris Brisbane Dick Fund, 1934; D-5: Biblioteca dell'Accademia Nazionale dei Lincei E. Corsiniana; D-6: Photo Hachette; D-7: The Metropolitan Museum of Art, Gift of Irwin Untermeyer, 1963; D-8: U.S. Navy/Photo Trends

ILLUSTRATIONS: Steele Savage

Preface

Our Latin Heritage: Book II is designed to follow *Book I* of the series. However, because of the complete review of first-year Latin contained in Part I, it may be used to complement the first book of most Latin series. Its immediate objective is the same as that of *Book I*, namely, to develop the student's ability to read and comprehend such Latin as is suited to his capacity and aptitude.

Parts I and II. Part I provides a thorough review of the vocabulary, inflections, and grammatical principles learned in first year. Part II develops such new facts of form and syntax as are essential for the reading of later selections in Parts III and IV. The twenty-two Units which comprise Parts I and II follow the method of presentation used in *Book I* of the series, with the Conversation, Practice Patterns, Sentence Patterns, and Latin reading in each Unit serving as the medium for the application and illustration of the explanatory material. Again, as in *Book I*, each of these Units contains a Building Word Power section. Here are introduced Latin roots and stems according to the frequency with which they appear in Latin root words and English derivatives. A comprehensive list of the most frequently used roots and stems can be found in the Appendix.

The present book is so organized that the reading of Caesar's *Gallic War* is postponed until near the end of the first semester. This arrangement allows ample time for the reading of the stories of Hercules, Ulysses, and Jason found as serials in Parts I and II. In these stories, adapted for the most part from Ritchie's *Fabulae Faciles*, there is a conscious imitation of the style, language, and syntax of Caesar's *Gallic War*. Thus the student is prepared to read Caesar's *Commentarii* with greater facility.

Part III. In the background sections introducing Part III, an attempt has been made to arouse interest in the personality and achievements of Caesar and in the age in which he lived. No effort has been spared to make the account of the Roman art of war intelligible and interesting.

In order that the student may become familiar with Caesar's work *in toto*, selections are given from all seven books of Caesar's *Gallic War* and from Book III of the *Civil War*, with summaries in English of the omitted portions of the Latin text. The major divisions of each book are preceded by a Preview in English to give the student a background knowledge of Caesar's purpose and of the incidents affecting the campaign described in that particular book.

The first twelve chapters of the first book of the *Gallic War* have been arranged in sense lines and have been simplified and abridged to furnish a gradual approach to the reading of the unmodified text of Caesar. Selections from Books II–VII, as well as the selections from the *Civil War*, preserve for the most part the original text.

The notes on the text of Caesar have been held to a minimum. They are limited to helping the student understand the particular chapter of the Latin text or to giving pertinent information of general educational value. The student's attention is called to the notes through the use of superior figures placed *before* the word or phrase being explained.

Following each chapter of the *Gallic War* there are questions in English which may serve as guides to comprehension of the Latin read. In addition, the selections from Books I, III, V, and VII of the *Gallic War* are followed by Latin questions to be answered in Latin from the text; there are also several sentences in English, based on the immediate chapter, to be translated into Latin. The selections from Books II, IV, and VI and from the *Civil War* are for sight translation.

Part IV. It is very necessary that the student be made aware that Latin literature did not begin and did not end in the age of Caesar. The Survey of Latin Literature found in this Part will focus attention on the fact that Latin literature extends for twenty-two and one-half centuries, from the third century B.C. to the present time. This survey consists of simple but interesting excerpts selected from a wide range of Latin authors. They are varied and attractive and are adapted as far as possible to the interest and capacity of the average high school student. The aim is to deepen and widen the student's knowledge of the life, language, and literature of the Romans.

The wealth of subject matter affords the teacher much freedom in the selection of material. The selections have been placed in chronological order, but the teacher may use them in whatever order best fits the needs of the class.

Appendix. Considerable supplementary material has been provided in the Appendix. This includes a glossary of literary terms, as well as a glossary of the proper names which appear in the myths, the *Gallic War*, the *Civil War*, and the Survey of Latin Literature.

Vocabulary. The entire mastery list for elementary Latin contained in the New York State Syllabus in Latin, 1956, is found in Units I–XXII either in the review lists or in the Words to Master sections appearing in all twenty-two Units. In the general vocabulary at the back of the book these words are marked with an asterisk. Many words in this vocabulary appear only once or twice in the text; they constitute a passive reading vocabulary for the wide range of reading selections and need not be assigned for memorization.

Contents

PART I Review of Forms, Functions, and Vocabulary

PART II New Syntax

vi

PART III   Julius Caesar

PART IV   Survey of Latin Literature

PART I

Review of Forms, Functions, and Vocabulary

The only use of a knowledge of the past is to equip us for the present.
—Alfred North Whitehead, 1861–1947

Unit I

CONVERSATION

PATER: Nēmō ex omnibus hominibus tam clārus quam (*as*) Herculēs erat.

PAULUS: Quis, pater, erat Herculēs?

PATER: Hic Alcmēnae fīlius validissimus erat.

ANNA: Ubi Herculēs habitābat?

MĀTER: In Graeciā (ut fāma est) Herculēs puer habitābat.

PETRUS: Nōnne Jūnō, rēgīna deōrum, Herculem īnfantem interficere temptāvit? Cūr id fēcit?

PATER: Jūnō Alcmēnam nōn amāvit. Itaque duās serpentēs ingentēs mīsit. Hae mediā nocte in cubiculum (*bedroom*) vēnērunt ubi Herculēs cum Īphicle frātre dormiēbat (*was sleeping*).

ANNA: Dīc nōbīs celeriter, māter! Quis parvōs puerōs servāvit?

MĀTER: Īphiclēs māgnā vōce clāmāvit; Herculēs ipse parvīs manibus serpentēs statim prehendit, et corpora eārum māgnā vī compressit.

PAULUS: Quid Alcmēna, māter puerōrum, fēcit?

MĀTER: Illa ad puerōs properāvit, sed ubi ad locum vēnit, Herculēs rīdēbat (*was laughing*) et serpentēs mortuās dēmōnstrābat.

PETRUS: Nōnne Herculēs īnfāns fortis erat et validus? Quid, Anna, putās?

1

SECTION 1 Nominative and Genitive Cases

NOMINATIVE CASE

USE	LATIN	ENGLISH
Subject	*Nūntius* clāmāvit.	The *messenger* shouted.
Pred. Noun	America est *patria* mea.	America is my *native land*.
	Lēgātus factus est *captīvus*.	The envoy was made *a prisoner*.
	Puer *Marcus* appellātus est.	The boy was called *Marcus*.
Pred. Adj.	Dux est *bonus*.	The leader is *good*.
	Mūrus *altus* vidētur.	The wall seems *high*.

GENITIVE CASE

USE	LATIN	ENGLISH
Possession	Fīlia *rēgīnae*.	The *queen's* daughter.
Description	Vir *magnī beneficī*.	A man *of great kindness*.
	Flūmen *trium pedum*.	A river *of three feet*.
Partitive (Whole)	*Puerōrum* fortissimī.	The bravest *of the boys*.

▶ PRACTICE PATTERNS

A. Select the word in parentheses that makes the sentence grammatically correct. Translate the sentence.

1. Urbs est (māgna, māgnīs). 2. Sīgnum (ducis, ducem) captum est. 3. Dux erat bonus (virum, vir). 4. (Rēx, Rēgem) ā populō appellātur. 5. Pars (urbī, urbis) dēlēta est. 6. Cicerō (cōnsulem, cōnsul) creātus est. 7. Vidēbāturne puer (bonum, bonus)? 8. Vallum decem (pedēs, pedum) aedificat.

B. Complete the following Latin sentences by translating the words in parentheses.

1. Līberī sunt (happy). 2. Partem (of the enemy) interfēcit. 3. (Of the soldiers) hī sunt fortissimī. 4. Urbs (large) vidēbātur. 5. (Leader) creātus est. 6. Vir (prisoner) factus est.

SECTION 2 First and Second Declension Nouns

▶ REVIEW OF MASTERY LIST

FIRST DECLENSION NOUNS

Feminine

amīcitia, friendship	**audācia**, boldness	**dīligentia**, care
aqua, water	**causa**, reason	**fāma**, report
aquila, eagle	**cōpia**, supply	**familia**, household

fēmina, woman
fīlia, daughter
fortūna, fortune
fossa, ditch
fuga, flight
glōria, fame
grātia, favor
hōra, hour
injūria, wrong
inopia, lack
īnsidiae (*pl.*), ambush

lingua, tongue
littera, letter
memoria, memory
mora, delay
nātūra, nature
patria, country
poena, punishment
porta, gate
praeda, booty
prōvincia, province
puella, girl

pūgna, fight
rīpa, bank
scientia, knowledge
silva, forest
terra, land
tuba, trumpet
via, road
victōria, victory
vigilia, watch
villa, country house
vīta, life

Masculine

poēta, poet   agricola, farmer   incola, inhabitant   nauta, sailor

SECOND DECLENSION NOUNS
Masculine (*–us*)

amīcus, friend
animus, mind
annus, year
captīvus, prisoner
cibus, food
deus, god
dominus, master
equus, horse

fīlius, son
gladius, sword
lēgātus, envoy
locus, place
modus, manner
mūrus, wall
numerus, number
nūntius, messenger

oculus, eye
populus, people
servus, slave
socius, ally
tribūnus, tribune
ventus, wind
vīcus, village

Masculine (*–er, –ir*)

ager, agrī, field
liber, librī, book

magister, –trī, teacher
puer, puerī, boy

vesper, vesperī, evening
vir, virī, man

Neuter (*–um*)

aedificium, building
arma (*pl.*), weapons
auxilium, help
bellum, war
beneficium, kindness
castra (*pl.*), camp
cōnsilium, plan
factum, deed
frūmentum, grain
hīberna (*pl.*), winter
  quarters

impedīmentum, hin-
  drance
imperium, command
initium, beginning
intervallum, space
jugum, yoke
negōtium, task
officium, duty
oppidum, town
perīculum, danger
praesidium, guard
pretium, price

praemium, reward
proelium, battle
rēgnum, kingdom
scūtum, shield
sīgnum, signal
spatium, space
studium, eagerness
tēlum, weapon
templum, temple
vallum, rampart
verbum, word

► PRACTICE PATTERNS

A. Identify the case and number of the following nouns. Translate.

1. fāmae	grātiās	vīcīs	magistrī	portās	amīcitia
2. equī	praemia	valla	officiīs	dominum	īnsidiae
3. factum	perīculī	nautīs	frūmentō	gladiō	oppidōrum
4. librī	captīvōs	viārum	ventōrum	familiā	castrōrum

B. Write in Latin these specified forms:

1. ablative singular and plural: wrong, wind, command
2. dative singular: food, price, sailor
3. nominative singular and plural: ditch, rampart, boy
4. genitive plural: teacher, shield, eagle
5. accusative singular and plural: gate, danger, envoy

SECTION 3 Third Declension Nouns

► REVIEW OF MASTERY LIST

CONSONANT STEMS

Masculine

cōnsul, cōnsulis, consul
dux, ducis, leader
homō, hominis, man
ōrdō, ōrdinis, order
pēs, pedis, foot
rēx, rēgis, king
sōl, sōlis, sun

eques, equitis, horseman
mīles, mīlitis, soldier
obses, obsidis, hostage
pedes, peditis, footsoldier

prīnceps, prīncipis, chief
frāter, frātris, brother
pater, patris, father
dolor, dolōris, grief
explōrātor, explōrātōris, scout
imperātor, imperātōris, general
labor, labōris, work
senātor, senātōris, senator
timor, timōris, fear
victor, victōris, conqueror

Feminine

aestās, aestātis, summer
aetās, aetātis, age
auctōritās, auctōritātis, influence
calamitās, calamitātis, disaster
celeritās, celeritātis, speed
cīvitās, cīvitātis, state
lībertās, lībertātis, freedom
potestās, potestātis, power
tempestās, tempestātis, storm

voluntās, voluntātis, will
condiciō, condiciōnis, terms
mūnītiō, mūnītiōnis, defenses
nātiō, nātiōnis, tribe
ōrātiō, ōrātiōnis, speech
legiō, legiōnis, legion
regiō, regiōnis, region
fortitūdō, fortitūdinis, bravery
lātitūdō, lātitūdinis, width

māgnitūdō, māgnitūdinis, size
multitūdō, multitūdinis, crowd
salūs, salūtis, safety
virtūs, virtūtis, courage
lēx, lēgis, law
lūx, lūcis, light
pāx, pācis, peace

vōx, vōcis, voice
hiēms, hiemis, winter
laus, laudis, praise
plēbs, plēbis, common people
soror, sorōris, sister
māter, mātris, mother

Neuter

agmen, agminis, line of march
flūmen, flūminis, river
nōmen, nōminis, name
caput, capitis, head

genus, generis, kind
latus, lateris, side
opus, operis, work
vulnus, vulneris, wound
iter, itineris, route

corpus, corporis, body
lītus, lītoris, shore
tempus, temporis, time
jūs, jūris, right

I-STEMS

Masculine

cīvis, cīvis, citizen
collis, collis, hill
fīnis, fīnis, boundary

hostis, hostis, enemy
īgnis, īgnis, fire
mēnsis, mēnsis, month
adulēscēns, adulēscentis, young man

mōns, montis, mountain
pōns, pontis, bridge

Feminine

caedēs, caedis, slaughter
vallēs, vallis, valley
classis, classis, fleet
nāvis, nāvis, ship

gēns, gentis, tribe
mēns, mentis, mind
pars, partis, part
cohors, cohortis, cohort

nox, noctis, night
urbs, urbis, city

Neuter

mare, maris, sea

▶ PRACTICE PATTERNS

A. Identify the case and number of the following nouns. Translate.

1.	vōcēs	gentium	capita	prīncipe	cīvium	flūminis
2.	sōlem	equitēs	laterī	legiōnēs	pedibus	regiōnibus
3.	rēgum	virtūtī	vallis	aestātum	agminis	imperātōre
4.	frātrī	vulnera	ōrdinī	patribus	dolōrum	tempestātem

B. Write in Latin these specified forms:

1. nominative singular and plural: sister, shore, man, month
2. ablative singular and plural: work, voice, time, city
3. dative singular and plural: tribe, consul, state, march
4. genitive plural: kind, praise, brother, hill
5. genitive and accusative singular: sun, safety, side, sea

5

SECTION 4 Fourth and Fifth Declension Nouns

▶ REVIEW OF MASTERY LIST

FOURTH DECLENSION NOUNS

Masculine

adventus, approach	**equitātus,** cavalry	**passus,** pace
cāsus, chance	**exercitus,** army	**reditus,** return
cōnspectus, sight	**impetus,** attack	**senātus,** senate

Feminine		*Neuter*
domus, home	**manus,** hand	**cornū,** horn, wing (of an army)

FIFTH DECLENSION NOUNS (*Feminine*)

aciēs, battle line	**fidēs,** faith	**speciēs,** appearance
diēs (*m.&f.*), day	**rēs,** thing	**spēs,** hope

▶ PRACTICE PATTERNS

A. Identify the case and number of the following nouns. Translate.

1. cornū	rē	senātum	reditus	speciē	cōnspectūs
2. rēbus	spem	speciem	adventū	cornua	exercituum
3. cāsuī	reī	cornuum	senātuī	diēbus	equitātibus
4. diēī	diē	impetū	manibus	rērum	adventum

B. Write in Latin these specified forms:

1. genitive singular: approach, faith, return
2. dative plural: chance, attack, thing
3. accusative singular: appearance, wing, hand
4. ablative plural: army, day, horn
5. nominative singular: hope, home, battle line

WORDS TO MASTER

arcus, –ūs, *m.*, bow (*arc*)

bracchium, –ī, *n.*, forearm, arm (*brachial*)

comprimō, –ere, –pressī, –pressus, squeeze (*compress*)

dēnsus, –a, –um, *adj.*, thick, close (*dense*)

expiō (1), atone for (*expiate*)

faucēs, –ium, *f.pl.*, throat, jaws (*faucal*)

īnfēstus, –a, –um, *adj.*, unsafe, dangerous (*infest*)

intendō, –ere, –tendī, –tentus, stretch, aim (*intend*)

leō, –ōnis, *m.*, lion (*leonine*)

ōrāculum, –ī, *n.*, oracle (*oracular*)

pellis, –is, *f.*, hide, skin (*pellicle*)

prehendō, –ere, –hendī, –hēnsus, grasp, seize (*prehensile*)

quotannīs, *adv.*, yearly

sagitta, –ae, *f.*, arrow (*sagittate*)

trānsfīgō, –ere, –fīxī, –fīxus, pierce through (*transfix*)

vestis, –is, *f.*, clothing, garment (*vest*)

6

BUILDING WORD POWER

Most of the difficult words you will meet in your textbooks this year have been derived from Latin. Thousands of these words came into English from Latin with no change whatsoever or with very minor changes in the endings. It is clear, therefore, that your knowledge of Latin can be a tremendous help to you in your efforts to improve your English vocabulary.

In the analysis of English words derived from Latin, the most important element is called the *root*. The syllable that precedes the root is the *prefix;* that which follows is called the *suffix*. In the first book of this Latin series, you learned all the important Latin prefixes and suffixes. In this second book you will study the most important Latin roots that help to form thousands of English words.

A root is the essential part of the word. Usually it is a monosyllable that gives the fundamental meaning of a particular word or group of words. It is not a real word; it is neither a noun naming something, nor a verb denoting action. It becomes a real word when a suffix is added. Almost all roots are noun or verb roots, that is, roots with meanings that may become parts of nouns or of verbs or of both.

Thus the monosyllable **rog–** is a root. It expresses the idea of asking. With the addition of *–ā–* it becomes **rogā–**, the present stem of **rogāre,** *to ask;* with *–āv–* it is the perfect stem of **rogāvit,** *he asked;* with *–āt–* it becomes the stem of the perfect passive participle, **rogātus,** *asked,* or of the supine, **rogātum.** The supine has the same spelling as the neuter singular of the perfect passive participle.

The shortest and surest way to learn the vocabulary of a language is to study its roots. Thousands of English and Latin words have been formed from a comparatively few Latin roots. Because these roots usually contain the central core of meaning, they can serve as very reliable memory pegs in the building up of English and Latin vocabulary.

Where are these Latin roots to be found? You will find them in Latin *root words*, of which you already know hundreds from your study of first-year Latin. Root words are words that cannot be broken down or analyzed into other words. **Portāre,** *to carry,* is a Latin root word.

As you have already learned, when the Romans wished to change the meaning of a word, they placed a prefix before it; but if they wished to change the function of a word in a sentence, that is, change its part of speech, they placed a suffix after it. By placing the prefix **ex–** before **portāre,** we form the word **exportāre,** *to carry out.* It is still a verb, but its meaning has been changed. By adding the suffix *–bilis* to the present stem, we form the word **portābilis,** with the meaning *able to*

7

be carried. The meaning of the root ***port–*** has been retained, but the function of the word in the sentence is no longer that of a verb but of an adjective.

Building Latin or English vocabulary should not be done at random. Real progress in vocabulary development requires an organized plan of study. The Building Word Power sections in this book provide such a plan. By learning the Latin prefixes, suffixes, and most important roots, you will have definite clues to the meanings of thousands of English words of which the Latin elements are component parts.

SENTENCE PATTERNS

A. Translate into English:

1. Herculēs ā puerō arcum intendere et tēla conjicere poterat.
2. Parvīs bracchiīs corpora eārum prehendit et ea māgnā vī compressit.
3. Omnibus vīribus faucēs leōnis percussit.
4. Lēgātī ad regiōnēs īnfēstās quotannīs mittēbantur.
5. Herculēs ā populō imperātor creātus est.
6. Nōnne vir nōbilis ad ōrāculum properāvit quod tantum scelus expiāre cupiēbat?
7. Ējus tamen pellem dēnsam trānsfīgere nōn potuit.
8. Omnēs incolae illīus terrae virum fortem māgnō in honōre habēbant.
9. Leōnis corpus ad urbem rettulit et pellem prō veste gerēbat.
10. Num Herculēs leōnis dēnsam pellem sagittīs trānsfīxit?

B. Translate into Latin:

1. The unhappy leader wished to expiate his evil deed.
2. Did he not stretch his bow and try to kill the lion with his arrows?
3. He squeezed the jaws of the lion with his huge arms, didn't he?
4. Did he want to wear the thick skin of the lion for a garment?
5. Every year they fought with the tribes of that region.

Living Mythology:
The Strong Man Who Loved Adventure

No Greek hero was more widely known in ancient times than the strong and adventurous Hercules. The career of this mighty hero was one of service to his fellow men. One day, while he was still a youth, there appeared to him at the meeting of the cross-roads (so the story goes) two women whom he had never seen before. One woman, named Pleasure, offered him ease and wealth, faithful friends, and a happy home with a life free from suffering and sorrow; the other, Duty, pointed the way to a career filled with pain, grief, and hardship in the service of mankind who would remember him with gratitude. Without hesitation Hercules chose the path of Duty.

After Hercules had grown to manhood, he was driven insane by the jealous goddess Juno. While in this unhappy and irresponsible state, he murdered his wife and children. As punishment for this crime, he was made subject to his cowardly cousin Eurytheus and was compelled to execute his cousin's harsh commands. The outstanding accomplishments of Hercules while under the orders of his cousin are known as the *Twelve Labors*.

Hercules' death was caused unintentionally by his wife Dejanira, who, fearing to lose his love, gave him a robe she did not know was soaked in the poisoned blood of Nessus the Centaur. After suffering terrible torments, Hercules died. The story of Hercules is begun in the Latin reading that follows.

Hercules: The Man of Might

Ōlim erat vir quīdam cūjus nōmen erat Herculēs. In Graeciā habitābat. Herculis pater fuit Juppiter, māter Alcmēna. Dīcitur etiam ā puerō fuisse omnium hominum validissimus. Īnfāns in cūnīs (*cradle*) duās serpentēs māgnās dextrā suā strangulāvit.

Adulēscēns Thēbīs habitābat ubi Creōn quīdam erat rex. Hōc tempore Minyae erant fīnitimī Thēbānīs et quod ōlim Thēbānōs superāverant, quotannīs ad eōs lēgātōs mittēbant et māgnum vectīgal (*tribute*) postulābant. Herculēs autem cupīvit cīvēs suōs hōc vectīgālī līberāre atque cum Minyīs pūgnāvit. Ē superiōre locō Thēbānī impetum in hostēs fēcērunt, quī salūtem fugā petīvērunt.

Creōn Herculī māgnōs honōrēs atque fīliam suam in mātrimōnium dedit. Hic cum uxōre suā vītam beātam agēbat, sed post paucōs annōs subitō in īnsāniam incidit (*became insane*), atque līberōs suōs ipse suā manū occīdit. Post breve tempus ad sānitātem reductus est. Tantum scelus expiāre māgnopere cupiēbat atque ad ōrāculum Delphicum īre cōnstituit. Apollō per Pythiam sacerdōtem (*priestess*) ācriter jūssit eum ad urbem Tīryntha īre et Eurystheō rēgī sē in servitūtem trādere. Itaque duodecim annōs in servitūte Eurystheī tenēbātur, et duodecim labōrēs, quōs ille imperāverat, cōnfēcit.

9

The First Labor: Slaying the Nemean Lion

Prīmum ab Eurystheō jūssus est Herculēs leōnem occīdere quī vallem Nemeaeam īnfēstam reddēbat. In silvās igitur in quibus leō habitābat statim properāvit. Mox leōnem vīdit et arcum suum intendit. Ējus tamen pellem dēnsam trānsfīgere nōn potuit. Tum clavā (*club*) māgnā quam semper gerēbat leōnem percussit. Frūstrā tamen; neque hōc modō eum occīdere potuit, neque sagittīs neque ūllō aliō tēlō mōnstrum vulnerāre potuit. Tandem Herculēs leōnem ingentibus bracchiīs suīs rapuit et faucēs ējus compressit. Hōc modō brevī tempore eum interfēcit. Tum leōnis corpus ad oppidum portāvit et pellem posteā prō veste gerēbat.

Omnēs incolae hōrum fīnium, ubi fāmam dē morte leōnis accēpērunt, erant laetissimī et Herculem māgnō in honōre habēbant.

Labor omnia vicit
Improbus et duris urgens in rebus egestas.
Never-flinching labor proved lord of all, and the
stress of need in a life of struggles.
—Virgil, 70–19 B.C.
Georgics

Unit II

CONVERSATION

HERCULĒS: Eurystheus mē Hydram necāre jūssit. Nōn negōtium timeō, sed auxilium cupiō. Venī mēcum, Īolāe.

ĪOLĀUS: Māgnopere timeō. Hoc mōnstrum novem capita habet.

HERCULĒS: Nōlī timēre, Īolāe. Ad palūdem Lernaeam quam Hydra incolēbat proficīscēmur.

ĪOLĀUS:	Brevī tempore nōs mōnstrum inventūrōs esse spērō.	
HERCULĒS:	Etsī rēs est perīculōsa, id sinistrā prehendam et dextrā capita novem abscīdere (*cut off*) statim incipiam.	
ĪOLĀUS	(*paucīs posteā diēbus*): Frūstrā labōrās, Herculēs. Māximē timeō. Quotiēns caput abscīdis, novum caput oritur. Auxilium Hydrae dat cancer (*crab*) ingēns.	
HERCULĒS:	Crūra (*legs*) mea mordet (*is biting*). Capita Hydrae cremābimus!	
ĪOLĀUS:	Octō capita dēlēta sunt, sed ūnum etiam vīvit!	
HERCULĒS:	Immortāle est, sed illud sub ingentī saxō pōnēmus et Hydra dēlēbitur! Mox possum sagittās meās sanguine ējus imbuere, itaque mortiferās (*deadly*) eās reddam!	

SECTION 1 Accusative Case

USE	LATIN	ENGLISH
Direct object (Verb) (Preposition)	**Frūmentum** portant. **In oppidum** frūmentum portant.	They are carrying *grain*. They are carrying grain into *the town*.
Duration of time	**Multās *hōrās*** exspectābat.	He waited for many *hours*.
Extent of space	**Sex *mīlia* passuum** nāvigāvit.	He sailed for six *miles*.
Place to which	**Ad *oppidum*** frūmentum portant.	They are carrying grain to *the town*.
Subject of inf.	***Tē*** discēdere jūssī. Dīxit *tē* discēdere.	I ordered *you* to leave. He said that *you* were leaving.
Predicate acc.	**Caesarem *ducem* vocant.**	They call Caesar their *leader*.
Double acc.	***Caesarem auxilium* rogāvit.**	He asked *Caesar* for *help*.

▶ PRACTICE PATTERNS

A. Choose the expression in parentheses that makes the sentence grammatically correct. Translate the sentence.

1. (Ad urbem, Urbī) ambulābant. 2. (Proelium, Proeliō) commīsit. 3. Ante (portīs, portās) stābant. 4. (Virō, Virum) aurum referre jūssit. 5. Dominum (pecūniae, pecūniam) ōrāvit. 6. (Multōs pedēs, Multīs pedibus) nōn nāvigābant. 7. Puellam pulchram (rēgīnae, rēgīnam) dēlēgērunt. 8. (Multīs hōrīs, Multās hōrās) nōn exspectābō. 9. Rēgem (auxilium, auxiliō) rogāvit. 10. (Mīlitēs, Mīlitis) discessisse dīxit.

B. Translate into Latin the words in italics:

1. The soldiers marched *for five hours*. 2. They marched *ten miles* through the *forest*. 3. The soldiers elected *Brutus* their *leader*. 4. The teacher ordered *him* to remain. 5. He announced that the *men* were leaving.

SECTION 2 Prepositions with Accusative

ad, to, toward, near, about
ante, before (*used of time more than of place*)
apud, near, at, among
circum, around
contrā, against
extrā, outside of, beyond
in, into, against
inter, between, among
intrā, within, inside of

ob, on account of
per, through
post, after, behind
praeter, besides, except
prope, near
propter, on account of
sub, under, close up to; (*of time*) just before
super, above, over
trāns, across

▶ PRACTICE PATTERNS

A. Translate into English:

1. in casam
2. ad rīpās
3. trāns mare
4. ob perīculum
5. ante diem
6. propter pūgnam
7. praeter pecūniam

sub pontem
post bellum
super aquam
per agrum
inter viās
apud fīnitimōs
contrā hostēs

intrā mūrōs
circum urbem
sub montem
extrā portam
prope ōram
in inimīcōs
ad flūmen

B. Translate into Latin:

1. into the temple
2. to that place
3. near the fields
4. before daybreak
5. between spaces
6. near the river
7. around the city
8. on account of the storm
9. through the mountains
10. except the women
11. against the enemy

across the roads
over the water
outside the city
among the baggage
within the town
under the bridge
after the battle
on account of the danger
behind the door
across the bridge
toward the hut

SECTION 3 First and Second Declension Adjectives

▶ REVIEW OF MASTERY LIST

ADJECTIVES IN –us, –a, –um

aequus, equal	**īgnōtus,** unknown	**posterus,** following
altus, high, deep	**inimīcus,** unfriendly	**proximus,** nearest
amīcus, friendly	**inīquus,** unjust	**pūblicus,** public
apertus, open	**lātus,** wide	**reliquus,** remaining
bonus, good	**longus,** long	**salvus,** safe
certus, certain	**māgnus,** great	**summus,** highest
clārus, clear	**malus,** wicked	**superus,** above
cupidus, desirous	**medius,** middle	**suus,** his, her, their (own)
extrēmus, farthest	**meus,** my	**tantus,** so great
fīnitimus, neighboring	**multus,** much, many	**tuus,** your
fīrmus, strong	**nōtus,** known	**validus,** strong
grātus, pleasing	**novus,** new	**vērus,** true
idōneus, suitable	**parvus,** small	**vīvus,** living
	paucī (*pl.*), few	

ADJECTIVES IN –er, –era, –erum

līber, free   **miser,** wretched

ADJECTIVES IN –er, –ra, –rum

dexter, right	**noster,** our	**sinister,** left
integer, whole	**pulcher,** beautiful	**vester,** your

▶ REVIEW HELPS

1. Adjectives of the first and second declensions are declined like nouns of these declensions.

  2. Adjectives of the first and second declensions follow three patterns:

    a. Adjectives in *–us, –a, –um: bon/us, bon/a, bon/um.* This is the pattern for the majority.

    b. Adjectives in *–er* that retain the *–e: miser/, miser/a, miser/um;* also *līber.*

    c. Adjectives in *–er* that drop the *–e: pulcher/, pulchr/a, pulchr/um;* also *dexter, sinister, integer, sacer, noster, vester.*

▶ PRACTICE PATTERNS

A. Identify the gender, number, and case of each of the following forms:

1. integer	nōta	certā	bonīs	grātae	vīvās
2. līberum	fīdō	māgnī	clārī	vestrī	bonae

13

3. pulchrō	alta	longam	vērās	multīs	amīcīs
4. miserōs	meās	tuōrum	lātōs	validō	meōrum

B. Choose the noun in parentheses with which the adjective agrees.

1. reliquam (agmen, nāvem, pedem, prīncipem)
2. nōtōrum (sorōrum, voluntātum, ducum, impetum)
3. inīquā (mare, parte, terra, īgnī)
4. fīnitimae (domūs, maria, flūmina, itinera)
5. proximīs (aestātis, regiōnibus, laudis, vallis)
6. īgnōtō (gente, cohorte, adulēscente, ōrdō)
7. inimīcī (imperātōris, mēnse, templō, nūntiīs)
8. vērae (rēs, castra, nātiōne, ōrdinēs)

C. Choose the adjective in parentheses that agrees with the noun.

1. genus (lātus, dextrā, nōtum, māgnus)
2. nātiōnem (fīnitimam, extrēmum, prīmum, pulchrum)
3. vulnera (integram, sinistrum, māgna, apertīs)
4. manūs (parvae, fīrmus, mediī, grātīs)
5. montibus (summīs, multī, prīmōs, propinquō)
6. speciē (pūblicō, idōneā, grātae, amīcī)
7. perīcula (certōs, malīs, tanta, quantō)
8. īnsidiīs (vīvōs, dextrārum, novīs, salvae)

SECTION 4 Adjectives of Special Declension

LATIN FORM	TRANSLATION	GEN. SING.	DAT. SING.
ūnus, ūna, ūnum	one, only	ūn/īus	ūn/ī
ūllus, ūlla, ūllum	any, some	ūll/īus	ūll/ī
nūllus, nūlla, nūllum	none, no	nūll/īus	nūll/ī
sōlus, sōla, sōlum	alone, only	sōl/īus	sōl/ī
tōtus, tōta, tōtum	all, entire, the whole	tōt/īus	tōt/ī
alius, alia, aliud	another (a different, an additional)	al/īus (alterius)	ali/ī
uter, utra, utrum	which (of two)	utr/īus	utr/ī
uterque, utraque, utrumque	each (of two); both	utr/īusque	utr/īque
neuter, neutra, neutrum	neither (of two)	neutr/īus	neutr/ī
alter, altera, alterum	the other (of two)	alter/ius	alter/ī

▶ REVIEW HELPS

1. These special adjectives are declined like adjectives of the first and second declensions, except for the genitive and dative cases singular.

2. *Alterius* (short –ĭ) is generally used for the genitive of *alius.*

▶ PRACTICE PATTERNS

A. Identify the case, number, and gender of these forms:

1. ūnī	utrī	utram	nūllīus	alteram
2. aliō	sōlum	ūllīs	neutram	neutrīs
3. tōtō	aliud	alterī	utrīque	utrāque

B. Write in Latin the genitive and dative cases singular of:

1. one life	neither way	whole province	no safety	each battle
2. any day	only island	the other name	which boy	another legion

SECTION 5 Third Declension Adjectives

▶ REVIEW OF MASTERY LIST

ADJECTIVES IN TWO ENDINGS (*–is, m.&f.; –e, n.*)

brevis, –e, short	**fortis**, –e, brave	**nōbilis**, –e, noble
difficilis, –e, difficult	**gravis**, –e, heavy, serious	**omnis**, –e, all, every
dissimilis, –e, unlike	**immortālis**, –e, immortal	**similis**, –e, similar
facilis, –e, easy	**levis**, –e, light	**ūtilis**, –e, useful

ADJECTIVES IN THREE ENDINGS (*–er, m., –(e)ris, f., –(e)re, n.*)

ācer, ācris, ācre, sharp, fierce   **celer, celeris, celere**, swift, quick

ADJECTIVES IN ONE ENDING

audāx, audācis, daring, bold   **dīligēns, dīligentis**, careful, diligent
fēlīx, fēlīcis, happy, fortunate   **potēns, potentis**, powerful, mighty

▶ REVIEW HELPS

1. Third declension adjectives with a few exceptions are declined like *i*-stem nouns of the third declension but with *–ī* in the ablative singular.

2. Adjectives of the third declension follow one of three patterns:

    a. One-ending adjectives have the same form for all genders in the nominative singular. The genitive singular is given in the vocabulary in order to show the base: *potēns, potēns, potēns (potent/is)*; also *dīligēns, audāx, fēlīx.*

    b. Two-ending adjectives have two different forms in the nominative singular, *–is* being used for the masculine and feminine, *–e* for the neuter: *fortis, fortis, forte*; also *brevis, gravis, levis, nōbilis, omnis, ūtilis, facilis, difficilis, similis, dissimilis.*

    c. Three-ending adjectives have three different forms in the nominative singular, one for each gender: *ācer, ācris, ācre* (the *–e–* is dropped); *celer, celeris, celere* (the *–e–* is retained).

15

▶ PRACTICE PATTERNS

A. Identify the gender, number, and case of the following:

1. fēlīcem   facilī   difficilēs   audācia   dissimilī   gravibus
2. fortium   celere   dīligentis   ūtilium   difficile   nōbilium
3. celeris   brevia   potentibus   ācribus   nōbilibus   potentēs

B. Choose the noun in parentheses which agrees with the adjective:

1. levis (imperiīs, injūriae, ventīs, intervallō)
2. gravia (inopia, sīgna, vigilia, sociō)
3. fēlīcēs (frātrēs, capita, obsidum, ōrdinibus)
4. fortem (initium, nōminum, captīvum, flūminum)
5. brevium (itinerum, praesidium, impedīmentum, spatium)
6. similī (aedificiō, negōtia, sociī, librī)
7. ācribus (salūs, tribūnus, ventus, equīs)
8. omnia (proelia, amīcitia, audācia, patria)

C. Choose the adjective in parentheses that agrees with the noun:

1. dolōris (brevī, ācris, māgnīs, potentēs)
2. dominō (nōbilī, facile, similis, omnem)
3. perīculī (levī, simile, fortium, gravis)
4. equōs (dissimilium, celerēs, potēns, dīligentis)
5. ducibus (audācibus, ūtilēs, difficilis, dīligentēs)
6. soror (gravia, brevium, fēlīx, forte)
7. equitātūs (omnis, nōbilium, brevia, levibus)
8. impetum (celeris, audācis, potentēs, ācrem)

SECTION **6 Numerals**

▶ REVIEW OF MASTERY LIST

Review the list of numerals and the declension of *one*, *two*, and *three* on pages 406–07 of the Appendix.

▶ REVIEW HELPS

1. *Ūnus*, *one*, is an adjective of special declension; *duo*, *two*, has a special declension and is declined only in the plural; *trēs*, *tria*, *three*, is declined like an adjective of the third declension in the plural.

2. All cardinal numbers from four to one hundred are indeclinable; *centī*, *–ae*, *–a*, the plural of *centum*, is declined like the plural adjectives of the first and second declensions; all ordinal numbers are declined like adjectives of the first and second declensions.

3. *Mīlle* in the singular is an indeclinable adjective; *mīlia*, plural

of *mīlle,* is a neuter plural noun of the third declension, and it is followed by another noun in the genitive case: *mīlle hominēs, a thousand men;* but *duo mīlia hominum, two thousand (of) men; tria mīlia passuum, three thousand (of) paces, three miles.*

▶ PRACTICE PATTERNS

A. Translate into English:

1. Homō ūnum caput, duās manūs, duōs pedēs, duōs oculōs, decem digitōs (fingers, toes) habet. 2. Dextra manus quīnque digitōs habet; sinistra manus quīnque digitōs habet; quīnque digitī et quīnque digitī sunt decem digitī. 3. Trēs et quattuor, quīnque et duo, ūnus et sex sunt septem. 4. Ūnus et septem sunt octō; duo et septem sunt novem; trēs et septem sunt decem. 5. Duo dē decem, ūnus dē novem octō sunt.

B. Write in Latin the cardinal numbers from ten to one; the ordinal numbers from one to ten; twelve thousands; twenty miles; one hundred soldiers; two hundred men.

SECTION 7 Comparison of Adjectives

▶ Review the regular comparison of adjectives, page 408 of the Appendix.

▶ REVIEW HELPS

1. Most Latin adjectives are compared like *lātus* or *fortis.*
2. All adjectives in *–er* are compared like *līber* or *ācer.*
3. Six adjectives are compared like *facilis: difficilis, similis, dissimilis, humilis, gracilis.*
4. All other adjectives in *–lis* are compared regularly: *nōbilis, ūtilis,* etc.
5. The formation of the comparative degree is the same for all adjectives of regular comparison.
6. The comparative degree of the adjectives is declined like third declension consonant stems: *honor, corpus.*
7. All superlative degree adjectives are declined like *bonus, –a, –um.*
8. With *quam,* the superlative denotes the highest possible degree: *quam plūrimī, as many as possible.*

▶ Review the irregular comparison of adjectives, page 408 of the Appendix.

▶ REVIEW HELPS

1. All adjectives in the comparative and superlative degree are declined regularly with the exception of *plūs.* (See Appendix, p. 409.)

2. *Plūs* as a singular neuter noun is regularly completed by the partitive genitive: *plūs pecūniae,* more (of) money.

3. *Plūrēs* as a plural adjective is placed in agreement with its noun, as: *plūrēs cōpiae,* more troops; *plūra nōmina,* more names.

4. *Novus, fīdus,* and *sacer* are rarely used in the comparative; *alacer* and *ingēns* have no superlative.

5. The following adjectives are comparatives and superlatives whose positive degree either does not exist or is rarely used.

COMPARATIVE	MEANING	SUPERLATIVE	MEANING
prior, –ius	*former*	prīmus, –a, –um	*first*
propior, –ius	*nearer*	proximus, –a, –um	*nearest, next*
ūlterior, –ius	*farther*	ūltimus, –a, –um	*farthest*
citerior, –ius	*nearer*	citimus, –a, –um	*nearest*
interior, –ius	*inner*	intimus, –a, –um	*inmost*
exterior, –ius	*outer*	extrēmus, –a, –um	*outermost, last*
īnferior, –ius	*lower*	īnfimus (īmus), –a, –um	*lowest*
posterior, –ius	*later*	postrēmus, –a, –um	*latest, last*
superior, –ius	*higher*	suprēmus (summus), –a, –um	*highest*

▶ PRACTICE PATTERNS

A. Identify the degree of each of the following adjectives and translate:

1. fortius	proprius	celerius
2. aequus	altius	minimus
3. melior	ācrior	ācerrimus
4. prius	clārius	facilior
5. clārum	miserior	celeris

B. Write the comparative and superlative forms of the following. Translate.

1. māgnus	fīrmus	nōtus	miser
2. levis	multus	ūtilis	nōbilis

C. Write in Latin:

1. highest	smallest	unfriendly
2. safer	outermost	rather wicked
3. worst	too long	most sacred
4. most unjust	very new	very desirous

SECTION 8 Summary of All Adjective Patterns

DECLENSION	MASC.	FEM.	NEUT.
First and Second	bonus līber pulcher	bona lībera pulchra	bonum līberum pulchrum
Special Genitive Dative	sōlus sōlīus sōlī	sōla sōlīus sōlī	sōlum sōlīus sōlī
Third	potēns fortis celer ācer	potēns fortis celeris ācris	potēns forte celere ācre
Comparative	–ior	–ior	–ius
Superlative	–issimus –errimus –illimus	–issima –errima –illima	–issimum –errimum –illimum
Irregular	(See p. 408.)		

▶ **REVIEW HELPS**

1. Latin adjectives regularly are declined like nouns of the first, second, or third declensions.

2. Latin adjectives agree in gender, number, and case with the nouns they modify.

3. Latin adjectives can modify nouns of all declensions.

▶ **PRACTICE PATTERNS**

A. Identify the gender, number, and case of the following forms. Translate.

1. flūmina duo
2. regiōnī tōtī
3. quīntum mēnsem
4. omnibus legiōnibus
5. tertiā diē
6. fīliae sōlīus
7. novīs rēbus

servī audācēs
bellum breve
cornū dextrō
reī pūblicae
uterque puer
spēs extrēma
mīlitum fortium

proximārum urbium
prīmā nocte
ōrātiōne longā
fīnibus suīs
equōs celerēs
nūllī captīvō
dolōrī ācerrimō

B. Choose the adjective in parentheses that agrees with the noun:

1. imperātōris (māgnīs, ūnīus, clārīs, uter)
2. nōminī (aliī, malī, simile, bonā)
3. lēgātōrum (industrium, sōlōrum, ācerrimum, tribus)
4. lēgēs (inīquissimae, aequī, omnibus, potēns)

19

5. via (facilia, breve, ūtilia, difficilior)
6. cōnsule (forte, aequī, nōbilī, dīligentis)
7. labōribus (difficillimīs, nōbilis, levis, facilī)
8. domūs (similium, novus, tōtīus, pūblicus)

C. Write in Latin the specified forms:

1. ablative plural: noble man; serious wound
2. accusative singular: suitable time; quick journey
3. genitive plural: fierce enemy; powerful weapons
4. ablative singular: very short name; bold captive
5. nominative plural: all the dangers; nine thousand
6. dative singular: the whole state; each province
7. genitive singular: brave cavalry; first legion
8. dative plural: five days; greatest sorrow
9. nominative singular: another part; top of the mountain
10. accusative plural: very difficult times; more enemies

WORDS TO MASTER

aper, aprī, *m.,* a wild boar
cervus, –ī, *m.,* stag, deer (*cervine*)
collum, –ī, *n.,* neck (*collar*)
cremō (1), burn, consume by fire (*cremate*)
cursus, –ūs, *m.,* a running, course (*cursive*)
extrahō, –ere, –trāxī, –trāctus, drag out (*extract*)
imbuō, –ere, –uī, –ūtus, wet, soak (*imbue*)
incolō, –ere, –uī, —, dwell in, inhabit (*with acc.*) (*arenicolous*)

occurrō, –ere, –currī, –cursūrus, meet, happen upon (*occur*)
orior, –īrī, ortus sum, rise, spring up (*orient*)
palus, –ūdis, *f.,* swamp (*paludal*)
quotiēns, *adv., interrog.,* how often? *rel.,* as often as (*quotient*)
sanguis, –inis, *m.,* blood (*sanguinary*)
saxum, –ī, *n.,* rock (*saxicoline*)
simul, *adv.,* at the same time; **simul atque,** as soon as (*simultaneous*)
vēstīgium, –ī, *n.,* footprint, track (*vestige*)

BUILDING WORD POWER

Notice the meaning of *do* or *make* in these English words, all of which are derived from the Latin word *facere, factum, to do or make.*

fact, that which is done, a deed
factor, a doer, a maker
factotum, a doer of all things
facsimile, something made like
facile, easy to do
facility, ease of doing
faculty, power to do

affect, to make a change, to alter
effect, to produce a result
perfect, to do completely
confect, to make by mixing
efficient, getting things done
proficient, highly competent to do
defection, failure to do

More than six hundred words in the English language are derived from the present stem of *facere,* or from its participial or supine stem, *fact-.* In Latin when *facere, factum* is compounded with the prepositional prefixes, the short *-a* in the present stem is changed to short *-i* in the present infinitive and to short *-e* in the supine: *in + facere, factum = inficere, infectum.*

Write the present infinitives and the supines of the compounds of this verb formed with the following prefixes: *ad-, de-, ex-, inter-, ob-, per-, prae-, pro-, re-, sub-.* Remember that in the English derivatives *ad-, ex-, ob-, sub-*became *af-, ef-, of-, suf-: affect, effect, officious, sufficient.*

From which of the compounds of *facere, factum* are the following English words derived: *affection, defect, effective, imperfect, confectionary, prefect, refectory, suffice?* Notice that *interficere, to kill,* is the only one of these compounds from which we have no derivatives in English.

SENTENCE PATTERNS

A. Translate into English:

1. Herculēs igitur profectus est ad palūdem quam Hydra incolēbat.
2. Quotiēns vir fortis hoc fēcerat, mōnstrum iterum orīrī temptābat.
3. Posteā octō Hydrae colla cremāvit.
4. Ingentī sub saxō nōnum caput posuit et dēlēvit.
5. Mōnstrum interfēcit et posteā sagittās suās sanguine imbuit.
6. Simul atque cervum vīdit, post eum summā celeritāte cucurrit.
7. Prīmō vēstīgiīs clāriōribus eum dēnsās in silvās sequēbātur.
8. Tandem, postquam tōtum annum cucurrit, cervum cursū dēfessum cēpit.
9. Postquam in silvās paulum prōgressus est, aprō occurrit.
10. Māximā cum difficultāte aprum ē palūde extrāxit.

B. Translate into Latin:

1. The very strong man set forth for the dangerous marsh.
2. How often did he meet the wild boar in the forest?
3. He soaked his arrows with its blood, didn't he?
4. Hercules dragged the boar out of the ditch and carried it back alive to the cruel king.
5. Did not the deer run for a whole year through the dense forest?

Second Labor: Destroying the Many-headed Hydra

Post haec jūssus est Herculēs ab Eurystheō Hydram quae novem capita habēbat necāre. Fortis vir igitur cum amīcō Īolāō profectus est ad palūdem Lernaeam quam Hydra incolēbat. Mox mōnstrum invēnit et summō cum perīculō collum ējus sinistrā manū prehendit. Tum dextrā capita novem abscīdere (*cut off*) incēpit; sed frūstrā diū labōrābat. Alia nova capita oriēbantur. Tandem cōnstituit capita īgne cremāre. Hoc celeriter fēcit.

Octō capitibus dēlētīs, invēnit extrēmum caput vulnerārī nōn posse, quod erat immortāle. Itaque illud sub ingentī saxō Herculēs posuit et ita labōrem cōnfēcit. Postquam tālī modō Hydram interfēcit, sagittās suās sanguine ējus imbuit et mortiferās eās reddidit.

Third Labor: Capture of the Cerynian Stag

Postquam Eurystheō caedēs Hydrae nūntiāta est, summus terror animum ējus occupāvit. Arbitrābātur sē tenēre tantum virum in rēgnō suō summō cum perīculō. Jūssit igitur Herculem cervum quendam, cūjus cornua aurea fuisse dīcuntur, capere. Hic cervus autem incrēdibilī fuit celeritāte et pedēs multō celeriōrēs ventō habēbat. Prīmum Herculēs vēstīgia ējus in silvā animadvertit. Deinde, cervō ipsō vīsō, Herculēs māximā cum celeritāte currere incēpit. Per plūrimōs diēs cucurrit nec noctū cessāvit (*did stop*). Frūstrā tamen; cervum cōnsequī nōn poterat. Tandem, postquam per tōtum annum cucurrit (ita dīcitur), cervum cursū dēfessum cēpit et vīvum ad Eurystheum rēgem rettulit.

Fourth Labor: Bringing Home a Live Boar

Deinde Eurystheus perterritus jūssit Herculem aprum quendam capere quī illō tempore agrōs Erymanthiōs vāstābat et hominēs illīus locī māgnopere terrēbat. Herculēs laetus negōtium suscēpit et in Arcadiam celeriter sē recēpit. Postquam in silvam paulum prōgressus est, aprō occurrit. Ille autem simul atque Herculem vīdit, statim summā celeritāte fūgit et timōre perterritus altā in fossā sē abdidit. Herculēs tamen eum ē fossā extrāxit nec aper ūllō modō sē līberāre potuit, sed vīvus ad Eurystheum relātus est.

Toil and pleasure, in their nature opposites, are yet linked together in a kind of necessary connection.
—Livy, 59 B.C.–A.D. 17

Unit III

CONVERSATION

PHOLUS: Salvē, viātor. Spēluncam meam intrā et quiētem cape.

HERCULĒS: Salvē et tū. Māgnās grātiās tibi agō; nox adest et dēfessus sum.

PHOLUS: Quō nōmine tū vocāris, advena?

HERCULĒS: Ego Herculēs sum, quī per multās terrās vagātus sum et multōs labōrēs cōnfēcī. Quis es tū?

PHOLUS: Pholus ego sum, prīnceps omnium Centaurōrum quī hanc regiōnem incolunt. Hāc in spēluncā habitō. Venī, cibum cape.

HERCULĒS: Bonus est cibus tuus, Phole, sed vīnum quoque mihi dā.

PHOLUS: Est vīnum quidem, sed hoc tibi dare nōn possum. Reliquī Centaurī mihi vīnum commīsērunt. Sī tibi hoc vīnum dabō, aliī Centaurī mē interficient.

HERCULĒS: Nōlī timēre! Ego tē dēfendam. (*Pōculum vīnī haurit et celeriter bibit.*) Optimum est vīnum!

VŌX PRĪMĪ CENTAURĪ: Odōrem vīnī sentiō!

VŌX ALTERIUS CENTAURĪ: Pholus vīnum nostrum bibit! Eum interficite!

HERCULĒS: Pholum nōn interficiētis. Ego eum dēfendam!

SECTION 1 Ablative Case

PREPOSITIONS WITH THE ABLATIVE CASE

ā, ab, away from, from, by
cum, with, together with
dē, down from, from; about, concerning
ē, ex, out of, from

in, in, on
prō, for, in behalf of; in front of; in defense of
sine, without
sub, under; at the foot of

USE	PREP.	LATIN	ENGLISH
Accompaniment	cum	*Cum amīcō* id scripsit.	He wrote it *with his friend.*
Manner	cum	*Cum cūrā* id scrīpsit.	He wrote it *with care.*
Personal agent	ā, ab	*Ab amīcō* id scrīptum est.	It was written *by his friend.*
Place in which	in, sub	*In nāve* id scrīpsit.	He wrote it *in the ship.*
Place from which	ab, dē, ex	*Ē nāve* id mīsit.	He sent it *from the ship.*
Separation	ab, dē, ex	*Ē nāve* eōs prohibuit.	He kept them *from the ship.*

ABLATIVE WITHOUT A PREPOSITION

USE	LATIN	ENGLISH
Means	*Tubā* sīgnum dedit.	He gave the signal *with a trumpet.*
Time	*Eō tempore* sīgnum dedit.	He gave the signal *at that time.*
	Ūnā hōrā sīgnum dedit.	He gave the signal *within an hour.*
Specification (Respect)	*Nōmine* et *factīs* fortēs erant.	They were brave *in name* and *in deeds.*
Description	*Homō ingentī corpore* erat.	He was a man *with a huge body.*
Comparison	Validior *frātre* erat.	He was stronger than *his brother.*
Degree of Difference	*Multō* validior *frātre* erat.	He was *much* stronger than *his brother.*
Absolute	*Sīgnō datō,* fūgērunt.	*When the signal was given,* they fled.
	Caesare duce, nōn fūgērunt.	*When Caesar was leader,* they did not flee.
Cause	Miser *timōre* fūgit.	*Because of fear,* the poor man fled.

ABLATIVE WITH OR WITHOUT A PREPOSITION

1. The ablative of manner may be expressed *without a preposition* when the noun is modified.

   Summā celeritāte fūgit.   He fled *with very great speed.*

2. The ablative of separation is used *without a preposition* after verbs meaning *to free, to lack,* and *to deprive;* after other verbs of separation a preposition (*ab, dē, ex*) may or may not be used, although it is regularly used with a person.

   Metū eōs **līberāvit.**   He freed them *from fear.*

24

3. The ablative of cause is sometimes expressed with a preposition (*dē, ex*).

> **Quā dē causā fūgit.** *For this reason* he fled.

▶ PRACTICE PATTERNS

A. Translate these expressions into English:

1. in agrīs	prō patriā	tēlīs superātī	paucīs mēnsibus
2. eā nocte	sine timōre	nōmine Pholus	summā cum laude
3. sub monte	ex hībernīs	multō fortior	itinere prohibēre
4. cum amīcīs	illō tempore	ācrior frātre	hīs rēbus gestīs
5. ab castrīs	metū līberātī	timōre commōtī	homō ingentī corpore

B. Translate the expressions in parentheses into Latin, and then translate the sentences into English:

1. (With whom) bellum gerunt? 2. (In two days) victus erat. 3. Exercitus (in Gaul) erat. 4. (From danger) eōs līberāvit. 5. (Within one hour) mortuus est. 6. Quis (by the leader) servātus est? 7. Hostēs (from the land) prohibēre vult. 8. (For many reasons) exspectābant. 9. Rōmānī (in courage) nōn superātī sunt. 10. (At daybreak) (from the city) discessit.

SECTION 2 Expressions of Place Without a Preposition

NAME	MOTION TOWARD	MOTION FROM	LOCATIVE
Rōma	**Rōmam,** *to Rome*	**Rōmā,** *from Rome*	**Rōmae,** *at, in Rome*
Brundisium	**Brundisium,** *to Brundisium*	**Brundisiō,** *from Brundisium*	**Brundisī,** *at, in Brundisium*
Carthāgō	**Carthāginem,** *to Carthage*	**Carthāgine,** *from Carthage*	**Carthāginī, –e,** *at, in Carthage*
Athēnae	**Athēnās,** *to Athens*	**Athēnīs,** *from Athens*	**Athēnīs,** *at, in Athens*
Pompējī	**Pompējōs,** *to Pompeii*	**Pompējīs,** *from Pompeii*	**Pompējīs,** *at, in Pompeii*
Gādēs	**Gādēs,** *to Cadiz*	**Gādibus,** *from Cadiz*	**Gādibus,** *at, in Cadiz*
Crēta	**Crētam,** *to Crete*	**Crētā,** *from Crete*	**Crētae,** *at, in Crete*
domus	**domum,** *home, to home* **domōs,** *to their houses*	**domō,** *from home* **domibus,** *from their houses*	**domī,** *at home* **domibus,** *at their houses*

1. With the names of cities, towns, small islands, **domus,** and a few other place words, the following rules must be noted:

    a. *Motion toward: accusative case* without a preposition.

    b. *Motion from: ablative case* without a preposition.

    c. *Place at* or *in: locative case.*

2. *Locative Case*

    a. The locative case of a singular noun of the first or second declension resembles the genitive singular: **Rōmae,** *at Rome;* **Brundisī,** *at Brundisium.*

    b. The locative case of singular nouns of the third declension resembles the dative or ablative singular: **Carthāginī** or **Carthāgine,** *at Carthage.*

    c. The locative case of all plural nouns resembles the ablative:

        Athēnīs, *at Athens;* **Pompējīs,** *at Pompeii;* **Gādibus,** *at Cadiz.*

▶ PRACTICE PATTERNS

A. Translate into English:

1. Domō discessit. 2. Rōmae habitābant. 3. Domum properāvērunt. 4. Nōnne domī mānsistis? 5. Crētae habitābāmus. 6. Crās Tarentum perveniēmus. 7. Athēnīs Brundisium nāvigāvērunt. 8. Quā dē causā Carthāginem iter fēcit?

B. Translate into Latin:

1. No one returned home. 2. When did they leave home? 3. Did they live at Pompeii? 4. Did anyone remain at home? 5. They used to live at Tarentum. 6. Why did they come back to Rome? 7. What men made a journey to Athens? 8. They sailed from Brundisium to Crete.

SECTION 3 Adverbs

FORMATION OF ADVERBS

DECLEN.	TYPE OF ADJ.	FORMULA	ADJ.	ADVERB	TRANSLATION
1st & 2nd	All regular adj.	base + –ē	altus līber pulcher	altē līberē pulchrē	*deeply* *freely* *beautifully*
3rd	Most regular adj.	base + –iter	fortis celer ācer	fortiter celeriter ācriter	*bravely* *swiftly* *sharply*
	audāx	base + –ter	**audāx**	**audācter**	*boldly*
	Adj. in **–ns**	base + –er	**potēns**	**potenter**	*mightily*

26

1. Adverbs modify verbs, adjectives, and other adverbs.

2. In Latin we sometimes use an adjective which is translated into English as an adverb.

Fēminae *laetae* **patriam adjūvē-**   The women *gladly* (*glad*) helped their
runt.   country.

3. Certain cases of nouns and adjectives are used as adverbs. *Forte* (abl.), *by chance; facile* (acc.), *easily; prīmum* (acc.), *first; prīmō* (abl.), *at first.*

▶ PRACTICE PATTERNS

A. Form adverbs from the following adjectives and translate the adverbs:

1. altus	amīcus	apertus	certus	clārus	cupidus
2. miser	fīrmus	validus	grātus	aequus	inimīcus
3. fēlīx	similis	ūtilis	gravis	brevis	dīligēns

B. Write in Latin the following adverbs:

wretchedly	publicly	easily	seriously	powerfully	unjustly

SECTION 4 Adverbs of Irregular Formation

▶ REVIEW OF MASTERY LIST

ADVERBS OF PLACE

hīc, here, in this place	**hinc,** hence, from this place	**hūc,** hither, here, to this place
ibi, there, in that place	**inde,** thence, from that place	**eō,** thither, there, to that place
ubi, where? in what place?	**unde,** whence? from what place?	**quō,** whither? where? to what place?

ADVERBS OF TIME

quando, when?	**hōdiē,** today	**prīmum,** first
nunc, now	**herī,** yesterday	**prīmō,** at first
tum (tunc), then	**crās,** tomorrow	**deinde,** next
mox, soon	**cōtīdiē,** daily	**posteā,** afterward
jam, already	**prīdiē,** the day before	**umquam,** ever
nōn jam, no longer	**postrīdiē,** the day after	**numquam,** never
quotiēns, how often?	**saepe,** often	**semper,** always
totiēns, so often	**quam prīmum,** as soon as possible	**dēnique,** at last

quam, how	**ita,** so	**circum,** around
tam, so	**sīc,** so	**contrā,** opposite
paene, almost	**quidem,** indeed	**prope,** near
magis, more	**cūr,** why?	**super,** over and above
vix, scarcely	**proptereā,** therefore	**suprā,** above
quoque, also	**nōn,** not	**subter,** beneath

▶ **REVIEW HELPS**

1. *Nunc* means *now, in the present,* and is rarely used when speaking of the past; *jam* means *now, already,* and may be used of any time.

2. *Etiam, also,* is stronger than *quoque, also,* and usually precedes the emphatic word, while *quoque* follows it. *Etiam* is a conjunction, while *quoque* is an adverb.

3. *Prīmum, first* (in order), implies a series of events; *prīmō, at first* (in time), is opposed to *afterward.*

▶ **PRACTICE PATTERNS**

A. Select the adverb that *cannot* be used with the given verb form:

1. veniet (herī, hodiē, crās, postrīdiē, mox)
2. iērunt (jam, herī, nunc, eō, posteā)
3. adest (hīc, hūc, ibi, saepe, numquam)
4. properābis? (Quandō, Cūr, Quō, Ibi, Mox)
5. ambulābat (saepe, numquam, semper, nōn jam, crās)

B. Write in Latin:

1. so bravely; how large?; from day to day; how often did he come?
2. in that place; as quickly as possible; afterward; to what place?
3. the women also; they came also; also by words; where are they?
4. the day before; at last they arrived; the day after; where are they going?

SECTION 5 Comparison of Adverbs

REGULAR COMPARISON OF ADVERBS

	POSITIVE	COMPARATIVE	SUPERLATIVE
Adjective	altus, –a, –um	altior, –ius	altissimus, –a, –um
Adverb	altē	altius	altissimē
Translation	*deeply*	*more (rather, too, quite) deeply*	*most (very) deeply*
Adjective	fortis, –e	fortior, –ius	fortissimus, –a, –um
Adverb	fortiter	fortius	fortissimē
Translation	*bravely*	*more (rather, too, quite) bravely*	*most (very) bravely*

POSITIVE	COMPARATIVE	SUPERLATIVE
bene, *well*	melius, *better*	optimē, *very well*
male, *badly*	pējus, *worse*	pessimē, *very badly*
multum, *much*	plūs, *more*	plūrimum, *most*
parum, *little*	minus, *less*	minimē, *not at all, least*
māgnopere, *greatly*	magis, *more, rather*	māximē, *very greatly, especially*
facile, *easily*	facilius, *more easily*	facillimē, *very easily*
prope, *near, nearly*	propius, *nearer*	proximē, *nearest, recently*
saepe, *often*	saepius, *oftener*	saepissimē, *most often*
diū, *for a long time*	diūtius, *for a longer time*	diūtissimē, *for a very long time*

▶ REVIEW HELPS

1. With the exception of *magis,* the comparative form of the adverbs is the same as the neuter comparative form of the adjective. *Magis* is frequently used to suggest degree: *magis idōneus, more suitable.*

2. With the exception of *plūrimum,* the superlative of the adverb is formed from the superlative of the adjective by changing *–us* to *–ē.*

3. With *quam,* the superlative of the adverb expresses the highest possible degree: *quam celerrimē,* as quickly as possible.

▶ PRACTICE PATTERNS

A. Write the comparative and translate:

1. bene   māgnopere   līberē   prope   parum   multum   diū   ācriter
2. male   fortiter   facile   grātē   clārē   miserē   lātē   saepe

B. Write the superlative and translate:

1. nōbiliter   cupidē   dīligenter   aequē   diū   bene   leviter   multum
2. māgnopere   facile   fēlīciter   prope   cārē   male   audācter   saepe

SECTION 6 Conjunctions

▶ REVIEW OF MASTERY LIST

COORDINATE

et, and
–que, and
atque (ac), and, and also
et . . . et, both . . . and
etiam, also
aut . . . aut, either . . . or
neque (nec) . . . neque (nec),
  neither . . . nor
itaque, and so, therefore
inde, thence, therefore

unde, whence, wherefore
igitur, therefore
sed, but
vērum, but
vērō, but
autem, but, however
tamen, but yet, nevertheless
nam, for
enim, for

sī, if	cum, although	cum, when
nisi, unless	etsī, although	quandō, when
ut, as	quamquam, although	ubi, when, where
quam, as, than	quod, because	ut, when
ut, that, so that	propterā quod, because	postquam, after
nē, that . . . not, lest	cum, because, since	dum, while

▶ REVIEW HELPS

1. *Et, and,* connects words or clauses; *–que* is always an enclitic to the word connected; *atque* is often equivalent to *and so.*

2. *Autem, enim,* and *vērō* are postpositive, that is, they do not stand first in the clause; *igitur* is generally postpositive.

3. Subordinate conjunctions are usually directional signals, indicating the type of clause introduced.

WORDS TO MASTER

aperiō, –īre, –uī, apertus, open (*aperture*); apertus, –a, –um, *adj.,* open

bibō, –ere, bibī, —, drink (*bibulous*)

dērīdeō, –ēre, –rīsī, –rīsus, mock, laugh at (*deride*)

diffundō, –ere, –fūdī, –fūsus, pour about, scatter (*diffuse*)

jūcundus, –a, –um, *adj.,* pleasant, agreeable (*jocund*)

labor, –ī, lapsus sum, glide, slip (*lapse*)

lacrima, –ae, *f.,* tear (*lacrimal*)

morior, morī, mortuus sum, die (*mortuary*)

nōlō, nōlle, nōluī, —, *irreg.,* not wish, be unwilling

pōculum, –ī, *n.,* drinking cup

somnus, –ī, *m.,* sleep (*insomnia*)

spēlunca, –ae, *f.,* cave (*speleology*)

vagor (1), wander about, roam (*vagary*)

vehementer, *adv.,* strongly, very much, violently (*vehemently*)

venēnum, –ī, *n.,* poison, drug, venom (*venomous*)

vīnum, –ī, *n.,* wine (*vintage*)

BUILDING WORD POWER

When the root word *facere, factum* was joined to nouns or adjectives to form compounds, it took the form of *–ficāre: amplus + –ficāre = amplificāre, to make large, to magnify.* From this compound of *facere,* we have the words *amplification, amplificator, amplify,* and *amplifier.* The first two came directly from the Latin words, the last two indirectly through the French. Almost two hundred English words are derived from Latin compounds formed with the verbal element *–ficāre,* the most important of which end in *–fy.*

A few adjectives and adverbs united with *facere* to give words like

30

satisfacere, from which we have our English words *satisfy* and *satisfaction.* Words like *horrific* and *terrific* came from adjectives such as **horrificus** and **terrificus.** Indirectly through the French came a few derivatives from **facere** such as *feat, defeat, feasible, surfeit, fashion,* and *affair.*

What English words are derived from: **clārificāre, glōrificāre, pācificāre, terrificāre, certificāre, simplificāre, deificāre, fortificāre, grātificāre, jūstificāre, nōtificāre, rēctificāre, sīgnificāre, specificāre, testificāre, vērificāre?** Can you use them correctly in sentences?

SENTENCE PATTERNS

A. Translate into English:

1. Diūtissimē Herculēs, postquam ad rēgem aprum rettulit, in Arcadiā longē vagābātur.
2. Vehementer dēfessus sum; cibum multōs diēs nōn habuī.
3. In spēluncā tamen cōnstitit et impetum fortissimē sustinēbat.
4. Nōnne Herculēs eum dērīsit et ipse pōculum vīnī bibit?
5. Ex manibus ējus sagitta lapsa est et pedem leviter vulnerāvit.
6. Multīs cum lacrimīs amīcum spectābat, et tum somnō sē dedit.
7. Brevī tempore vī venēnī mortuus est.
8. Pholus jūcundum vīnum dare nōlēbat quod reliquōs timēbat.
9. Simul atque spēlunca aperta est, odor vīnī undique diffūsus est.
10. Postquam multōs sagittīs suīs vulnerāvit, cum reliquīs pūgnāvit.

B. Translate into Latin:

1. The rest fled from the cave with great speed.
2. The man, Hercules by name, was much stronger than his friends.
3. Was not the door opened by a very pleasant woman?
4. Did the man who surpassed all in courage ever live at Athens?
5. He laughed at the good man who was not willing to give him a cup of wine.

The Fatal Wine

Herculēs dum in Arcadiā vagātur ad eum locum pervēnit ubi Centaurī habitābant. Centaurus erat equus sed hominis caput habēbat. Mox, quod nox jam appropinquābat, ad spēluncam properāvit, in quā Centaurus quīdam, nōmine Pholus, habitābat. Ille Herculem benīgnē excēpit et cibum parāvit. "Bonus est cibus tuus, amīce; vehementer autem sitiō (*am thirsty*). Vīnum quoque mihi dā!"

Erat in spēluncā māgna amphora (*jar*) vīnī optimī quam Cen-

Hercules attacking the centaurs.

taurī ibi dēposuerant. Pholus hoc vīnum dare nōlēbat quod reliquōs Centaurōs timēbat. "Hoc vīnum," inquit, "mihi commissum est. Sī id tibi dabō, Centaurī mē interficient." Herculēs tamen eum dērīsit et ipse pōculum vīnī ex amphorā hausit (*drew*).

Simul atque amphora aperta est, odor jūcundissimus undique diffūsus est. Centaurī nōtum odōrem sēnsērunt et omnēs statim ad locum convēnērunt. "Quid est? Quis est hic homō quī vīnum nostrum bibit?" alius alium rogābat. Māximē īrātī erant, quod Herculem vīnum bibentem vīdērunt, ac Pholum interficere volēbant. Herculēs Pholum amīcum dēfendit et impetum eōrum fortissimē sustinēbat. Multōs sagittīs suīs vulnerāvit. Hae autem sagittae eaedem erant quae sanguine Hydrae ōlim imbūtae erant. Omnēs quōs ille sagittīs vulnerāverat venēnō cōnsūmptī sunt. Hōc vīsō, reliquī fugā salūtem petīvērunt.

Pholus' Fate

Postquam reliquī fūgērunt, Pholus ex spēluncā ēgressus est et corpora mortua spectābat. "Cūr propter tam leve vulnus ā vītā discessērunt? Quae est causa?" Sagittam ē vulnere cūjusdam Centaurī extrāxit. Ē manibus ējus lapsa est et pedem leviter vulnerāvit. Ille statim dolōrem gravem per omnia membra sēnsit, et post breve tempus vī venēnī mortuus est.

Mox Herculēs, quī reliquōs Centaurōs secūtus erat, ad spēluncam rediit et māgnō cum dolōre Pholum mortuum vīdit. Multīs cum lacrimīs corpus amīcī sepelīvit (*buried*). Deinde in spēluncam rediit, et alterum pōculum vīnī bibit; tum dēfessus somnō sē dedit.

The obscene ravens, clamorous o'er the dead.
      —Percy Bysshe Shelley, 1792–1822

CONVERSATION

ĪOLĀUS: Nē centum quidem hominēs hunc labōrem cōnficere possunt.

HERCULĒS: Eurystheus perterritus est. Hic labor quem mihi imposuit multō est gravior quam alterī. Quis est Augēās?

ĪOLĀUS: Augēās rēx Ēlidis est.

HERCULĒS: Tria mīlia boum in stabulō ingentis māgnitūdinis inclūsit. Ad hoc tempus stabulum numquam pūrgātum est!

ĪOLĀUS: Trīgintā annōs in stabulō bovēs incoluērunt. Num intrā spatium ūnīus diēī illud pūrgāre potes?

HERCULĒS: Etsī negōtium est difficillimum, bonum cōnsilium cēpī.

ĪOLĀUS: Tē adjuvābō, Herculēs. Quid est istud cōnsilium?

HERCULĒS: Prīmum fossam duodēvīgintī (*eighteen*) pedum dūcēmus. Tum per hanc fossam flūminis aqua dē montibus ad mūrum stabulī fluet.

ĪOLĀUS: Hoc cōnsilium nōn intellegō. Cui bonō est tantus labor?

HERCULĒS: Parte mūrī parvā dēlētā, aqua per stabulum fluet. Hōc modō fīnem operis ūnō diē facillimē cōnficiam!

SECTION 1 Dative Case

USE	LATIN	ENGLISH

Indirect Object
  With trans. verbs
	Amīcō **pecūniam dedit.**	He gave money
		  to his friend.

With intrans. verbs	*Hostibus* **fortiter resistent.**	They will resist *the enemy* bravely.
With compound verbs	**Legātus** *cōpiīs* **praeerat.**	The lieutenant was in command of *the troops.*
With Special adjs.	**Locus** *castrīs* **idōneus erat.**	The place was suitable *for a camp.*

▶ PRACTICE PATTERNS

A. Complete these sentences by translating the words in the parentheses into Latin. Translate the completed sentences.

1. (messenger) nōn crēdō. 2. (the soldier) gladium dedit. 3. Lēgātus (the camp)

praeest. 4. Facile (the boy) persuāsit. 5. Belgae proximī (Germans) sunt. 6. Lēgātum (the camp) praefēcit. 7. Victōriam (the Romans) nūntiāvit. 8. Fīliae similēs (their mother) sunt.

B. Translate into Latin:

1. Who gave the food to the birds? 2. The oxen did not injure the king. 3. The stable was not suitable for oxen. 4. Why did they wish to harm the birds? 5. Was the man in charge of the troops? 6. The king was not friendly to Hercules. 7. They showed him the spacious stable. 8. When did they wage war against the enemy? 9. Who placed him in command of the troops? 10. He did not try to persuade the king, did he?

SECTION 2 Horizontal Comparison of Case Indicators

1. The nominative singular is often irregular and must be learned from the vocabulary. The nominative singular of *masculine* and *feminine* nouns originally ended in *–s*, but the *–s* has disappeared from the first declension, from second declension nouns like *ager* and *vir*, and from some third declension consonant-stem nouns like *cōnsul.*

2. The accusative singular of masculine and feminine nouns ends in *–m* in all declensions, with the preceding vowel short.

3. The accusative plural of masculine and feminine nouns ends in *–s* in all declensions, with the preceding vowel long.

4. In neuters the nominative and accusative singular are alike, and the nominative and accusative plural are alike and always end in short *–a.*

5. The ablative singular ending is the stem vowel, except in consonant stems and most masculine and feminine *i*-stems, which end in *–e.*

6. In each declension the dative plural is like the ablative plural. The ending is *–īs* in the first and second declensions, *–bus* in the others.

7. In all declensions the genitive plural ends in *–um,* which is preceded by *–r* in the first, second, and fifth declensions.

8. The vocative is like the nominative except in the singular of second declension nouns in *–us* (vocative *–e*) and *–ius* (vocative *–ī*).

9. With names of cities, towns, small islands, *domus,* and other place names, *place where* is expressed by the locative case. The locative has the same form as the genitive in the singular nouns of the first and second declensions. In the singular of nouns of the third declension and in all plural nouns, it has the same form as the ablative.

Declension	First	Second		Third Cons. Stems		Third i-Stems		Fourth		Fifth
Stem Vowel	−a	−o						−u		−e
Gender	F.	M.	N.	M.&F.	N.	M.&F.	N.	M.	N.	F.
SINGULAR										
Subject — Nom.	−a	−us	−um	(as in vocabulary)		(as in vocabulary)		−us	−ū	−ēs
Possession (of) — Gen.	−ae	−ī		−is		−is		−ūs		−ēī, −eī
To, for — Dat.	−ae	−ō		−ī		−ī		−uī	−ū	−ēī, −eī
Object; in, into; **ad,** to, toward — Acc.	−am	−um		−em	(nom.)	−em	(nom.)	−um	−ū	−em
From, with, by; in, on, at; **ā, ab;** from, by; **ē, ex,** out of, from; **cum,** with; **in,** in, on — Abl.	−ā	−ō		−e		−e, −ī	−ī	−ū		−ē
PLURAL										
Nom.	−ae	−ī	−a	−ēs	−a	−ēs	−ia	−ūs	−ua	−ēs
Gen.	−ārum	−ōrum		−um		−ium		−uum		−ērum
Dat.	−īs	−īs		−ibus		−ibus		−ibus		−ēbus
Acc.	−ās	−ōs	−a	−ēs	−a	−ēs, −īs	−ia	−ūs	−ua	−ēs
Abl.	−īs	−īs		−ibus		−ibus		−ibus		−ēbus

► PRACTICE PATTERNS

A. Identify the case and number of the following nouns. Translate.

1. aetās	vallēs	nāvium	aciēī	hominibus	cohortī
2. ducum	timōrī	speciē	poena	celeritāte	itinera
3. fīliās	impetū	mīlitis	rēbus	exercitūs	vītārum
4. verbīs	patris	glōriae	vīcōs	cōnsiliōrum	adventum
5. urbium	proelī	imperiō	ventī	pecūniam	urbibus
6. villīs	poenae	senātuī	sīgna	nātiōnēs	vulnera

B. Write in Latin these specified forms:

1. accusative plural: punishment, son, book, soldier, day
2. ablative singular: hope, approach, sea, right, deed
3. nominative plural: disaster, guard, number, flight, teacher
4. accusative singular: horseman, kind, inhabitant, people, slave
5. genitive plural: thing, army, side, month, duty
6. nominative singular: ship, sign, wall, hostage, weapon
7. dative plural: state, legion, manner, eagle, place
8. genitive singular: faith, head, impediment, mountain, death
9. ablative plural: road, eye, march, pace, day
10. dative singular: body, ally, evening, tongue, enemy

SECTION 3 Personal Pronouns

	FIRST	SECOND	THIRD (DEMONSTRATIVE)		
			SINGULAR		
Nom.	ego, *I*	tū, *you*	is, *he*	ea, *she*	id, *it*
Gen.	meī	tuī		ējus	
Dat.	mihi	tibi		eī	
Acc.	mē	tē	eum	eam	id
Abl.	mē	tē	eō	eā	eō
			PLURAL		
Nom.	nōs, *we*	vōs, *you*	eī (iī), *they*	eae, *they*	ea, *they*
Gen.	nostrum (nostrī)	vestrum (vestrī)	eōrum	eārum	eōrum
Dat.	nōbīs	vōbīs	eīs (iīs)		
Acc.	nōs	vōs	eōs	eās	ea
Abl.	nōbīs	vōbīs	eīs (iīs)		

► REVIEW HELPS

1. When a compound subject includes more than one person, the order in Latin is first person, second person, third person. Notice that this

is the opposite of the usual English order. The verb agrees with the first person rather than the second, and the second person rather than the third.

Ego et tū in urbem vēnimus. *You and I came* to the city.
Tū et puer in urbem vēnistis. *The boy and you came* to the city.

2. *Nostrum* and *vestrum* are used only for the partitive genitive.

3. *Nostrī* and *vestrī* are genitives used either as reflexive pronouns or as objective genitives.

▶ PRACTICE PATTERNS

A. Translate into English:

1. Ego et tū eōs vidēmus. 2. Eī multam pecūniam habent. 3. In māgnō oppidō cum eīs sumus. 4. Ego tē et eum et eam spectābam. 5. Equī nōs et vōs et eōs portābant. 6. Ego sum laetus; cūr tū es nōn laeta? 7. Nōn mēcum et tēcum sed cum eō pūgnat. 8. Multī nostrum et vestrum sunt miserī. 9. Nōn vōbīscum sed cum eīs nunc ambulāmus. 10. Castra spectant; circum ea sunt et mūrus et vallum.

B. Translate into Latin:

1. We, not you, are free. 2. I gave him the weapons. 3. The town is large; I see it. 4. The wall is high; I see it. 5. The camp is large; I see it. 6. The city is large; you see it. 7. The cities are large; I see them. 8. The walls are high; I see them. 9. They are watching you and us and them. 10. Many of us and many of you live in the city.

SECTION 4 Reflexive Pronouns

	SINGULAR				PLURAL			
	Gen.	Dat.	Acc.	Abl.	Gen.	Dat.	Acc.	Abl.
First	**meī**, *of myself*	**mihi**	**mē**	**mē**	**nostrī**	**nōbīs**	**nōs**	**nōbīs**
Second	**tuī**, *of yourself*	**tibi**	**tē**	**tē**	**vestrī**	**vōbīs-**	**vōs**	**vōbīs**
Third	**suī**, *of himself*	**sibi**	**sē**	**sē**	**suī**	**sibi**	**sē**	**sē**

▶ REVIEW HELPS

1. A reflexive pronoun has no nominative case.

2. In the first and second persons the forms of the reflexive pronouns are the same as those of the personal pronouns. *Nostrum* and *vestrum* are not used as reflexive pronouns.

3. The third person has a separate reflexive pronoun. The forms for all genders are alike in both the singular and plural. *Suī* may mean: *of*

himself, of herself, of itself, of themselves, depending on the subject to which it refers.

4. A reflexive pronoun occurs in the predicate of the sentence and refers usually to the subject of the verb in its clause.

5. The preposition *cum* is attached to the ablative case, singular and plural, of the reflexive pronouns: *mēcum, tēcum, sēcum, nōbīscum, vōbīscum.*

▶ PRACTICE PATTERNS

A. Translate into English:

1. Vir sē laudat. 2. Vōs accūsātis. 3. Fēmina sē laudat. 4. Nōs dēfendēbāmus. 5. Rēx sē interfēcit. 6. Ego mē numquam laudō. 7. Tū tē laudāre nōn dēbēs. 8. Agrum optimum sibi dēligunt. 9. Multōs comitēs sēcum habēbat. 10. Puerī sē laudant; puellae sē laudant.

B. Translate into Latin:

1. We praised ourselves. 2. He spoke about himself. 3. The boy wounded himself. 4. The girl praised herself. 5. They gave gifts to themselves. 6. You ought to help yourself. 7. You chose the best for yourselves. 8. He led the soldiers with him into Italy. 9. He saved others; himself he did not save. 10. We never see ourselves as (*ut*) our neighbors see us.

SECTION 5 Summary of Personal Pronouns and Possessive Adjectives

PRONOUNS	USE	ADJECTIVES
ego, *I* **nōs,** *we*	1st Personal and Reflexive	**meus, mea, meum,** *my, my own* **noster, nostra, nostrum,** *our, our own*
tū, *you* **vōs,** *you*	2nd Personal and Reflexive	**tuus, tua, tuum,** *your, your own* **vester, vestra, vestrum,** *your, your own*
is, ea, id, *he, she, it* **eī, eae, ea,** *they*	3rd Personal only	(No adjectives. Genitive of **is, ea, id** is used instead.) **ējus,** *of him, of her, of it, her, his, its* **eōrum, eārum,** *of them, their*
suī, *of himself, herself, itself, themselves* **sibi,** *to, for himself, etc.* **sē,** *himself, etc.* **sē,** *from, by, with himself, etc.*	3rd Reflexive only	**suus, sua, suum,** *his own, her own, its own, their own*

1. The possessive adjective agrees with the noun it modifies in gender, number, and case, except that *meus* forms its vocative masculine singular in –*ī:*

mī amīce, *O my friend!*

2. The possessive *suus* is reflexive. It stands in the predicate and refers to the subject, indicating that the subject is the possessor.

3. The Latin possessives are omitted whenever the meaning is clear without them.

4. Possessive adjectives, when not emphatic, follow their nouns; when emphatic, they precede.

5. If they do not refer to the subject, *his, her, its* are expressed by the genitive *ējus; their* is expressed by the genitives **eōrum, eārum.**

▶ PRACTICE PATTERNS

A. Translate into English:

1. Avis mea āvolāvit. 2. Vōcem suam nōn audit. 3. Puer suōs librōs habet. 4. Puer librum ējus habet. 5. Puella librōs suōs habet. 6. Puella librum eōrum habet. 7. Domus eārum antīqua est. 8. Meum stabulum est amplius quam tuum. 9. Nostrī bovēs in vestrō agrō inclūsī sunt. 10. Dominus tuus crepitum avium meārum audit.

B. Translate into Latin:

1. Your birds flew away. 2. I did this with my own hand. 3. He did not kill your birds. 4. We heard the noise of their birds. 5. The king will lead his own troops. 6. The girl could not hear her own voice. 7. The man did not cleanse his own stables. 8. They heard the noise of their own birds. 9. The king enclosed the oxen in his own stable. 10. The boy was blamed by his own father.

SECTION 6 Demonstrative Pronouns and Adjectives

▶ Review the declension of *hic, ille, idem,* Appendix, pages 410–11.

▶ REVIEW HELPS

1. *Hic* is an emphatic word for *this; ille* is an emphatic word for *that:*

Hic mīles erat fortior illō (quam   *This* soldier was braver than *that.*
ille).

2. *Hic* means *the latter, ille, the former:*

Sextus et Lūcius erant mīlitēs Rō-   Sextus and Lucius were Roman sol-
mānī; *ille* erat fortis, *hic* nōn   diers; *the former* was brave, *the latter*
erat.   was not.

3. *Ille* is used to show a change of subject:

Captīvōs cōnsistere jussērunt; *illī* They ordered the prisoners to stand;
fūgērunt. *they* fled.

4. *Haec, illa, eadem,* neuter plurals, are frequently translated *these things, those things, the same things.* In the genitive, dative, and ablative cases, forms of the noun *rēs* are used with these demonstratives in order to avoid ambiguity.

PLURAL	*these things*	*those things*	*the same things*
Nom.	**haec** (*neut. pl.*)	**illa** (*neut. pl.*)	**eadem** (*neut. pl.*)
Gen.	**hārum rērum**	**illārum rērum**	**eārundem rērum**
Dat.	**hīs rēbus**	**illīs rēbus**	**eīsdem rēbus**
Acc.	**haec** (*neut. pl.*)	**illa** (*neut. pl.*)	**eadem** (*neut. pl.*)
Abl.	**hīs rēbus**	**illīs rēbus**	**eīsdem rēbus**

▶ PRACTICE PATTERNS

A. Translate into English:

1. Hī pūgnant. 2. Eadem laudō. 3. Illī cibum vorant. 4. Eīdem crepitum audiunt. 5. Incolās hūjus oppidī timent. 6. Eundem crepitum audīvērunt. 7. Hic puer adest; illa puella abest. 8. Haec erat causa illīus bellī. 9. Haec laudō; illa nōn laudō. 10. Romulus et Numa erant rēgēs; ille erat audāx, hic bonus.

B. Translate into Latin:

1. I saw the same oxen. 2. That was a long battle. 3. We saw the same things. 4. The same birds flew away. 5. The men of the legion were brave. 6. These were inhabitants of the same city. 7. These were the same causes of that war. 8. These things I like; those I do not like. 9. The soldier was informed about these things. 10. Fabius and Coriolanus were Romans; the former was a consul, the latter an exile.

SECTION 7 The Intensive Pronoun *ipse*

▶ Review the declension of *ipse,* page 411 of the Appendix.

▶ REVIEW HELPS

1. *Ipse* is an intensive pronoun or adjective. It emphasizes nouns or pronouns of any person.

2. *Ipse* is translated *myself, yourself, himself,* etc., depending upon its reference. Sometimes it is best translated by other intensive words as *very, actual, mere,* etc.

▶ PRACTICE PATTERNS

A. Translate into English:

1. Ipsa vēnit. 2. Ego ipse eōs vīdī. 3. Lēgātus ipse haec dīxit. 4. Ipsī crepitum audīvimus. 5. Ipsō dīe stabulum pūrgāvit. 6. Haec erat ipsa causa illīus bellī. 7. Nūllus erat ipsā in urbe terror. 8. Crepitū avium ipsī territī sunt. 9. Bovēs rēgis ipsīus inclūdēbantur. 10. Hostium ipsōrum multī eī grātiās ēgērunt.

B. Translate into Latin:

1. I myself came with him. 2. I saw the girl herself. 3. I came with him himself. 4. The birds themselves flew away. 5. The business itself was difficult. 6. We ourselves attacked the birds. 7. On that very day we heard the noise. 8. The king himself enclosed the oxen. 9. He gave the books to the men themselves. 10. One man alone cleansed that very stable.

WORDS TO MASTER

aes, aeris, *n.*, copper, bronze, brass (*aeruginous*)

aggredior, –gredī, –gressus sum, attack (*aggression*)

amplus, –a, –um, *adj.*, large, spacious (*ample*)

avis, –is, *f.*, bird (*aviary*)

āvolō (1), fly away (*volatile*)

bōs, bovis, *m.&f.*, ox, bull, cow; *gen. pl.*, **boum** *or* **bovum;** *dat. and abl. pl.*, **bōbus** *or* **būbus** (*bovine*)

carō, carnis, *f.*, flesh (*carnal*)

cōnsistō, –ere, –stitī, —, take one's stand, be formed of (*consist*)

crepitus, –ūs, *m.*, rattle, noise (*crepitant*)

inclūdō, –ere, –clūsī, –clūsus, shut in, enclose (*include*)

līmus, –ī, *m.*, mud (*limicolous*)

opīniō, –ōnis, *f.*, conjecture, supposition (*opinion*)

pūrgō (1), make clean, cleanse (*purge*)

quidem, *adv.*, in fact, indeed; **nē . . . quidem,** not even

stabilis, –e, *adj.*, firm (*stable*)

stabulum, –ī, *n.*, standing place, stall (*stable*)

vorō (1), devour (*voracious*)

BUILDING WORD POWER

Second only to *facere, factum* in the number of words it has given to the English language is the root word *capere, captum, to take* or *to seize.* When it was compounded with the prepositional prefixes, it was changed to *–cipere,* and thus we have the verbs *accipere, concipere, dēcipere, excipere, incipere, intercipere, occipere, percipere, praecipere, recipere, suscipere. Anticipāre* and *occupāre* are also compounds of *capere.* English words derived directly from Latin contain the syllables *cap–, capt–, cip–, cept–.* Those that came into our language indirectly through the French have the syllables *ceiv–, ceipt–, ceit–.*

41

Note how the following derivatives contain the original meaning of *take, seize, receive.*

capacious, capable of receiving, large
captive, one taken
capture, a seizure
accept, to take, receive
except, to take out, exclude
intercept, to seize on the way
perceive, to take hold of, take note of

incipient, taking up, beginning
receive, to take into one's possession
receipt, a receiving; written acknowledgment of receiving
preceptor, one who takes up before the pupils, hence, a teacher
occupy, to seize, take possession of

What are etymological meanings of: *anticipate, participate, susceptibility, emancipate, deceive, deceit?*

Originally a **capsa** (**capiō**) was a box, and **capsula** (**capsule**) was a little box. Our word *cash* was derived from **capsa** because money was kept in a box.

SENTENCE PATTERNS

A. Translate into English:

1. Rēx quidem Herculī labōrem gravem imposuit.
2. Nē centum quidem servī intrā spatium ūnīus diēī id cōnficere poterant.
3. Ubi virī cum illō nāvigant, māximō perīculō occurrunt.
4. Augēās rēx tria mīlia boum in amplō stabulō inclūserat.
5. Neque ad id tempus umquam pūrgātum est.
6. Contrā opīniōnem omnium stabulum ūnō diē aquā pūrgāvit.
7. Num avēs aggredī poterat quod lacus ē līmō cōnstitit?
8. Nōnne eae ācrī crepitū perterritae sunt?
9. Ipse haec ex aere fēcerat postquam Minerva auxilium ab eō petīvit.
10. Hae avēs postquam carnem hominum vorāvērunt celeriter āvolāvērunt.

B. Translate into Latin:

1. The noise frightened the large birds, and they flew away.
2. This huge stable had not been cleansed for many years, had it?
3. The lake consisted not of water but of mud.
4. These oxen had been enclosed in that stable for a very long time.
5. He attacked a great number of them with arrows while they were flying away.

Fifth Labor: Cleaning Up the Augean Stables

Deinde Eurystheus Herculī hunc labōrem multō graviōrem imposuit. Māximā māgnitūdine erat hic labor; nē centum quidem hominēs id cōnficere potuerant. Augēās quīdam, quī illō tempore rēgnum in Ēlide obtinēbat, tria mīlia boum habēbat. Hī in stabulō ingentis māgnitūdinis inclūdēbantur. Hoc stabulum, quod per trīgintā annōs nōn pūrgātum erat, Herculēs intrā spatium ūnīus diēī pūrgāre jūssus est. Ille, etsī rēs erat difficillima, negō-tium suscēpit. Prīmum fossam fēcit per quam flūminis aquam dē montibus ad mūrum stabulī dūxit. Tum parte parvā mūrī dēlētā, aqua per stabulum flūxit. Hōc modō fīnem operis contrā opīni-ōnem omnium ūnō diē facillimē cōnfēcit.

Hercules shooting the Stymphalean birds.

Sixth Labor: Scaring the Birds with the Brazen Beaks

Post paucōs diēs Herculēs ad oppidum Stymphālum iter fēcit. Jūsserat eum Eurystheus avēs necāre quae rostra aenea (*brass*) habēbant et hominēs miserōs vorābant. In hōc lacū quī nōn longē erat ab oppidō Stymphālō, avēs incolēbant. Lacus autem nōn ex aquā sed ex līmō cōnstitit; Herculēs igitur neque pedibus neque nāve prōgredī neque eās aggredī potuit.

Tandem postquam māgnam partem diēī frūstrā cōnsūmpsit, ad Vulcānum properāvit et auxilium ab eō petīvit. Vulcānus cre-pundia (*rattles*) quae ipse ex aere fēcerat Herculī dedit. Eīs Her-culēs ācrem crepitum fēcit et avēs perterritae āvolāvērunt. Ille autem dum āvolant, māgnum numerum eārum sagittīs trānsfīxit.

Courage is resistance of fear, mastery
of fear—not absence of fear.
—Mark Twain, 1835–1910

Unit V

CONVERSATION

PRĪMUS NAUTA: Cūr, comes, ad īnsulam Crētam nāvigāmus?

SECUNDUS NAUTA: Nōnne rēgis imperia audīvistī?

PRĪMUS: Nihil audīvī. Dīc mihi, bone amīce, causam itineris.

HERCULĒS: Colloquium vestrum cāsū audīvī, comitēs fīdī. Eurystheus
mē taurum ferōcem ex īnsuiā Crētā vīvum referre jūssit.
Rēs est perīculōsa, sed quīcumque mēcum nāvigant, in perīculō semper vīvunt!

SECUNDUS: Quācumque possumus ratiōne tibi auxilium dabimus.

HERCULĒS: Ad īnsulam jam appropinquāmus, sed tempestās est māgna.
Nāvis cursum tenēre nōn potest.

TERTIUS: Quid faciēmus? Timor animōs nostrōs occupāvit et omnem
spem salūtis dēposuimus.

HERCULĒS: Nōlīte timēre. Tranquillitās mox tempestātem cōnsequētur
et nāvem incolumem ad lītus appellēmus. Rēx Crētae erit
nōbīs amīcus.

PRĪMUS: Deinde ad eam regiōnem quam taurus vāstat contendere
dēbēmus.

SECUNDUS: Incolumēs mōnstrum ferōx ad nāvem trahēmus, et cum
praedā in Graeciam redībimus. Herculēs dux noster negōtium fēlīciter cōnficiet.

SECTION 1 Relative Pronouns

▶ Review the declension of the relative pronoun *quī, quae, quod,*
page 411 of the Appendix.

▶ REVIEW HELPS

1. A relative pronoun connects a subordinate clause, of which it is a
part, with its antecedent in the same sentence. The *antecedent* is the noun
or pronoun to which the relative pronoun refers and which generally
precedes the relative pronoun.

2. The relative pronoun agrees in gender and number with its antecedent, but its case is determined by its use in the clause in which it
stands.

44

Agreement of Relative Pronouns

Nom.	Mīles (*quī pūgnat*) est fortis.	The soldier (*who is fighting*) is brave.
Gen.	Mīles (*cūjus amīcus sum*) est fortis.	The soldier (*whose friend I am*) is brave.
Dat.	Mīles (*cui pecūniam dedī*) est fortis.	The soldier (*to whom I gave the money*) is brave.
Acc.	Mīles (*quem vidēs*) est fortis.	The soldier (*whom you see*) is brave.
Abl.	Mīles (*ā quō hostis est interfectus*) est fortis.	The soldier (*by whom an enemy was killed*) is brave.

Nom.	Mīlitēs (*quī pūgnant*) sunt fortēs.	The soldiers (*who are fighting*) are brave.
Gen.	Mīlitēs (*quōrum amīcī sumus*) sunt fortēs.	The soldiers (*whose friends we are*) are brave.
Dat.	Mīlitēs (*quibus pecūniam dedī*) sunt fortēs.	The soldiers (*to whom I gave the money*) are brave.
Acc.	Mīlitēs (*quōs vidēs*) sunt fortēs.	The soldiers (*whom you see*) are brave.
Abl.	Mīlitēs (*ā quibus hostēs sunt interfectī*) sunt fortēs.	The soldiers (*by whom the enemy were killed*) are brave.

3. The preposition *cum* is attached to the ablative of the relative pronoun: *quōcum, quācum, quibuscum, with whom.*

4. The relative pronoun is never omitted in Latin as it sometimes is in English:

> the present you gave me   **dōnum *quod* mihi dedistī**

5. *He, she, they, that,* or *those* as the antecedents of relative pronouns are usually expressed with the pronoun *is:*

> **is quī** = *he who;* **ea quae** = *she who;* **eī quī** = *those who*
> **id quod** = *that which* (*what*); **ea quae** = *those things which* (*what*)

6. *Quī, quae, quod* is sometimes used at the beginning of a sentence to serve as a connection with the preceding sentence.

> **Mē īre jūssit. *Quod* fēcī.**   He ordered me to go. *This* (literally *which*) I did.

45

▶ PRACTICE PATTERNS

A. State the antecedent and account for the gender, number, and case of every relative pronoun in the following:

1. Is quī incolit ... 2. Ea quae fēcērunt ... 3. Eī quibuscum solvō ... 4. Supplicium quod cēpit ... 5. Advenae quī vēnerant ... 6. Comes ā quō vulnerātus est ... 7. Lītus ad quod pervēnimus ... 8. Eae quārum līberī aderant ... 9. Advenās quōs certiōrēs fēcī ... 10. Sagittae quibus interfectī sunt ...

B. Translate into Latin; state the antecedent and account for the gender, number, and case of every relative pronoun:

1. The comrade who came ... 2. The storms which began to blow ... 3. The shore near which they sailed ... 4. The sailors whom he set ashore ... 5. The strangers to whom he gave ... 6. The ships on which they set sail ...

SECTION 2 Interrogative Pronouns and Adjectives

▶ Review the declension of the interrogative pronouns and adjectives, page 411 of the Appendix.

▶ REVIEW HELPS

1. The interrogative adjective *quī, quae, quod, which? what?* is declined like the relative pronoun *quī, quae, quod, which, that.*

2. The interrogative pronoun has in the nominative singular *quis, who?* for the masculine and feminine, and *quid, what?* for the neuter singular. The rest is declined like the relative pronoun.

▶ PRACTICE PATTERNS

A. Translate these sentences:

1. Quem audīs? 2. Quis nāvem solvit? 3. Quod lītus vīdistī? 4. Quid tū faciēbās? 5. Quam nāvem appulit? 6. Quae ratiō data est? 7. Cui pecūnia data est? 8. Cūjus equōs interfēcit? 9. Ad quem rēgem advenās mīserās? 10. Ad quae castra comitēs contendērunt?

B. Distinguish between the relative pronouns and the interrogative pronouns and adjectives. Translate into Latin:

1. Who comes? 2. The stranger who comes ... 3. What can you do? 4. The ships which set sail ... 5. Which shore is dangerous? 6. Whose comrade was with you? 7. The storm which began to blow ... 8. The stranger with whom you sailed ... 9. The ship in which they were setting sail ... 10. To whom was he explaining the reason of the journey?

SECTION 3 Indefinite Pronouns and Adjectives

PRONOUNS	ADJECTIVES
quis, quid, *someone, something anyone, anything*	**quī, quae (qua), quod,** *some, any*
aliquis, aliquid, *someone, something anyone, anything*	**aliquī, aliqua, aliquod,** *some, any*
quīdam, quaedam, quiddam, *a certain one*	**quīdam, quaedam, quoddam,** *a certain*

▶ REVIEW HELPS

1. The indefinite pronouns and adjectives are used to indicate that some person or thing is meant, without stating what one.

2. The indefinite pronoun **quis, quid** and its compound **aliquis, aliquid** (**ali–** + **quis, quid**) are identical in declension with the interrogative pronoun **quis, quid,** except that **aliqua** is generally used for the feminine singular nominative.

3. The indefinite adjectives of **quis** and **aliquis** are declined like the interrogative adjective and the relative pronoun **quī, quae, quod.**

4. **Quis,** *anyone,* is least definite, and **quīdam,** *a certain one,* is most definite; **aliquis,** *someone,* stands between the two.

5. The indefinite pronoun **aliquis, aliquid,** is generally used in the singular to mean *some* or *other,* as opposed to *none.*

6. The indefinite pronoun **quis, quid** is used only in a clause introduced by **sī, nisi, nē, num.**

> **Sī quis vēnerit,** nōn vidēbitur.   *If anyone comes,* he will not be seen.

▶ PRACTICE PATTERNS

A. Decline, giving a translation of the nominative singular:

> quīdam homō   aliqua ratiō (sing. only)   quod flūmen

B. Translate into Latin:

1. I see someone. 2. If anyone comes, tell me. 3. He called a certain comrade. 4. Some wish to go away.

SECTION 4 Review of All Pronoun Patterns

▶ PRACTICE PATTERNS

A. Identify the case and number of the following forms:

1. sē	vōs	sibi	ipsīs	istīus	mē	quem	quibus
2. hī	tuī	quid	nōbīs	alicui	id	quod	eādem

47

3.	tē	suī	hanc	eadem	quendam	cui	tibi	cūjus
4.	hoc	hae	mihi	eārum	ipsōrum	hāc	idem	illae
5.	hōc	quā	quōs	illīus	alicūjus	eīs	haec	istud

B. Change the adjectives in parentheses if they need to be changed to agree with the given noun:

1. lītora (haec, ipsa, illae, eadem)
2. advenam (quendam, aliquem, quod, ipsum)
3. terrōrī (alicui, ipsō, eīdem, illī)
4. ratiōnis (illīus, alicūjus, cūjusdam, tuīs)
5. comitibus (quibusdam, hīs, eās, illīs)
6. tempestātum (eārum, quārundam, ipsum, hārum)
7. supplicium (id, ipsum, illum, quod)
8. aeris (alicūjus, ipsīus, cūjusdam, hīs)
9. opiniōnem (eam, hanc, quaedam, illam)
10. spēluncārum (eārum, quārundam, illārum, aliquōrum)

C. Write in Latin the specified forms:

1. genitive singular and plural: this wound; that night
2. ablative singular and plural: the very shield; this mountain
3. dative singular and plural: any village; which part?
4. accusative singular and plural: the same horn; that horse of yours
5. nominative singular and plural: a certain route; some part

SECTION 5 Questions

PRONOUN QUESTIONS

Interrogative Pronouns and Adjectives		Interrogative Adverbs	
LATIN	ENGLISH	LATIN	ENGLISH
quis	*who?*	ubi	*where?*
quid	*what?*	quō	*whither?*
uter	*which (of two)?*	unde	*whence?*
quot (indecl.)	*how many?*	quandō	*when?*
quantus	*how large?*	quotiēns	*how often?*
quālis	*of what sort?*	quā	*by what way?*
quī, quae, quod	*which? what?*	quam	*how?*
		cūr	*why?*
Interrogative Phrases		quamdiū	*how long?*
		quōmodo	*how?*
quā dē causā	*why?*		
quam ob rem	*why?*		
quā rē	*why?*		

YES AND NO QUESTIONS

EXPECTED ANSWER	INTROD. WORD	LATIN	ENGLISH
Yes	Nōnne	Nōnne virum vidēs?	*You see the man, don't you?* *Don't you see the man?* *Of course, you see the man!*
No	Num	Num virum vidēs?	*You don't see the man, do you?* *Of course, you don't see the man!*
Yes or *No*	–ne	Virumne vidēs?	*Do you see the man?*

▶ REVIEW HELPS

1. Pronoun questions are introduced by interrogative pronouns or by words derived from interrogative pronouns.

2. *Yes* and *no* questions require the answer *yes* or *no* in English.

▶ PRACTICE PATTERNS

A. Translate into English:

1. Quō is? 2. Quid tenēs? 3. Quamdiū aberās? 4. Quālis dux erat? 5. Quanta est urbs? 6. Vidēsne comitem? 7. Quis portat aquam? 8. Nōnne nāvem solvit? 9. Quōmodo oppūgnāvērunt? 10. Quantās cōpiās vīcērunt?

B. Translate into Latin:

1. How did they embark? 2. Where are my comrades? 3. Whither did they sail? 4. When did the storm blow? 5. How long did they remain? 6. How many strangers came? 7. Whence did they come? 8. How often were they present? 9. At what shore did they arrive? 10. Which of the ships did they board?

WORDS TO MASTER

advena, –ae, *m.&f.,* stranger

appellō, –ere, –pulī, –pulsus, drive to, bring to; (of ships) to land

comes, –itis, *m.&f.,* comrade

cōnscendō, –ere, –scendī, –scēnsus, climb; (of ships) embark

expōnō, –ere, –posuī, –positus, put out, explain, set ashore (*expose*)

ferōx, –ōcis, *adj.,* fierce, savage (*ferocious*)

flō (1), blow (*flatulent*)

incolumis, –e, *adj.,* unhurt, safe and sound

lītus, –oris, *n.,* shore (*littoral*)

perīculōsus, –a, –um, *adj.,* dangerous (*perilous*)

quīcumque, quae–, quod–, *indef. pronoun,* whoever, whichever, whatever

ratiō, –ōnis, *f.,* plan, means, method, manner (*ratio*)

solvō, –ere, solvī, solūtus, release, set free; pay; (of ships) set sail (*solve*)

supplicium, –ī, *n.,* punishment, death penalty

tempestās, –tātis, *f.,* weather, storm (*tempest*)

terror, –ōris, *m.,* fright, panic (*terror*)

49

BUILDING WORD POWER

Three closely related root words have about two hundred English relatives in the dictionary. They are *stāre, statum, to stand, sistere, statum,* to cause to stand, to bring to a stand, to check, and *statuere, statūtum,* to cause to stand, to decide. The roots of these verbs are found in English under these forms: *–sta–, –stat–, –st–, –stet–, –sist–, –statu–, –stitu–.*

Name English words that are derived from the following Latin verbs. Notice the underlying meaning of *stand* in all of them.

circumstāre, *to stand around*
cōnstāre, *to stand firm*
distāre, *to stand apart*
exstāre, *to stand out*

assistere, *to stand by, defend*
cōnsistere, *to stand still*
dēsistere, *to stand away, stop*
exsistere, *to stand forth, appear*

cōnstituere, *to cause to stand, set up, establish*
dēstituere, *to stand alone, desert*

instāre, *to stand on, close to*
obstāre, *to stand in the way*
restāre, *to stand against, remain*
substāre, *to stand firm, exist*

īnsistere, *to stand still on*
persistere, *to stand constant*
resistere, *to withstand, oppose*
subsistere, *to make a stand against*

īnstituere, *to stand in place, introduce, determine*
substituere, *to stand next, to put in the place of*

Explain the italicized words: a *stable* government; a large *stable;* a *stanza* of poetry; the *stamen* of a flower; the *statue* was *stationary;* engraved *stationery;* the *statutes* of the *state.*

SENTENCE PATTERNS

A. Translate into English:

1. Ille quī taurum quendam ferōcem referre jūssus est statim nāvem solvit.
2. Māgnus terror animōs comitum occupāvit, plūrimī quōrum omnem spem salūtis dēposuerant.
3. Paulō post comitēs Herculis, quī nāvem cōnscendērunt, ex īnsulā Crētā nāvigāvērunt.
4. Nōnne dux ipse comitibus quandam ratiōnem itineris exposuit?
5. Quī nāvem incolumem ad terram appulērunt?
6. Quācumque possumus ratiōne equōs in lītus expōnēmus.
7. Māgna tempestās perīculōsa facta est ubi ventī flāre subitō incēpērunt.
8. Is quī anteā multōs advenās necāverat, ipse eōdem suppliciō jūstē necātus est.
9. Num terror animōs nautārum occupāvit quōs in lītus exposuit?
10. Quibusdam comitibus praedam dedit quam cēperat.

B. Translate into Latin:

1. Who ordered Hercules to bring back the savage bull?
2. Panic seized the minds of certain comrades who had boarded the ship.
3. We shall help our leader in whatever way we can.
4. The task was dangerous for the sailors whom he had set ashore.
5. To which men did he give the booty that he took from the strangers?

Seventh Labor: Taking the Bull by the Horns

Tum Eurystheus Herculem jūssit taurum quendam ferōcissi-
mum ex īnsulā Crētā vīvum referre. Simul atque ventus idōneus
fuit, ille nāvem cōnscendit et statim solvit. Ubi tamen ad īnsulam
jam appropinquābat, māgna tempestās subitō flāre incēpit, neque
nāvis cursum tenēre potuit. Māgnus terror animōs nautārum occupāvit; paene omnem spem salūtis dēposuērunt. Herculēs tamen
nūllō modō territus est.

Post breve tempus fuit summa tranquillitās, et nautae, quī sē
ex terrōre jam recēperant, nāvem incolumem ad terram appu-

lērunt. Herculēs quī ē nāvī ēgressus est ad rēgem Crētae properāvit quem causam itineris docuit. Deinde postquam omnia parāta
sunt, ad eam regiōnem contendit quam taurus vāstābat. Brevī
tempore ipse taurum vīdit, et etsī rēs erat perīculōsa, cornua ējus
prehendit. Tum ingentī labōre mōnstrum ad nāvem trāxit et cum
praedā in Graeciam rediit.

Eighth Labor: The Man-eating Horses of Diomedes

Postquam ex īnsulā Crētā rediit, Herculēs ab Eurystheō in Thraciam missus est et equōs Diomēdis redūcere jūssus est. Hī equī carnem hominum vorābant; Diomedēs, autem, vir crūdēlissimus, eīs prōjiciēbat advenās omnēs quī in eam regiōnem vēnerant. Herculēs igitur māgnā celeritāte in Thraciam contendit et ab Diomēde hōs equōs postulāvit. Diomedēs tamen hoc facere nōlēbat et Herculēs īrā commōtus eum interfēcit. Corpus ējus mortuum equīs prōjicī jūssit.

Ita is quī anteā multōs cum cruciātū (*torture*) necāverat, ipse eōdem suppliciō necātus est. Ubi omnia haec nūntiāta sunt, omnēs quī eam regiōnem incolēbant, māgnā laetitiā permōtī sunt. Herculēs equōs in nāvem dūxit; deinde sine morā solvit et mox equōs in lītus Graecum exposuit.

Woman is woman's natural ally.
—Euripides, 484–406 B.C.

Unit VI

CONVERSATION

PAULUS: Audīvistīne, Lūcī, umquam fābulam dē Amāzonibus?

LŪCIUS: Antīquīs temporibus erat gēns, quae dīcitur omnīnō ex mulieribus cōnstitisse. Amāzonēs appellābantur.

PAULA: Habēbantne prīncipem et exercitum?

LŪCIUS: Rēgīnam habēbant cui erat nōmen Hippolytē. Omnēs Amāzonēs māgnam scientiam reī mīlitāris habēbant, et saepe cum virīs proelium committere audēbant.

ANNA: Quam ob rem Herculēs contrā Amāzonēs bellum gerēbat?

LŪCIUS: Hippolytē balteum pulcherrimum habuit, quem Mārs, bellī deus, eī dōnāverat. Admēta, Eurystheī fīlia, hunc balteum possidēre vehementer cupiēbat.

PAULUS: Num Hippolytē hunc balteum rēgis fīliae dedit?

LŪCIUS: Eurystheus Herculem cōpiās cōgere jūssit et in fīnēs Amāzonum prōcēdere ac balteum postulāre.

PAULA: Mandātum rēgis erat inīquum. Pūgnāvēruntne Amāzonēs?

LŪCIUS: Prīmō Amāzonēs cōpiās Herculis superāvērunt, sed posteā Herculī balteum concēdere coāctae sunt. Nōn gāvīsae sunt.

SECTION 1 Regular Verbs of All Conjugations

▶ REVIEW OF MASTERY LIST

FIRST CONJUGATION VERBS

aedificō, build
*ambulo, walk
amō, like, love
appellō, call, name
appropinquō, draw
        near
armō, arm
†circumdō, surround
*clāmō, shout
comparō, prepare
cōnfīrmō, strengthen
convocō, summon
cūrō, take care of
†dō, give
dubitō, hesitate
exīstimō, think
expūgnō, take by storm

exspectō, wait for
*habitō, inhabit
imperō, command
incitō, urge on
labōrō, work
laudō, praise
līberō, set free
locō, place
narrō, tell
nāvigō, sail
nūntiō, announce
occupō, seize
oppūgnō, attack
ōrō, beg, pray
parō, prepare
portō, carry
postulō, demand

properō, hasten
*pūgnō, fight
putō, think
rogō, ask
servō, save
spectō, look at, watch
spērō, hope
‡stō, stand
superō, conquer
temptō, try
trānsportō, carry over
vāstō, lay waste
*vigilō, be awake, watch
vītō, avoid
*volō, fly
vulnerō, wound

SECOND CONJUGATION VERBS

augeō, increase
commoveō, alarm
dēbeō, ought, owe
doceō, teach
habeō, have, hold
jubeō, order
*maneō, remain
moveō, move
obtineō, possess

oportet, it is necessary
permoveō, arouse
*persuādeō, persuade
perterreō, frighten
*pertineō, reach
prohibeō, prevent
*remaneō, remain
respondeō, answer
retineō, hold back

*sedeō, sit
*studeō, be eager for
sustineō, withstand
teneō, hold
terreō, frighten
timeō, fear
video, see

THIRD CONJUGATION VERBS

agō, drive, do
   cōgō, force, collect
cadō, fall
   accidō, happen
capiō, take, seize
   accipiō, receive

excipiō, take out,
      receive
*incipiō, take on,
      begin
recipiō, take back,
      receive

suscipiō, undertake
*cedō, yield, go away
*discēdō, go away
*excēdō, go out
*prōcēdō, go for-
      ward

---

* Intransitive; future participle for fourth principal part
† Irregular formation of principal parts
‡ Irregular formation of principal parts; intransitive

53

crēdō, believe
  dēdō, give up
  reddō, give back
  trādō, give over
dūcō, lead
  addūcō, lead to, influence
  ēdūcō, lead out
  indūcō, lead on, induce
  prōdūcō, lead forth, produce
  redūcō, lead back
  trādūcō, lead across
faciō, make, do
  cōnficiō, accomplish
  efficiō, bring about
  interficiō, kill
  perficiō, accomplish
  praeficiō, place in command
jaciō, throw, hurl
  conjiciō, throw, hurl
  dējiciō, throw down
legō, read, choose

intellegō, understand
ēligō, choose
mittō, send
  committō, entrust, begin
  dīmittō, send away
  intermittō, interrupt
  praemittō, send ahead
pellō, strike, drive out
  expellō, drive out
  impellō, drive on
  repellō, drive back
premō, press, crush
  opprimō, crush, overwhelm
statuō, place, decide
  cōnstituō, decide
sūmō, take, put on
  cōnsūmō, use up, destroy
vertō, turn
  animadvertō, turn the mind to, notice

claudō, close
cōgnōscō, learn
cōnsīdō, sit down
contendō, struggle, hasten
*****currō**, run
dēfendō, defend
dīcō, say, tell
dīvidō, divide
gerō, bear, carry
incendō, set on fire
īnstruō, draw up, build
jungō, join
occīdō, cut down, kill
ostendō, show
petō, seek, beg
pōnō, place, put
quaerō, seek, ask
regō, rule
relinquō, abandon
*****resistō**, resist
scrībō, write
trahō, draw, drag
vincō, conquer, win

FOURTH CONJUGATION VERBS

audiō, hear
fīniō, finish
impediō, hinder

mūniō, fortify
sciō, know
sentiō, feel, perceive

*****veniō**, come
  *****conveniō**, assemble
  inveniō, find
  *****perveniō**, arrive at

SECTION 2 Regular Verbs, Indicative Active

PRINCIPAL PARTS

CONJUGATION	FIRST	SECOND	THIRD	THIRD–io	FOURTH
Present Indicative	vocō	moneō	regō	capiō	audiō
Present Infinitive	vocāre	monēre	regere	capere	audīre
Perfect Indicative	vocāvī	monuī	rēxī	cēpī	audīvī
Perfect Passive Participle	vocātus	monitus	rēctus	captus	audītus

---

* Intransitive; future participle for fourth principal part

54

Verb Stems

Present	vocā–	monē–	rege–	cape–	audī–
Perfect	vocāv–	monu–	rēx–	cēp–	audīv–
Participial	vocāt–	monit–	rēct–	capt–	audīt–
Inflection Vowel	–ā	–ē	–e	–e	–ī

Formation of Tenses

Present Tense
 	
I call, do call, am calling, etc.
	Formula: Present Stem + Active Person Indicators
	  –ō –mus
	  –s –tis
	  –t –nt

Imperfect Tense
 	
I was calling, used to call, etc.
	Formula: Present Stem + –bam –bāmus
	  –bās –bātis
	  –bat –bant

Future Tense
 	
I shall call, etc.
	First and Second Conjugations:
	Formula: Present Stem + –bō –bimus
	  –bis –bitis
	  –bit –bunt
	
	Third and Fourth Conjugations:
	Formula: Present Stem + –am –ēmus
	  –ēs –ētis
	  –et –ent

Perfect Tense
 	
I carried, have carried, etc.
	Formula: Perfect Stem + –ī –imus
	  –istī –istis
	  –it –ērunt

Pluperfect Tense
 	
I had carried, etc.
	Formula: Perfect Stem + –eram –erāmus
	  –erās –erātis
	  –erat –erant

Future Perfect Tense
 	
I shall have carried, etc.
	Formula: Perfect Stem + –erō –erimus
	  –eris –eritis
	  –erit –erint

▶ REVIEW HELPS

1. In the present tense –*a* drops out before –*o* in the first conjugation; short –*e* of the stem changes to –*i* in the third conjugation.

2. In the imperfect tense –*m* is used instead of –*o* in the first person singular.

3. In the future tense short –*e* drops out before –*a* in the first person singular of the third conjugation.

4. The formation of the imperfect, perfect, pluperfect, and future perfect tenses active is the same for all Latin verbs.

5. Long vowels become short before final –*m*, –*t*, and –*nt*.

► PRACTICE PATTERNS

A. Write the second verb in the same form (voice, mood, tense, person, number) as the first verb.

1. stābunt — sciō
2. cēperant — teneō
3. mīsērunt — parō
4. capis — exīstimō
5. mūnit — regō
6. monet — petō
7. coēgit — persuādeō
8. vocābis — faciō
9. pūgnābāmus — dūcō
10. vīcerātis — timeō
11. posueritis — jaciō
12. gerētis — videō

B. Write in Latin the specified forms in the indicative active:

1. present third singular: hear, lead, have, overcome
2. future third plural: think, fortify, move, receive
3. perfect second singular: remain, send, arrive, attack
4. imperfect first plural: give, advise, leave, know
5. pluperfect second plural: run, ask, hold, depart

SECTION 3 Regular Verbs, Indicative Passive

FORMATION OF TENSES

Present Tense
I am called,
  am being called, etc.
	Formula: Substitute passive person indicators for active ones.
	
	  –r –mur
	  –ris (–re) –minī
	  –tur –ntur

Imperfect Tense *I was called,* *was being called,* etc.	*Note:* 1. –r is added directly to the full active form: **vocor, vocābor.**

Future Tense
I shall be called, etc.
	2. Careful attention should be given to the forms of the second person singular of the 3rd conjugation:
	
	  Present: **reg + eris** = *you are ruled*
	  Future: **reg + ēris** = *you will be ruled*

Perfect Tense
I was called,
  have been called, etc.
	Formula: Perfect Passive Participle + *Present* Tense of **sum**
	  vocātus, –a, –um sum, etc.

Pluperfect Tense *I had been warned,* etc.	*Formula:* Perfect Passive Participle + *Imperfect* Tense of **sum** **monitus, –a, –um eram,** etc.
Future Perfect Tense *I shall have been ruled,* etc.	*Formula:* Perfect Passive Participle + *Future* Tense of **sum** **rēctus, –a, –um erō,** etc.

► PRACTICE PATTERNS

A. Translate into English:

1. possēdit	expiāris	appellērīs	concesserint
2. aperiunt	expōnētur	trānsfīgis	inclūdēbātur
3. pūrgābat	extrahitur	ēvocāverant	cōnstitūtus est
4. vorābunt	appelleris	solūtī sunt	compressī erunt

B. Write the following verbs in the plural and translate:

1. imbuet	occurram	dēsperāvī	inclūsum est
2. solvis	concēdit	perturbat	prehēnsus est
3. intendit	incolēbās	possidēbit	dōnātum erit
4. cremābis	āvolāverō	diffūsa erat	appellātus erit

C. Select from the parentheses the form indicated:

1. future indicative passive: (possedit, comprimēris, perturbāmus)
2. imperfect indicative active: (expiābat, perturbat, bibitur)
3. present indicative passive: (prehendet, comprimitur, occurrēbat)
4. perfect indicative active: (possident, diffūdit, expōnit)
5. pluperfect indicative passive: (incoluerat, solūtī erant, dēsperāverat)

D. Translate into Latin:

1. he mocked	I had yielded	she had called out
2. we had met	they were called	they were devouring
3. they despair	they are opening	he had been disturbed
4. it was opened	it was enclosed	they were being seized

SECTION 4 Deponent and Semideponent Verbs

► Review the conjugation of deponent verbs, pages 419–21 of the Appendix.

PRINCIPAL PARTS OF DEPONENT VERBS

CONJ.	PRES. INDIC.	PRES. INFIN.	PERF. INDIC.
I	cōnor, *I try*	cōnārī, *to try*	cōnātus, −a, −um sum, *I tried*
II	vereor, *I fear*	verērī, *to fear*	veritus, −a, −um sum, *I feared*
III	sequor, *I follow*	sequī, *to follow*	secūtus, −a, −um sum, *I followed*
III–io	patior, *I suffer*	patī, *to suffer*	passus, −a, −um sum, *I suffered*
IV	largior, *I bestow*	largīrī, *to bestow*	largītus, −a, −um sum, *I bestowed*

► REVIEW HELPS

1. The term deponent derives from *dē + pōnō*, *lay aside*. The deponent verbs, *passive* in form, have laid aside their passive meaning and have taken an *active* one.

2. Deponent verbs have only three principal parts, each of which is passive in form and active in meaning. They are conjugated according to the rules for the passive of regular verbs.

PRINCIPAL PARTS OF SEMIDEPONENT VERBS

CONJ.	PRES. INDIC.	PRES. INFIN.	PERF. INDIC.
II	audeō, *I dare*	audēre, *to dare*	ausus, –a, –um sum, *I dared*
II	gaudeō, *I rejoice*	gaudēre, *to rejoice*	gāvīsus, –a, –um sum, *I rejoiced*

▶ REVIEW HELPS

1. Semideponent (half-deponent) is the name given to a few verbs that have active forms in the present, imperfect, and future tenses, but passive forms with active meanings in the perfect, pluperfect, and future perfect.

2. The following is a synopsis of *audeō,* in the six tenses of the indicative mood.

SYNOPSIS OF SEMIDEPONENT VERBS

TENSE	LATIN	ACTIVE MEANING
Present	**audeō**	*I dare*
Imperfect	**audēbam**	*I was daring*
Future	**audēbō**	*I shall dare*
Perfect	**ausus sum**	*I dared*
Pluperfect	**ausus eram**	*I had dared*
Future Perfect	**ausus erō**	*I shall have dared*

▶ PRACTICE PATTERNS

A. Write in Latin and translate the specified synopses in the indicative.

1. arbitror (third person singular)
2. polliceor (first person plural)
3. gaudeō (third person plural)

B. Choose the correct translation of the Latin verb:

1. largiēbātur (he bestows, is bestowing, was bestowing, will bestow)
2. cohortātus est (he is encouraged, is encouraging, encourages, encouraged)
3. gāvīsa eram (I am delighted, was delighted, will be delighted, had been delighted)
4. audent (they will dare, dare, dared, were daring)
5. loquētur (it is spoken, he speaks, she will speak, we are speaking)
6. lapsus sum (I am slipping, slipped, had slipped, will slip)
7. secūtī erunt (they follow, have followed, will follow, will have followed)
8. mortuus erat (he died, will have died, had died, was dying)

58

SECTION 5 Irregular Verbs

▶ Review the conjugation of the irregular verbs, pages 422–26.

PRINCIPAL PARTS OF IRREGULAR VERBS

Pres. Ind.	sum	possum	eō	ferō	volō	nōlō	fīō
Pres. Inf.	esse	posse	īre	ferre	velle	nōlle	fierī
Perf. Ind.	fuī	potuī	iī	tulī	voluī	nōluī	factus sum
Perf. Pass. Part.	(futūrus)	—	(itūrus)	lātus	—	—	factus

▶ REVIEW HELPS

1. **Eō** as an intransitive verb is found only in the active voice, except when used impersonally in the third person singular of the various tenses. Transitive compounds (**trānseō, ineō**) form their passives regularly.

2. The –v– in the perfect system of the verb **eō** is seldom used.

3. **Fīō** is used for the passive of the verb *faciō* in the three simple tenses. Compounds of *faciō* form their passives regularly.

4. **Ferō** is transitive and, with the exception of the present tense, forms its passive regularly.

▶ PRACTICE PATTERNS

A. Change to the tenses indicated without changing mood or voice.

1. Future: abeunt, volēbat, eunt, fīō, fert, nōlō, potueram, es
2. Perfect: cōnferēbam, fuerō, trānsit, fiēbant, nōlunt, potes, vult, estis

B. Translate into Latin:

1. he will be able; you had been; to go; he did not want; it became
2. it was carried; they wanted; we were present; you (pl.) have been; they went

WORDS TO MASTER

audeō, –ēre, ausus sum, *semidep.,* dare (*audacious*)

balteus, –ī, *m.,* belt (*belt*)

clēmentia, –ae, *f.,* mercy, kindness (*clemency*)

cohortor (1), encourage, exhort

concēdō, –ere, –cessī, –cessūrus, grant, yield (*concede*)

dēspērō (1), despair (*desperation*)

dōnō (1), give, reward (*donate*)

enim, *conj.* (*postpositive*), for, indeed

ēvocō (1), call out, call forth (*evoke*)

gaudeō, –ēre, gāvīsus sum, *semidep.,* be delighted, rejoice

mulier, –eris, *f.,* woman (*muliebrity*)

occāsus, –ūs, *m.,* setting (*occasion*); **sōlis occāsus,** sunset, the west

ōstium, –ī, *n.,* mouth, door (*ostiary*)

perturbō (1), throw into confusion, disturb (*perturbation*)

possideō, –ēre, –sēdī, –sessūrus, hold, own, possess (*possession*)

ūsus, –ūs, *m.,* use, practice, experience (*use*)

59

BUILDING WORD POWER

A Latin root word very important in both Latin and English is the irregular verb **ferre, lātum**, *to bear, bring, carry, cause*. The derivatives of this verb appear in English under the forms *fer–, lat–*. Several important English verbs end in *–fer: confer, defer, differ, infer, offer, prefer, proffer, refer, suffer, transfer*. Write the Latin verbs from which these compounds are directly derived, and show that in both English and Latin they retain the meaning of *bear, bring, carry,* or *cause*.

You will notice that the English word *defer* has two different meanings and two different origins. *Defer*, to submit, is derived from **dēferre,** *to bring down; defer*, to postpone, has the same origin as *differ,* **differre,** which is composed of the prefix **dis–,** *apart*, and *ferre, to carry*.

In science we have a number of words ending in *–ferous*, as *auriferous*, gold-bearing. What is the difference between *afferent* and *efferent* nerves? What do *lucifer* and *conifer* mean?

What is the Latin origin and meaning of: *dilate, relate, prelate, oblate, prolate, elate?* What is a *circumferential* highway; a *vociferous* individual; a *fertile* field; the *ablative* case?

SENTENCE PATTERNS

A. Translate into English:

1. Quae rēgīna cum validīs virīs bellum gerere audēbat?
2. Quī rēx Herculem jūssit cōpiās cōgere et bellum mulieribus īnferre?
3. Quā dē causā eōs dēlēgit quī ūsum in rē mīlitārī habēbant?
4. Paucīs post diēbus ad ōstium flūminis nāvem appulit.
5. Concēde, Ō rēgīna, fortissimō ducī balteum quem possidēs!
6. Nōnne rēgīna, quae fāmam dē Herculis virtūte accēperat, balteum trādere volēbat?
7. Amāzonēs gāvīsae sunt quod virī novō genere pūgnae perturbātī sunt.
8. Ad sōlis occāsum mulierēs dē suīs fortūnīs dēspērābant.
9. Dōnāvitne rēgīna Herculī balteum quod clēmentiam dēmōnstrāvit?
10. Dux fortis enim cōpiās ēvocāvit et mīlitēs cohortātus est.

B. Translate into Latin:

1. Don't yield the belt to the powerful stranger, brave woman!
2. He called forth to battle the enemy, who were beginning to despair.
3. They took many prisoners, among whom was the queen.
4. Did these women dare to wage war with powerful men?
5. The men were delighted at first, but afterward they were disturbed by this new kind of battle.

60

Hercules and his men battling the Amazons.

Ninth Labor: Regiment for Women Only

Illō tempore erat gēns Amāzonum quae dīcitur omnīnō ex mulieribus cōnstitisse. Hae summam scientiam reī mīlitāris habēbant. Etiam cum virīs proelium committere audēbant. Hippolytē, Amāzonum rēgīna, balteum nōtissimum habuit, quem Mārs eī dederat. Admēta autem, Eurystheī fīlia, fāmam dē hōc balteō accēperat et eum possidēre vehementer cupiēbat. Eurystheus igitur jūssit Herculem cōpiās cōgere et bellum cum Amāzonibus gerere. Ille nūntiōs in omnēs partēs dīmīsit. Herculēs postquam māgna multitūdō convēnit eōs dēlēgit quī māximum ūsum reī mīlitāris habēbant. Hīs virīs causam itineris exposuit.

Fortissimī eōrum, auctōritāte ējus adductī, cum eō iter facere cōnstituērunt. Tum cum eīs quibus persuāserat nāvem cōnscendit, et post paucōs diēs ad ōstium flūminis Thermōdontis pervēnit. Postquam in fīnēs Amāzonum vēnit, nūntium ad Hippolytam mīsit; ille causam itineris docuit et balteum postulāvit. Ipsa Hippolytē balteum trādere volēbat, quod dē Herculis virtūte fāmam accēperat, sed reliquae Amāzonēs illī balteum concēdere nōlēbant et negāvērunt. Herculēs, ubi haec nūntiāta sunt, bellī fortūnam cōnārī cōnstituit. Proximō diē cōpiās ēdūxit, locum idōneum dēlēgit atque hostēs ad pūgnam ēvocāvit. Amāzonēs quoque cōpiās suās ex castrīs ēdūxērunt.

Palūs erat nōn māgna inter duōs exercitūs; neutrī tamen initium trānseundī (*of crossing*) facere volēbant. Tandem Herculēs sīgnum dedit et, ubi palūdem trānsiit, proelium commīsit. Amāzonēs impetum virōrum fortiter sustinuērunt, et contrā omnium

61

opīniōnem summam fortitūdinem dēmōnstrāvērunt; multōs eōrum occīdērunt, multōs etiam in fugam conjēcērunt. Virī enim novō genere pūgnae perturbātī sunt nec māgnam virtūtem dēmōnstrāvērunt. Mulierēs gāvīsae sunt, sed Herculēs dē suīs fortūnīs dēspērāre incēpit. Mīlitēs igitur vehementer cohortātus est.

Verbīs suīs animōs omnium cōnfīrmāvit, et tandem ad sōlis occāsum mulierēs fugā salūtem petīvērunt. Multae autem vulneribus dēfessae dum fugiunt captae sunt, in quō numerō erat Hippolytē. Herculēs captīvīs summam clēmentiam dēmōnstrāvit, et postquam balteum accēpit, lībertātem omnibus Amāzonibus dedit. Tum sociōs ad mare redūxit et in Graeciam proficīscī properāvit. Dōnāvitne balteum, quem Mārs rēgīnae fortī dederat, rēgis fīliae Admētae?

Throughout his life Hercules had this perfect confidence that no matter who was against him he could never be defeated, and facts bore him out.
—Edith Hamilton, 1867–1963

Unit VII

CONVERSATION

HERCULĒS:	Eurytiōn mortuus est. Bovēs per Hispāniam et Liguriam nōs compellere necesse est. Omnia parāte, comitēs.
PRĪMUS COMES:	Bovēs ex īnsulā ad continentem trānsportāre facile nōn erit. Ligurēs bellicōsī nōs prōgredī prohibēre cōnābuntur.
HERCULĒS:	Saxa tēlaque in nōs conjicient sed fortasse (*perhaps*) Juppiter ipse nōbīs auxilium feret!
SECUNDUS COMES:	Exīstimō eum imbrem lapidum ingentium dēmissūrum esse.
PRĪMUS COMES:	Hī māgnā vī māgnum numerum Ligurum occīdere dēbent.
HERCULĒS:	Ego spērō nōs nihil incommodī captūrōs esse.
TERTIUS COMES:	Post paucōs diēs ad Alpēs perveniēmus. Necesse erit hōs trānsīre quod in Ītaliam bovēs dūcere volumus.
PRĪMUS COMES:	Rēs summae erit difficultātis. Neque frūmentum neque pābulum in eīs regiōnibus invenīrī potest.
HERCULĒS:	Nōlīte timēre! Māgnam cōpiam frūmentī et pābulī bovēs ipsī trāns Alpēs trānsportābunt. Satis erit.
PRĪMUS COMES:	Bovēs incolumēs in Ītaliam pervenient. Avē, māgne Herculēs!

SECTION 1 Imperative Mood

PRESENT IMPERATIVE

CONJUGATION		I	II	III	III–io	IV	sum
Present Stem		vocā–	monē–	rege–	cape–	audī–	es–
Active	Sing.	vocā	monē	rege	cape	audī	es
	Pl.	vocāte	monēte	regite	capite	audīte	este

▶ REVIEW HELPS

1. The imperative (**imperō** = give orders) is used to give a direct command.

2. The singular form of the present imperative active is equivalent to the present stem of the verb; the plural adds –*te* to the present stem.

3. In verbs of the third conjugation, both types, the –*e* of the present stem is shortened to –*i* in the plural form of the imperative.

4. Four Latin verbs of the third conjugation drop the final –*e* of the present stem to form the present imperative active.

VERB	PRESENT STEM	PRESENT IMPERATIVE ACTIVE	
dīcō, *say, tell*	**dīce–**	**dīc**	**dīcite**
dūcō, *lead*	**dūce–**	**dūc**	**dūcite**
faciō, *do, make*	**face–**	**fac**	**facite**
ferō, *bear, carry*	**fere–**	**fer**	**ferte**

5. In the plural form *ferte* the short –*i* has been dropped.

▶ PRACTICE PATTERNS

A. Change the following forms to the plural:

1. dā	rege	es	properā	dīc
2. monē	fac	ī	venī	accipe

B. Change the following forms to the singular:

1. ferte	temptāte	nōlīte	este	vidēte
2. mūnīte	currite	dūcite	suscipite	īte

C. Write in Latin the present imperative singular and plural:

1. run	stay	drive	look	be present
2. go away	prepare	try	hear	read

63

SECTION 2 Negative Commands

▶ REVIEW HELPS

Negative commands may be expressed in Latin by using the present imperative of **nōlō**, *be unwilling, refuse*, with the present infinitive, active or passive. The present imperative of **nōlō** is:

nōlī (sing.), *be unwilling*   **nōlīte** (pl.), *be unwilling*

Do not (*Don't*) *fear* is translated into Latin as if it were *be unwilling to fear:*

Nōlī (Nōlīte) timēre.

SECTION 3 Vocative Case

DECLENSION	I	II	II	III	IV	V
Nominative	**Galba**	**Mārcus**	**Lūcius**	**Hector**	**Senātus**	**diēs**
Vocative	**Galba**	**Mārce**	**Lūci**	**Hector**	**Senātus**	**diēs**

▶ REVIEW HELPS

1. The vocative case in Latin is equivalent to the nominative of address in English. It is used when a person is directly addressed.

2. The vocative case is always the same in form as the nominative case, except in the singular of *–us* nouns and adjectives of the second declension. If the nominative singular ends in *–us*, the vocative singular ends in *–e*; if the nominative singular of a *proper noun* ends in *–ius*, the *–us* is dropped and the *–i* of the stem is lengthened. *Fīlius* is treated as if it were a proper noun. The vocative of adjectives in *–ius* is *–ie*.

3. The vocative of *deus* is the same as the nominative.

4. The vocative of *meus*, singular masculine, is *mī*, except with *deus;* the vocative plural of *meus* is *meī*.

5. Latin sentences rarely begin with a vocative case.

▶ PRACTICE PATTERNS

A. Translate into English:

1. Cūstōdīte canēs. 2. Dēdūc, nauta, nāvem. 3. Trahite caudīs bovēs. 4. Fer auxilium, Cornēlī. 5. Temptāte pābulum invenīre. 6. Dēmitte, Juppiter, imbrem lapidum. 7. Nōlī abripere, Cāce, quattuor bovēs. 8. Compelle, fortis homō, bovēs per montēs. 9. Nōlīte, mīlitēs, audāciam virī admīrārī. 10. Ferte, virī fēminaeque, ad bovēs pābulum.

64

B. Translate into Latin:

1. Help us, master! 2. Be brave, comrades! 3. Son of the king, hear us! 4. Make an attack, soldier! 5. Tell us a story, father! 6. Don't be afraid of difficulties, young men! 7. Do not carry off the stones, young man! 8. Guard the dog and the oxen, boy! 9. Launch the ship, brave comrades! 10. Don't admire evil, boys!

SECTION 4 Formation of Infinitives

▶ Review the formation of the infinitives of regular verbs, page 418 in the Appendix.

FORMATION OF INFINITIVES

TENSE	ACTIVE	PASSIVE
Present	Second Principal Part	1st, 2nd, 4th conj., change –e of act. infin. to –ī 3rd conj., change –ere of act. infin. to –ī
Perfect	Perfect Stem + –isse	Perf. Pass. Part. + esse
Future	Future Part. + esse	——————

▶ REVIEW HELPS

1. Infinitives are verbal nouns. They express the basic meaning of the verb, but they are not limited by the person and number of the subject.

2. In their verbal use infinitives have tense and voice; they may be modified by adverbs; and they may take the same case as other parts of the verb.

3. In their noun use infinitives are neuter in gender and singular in number, and they may be used as subjects or objects of other verbs.

INFINITIVES OF DEPONENT VERBS

TENSE	CONJ.	FORMULA	PASSIVE FORM, ACTIVE MEANING
Pres.	I II III III–io IV	Second Principal Part	cōnārī, *to try* verērī, *to fear* sequī, *to follow* patī, *to permit* largīrī, *to bestow*
Perf.	I–IV	Perf. Part. + esse	cōnātus esse, *to have tried*, etc.
Fut.	I–IV	Fut. Part. + esse	cōnātūrus esse, *to be about to try*

65

Infinitives of Irregular Verbs

TENSE	sum	possum	volō	ferō	eō
Present	esse, *to be*	posse, *to be able*	velle, *to wish*	ferre, *to carry*	īre, *to go*
Perfect	fuisse, *to have been*	potuisse, *to have been able*	voluisse, *to have wished*	tulisse, *to have carried*	īsse, iisse, *to have gone*
Future	futūrus esse, *to be about to be*	——	——	lātūrus esse, *to be about to carry*	itūrus esse, *to be about to go*

NOTE: For the infinitives of **nōlō, mālō,** and **fīō,** see pages 425–26 of the Appendix.

▶ PRACTICE PATTERNS

A. Identify the following infinitives and translate:

1. adesse nōluisse exitūrus esse arbitrātus esse
2. gessisse mūnītus esse fierī accipī
3. doctūrus esse clāmāvisse amāre vīsus esse

B. Write in Latin:

1. to come; to have gone; to be about to ask; to have been seized
2. to be carried; to follow; to be about to bestow; to be led
3. to suffer; to have been able; to have wished; to be about to go
4. to be praised; to have been; to be heard

SECTION 5 Uses of the Infinitive

CATEGORY		USE	TENSE OF INFINITIVE
Complementary	without subject	completes other verb	present
Subjective	with or without acc. subject	subject of impersonal verbs	present, perfect
Objective	with acc. subject	object of certain verbs	present
Indirect Statement	with acc. subject	object of certain verbs	present: same time as perfect: time before future: time after that of main verb

▶ REVIEW HELPS

1. The following verbs regularly use the *complementary infinitive:* **cōnor, cōnstituō, contendō, cupiō, dēbeō, dēsīderō, parō, possum, studeō, temptō, volō, nōlō.**

66

2. The following impersonal verbs regularly use the *subjective infinitive:* **est, erat, erit, oportet, necesse est.**

3. The following verbs frequently use the *infinitive as object:* **cōgō, cupiō, doceō, jubeō, patior, prohibeō, vetō.**

4. Verbs of mental action, such as saying, knowing, thinking, hearing, believing, seeing, and the like, are followed by an *indirect statement;* the subject of the clause is in the accusative case and the verb in the infinitive.

VERBS FOLLOWED BY INDIRECT STATEMENT

SAYING	KNOWING	THINKING	PERCEIVING
dīcō, *say*	**cōgnōvi,** *know*	**arbitror,** *think*	**audiō,** *hear*
negō, *deny*	**sciō,** *know*	**exīstimō,** *think*	**sentiō,** *perceive*
respondeō, *reply*		**putō,** *think*	**videō,** *see*
nūntiō, *announce*		**jūdicō,** *judge*	**intellegō,** *understand*
loquor, *speak*		**crēdō,** *believe*	**animadvertō,** *notice*
jūrō, *swear*		**spērō,** *hope*	**cōgnōscō,** *find out*
certiōrem faciō, *inform*			

5. In indirect statement:

    a. The *present* infinitive indicates the *same time* as the main verb.

    b. The *perfect* infinitive indicates *time before* that of the main verb.

    c. The *future* infinitive indicates *time after* that of the main verb.

6. Verbs of hoping, promising, and swearing are always followed by the future infinitive.

7. **Dīco,** *say,* cannot be used if it is followed by the negative; it must be replaced by **negō,** *say not, deny.*

8. The participle of the compound infinitive in indirect discourse is always in the accusative case and agrees with its subject in gender and number.

9. A predicate noun or adjective used with an infinitive in indirect discourse is always in the accusative case and agrees with its subject in gender and number.

10. When the speaker makes a statement about himself in indirect discourse, the reflexive pronoun is used.

▶ PRACTICE PATTERNS

A. Translate into English. Identify the infinitives.

1. Facile est nāvem dēdūcere. 2. Cōnstituit montēs trānsīre. 3. Coēgit bovēs montēs trānsīre. 4. Bovēs montēs trānsīre oportet. 5. Gēryōn jūrāvit sē bovēs nōn trāditūrum esse. 6. Intellēxit bovēs ā Cācō abreptōs esse. 7. Dīxit tria corpora inter sē conjungī. 8. Dīcitur Cācus bovēs caudīs trāxisse.

67

B. Translate into Latin. Identify the infinitives.

1. We hoped that he would find the oxen. 2. Did you think that the men were sleeping? 3. Hercules ordered the men to launch the ship. 4. Who perceived that the food had been carried off? 5. Was the god able to send down a shower of stones? 6. Does he not know that the dogs have been carried off? 7. It was necessary to drive the dogs through the streets. 8. He understood that there would be a shower of stones.

WORDS TO MASTER

abripiō, –ere, –uī, –reptus, snatch away, carry off

admīror (1), wonder at, admire (*admiration*)

canis, –is, *m.&f.,* dog (*canine*)

cauda, –ae, *f.,* tail (*caudal*)

compellō, –ere, –pulī, –pulsus, drive together, force back, drive (*compel*)

conjungō, –ere, –jūnxī, –jūnctus, join together, join (*conjunction*)

dēdūcō, –ere, –dūxī, –ductus, lead down or away, bring; **nāvem dēducere,** to launch a ship (*deduce*)

dēmittō, –ere, –mīsī, –missus, send down, let fall (*demise*)

difficultās, –tātis, *f.,* difficulty

dormiō, –īre, –īvī, –itūrus, sleep (*dormitory*)

fretum, –ī, *n.,* strait

imber, imbris, *m.,* rain, shower (*imbricate*)

incommodum, –ī, *n.,* inconvenience, harm (*incommodious*)

lapis, –idis, *m.,* stone (*lapidary*)

pābulum, –ī, *n.,* food, fodder (*pabulum*)

satis, *adv.,* enough, sufficiently (*satisfy*)

BUILDING WORD POWER

The fundamental meaning of *agere, āctum* is *to set in motion.* It has also the meanings *drive, do, treat, wear,* and *go.* Because it has many compounds in Latin, it has many derivatives in English. These can be recognized by the roots and stems *ag–, agit–, git–, ig–, g–, act–, actu–.*

From *ag–* we have the English words *agent, agenda, agile;* from *āct–* we have *act, actor, action, active, actual.* From *cōgere* (*cum + agere*) we derive the words *cogent* and *cogency;* from *exigere* (*ex + agere*), *exigency, exact;* from *redigere* (*re + d + agere*), *redactor;* **retroagere** (*retrō + agere*), *retroact;* **trānsigere** (*trāns + agere*), *transact.*

A new verb was formed to make *agitāre, to keep doing, disturb.* With *cum* it became. *cōgitāre, to turn over in the mind, to consider.* What English words were derived from these Latin verbs?

When a verb is compounded with anything other than a preposition, the verb formed is of the first conjugation. What English verbs are derived from these compounds of *agere: nāvigāre, fūmigāre, castigāre, lītigāre, mītigāre, variegāre?* If **ambigere** (*amb* + *agere*) means *to go from side to side, to be doubtful,* what does *ambiguous* mean? How did the *prodigal* (**prodigere, pro** + **d** + **agere,** *to spend*) waste his money? Does jelly *coagulate?*

SENTENCE PATTERNS

A. Translate into English:

1. Intellege, Herculēs, rem esse satis difficilem.
2. Nōlī putāre necesse esse mīlitem per multās terrās iter facere.
3. Dīcitur Herculēs māgnum incommodum ex sōle accēpisse.
4. Exīstimāsne sōlem summam audāciam virī admīrārī?
5. Dīc nūllam nāvem in hīs regiōnibus invenīrī posse.
6. Num nautās nāvem dēdūcere et bovēs caudīs trahere jūssit?
7. Nōlīte nūntiāre, comitēs, deum imbrem lapidum ē caelō dēmīsisse.
8. Nōlī crēdere tria corpora mōnstrī inter sē conjūncta esse.
9. Nōn crēdō Herculem in utrōque lītore fretī columnās cōnstituisse.
10. Bovēs sine pābulō compellere trāns montēs erat rēs summae difficultātis.

B. Translate into Latin:

1. Announce to the king, my son, that Cacus snatched away the oxen and dragged them by their tails into the cave.
2. Don't say, boys, that the oxen were guarded by a dog.
3. Neither grain nor fodder was able to be found on the mountains.
4. To launch a ship was difficult enough, but to drive oxen across the mountains was much more difficult.
5. Bring help, Cornelius, and try to save the ship!

Tenth Labor: The Capture of Geryon's Oxen

Tum vērō missus est Herculēs ad īnsulam Erythēam et bovēs Gēryonis redūcere jūssus est. Rēs erat satis difficilis quod bovēs ab Eurytiōne et ā cane bicipite (*two-headed*) cūstōdiēbantur. Ipse autem Gēryon horribilem aspectum habēbat; tria corpora inter sē conjūncta sunt. Herculēs etsī intellēxit māxımum perīculum esse tamen negōtium suscēpit. Per multās terrās iter fēcit et tandem ad eam partem Āfricae pervēnit quae Eurōpae proxima est. Ibi in utrōque lītore fretī, quod Eurōpam ab Āfricā dīvidit, columnās cōnstituit, quae posteā Herculis Columnae appellābantur.

Herculēs dum hīc manet, māgnum incommodum ex calōre (*heat*) sōlis accipiēbat. Tandem īrā commōtus, arcum suum intendit et

Hercules fighting the three-bodied Geryon.

sōlem sagittīs petīvit. Sōl tamen audāciam virī admīrātus est et eī
nāvem auream dedit. Herculēs hoc dōnum laetē accēpit, quod
nūllam nāvem in hīs regiōnibus invenīre potuerat. Tum nāvem
dēdūxit et post breve tempus ad īnsulam pervēnit. Postquam ex
incolīs locum ubi bovēs abditī sunt cōgnōvit, in eam partem statim
profectus est, atque ā rēge Gēryone bovēs postulāvit. Quod tamen
ille hōs trādere nōlēbat, Herculēs et rēgem ipsum et Eurytiōnem
statim interfēcit. Tum per Hispāniam et Liguriam bovēs compellere cōnstituit.

Ligurēs autem, dum ille per fīnēs eōrum iter facit, māgnās
cōpiās coēgērunt atque eum longius prōgredī prohibēbant. Ille
paene omnem spem salūtis āmīserat, sed Juppiter imbrem lapidum
ingentium ē caelō dēmīsit et māgnus numerus Ligurum interfectus est.

Postquam Ligurēs hōc modō superātī sunt, Herculēs celerrimē
prōgressus est et post paucōs diēs ad Alpēs pervēnit. Eās trānsīre
erat rēs summae difficultātis. In hīs regiōnibus neque frūmentum
neque pābulum invenīrī poterat. Herculēs autem māgnam cōpiam
frūmentī et pābulī comparāvit et, contrā omnium opiniōnem, bovēs
in Ītaliam trādūxit.

Brevī tempore ad flūmen Tiberim vēnit. Nōn longē ā flūmine
erat spēlunca in quā Cācus, horribile mōnstrum, tum habitābat.
Dum Herculēs dormit, Cācus quattuor bovēs abripuit. Etsī bovēs
caudīs in spēluncam trāxit, Herculēs tamen eōs invēnit quod ūnus
ē būbus quōs sēcum habuit mūgīre (*to bellow*) incēpit et eī quī in
spēluncā erant mūgītum reddidērunt. Horribilī mōnstrō ab Hercule interfectō, cum omnibus būbus ille domum profectus est.

70

The emptiness of ages in his face
And on his back the burden of the world.
—Edwin Markham, 1852–1940

Unit **VIII**

CONVERSATION

ATLĀS: Salvē, advena! Quis es tū quī ad hanc extrēmam partem orbis terrārum venīs? Quā dē causā hūc properās?

HERCULĒS: Herculēs appellor. Ego per multās terrās vagātus multōs hominēs rogāvī: "Ubi est hortus Hesperidum?" Sed quis es tū? Cūr tam ingēns corpus habēs?

ATLĀS: Ego Atlās sum, quī caelum umerīs meīs sustinēns terram servō.

HERCULĒS: Tantus labor est! Sed auxilium mihi petentī fer! Audīvistīne cāsū aliquid dē hortō Hesperidum?

ATLĀS: Quō cōnsiliō hunc hortum reperīre vīs?

HERCULĒS: Eurystheus, dominus meus, multīs labōribus ā mē jam cōnfectīs, nunc mē pōma aurea ex hortō Hesperidum referre jubet.

ATLĀS: Hortum bene sciō; nam Hesperidēs sunt fīliae meae. Sed difficillimum est pōma ex hortō auferre. Tē adjuvante, bonum cōnsilium cēpī! Sī tū hoc pondus sustinēbis, ego ipse ad hortum properābō et mox hūc cum pōmīs redībō. Quid dīcis?

HERCULĒS: Gaudeō negōtium suscipere sī tū pōma referēs! Properā! (*Atlās, caelō umerīs Herculis impositō, discēdit.*)

SECTION 1 Participles

▶ Review the participles of regular transitive verbs, page 418 of the Appendix.

FORMATION OF PARTICIPLES

TENSE	ACTIVE	PASSIVE
Present	Pres. Stem + –ns, –ntis	
Perfect	——	Fourth Principal Part of Verb
Future	Part. Stem + –ūrus, –a, –um	

▶ REVIEW HELPS

1. Participles are verbal adjectives; the future and perfect participles are declined like adjectives of the first and second declensions; the present

71

participle, when used as an adjective, is declined like *potēns,* page 407; as a participle, the ablative singular regularly ends in –*e: vocante.*

2. Participles can themselves govern the same case as the verbs from which they are derived.

PARTICIPLES OF DEPONENT VERBS

TENSE	CONJ.	LATIN	ENGLISH
Present	I II III III–io IV	cōnāns, cōnantis verēns, verentis sequēns, sequentis patiēns, patientis largiēns, largientis	*trying, while trying* *fearing, while fearing* *following, while following* *permitting, while permitting* *bestowing, while bestowing*
Perfect	I–IV	cōnātus, –a, –um	*having tried, after trying*
Future	I–IV	cōnātūrus, –a, –um	*about to (going to, intending to) try*

▶ REVIEW HELPS

1. The present and future participles of deponent verbs are formed regularly and are active in meaning. The perfect participle is passive in form but active in meaning.

2. The perfect participle of a deponent verb may be used to express the same idea as an English perfect active participle: *cōnātus = having tried.*

PARTICIPLES OF IRREGULAR VERBS

TENSE	sum	volō	eō	fīō
Pres.	——	volēns, –entis, *wishing, willing,* *while wishing*	iēns, euntis, *going,* *while going*	——
Perf.	——	——	——	factus, –a, um, *having been done*
Fut.	futūrus, –a, –um, *about to be*	——	itūrus, –a, –um, *about to go*	

▶ REVIEW HELPS

1. The verb *sum* has no present participle. *Absēns* and *praesēns* are from compounds of *sum: absum* and *praesum. Potēns,* from *possum,* is used only as an adjective meaning *powerful.*

2. The participles of the irregular verb *ferō* are formed regularly.

3. The participle of the verb *nōlō* is similar in form to *volō.*

72

▶ PRACTICE PATTERNS

A. Write in Latin and translate the participles of: spectō, conjungō, abripiō, dormiō, admīror, auferō, augeō, audeō.

B. Translate into Latin the italicized words:

1. The soldier *fighting* bravely was wounded. 2. They captured the *fleeing* soldiers. 3. The enemy took the city *fortified* by a ditch. 4. The *conquered* leaders were sent to Caesar. 5. *Wishing* to escape, the slaves hid in the woods. 6. They saw the master *about to follow* the slaves. 7. The *fugitives* (Those fleeing) were caught. 8. *Having been alarmed* by these things, the enemy fled.

SECTION 2 Use of the Present Participle

Fugientēs servī captī sunt.

As adjective:	a. The *fleeing* slaves were caught.
As participle:	b. *While fleeing* ⎫ the slaves were caught. c. *Fleeing* ⎭
As subordinate clause: (temporal) (concessive) (conditional) (relative)	d. *While they were fleeing* ⎫ e. *When they were fleeing* ⎪ f. *As they were fleeing* ⎬ the slaves were caught. g. *Although they were fleeing* ⎪ h. *If they were fleeing* ⎭ i. The slaves *who were fleeing* were caught.
As principal clause:	j. The slaves *were fleeing* and they were caught.

▶ REVIEW HELPS

1. The present participle may be the equivalent of a relative clause or a noun:

fugiēns = *he who flees, a fugitive*

2. In English a present participle is sometimes used when it refers to an action completed before the time of the main verb. In translating this *false present* into Latin, the ablative absolute construction is used.

Receiving his reward, he departed.   *Praemiō acceptō*, **discessit.**

3. Since there is no present passive participle in Latin, **dum** with the passive indicative, present tense, must be used to express *while* if the verb is passive.

Dum haec geruntur, **cōpiās coēgit.**   *While this (these things) was going on, he mobilized the troops.*

73

4. The perfect participle of a deponent verb is often translated as if it were a present participle, but it regularly denotes an action that was begun *before* the time of the main verb.

> **Virōs *cohortātus*, discessit.**   *Having encouraged (After encouraging)*
>   *the men, he departed.*

▶ PRACTICE PATTERNS

A. Translate into English the italicized words:

1. *Dēcidentī* auxilium tulit. 2. Clāmor *fugientium* audītus est. 3. Nōnne vīdit virōs pōma *auferentēs?* 4. Fortiter *pūgnāns* bovēs superat. 5. Iter *facientēs* vidēre nōn poterat. 6. Eum fīliābus *persuādentem* repperimus. 7. Ā mercātōribus dōna *offerentibus* inducuntur. 8. Num hominem pondus caelī *sustinentem* vidit?

B. Translate into Latin the italicized words or phrases:

1. The merchant, *while offering* the gift, was captured. 2. He saw the man *fleeing* from the garden. 3. *Desiring* rest, he nevertheless obeyed the king. 4. *Trying* to find the apples, he arrived at the end of the world. 5. He saved the world *while bearing* the weight of the sky.

SECTION 3 Use of the Future Active Participle

▶ REVIEW HELPS

1. The combination of the future active participle with *esse* forms the future active infinitive. (See p. 65.)

2. The Latin future active participle is translated into English, which has no future participle, by such roundabout expressions of the future as *about to, going to, intend to.* The word we use for *roundabout* in Latin grammar is *periphrastic.* The combination of the *future active participle* with *sum* is called the *active periphrastic conjugation.*

> **Discessūrus est.**   *He is about to leave.*
> **Discessūra erat.**   *She was going to leave.*
> **Discessūrī fuerant.**   *They had intended to leave.*

▶ PRACTICE PATTERNS

A. Translate into English:

1. Vir ad Graeciam profectūrus est. 2. Avē Imperātor! Nōs moritūrī tē salūtāmus! 3. Num mercātōrēs hortum repertūrī sunt? 4. Fīliae patrī pōma trāditūrae erant. 5. Atlās discessūrus caelum umerīs Herculis imposuit.

B. Translate into Latin:

1. We were about to offer you a gift. 2. They saw the man who was about to carry away the apples. 3. He is going to sustain the weight on his shoulders. 4. Does he intend to ask the merchants about the garden? 5. They were about to depart from home.

SECTION 4 Use of the Perfect Passive Participle

Cōpiae _victae_ erant miserae.

As adjective:	a. The _conquered_ troops were unhappy.		
As participle:	b.	_conquered_	
	c.	_being conquered_	
	d. The troops	_on being conquered_	were unhappy.
	e.	_after being conquered_	
	f.	_having been conquered_	
As subordinate clause: (temporal)	g.	_when they were conquered_	
	h.	_after they had been conquered_	
(causal)	i. The troops	_since they had been conquered_	were unhappy.
(concessive)	j.	_although they had been conquered_	
(conditional)	k.	_if they had been conquered_	
(relative)	l.	_who had been conquered_	
As principal clause:	m. The troops _were conquered_ and were unhappy.		

▶ REVIEW HELPS

1. Combined with the various tenses of **_sum_,** the perfect passive participle forms the perfect passive system of the indicative and the subjunctive:

vocātus sum, eram, erō; sim, essem

2. Combined with **_esse_,** the perfect passive participle forms the perfect passive infinitive: **_vocātus esse._**

3. The perfect participle of a deponent or semideponent verb usually has an active meaning.

Pūgnāre _ausus_ cōnsul hostēs superāvit.   The consul _having dared_ to fight defeated the enemy.

4. Participles may be used as predicate adjectives.

Gallia est _dīvīsa._   Gaul is _divided._

75

5. Latin seldom uses short sentences joined by **et.** Instead, the most important action in an English compound sentence is translated into Latin by the main verb, and all previous actions become participles or subordinate clauses.

The soldiers *were seen* and *captured.*	**Mīlitēs *vīsī captī sunt.***
He *led* the men into the camp and *left* them.	**Virōs in castra *ductōs relīquit.***

▶ PRACTICE PATTERNS

A. Translate into English:

1. Vīsus ab hostibus fūgī. 2. Oblāta pōma accēpit. 3. Vir ausus circum orbem terrārum iter facere hortum repperit. 4. Sententiā mercātōrum graviter commōtī erant. 5. Multī aurī cupiditāte inductī in terram longinquam profectī sunt.

B. Translate into Latin:

1. The conquered man tried to escape. 2. The garden, surrounded on all sides by a huge wall, was easily seen. 3. Having tried in vain to find the garden, he asked for help. 4. The man had sustained the weight for a long time and was exhausted. 5. He rejoiced to undertake the business.

SECTION 5 Ablative Absolute

▶ REVIEW HELPS

1. An ablative absolute phrase consists of two words in the ablative case:

    a. A *noun* or *pronoun* with a *perfect passive participle:*

Hortō repertō, pōma abstulit.	*When he had found the garden,* he carried away the apples.

    b. A *noun* or *pronoun* with a *present participle:*

Fīliābus spectantibus, Atlās pōma auferēbat.	*While his daughters were watching,* Atlas was carrying away the apples.

    c. A *noun* or *pronoun* with a *noun* or *adjective*: (**Sum** has no present participle.)

Eō duce, pōma abstulērunt.	*Under his leadership,* they carried away the apples.
Amīcō meō vīvō, Rōmānī nōn superātī sunt.	*In the lifetime of my friend,* the Romans were not defeated.

76

2. The ablative absolute phrase has no grammatical connection with the rest of the sentence.

TRANSLATION OF THE ABLATIVE ABSOLUTE

Pōmīs acceptīs, discessit.

Literal translation:	a. *The apples having been received*, he departed.

As subordinate clause:
    (temporal)
 	
    (causal)
 	
    (concessive)
    (conditional)
	b. *When the apples had been received*
	c. *After the apples had been received*
	d. *Since the apples had been received*
	e. *Because the apples had been received* ⎫ he departed.
	f. *As the apples had been received*
	g. *Although the apples had been received*
	h. *If he received the apples*

As principal clause:	i. *The apples were received*, and he departed.

▶ REVIEW HELPS

1. Ablative absolute phrases in Latin are best translated into English by subordinate adverbial clauses.

2. An English subordinate adverbial clause is often best expressed in Latin by an ablative absolute phrase.

3. Many English participial phrases containing a perfect active participle cannot be translated literally into Latin. Methods of translating such phrases are as follows:

    a. If the participle is from a *transitive verb* (for example, *Having received the apples*, he departed), change the participial phrase into passive form and use the *ablative absolute* construction:

When he had received the apples, he departed.   **Pōmīs acceptīs**, discessit.

    b. When a *deponent verb* is available, the sentence may be translated literally:

Having tried to carry off the apples, he departed.   **Pōma auferre cōnātus**, discessit.

    c. If the participle is from an intransitive verb and no deponent verb is available, such phrases *must* be translated into Latin by a clause with **ubi** + *the perfect indicative* or **cum** + *the pluperfect subjunctive.*

Hercules, *having arrived* at the garden, took away the apples.   **Hercülēs, *ubi* ad hortum *pervēnit*, pōma abstulit.**
Hercules, *cum* ad hortum *pervēnisset*, pōma abstulit.

77

► PRACTICE PATTERNS

A. Translate into English. Identify the ablative absolute constructions.

1. Ipse, cōgnitā locōrum nātūrā, ad nāvem sē recēpit. 2. Hāc sententiā nūntiātā, ex urbe discessit. 3. Hercule prīncipe, hortus repertus est. 4. Rēge mortuō, fīlia rēgnum occupāvit. 5. Nautīs volentibus, dux in īnsulā mānsit.

B. Using the ablative absolute, express the following in Latin.

1. since our men are unwilling 2. after the garden was found 3. when the serpent was killed 4. if the island is distant 5. although the apples were carried away 6. under the leadership of Hercules 7. while the merchants were watching 8. after the signal had been given

WORDS TO MASTER

at, *conj.,* but, yet
auferō, –ferre, abstulī, ablātus, *irreg.,* carry away (*ablative*)
dēcidō, –ere, –cidī, —, fall, fall down (*deciduous*)
dracō, –ōnis, *m.,* dragon, serpent
hortus, –ī, *m.,* garden (*horticulture*)
longinquus, –a, –um, *adj.,* remote, distant
mercātor, –ōris, *m.,* merchant, trader (*mercantile*)
offerō, –ferre, obtulī, oblātus, *irreg.,* present, proffer (*offer*)

orbis, –is, *m.,* circle (*orbit*); **orbis terrārum,** the world
pareō, –ēre, –uī, —, obey
pōmum, –ī, *n.,* apple, fruit (*pomiculture*)
pondus, –eris, *n.,* weight (*ponderous*)
quiēs, –ētis, *f.,* rest, sleep (*quiet*)
reperiō, –īre, repperī, repertus, find, discover
sententia, –ae, *f.,* feeling, thinking, view (*sentence*)
umerus (humerus), –ī, *m.,* shoulder, upper arm (*humeral*)

BUILDING WORD POWER

Vertere, versum, to turn, to turn around, is another important Latin root word, both in Latin and in English. Write the present infinitives of the Latin verbs that gave the following words to English: *advert, avert, convert, divert, evert, invert, obvert, pervert, revert, subvert. Extrovert* and *introvert* have been coined in modern times. What do they mean?

Vertex was the turning point about which something turns, the top. (*Vortex,* another form of the same word, came to mean a *whirlpool.*) *Vertigo* is *a whirling around, a dizziness. Vertebra (–ae),* something on which to turn, *a joint,* is a joint or a bone of the spine. The noun **versus,** from meaning a *turning,* came to mean *a line of writing, of poetry,* hence, our word *verse.* **Prōversus,** *turned forward,* was shortened to **prōsus,** and we have our word *prose* from **prōsa ōrātiō,** straightforward or unmetrical speech. **Adversus,** *turned opposite,* became *adverse, unfavorable.* The face of a coin is the *obverse* (turned toward one) side, the other is the *reverse* (turned back) side. Explain *inverse, divers, diverse.*

The frequentative (formed on the fourth principal part) verb **versō,** *to turn about often,* and the deponent **versor,** *to remain, to be engaged in,* and their compounds gave us a few English words.

What do the italicized words mean: *controversial* subject; pleasant *conversation; versatile* student; *universal* interest; biased *version; invertebrate* animal; happy *anniversary?*

SENTENCE PATTERNS

A. Translate into English:

1. Quis virum fortem jūssit pōma puellīs pulchrīs commissa referre?
2. Opus, quod rēx Herculī imperāverat, erat summae difficultātis.
3. Multī hominēs pecūniae cupiditāte inductī nihil certum reperīre poterant.
4. Tōtō annō intermissō, ad extrēmam partem orbis terrārum pervēnit.
5. Caelum dēcidere nōn poterat, quod vir quīdam umerīs suīs id sustinēbat.
6. Nōnne gāvīsus est oblātum auxilium accipere?
7. Cui nūntiāvit necesse esse aliquem pondus caelī umerīs sustinēre?
8. Herculēs hāc morā graviter commōtus, tandem quīntō diē patrem puellārum redeuntem vīdit.
9. Hae patrī suō paruērunt quī pōma ex hortō longinquō auferre poterat.
10. Mercātor eum sententiam rogāvit at vir, quiētem vehementer cupiēns, respondēre nōlēbat.

B. Translate into Latin:

1. Why did anyone wishing to find apples come to the end of the world?
2. I know the garden well, but it is very difficult to take away the apples, which are guarded by a dragon with a hundred heads.
3. We cannot give you these apples entrusted to us by the goddess.
4. You yourself sustain the weight of the heaven a little longer.
5. The brave man, about to despair, accepted the proffered help.

Eleventh Labor: Search for the Golden Apples

Undecimus labor quem Eurystheus Herculī imposuit multō erat gravior quam eī quōs suprā narrāvimus. Jūssit eum aurea pōma ex hortō Hesperidum auferre. Hesperidēs erant pulcherrimae nymphae quae in terrā longinquā habitābant et quibus aurea pōma ā Jūnōne commissa erant. Multī hominēs, aurī cupiditāte inductī, haec pōma auferre jam anteā cōnātī erant. Rēs tamen difficillima erat, quod hortus in quō pōma erant mūrō ingentī undique circumdatus est. Praetereā dracō quīdam, quī centum capita habēbat, portam hortī dīligenter cūstōdiēbat.

Herculēs, etsī quiētem vehementer cupiēbat, cōnstituit tamen Eurystheō parēre. Multōs mercātōrēs sententiam rogāvit; nihil certum dē domiciliō Hesperidum scīvērunt. Frūstrā per multās terrās iter fēcit. Tandem ad extrēmam partem terrae, quae proxima erat Oceānō, pervēnit. Hīc stābat vir quīdam, nōmine Atlās, quī caelum (ita fāma erat) umerīs suīs sustinēbat et in terram dēcidere prohibēbat. Herculēs statim in colloquium cum Atlante vēnit et, postquam causam itineris exposuit, auxilium ab eō petīvit.

Atlās Herculem māximē adjuvāre potuit, quod ipse erat pater Hesperidum et locum hortī bene scīvit. "Ipse," inquit, "ad hortum ībō; fīliae meae certē mihi pōma dabunt." Herculēs, ubi haec

Atlas bringing Hercules the golden apples.

audīvit, gāvīsus est; rem sine vī cōnficere māximē cupiēbat. Cōnstituit igitur oblātum auxilium accipere. Sed quod Atlās discessūrus erat, necesse erat aliquem caelum umerīs sustinēre. Hoc negōtium Herculēs laetus suscēpit, et tōtum pondus caelī complūrēs diēs sōlus sustinuit.

Atlās intereā ad hortum Hesperidum, quī pauca mīlia passuum aberat, sē quam celerrimē contulerat. At fīliae ējus diū dubitāvērunt patrī pōma ab ipsā Jūnōne accepta dare. Atlās tamen eīs persuāsit ac pōma ad Herculem rettulit.

Dum haec geruntur, Herculēs, quī plūrēs diēs exspectāverat neque ūllam fāmam dē reditū Atlantis accēperat, hāc morā graviter commōtus est. Tandem quīntō diē Atlantem vīdit redeuntem, et mox pōma māgnā cum laetitiā accēpit. Tum postquam Atlantī grātiās prō tantō beneficiō ēgit, ad Graeciam proficīscī properāvit.

PART II
New Syntax

Rather would I, in the sun's warmth divine,
Serve a poor churl who drags his days in grief,
Than the whole lordship of the dead were mine.
—Homer, circa 850 B.C.

CONVERSATION

HERCULĒS (*sēcum loquitur*): Eheu! (*Alas!*) Redeat tandem Atlās iste! Tot labōrēs cōnfēcī sed hic pessimus omnium vidētur! Umerī et tergum et membra mea dolent (*ache*)!

ATLĀS (*nōn longē abest*): Avē, Herculēs! Pōma reportāvī!

HERCULĒS: Revēnistī tandem! Diū tē exspectāvī! Quae est causa morae?

ATLĀS: Fīliae meae pōma mihi trādere diū dubitāvērunt. Hoc mūnus ā Jūnōne accēperant; deam timent. Sed tamen postquam ego eīs persuāsī, pōma mihi trādidērunt. Laudentur!

HERCULĒS: Dā mihi pōma, et hoc pondus removeātur!

ATLĀS: Sī tibi placet, caelum paulō diūtius sustinē, dum ego haec pōma aurea ad Eurystheum reportō. Es (*Be*) tranquillus! Reveniam!

HERCULĒS: Cōnsilium tuum bonum vidētur, sed prīmum cape hoc pondus dum pulvīnum (*cushion*) umerīs meīs impōnō!

ATLĀS: Certē! Sed properēmus! Ego ad Eurystheum quam prīmum proficīscī cupiō.

HERCULĒS (*pōma accipiēns*): Tū caelum sustinē, dum ego ad rēgem cum hīs pōmīs proficīscor. Valē! Et māximās grātiās tibi agō.

SECTION 1 Subjunctive Mood

▶ DISCUSSION

1. In both English and Latin there are three finite moods: the *indicative*, the *imperative*, and the *subjunctive*. The *indicative* in both languages is commonly used to state a fact or to ask a direct question. The *imperative* in both languages expresses a command.

2. In English the *subjunctive* mood is not so commonly used as formerly,

but it is still often heard in such sentences as: *If this be true . . ., If I were he . . ., Long live the King!* In Latin, however, forms of the verb in the subjunctive appear on almost every page of normal text.

3. The subjunctive may be used in principal (independent) and subordinate (dependent) clauses. It can express the ideas of command, purpose, result, indirect question, and the like, and the English translation must contain these ideas.

4. Sometimes the Latin subjunctive may be translated by the English indicative, and sometimes with the aid of auxiliary verbs such as *may, might, can, could, would,* and *should.*

5. The subjunctive mood in Latin has four tenses. It has no future or future perfect.

6. The person indicators (P.I.), active and passive, are the same as in the indicative, except that *–m,* never *–ō,* is always used in the first person active. The indicators of the perfect indicative active differ from those of the other tenses, as has been noted before.

SECTION 2 Formation of the Present Subjunctive

▶ DISCUSSION

1. The *base,* or *root,* of a verb is the same as the present stem minus the inflection vowel: *vocā–, monē–, rege–, cape–, audī–* are *present stems; voc/, mon/, reg/, cap/, aud/* are bases, or roots.

2. Each tense of the subjunctive has its own indicator by which the particular form can be easily identified. In the first conjugation the tense indicator (T.I.) for the present tense is long *–ē,* and for the second, third, and fourth conjugations it is long *–ā.*

PRESENT SUBJUNCTIVE ACTIVE, FIRST CONJUGATION

	Base + T.I. + P.I. =	*Form*	*Possible Translation*
	SINGULAR		
First	**voc**/ + **ē** + **m**	= **vocem**	*I may call*
Second	**voc**/ + **ē** + **s**	= **vocēs**	*you may call*
Third	**voc**/ + **ē** + **t**	= **vocet**	*he, she, it may call*
	PLURAL		
First	**voc**/ + **ē** + **mus**	= **vocēmus**	*we may call*
Second	**voc**/ + **ē** + **tis**	= **vocētis**	*you may call*
Third	**voc**/ + **ē** + **nt**	= **vocent**	*they may call*

The Latin present subjunctive is translated into English not only by *may*, but by *let, should, would,* or by the indicative present or future, according to the nature of the clause in which the subjunctive stands.

PRESENT SUBJUNCTIVE ACTIVE

CONJUGATION:	SECOND	THIRD	THIRD –io	FOURTH
	Base + **eā**	*Base* + **ā**	*Base* + **iā**	*Base* + **iā**
		SINGULAR		
First	moneam	regam	capiam	audiam
Second	moneās	regās	capiās	audiās
Third	moneat	regat	capiat	audiat
		PLURAL		
First	moneāmus	regāmus	capiāmus	audiāmus
Second	moneātis	regātis	capiātis	audiātis
Third	moneant	regant	capiant	audiant

▶ STUDY HELPS

1. The vowel before the personal ending remains the same throughout.
2. The quantity of vowels changes as in the indicative mood.
3. The passive voice is formed regularly by substituting the passive indicators for the active ones. (See Appendix, pp. 416–17, or the paradigm for deponents below.)

PRESENT SUBJUNCTIVE, DEPONENT VERBS

CONJUGATION:	FIRST	SECOND	THIRD	THIRD –io	FOURTH
	Base + **ē**	*Base* + **eā**	*Base* + **ā**	*Base* + **iā**	*Base* + **iā**
			SINGULAR		
First	cōner	verear	sequar	patiar	oriar
Second	cōnēris	vereāris	sequāris	patiāris	oriāris
Third	cōnētur	vereātur	sequātur	patiātur	oriātur
			PLURAL		
First	cōnēmur	vereāmur	sequāmur	patiāmur	oriāmur
Second	cōnēminī	vereāminī	sequāminī	patiāminī	oriāminī
Third	cōnentur	vereantur	sequantur	patiantur	oriantur

PRESENT SUBJUNCTIVE, IRREGULAR VERBS

Sum	Possum	Volō	Eō	Ferō	Fīō
sim	possim	velim	eam	feram	fīam
sīs	possīs	velīs	eās	ferās	fīās
sit	possit	velit	eat	ferat	fīat
sīmus	possīmus	velīmus	eāmus	ferāmus	fīāmus
sītis	possītis	velītis	eātis	ferātis	fīātis
sint	possint	velint	eant	ferant	fīant

83

Volō, nōlō, mālō, and **sum** and its compounds are the only Latin verbs that have an *–i* in the present subjunctive. For **nōlō** and **mālō,** see page 426 of the Appendix.

▶ PRACTICE PATTERNS

A. Write the third person singular of the present subjunctive, active and passive, of the following verbs: mergō, reportō, parcō, corripiō, reperiō. Translate by using *let.*

B. Write the third person plural of the present subjunctive of the following verbs. Translate by using *may.*

1. adeō	cōnferō	polliceor	proficīscor
2. adsum	vagor	cohortor	ēgredior

C. Using *let* or *may*, translate into English:

1. sequāmur	vereantur	fiat	eant	vocēminī
2. cōnētur	oriātur	ferāminī	patiāris	moneātur

D. Translate into Latin:

1. they may offer	he may run away	let them be surrounded
2. let him descend	let us approach	it may be carried back
3. you (sing.) may be	let it be sunk	they may be unwilling
4. let him be	they may become	you (pl.) may be carried
5. let us go	we may be able	you (sing.) may be carried

SECTION 3 Subjunctive Used in the Main Verb

▶ DISCUSSION

1. The subjunctive mood in independent sentences expresses the action of the verb *not as a fact* but as an *idea.* The action is willed or wished for; it indicates possibility; or it implies uncertainty.

2. These subjunctives are classified as *volitive* (willed), *optative* (wished for), *potential* (possible), *deliberative* (question in which uncertainty is implied).

PATTERNS	LATIN	ENGLISH	NEGATIVE
Volitive			
a. Hortatory	**Exeāmus.**	*Let us go out.*	**Nē**
b. Jussive	**Exeant.**	*Let them go out.*	**Nē**
Optative	**Exeās!**	*May you go out!*	**Nē**
Potential	**Aliquis exeat.**	*Someone may go out.*	**nōn**
Deliberative	**Quid faciam!**	*What shall I do!*	**nōn**

84

▶ **PRACTICE PATTERNS**

A. Translate into English:

1. Adeāmus	Quid dīcam!	Nē dīcātur	Corripiantur
2. Adeant	Fīat	Ferantur	Reportēmus
3. Adeās	Velīmus	Cingāmur	Nē polliceāmur
4. Aliquis adeat	Sīmus	Dēscendant	Nē refugiātis

B. Translate into Latin.

1. Let us go. 2. Let us not join. 3. Whom shall we seize! 4. Let him run away 5. Let them go. 6. Someone may think. 7. Let us not promise. 8. Don't let him go. 9. May you depart. 10. Let him promise. 11. Don't let it sink. 12. Someone may escape. 13. Let it be done. 14. Let him go out. 15. Let us descend. 16. What shall we say!

WORDS TO MASTER

adeo, –īre, –iī, –itūrus, *irreg.,* go to, approach; **aditus, –ūs,** *m.,* approach, entrance

adjungō, –ere, –jūnxī, –jūnctus, join to, unite with (*adjunct*)

atrium, –ī, *n.,* hall (*atrium*)

cingo, –ere, cīnxī, cīnctus, surround, encircle (*cincture*)

corripiō, –ere, –uī, –reptus, snatch up, seize

dēscendō, –ere, –scendī, –scēnsus, climb down, descend (*descent*)

exitus, –ūs, *m.,* a going out, way out, result (*exit*)

facultās, –tātis, *f.,* ability, means, power, opportunity (*faculty*)

manēs, –ium, *m.pl.,* a departed spirit, soul of the dead

mergō, –ere, mersī, mersus, cause to sink, sink (*merge*)

minae, –ārum, *f.pl.,* threats

polliceor, –ērī, pollicitus sum, *dep.,* promise

refugiō, –ere, –fūgī, —, fly back, run away from (*refuge*)

reportō (1), carry back (*report*)

tergum, –ī *n.,* back

tot, *indecl. adj.,* so many

BUILDING WORD POWER

A *dirge* is far distant in meaning from a *ruler*, yet both trace their origin to the root word **regere, rēctum,** *to guide, direct, rule, govern,* or *administer.* **Dīrige** is the imperative singular of **dīrigere** (**dis + regere**), *to direct.* It is the first word in the funeral hymn *Dīrige, Domine,* taken from the fifth psalm. Eventually the second –*i* dropped out, and the hymn itself was called the **dirge.** Now it means a plaintive song or lament.

The noun **regula,** *a straight stick,* became in Latin a pattern, a model, a ruler. The word *ruler* itself came into English through a French word originating in **regula.** The Latin verb **regulāre, regulātum** developed from **regula,** and it means to control according to a rule, as to regulate the heat, a clock, etc.

From *reg–*, the root of *regere*, we have the Latin words **rēx, rēgis**, *king;* **rēgīna**, *queen;* **regiō, regiōnis**, *region;* **rēgālis**, *regal;* **rēgnum**, *kingdom;* **rēgnāre**, *to reign;* **regimen**, *a rule;* **rēgula**, *a ruler;* **rēgius**, *royal;* **rēgia**, *palace.* From which of the above words did the following English words come: *Regina, region, regal, reign, regnant, regent, regency, regimen, regime?*

Rēctus, *ruled*, means *right, straight.* What do *rector, rectify, rectitude* mean? **Rēcti–** is a combining form meaning *straight*, as in rectilinear. From what compounds of **regere** are these words formed: *correct, direct, erect, resurrection?*

SENTENCE PATTERNS

A. Translate into English:

1. Nē adeat rēgis atrium cum cane ferōcī in tergō suō!
2. Inveniāmus spēluncam ubi omnēs ad Orcum dēscendunt.
3. Mox intellēxit deum atque deam sē eī adjūnctūrōs esse.
4. Cingēmus canem quī aditum atque exitum Orcī cūstōdit.
5. Nēmō propter pondus nāvem in mediō flūmine mergat!
6. Nōnne pollicitus est sē facultātem illī datūrum esse?
7. Nē rēx ex atriō refugiat!
8. Nē minīs rēgis territī servī canem ferōcem corripiant!
9. Aliquī locum reperiant ubi manēs mortuōrum nāvem parvam exspectant.
10. Nē tot tēla ab homine reportentur!

B. Translate into Latin:

1. As soon as we find the entrance, let us descend without delay!
2. Let him not be terrified by the threats of the king!
3. May you never run away from danger on account of fear!
4. Let the dog be seized and carried back to the atrium of the king!
5. May the god give him the opportunity which he seeks!

Twelfth Labor: A Visit to the Realms of Pluto

Ūnus relinquēbātur ē duodecim labōribus quōs Pythia Herculī imperāvit. Eurystheus Herculem māgnopere timēbat et sē ab eō in perpetuum līberāre volēbat. Jūssit igitur eum canem Cerberum ex Orcō (*the underworld*) in lūcem trahere. Is canis aditum atque exitum Orcī cūstōdiēbat. Et Herculēs et Eurystheus intellēxērunt hunc labōrem omnium difficillimum esse; nēmō umquam ex Orcō redierat. Praetereā, Cerberus ipse mōnstrum erat horribilī aspectū, quī tria capita serpentibus cīncta habēbat.

Herculēs postquam imperia rēgis accēpit, statim in Lacōniam

Hercules and Charon crossing the river Styx.

sē contulit. Ibi invēnit spēluncam ingentī māgnitūdine per quam
hominēs ad Orcum dēscendēbant. Eō ubi vēnit et ex incolīs locum
spēluncae quaesīvit ac repperit, sine morā dēscendere cōnstituit.
Nec tamen sōlus iter fēcit; Mercurius et Minerva sē eī adjūnxē-
runt Ubi ad rīpam Stygis pervēnit, cōgnōvit nūllum pontem in
flūmine esse. Manēs mortuōrum trāns flūmen ā Charonte quōdam
trānsportātī sunt, quī ad rīpam cum parvā nāve exspectābat.
Charōn prō hōc officiō praemium postulābat. Hanc ob causam
mōs erat apud antīquōs nummum (*coin*) in ōre mortuī pōnere.

Quod Herculēs erat vir ingentī māgnitūdine corporis, Charōn
nāvem solvere nōlēbat. Arbitrābātur tantum pondus nāvem suam
in mediō flūmine mersūrum esse. Tandem tamen minīs Herculis
territus, Charōn nāvem solvit et eum incolumem ad ūlteriōrem
rīpam trādūxit.

Postquam Stygem hōc modō trānsiit, Herculēs in rēgnum ipsīus Plūtōnis pervēnit. Ibi Plūtōnem causam itineris docuit, et
Plūtō, quī dē clārō Hercule audīverat, eum benīgnē excēpit.
Facultātem quam ille petēbat dedit, sed jūssit Herculem imperia
rēgis facere et posteā Cerberum in Orcum rūrsus redūcere. Herculēs haec pollicitus est. Cerberum correptum summō cum labōre
ex Orcō in lūcem atque ad urbem Eurystheī trāxit.

Eō ubi vēnit, māgnus terror animum rēgis occupāvit, quī ex
atriō statim refūgit. Multīs lacrimīs Herculem jūssit mōnstrum
sine morā in Orcum redūcere. Sīc contrā omnium opīniōnem duodecim labōrēs, quōs ōrāculum jūsserat, intrā duodecim annōs
cōnfectī sunt. Herculēs, servitūte tandem līberātus, magnō cum
gaudiō Thēbās rediit.

CONVERSATION

PAULA: Respondē mihi, Paule. Cūr Herculēs ē cīvitāte suā in exsilium excēdere jūssus est? Prō cīvitāte multa facta īnsīgnia perfēcit.

PAULUS: Puer quīdam, nōmine Eunomus, ab Hercule cāsū occīsus est. Cīvēs tam īrātī erant ut eum ex urbe expellerent.

LŪCIUS: Nōnne scīvērunt puerum cāsū occīsum esse?

PAULUS: Certē. Herculēs tamen cum uxōre Dējanīrā ē patriā exīvit.

LŪCIA: Dum iter quaerunt quō flūmen trānsīre possent, Centaurus quīdam, cui nōmen erat Nessus, eīs auxilium obtulit.

PAULA: Quid Nessus fēcit ut Herculem et Dējanīram adjuvāret?

PAULUS: Herculēs nāvem invenīre cōnātus erat ut flūmen cum Dējanīrā trānsīre posset. Nūlla nāvis erat. Nihil suspicāns, uxōrem suam in tergum Nessī imposuit, dum ipse flūmen trānat.

LŪCIA: Nessus paulum in aquam progressus est, sed subitō ad rīpam revertit ut Dējanīram auferret.

PAULA: Quid fēcit Herculēs ut uxōrem suam cōnservāret?

PAULUS: Nē Centaurus cum Dējanīrā fugeret, Herculēs pectus Nessī sagittā trānsfīxit. Centaurus moriēns erat tam īrātus ut mortem Herculis efficere per uxōrem cōnsilium caperet.

SECTION 1 Formation of the Imperfect Subjunctive

▶ DISCUSSION

The imperfect subjunctive, active and passive, for all Latin verbs is formed by adding the regular person indicators, active and passive, to the present active infinitive.

IMPERFECT SUBJUNCTIVE ACTIVE, FIRST CONJUGATION

Pres. Act. Inf. + P.I. =			*Form*	*Possible Translation*
SINGULAR				
First	vocāre	+ m	= vocārem	*I might call*
Second	vocāre	+ s	= vocārēs	*you might call*
Third	vocāre	+ t	= vocāret	*he, she, it might call*
PLURAL				
First	vocāre	+ mus	= vocārēmus	*we might call*
Second	vocāre	+ tis	= vocārētis	*you might call*
Third	vocāre	+ nt	= vocārent	*they might call*

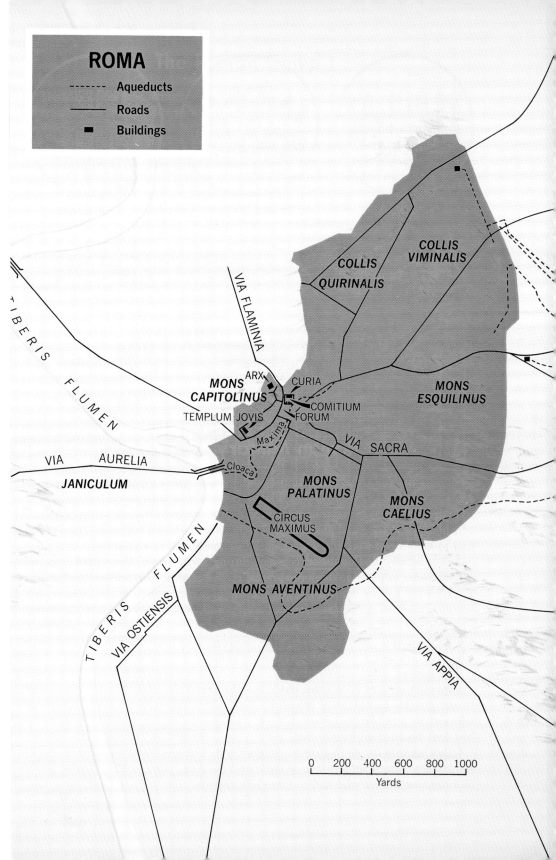

ROMA

- - - - - Aqueducts
——— Roads
■ Buildings

TIBERIS FLUMEN

VIA FLAMINIA

COLLIS QUIRINALIS

COLLIS VIMINALIS

MONS ESQUILINUS

ARX

MONS CAPITOLINUS

CURIA

COMITIUM

TEMPLUM JOVIS

FORUM

Maxima

VIA SACRA

VIA AURELIA

JANICULUM

Cloaca

MONS PALATINUS

MONS CAELIUS

CIRCUS MAXIMUS

MONS AVENTINUS

TIBERIS FLUMEN

VIA OSTIENSIS

VIA APPIA

0   200   400   600   800   1000

Yards

The ROMAN REPUBLIC: 44 B.C.

ROMAN DOMINION

ROMAN ALLIES

PARTHIAN EMPIRE

SARMATIA

DACIA

JM

Danuvius

PONTUS   EUXINUS

THRACIA

MACEDONIA

BITHYNIA

PONTUS

ARMENIA

GALATIA

ASIA

CAPPADOCIA

LYCAONIA

PAMPHYLIA

CILICIA

GRAECIA

MARE
AEGAEUM

LYCIA

SYRIA

CYPRUS

CRETA

I N T E R N U M

CYRENAICA

ARABIA

AEGYPTUS

Roman Ships and Shipping

Nāvis longa was the general name for a Roman warship, of which there were two standard types: (1) the *quīnquerēmis*, and (2) the *trirēmis*. Both ships were designed especially for speed and hence were comparatively narrow for their length.

The quinquereme accommodated a crew of three hundred, plus a detachment of heavily armed Roman infantry. The arrangement of the rowers is uncertain. It was either one tier of oars, with five men to an oar, or three tiers of oars, with two men pulling the two upper oars and one man pulling the lowest oar.

The trireme accommodated a crew of approximately two hundred, plus a detachment of Roman infantry. The oars came through the sides of the ship in three tiers. Three men were probably seated on each rowing bench, which was braced obliquely to the side of the ship. Both the quinquereme and the trireme were equipped with bronze-covered rams or beaks, level with or below the surface of the water.

The Romans won their first naval victory against Carthage in 260 B.C. The decisive weapon was a swinging boarding bridge called the *corvus* (raven), one end of which had a heavy iron beak resembling that of a raven. The base of this footbridge was hinged to the prow of the Roman ship, and when the enemy ship drew near, the Romans let the iron beak crash down on the enemy deck. The Roman marines then charged across the bridge, engaged the Carthaginian sailors in hand-to-hand fighting, and easily captured the ship. This signal victory was later celebrated in Rome by a monument, the *columna rōstrāta*, a column decorated with the beaks of the captured Cathaginian ships.

Nāvis Longa

Nāvis onerāria was the general name for the heavy, slow merchant ship. This was shorter, broader, and deeper than a war galley, was more seaworthy, and could carry greater loads. An ordinary cargo ship had a carrying capacity of about two hundred tons. Although it had oarsmen, it relied for motion chiefly on a large, square sail, made from linen or hide.

In the late Republic and the early Roman Empire, much traffic and trade flowed to and from Rome's chief seaports: Puteoli, on the Bay of Naples, and Ostia, at the mouth of the Tiber. From every port of the Mediterranean, from the Rhine and the Danube, from India, and eventually from China, merchants came with their wares. They brought raw materials and a variety of luxuries, although grain and slaves were the chief Roman imports. These imports greatly exceeded the Roman exports of ironware, bronzeware, pottery, ointments, wine, and olive oil.

Columna Rōstrāta

The Roman aristocracy was forbidden by law to engage in commerce. Control of commercial trade therefore remained for the most part in the hands of the knights, although the actual buying and selling of goods and the manning of the ships were in the control of foreigners, generally from Greece and the Middle East.

Nāvis Onerāria

ITALIA
- - - - - - - Roman roads

ALPES

VENETIA
Aquileia

Mediolanum
(Milan)
Verona
GALLIA
Patavium
CISALPINA
Mantua

LIGURIA
APPENINUS MONS
Genua

Ariminum

Luca
Faesulae
Pisae
UMBRIA
Ancona
Arretum

L. Trasimenus
PICENUM

ETRURIA
MARE ADRIATICUM

CORSICA
Falerii
SABINI
SAMNIUM

Roma
Praeneste
APULIA
Ostia
Alba Longa
Cannae
Ardea
LATIUM
Beneventum
Capua
Venusia
Brundis
Herculaneum
M. Vesuvius
SARDINIA
Pompeii
CAMPANIA
Tarentu
LUCANIA

MARE TYRRHENUM
Heraclea

CALABRIA

BRUTIUM

Mylae
Rhegium
Messana

Lilybaeum
SICILIA
M. Aetna

Carthago
Agrigentum
Syracusae

0   50   100
Miles

MARE   AFRICUM

The Latin imperfect subjunctive is translated into English not only by *might* but also by *would* and the past tenses of the indicative, according to the nature of the clause in which the subjunctive stands.

IMPERFECT SUBJUNCTIVE ACTIVE

Pres. Act. Inf. + P.I. = Form

CONJUGATION:	SECOND	THIRD	THIRD –io	FOURTH
		SINGULAR		
First	monērem	regerem	caperem	audīrem
Second	monērēs	regerēs	caperēs	audīrēs
Third	monēret	regeret	caperet	audīret
		PLURAL		
First	monērēmus	regerēmus	caperēmus	audīrēmus
Second	monērētis	regerētis	caperētis	audīrētis
Third	monērent	regerent	caperent	audīrent

▶ STUDY HELPS

1. The passive voice of the imperfect subjunctive is formed regularly by substituting passive indicators. (See Appendix, p. 417.)

2. The syllable *–re* may be considered the tense indicator.

IMPERFECT SUBJUNCTIVE, DEPONENT VERBS

The imperfect subjunctive of the deponent verbs is formed regularly as in the passive voice of regular verbs.

cōnārer   verērer   sequerer   paterer   largīrer

IMPERFECT SUBJUNCTIVE, IRREGULAR VERBS

The imperfect subjunctive of the irregular verbs is formed regularly.

essem   possem   vellem   īrem   ferrem   fierem

▶ PRACTICE PATTERNS

A. Write the third person plural of the imperfect subjunctive, active and passive, of the following verbs. Translate by using *might:* cōnservō, haereō, perscrībō, īnficiō, reperiō, caedō, rejiciō, impedīō, incūsō, auferō.

B. Write the third person singular of the imperfect subjunctive, active, of the following verbs. Translate by using *would:* dōnō, habeō, dūcō, jaciō, mūniō, absum, repōnō, īnferō, haereō, īnficiō.

C. Using *might* or *would*, translate into English: suspicārentur, loquerēmur, orīrētur, ēgrederēminī, pollicērēris, arbitrārer.

D. Translate into Latin:

1. they might save; we might turn back; it might be fortified
2. he would be; they would put aside; we would be saved
3. I might be present; you (sing.) might suspect; you (pl.) might turn back

89

4. we might swim; it would be fortified; he might be poisoned
5. it might stick fast; they would be returned; it would be written in full

SECTION 2 Clauses Expressing Purpose

▶ DISCUSSION

1. In English when we say *He is coming to see me*, the infinitive *to see* expresses the purpose of his coming. Instead of an infinitive in a simple sentence, we may use a clause in a complex sentence: *He is coming in order that he may see me.*

2. In Latin prose we do not use an infinitive to express purpose. We often use a subordinate clause introduced by **ut** if the clause is positive; by **nē,** if negative. Instead of **ut,** the relative pronoun **quī** may be used as the connective if the antecedent is a noun or pronoun. **Quō** (ablative of the relative pronoun) is used with the subjunctive in a clause containing a comparative adjective or adverb.

PURPOSE CLAUSES INTRODUCED BY Ut

Venit, He comes
Veniet, He will come } ***ut mē videat.*** {
Vēnit, He has come

to see me.
so as to see me.
in order to see me.
so that he may see me.
in order that he may see me.

Vēnit, He came
Veniēbat, He was coming } ***ut mē vidēret.*** {
Vēnerat, He had come

to see me.
so as to see me.
in order to see me.
so that he might see me.
in order that he might see me.

PURPOSE CLAUSES INTRODUCED BY Nē

Fugit, He flees
Fugiet, He will flee } ***nē capiātur.*** {
Fūgit, He has fled

so as not to be taken.
in order not to be taken.
so that he may not be taken.
in order that he may not be taken.
lest he be taken.
to avoid being taken.

Fūgit, He fled
Fugiēbat, He was fleeing } ***nē caperētur.*** {
Fūgerat, He had fled

so as not to be taken.
in order not to be taken.
so that he might not be taken.
in order that he might not be taken.
lest he be taken.
to avoid being taken.

90

Mīlitēs mīsit *quī* **urbem caperent.**	He sent soldiers *to take the city.*
Legiōnem mittit *quae* **urbem dēfendat.**	He is sending a legion *to defend the city.*
Plūrēs mīlitēs mīsit *quō celerius* **urbs caperētur.**	He sent more soldiers *in order that the city might be taken more quickly.*

▶ STUDY HELPS

1. After verbs meaning *choose, send,* or *leave,* purpose may be expressed by a relative clause with its verb in the present or imperfect subjunctive.

2. The antecedent of the relative pronoun is usually the object of the main verb.

SECTION 3 Clauses Expressing Result

▶ DISCUSSION

1. In English the verb in a clause of result is expressed by the indicative mood because a result is something that has actually happened. A fact is stated. In Latin the verb is in the subjunctive mood; and the clause, whether affirmative or negative, is introduced by **ut.** In a negative clause the negative adverb **nōn** is placed before the verb. In the English translation the auxiliary verbs *may, might, should,* and *would* are never used.

2. In Latin as in English, some word in the main clause serves as a warning *indicator* that a result clause is coming.

So, such before adjectives and adverbs are translated by the adverbs **tam** or **ita.**

Tam (*Ita*) **fortis erat**	He was *so* brave
ut omnēs puerī eum laudārent.	*that all the boys praised him.*

So before verbs is translated by the adverb **sīc** or **ita.**

Sīc (*Ita*) **verentur**	They are *so* afraid
ut ab urbe discēdant.	*that they are leaving the city.*

So great, **tantus,** and *such,* **tālis,** are adjectives.

Tanta est potestās dictātōris	*So great* is the dictator's power
ut plēbs eum timeat.	*that the common people fear him.*
Tālis erat terror	*Such* was the terror
ut virī fugerent.	*that the men fled.*

So many, **tot,** is an indeclinable adjective.

Tot hostēs adsunt	*So many enemies are present*
ut fugere nōn possīmus.	*that we cannot escape.*

NEGATIVE RESULT CLAUSES WITH **Ut . . . Nōn**

Ita ācer erat impetus	*So* fierce was the attack
ut oppidum dēfendī nōn posset.	*that the town could not be defended.*
Ita verentur	They are *so* afraid
ut nōn clāment.	*that they do not shout.*
Tantus erat timor hostium	*So great* was the fear of the enemy
ut fortiter pūgnāre nōn possent.	*that they could not fight bravely.*
Tālēs erant condiciōnēs pācis	The conditions of peace were *such*
ut Rōmānī eās nōn probārent.	*that the Romans did not approve them.*

PURPOSE AND RESULT CLAUSES: COMPARISON

PURPOSE	RESULT
1. **ut,** positive; **nē,** negative	1. **ut,** positive; **ut . . . nōn,** negative
2. *that, in order that; that . . . not; lest*	2. *that, so that; that . . . not*
3. sometimes with an infinitive	3. never with an infinitive
4. *may* or *might*	4. never *may* or *might*
5. incomplete action: possibility	5. complete action: fact
6. for what purpose? why?	6. with what result?

PURPOSE

Rōmānī fortiter pūgnāvērunt *ut hostēs superārent.* The Romans fought bravely *that they might overcome the enemy.*

RESULT

Rōmānī *tam* **fortiter pūgnāvērunt** *ut hostēs superārent.* The Romans fought *so* bravely *that they did overcome the enemy.*

SECTION 4 Sequence of Tenses

▶ DISCUSSION

The tense of the subjunctive in a subordinate clause depends on the tense of the main verb. This tense relationship between the verbs in the principal and subordinate clauses is called *sequence of tenses.*

SEQUENCE	IF THE MAIN VERB IS:	THE SUBORDINATE CLAUSE USES:
Primary	present future present perfect (*has, have*) future perfect imperative present subjunctive	1. the *present subjunctive* (to express same time as, *or* time future to that of the main verb) 2. the *perfect subjunctive* (to express time before that of the main verb)
Secondary	imperfect perfect (simple) pluperfect	1. the *imperfect subjunctive* (to express same time as, *or* time future to that of the main verb) 2. the *pluperfect subjunctive* (to express time before that of the main verb)

▶ STUDY HELPS

1. Primary tenses follow primary tenses; secondary follow secondary.

2. The *present perfect* in English always uses *has* or *have; it is a primary* tense. The *simple* or *historical perfect* expresses past time without auxiliary verbs; it is a secondary tense: primary = *I have called;* secondary = *I called.*

3. Purpose and result clauses use the present and imperfect subjunctive, but in a result clause the perfect subjunctive is frequently used to emphasize a single past action.

▶ PRACTICE PATTERNS

A. Identify the purpose or result clauses, primary or secondary sequence, in the following sentence. Translate into English.

1. Nūntiī veniunt ut rēgem videant. 2. Fugit nē interficiātur. 3. Tam fortiter pūgnābat ut omnēs vinceret. 4. Mīsit explōrātōrēs quī agrōs vāstārent. 5. Tantus erat terror ut juvenēs fūgerent. 6. Rēx cīvēs sīc terret ut eum māximē timeant. 7. Virtūs sociōrum tanta erat ut superārī nōn possent.

B. Translate into Latin.

1. So many were the attacks that the inhabitants were terrified. 2. Hercules fought so bravely that he saved his wife. 3. Hercules fought bravely to save his life. 4. He is going into exile so as not to be taken prisoner. 5. Hercules drove his ship to the island in order to offer sacrifice to the god. 6. So great is the king's power that all fear him. 7. Such is the noise that the sailors cannot hear the leader's instructions.

BUILDING WORD POWER

Most derivatives from the Latin root word **vidēre, vīsum,** *to see, perceive,* contain the syllable *–vis–,* but a few have *vid–.* From **invidēre,** *to look at with evil eye,* we have *invidious* as well as *envy;* from **prōvidēre,** *to foresee,* came *provide* and *provision.* The English word *evident* is derived from **ēvidēns,** meaning *evident, apparent. Prevision* is from **praevidēre,** *to see before; revision* is from **revidēre,** *to see again.* We have no English derivatives from **pervidēre,** *to see through. Vision, visible,* and *visual* are from **vīsus,** *seen.*

Vīsere, vīsum, *to look at carefully,* is one of the few frequentative verbs that is not of the first conjugation. A frequentative verb denotes repeated or intensified action. **Vīsitāre, vīsitātum,** *to see often, to visit,* is a frequentative of **vīsere.** It is easy to understand how *visit* and *visitation* came from **vīsitāre, vīsitātum,** but we have some derivatives from **vidēre, vīsum** whose origin is not so easily traced because of their detour through French. *Survey* means to look over; *supervision* is from the same origin, **super + vidēre.** *Purvey,* to furnish, and *proviso,* a condition, are from **prōvidēre,** as is also *prudent* (**prōvidentia**). *Advice* and *advise* are doublets from **advidēre,** *to look at.* A *vista* (Italian, from **vīsum**) is a *view* (French, from **vidēre**) through an avenue of trees.

WORDS TO MASTER

amor, –ōris, *m.,* love, (*amorous*)
cōnservō (1), keep, save (*conserve*)
ergā, *prep. with acc.,* toward
exsilium, –ī, *n.,* exile, banishment (*exile*)
fūmus, –ī, *m.,* smoke (*fume*)
haereō, –ēre, haesī, haesūrus, stick fast, adhere; hesitate (*adhesive*)
īnficiō, –ere, –fēcī, –fectus, work in, stain, dye, poison (*infect*)
misericordia, –ae, *f.,* pity, mercy, compassion

nūbēs, –is, *f.,* cloud (*nubilous*)
pectus, –oris, *n.,* breast (*pectoral*)
perscrībō, –ere, –scrīpsī, –scrīptus, write in full, recount
repōnō, –ere, –posuī, –positus, put aside, keep (*repose*)
revertō, –ere, –vertī, –versus, turn back, return (*revert*)
suspicor (1), *dep.,* suspect, surmise
trānō (1), swim across
viātor, –ōris, *m.,* traveler, stranger (*viator*)

SENTENCE PATTERNS

A. Complete the following sentences with the correct form in Latin of the word in parentheses and translate:

1. Ad rīpam tam subitō revertit ut Dējanīram paene (auferō).
2. Tālis erat virī īra ut arcum (intendō) et pectus Nessī sagittā (vulnerō).
3. Repōne aliquid sanguinis hūjus nē amōrem conjugis tuī (āmittō).
4. Ipse flūmen celeriter trānāvit quō facilius uxor (cōnservō).
5. (Viātor) miserīs auxilium offerāmus!

94

6. Nē uxor vestem virī (īnficiō) ut amōrem conjugis suī (cōnservō).
7. In exsilium eant! Nē ergā illōs ūllam (misericordia) habeāmus!
8. Deī nūntium ad terram mīsērunt quī corpus, fūmō et nūbe abditum, (abripiō).
9. Vestem quae in corpore haeret dētrahere cōnātur ut dolōrem (fugiō).
10. Ita ea perscrīpsit ut dux nihil malī (suspicor).

B. Translate into Latin:

1. Did he not place his wife on the back of the horse so that he himself could swim across the river?
2. So great is his anger that he is turning back to punish his enemy.
3. Let her put the clothing aside so that it may not be poisoned.
4. The smoke and the clouds were so dense that he did not see the man.
5. Let us send a messenger to bring back the white garment.

Last Days of a Hero

Posteā Herculēs tot alia facta īnsīgnia perfēcit ut ea perscrībere longius esset. Tandem post multōs annōs Dējanīram, Oeneī fīliam, in mātrimōnium dūxit. Tribus annīs intermissīs, puerum quendam, nōmine Eunonum, cāsū occīdit. Ob hanc rem cīvitās Herculem in exsilium īre jūssit. Herculēs igitur cum uxōre suā ē fīnibus ējus cīvitātis exīre properāvit. Dum iter faciunt, ad flūmen quoddam pervēnērunt in quō nūllus pōns erat. Prīmum nāvem invenīre cōnābantur ut flūmen trānsīre possent.

Tum Centaurus quīdam, nōmine Nessus, ad viātōrēs appropinquāvit ut auxilium eīs offerret. Herculēs uxōrem suam in tergum Nessī imposuit; tum ipse flūmen trānāvit. At Nessus paulum in aquam prōgressus ad rīpam subitō revertit ut Dējanīram auferret. Quod ubi Herculēs vīdit, ipse celeriter revertit, et nē Nessus cum uxōre ējus fugeret, arcum intendit et pectus Nessī sagittā trānsfīxit.

Nessus moriēns, nē occāsiō Herculem pūniendī (*of punishing*) dīmitterētur, ita locūtus est: "Tū, Dējanīra, verba morientis audī. Sī amōrem conjugis tuī cōnservāre vīs, aliquid sanguinis hūjus sūme et repōne; tum, sī umquam suspiciō in mentem tuam vēnerit, vestem conjugis hōc sanguine īnficiēs." Dējanīra, nihil malī suspicāns, imperia fēcit.

Post breve tempus, Herculēs bellum contrā Eurytum, rēgem Oechaliae, suscēpit. Rēgem ipsum cum fīliīs interfēcit, et Iolēn ējus fīliam captīvam sēcum redūxit. Tum āram cōnstituit ut Jovī

Nessus, with Hercules' arrow in his chest.

sacrificium faceret. Dum tamen sacrificium parat, Licham comitem suum domum mīsit, quī vestem albam referret; mōs enim
erat apud antīquōs, dum sacrificium faciunt, vestem albam gerere.
Dējanīra, arbitrāta Herculem amōrem ergā Iolēn habēre, vestem
quam Lichae dedit, sanguine Nessī īnfēcit.

Herculēs nūllum malum suspicāns vestem quam Lichās tulerat
celeriter induit (*put on*). Statim dolōrem per omnia membra
sēnsit. Vestem dētrahere cōnātus est ut dolōrem fugeret; illa
tamen in corpore haesit neque eam ūllō modō abscindere (*cut off*)
potuit. Tum in montem Oetam sē contulit et in rogum (*funeral
pyre*), quem summā celeritāte cōnstituit, sē imposuit. Hoc ubi
fēcit, pastor quīdam, ad misericordiam inductus, rogum incendit.
Tum Herculēs, fūmō ac dēnsā nūbe abditus, ā Jove in Olympum
abreptus est ut inter deōs habitāret.

Living Mythology:
Quiz

A. Complete the following:

1. The accomplishments of Hercules are known as ＿＿
2. A river so named because its discoverers claimed they had seen huge
   female warriors along its bank ＿＿
3. A book which contains the maps of the world ＿＿
4. The rocks at either side of the Strait of Gibraltar ＿＿

5. The waters adjacent to the Strait of Gibraltar ____
6. Mountain range in northern Africa ____
7. A gift which causes pain and trouble ____
8. A bone just back of the neck which supports the head ____

B. Match the terms on the right with the proper adjectives or nouns on the left:

1. Nemean __	a. horses
2. Lernean __	b. stables
3. Erymanthian __	c. swamp
4. Cerynean __	d. belt
5. Stymphalean __	e. cattle
6. Augean __	f. stag
7. Cretan __	g. lion
8. Diomedes __	h. boar
9. Hippolyte __	i. birds
10. Geryon __	j. bull
11. Hesperides __	k. three-headed dog
12. Cerberus __	l. poisoned shirt
13. Nessus __	m. golden apples

C. Explain the meaning of the following phrases:

a. an infant Hercules
b. hydra-headed evils
c. Herculean task
d. Hercules' choice
e. shirt of Nessus
f. like the club of Hercules
g. the golden apples of the Hesperides
h. even the ghosts in Hades fear Hercules
i. as bad as cleaning the Augean stables
j. Herculean vigor

Read Homer once and you can read no more;
For all books else appear so mean, so poor.
—John Sheffield, Duke of Buckinghamshire, 1648–1721

Unit XI

CONVERSATION

MAGISTER: Loquēmur dē itinere Ulixis clārī! Scītisne quī poēta dē bellō Trōjānō opus nōtum scrīpserit?

PAULUS: Audīvī Homerum, māximum poētārum Graecōrum, dē bellō Trōjānō Iliāda (the *Iliad*), opus nōtissimum, perscrībere.

MAGISTER: Dīc nōbīs quam diū Graecī contrā Trōjānōs pūgnāverint.

PAULA: Urbem Trōjam ā Graecīs decem annōs obsessam esse satis cōnstat. Trōja tandem per īnsidiās ā Graecīs capta est.

MAGISTER: Quis dolum istum cōgitāvit quō Trōjam captam esse cōnstat?

PAULUS:	Ulixēs, summae virtūtis ac prūdentiae vir, erat dux clārus Graecōrum quī cōnsilium fēcit.
MAGISTER:	Quis dīcere potest quid Graecī post bellum facere statuerint?
PAULA:	Dīxērunt: "Domum redeāmus! Bellō dēfessī sumus!"
MAGISTER:	Ad quam terram, Trōjā relictā, nāvis Ulixis vī tempestātis appulsa est?
PAULUS:	Ad lītus Āfricae appulsa est. Tum Ulixēs locūtus est: "Paucōs ē sociīs in terram expōnāmus! Aquam ad nāvem referant! Quālis sit nātūra hūjus regiōnis cōgnōscant!"

SECTION 1 Formation of the Perfect Subjunctive Active

▶ DISCUSSION

The perfect subjunctive active for all Latin verbs is formed by adding the tense indicator *-eri* plus the person indicators to the perfect stem.

PERFECT SUBJUNCTIVE ACTIVE, FIRST CONJUGATION

Perf. Stem. + *T.I.* + *P.I.* =				*Form*	*Possible Translation*
			SINGULAR		
First	vocāv	+ eri +	m	= vocāverim	*I may have called*
Second	vocāv	+ eri +	s	= vocāverīs	*you may have called*
Third	vocāv	+ eri +	t	= vocāverit	*he, she, it may have called*
			PLURAL		
First	vocāv	+ eri +	mus	= vocāverīmus	*we may have called*
Second	vocāv	+ eri +	tis	= vocāverītis	*you may have called*
Third	vocāv	+ eri +	nt	= vocāverint	*they may have called*

PERFECT SUBJUNCTIVE ACTIVE

CONJUGATION:	SECOND	THIRD	THIRD -io	FOURTH
		SINGULAR		
First	monuerim	rēxerim	cēperim	audīverim
Second	monuerīs	rēxerīs	cēperīs	audīverīs
Third	monuerit	rēxerit	cēperit	audīverit
		PLURAL		
First	monuerīmus	rēxerīmus	cēperīmus	audīverīmus
Second	monuerītis	rēxerītis	cēperītis	audīverītis
Third	monuerint	rēxerint	cēperint	audīverint

1. The perfect subjunctive active is like the future perfect indicative active except for the long –ī in the first person plural and the second person singular and plural, and for the use of –*m* instead of –*ō* in the first person singular for the person indicator.

2. The Latin perfect subjunctive is translated into English not only by *may have* but by other forms, according to the nature of the clause in which the subjunctive is found.

PERFECT SUBJUNCTIVE, IRREGULAR VERBS

The perfect subjunctive of the irregular verbs is formed regularly:

fuerim   potuerim   voluerim   ierim (īverim)   tulerim

▶ PRACTICE PATTERNS

A. Write in Latin the specified forms:

1. perfect subjunctive active first person plural: collocō, disjiciō, vinciō, mergō, haereō
2. perfect subjunctive active third person plural: absum, possum, volō, nōlō, adeō, referō
3. imperfect subjunctive passive third person singular: obsideō, disjiciō
4. present subjunctive active third person plural: cōnstō, gustō, vinciō

B. Write in Latin the specified forms:

1. perfect subjunctive active second person singular: taste, sink, stick to, bind
2. perfect subjunctive active second person plural: open, offer, perish, consist of

SECTION 2 Formation of the Pluperfect Subjunctive Active

▶ DISCUSSION

The pluperfect subjunctive active for all Latin verbs is formed by adding the tense indicator –*isse* plus the regular person indicators to the perfect stem.

PLUPERFECT SUBJUNCTIVE ACTIVE, FIRST CONJUGATION

Perf. Stem. + *T.I.* + *P.I.* =				*Form*	*Possible Translation*
		SINGULAR			
First	**vocāv**	+ **isse** +	**m**	= **vocāvissem**	*I might have called*
Second	**vocāv**	+ **isse** +	**s**	= **vocāvissēs**	*you might have called*
Third	**vocāv**	+ **isse** +	**t**	= **vocāvisset**	*he, she, it might have called*

99

First	vocāv	+ isse + mus = vocāvissēmus	*we might have called*
Second	vocāv	+ isse + tis = vocāvissētis	*you might have called*
Third	vocāv	+ isse + nt = vocāvissent	*they might have called*

PLUPERFECT SUBJUNCTIVE ACTIVE

CONJUGATION:	SECOND	THIRD	THIRD –io	FOURTH
		SINGULAR		
First	monuissem	rēxissem	cēpissem	audīvissem
Second	monuissēs	rēxissēs	cēpissēs	audīvissēs
Third	monuisset	rēxisset	cēpisset	audīvisset
		PLURAL		
First	monuissēmus	rēxissēmus	cēpissēmus	audīvissēmus
Second	monuissētis	rēxissētis	cēpissētis	audīvissētis
Third	monuissent	rēxissent	cēpissent	audīvissent

▶ STUDY HELPS

1. The pluperfect subjunctive active may also be formed by adding person indicators to the perfect active infinitive: *vocāvisse + m*, etc.

2. The Latin pluperfect subjunctive may be translated into English by *might have, would have,* and by other forms, according to the nature of the clause in which the subjunctive is found.

PLUPERFECT SUBJUNCTIVE, IRREGULAR VERBS

The pluperfect subjunctive of the irregular verbs is formed regularly:

fuissem   potuissem   voluissem   īssem (īvissem)   tulissem

▶ PRACTICE PATTERNS

A. Write in Latin the second person plural pluperfect subjunctive active of the following verbs: explōrō, obsideō, dīcō, accipiō, mūniō, trānseō, praesum, nōlō, possum, cōnferō, volō.

B. Write synopses in the subjunctive active only:

1. collocō (first person singular)
2. disjiciō (third person plural)
3. obsideō (second person singular)
4. adeō (second person plural)
5. ferō (third person singular)
6. absum (first person plural)

C. Write in Latin:

1. they might have found
2. he would have laid aside
3. we might have encircled
4. you (sing.) would have besieged
5. you (pl.) might have possessed
6. he would have gone
7. she might have tasted
8. they would have snatched away

SECTION 3 Indirect Questions

▶ DISCUSSION

1. In English and in Latin there are two kinds of questions:

Direct:	*What are you making?*	**Quid facis?**
Indirect:	*I ask what you are making.*	**Rogō quid faciās.**

A *direct* question becomes *indirect* when it is used as the direct object of verbs meaning: *ask, know, perceive, show.* It is always introduced by an interrogative word. In English the verb of an indirect question is in the indicative mood; in Latin it is in the subjunctive, although the English translation is like the indicative.

2. Definite futurity in an indirect question is expressed by the future participle with the required form of the subjunctive of **sum.**

Quandō venient?	*When will they come?*
Rogat quandō ventūrī sint.	*He asks when will they come.*
Rogāvit quandō ventūrī essent.	*He asked when they would come.*

3. A single English indirect question beginning with *whether* or *if* is introduced in Latin either by **num** or by **–ne** added to the first word of the indirect question.

Validusne est?	*Is he strong?*
Quaerō num validus sit.	*I ask whether (or if) he is strong.*
Quaerō validusne sit.	

▶ STUDY HELPS

1. It is necessary to distinguish between indirect questions and indirect statements.

INDIRECT STATEMENT	INDIRECT QUESTION
Sciō *eum vēnisse.*	**Sciō *cūr vēnerit.***
I know (*that*) he came.	I know *why* he came.
1. Introduced by *that* in English but *no introductory word* in Latin.	1. Introduced in both English and Latin by a *question* word or phrase.
2. Verb in the *infinitive.*	2. Verb in the *subjunctive.*
3. Subject in the *accusative.*	3. Subject in the *nominative.*

2. There are three words in Latin which mean *ask:*

rogō	+ — + two accusatives	= *ask (in any sense)*
quaerō + ā, ab + ablative		= *ask (a question)*
petō + ā, ab + ablative		= *ask (a favor)*

101

► PRACTICE PATTERNS

A. Translate into English:

1. Rogant quid puer videat. 2. Nēsciēbant quid mīles faceret. 3. Quaerunt num sit amīcus. 4. Scīmus quandō profectūrus sit. 5. Ab eīs quaesīvī essentne inimīcī. 6. Cōgnōvēruntne quālis esset nātūra ējus locī? 7. Mīrātus est cūr regiōnem nōn explōrāvissent. 8. Scīsne quā dē causā nautās vīnxerint? 9. Num nēscīs quōs frūctūs vorāverint? 10. Nōnne audīvistī quae dīcerent?

B. Change the following direct questions to indirect questions using verbs of asking, knowing, perceiving, or showing. Translate into Latin:

1. Who was tasting the wonderful fruit? 2. What town was besieged by the enemy? 3. In what manner were the ships scattered? 4. Why did the Trojans wage war with the Greeks? 5. Where did they place their unwilling comrades?

SECTION 4 Optative Subjunctive

► DISCUSSION

A wish may be expressed by the optative subjunctive in any person or number (see p. 84). The negative is always **nē**. The adverb **utinam,** which means *would that, oh that, if only, I wish that,* is generally used with the optative subjunctive.

There are three uses of the optative subjunctive:

1. *Possible wishes for the future.* The *present subjunctive,* with or without **utinam,** is used to express a wish that may be realized.

Domum redeātis!	*May you return home!*
Utinam domum redeātis!	*Would that you may return home!*
Nē hoc fiat!	*May this not be done!*

2. *Impossible wishes for the present.* The *imperfect subjunctive* preceded by *utinam* is used to express a wish referring to present time which cannot be realized.

Utinam adessēs!	*Would (I wish) that you were here!*
Utinam nē adessēs!	*Would that you were not here!*

3. *Impossible wishes for the past.* The *pluperfect subjunctive* preceded by *utinam* is used to express a wish referring to past time which cannot be realized.

Utinam vēnissētis!	*Would that (If only) you had come!*
Utinam nē vēnissētis!	*Would that you had not come!*

▶ PRACTICE PATTERNS

A. Translate into English:

1. Pecūnia nōbīs dētur! 2. Utinam nē adesset! 3. Utinam domī essem! 4. Nē eum videam! 5. Utinam vēnisset! 6. Utinam brevius iter invēnissēmus! 7. Tūtī reveniātis! 8. Utinam nē adfuissent! 9. Utinam domō discēdat!

B. Translate into Latin:

1. May they hear me! 2. I wish I had not come! 3. I wish I were a bird! 4. May you be heard! 5. Oh that the war would end! 6. If only I had not come! 7. May we not be seen! 8. Would that he were safe! 9. May you return soon!

WORDS TO MASTER

avidus, –a, –um, *adj.,* greedy (*avid*); **avidē,** *adv.,* eagerly, greedily

clāmor, –ōris, *m.,* shout, cry (*clamor*)

collocō (1), place, place together, station (*collocate*)

cōnstō, –stāre, –stitī, –statūrus, *irreg.,* stand firm, consist of; **cōnstat,** *impers.,* it is agreed, it is well known (*constant*)

disjiciō, –ere, –jēcī, –jectus, throw apart, scatter

explōrō (1), find out, investigate (*explore*)

frūctus, –ūs, *m.,* fruit (*fructify*)

gustō (1), taste (*gusto*)

mīror (1), *dep.,* wonder, be astonished at (*miracle*); **mīrus, –a, –um,** *adj.,* wonderful

obsideō, –ēre, –sēdī, –sessus, blockade, besiege (*obsession*)

portus, –ūs, *m.,* harbor, port (*port*)

praecipuē, *adv.,* especially

priusquam, *conj.,* before, sooner than

prūdentia, –ae, *f.,* foresight, good judgment (*prudence*)

sponte, *abl. sing., f., with* **suā,** of his (her, their) own accord, voluntarily (*spontaneous*)

vinciō, –īre, vīnxī, vīnctus, bind (*vinculum*)

BUILDING WORD POWER

Most of the more than one hundred derivatives from **tenēre, tentum,** *to hold,* have the memory peg *–ten–, –tin–,* or *–tain.*

abstinēre, abstentum, to keep away from: *abstain, abstention, abstinent*
continēre, contentum, to hold together: *contain, contention, continent*
dētinēre, dētentum, to hold back: *detain, detention*
obtinēre, obtentum, to hold, possess: *obtain*
pertinēre, pertentum, to belong to: *pertain, pertinent*
retinēre, retentum, to hold back: *retain, retention*
sustinēre, sustentum, to hold up: *sustain*

All the compounds with *–tain* came into English via French. Strangely enough, *attain* is not derived from **tenēre** but from **tangere,** *to touch.*

What is the meaning of the italicized words: *tenure* of office; *continuity* of thought; *retentive* memory; *tenacious* grip; even *tenor* of his ways; *tenement district; pertinent* argument; inconsistent *tenet;* pay for their *sustenance;* to be a *malcontent?*

SENTENCE PATTERNS

A. Translate into English:

1. Utinam in hāc terrā mīrā semper manēre possēmus!
2. Urbem Trōjam ā Graecīs decem annōs obsessam esse satis cōnstat.
3. Exposuēruntne quam ob rem Graecī domum redīre properāvissent?
4. Tanta tempestās subitō orta est ut nāvēs disjicerentur.
5. Explōrēmus regiōnem et cōgnōscāmus quālis sit nātūra ējus locī.
6. Manūs eōrum vīnciantur et eī invītī ad nāvem trahantur.
7. Utinam sociī atque comitēs mīrum frūctum numquam gustāvissent!
8. Mīrātus est quae causa esset morae.
9. Māgnō cum clāmōre avidōs sociōs in nāve collocāvērunt ut ex portū quam prīmum solverent.
10. Dux erat vir tālis prūdentiae ut praecipuē cuperet virōs ad nāvem sponte redīre.

B. Translate into Latin:

1. It is well known that Troy was taken by a trick.
2. Such was the prudence of the leader that he did not wish his comrades to taste the wonderful fruit.
3. The greedy sailors asked with a loud shout why they ought to set sail from the harbor voluntarily.
4. Let their hands be bound and let them be placed near the shore.
5. Would that we had some fruit! Let us return to the island.

Living Mythology:
Ulysses

The *Odyssey*, written by a Greek poet named Homer, is one of the most famous poems in the world. It relates the wanderings of Odysseus, or, as he is called in English, Ulysses, after the destruction of Troy. Ulysses was one of the bravest of the Greek leaders in the Trojan War, but he was particularly noted for his craftiness and keenness of mind. It was his clever stratagem of the wooden horse that won the war for the Greeks.

After the fall of Troy, Ulysses, laden with booty, set out with many companions for his kingdom, Ithaca, a small island off the coast of western Greece. The return voyage was a stormy one, and again and again the ships were driven off their course. They wandered south as far as Africa and west as far as Sicily. So varied were their fortunes and so long their wanderings that it was ten years before Ulysses, the only survivor, finally reached Ithaca. Since the Trojan War lasted ten years, he was away twenty years altogether. We shall read in this and the succeeding units about the many strange adventures that befell him on the way to Ithaca.

Ulysses, hero of Homer's *Odyssey*.

Homeward Bound

Per decem annōs Trōjānī cum Graecīs bellum gesserant. Trōjā tandem per īnsidiās captā, Graecī bellō dēfessī ad domicilia sua redīre praecipuē cupīvērunt. Omnibus rēbus ad iter parātīs, nāvēs dēdūxērunt et māgnō cum gaudiō solvērunt.

Erat inter Graecōs Ulixēs quīdam, vir summae prūdentiae ac virtūtis, quī rēgnum īnsulae Ithacae obtinuerat. Paulō priusquam ad bellum cum reliquīs Graecīs profectus est, puellam pulcherrimam, nōmine Pēnelopēn, in mātrimōnium dūxerat. Post bellum igitur māgnā cupiditāte patriam uxōremque vidēre volēbat.

Lost Time in the Land of the Lotus-Eaters

Postquam Graecī pauca mīlia passuum ā lītore Trōjae prōgressī sunt, tanta tempestās subitō orta est ut nūlla nāvium cursum tenēre posset, sed aliae aliam in partem disjicerentur. Nāvis Ulixis vī tempestātis ad Āfricae lītus appulsa est. Ulixēs cōnstituit paucōs ē comitibus in terram expōnere, quī regiōnem explōrārent atque aquam ad nāvem referrent, et quālis esset nātūra ējus locī cōgnōscerent.

Hī ē nāve ēgressī mandāta facere parābant. At dum aquam quaerunt, quōsdam ex incolīs invēnērunt atque ab eīs benīgnē acceptī sunt. Cibus eōrum hominum paene omnīnō ē quōdam mīrō frūctū cōnstābat, quem lōtum appellābant. Graecī, simul atque hunc cibum gustāvērunt, memoriam patriae et sociōrum statim dēposuērunt. Māgnīs cum clāmōribus cōnfīrmāvērunt sē semper in illā terrā mānsūrōs esse ut illum cibum in perpetuum vorārent. "Maneāmus in hāc mīrā terrā! Domum redeant quī redīre dēsīderant!"

Intereā Ulixēs, mīrāns cūr comitēs ējus nōn redīrent, ab hōrā septimā ad vesperum exspectāvit. Tandem complūrēs nautae in eandem regiōnem missī sunt, quī quae causa esset morae cōgnōscerent. Itaque hī in terram expositī ad vīcum quī nōn longē aberat sē contulērunt. Mox sociōs suōs lōtum avidē vorantēs invēnērunt, sed neque patriam neque domōs neque amīcōs memoriā jam tenēbant. Nihil praeter lōtum praecipuē dēsīderābant. Clāmābant vehementer sē numquam ex illō locō exitūrōs esse.

Hīs rēbus cōgnitīs, Ulixēs ipse cum reliquīs quī in nāve relictī erant ad eum locum vēnit. Sociōs suōs frūstrā jūssit suā sponte redīre. "Utinam nāvem numquam relīquissent!" inquit Ulixēs. "Vinciāmus manūs eōrum et ad nāvem comitēs invītōs trahāmus!" Invītōs vīnctōsque sociōs in nāve collocāvērunt et posteā quam celerrimē ex portū solvērunt.

They hear like ocean on a western beach
The surge and thunder of the Odyssey
—Andrew Lang, 1844–1912

Unit XII

CONVERSATION

ULIXĒS:	Quālem ad terram pervēnimus? Explōrēmus! Hīc manēte prope lītus dum ego paucīs cum comitibus ad interiōrem partem terrae prōcēdō. Cum prīmum reperīmus quālis sit regiō quālēsque incolae sint, reveniēmus. Intereā nōlīte abīre!
PRĪMUS COMES:	Nōs vērō hīc manēbimus. Nōlīte in perīculum venīre!
ULIXĒS:	Perīculum vītābimus. Quis vult mē sequī?

COMITĒS:	Tē sequēmur quōcumque nōs dūcere vīs, Ulixēs!
ULIXĒS:	Venīte igitur mēcum, comitēs! (*Ulixēs paucīs cum comitibus ad interiōrem īnsulae partem proficīscitur.*) Spēluncam videō. Multa pecora prope spēluncam stant!
SECUNDUS COMES:	Spēluncam intrēmus! Quid īnsit cōgnōscere volō!
ULIXĒS (*in spēluncā*):	Quot rēs adsunt! Optima invēnimus!
TERTIUS COMES:	Omnia in nāvem reportēmus!
ULIXĒS:	Nōlīte ita facere! Videō gigantem (*giant*) ad spēluncam redeuntem!
PRĪMUS COMES:	In interiōre spēluncae parte maneāmus! Timeō!
TERTIUS COMES:	Ut prīmum possumus, abeāmus! (*Gigās intrat.*)
GIGĀS:	Vōcem hominis audiō! Quis adest? Quis es tū?

SECTION 1 Formation of the Perfect Subjunctive Passive

▶ DISCUSSION

The perfect subjunctive passive for all transitive Latin verbs is composed of the perfect passive participle and the present subjunctive of *sum*.

PERFECT SUBJUNCTIVE PASSIVE, FIRST CONJUGATION

Perf. Pass. Part. + **sim** = *Form*		*Possible Translation*
	SINGULAR	
First	**vocātus, –a, –um sim**	*I may have been called*
Second	**vocātus, –a, –um sīs**	*you may have been called*
Third	**vocātus, –a, –um sit**	*he, she, it may have been called*
	PLURAL	
First	**vocātī, –ae, –a sīmus**	*we may have been called*
Second	**vocātī, –ae, –a sītis**	*you may have been called*
Third	**vocātī, –ae, –a sint**	*they may have been called*

PERFECT SUBJUNCTIVE PASSIVE

CONJUGATION:	SECOND	THIRD	THIRD –io	FOURTH
		SINGULAR		
First	**monitus sim**	**rēctus sim**	**captus sim**	**audītus sim**
Second	**monitus sīs**	**rēctus sīs**	**captus sīs**	**audītus sīs**
Third	**monitus sit**	**rēctus sit**	**captus sit**	**audītus sit**

107

First	monitī sīmus	rēctī sīmus	captī sīmus	audītī sīmus
Second	monitī sītis	rēctī sītis	captī sītis	audītī sītis
Third	monitī sint	rēctī sint	captī sint	audītī sint

▶ STUDY HELPS

The Latin perfect subjunctive passive is translated into English not only by *may have been*, but by other forms, according to the nature of the clause in which the subjunctive is formed.

PERFECT SUBJUNCTIVE DEPONENT VERBS

The perfect subjunctive of deponent verbs is formed regularly:

cōnātus sim   veritus sim   secūtus sim   passus sim   ortus sim

SECTION 2 Formation of the Pluperfect Subjunctive Passive

▶ DISCUSSION

The pluperfect subjunctive passive for all transitive verbs is composed of the perfect passive participle and the imperfect subjunctive of *sum.*

PLUPERFECT SUBJUNCTIVE PASSIVE, FIRST CONJUGATION

Perf. Pass. Part. + **essem** = *Form*   *Possible Translation*

SINGULAR

First	vocātus, –a, –um essem	*I might have been called*
Second	vocātus, –a, –um essēs	*you might have been called*
Third	vocātus, –a, –um esset	*he, she, it might have been called*

PLURAL

First	vocātī, –ae, –a essēmus	*we might have been called*
Second	vocātī, –ae, –a essētis	*you might have been called*
Third	vocātī, –ae, –a essent	*they might have been called*

PLUPERFECT SUBJUNCTIVE PASSIVE

CONJ.	SECOND	THIRD	THIRD –io	FOURTH
		SINGULAR		
First	monitus essem	rēctus essem	captus essem	audītus essem
Second	monitus essēs	rēctus essēs	captus essēs	audītus essēs
Third	monitus esset	rēctus esset	captus esset	audītus esset

First	moniti essēmus	rēctī essēmus	captī essēmus	audītī essēmus
Second	moniti essētis	rēctī essētis	captī essētis	audītī essētis
Third	moniti essent	rēctī essent	captī essent	audītī essent

▶ STUDY HELPS

The Latin pluperfect subjunctive passive is translated into English not only by *might have been*, but by other forms according to the nature of the clause in which the subjunctive is found.

PLUPERFECT SUBJUNCTIVE, DEPONENT VERBS

The pluperfect subjunctive of deponent verbs is formed regularly:

cōnātus essem   veritus essem   secūtus essem
passus essem   ortus essem

▶ PRACTICE PATTERNS

A. Translate into English, using *may have been* for the *perfect passive subjunctive* and *might have been* or *would have been* for the *pluperfect passive subjunctive*:

1. audīta sit	complētī sint	āmōta sint
2. cīncta essent	sublātus essem	vīnctus esset

B. Write in Latin the third person plural, perfect and pluperfect subjunctive of:

vagor   polliceor   sequor   ēgredior   orior   cohortor

C. Write in Latin:

1. he may have called; he may have been called; they might have moved away
2. you may have tried; they might have lifted; it might have been filled
3. he might have risen; you might have followed; we might have been blamed

SECTION 3 *Cum* Temporal Clauses

▶ DISCUSSION

1. *Cum,* meaning *when,* referring to *present* or *future* time, is used with the *indicative* mood:

PRESENT TIME

Cum pictūram tuam spectō,   When I am looking at your picture,
tēcum esse videor.   I seem to be with you.

109

The *future tense* is used in the subordinate clause if the action or state expressed by the verb continues during the action or state expressed by the verb in the principal clause.

Tē cum in urbe eris vidēbō. I shall see you *when you are in the city.*

The *future perfect tense* is used in the subordinate clause if the action or state expressed by the verb is completed before the action or state expressed by the verb in the principal clause.

Tē cum in urbem vēneris vidēbō. I shall see you *when you come to the city.*

2. **Cum,** meaning *when,* referring to *past time,* is used with the *indicative* or *subjunctive* mood:

INDICATIVE

Referring to *definite past time,* **cum** is used with the *indicative* mood:

Cum in urbem vēnistī, tē vīdī. At the time *when you came into the city,* I saw you.

SUBJUNCTIVE

Referring to *past time,* **cum** is used with the *subjunctive* mood in a subordinate clause describing the situation or circumstances under which the principal action takes place.

The *imperfect subjunctive* is used when the subordinate action is *contemporary* with the principal action:

Cum id facerent, *When they were doing this,*
sonitus terribilis audītus est. a terrible sound was heard.

The *pluperfect subjunctive* is used when the subordinate action is *prior* to the principal action.

Cum id fēcissent, *When they had done this,*
sonitus terribilis audītus est. a terrible sound was heard.

▶ STUDY HELPS

1. A clause which may be translated by **cum** with the imperfect subjunctive may also be expressed by the *present participle* or by **dum** with the *present indicative.*

Cum id facerent,
Eīs id facientibus, *When they were doing this,*
Dum id faciunt,
sonitus terribilis audītus est. a terrible sound was heard.

2. A clause translated by **cum** with the pluperfect subjunctive may also be expressed by **postquam, ubi,** or **ut** with the *perfect indicative*.

$$\left. \begin{array}{l} \textbf{\textit{Cum id fēcissent,}} \\ \textbf{\textit{Postquam (Ubi, Ut) id fēcērunt,}} \end{array} \right\} \left. \begin{array}{l} \textit{After} \\ \textit{When} \end{array} \right\} \textit{they} \left\{ \begin{array}{l} \textit{did} \\ \textit{had done} \end{array} \right\} \textit{this,}$$

sonitus terribilis audītus est.   a terrible sound was heard.

3. **Cum prīmum (Ubi prīmum, Ut prīmum, Simul atque),** *as soon as; **ubi,** when;* and **ut,** *when,* are used with the *perfect indicative* when referring to a single act or an actual occurrence in past time.

▶ PRACTICE PATTERNS

A. Translate into English:

1. Cum spēluncam intrāvissent, cōpiam lactis animadvertērunt. 2. Cum prīmum lac animadvertērunt, fūgērunt. 3. Cum explōrārent, sonitum audīvērunt. 4. Cum in spēluncā erunt, cōpiam lactis vidēbunt. 5. Cum ad spēluncam pervēnerint, intrābunt. 6. Illō tempore cum in spēluncam intrāvērunt, lac vīdērunt. 7. Haec eō dīcente, silentium fuit. 8. Hīs rēbus ab eō dictīs, silentium fuit. 9. Cum adsunt, timēmus. 10. Haec cum dīcerentur, silentium fuit.

B. Translate into Latin:

1. As soon as they saw the soldiers, they went away. 2. That night when they arrived at Rome, they talked with the leader. 3. I advise my friend when I see him. 4. When he was entering the cave, he did not notice the milk. 5. When he had moved away the stone, the cattle went out. 6. They will go away when the monster removes the stone. 7. When he is absent, they will prepare a sharpened stake. 8. As soon as he had tasted the wine, he ordered the cup to be filled again. 9. They surrounded the monster when he was oppressed with sleep. 10. When he notices the men, he will shout with a loud voice.

SECTION 4 Objective Genitive and Subjective Genitive

▶ DISCUSSION

1. The *objective genitive* is often used to indicate the receiver or the object of the action suggested by the noun on which it depends.

spēs praemī   *the hope of reward*
amor lībertātis   *the love of liberty*

The meaning of the noun the genitive modifies can readily be expressed in English by a verb. The genitive becomes the object of a verb.

Praemium spērat.   *He hopes for a reward.*
Lībertātem amat.   *He loves liberty.*

111

Some common nouns completed by the objective genitive are: **cupidi-tās, dēsīderium, facultās, occāsiō, potestās.**

cupiditās pācis	*eagerness for peace*
occāsiō fugae	*chance for escape*

These nouns translated into English are often followed by *for.*

Certain adjectives denoting *desire, knowledge, memory, fullness, power, skill, sharing, guilt,* and their opposites are completed by the objective genitive.

jūris perītus	*skilled in law*
laudis avidus	*greedy for praise*

2. The *subjective genitive* is often used to indicate the doer or the subject of the action suggested by the noun on which it depends.

adventus Caesaris	*the arrival of Caesar*
mora exercitūs	*the delay of the army*

The meaning of the noun the genitive modifies can easily be expressed in English by a verb. Notice that the genitive becomes the subject of the verb.

Caesar advenit.	*Caesar arrives.*
Exercitus morātur.	*The army delays.*

▶ PRACTICE PATTERNS

A. Translate into English and explain each italicized genitive.

1. Sunt perītī *nāvium.* 2. Amor *patriae* est bonus. 3. Laudēmus victōriam *Caesaris.* 4. Sunt cupidī *pecūniae.* 5. Imperium *Rōmānōrum* erat māgnum. 6. Erat māgnum dēsīderium *pācis.*

B. Translate into Latin and explain each genitive.

1. They were skilled in war. 2. They showed great fear of death. 3. He had great desire for knowledge. 4. The love of the mother was great. 5. The flight of the enemy was quick. 6. The envy of the citizens harmed Caesar.

BUILDING WORD POWER

There seems to be a close relationship between **tenēre, tentum,** *to hold,* and **tendere, tentum** (or **tēnsum**), *to stretch, extend.* Write the Latin compounds for: *attend, contend, distend, extend, intend, portend, pretend, subtend.* Notice the use of *tent–* and *tens–* in these nouns: *attention, contention, distention, intention, extension, pretension, tension.* What do we mean by a *tense* silence; *tensile* strength of steel; a *tendency* to tears; legal *tender;* the *tender* was overloaded; *ostensible* bravery; a *contentious* character?

Tentāre or *temptāre* is a frequentative of *tendere*, and it means *to try the strength of, to test, to prove.* What is a *tentative* program, the *tentacle* of a jelly fish, a violent *temptation?*

The adjective *tenuis, –e* seems to be a relative of *tendere, to stretch.* It means *fine, thin, slender,* as something stretched out is apt to be. The two compounds *attenuāre* and *extenuāre* have approximately the same meaning in both English and Latin, *to make thin, to reduce.* Explain: *extenuating* circumstances; a *tenuous* plot; to *attenuate* a virus.

WORDS TO MASTER

abeō, –īre, –iī, –itūrus, *irreg.,* go away, depart

acūtus, –a, –um, *adj.,* sharp, sharpened, pointed (*acute*)

āmoveō, –ēre, –mōvī, –mōtus, move away

circumveniō, –īre, –vēnī, –ventus, come around, surround (*circumvent*)

compleō, –ēre, –plēvī, –plētus, fill full, fill up (*complete*)

cum, *conj.,* when, while, after, since, because, although; **cum prīmum,** as soon as

frōns, frontis, *f.,* forehead (*front*)

incidō, –ere, –cidī, —, fall into *or* upon (*incident*)

lac, lactis, *n.,* milk (*lactic*)

nesciō, –scīre, –scīvī, —, not to know, be ignorant of (*nescience*)

pālus, –ī, *m.,* stake, pale (*palisade*)

pecus, –oris, *n.,* cattle, herd, flock (*peculiar*)

rēmus, –ī, *m.,* oar

sonitus, –ūs, *m.,* sound, noise

speciēs, –ēī, *f.,* sight, appearance, shape (*species*)

tollō, –ere, sustulī, sublātus, *irreg.,* lift, raise, remove

SENTENCE PATTERNS

A. Complete the following sentences by selecting the correct word in parentheses. Translate the completed sentences.

1. Graecōrum animōs tantus terror occupāvit ut nē loquī quidem (possent; potuerant).
2. Cum (intellēxissent; intellēxerint) quō in locō rēs esset, māgnum clāmōrem sustulērunt.
3. Cum prīmum vīnum (gustat; gustāvit), iterum pōculum complērī jūssit.
4. Ut prīmum saxum āmōvit, pecora ex spēluncā (cucurrērunt; currerent).
5. Tum cum virī Polyphēmum circumveniēbant, aliquī pālum acūtum (parārent; parābant).
6. Nōnne horribile mōnstrum hūmānā speciē sed ūnō oculō in mediā fronte positō (vīdērunt; vidērent)?
7. Abeāmus! Nē (āmoveāmus; āmoveāmur) māgnam cōpiam lactis!
8. Ut prīmum sonitum (audiant; audīvērunt) nescīvērunt quid facerent.

9. Rēmīs contendēbant ut quam prīmum ad terram nāvem (appulērunt; appellerent).
10. Forte ita inciderat ut Graecī tūtī ad nāvēs (contenderent; contendant).

B. Translate into Latin:

1. As soon as they saw the man with one eye set in the middle of his forehead, they knew who he was.
2. When he knew that there were men in the cave, he shouted with a loud cry.
3. As soon as he heard this, he spoke thus.
4. Let him move away the stone so that we may go away.
5. When they had done this, they wondered who lived in the cave.

Unwelcome Guests

Illā tōtā nocte rēmīs contendērunt et postrīdiē ad īgnōtam terram nāvem appulērunt. Ipse Ulixēs cum duodecim sociīs in terram ēgressus est ut locum explōrāret. Paulum ā lītore prōgressī, ad spēluncam ingentem pervēnērunt. Etsī intellegēbant sē nōn sine perīculō hoc factūrōs esse, tamen spēluncam intrāvērunt. Cum id fēcissent, māgnam cōpiam lactis in vāsīs (*vessels*) ingentibus animadvertērunt. Dum mīrantur quis in eō locō habitāret, sonitum terribilem audīvērunt, et ad ōstium mōnstrum horribile vīdērunt, hūmānā speciē et figūrā sed ingentī māgnitūdine corporis. Cum autem spectāvissent mōnstrum ūnum modō oculum habēre in mediā fronte positum, intellēxērunt hunc esse ūnum ex Cyclopibus dē quibus jam audīverant.

Cyclopēs pastōrēs erant quī īnsulam Siciliam praecipuēque montem Aetnam incolēbant. Ibi Vulcānus, protector fabrōrum (*of blacksmiths*) īgnisque inventor, cūjus servī Cyclopēs erant,

Ulysses and his men about to blind the Cyclops.

114

officīnam (*shop*) suam habēbat. Cum prīmum nautae mōnstrum vīdērunt, perterritī in interiōrem spēluncae partem fūgērunt, et sē abdere cōnābantur. Polyphēmus (sīc enim Cyclops appellābātur) cum sēnsisset hominēs in interiōre spēluncae parte esse abditōs, māgnā vōce exclāmāvit. Sine morā duōs hominēs miserōs corripuit et interfēcit. Tum carnem eōrum avidē vorāvit. Graecōrum animōs tantus terror occupāvit ut, omnī spē salūtis dēpositā, praesentem mortem exspectārent. Posterō diē duōs aliōs interfectōs vorāvit. Deinde, cum saxō ingentī ōstium clausisset, ex spēluncā excessit et pecus ad montes ēgit.

Sub vesperum Polyphēmus in spēluncam rediit. Deinde Ulixēs mōnstrō māximum pōculum vīnī dedit. Numquam anteā Cyclōps vīnum gustāverat. Iterum iterumque pōculum complērī jūssit. Cum quaesīvisset quō nōmine Ulixēs appellārētur, ille respondit: "Nēmō appellātus sum." Polyphēmus, cum id audīvisset, ita locūtus est: "Prō tantō beneficiō, tē postrēmum (*last*) omnium vorābō." Brevī tempore mōnstrum somnō oppressum est.

Tum Ulixēs et sociī ējus Polyphēmum circumvēnērunt; pālō (*stake*) acūtō oculum ējus perfōdērunt (*pierced*). Tantum clāmōrem sustulit ut reliquī Cyclōpēs undique ad spēluncam convenīrent. Cum quaesīvissent quis eī vim intulisset, respondit: "Nēmō id fēcit!" Cyclōpēs eum in īnsāniam incidisse arbitrātī abiērunt.

Posterō diē Polyphēmus saxum āmōvit ut pecora ex spēluncā mitteret. Tum ex spēluncā horribilī Graecī dolō fūgērunt et tūtī ad nāvēs contendērunt.

Fair laughs the morn, and soft the zephyr blows
While proudly riding o'er the azure realm.
        —Thomas Gray, 1716–1771

Unit XIII

CONVERSATION

ULIXĒS: Haec patria est ventōrum. Rēx ventōrum Aeolus appellātur.

EURYLOCHUS: Aliī ventī nōbīs auxiliō, aliī impedīmentō sunt.

ULIXĒS: Paucōs diēs hīc manēbimus cum comitēs meī, aegrī anxiīque, quiētem cupiant.

AEOLUS: Salvēte, advenae! Ancoram jacite! Nōlīte virōs praesidiō nāvī relinquere! Nāvis erit tūta! Comitēs cēnent (*let them dine*) et quiētem capiant!

ULIXĒS: Grātiās agimus tibi, Aeole! Septem diēs in īnsulā tuā commorābimur, quod necesse est virōs ē labōribus sē recipere et omnia ad nāvigātiōnem parāre.

AEOLUS   (*septimō diē*): Nē annī tempore ā nāvigātiōne exclūdāris, Ulixēs, nāvem solvere statim dēbēs.

ULIXĒS: Abīre jam parātī sumus, quod patriam nostram vidēre māgnopere volumus.

AEOLUS: Tibi, Ulixēs, saccum dō, in quō omnēs ventī praeter ūnum inclūsī sunt. Zephyrum modo solvī, quod ille ventus ab īnsulā Aeoliā nāvigantī Ithacam est secundus.

SECTION 1 Causal Clauses

▶ DISCUSSION

A causal clause is a subordinate clause that states a cause or reason. Either the indicative or subjunctive mood is used.

1. Causal clauses introduced by the conjunctions *quod, quia,* or *quoniam, because, since,* and stating the reason as a definite fact on the authority of the speaker or the writer, take the indicative.

Domī mānsit *quod aeger erat.*   He stayed at home *because he was sick.*

2. *Quod* or *quia* is followed by the *subjunctive* when the reason is alleged, assumed, or indirectly quoted, i.e., when the reason is not that of the speaker or the writer but represents the thought of someone else.

Impērātor accūsāvit mīlitēs   The general blamed the soldiers
 quod fortēs nōn essent.   *on the grounds that (on the charge that; because, as was said) they were not brave.*

3. Causal clauses introduced by *cum, since,* take the *subjunctive* in whatever tense is required by the English.

Cum fortis sit, nihil timet.   *Since he is brave,* he fears nothing.
Cum fortis esset, nihil timēbat.   *Since he was brave,* he feared nothing.

4. *Cum* with the *subjunctive* may be used in *all* causal clauses.

Domī mānsit *cum aeger esset.*   He stayed at home *because he was sick.*
Imperātor accūsāvit mīlitēs   The general blamed the soldiers
 cum fortēs nōn essent.   *because they were not brave.*

▶ PRACTICE PATTERNS

A. Translate into English:

1. Cum vēnerit, abībunt. 2. Quia victī sunt, fūgērunt. 3. Cum audāx sit, nihil timet. 4. Ē somnō excitātus est quod comitēs saccum solverant. 5. Cum haec

116

facere nōn posset, domō fūgit. 6. Cum dēfessus esset, recumbere cōnstituit.
7. Quod haec facere potuit, pācem fēcit. 8. Quod aurum in saccō latēre crēderent,
ducī nōn paruērunt.

B. Translate into Latin:

1. Since he was ill, he decided to remain on the boat. 2. Because the winds
burst from the sack, a great storm arose. 3. The leader was very angry because
the men had not obeyed him. 4. They drew lots because no one was willing to
explore the region. 5. Since they had loosened the sack and set free the winds,
they could not hold their course. 6. The king of the winds was unwilling to help
the Greeks again because all the gods were hostile to them.

SECTION 2 Special Datives: Purpose; Reference; Double Dative

▶ DISCUSSION

1. *Dative of purpose.* The dative singular of many abstract nouns is
sometimes used in Latin with certain verbs (most frequently **sum**) to
indicate what something is for, what purpose it serves, or what effect
it produces.

Hanc pecūniam *praemiō* **dedī.**	I gave this money *as a reward* (*for a reward*).
Mīlitēs *praesidiō* **relīquit.**	He left the soldiers *as a guard* (*for a guard*).

The dative of purpose is sometimes used in Latin where English would
employ a predicate nominative.

Scūtum *impedīmentō* **erit.**	The shield will be a *hindrance* (*for a hindrance*).

2. *Dative of reference.* The dative may denote the person or thing with
reference to whom a statement is true. The person or thing may be
interested, benefited, or harmed by the action of the verb.

Imperātōrī **fortiter pūgnāvit.**	He fought bravely *for the general.*
Praesidium *oppidō* **reliquit.**	He left a garrison *for the town.*

3. *Double dative.* The double dative consists of a combination of the
datives of purpose and reference.

Auxiliō sociīs **vēnimus.**	We have come *as an aid to our allies.*
Tertiam aciem *hostibus impedīmentō* **mīsit.**	He sent the third line *as a hindrance to the enemy.*
Est māgnae *cūrae* **patrī.**	He is a great *care to his father.*

► PRACTICE PATTERNS

A. Translate into English and explain each italicized dative:

1. Auxilium *urbī* fert. 2. Locum *castrīs* dēligit. 3. Mīlitēs *subsidiō* mīsit. 4. Servus nōn est *ūsuī nōbīs*. 5. Illud est *māgnō auxiliō eī*. 6. Fīlius meus est *cūrae mātrī*.

B. Translate into Latin and give the reason for the dative case:

1. This is a great worry to us. 2. The weather was a hindrance. 3. He was of little service to me. 4. We chose a place for the meeting. 5. He was left as a protection for you. 6. The winds were favorable for sailing.

WORDS TO MASTER

aeger, –gra, –grum, *adj.,* sick; **aegrē,** *adv.,* ill, with difficulty

anxius, –a, –um, *adj.,* anxious, uneasy (*anxiety*)

argentum, –ī, *n.,* silver (*argentiferous*)

ērumpō, –ere, –rūpī, –ruptus, break open, burst forth (*erupt*)

excitō (1), cry out, arouse, raise up (*excite*)

exclūdō, –ere, –clūsī, –clūsus, shut out (*exclude*)

hortor (1), *dep.,* exhort, encourage, urge (*exhort*)

incertus, –a, –um, *adj.,* uncertain, doubtful, not sure (*uncertain*)

lateō, –ēre, –uī, —, lie hidden, be concealed (*latent*)

modo, *adv.,* only, just now, lately

nāvigātiō, –ōnis, *f.,* sailing, voyage (*navigation*)

recēns, –entis, *adj.,* new, fresh, young (*recent*)

recumbō, –ere, –cubuī, —, lie back, recline (*recumbent*)

saccus, –ī, *m.,* bag, sack, money bag (*sack*)

sors, sortis (*abl.* **sortī**), *f.,* a lot, casting of lots (*sort*)

sortior, –īrī, –ītus sum, *dep.,* cast or draw lots

BUILDING WORD POWER

Many interesting and useful words came into English from the root word ***plicāre, plicātum,*** *to fold, to fold together,* and its compounds. Explain the meanings of the words in the column on the right.

applicāre, to join, apply to: *application* — *appliqué*
complicāre, to fold together: *complication* — *accomplice*
duplicāre, to double: *duplication* — *duplicity*
explicāre, to unfold: *explication* — *explicit*
implicāre, to enfold: *implication* — *implicit*
multiplicāre, to multiply: *multiplication* — *multiplier*
quadruplicāre, to make fourfold: *quadruplication* — *quadruple*
replicāre, to fold back: *replication* — *replica*
simplicāre, to make simple — *simplicity*
supplicāre, to kneel down: *supplication* — *supple*
triplicāre, to make threefold: *triplication* — *triple*

118

Notice that *apply, imply, multiply,* and *reply* are derived from **plicāre,** *to fold,* but *comply* and *supply* have come through the French from **plēre,** *to fill. Duplex, multiplex, simplex,* and *triplex* are Latin words formed from **plicāre,** *to fold,* whereas *complex* and *perplex* are derived from the root word **plectere, plexum,** *to weave.* A **plexus** is a *network.* Where is the solar *plexus?* Distinguish between **plicāre** and **plectere,** *to weave.*

SENTENCE PATTERNS

A. Translate into English:

1. Quod Aeolus, rēx ventōrum, eōs benīgnē accēpit, paucōs diēs in īnsulā mānsērunt.
2. Graviter eōs accūsāvit quod ventōs solverent.
3. Cum crēderent argentum in saccō latēre, ducī pārēre nōlēbant.
4. Ulixēs, nē propter tempus annī ā nāvigātiōne exclūderētur, omnia quae nāvigantī auxiliō erant parāre cōnstituit.
5. Quod somnō oppressus est, recumbere statuit.
6. Jam Graecī cursum aegrē tenēbant quod ventī eīs impedīmentō erant.
7. Dux ē somnō excitātus, quod recēns perīculum statim intellēxit, erat īrātissimus.
8. Haec cum ita essent, inter sē sortītī sunt.
9. Comitēs suōs, quī sorte in incertam terram ēgrediēbantur, hortātus est et reditum eōrum anxiō animō exspectāvit.
10. Nōn modo ventī ērūpērunt sed nāvem in eandem partem unde nautae profectī erant etiam appulsērunt.

B. Translate into Latin:

1. They departed immediately because the weather was a help to those sailing to Ithaca.
2. Since these things are so, we do not wish to draw lots.
3. When they had advanced a few miles from that place, the winds burst forth from the sack.
4. Because their leader was overwhelmed with sleep, they opened the sack.
5. They remained on the shore as a guard to the ship.

The Price of Curiosity

Pauca mīlia passuum ab eō locō prōgressus, Ulixēs ad īnsulam Aeoliam pervēnit. Aeolus, rēx ventōrum, hīc habitābat, et Graecōs benīgnē accēpit. Paucōs diēs in īnsulā mānsērunt. Septimō diē, cum omnēs ē labōribus sē refēcissent *(recovered),* Ulixēs, nē annī tempore ā nāvigātiōne exclūderētur, iterum proficīscī volēbat. Tum rēx Aeolus, quod sciēbat Ulixem patriam vidēre māgnopere

cupere, eī māgnum saccum dedit in quō omnēs ventōs praeter
ūnum inclūserat. Zephyrum modo solverat quod ille ventus nāvigantī ab īnsulā Aeoliā Ithacam est auxiliō. Ulixēs laetus hoc
dōnum accēpit, et rēgī grātiās prō tantō beneficiō ēgit.

Novem diēs Graecī secundissimō ventō cursum tenuērunt atque
jam in cōnspectum patriae suae vēnerant. Tum Ulixēs labōre
dēfessus recumbere cōnstituit; at sociī, quī jam diū mīrābantur
quid in illō saccō esset, cum ducem somnō oppressum vidērent,
saccum solvērunt. Crēdēbant enim aurum et argentum in saccō
latēre. Itaque spē praedae adductī, ducī suō nōn paruērunt. Statim ē saccō ventī ērūpērunt et tanta tempestās orta est ut illī
cursum tenēre nōn possent, sed in eandem partem unde erant
profectī referrentur.

Ulixēs ē somnō excitātus quō in locō rēs esset statim intellēxit.
Īrātissimus erat cum nāvem māgnō in perīculō esse vidēret. Tem-

Ulysses and Aeolus, king of the winds.

pestās Graecōs ad īnsulam Aeolī rettulit. Aeolus māgnā cum īrā
dīxit omnēs deōs Ulixī et sociīs ējus inimīcōs esse, neque Graecōs
iterum juvāre volēbat.

Brevī spatiō intermissō, Graecī īnsulae cuidam appropinquāvērunt, in quā Circē, fīlia Sōlis, habitābat. Eō cum Ulixēs nāvem
appulisset, ibi frūmentum petere cōnstituit. Itaque sociīs ad sē
convocātīs, quō in locō rēs esset et quid fierī vellet ostendit. Cum
tamen omnēs memoriā tenērent recentem et crūdēlem mortem
eōrum quī anteā ē nāvī ēgressī essent, nēmō repertus est quī hoc
negōtium suscipere vellet. Tandem Ulixēs sociōs in duās partēs
dīvīsit, quārum alterī Eurylochus, vir summae virtūtis, alterī
ipse praeesset. Tum hī duo inter sē sortītī sunt uter in terram in-

120

certam ēgrederētur. Eurylochus sorte cum duōbus et vīgintī sociīs
rem aegrē suscēpit dum Ulixēs reditum eōrum anxiō animō exspectat.

Besides 'tis known he could speak Greek
As naturally as pigs squeak;
— Samuel Butler, 1600–1680

Unit XIV

CONVERSATION

EURYLOCHUS: Comitēs meī, Ulixēs, mēcum nōn revēnērunt quamquam
eōs relinquere nōlēbam. Hīs virīs fortūna mala accidit.

ULIXĒS (*commōtus*): Ubi sunt? Ad eōs statim eāmus!

EURYLOCHUS: Hōs virōs līberāre difficillimum erit! Quamquam, Ō dux,
vir fortis es, tamen huic operī es nōn pār.

ULIXĒS: Fortēs hī virī semper fuērunt. Sī mēcum nōn veniēs, sōlus
ad eōs ībō. Sociōs meōs redūcere est officium meum.
(*Ante lucem ē nāve contendit dux fortis quī cēterōs animō
superāvit.*)

MERCURIUS: Quō properās? Nōnne scīs quantum sit perīculum tuum?
Virī tuī cantum fēminae malae cui nōmen est Circē audīvērunt. Ab illā in porcōs (*pigs*) conversī sunt. Num villam
inīre audēs?

ULIXĒS: Cum māgnum sit perīculum, prō sociīs meīs pūgnābō!

MERCURIUS: Hanc herbam cape. Tum Circē tibi injūriās facere nōn
poterit. Nōlī tardāre! Tardius vēneris! Jānua patet!

ULIXĒS (*posteā ad mēnsam cōnsidēns*): Nōlī mē tangere, Circē, virgā tuā!
Contrā mē ars magica tua nihil valet! In fōrmam hūmā-
nam statim sociōs meōs converte vel tē gladiō interficiam!

SECTION 1 Concessive Clauses

▶ DISCUSSION

1. A concessive (**concēdere**, *to yield*) clause is a subordinate adverbial
clause. In English such clauses are introduced by *although, granted that,
in spite of the fact that*, etc. In Latin they are introduced by **quamquam,
etsī, cum, quamvīs**, etc.

2. **Quamquam, etsī**, *although*, introduce a statement of fact, and are
followed by the indicative (of any tense, as required by the meaning).

Quamquam (Etsī) māgnum est   *Although the danger is great*, I shall stay
perīculum, in īnsulā morābor.   on the island.

3. **Quamvīs,** *although,* does not introduce a statement of fact, but represents an act merely as conceived. It is followed by the subjunctive, usually of the present tense.

Quamvīs māgnum sit perīculum,   *Although the danger may be great,* I shall
in īnsulā morābor.   stay on the island.

4. **Cum,** *although,* is always followed by the subjunctive (of any tense, as required by the meaning).

Cum māgnum sit perīculum, in   *Although the danger is great,* I shall
īnsulā morābor.   stay on the island.

5. After a concessive clause, Latin often inserts the word **tamen,** *yet, nevertheless,* in the main clause.

Quamquam fortiter pūgnāvit, (ta-
men) victus est.   *Although he fought bravely, (neverthe-*
Cum fortiter pūgnāvisset, (tamen) *less) he was defeated.*
victus est.

▶ PRACTICE PATTERNS

A. Translate into English:

1. Quamquam multum valēbat, tamen cōnsul nōn creātus est. 2. Etsī ad sōlis occāsum exspectāvit, comitēs ējus nōn rediērunt. 3. Cum fēmina mala virgā ducem tangeret, nihil efficere potuit. 4. Cum fēmina nautās benīgnē acciperet, tamen dux cum reliquīs nōn intrāvit. 5. Cum virī in hūmānam speciem iterum conversī essent, tamen per tōtum annum in īnsulā morābantur.

B. Translate into Latin:

1. They remained on the island although they were afraid. 2. Although they were in great danger, they entered the villa. 3. He will try to help his comrades although he will be too late. 4. Although she is touching him with her wand, his appearance is not changing. 5. Although they had approached the villa in the silence of the night, they did not save their friends.

SECTION 2 Dative of Possession

▶ DISCUSSION

1. The dative case is used in the predicate with **sum** to indicate the possessor; the thing possessed is then in the nominative case as the subject of a form of **sum.** This is called the dative of possession.

Sunt *tibi* multī librī.   *You* have many books. (Many books
                             are *to you.*)
Sī *tibi* est aequus animus, . . .   If *you* have a calm mind, . . .

2. This dative emphasizes the fact of ownership, not the owner.

3. This dative is often used with **nōmen est.**

> **Mihi nōmen est Paulus.** *I* have the name Paul. Paul is *my* name.

▶ PRACTICE PATTERNS

A. Translate into English:

1. Est eī fīlius. 2. Illī nōmen erat Circē. 3. Erat rēx cui erant trēs fīliae. 4. Māgnae dīvitiae huic virō erant. 5. Imperātōrī sunt multī fortēs mīlitēs. 6. Est mihi domī pater cārus.

B. Translate into Latin:

1. He has a sword. 2. The man's name is Ulysses. 3. This farmer has a large field. 4. His brother had great influence. 5. The woman had great knowledge and power. 6. There was a queen who had three wonderful wands.

SECTION 3 Summary of Uses of *cum* with the Indicative and the Subjunctive

TYPE OF **cum**-CLAUSE	LATIN	ENGLISH
Cum-causal *Subjunctive.* Tense as required by English.	*Cum veniat, exeunt.* *Cum venīret, exiērunt.* *Cum vēnerit, exeunt.* *Cum vēnisset, exiērunt.*	*Since he is coming,* they are leaving. *Since he was coming,* they left. *Since he has come,* they are leaving. *Since he had come,* they left.
Cum-concessive *Subjunctive.* Tense as required by English.	*Cum veniat, eximus.* *Cum venīret, exiimus.* *Cum vēnerit, eximus.* *Cum vēnisset, exiimus.*	*Although he is coming,* we are leaving. *Although he was coming,* we left. *Although he has come,* we are leaving. *Although he had come,* we left.
Cum-temporal *Subjunctive.* Used only in past time. Imperf. or pluperf.	*Cum venīret, exiērunt.* *Cum vēnisset, exiērunt.*	*When he was coming,* they left. *When he had come,* they left.
Indicative. Used when referring to present time.	*Cum venit, exeunt.*	*When he comes,* they leave.
Indicative. Used when referring to future time.	*Cum veniet, exībunt.* *Cum vēnerit, exībunt.*	*When he will come,* they will leave. *When he comes,* they will leave. *When he will have come,* they will leave. *When he comes,* they will leave.
Indicative. Used when referring to definite past time.	*Cum vēnit, exiērunt.*	*When he came,* they left.

123

1. In expressing past time with *cum,* the indicative in a past tense states a definite time when something happened; and the subjunctive in the imperfect or pluperfect states the circumstances.

2. With the indicative the time is dated; with the subjunctive the time is described.

Cum — pure temporal: **Cum vēnit, exiērunt.** When he *came,* they left.

Cum — circumstantial: **Cum venīret, exiērunt.** When he *was coming,* they left.

▶ PRACTICE PATTERNS

A. Translate into English. Note the reason for the mood of the verb in the subordinate clause.

1. Cum virī essent māgnō in perīculō, Ulixēs illōs servāvit. 2. Cum dux ē nāve excessit, nautae māgnopere timēbant. 3. Haec cum dīxisset, ad jānuam appropinquāvit. 4. Cum sītis in meā potestāte, tamen vōbīs nōn nocēbō. 5. Nautae, cum tēla habeant, fēminam malam nōn timēbunt. 6. Cum Circē virōs virgā tetigerit, hūmānī nōn jam sunt. 7. Cōnsul, cum fīliōs amāret, tamen eīs nōn pepercit. 8. Cum Ulixēs ad fēminam cum herbā accēdet, perterrēbitur. 9. Deus cum virō herbam dedisset, tamen domicilium nōn iniit. 10. Cum Ulixēs adest, nautae sunt fortēs.

B. Translate into Latin:

1. Since he was leaving, they remained. 2. Although they had fought bravely, nevertheless they did not take the town. 3. When the leader was approaching the house, he saw the god. 4. Since the sailors have been absent for a long time, Ulysses fears for their safety. 5. When their leader comes, the men will be saved.

WORDS TO MASTER

accēdō, –ere, –cessī, –cessūrus, approach, move toward (*accede*)

bis, *adv.,* twice, in two ways (*bisect*)

campus, –ī, *m.,* plain, field (*camp*)

canō, –ere, cecinī, —, sing; **cantus, –ūs,** *m.,* song (*cant*)

herba, –ae, *f.,* herb, plant (*herbaceous*)

hūmānus, –a, –um, *adj.,* of man, human, civilized (*humanity*)

jānua, –ae, *f.,* door (*janitor*)

moror (1), *dep.,* delay, linger, stay (*moratorium*)

pateō, –ēre, –uī, —, lie open, spread, extend (*patent*)

quamquam, *conj.,* although, though, and yet

silentium, –ī, *n.,* stillness, silence

tangō, –ere, tetigī, tactus, touch (*tangent, tact*)

tardus, –a, –um, *adj.,* slow, tardy; **tardō** (1), slow down, hinder, delay (*retard*)

valeō, –ēre, –uī, –itūrus, be strong, be powerful; **multum valeō,** have much power, influence (*value*)

vel, *conj.,* or; **vel . . . vel,** either . . or

virga, –ae, *f.,* twig, rod, wand (*virgule*)

BUILDING WORD POWER

The verb **dicāre, dicātum,** *to proclaim, show, dedicate,* seems to have been originally the same verb as **dīcere, dictum,** *to say, tell, declare.* From **dicāre, dicātum** we have *abdicate, dedicate, indicate, predicate, vindicate,* with their close relatives coming into the English language either directly or indirectly. From **dīcere, dictum** came *addict, Benedict, contradict, edict, indict, interdict, predict, verdict, diction, dictionary, valedictory;* and from the frequentative **dictāre** we have *dictate.* Notice that **dicāre** is a verb of the first conjugation, **dīcere,** of the third; the –*i*– in **dicāre** is short, in **dīcere,** long; the word *indict,* to charge with an offense, is pronounced as if it were *indite,* to compose and write.

Explain the meaning of: pure *diction; dictatorial* manner; *contradictory* reports; *Edict* of Nantes; the antonyms *benediction* and *malediction;* a lively *ditty* (**dictātum**); *ditto* (**dictum**) marks; unreasonable *conditions* (**condiciō**); under the bishop's *jurisdiction;* the *abdication* of the king; blind *prejudice; vindicate* one's honor; the *dedication* of a church.

Note that a *verdict* (**vērē,** *truly,* + **dictum**), a *decision,* is a *saying of the truth;* to *preach* (**prae** + **dicāre**), *to proclaim before,* is derived from the same compound as *predicament* and *predicate; judge* is from **jūdicāre** (**jūs,** *right, law,* + **dicāre**), *to proclaim the law;* a *valedictory* (**valē,** *farewell,* + **dīcere**) is a *farewell speech.*

SENTENCE PATTERNS

A. Supply the Latin form of the verb. Then translate the sentence.

1. Quamquam eīs quid fierī (volō, *he wished*) ostendit, ducī parēre nōlēbant.
2. Hī duo inter sē (sortior) ut statuerētur uter in nāve (maneō).
3. Cum tardius (sum), dux fortis comitēs suōs adjuvāre properat.
4. Vir summae virtūtis cui erat nōmen Eurylochus rem (suscipiō).
5. Cum cantum (audiō), ad jānuam accessērunt.
6. Cum prīmum virī virgā (tangō) sub potestāte fēminae malae erant.
7. Tam celeriter per campum currēbat ut advenam vix (video).
8. Quamquam Ulixēs domum redīre māgnopere (volō), per tōtum annum in īnsulā morābātur.
9. Nē tardēmus! Utinam herba contrā artem fēminae canentis multum (valeō)! Sociī nostrī in fōrmam hūmānam convertentur!
10. Bis in silentiō noctis ad jānuam accessērunt sed jānua nōn (pateō) vel nēmō respondit.

B. Translate into Latin:

1. Although they knew there was no grain on the ship, the sailors did not wish to approach the unknown island.

2. Twice they asked why the man named Eurylochus waited near the door.
3. Indeed those in the ship were scarcely able to hold back their tears because they believed they would never see their companions again.
4. Although they feared greatly, they approached and entered the door of the villa.
5. He gave him a certain herb which he said had much effect against the woman's song.

A Charm and Its Countercharm

His rēbus ita cōnstitutīs, Eurylochus cum sociīs in interiōrem partem īnsulae profectus est. Tantus tamen timor animōs eōrum occupāverat ut exīstimārent sē ad mortem appropinquāre. Illī quī in nāve relictī erant crēdēbant sē sociōs numquam posteā vīsūrōs esse. Hī autem post breve iter per campum ad villam pulcherrimam pervēnērunt.

Ad ōstium cum adissent, vōcem fēminae canentis audīvērunt. Postquam jānuam bis pulsāvērunt (*knocked*), pulcherrima fēmina,

Circe offering drugged wine to Ulysses.

cui nōmen erat Circē, exiit et summā cum benīgnitāte (*kindness*) eōs salūtāvit atque accēpit. Eurylochus īnsidiās veritus nōn cum reliquīs intrāvit sed prope jānuam sedēbat. Ibi ad sōlis occāsum anxiō animō exspectāvit; deinde sōlus ad nāvem contendit.

Eō cum Eurylochus vēnisset, timōre ita perturbātus fuit ut quae vīdisset vix narrāre posset. Intereā eī quī villam intrāverant convīvium (*feast*) parātum invēnērunt. At Circē, quae artis magicae summam scientiam habēbat, vīnum eīs dedit in quō medicāmentum (*drug*) quoddam posuerat. Postquam Graecī vīnum bibērunt, Circē capita eōrum virgā aureā tetigit. Hōc factō, omnēs in porcōs conversī sunt.

Ulixēs, cum intellegeret sociōs suōs māgnō in perīculō esse, gladium cēpit et in īnsulam prōgressus est. Ad villam Circēs (–ae) statim accessūrus erat. Subitō deus Mercurius eum domum intrantem manū prehendit. "Quō," inquit, "contendis? Nōnne scīs hoc esse Circēs domicilium? Hīc sunt amīcī tuī, quamquam ex hūmānā speciē in porcōs conversī sunt. Num vīs ipse in eandem calamitātem venīre?" Tamen hīs dictīs, herbam quandam deus eī dedit, quae contrā artem magicam multum valēbat. Brevī intermissō spatiō, Ulixēs jānuam pulsāvit et ab ipsā Circē benīgnē acceptus est.

Omnia eōdem modō atque anteā facta sunt. Quamquam Circē per magicam artem suam Ulixem in porcum vertere cōnāta est, propter herbam nihil efficere potuit. Deinde Ulixēs eam gladiō interfectūrus erat. Circē perterrita veniam petīvit et porcōs quī hominēs fuerant in fōrmam hūmānam statim convertit.

Cum Ulixēs ex hāc īnsulā quam celerrimē discēdere in animō habēret, Circē tamen eum paucōs diēs apud sē manēre māgnopere volēbat. Ab odiō (*hatred*) ad amōrem conversa, māgna beneficia Ulixī atque sociīs ējus dabat. Itaque per tōtum annum apud Circēn (Circam) morābantur.

Farther than the arrow, higher than wings, fly
poet's song and prophet's word.
—Rosco Conkling, 1867–1946

Unit XV

CONVERSATION

CIRCĒ: Quā dē causā Ulixēs omnia quae ad nāvigandum ūsuī sunt comparārī jūssit?

EURYLOCHUS: Ulixēs māgnō dēsīderiō patriae videndae movētur. Cum tōtum jam annum hīc morātus sīt, comitēs ējus Ulixem iter intermissum repetere (*resume*) volunt.

CIRCĒ: Rem aegrē ferō, sed māgnum subsidium Graecīs dabō.

ULIXĒS: Grātiās agāmus Circī, dominae benīgnae īnsulae pulchrae.

CIRCĒ: At prīmum necesse est Ulixem ad īnferōs adīre caecī Tīresiae videndī atque cōnsulendī causā.

ULIXĒS: Ad īnferōs adīre est difficillimum. Iter nēsciō.

CIRCĒ: Ego tibi iter quō celerius adeās expōnam. Hūc revenī cum loquendī fīnem cum Tīresiā fēcissēs. Multa quidem perīcula tē atque virōs tuōs ante itineris fīnem exspectant. Quōmodo omnia haec vītēs, tē docēbō.

ULIXĒS: Tē nōs adjuvante admonitū tuō, negōtium facillimum erit.

CIRCĒ: Valē, Ulixēs! Tē atque comitēs tuōs iterum vidēbō!

SECTION 1 Formation of the Gerund

▶ DISCUSSION

1. In English the gerund is an active verbal noun ending in *-ing* (I like *reading;* the art of *writing,* etc.).

2. In Latin the gerund is an active verbal noun formed on the present stem, to which is added the characteristic indicator *–nd–* + the singular case indicators of a second declension neuter noun. It is found only in the genitive, dative, accusative, and ablative singular. In the nominative case the infinitive is used instead.

3. In the third *–iō* conjugation and the fourth conjugation, an *–e–* is inserted between the present stem and characteristic indicator *–nd–*.

4. The gerunds of the deponent verbs are regularly formed and are active in meaning.

5. Of the irregular verbs only *ferō* and *eō* have the gerund.

FORMATION AND MEANING OF THE GERUND

	I	II	III	III–io	IV
Nom.	(*Infinitive is used*)				
Gen.	vocandī	monendī	regendī	capiendī	audiendī
Dat.	vocandō	monendō	regendō	capiendō	audiendō
Acc.	vocandum	monendum	regendum	capiendum	audiendum
Abl.	vocandō	monendō	regendō	capiendō	audiendō
Translation of genitive	*of calling*	*of warning*	*of ruling*	*of taking*	*of hearing*

SECTION 2 Uses of the Gerund

▶ DISCUSSION

1. Because a gerund is partly a noun and partly a verb, it has the attributes of a noun and, as a verb, may take an object.

128

2. The *nominative case* is supplied by the infinitive:

Vidēre est crēdere.   *Seeing (To see) is believing (to believe).*

3. The *genitive case* of the gerund is used in three ways. With nouns it is used as objective genitive:

fīnis pūgnandī   *the end of fighting*

With adjectives it is used to complete the meaning:

cupidus discēdendī   *desirous of leaving*

With **causā** or **grātiā** it is used to denote purpose:

videndī causā   *for the purpose of seeing*

Notice that **causā** and **grātiā** are in the ablative case.

4. The *dative case* of the gerund is rarely used. It is sometimes used with adjectives that take the dative:

Aqua ūtilis est bibendō.   Water is *useful for drinking.*

5. The *accusative case* of the gerund is used only with prepositions, chiefly **ad** to express purpose:

Ad pūgnandum vēnērunt.   They came *to fight.*

6. The *ablative case* of the gerund is used in two ways. It can be used as an ablative of means:

Nihil morandō cōnfēcit.   He accomplished nothing *by delaying.*

It can also be used after the prepositions **ab, dē, ex,** or **in:**

Occupātī sunt in labōrandō.   They were engaged *in working.*

7. As a noun the gerund is itself governed by other words; as a verb it may take an object in the proper case. When the gerund would have an object in the accusative, the gerundive is generally used instead (see p. 131).

▶ STUDY HELPS

The English suffix *–ing* is used in several different ways:
(a) in the progressive form of the verb: *I am calling;* (b) as a present participle or verbal adjective: *the boy running away, the running boy;* (c) as a gerund or verbal noun: *I like skating.*

▶ PRACTICE PATTERNS

A. Translate into English:

1. Perītus est scrībendī. 2. Cupidus vincendī est. 3. Vincere erat difficile. 4. Occupāta erat in legendō. 5. Erat difficultās trānseundī. 6. Est nūlla occāsiō

fugiendī. 7. Dux fīnem oppūgnandī fēcit. 8. Currendō celeriter vēnimus. 9. Mīlitēs pūgnandī grātiā vēnērunt. 10. Cōpiae erant parātae ad currendum.

B. Translate into Latin:

1. Flying is not easy. 2. She is desirous of leaving. 3. They are skilled in teaching. 4. The farmers are occupied in working. 5. This weather is suitable for sailing. 6. The soldiers came to fight.

SECTION 3 Formation of the Gerundive

▶ DISCUSSION

1. The gerundive is a verbal adjective of the passive voice. It is declined like adjectives of the first and second declensions.

2. It is formed on the present stem, to which is added the characteristic *–nd + us, –a, –um.* Verbs of the fourth conjugation and *–io* verbs of the third conjugation have *–ie* before the *–nd–.*

3. The gerundive is used to express the notion of duty, obligation, and necessity.

4. It is totally unlike any usage in English.

5. The gerundives of deponent verbs are regularly formed and are passive in meaning, as are the gerundives of all verbs.

FORMATION AND MEANING OF THE GERUNDIVE

CONJ.	Pres. Stem + –ndus, –a, –um =		Form	Possible Translation
I	vocā	+ –ndus, –a, –um =	vocandus, –a, –um	to be called
II	monē	+ –ndus, –a, –um =	monendus, –a, –um	to be warned
III	rege	+ –ndus, –a, –um =	regendus, –a, –um	to be ruled
III–io	cap(i)e	+ –ndus, –a, –um =	capiendus, –a, –um	to be taken
IV	audi(e)	+ –ndus, –a, –um =	audiendus, –a, –um	to be heard

SECTION 4 Uses of the Gerundive

▶ DISCUSSION

1. The gerundive is used as a verbal adjective limiting directly an expressed noun or pronoun. The meaning of the gerundive phrase is generally expressed in English by an active verbal form ending in *–ing* with an object expressed.

difficultās nāvium *faciendārum*   the difficulty *of making* ships
    (Literally: the difficulty of ships *to be made*)

2. As a rule, only the genitive of the gerund (without a preposition) may use a direct object. Instead of the genitive or ablative of the *gerund*, the *gerundive* construction is generally used to replace a transitive gerund, i.e., a gerund that governs an object in the accusative case. The direct object in English takes the case in Latin that would be required by the gerund, and the gerundive is placed in agreement:

    cupidus *urbis videndae*   desirous *of seeing the city*
    (not **cupidus *urbem videndī*)**

    nāvibus faciendīs   *by making ships*
    (not ***nāvēs faciendīs*)**

3. If the object is a neuter pronoun or a neuter adjective used substantively (as a noun), the gerund should be used to avoid ambiguity.

    cupidus *hoc faciendī*   desirous *of doing this*

4. The gerund should always be used with intransitive verbs.

    spēs *ducī persuādendī*   the hope *of persuading the leader*

5. For verbs that govern the ablative case (***ūtor, fruor,*** etc.), the gerundive construction is generally used.

6. The accusative of the gerund and the gerundive is used after the preposition ***ad*** to express purpose. If an object is expressed, the gerundive construction is used.

    ad *nāvēs faciendās*   for the purpose *of making ships*
    (not **ad *nāvēs faciendum*)**

7. The genitive of the gerund or gerundive with ***causā*** or ***grātiā*** expresses purpose. If an object is expressed, the gerundive construction is used.

    causā *nāvium faciendārum*   for the purpose *of making ships*
    (not **causā *nāvēs faciendī*)**

▶ STUDY HELPS

1. The gerundive cannot be used as a substitute for the gerund unless the gerund has an object in the accusative or the ablative case. (See 2, 5, and 6 above.)

2. Transitive verbs govern an object in the accusative case; intransitive verbs in Latin either require no object or govern an object in a case other than the accusative. (See 2, 4, and 5 above.)

131

GERUND AND GERUNDIVE COMPARED

GERUND	GERUNDIVE
1. verbal noun	1. verbal adjective
2. active voice	2. passive voice
3. neuter gender	3. all genders
4. singular only	4. singular and plural
5. no nominative case	5. all cases
6. used with transitive and intransitive verbs	6. used with transitive verbs only

▶ **PRACTICE PATTERNS**

A. Translate into English. Distinguish between the gerund and the gerundive.

1. Mox fīnem loquendī facient. 2. Est cupidus pontis faciendī. 3. Nōn parātī sunt ad nāvigandum. 4. Est perītus virīs persuādendī. 5. Saxīs trahendīs mūrōs renovāvērunt. 6. Ad rēgem cōnsulendum in urbem vēnit. 7. Hostēs in spem castrōrum oppūgnandōrum vēnerant. 8. Māgnās cōpiās parābant hostibus resistendī causā. 9. Omnia comparārī nāvium renovandārum causā jūssit. 10. Haec ōrātiō fuit inūtilis ad animōs comitum cōnfīrmandōs.

B. Translate into Latin. Use more than one way where the sentence permits more than one way of expressing the thought correctly.

1. He lost the chance to leave the city. 2. We knew the difficulties of waging war. 3. They came for the purpose of seeing the games. 4. He had a great desire to see his fatherland. 5. He went to the underworld to consult the poet.

WORDS TO MASTER

adhibeō, –ēre, –uī, –itus, hold to, employ, show

admoneō, –ēre, –uī, –itus, warn, advise; **admonitum, –ī,** *n.,* warning (*admonition*)

alligō (1), tie to, bind to

cōnsulō, –ere, –uī, –sultus, take counsel, consult

dēns, dentis, *m.,* tooth (*dental*)

dēsīderium, –ī, *n.,* desire, longing

frangō, –ere, frēgī, fractus, break, shatter, wreck (*fracture*)

īnfēlīx, –īcis, *adj.,* unfortunate, unhappy (*infelicitous*)

īnferus, –a, –um, below, of the underworld; **īnferī, –ōrum,** *m.pl.,* the lower world (*inferior*)

inūtilis, –e, *adj.,* of no use, useless (*inutility*)

mālus, –ī, *m.,* mast

praētereō, –īre, –iī, –itūrus, *irreg.,* pass by, go by (*preterite*)

renovō (1), renew, repair (*renovate*)

rūpēs, –is, *f.,* rock, cliff

subeō, –īre, –iī, –itūrus, *irreg.,* go under, undergo, endure

subsidium, –ī, *n.,* support, help, assistance (*subsidy*)

BUILDING WORD POWER

Almost all English words derived from **mittere, missum,** *to send, let go, release,* can be recognized by the syllables *mit-, mitt-, mis-, miss-.* The underlying meaning is usually *to send, to let go, to release,* as in the Latin root word. Notice the similarity in the formation of the Latin and the English compounds. Only one Latin compound given here has no English derivative.

admittere, to send to, let in: *admit, admission*
committere, to unite, begin, combine: *commit, commission*
dēmittere, to send down, let down: *demit, demission, demise*
dīmittere, to send in different directions: *dismiss, dismission*
ēmittere, to send out: *emit, emission*
immittere, to send in, let go: —
intermittere, to leave a space: *intermit, intermission*
manūmittere, emancipate (a slave): *manumit, manumission*
ōmittere, to let go, to leave out: *omit, omission*
permittere, to let go through: *permit, permission*
praemittere, to send before: *premise*
praetermittere, to let go by: *pretermit, pretermission*
prōmittere, to send forth, promise: *promise*
remittere, to send back or again: *remit, remission*
submittere, to send under, lower: *submit, submission*
trānsmittere, to send across: *transmit, transmission*

A few of these English words derived from Latin **mittere** are not in common use, but over one hundred are. Notice *missal, missile, missive, mission, missionary, missioner. Mess, message,* and *messenger* came into English via French.

SENTENCE PATTERNS

A. Translate into English:

1. Cum dux fīnem loquendī fēcisset, īnfēlīx fēmina sē ad pedēs ējus prōjēcit.
2. Mox ad omnia perīcula subeunda parābantur.
3. Cum tālem dīligentiam comitēs ējus adhibuissent, tertiā diē omnia ad proficīscendum cōnficiēbantur.
4. Nōnne tantō dēsīderiō patriae suae mōtī sunt ut tribus diēbus nāvem renovāvissent?
5. Adiitne ad īnferōs caecī poētae videndī atque cōnsulendī causā?
6. Circē Graecīs māgnō subsidiō erat.
7. Cum ad rūpēs adīrent, quās Sīrēnēs incolēbant, comitēs ējus ducem ad mālum alligāvērunt, quod admonitum ējus memoriā tenuērunt.
8. Tempestās nāvem ita frēgit ut ad nāvigandum inūtilis esset.

9. Quamquam sex nautae ā mōnstrō correptī sunt, reliquī hoc perīculum tūtō praeteriērunt.
10. Admoneāmus comitēs quī mōnstrum spectant. Sex capita habet in quibus omnibus trēs ōrdinēs dentium sunt.

B. Translate into Latin:

1. He ordered all baggage which was useless for sailing to be left behind.
2. Let us thank the unhappy woman who was such a help to us!
3. He went to the lower world to see and to consult the blind poet.
4. Would that they would prepare all things for the renovating of the ship!
5. Although the ship be shattered by the storm, we shall soon be ready for sailing.

Another Visitor to Hades

Postquam tōtum annum apud Circēn cōnsūmpsit, Ulixēs māgnō dēsīderiō patriae suae mōtus est. Itaque sociīs ad sē convocātīs, quid in animō habēret ostendit. At ubi ad lītus dēscendit, nāvem suam tempestātibus ita fractam invēnit ut ad nāvigandum paene inūtilis esset. Omnia quae ad nāvem renovandam ūsuī erant comparārī jūssit. Tantam dīligentiam omnēs adhibēbant ut tertiā diē opus cōnficerent.

Circē, cum omnia ad proficīscendum parāta esse vidēret, rem aegrē tulit, sed māgnum subsidium Graecīs dedit. Ulixem certiōrem fēcit necesse esse eum ad īnferōs adīre ut vātem (*prophet*) caecum Tīresiam vidēret atque cōnsuleret. Ad īnferōs adīre erat difficillimum sed Circē exposuit Ulixī iter quō celerius īret.

Sine morā sed māgnā cum difficultāte ad īnferōs dux fortis iit. Diū cum Tīresiā mānsit. Cum loquendī fīnem fēcisset, ad Circēn rediit, sed in īnsulā breve tempus mānsit. Deinde Ulixēs et eīdem sociī, quī sēcum trāns mare nāvigāverant, ex īnsulā excessērunt.

The Song of the Sirens

Mox ad rūpēs appropinquābant, ubi Sīrēnēs habitābant. Hae erant pulcherrimae fēminae quōrum cantus fascināvit (*bewitched*) omnēs quī eum audīvit. Cum Circē Ulixem dē perīculō māximō monēret, ille nautās suōs eum ad mālum alligāre jūssit. Aurēs eōrum cērā (*wax*) complēvit nē cantum audīrent. Cum Sīrēnēs cantum suum canerent, frūstrā Ulyssēs sē līberāre cōnātus est. Frūstrā hominēs eum līberāre jūssit. Neque cantum Sīrēnum neque imperia Ulixis audīvērunt. Sīc is et illī hoc perīculum tūtō praeteriērunt.

Ulysses and his crew sailing past the Sirens.

Between Scylla and Charybdis

Inter Ītaliam atque Siciliam est fretum quod (ita trādunt) cūstōdiēbātur ā mōnstrīs, quibus nōmina erant Scylla et Charybdis. Scylla, terribilis aspectū, corpus fēminae habēbat, sed duodecim pedēs et sex longa colla cum sex capitibus. In omnī capīte erant trēs ōrdinēs dentium. Charybdis erat vortex rapidus quī nāvēs īnfēlīcēs vorāvit. Nāvis Ulixis māximā arte perīculum vorticis avidī (*greedy*) vītāvit, sed Scylla perīculōsa sex nautās manibus crūdēlissimīs corripuit dum Ulixēs hominēs suōs servāre frūstrā cōnātur.

A daughter of the gods, divinely tall,
And most divinely fair.
—Alfred, Lord Tennyson, 1809–1892

Unit XVI

CONVERSATION

ULIXĒS: Nōs ad īnsulam Thrināciam, comitēs, perventūrī sumus. Memoriā tenēte bovēs in īnsulā habitantēs deō Sōlis sacrōs esse. Hī nōbīs nōn necandī sunt.

COMITĒS: Jūrāmus nōs būbus nōn nocitūrōs esse.

ULIXĒS: Mandāta mea vōbīs servanda sunt, aut māximō in perīculō erimus. Sīc Tīresiās atque Circē mihi praedīxērunt.

PRĪMUS COMES	(*multīs post diēbus*): In hāc īnsulā per ūnum mēnsem commorātī sumus, quod ventī secundī nōn fuērunt.
SECUNDUS COMES:	Nunc nūllum cibum habēmus.
TERTIUS COMES:	Neque in īnsulā cibus invenīrī potest.
EURYLOCHUS:	Necesse est nōs cibum habēre. Bovēs Sōlis nōbīs necandī sunt. Mālō in marī quam in terrā morīrī!
ULIXĒS	(*postrīdiē*): Quid fēcistis, virī, mē absente! Portenta terribilia sunt! Nāvem ad nāvigandum statim parāte!
EURYLOCHUS:	Omnia nautīs quam celerrimē agenda sunt, sed tempestāte secundā, ab īnsulā hāc diē nāvigābimus!
ULIXĒS:	Tardius! Deī īrātī nōs pūnītūrī sunt!

SECTION 1 Gerundive with *sum;* Dative of Agent

▶ DISCUSSION

1. The gerundive, also called the future passive participle, in combination with the present, imperfect, perfect, or future tense of *sum,* expresses obligation, duty, or necessity in Latin. This combination is called the *passive periphrastic conjugation,* just as the combination of the future active participle with *sum* has been called the *active periphrastic conjugation* (see p. 74).

2. The gerundive agrees with the subject in gender, number, and case.

Auxilium mittendum est.   Help must be sent (is to be sent).

3. The tense of *sum* in the passive periphrastic depends on the time of the obligation.

TENSE	PASSIVE PERIPHRASTIC	POSSIBLE TRANSLATION
Present	**Auxilium mittendum est.**	*Help is to be sent.* *Help ought to be sent.* *Help must be sent.* *Help has to be sent.* *Help should be sent.*
Past	**Auxilium mittendum erat (fuit).**	*Help was to be sent.* *Help ought to have been sent.* *Help had to be sent.* *Help should have been sent.*
Future	**Auxilium mittendum erit.**	*Help will have to be sent.*

4. With the gerundive, the word denoting the person by whom the act must be done is regularly expressed by the dative of agent.

Auxilium *ducī* mittendum est.   Help ought to be sent *by the leader.*

136

5. Expressions that contain the passive periphrastic construction are often best translated by changing the verb to the active voice in English. The Latin dative of agent is then represented in English by the subject of the active verb.

TENSE	PASSIVE PERIPHRASTIC	ACTIVE TRANSLATION
Present	**Auxilium ducī mittendum est.**	*The leader has to send help.*
Past	**Auxilium ducī mittendum erat (fuit).**	*The leader had to send help.*
Future	**Auxilium ducī mittendum erit.**	*The leader will have to send help.*

6. The passive periphrastic may be used in indirect discourse.

Putō *hoc faciendum esse.*   I think *this should be done.*
Putō *hoc faciendum fuisse.*   I think *this should have been done.*
Mīror *cūr hoc faciendum sit.*   I wonder *why this should be done.*

7. The passive periphrastic of an intransitive verb can be used only in the impersonal form, with the gerundive in the neuter singular and the verb in the third person singular.

Nōbīs fortiter pūgnandum est.   *We must fight bravely.*
(Literally: *It must be fought bravely by* [*to*] *us.*)

▶ STUDY HELPS

1. The active sentence in English must be changed into its corresponding passive form before translating into Latin.

The Romans had to do this.
This had to be done by the Romans.   **Hoc Rōmānīs faciendum erat.**

2. The *will have* in the future tense does not indicate the future perfect. The *will* denotes the future; the *have to* denotes obligation.

3. Obligation may also be expressed by the verb **dēbeō,** *ought,* with the complementary infinitive (see p. 66).

Domōs suās dēfendere dēbent.
Domūs suae eīs dēfendendae sunt.   *They ought to defend their own homes.*

4. Obligation may also be expressed by the impersonal **oportet,** *it is fitting,* with the passive infinitive as subject.

Captīvōs interficī nōn oportet.
Captīvī nōn sunt interficiendī.   *The prisoners ought not to be killed.*

▶ PRACTICE PATTERNS

A. Translate into English:

1. Mūrī oppidī dēfendendī sunt. 2. Haec nautīs comportanda erant. 3. Servanda est cīvibus lībertās. 4. Lībertās cīvibus servanda erit. 5. Nōbīs venien-

dum est. 6. Brevī tempore respondendum est. 7. Crēdō lībertātem cīvibus servandam esse. 8. Lēgātus rogāvit quid virīs faciendum esset. 9. Dīcit võbīs nōn nocendum esse. 10. Tibi currendum est.

B. Translate into Latin:

1. The city must be destroyed. 2. Caesar had to do everything. 3. You ought to carry the wood. 4. They will have to come. 5. He says that you must run. 6. They will have to exercise the horses. 7. We ought to love and praise him. 8. Did not the men have to take an oath? 9. The prisoners had to be freed. 10. We had to fight on the fifth day.

SECTION 2 Supine

▶ DISCUSSION

1. Besides the infinitive and the gerund some Latin verbs have another form called the *supine*. It is formed from the participial stem and is found only in the accusative singular and ablative singular of the fourth declension.

CONJ.	I	II	III	III–io	IV
Acc.	vocātum	monitum	rēctum	captum	audītum
Abl.	vocātū	monitū	rēctū	captū	audītū

2. The accusative supine in –*um* may be used with verbs meaning motion toward to express purpose. The supine in –*um* may take an object.

> **Vēnērunt *pācem petītum*.**   They came *to seek peace*.

3. The ablative supine in –*ū* is used with certain adjectives as an ablative of specification or respect. The supine in –*ū* never takes an object.

facile factū	difficile vīsū	mīrābile dictū
easy to do	*hard to see*	*wonderful to relate*
(*easy in the doing*)	(*hard in the seeing*)	(*wonderful in the relating*)

▶ PRACTICE PATTERNS

A. Translate into English:

1. Hoc erat facile dictū. 2. Pecūniam postulātum vēnit. 3. Pācem petītum vēnērunt. 4. Eratne horribile vīsū? 5. Nōnne est optimum factū? 6. Lēgātōs mittunt rogātum auxilium. 7. Difficile vīsū et etiam audītū erat. 8. Nōbīs subsidium lātum currit. 9. Mīrābile dictū praemium accēpit. 10. Oppidum oppūgnātum illōs remīsit.

B. Translate into Latin:

1. He went to ask for help. 2. It is not the best thing to do. 3. They came to take away the booty. 4. That is easy to say but difficult to do. 5. He is leaving the city to seek help. 6. He sent the slaves back to collect grain.

WORDS TO MASTER

citerior, –ōris, *adj.,* on this side, nearer

commūnis, –e, *adj.,* common, in common, general, public (*community*)

comportō (1), carry, bring together, collect (*comport*)

concilium, –ī, *n.,* meeting, assembly (*council*)

continuus, –a, –um, *adj.,* continuous, successive (*continuous*)

ēnuntiō (1), report, tell, announce (*enunciation*)

exerceō, –ēre, –uī, –itus, keep at work, practice, exercise

hiemō (1), pass the winter, keep in winter quarters

īnstituō, –ere, –uī, –ūtus, put in place, build, construct, train (*institute*)

jūrō (1), swear, take an oath (*jury*)

māteria, –ae, *f.,* wood, lumber (*material*)

pereō, –īre, –iī, –itūrus, *irreg.,* perish, be killed (*perish*)

praedīcō, –ere, –dīxī, –dictus, predict, foretell (*predict*)

ratis, –is, *f.,* raft, ship

singulī, –ae, –a, *distributive num. adj., pl.,* one at a time, one by one (*single*)

sōlum, *adv.,* alone, only; **nōn sōlum ... sed etiam,** not only ... but also

BUILDING WORD POWER

The majority of words derived from ***dūcere, ductum*** contain the memory peg *duc* or *duct*, but a few have *duk, duch,* or *duit.* The general meaning is *to draw, lead, consider.* Form the Latin verbs from which these English words are derived, and show the similarity of meaning: *adduce, conduce, deduce, educe, induce, introduce, produce, reduce, seduce, subduce, traduce, abduct.*

Show the underlying meaning of *lead* or *draw* in the italicized words: insecurity often *conduces* to fear; wire *conducts* electricity; the boy was *induced* to enlist; he was *inducted* into the army; they easily *deduced* the cause of the crime; they *deducted* the discount; he *adduced* his absence as a proof of his innocence; *abduction* is a criminal offense; the tear *duct* was injured; copper is *ductile;* the editor of the paper *traduced* the candidate; the girl *produced* the evidence; the cast *reproduced* the play. The *Doge* of Venice met the *Duke* of York; Shylock lost his *ducats* and his daughter; they *introduced* him to city life.

The verb ***ēducāre, ēducātum,*** *to rear, bring up,* is closely related to

139

ēdūcere, *to lead* or *draw out*. A sound American *education* is almost a necessity in these days. We must have *educated* leaders and *educators* who lead.

SENTENCE PATTERNS

A. Write the correct form of the verb in parentheses, and then translate the sentence into English.

1. Mīror cūr Ulixēs admonitum poētae memoriā nōn (teneō).
2. Pecora nōbis nōn necanda sunt, nē mala fortūna nōbīs (accidō).
3. Nōnne singulī jūrāvērunt sē advenās dē commūnī perīculō (admoneō — would warn)?
4. Nautae perītūrī erant quod Sōlis bovēs (occīdō).
5. Tempestātēs tam continuae erant ut ratis (frangō).
6. Omnia ad nāvem cōnservandam nautīs statim agenda erant, quamquam poēta omnēs praeter Ulixem perītūrōs esse (praedīcō).
7. Cum ab īnsulā dux abitūrus erat, Calypsō māteriam et aliās cōpiās (comportō) jūssit.
8. Nōn sōlum nāvēs īnstituērunt sed etiam nautās (exerceō).
9. Concilium nautārum habendum est ut hīs quid (sentiō) ēnuntiem.
10. Ulixēs cum comitibus in citeriōre parte īnsulae (hiemō — intends to winter).

B. Translate into Latin:

1. The inhabitants of the island had to gather supplies and construct rafts.
2. He was about to announce the warning of the poet to his comrades.
3. They were about to pass by the dangerous cliffs when six men were seized.
4. One by one the men swore that they would not touch the oxen.
5. All the soldiers had to be trained and warned.

The Cattle of the Sun

Cum nāvis ad deī Sōlis īnsulam perventūra esset, Ulixēs admonitum Tīresiae memoriā tenuit. "Bovēs Sōlis nōbīs nōn necandī sunt, nē eadem fortūna nobis iterum accidat," admonuit ille dux fortis. "Ad patriam nostram atque uxōrēs līberōsque properēmus! Diū nōs exspectāvērunt!" Singulī comitēs jūrāvērunt sē Sōlis bovēs nōn necātūrōs esse.

In hāc īnsulā per ūnam noctem manēre in animō habēbat, cum ad patriam Ithacam et uxōrem et familiam suam quam prīmum pervenīre vellet, sed per ūnum mēnsem mānsērunt, quod ventī secundī nōn erant. Brevī tempore nūllum cibum habēbant neque in īnsulā cibus invenīrī poterat. Triste dictū,

140

dum Ulixēs abest, sociī illīus ducis fortis paucōs dē Sōlis būbus occidērunt. Cum dux redīret, timōre captus est. Conciliō nautārum convocātō, nāvem statim ad nāvigandum parārī jūssit. Omnia nautīs quam celerrimē agenda erant, sed illā diē ab īnsulā nāvigāvērunt.

Brevi tempore tantae atque tam continuae erant tempestātēs ut nāvis frangerētur et omnēs praeter Ulixem perīrent. Fēlīx Ulixēs in lītus īnsulae jactus est. Hīc Nympha, cui erat nōmen Calypsō, incolēbat. Eum tam benīgnē excēpit ut in hūjus nymphae īnsulā per septem annōs manēret. Tandem ducem fortem sē in mātrimōnium dūcere cupiēbat, sed Nympham eum līberāre Juppiter jūssit. Hoc aegrē fēcit, sed cibum, vestem, māteriam comportārī et ratem aedificārī jussit. Haec Ulixī dōnāvit.

Cum discessūrus erat, Calypsō eum sīc admonuit: "Hoc iter, quod tibi nunc patet, erit summae difficultātis. Multī labōrēs atque ācrēs dolōrēs tibi patiendī sunt. Neptūnus, maris deus, tibi est inimīcus quod Polyphēmō nocuistī, sed Minerva tē perītūrum servābit et adjuvābit. Ad terram novam perveniēs. Ā rēge benīgnō accipiēris. Eī et familiae ējus multae fābulae dē bellō Trōjānō tibi narrandae sunt. Tē adjuvābit. Nunc, dux nōbilis, valē!"

Multōs diēs Ulixēs nāvigāvit. Iterum fuit tempestās, ab īrātō Neptūnō missa. Rate fractā, per duōs diēs atque duās noctēs trānāvit, sed Minerva eum adjūvit et brevī tempore in īnsulae

Calypso waving to the departing Ulysses.

amīcae lītus jactus est. Ā fīliā rēgis Alcinoī, quī īnsulam regēbat, Ulixēs inventus est. Haec puella, cui erat nōmen Nausicaa, eum ad patris domicilium dūxit. Tam amīcus erat Alcinous ut ducī fortī nōn sōlum nāvem sed etiam virōs daret.

Ulixēs rēgī benīgnō māximās grātiās ēgit et mox ab īnsulā amīcā nāvigāvit. Diū homō dēfessus dormiēbat et, cum ē somnō excitārētur, in patriae Ithacae lītore erat.

So ends the bloody business of the day.
—Homer, 850 B.C.
last line of the *Odyssey*

Unit XVII

CONVERSATION

ULIXĒS:	Quandō, Ō dī immortālēs, patriam meam rūrsus vidēbō?
MINERVA	(*intrat*): Salvē, advena!
ULIXĒS:	Salvē et tū! Ubi sum? Ubi sunt virī mēcum ā rēge bonō missī? Cūr ab illīs relictus sum?
MINERVA:	Nōnne nōmen hūjus īnsulae quae ab Ulixe nōbilī rēcta est memoriā tenēs? In lītore Ithacae nunc stās.
ULIXĒS:	Num est patria mea? Estne haec terra Ithaca?
MINERVA:	Dea Minerva ego sum. Haec vērō, Ulixēs, est patria tua. Mox rēgnō tuō potiēris, et familiā atque amīcīs tuīs fruēris.
ULIXĒS:	Suntne conjunx Pēnelopē atque fīlius Tēlemachus incolumēs?
MINERVA:	Incolumēs sunt, sed difficile opus tibi administrandum est. Dum tū abes, multī virī postulāvērunt ut Pēnelopēn in mātrimōnium dūcerent. Hī procī domiciliō tuō ūtēbantur et cibō tuō vescēbantur, sed Pēnelopē bona et pulchra tibi fīda etiam est. Frūstrā multōs annōs Tēlemachus tē quaerēbat.
ULIXĒS:	Ad Pēnelopēn et domicilium meum statim redībō. Ōrō, dea benīgna, ut mihi auxilium ferās! Eāmus!

SECTION 1 *Volō, Nōlō, Mālō*

PRINCIPAL PARTS

volō, velle, voluī	**nōlō, nōlle, nōluī**	**mālō, mālle, māluī**
I wish, am willing	*I do not wish, am unwilling, refuse*	*I prefer, wish rather, had rather, would rather*

142

Pres.	**volō**	**nōlō**	**mālō**
	vīs	**nōn vīs**	**māvīs**
	vult	**nōn vult**	**māvult**
	volumus	**nōlumus**	**mālumus**
	vultis	**nōn vultis**	**māvultis**
	volunt	**nōlunt**	**mālunt**
Imperf.	**volēbam,** etc.	**nōlēbam,** etc.	**mālēbant,** etc.
Fut.	**volam,** etc.	**nōlam,** etc.	**mālam,** etc.
Perf.	**voluī,** etc.	**nōluī,** etc.	**māluī,** etc.
Pluperf.	**volueram,** etc.	**nōlueram,** etc.	**mālueram,** etc.
Fut. perf.	**voluerō,** etc.	**nōluerō,** etc.	**māluerō,** etc.

SUBJUNCTIVE MOOD

Pres.	**velim,** etc.	**nōlim,** etc.	**mālim,** etc.
Imperf.	**vellem,** etc.	**nōllem,** etc.	**māllem,** etc.
Perf.	**voluerim,** etc.	**nōluerim,** etc.	**māluerim,** etc.
Pluperf.	**voluissem,** etc.	**nōluissem,** etc.	**māluissem,** etc.

INFINITIVES

Pres.	**velle,** *to wish*	**nōlle,** *to be unwilling*	**mālle,** *to prefer*
Perf.	**voluisse,** *to have wished*	**nōluisse,** *to have been unwilling*	**māluisse,** *to have preferred*

PARTICIPLES

Pres.	**volēns, volentis,** *wishing, willing*	**nōlens, nōlentis** *refusing, being unwilling*	

▶ STUDY HELPS

1. **Volō** has no imperative, no future infinitive, and no participle except the present.

2. **Nōlō** has no future infinitive and no participle except the present; the present imperatives are **nōlī, nōlīte,** *be unwilling.*

3. **Mālō** has no imperative, no future infinitive, and no participle.

4. **Volō, nōlō,** and **mālō** are completed by the complementary infinitive.

▶ PRACTICE PATTERNS

A. Translate into English:

1. Discēdere vult. 2. Discēdere nōn vult. 3. Discēdere māvult. 4. Nōlī discēdere. 5. Volumus rogāre. 6. Vīsne respondēre? 7. Domum cernere voluī. 8. Statim

143

proficīscī volunt. 9. Currere nōluerat. 10. Manēre mālēbat. 11. Vīsne in urbe habitāre? 12. Cum venīre velīs, discēdam. 13. Cum redīre māllet, tamen mānsit. 14. Nōlīte pecūniam remittere. 15. Voluimus rēgem vidēre.

B. Translate into Latin:

1. Do not fear to speak. 2. I am willing to remain. 3. I prefer to walk alone. 4. Don't stand near the door. 5. Since he wished to leave . . . 6. Although he refuses to help . . . 7. Did they wish to escape? 8. They refused to set forth. 9. We shall have wished.

SECTION 2 Substantive Clauses of Purpose

▶ DISCUSSION

1. *Substantive* means *noun;* therefore a substantive clause must be used as a noun. It may be the subject or the object of a verb, or it may be in apposition.

2. A *substantive clause of purpose* may be considered an indirect command or request that in its original form was an imperative. The imperative *Leave!* in a quoted clause after a verb of commanding, urging, asking, etc., becomes *that we leave.*

3. After verbs meaning *command, ask, decree, exhort, urge,* etc., where English frequently uses the infinitive with *to,* Latin generally uses the subjunctive mood with *ut* to introduce a positive clause and *nē* to introduce a negative clause.

Ōrāvērunt (nōs) *ut discēderēmus.* They begged us *to leave.*
Rogābit (nōs) *nē discēdāmus.* He will ask us *not to leave.*

4. When the English verb takes a pronoun as a direct object, this pronoun may be omitted, as in the sentences above, since it is expressed in the verb of the subordinate clause.

5. The tense of the subjunctive to be used in the subordinate clause is the present or imperfect, depending on the tense of the main verb.

6. Some important verbs are regularly followed by substantive clauses of purpose.

Those taking the *accusative* of the person commanded are: ***hortor,*** *urge;* ***rogō,*** *ask;* ***moneō,*** *warn, advise;* ***ōrō,*** *beg, ask.*

Those taking a *dative* of the person commanded are: ***imperō,*** *command;* ***mandō,*** *order;* ***persuādeō,*** *persuade;* ***permittō,*** *allow.*

Those taking *ā* or *ab* and *ablative* of person commanded are: ***petō,*** *seek;* ***postulō,*** *demand.*

144

7. There are very important exceptions to these rules. The following verbs meaning *to order, forbid, permit* take the accusative of the person and the objective infinitive:

Jubeō, *order:* **Jūssī tē venīre.** I ordered *you to come.*
Vetō, *forbid:* **Vetuī tē venīre.** I forbade *you to come,* I ordered *you not to come.*
   (Never **jubeō . . . nōn.**)
Patior, *permit, allow:* **Passus est eōs īre.** He permitted *them to go.*

8. **Volō,** *wish;* **nōlō,** *am unwilling;* **mālō,** *prefer;* **cupiō,** *desire;* **studeō,** *am eager,* take the objective infinitive and the accusative of the person if a subject of the infinitive is expressed.

      Cupiō eōs īre.   I desire *them to go.*

▶ PRACTICE PATTERNS

A. Translate into English:

1. Ōrat ut veniāmus. 2. Nōbīs imperat nē veniāmus. 3. Ā nōbīs petet ut veniāmus. 4. Nōs discēdere jūssit. 5. Nōs discēdere vetuit. 6. Virīs imperāvit nē discēderent.

B. Translate into Latin:

1. He orders us to leave. 2. He demands that we leave. 3. He ordered us not to leave. 4. They begged us not to leave. 5. She will ask us to leave. 6. We advised the men to leave.

SECTION 3 Ablative with Certain Deponent Verbs

▶ DISCUSSION

Five deponent verbs and their compounds are used with the ablative case in Latin, but they are translated with the objective case in English.

PRES. INDIC.	PRES. INFIN.	PERF. INDIC.	TRANSLATION
ūtor	**ūtī**	**ūsus sum**	*use, employ*
fruor	**fruī**	**frūctus sum**	*enjoy*
fungor	**fungī**	**fūnctus sum**	*perform*
potior	**potīrī**	**potītus sum**	*gain possession of*
vescor	**vescī**	—	*feed on, live on*

    Ulixēs *arcū* gravī ūsus est.   Ulysses used the heavy *bow.*
           Rēgnō potiēris.   You will gain possession of *a kingdom.*
Nautae *cibō* mīrō vescēbantur.   The sailors lived on marvelous *food.*

A. Translate into English:

1. Vītā fruitur. 2. Castrīs potītus est. 3. Hostēs urbe potītī sunt. 4. Mīlitēs frūmentō vescuntur. 5. Imperātor novā bellī ratiōne ūtēbātur. 6. Herculēs māgnīs labōribus fūnctus est.

B. Translate into Latin:

1. He enjoyed good food. 2. The inhabitants lived on grain. 3. He used the same sword in battle. 4. He always performs his duties well. 5. The suitors will not gain possession of the kingdom. 6. Did he use the huge ancient bow?

SECTION 4 Summary of Purpose Constructions

▶ DISCUSSION

1. In Latin as in English there are several ways to express purpose.

2. In Latin prose the infinitive cannot be used to express purpose, although in English this construction is regularly used.

LATIN CONSTRUCTION	LITERAL TRANSLATION	BETTER TRANSLATION
ut + subjunctive	*in order that . . .*	*to . . .*
nē + subjunctive	*in order that . . . not*	*not to . . .*
quī + subjunctive	*who should . . .*	*to . . .*
quō + subjunctive and a comparative	*in order . . . the more*	*to . . . more*
ad + gerund	*for . . .ing*	*to . . .*
ad + gerundive phrase	*for . . . to be . . .*	infinitive ⎰ *to . . .*
causā ⎱ + gerund **grātiā** ⎰	*for the sake of . . .ing*	*to . . .*
causā ⎱ + gerundive phrase **grātiā** ⎰	*for the sake of . . . to be . . .*	*to . . .*
accusative supine	*infinitive (to . . .)*	*to . . .*

The sentence *They came to seek peace* may be translated into Latin as follows:

Venērunt *ut pācem peterent.*   **ut** + subjunctive
Venērunt *quī pācem peterent.*   **quī** + subjunctive
Venērunt *ad pācem petendam.*   **ad** + gerundive phrase
Venērunt *pācis petendae causā (grātiā).*   **causā**   **(grātiā)** + gerundive phrase
Venērunt *pācem petītum.*   accusative supine

▶ PRACTICE PATTERNS

A. Translate into English three ways:

1. Vir vēnit ut mē vidēret. 2. Fugiunt nē interficiantur. 3. Dōna offerunt pācis

cōnfīrmandae causā. 4. Conjūrātiōnem ad rem pūblicam dēlendam fēcit. 5. Nūntiōs mīsērunt quī praedam postulārent. 6. Veniēbat pecūniam rogātum.

B. Translate into Latin three ways:

1. They went to Gaul to wage war. 2. He sent scouts ahead to learn the nature of the place. 3. They fled so that they might not be seized. 4. They built high walls in order more easily to keep out their neighbors. 5. Are they fighting for the sake of obtaining glory? 6. He left a legion to defend the city.

WORDS TO MASTER

agnōscō, –ere, –gnōvī, –gnitus, recognize

cernō, –ere, crēvī, crētus, separate; perceive, see (*discern*)

currus, –ūs, *m.,* chariot (*curule*)

dēfēnsor, –ōris, *m.,* defender (*defense*)

digitus, –ī, *m.,* finger, toe (*digit*)

facilitās, –tātis, *f.,* ease (*facility*)

flectō, –ere, flēxī, flexus, bend, turn (*flex*)

mandō (1), entrust, command (*mandatory*)

mendicus, –ī, *m.,* beggar (*mendicant*)

nāscor, nāscī, nātus sum, *dep.,* be born, arise; **nātus, –a, –um,** *adj.,* sprung, born (*natal*)

potior, –īrī, –ītus sum, *dep.,* get possession of, *with abl. or gen.*

procus, –ī, *m.,* suitor

remittō, –ere, –mīsī, –missus, send back (*remit*)

rōbur, –oris, *n.,* oak, strength (*robust*)

spargō, –ere, sparsī, sparsus, scatter, sprinkle (*sparse*)

ūtor, –ī, ūsus sum, *dep.,* use, exercise, *with abl.*

BUILDING WORD POWER

Do you know that almost all Latin derivatives in the English language that contain the syllables *spec–* or *spic–* or *spect–* originated with the root word *specere* (*–spicere*) and its frequentative *spectāre, spectātum, to look at, watch, observe?* The few exceptions came from the Latin word *spīca,* meaning a *spike.* In biology you will meet the word *spīcula, a little spike,* when you study the sponge, and you will come across its doublet, *spīculum,* in the dissection of the starfish. They are small pieces of bony material.

Specere has formed compounds with:

ad– (aspicere, aspectum, *to look at*)

circum– (*to look around*)

con– (*to catch sight of;* in the passive, *to attract notice*)

dē– (*to look down on*)

in– (*to look into*)

intro– (*to look into carefully*)

per– (*to look through*)

prō– (*to look forward*)

re– (*to look back* or *again*)

sub– (*to look from below*)

trāns– (*to see through*)

Most of these compound verbs had frequentatives, but only two gave derivatives to English; *spectāre, spectātum, to look at carefully, watch,* and *exspectāre, exspectātum, to look out for, to wait for.*

Explain the meaning of the italicized words: a joyful *aspect;* a *circumspect* speaker; pleasant *prospects;* great *expectations; suspicious* circumstances; *conspicuous* dress; awe-inspiring *spectacle; introspective* character; *despicable* traits; great *respect;* correct *perspective;* unusual *perspicacity; prospectus* of a college; rare *species;* fine *specimen; specific* proofs; gold *specie;* carefully *inspected; perspicuity* of expression; a *special* case.

SENTENCE PATTERNS

A. Supply in Latin the correct form of the verb in parentheses. Then translate the sentence.

1. Rēx est tam pauper ut puer patrem suum nōn (agnōscō).
2. Audācibus procīs imperāvit ut arcū gravī (ūtor).
3. Mendicus arcum gravem tantā facilitāte flēxit ut omnēs fugere (cōnor).
4. Nōnne postulāvit ut fīlius nūllī reditum ējus (praedīcō)?
5. Mīrābile dictū, nēsciēbant ubi advenae (nāscor).
6. Num dux mandāvit ut currus ad urbem (remittō)?
7. Dēfēnsōribus captīs, hostēs ācrēs oppidō (potior).
8. Cum procī commūne perīculum nōn (cernō), ad pūgnandum nōn parantur.
9. Digitīs celeribus et māximō rōbore arcum intendit ut inter virōs fugitūrōs sagittās (spargō).
10. Mendicus servōs admonuit nē jānuās (aperiō).

B. Translate into Latin:

1. Telemachus asked that all the young men use his father's bow.
2. Did not the king advise his son not to send back the chariot?
3. May the greedy suitors not recognize their master nor perceive their common danger!
4. He must not scatter his enemies lest they escape one by one.
5. I wonder why so many suitors tried to get possession of the queen's riches!

Home from Foreign Shores

Cum Ulixēs, in mendicum humilem ā Minervā conversus ad domicilium redīret, ibi fīlium Tēlemachum vīdit. Prīmum adulescēns patrem suum nōn āgnōvit, cum per vīgintī annōs eum nōn vīdisset. Māgnopere mōtus clāmāvit: "Esne tū vērō pater meus? Multōs annōs atque multīs in terrīs tē quaesīvī. Dēnique revēnistī!" Ulixēs fīlium suum monuit nē ūllī reditum ējus nūntiāret.

Ulysses slays Penelope's suitors.

Uxor Ulixis, cui erat nōmen Pēnelopē, per vīgintī annōs fīda conjugī mānserat. At illa erat pulcherrima; lātās terrās, multōs gregēs, multitūdinem servōrum possidēbat. Inter prīncipēs Ithacae erat eō tempore māgna aemulātiō (*rivalry*). Omnēs Pēnelopē atque dīvitiīs ējus potīrī cupīvērunt. In domiciliō ējus habitābant, et cibum ējus vorāvērunt et servīs ējus mandāta dedērunt. Diem ex diē fīda Pēnelopē reditum conjugis suī spērābat, sed tandem, cum Ulixēs nōn rediisset, coācta est prōmittere sē alium conjugem dēlēctūram esse.

Ulixēs, cum haec cōgnōsceret, cōnsilium cēpit, quod fīliō Tēlemachō exposuit. Procīs Tēlemachus nūntiāvit: "Quī et arcum flectere et sagittam perītissimē mittere potest, Pēnelopēn in mātrimōnium dūcet." Tēlemachus arcum gravem, quō jam prīdem Ulixēs ipse ūterētur, sine ūllā morā dēlēgit. Audācibus procīs quī perīculum nōn crēvērunt, hunc arcum dedit.

Cum nēmō eum flectere posset, Tēlemachus mendicō prope jānuam stantī arcum trādidit. Procī superbī mendicum pauperem dērīsērunt quī digitīs perītīs sibi arcum parāvit et eum facile flectere potuit. Eōdem arcū in proeliō saepe ūsus erat. Tum māgnā cum facilitāte per duodecim forāmina (*holes*) sagittās mīsit. Statim omnēs cōgnōvērunt dominum ante eōs stāre. Cum procī malī fugere cōnārentur, Ulixēs sagittīs celeribus interfēcit eōs quī eō absente Pēnelopēn in mātrimōnium dūcere cupīverant.

Sīc fīda Pēnelopē līberāta est ā procīs quī multōs annōs servīs

149

ūsī erant et cibum vorāverant atque dīvitiīs ējus potīrī cōnāti erant. Māgnō cum gaudiō Ulixēs domiciliō, uxōre, fīliō, rēgnō suō potītus est. Pēnelopē eum ōrāvit nē eam umquam iterum relinqueret. Id māgnō cum gaudiō pollicitus est.

Living Mythology:
Quiz

A. Complete the following statements with one word:

1. The famous poem that relates the wanderings of Ulysses is called ____. It was written by ____, the Greek poet.
2. After the fall of Troy, Ulysses set out for his home at ____.
3. ____, wife of Ulysses, waited ____ years for his return.
4. ____, son of Ulysses, traveled in search of his father.
5. The ____ were giants with one eye.
6. Ulysses told ____ that his name was ____.
7. ____, king of the winds, gave Ulysses a bag of ____.
8. The enchantress, ____, changed the sailors into ____.
9. The god ____ gave Ulysses the magic herb called moly.
10. After leaving Circe's island, Ulysses heard the song of the ____.
11. Ulysses remained on the island of ____ for seven years.
12. Alcinous, the father of ____, gave a feast in honor of Ulysses.

B. What is the meaning of the following expressions?

1. to go on an odyssey
2. wily Ulysses
3. faithful Penelope
4. a feast of Alcinous
5. to dally in a lotus-eater's land
6. between Scylla and Charybdis
7. to bend Ulysses' bow
8. the spell of the sirens

A loftier Argo cleaves the main,
Fraught with a later prize;
Another Orpheus sings again
And loves, and weeps, and dies.
—Percy Bysshe Shelley, 1792–1822

Unit XVIII

CONVERSATION

PAULUS: Narrā nōbīs, magister, fābulam dē vellere aureō.
MAGISTER: Ōlim in terrā longinquā incolēbant frāter sororque, Phrixus et Hellē. Līberī rēgis Thēbānī erant. Accidit ut Phrixus propter crūdēlitātem novercae (*of his stepmother*) ā patriā fugitūrus esset et deōs auxilium ōrāret.

JOANNĒS:	Nōnne deī līberīs auxilium tulērunt?
MAGISTER:	Mercurius, precibus puerī ad misericordiam mōtus, arietem (*ram*) sacrum aureō vellere mīsit ad agrum ubi Phrixus et Hellē saepe lūdēbant. Līberī arietem ascendērunt, quī subitō cum līberīs per nūbēs celeriter volāvit.
ANNA:	Mīrābile dictū! Incolumēsne ad terram pervēnērunt?
MAGISTER:	Eheu (*Alas*)! Hellē dēfessa in pontum (*sea*) angustum cecidit, quī posthāc Hellespontus (*the Hellespont*) appellātus est.
PAULUS:	Quid frātrī ējus Phrixō accidit?
MAGISTER:	Mercurius effēcit ut Phrixus ad Colchōs incolumis pervenīret. Ibi deō arietem sacrificāvit; vellus ējus aureum in arbore sacrā suspendit quam dracō horribilī speciē cūstōdiēbat.

SECTION 1 Substantive Clauses of Result

▶ **DISCUSSION**

1. You are already familiar with *adverbial clauses of result* introduced by *ut* (*that, so that*), and, in the negative, by *ut . . . nōn* (*so that . . . not*). The main clause usually contains signal words, such as *tam, ita, sīc, tantus, tālis,* and the like (see pp. 91–92). The subjunctive mood is used in the subordinate clause, but the English translation is like the indicative.

2. *Substantive clauses of result* are also introduced by *ut* or *ut . . . nōn,* but they are used as *nouns.* Such clauses can be used as *objects* of verbs meaning *to accomplish* or *to bring about,* especially *faciō* and its compounds, *efficiō, cōnficiō, perficiō,* etc.

Rēx effēcit ut Jāsōn in urbe nōn commorārētur.   The king brought it about *that Jason did not remain in the city.*

They can be used as *subjects* of impersonal verbs, such as *accidit, ēvenit, fit,* etc., meaning *it happens, it comes about,* etc.

Accidit ut incolumēs pervenīrent.   It happened *that they arrived unharmed.*

They can also be used as *predicate nominatives* with expressions like *jūs est, it is right; mōs est, it is the custom.*

    Jūs est ut ducem laudēmus.   It is right *that we praise the leader.*

3. The translation of the subordinate clause is as if it were in the indicative.

► PRACTICE PATTERNS

A. Translate into English:

1. Jūs est ut amīcī eum adjuvent. 2. Ita ēvenit ut nāvem facere nōn possit. 3. Accidit ut Peliās sacrificium factūrus esset. 4. Hīs rēbus fiēbat ut Jāsonem ad sē arcesseret. 5. Accidit ut Jāsōn ūnum calceum (shoe) āmitteret.

B. Translate into Latin:

1. It happens that he is not present. 2. It is right that evil be punished. 3. It is the custom of men that they do these things. 4. She brought it about that Jason found the fleece. 5. By chance it turned out that he arrived with one foot bare.

SECTION 2 The Ablative with Adjectives

► DISCUSSION

1. The ablative case is used with adjectives meaning *worthy of, relying on, contented with, full of,* etc.

2. Such adjectives are: **dīgnus, –a, –um,** *worthy of;* **indīgnus, –a, –um,** *unworthy of;* **frētus, –a, –um,** *relying on;* **contentus, –a, –um,** *contented with;* **plēnus, –a, –um,** *full of.* However, **plēnus** more frequently takes the genitive.

Vir *laude dīgnus* est.	He is a man *worthy of praise.*
Ille **plēnus annīs** vīxit, **plēnus honōribus.**	He lived *full of years, full of honors.*
Bellum est *perīculōrum plēnum.*	War is *full of dangers.*

► PRACTICE PATTERNS

A. Translate into English:

1. frētus nōbīs   fide vestrā indīgnus   plēnus timōris
2. paucīs contentus   summō honōre dīgnī   plēnus jūstitiā

B. Translate into Latin:

1. full of joy   filled with horror   relying on your help
2. worthy of reward   contented with life   unworthy of the praise

BUILDING WORD POWER

Most of the ninety English words derived from **trahere, trāctum,** *to draw, drag,* contain the participial stem *trāct–.* Form the Latin compounds of **trahere, trāctum** with the following prefixes, and write one English derivative from each which ends in *–tract:* **ab(s)–, ad (at)–, con–, dē–,**

152

dis–, ex–, prō–, re–, sub–. Show the similarity in meaning between the English derivative and the original Latin verb.

The Latin noun **trāctus, –ūs** means a *track*, a *trail, tract of country, dragging, drawing*. From this noun we have our English words *trace, tract, tractile, traction, tractive, tractor;* and, via French, *trail, train, trait, treat, treatise, treaty, portray, portrait, mistreat, retreat, entreat, maltreat, distrait, distraught*.

Explain the original meaning of the italicized words: a state of constant *abstraction;* the *attraction* of gravity; a signed *contract;* guilty of *detraction;* numerous *distractions; extraction* of a tooth; lemon *extract; extract* from a book; to demand a *retraction;* a *protracted* discussion; *subtraction* of discount; a *tractile* metal; characteristic *traits; treatise* on democracy; *distraught* mother; *tractable* child; *traction* engine; *tractor* propeller; strong *counterattraction; treaty* of peace.

WORDS TO MASTER

arcessō, –ere, –īvī, –ītus, summon, send for

armō (1), equip, arm; **armātus, –a, –um,** *adj.,* armed; **armātī,** *m.pl.,* armed men

centuriō, –ōnis, *m.,* centurion, captain of a century

circiter, *adv.,* about, near

commoror (1), *dep.,* delay, stay temporarily, remain

dīgnus, –a, –um, *adj.,* worthy, *with abl.* (*dignity*)

frētus, –a, –um, *adj.,* relying on, *with abl.*

novitās, –tātis, *f.,* newness, novelty

nūdus, –a, –um, *adj.,* naked, bare (*nude*)

pācō (1), subdue, pacify; **pācātus, –a, –um,** *adj.,* peaceable, quiet

perferō, –ferre, –tulī, –lātus, *irreg.,* carry through, endure

plēnus, –a, –um, *adj.,* full, *with gen. or abl.* (*plenary*)

rēgius, –a, –um, *adj.,* royal; **rēgia, –ae,** *f.,* palace

subsequor, –sequī, –secūtus sum, *dep.,* follow on, follow (*subsequent*)

vacuus, –a, –um, *adj.,* empty, vacant, free from, *with abl.* (*vacuum*)

vellus, –eris, *n.,* fleece

SENTENCE PATTERNS

A. Translate into English:

1. Ōlim habitābant in Thessaliā duo frātrēs, quōrum alter Aesōn, Peliās alter appellābātur.
2. Accidit ut Aesōn prīmō rēgnum obtinēret.
3. Post paucōs annōs Peliās frātrem expulit et Jāsonem, Aesonis fīlium, interfectūrus erat.
4. Forte ēvēnit ut quīdam ex amīcīs Aesonis puerum ēriperet.

153

5. Nōnne rēx amīcum quendam arcessīvit et quae causa mortis fuisset ex illō quaesīvit?
6. Illum Delphōs mīsit quī Apollinem cōnsuleret.
7. Pythia monuit Peliam ut aliquem cum ūnō pede nūdō vītāret.
8. Mōs est ut nāvis ē rōbore fiat ad vim tempestātum perferendam.
9. Sīc rēx, dolō plēnus, effēcit ut Jāsōn in rēgiā diū nōn commorārētur.
10. Diēs circiter decem cōnsūmptī sunt in nāvibus armandīs.

B. Translate into Latin:

1. Relying on his own courage and strength, he set forth to find the golden fleece.
2. By chance it was brought about that he delayed there for a few days.
3. The newness of the affair and the hope of glory moved many men who were worthy of very great praise.
4. The centurion was about to pacify a town empty of (free from) defenders.
5. Many men, worthy of praise, followed their daring leader.

Living Mythology:
The *Argo* and the Argonauts

Once upon a time in Thessaly there were two brothers, Aeson and Pelias. At first Aeson ruled the kingdom, but after a few years he was driven out by his brother, Pelias, who even tried to kill Jason, Aeson's son. Some friends, wishing to save Jason, took the boy out of the city and reported to the king that he had been killed.

After a brief period Pelias, fearing that he might lose the kingdom that he had seized with such violence and fraud, sent a friend to Delphi to consult the oracle. The priestess Pythia said there was no danger for the present, but that if anyone should come wearing one shoe, the king should beware.

After a few years Pelias decided to make a great sacrifice to the gods. He sent messengers far and wide to bring a multitude together. On the appointed day a large crowd gathered. Among these was Jason, who from boyhood had been living with a centaur. While making the journey, however, Jason had lost one of his shoes in crossing a river. Our Latin story begins with Jason's arrival at the palace of Pelias.

A Prophecy Comes True

Itaque accidit ut Jāsōn, cum calceum (*shoe*) āmissum nūllō modō recipere posset, ūnō pede nūdō in domicilium rēgium pervēnit. Cum prīmum Peliās eum vīdit, perterritus est. Intellēxit enim ōrāculum sē dē hōc virō monuisse. Ille dolō plēnus hoc cōnsilium iniit. Erat rēx quīdam, Aeētēs, quī rēgnum Colchidis illō tempore obtinēbat. Huic commissum erat vellus aureum quod Phrixus ōlim ibi relīquerat. Cōnstituit igitur Peliās Jāsonem mittere ut hoc vellere potīrētur. Cum perīculum esset māgnum, eum in itinere perītūrum esse spērābat. Jāsonem igitur ad sē arcessīvit, et eum dē vellere certiōrem fēcit. Ille cum intellegeret rem esse summae difficultātis, tamen virtūte suā frētus negōtium māgnō cum studiō suscēpit.

The Good Ship *Argo* Is Built

Cum Colchis multa mīlia passuum ab eō locō abesset, sōlus Jāsōn īre nōluit. Nūntiōs igitur in omnēs partēs dīmīsit, quī causam itineris expōnerent et multōs virōs convocārent. Intereā omnia quae sunt ūsuī ad armandās nāvēs comportārī jūssit. Tum Argō cuidam negōtium dedit ut nāvem aedificāret. Argus summam scientiam nauticārum rērum habēbat. In hīs rēbus circiter decem diēs cōnsūmptī sunt; Argus enim tantam dīligentiam adhibēbat ut nē nocturnum quidem tempus ad labōrem intermitteret. Effēcit ut nāvis tōta ē rōbore fieret. Hoc factum est quō vim tempestatum facilius perferre posset.

The building of the ship *Argo*.

Anchors Aweigh

Intereā ea diēs aderat quam Jāsōn per nūntiōs dīxerat, et ex omnibus regiōnibus Graeciae multī, quōs aut reī novitās aut spēs glōriae commovēbat, undique conveniēbant. In hōc numerō erant Herculēs, Orpheus, Thēseus, multīque aliī quōrum nōmina sunt nōtissima. Ex hīs Jāsōn, quōs ad omnia perīcula subeunda parātissimōs esse arbitrābātur quīnquāgintā (*fifty*) fortēs virōs dēlēgit. Tum paucōs diēs commorātus, nāvem dēdūxit et, tempestāte idōneā ad nāvigandum, māgnō cum plausū (*applause*) omnium solvit.

—The blades of the oars
moving together like the feet of water spiders
as if there were no such thing as death.
   —Marianne Moore, 1887–1972

Unit **XIX**

CONVERSATION

MAGISTER: Nōn multō post Argonautae ad īnsulam quandam, nōmine Cyzicum, pervēnērunt. Ā rēge benīgnō illīus regiōnis acceptī sunt.

VICTŌRIA: Quam diū ibi commorātī sunt?

MAGISTER: Paucās hōrās ibi commorātī ad sōlis occāsum solvērunt.

VICTOR: Eratne tempus ad nāvigandum idōneum?

MAGISTER: Postquam pauca mīlia passuum prōgressī sunt, tanta tempestās subitō orta est ut cursum tenēre nōn possent.

PETRUS: Quid fēcērunt? Nōn longē ab īnsulā amīcā erant.

MAGISTER: Ad eandem partem īnsulae unde modo profectī erant relātī sunt. Incolae, cum nox esset obscūra, Argonautās nōn agnōscēbant et eōs ēgredī prohibēbant.

ANNA: Cūr rēgem īnsulae arcessīvērunt?

MAGISTER: Priusquam rēx, quī ad lītus cucurrerat, agnōscerētur, ab Argonautīs cāsū occīsus est. Argonautae cum rēgem occīsum esse vidērent, māgnum dolōrem cēpērunt.

PAULUS: Antequam vellus aureum obtinērent, Argonautae multō plūrēs mājōrēsque dolōrēs cēpērunt.

SECTION 1 Temporal Clauses: *dum* meaning *while*

▶ DISCUSSION

1. **Dum,** meaning *while,* introduces adverbial clauses of time.

156

2. If the *while* means *as long as* (*all the time that*), we use **dum** with whatever tense of the indicative is required by the sense.

> **Dum scrībēbant, legēbam.**   *While they were writing,* I was reading.
> **Dum vīxit, bene vīxit.**   *While he lived,* he lived well.

3. If the *while* introduces a clause in which the time is longer than that denoted by the verb of the main clause, we use **dum** with the present indicative, even if the main verb is a past tense.

> **Dum haec geruntur, victōria ducī**   *While these things were going on,* the
> **nūntiātā est.**   victory was announced to the leader.

4. There is no present passive participle in Latin. A **dum** clause with its verb in the present passive indicative may be used to express the intended idea.

> **Oppidum, *dum oppūgnātur*, sē dē-**   The town *being attacked* surrendered.
> **didit.**

5. It is preferable to use the present participle, instead of **dum** with the present indicative, if the expression is active.

> **Captīvī fugientēs interfectī sunt.**   *While the prisoners were fleeing,* they
>   were killed.

▶ PRACTICE PATTERNS

A. Translate into English:

1. Dum vīvō, spērō. 2. Dum pūgnat, interfectus est. 3. Castra, dum mūniuntur, capta sunt. 4. Dum in hortō ambulābās, epistulās legēbam. 5. Mīlitēs pūgnantēs ab imperātōre spectābantur. 6. Dum ea geruntur, dux Rōmam pervēnit.

B. Translate into Latin:

1. As long as he lived, he remembered your brave deeds. 2. The ship, while being renovated, was captured by the enemy. 3. While standing in the prow of the ship, the sailor sent forth the dove. 4. While the king was reclining at table, the birds were descending from above. 5. While the sailors were sitting with the king, the birds were carrying off the food.

SECTION 2 Temporal Clauses: *dum* meaning *until*

▶ DISCUSSION

1. **Dum,** meaning *until*, introduces adverbial clauses of time.
2. If the clause states a fact, the perfect indicative is used.

> **Exspectābant *dum nāvis facta est.***   They waited *until the ship was built.*

157

3. In a purely temporal clause, if the main verb is present, future, or imperative, we use *dum* with the present subjunctive.

Exspectāmus *dum veniant.*   We are waiting *until they come.*
Exspectābimus *dum veniant.*   We shall wait *until they come.*
Exspectāte *dum veniant.*   Wait *till they come.*

4. If the *dum*-clause implies anticipation, expectancy, or purpose, we use *dum* with the subjunctive, following the rules of sequence of tenses.

Dum nāvēs convenīrent, **exspectā-**   They waited *until the ships should as-*
vērunt.   *semble.*

Dux, *dum imperātōrem* **cōnsu-**   The leader delayed *until he could con-*
leret, morātus est.   *sult the general.*

▶ PRACTICE PATTERNS

A. Translate into English:

1. In īnsulā mānsimus dum columba ₁ ēvāsit. 2. In īnsulā manēbimus dum columba ēvadat. 3. Dum columba ēvaderet, in īnsulā mānsimus.

B. Translate into Latin:

1. They waited until the rocks dashed together again. 2. They will wait until the rocks dash together again. 3. They waited until the rocks could dash together again.

SECTION 3 Temporal Clauses: *antequam* and *priusquam*

▶ DISCUSSION

1. If a *before*-clause is purely temporal, we use *antequam* or *priusquam* with the indicative mood in the subordinate clause.

The subordinate clause uses the present indicative if the verb in the main clause is present, future, or imperative.

Antequam abeō, **tibi pecūniam**   *Before I go away,* I shall give you the
dabō.   money.

The subordinate clause uses the future perfect indicative if the main verb is negative and future.

Nōn abībō *antequam* **tibi pecū-**   I shall not go away *before I give (shall*
niam dederō.   *have given) you the money.*

The subordinate clause uses the perfect indicative if the main verb states a fact in past time.

Antequam abiit, tibi pecūniam dedī.

Before he went away, I gave you the money.

2. If the *before*-clause implies expectancy in past time, we use **antequam** or **priusquam** with the subjunctive (usually the imperfect).

Antequam abīrem, tibi pecūniam dedī.

Before I could go away, I gave you the money.

▶ STUDY HELPS

Antequam and *priusquam* often become *ante . . . quam* and *prius . . . quam*, especially in negative sentences and with intervals of time.

Paucīs *ante* diēbus *quam* abiī, tibi pecūniam dedī.

A few days *before* I went away, I gave you the money.

▶ PRACTICE PATTERNS

A. Translate into English:

1. Antequam venit, litterās mittet. 2. Nōn respondēbō tibi antequam tū ipse mihi responderis. 3. Priusquam nāvēs incolumēs ēvaderent, rūpēs cōnflīxērunt. 4. Antequam rūpēs concurrerent, Argonautae nāvem perdūxērunt. 5. Priusquam cibus appositus est, volucrēs dēsuper vēnērunt.

B. Translate into Latin:

1. Come before I go away. 2. A few days before I came, he had departed. 3. We reached the city before the gates were shut. 4. I shall not come before you send for me. 5. Before we could prevent him, he crossed the river.

WORDS TO MASTER

afferō, –ferre, attulī, allātus, *irreg.,* bring to, offer, report (*afferent*)

afficiō, –ere, –fēcī, –fectus, do something to, affect, afflict (*affect*)

antequam, *conj.,* before

appōnō, –ere, –posuī, –positus, set before, serve (*apposition*)

columba, –ae, *f.,* dove, pigeon (*columbarium*)

concurrō, –ere, –currī, –cursūrus, run together, dash together (*concur*)

cōnflīgō, –ere, –flīxī, –flīctus, dash together, harass (*conflict*)

dēsuper, *adv.,* from above

dum, *conj.,* while, as long as, till, until

ēmittō, –ere, –mīsī, –missus, send out, let go, throw, hurl (*emit*)

ēvadō, –ere, –vāsī, ēvāsūrus, go forth, escape (*evade*)

perdūcō, –ere, –dūxī, –ductus, lead through, lead, bring

praebeō, –ēre, –uī, –itus, hold forth, offer, present, show

prōra, –ae, *f.,* prow, bow (*prow*)

sublevō (1), lighten, raise, raise up, assist

volucer, –cris, –cre, *adj.,* winged; **volucris, –cris,** *f.,* bird

159

BUILDING WORD POWER

The Latin root word *legere, lēctum,* *to collect, choose, read, pick,* and its compounds in *–ligere* have derivatives in English with widely different meanings. The word *select* is far removed from *legible* in meaning but not in origin. The derivatives in English directly from Latin may be recognized by the syllables *leg–, lect–, lig–.*

What English words are derived from the following Latin words?

intellegere (inter + legere), *to choose between, perceive, understand*
dīligere (dis + legere), *to choose out carefully, prize, love*
ēligere (ex + legere), *to pick out, choose*
neglegere (nec + legere), *to fail to choose, to pass over*
sēligere (sē + legere), *to choose*
praelegere (prae + legere), *to read before others*

Notice the following:

legion (**legiō**), *a chosen body of men*
college (**collegium**), *a collection of persons, a society*
legend (**legendum**), *appointed to be read, a mythical story*
eligible (**ēligibilis**), *qualified to be chosen*
diligent (**dīligēns**), *careful in the matter chosen; opposite of* negligent (**negligēns**), *not careful*
intellect (**intellectum**), *the faculty of choosing, knowing*
elegant (**ēlegāns**), *well-chosen*

Do not confuse *lēgāre,* *to send on an embassy,* with *legere,* *to choose.* *Lēgāre, lēgātum,* is derived from *lēx, lēgis,* law. *Legal, legacy, legislate, legitimate,* and *privilege* are the important derivatives from *lēx, lēgis;* and *allegation, delegate, legate,* and *relegate* come from *lēgāre.*

SENTENCE PATTERNS

A. Supply in Latin the correct form of the word in parentheses. Translate the sentence into English.

1. Antequam Argonautae multa mīlia passuum prōgressī erant, ad īnsulam quandam, nōmine Cyzicum, (perveniō).
2. Paucās hōrās ibi commorābantur dum tempestās satis idōnea (sum).
3. Ad eandem partem īnsulae unde modo profectī erant (referō).
4. Incolae, cum nox esset, Argonautās nōn agnōscēbant eōsque ēgredī (prohibeō).
5. Nōnne advenae māgnō dolōre affectī sunt cum intellegerent sē rēgem benīgnum (occīdō)?
6. Cum Hylās speciem pulcherrimam praebēret, Nymphae eī persuādēre cōnātae sunt ut apud sē (maneō).

7. Priusquam cibum quem ante eum apposuerant caperet, volucrēs dēsuper dēscendēbant et eum (auferō).
8. Dum in prōrā nauta (stō), columbam ēmīsit quae posteā incolumis ēvāsit.
9. Antequam rūpēs rūrsus (concurrō) et cōnflīgerent, nāvem perdūxit.
10. Nautae sē sublevāvērunt ut dēsuper volucrēs quae tantum timōrem afferēbant (interficiō).

B. Translate into Latin:

1. While he was seeking for water, he departed a little from his comrades.
2. Before his comrades could return to the shore, Jason set sail.
3. Before the Argonauts arrived, these birds brought great fear to the king.
4. They waited until they should raise themselves in order to kill the birds from above.
5. Before the rocks could run together, the dove escaped unharmed.

Living Mythology:
A Fatal Mistake

The Argonauts (*Argus* + *nautae*) soon reached an island called Cyzicus and were hospitably received by the king. At sunset they again set sail, but were driven back by a sudden storm. The inhabitants of Cyzicus, thinking it was an enemy ship, seized arms in order to prevent the supposed enemy from landing. A fierce battle was fought on the shore, and in the darkness of the night, the Argonauts killed the king who had been so kind to them. At daybreak, when they realized their grievous mistake, they were filled with great sorrow.

The next day Jason again set sail, and before night he reached Mysia. He sent a few sailors to get fresh water because their supply was failing. Among these was a handsome boy named Hylas, who accidentally wandered away from his companions. The Nymphs whose duty it was to guard the fountain fell in love with him and detained him by force. His companions sought for him in vain. With great sorrow they retraced their steps to the shore only to learn that Jason had already sailed.

The Deliverance of Phineus

Ab eō locō Argonautae ad Thrāciam cursum tenuērunt, et postquam ad oppidum Salmydessum nāvem appulērunt, ē nāve ēgressī sunt. Virī in terram prōgressī ab incolīs quaesīvērunt quis rēgnum ējus regiōnis obtinēret. Certiōrēs factī sunt Phīneum quendam tum rēgem esse. Cōgnōvērunt etiam hunc caecum esse et gravissimō quōdam suppliciō afficī quod sē ōlim crūdēlissimum in fīliōs suōs praebuisset. Hūjus generis erat supplicium. Juppiter mōnstra quaedam speciē horribilī mīserat, quae capita virginum, corpora volucrum habēbant. Hae volucrēs, quae Harpȳiae appellābantur, summam molestiam (*annoyance*) afferēbant. Quotiēns ille accubuerat (*reclined at table*) statim veniēbant et cibum appositum auferēbant.

Rēs igitur in hōc locō erant cum Argonautae ad Thrāciam nāvem appulērunt. Phīneus autem simul atque audīvit eōs in fīnēs

Jason and his men passing through the Symplegades.

suōs pervēnisse, māgnopere gāvīsus est. Sciēbat quantam opīniōnem virtūtis habērent et putābat eōs sibi auxilium lātūrōs esse. Nūntium igitur ad nāvem mīsit quī Jāsonem sociōsque ad rēgiam vocāret. Eō cum vēnissent, Phīneus pollicitus est sē prō auxiliō sibi ab Argonautīs datō, eīs māgna praemia datūrum esse. Argonautae negōtium māgnō cum studiō suscēpērunt, et ubi hōra vēnit cum rēge accubuērunt. At simul ac cibus appositus est, Harpȳiae vēnērunt et cibum auferre cōnābantur. Argonautae prīmum gladiīs volucrēs petīvērunt, sed frūstrā pūgnāvērunt. Deinde Zētēs et Calais, quī ālīs erant īnstrūctī, in āera sē sublevāvērunt ut dēsuper impetum facerent. Hoc cum Harpȳiae sēnsissent, reī novitāte perterritae statim fūgērunt, neque posteā umquam rediērunt.

Hōc factō Phīneus, ut prō tantō beneficiō māximam grātiam referret, Jāsōnī dēmōnstrāvit quā ratiōne Symplēgadēs vītāre posset. Symplēgadēs erant duae rūpēs ingentī māgnitūdine, quae erant impedīmentīs illīs cōnantibus ad Colchida pervenīre. Hae parvō intervallō in marī natābant (*floated*). Cum prīmum in medium spatium aliquid vēnit, incrēdibilī celeritāte concurrēbant. Postquam igitur ā Phīneō doctus est quid faciendum esset, Jāsōn nāvem solvit et mox ad Symplēgadēs appropinquāvit; tum in prōrā stāns, columbam quam in manū tenēbat ēmīsit. Illa rēctā viā per medium spatium volāvit et, priusquam rūpēs cōnflīxērunt, incolumis ēvāsit, caudā tantum (*only*) āmissā. Tum rūpēs utrimque discessērunt; antequam tamen rūrsus concurrerent, Argonautae, bene intellegentēs omnem spem salūtis in celeritāte positam esse, summā vī rēmīs contendērunt et nāvem incolumem perdūxērunt.

| In such a night | *Unit* XX |

In such a night
Medea gather'd the enchanted herbs
That did renew old Aeson.
          —Shakespeare
          Merchant of Venice

CONVERSATION

JĀSŌN: Mox ad flūmen Phāsim, quod in fīnibus Colchōrum est, perveniēmus. Nōn dubium est quīn Aeētēs vellus possideat.

COMES: Vereor nē nōbīs impedīmentō sit! Vellere aureō potītus est, et ubi sit nēscīmus.

JĀSŌN: Ego, frētus auxiliō deōrum et fortibus sociīs meīs, postulābō ut vellus nōbīs trādātur.

COMES: Ut prīmum ē nāve ēgressī sumus, ad rēgem Aeētem nōs cōnferāmus!

JĀSŌN: Ille cum audiet quam ob causam vēnerīmus īrā commovēbitur.

AEĒTĒS: (*paucīs post hōrīs*): Salvēte, viātōrēs. Cūr hūc vēnistis?

JĀSŌN: Salvē, rēx Aeētēs. Vēnimus ut vellere aureō potiāmur.

AEĒTĒS: (*māgnā cum īrā*): Tibi vellus trādere nōlō. At cum nōn sine auxiliō deōrum hoc negōtium suscēperis, mūtātā sententiā meā, polliceor mē vellus trāditūrum esse, sī labōrēs duōs difficillimōs perfēceris.

JĀSŌN: Ad omnia perīcula subeunda parātus sum. Ostende quid mihi faciendum sit. Nihil potest prohibēre quīn fīat.

SECTION 1 Substantive Clauses as Objects of Verbs of Fearing

▶ DISCUSSION

1. As a general rule, when an English verb of fearing is completed by an infinitive, the Latin translation also uses the infinitive.

Timēbat īre.   He was afraid to go.

2. When an English verb of fearing is completed by an objective substantive clause, a subordinate clause is used also in Latin.

3. In English the subordinate clause is introduced by *that* or *lest*. In Latin a positive subordinate clause is introduced by *nē,* and the verb in the clause is in the subjunctive mood.

Timet *nē audācior sīs.*	He is afraid *that you are (will be, may be) too daring.*
	He is afraid *lest you be too daring.*
Timet *nē audācior fuerīs.*	He is afraid *that you were too daring.*
Timēbat *nē audācior essēs.*	He was afraid *that you were (would be, might be) too daring.*
Timēbat *nē audācior fuissēs.*	He was afraid *that you had been too daring.*

4. A negative subordinate clause after verbs of fearing in Latin is introduced by *ut* or by *nē nōn (nē nēmō, nē numquam,* etc.).

Vereor *ut veniat.*	
Vereor *nē nōn veniat.*	I fear *that he will not (may not) come.*
Timēbam *nē nēmō venīret.*	I feared *that no one would come.*

▶ STUDY HELPS

1. A passive infinitive cannot be used in Latin after a verb of fearing. A subordinate clause must be used.

Timēbat *nē agnōscerētur.*   He was afraid *to be recognized.*

2. If the verb of fearing is **vereor** and is positive, **ut** rather than **nē nōn** introduces the clause. But if **vereor** is negative, only **nē nōn (nē nēmō, nē numquam,** etc.) may introduce the clause.

Nōn vereor *nē nōn veniat.*   I do not fear *that he will come.*

▶ PRACTICE PATTERNS

A. Translate into English:

1. Haec facere timēbat. 2. Timēbam nē nēmō servārētur. 3. Nōn vereor nē nōn

164

perveniat. 4. Id vereor ut tibi concēdere possim. 5. Veritī erant ut sociī sibi auxilium ferrent. 6. Numquam timēbant nē vellere aureō nōn potīrentur.

B. Translate into Latin:

1. He was afraid to be seen. 2. Don't be afraid to tell the truth. 3. We feared that the king would overtake us. 4. He did not fear that the leader would not come. 5. I am not afraid that my evil deeds will be discovered. 6. Jason feared that he might not be able to get possession of the Golden Fleece.

SECTION 2 Substantive Clauses as Objects of Verbs of Hindering, Preventing, etc.

▶ DISCUSSION

1. Certain verbs of hindering, preventing, opposing, or their equivalents govern a substantive clause with the verb in the subjunctive, present or imperfect tense.

The most common verbs thus used are: **impediō,** *hinder;* **dēterreō,** *deter, frighten from;* **retineō,** *restrain;* **recūsō,** *object to, protest against;* **obsistō** and **obstō,** *oppose.*

2. The subordinate clause is introduced by **quōminus** (*by which the less*), *so that not.* If the main verb is affirmative, the subordinate clause may be introduced by **nē** instead of **quōminus;** if negative, by **quīn,** *but that, that not, without,* instead of **quōminus.**

Nōs impedīvērunt *quōminus* **(nē) abīrēmus.**	They hindered us *from going away.*
Nōs nōn impedīvērunt *quōminus* **(quīn) abīrēmus.**	They did not hinder us *from going away.*
Tē nōn dēterrent *quōminus* **(quīn) abeās.**	They are not deterring you *from going away.*

3. The most common verb of preventing is **prohibeō,** which regularly takes the accusative and the infinitive.

Prohibent nōs abīre.	They are preventing *us from going away.*

▶ STUDY HELPS

The verb **recūsō** also means *refuse,* but it is not used in expressions such as: *He refuses to go.* This sentence is translated into Latin: **Īre nōn vult,** or **Negat sē itūrum esse.**

165

► PRACTICE PATTERNS

A. Translate into English:

1. Recūsō quōminus eat. 2. Rēx nostrōs nāvibus ēgredī prohibēbat. 3. Eōs dē-terret nē abeant. 4. Tē nōn impedīvērunt quōminus loquerēris. 5. Jāsōn re-tinērī nōn poterat quīn vellus aspiceret. 6. Dolōrēs tē impediēbant quōminus mēcum essēs.

B. Translate into Latin:

1. He objected to my doing that. 2. Who prevents you from coming? 3. He hindered you from replying. 4. I shall oppose your setting out. 5. No one de-terred you from returning. 6. He restrained the leader from seizing the fleece.

SECTION 3 Substantive Clauses with Expressions of Doubt

► DISCUSSION

1. With negative expressions of doubt or questions of doubt implying a negative answer, the subjunctive is used in a substantive clause intro-duced by *quīn.*

Nōn dubitō *quīn vērum sit.* I do not doubt *that it is true.*

2. Affirmative expressions of doubt take indirect question introduced by *num, whether; an, whether, or;* or *sī, if.*

Dubitat *num veniat.* He doubts *whether he will come.*

3. *Dubitō, hesitate,* takes the complementary infinitive.

Pūgnāre **nōn dubitāvit.** He did not hesitate *to fight.*

► PRACTICE PATTERNS

A. Translate into English:

1. Dubitō num vērum sit. 2. Haec facere dubitābat. 3. Nēmō dubitāvit quīn adessent. 4. Nōn dubium erat quīn adessent. 5. Quis dubitat num adfuerint? 6. Nōn dubium est quīn illīs auxilium ferat.

B. Translate into Latin:

1. There is no doubt that they will escape. 2. No one doubts that she pressed out the juice. 3. He did not hesitate to propose the evil deed. 4. They doubt whether she will seize the fleece. 5. Who doubted that the juice could nourish the body? 6. We did not doubt that he would arrive at Rome safely.

alō, –ere, –uī, altus, nourish, sustain (*alimentary*)

aspiciō, –ere, –spēxī, –spectus, look on (*aspect*)

carpō, –ere, carpsī, carptus, pluck, seize (*excerpt*)

dubium, –ī, *n.*, doubt (*dubious*)

ēdīcō, –ere, –dīxī, –dictus, proclaim, appoint (*edict*)

exprimō, –ere, –pressī, –pressus, press out (*express*)

galea, –ae, *f.*, helmet

īnsciēns, –entis, *adj.*, not knowing, unaware

merīdiēs, –ēī, *m.*, midday, south (*meridian*)

paulisper, *adv.*, a little while, for a short time

praecipiō, –ere, –cēpī, –ceptus, instruct beforehand, command (*precept*)

prōpōnō, –ere, –posuī, –positus, place before, propose, set forth (*propose*)

quīn, *conj.*, why not, that not, but that, without, that

quōminus, *conj.*, that not, so that not, from

sūcus, –ī, *m.*, juice, sap

vereor, –ērī, –itus sum, *dep.*, fear, be afraid of, dread

BUILDING WORD POWER

Several groups of Latin derivatives in common use trace their origin back to the root word *nōscere, nōtum, to know.* From the root *nō–* was formed the Latin word *nōmen, nōminis,* the result of knowing, the *name* by which something is known, and then the verb *nōmināre, nōminātum, to name.* From the same root we have the adjective *nōbilis, noble, well known.*

From *nōtum, known,* is derived the Latin noun *nota, –ae,* meaning *note,* from which developed *notāre, notātum, to mark, to note.* We likewise have *nōtiō, –ōnis,* notion; *nōtitia,* notice; *nōtābilis,* notable; *notātiō, –ōnis,* notation; *notārius,* notary.

Agnōscere, agnitum, (*ad + gnōscere*), *to recognize; cōgnōscere, cōgnitum,* (*cum + gnōscere*) *to get to know,* and in the perfect, *to know;* and *recōgnōscere, recōgnitum, to know again;* and the adjective *incōgnitus, unknown,* are the important compounds of *nōscere* in Latin. *Cognizant* and *recognize* came into English through the French. So did *connoisseur* and *reconnoiter, acquaint,* and *noun.*

Explain the italicized words: *nominal* peace; *notorious* bandit; *connoisseur* of art; religious *denomination;* travel *incognito* (the accent is on the *cog–*); communism is a *misnomer; nominating* committee; some Romans had a *praenomen, nomen, cognomen,* and *agnomen;* immediate *recognition;* biological *nomenclature.*

SENTENCE PATTERNS

A. Translate into English:

1. Brevī intermissō spatiō, ā rēge postulāvērunt ut vellus aureum sibi trāderētur.
2. Ille, cum audīvisset quam ob rem Argonautae vēnissent, īrā commōtus est et diū negāvit sē vellus trāditūrum esse.
3. Tandem tamen, cum timēret nē deī eum pūnīrent, sententiam mūtāvit.
4. Nōnne labōrēs duōs difficillimōs prōposuit ut Jāsōn interficerētur?
5. Nōn dubium est quīn Mēdēa, īnsciente patre, herbās quāsdam carpserit et ex eīs sūcum expresserit, quī corpus alit.
6. Comitibus aspicientibus, tantam dīligentiam praebuit ut ante merīdiem agrum arāvisset.
7. Cūr rēx cōnātur virum fortem impedīre quōminus vellus obtineat?
8. Nōn dubitābat quīn fīlia rēgis auxilium advenae tulisset.
9. Illō diē quem rēx ēdīxerat Jāsōn virōs gladiīs galeīsque armātōs interfēcit, ut eī praeceptum erat.
10. Verēbātur nē pater eam exīre domō prohibēret.

B. Translate into Latin:

1. He did not hesitate to throw the stone into the middle of the men.
2. Did she fear that Jason would not get possession of the fleece?
3. He did not doubt but that he would kill the men armed with helmets.
4. When she heard that he was about to undergo such a danger, she proposed a good plan.
5. She did not prevent Jason from escaping, did she?

Living Mythology:
More Frustrations

Within a short time, the Argonauts arrived at the river Phasis which was in the territory of the Colchians. As soon as they had landed, the Argonauts hurried to King Aeetes and demanded the Golden Fleece. He became very angry and said that he would not give up the fleece. Finally, however, when he realized that Jason had the help of the gods behind him, he changed his mind and promised that he would give up the fleece, provided Jason first performed two very difficult tasks. When Jason answered that he was ready to undergo these dangers for the sake of getting possession of the fleece, the king explained what he wished to be done.

First Jason must yoke two bulls, which were dreadful in appearance and belched forth flames; when the bulls were yoked, a certain field must be plowed and then sowed with the teeth of a dragon. Jason realized that these were tasks of extreme danger; nevertheless, because he was not willing to lose this opportunity of reaching his goal, he accepted the conditions.

Medea's Magic

At Mēdēa, rēgis fīlia, Jāsōnem māximē amābat et, ubi audīvit eum tantum perīculum subitūrum esse, vērita est nē ducī fortī nocērētur. Nōn dubium erat quīn pater ējus labōrem difficilem prōposuisset ut Jāsōn interficerētur. Mēdēa, quae summam scientiam artis magicae habēbat, hoc cōnsilium inīre ausa est. Mediā nocte, īnsciente patre, ex urbe ēvāsit et postquam in montēs fīnitimōs vēnit, herbās quāsdem carpsit; tum, sūcō (*sap*) expressō, unguentum (*ointment*) parāvit quod vī suā corpus aleret et cōnfīrmāret. Hōc factō, Jāsōnī unguentum dedit. Jūssit ducem autem eō diē quō istōs labōrēs cōnfectūrus erat, corpus suum et arma māne oblinere (*to smear*). Jāsōn, quamquam paene omnēs hominēs māgnitūdine et vīribus corporis superābat, tamen hoc cōnsilium nōn neglegendum sibi esse cēnsēbat.

The Dragon's Teeth and How They Grew

Ubi is diēs vēnit quem rēx ad agrum arandum ēdīxerat, Jāsōn, ortā lūce, cum sociīs ad locum cōnstitūtum sē contulit. Ibi stabulum ingēns repperit, in quō taurī erant inclūsī; tum portīs apertīs, taurōs in lūcem trāxit, et summā cum difficultāte eīs jugum imposuit. At Aeētēs, cum vidēret taurōs nihil contrā Jāsōnem valēre, māgnopere mīrātus est; nēsciēbat enim fīliam suam auxilium eī dedisse. Tum Jāsōn, omnibus aspicientibus, agrum arāre incēpit. Tantam dīligentiam praebuit ut ante merīdiem tōtum opus cōnficeret. Hōc factō, ad locum ubi rēx sedēbat properāvit et dentēs dracōnis postulāvit. Hōs ubi accēpit, in agrum quem arāverat māgnā cum dīligentiā sparsit. Hōrum autem dentium nātūra erat tālis ut in eō locō ubi sparsī erant, virī armātī mīrō quōdam modō orīrentur.

Imperāverat enim eī Aeētēs ut armātōs virōs sōlus interficeret. Paucās hōrās Jāsōn dormiēbat; sub vesperum saxum ingēns, ut

Jason sowing the dragon's teeth.

(*as*) Mēdēa praecēperat, in mediōs virōs gladiīs galeīsque armātōs conjēcit. Statim māgna contrōversia orta est. Sibi quisque id saxum habēre voluit. Brevī tempore gladiīs inter sē pūgnāre incēpērunt. Cum hōc modō plūrimī occīsī essent, reliquī, vulneribus cōnfectī, ā Jāsōne sine difficultāte interfectī sunt.

It is impossible to please all the world and one's father.
—Jean de la Fontaine, 1621–1695
Fables

Unit XXI

CONVERSATION

ROBERTUS: Cum rēx Aeētēs Jāsonem labōrem prōpositum cōnfēcisse cōgnōsceret, quid fēcit?

MAGISTER: Statim graviter commōtus est. Id enim per dolum factum esse intellegēbat. Nōn dubitābat quīn Mēdēa Jāsonī auxilium tulisset.

ROBERTA: Nōnne Mēdēa intellēxit sē in māgnō futūram esse perīculō, sī in rēgiā manēret?

MAGISTER: Mēdēa perīculum suum bene intellēxit et fugā salūtem petere cōnstituit. Omnibus rebus ad fugam parātīs, mediā nocte, īnsciente patre, cum frātre Absyrtō ēvāsit.

ROBERTUS: Sī pater ējus haec cōnsilia cōgnōvisset, eam persecūtus esset.

170

MAGISTER: Quam celerrimē ad locum ubi Argō subducta erat Mēdēa sē contulit. Eō cum vēnisset, sē ad pedēs Jāsonis prōjēcit. Multīs cum lacrimīs eum ōrāvit nē mulierem relinqueret quae eī tantum auxilium tulisset. Jāsōn postquam causam veniendī repperit, hortātus est nē patris īram timēret; eam sēcum nāve suā ēvāsūram esse pollicitus est.

SECTION 1 Conditional Sentences

▶ DISCUSSION

1. In English and in Latin conditional sentences have two parts, the condition and the conclusion. The *condition* is expressed in a subordinate, adverbial clause introduced in English by *if*, *if not*, *unless* and in Latin by **sī, nisi.** The *conclusion* is expressed in the principal clause.

TYPES OF CONDITIONAL SENTENCES

TYPE	ENGLISH		LATIN
			Both clauses Indicative; Tense required by sense
	Present: *If he is here, it is well.*		**Sī adest, bene est.**
Conditions of fact	Past:	*If he was here, it was well.* *If he has been (was) here, it has been (was) well.*	{ **Sī aderat, bene erat.** **Sī adfuit, bene fuit.**
	Future:	*If he is (will be) here, it will be well.* *If he is (will have been) here, it will be well.*	{ **Sī aderit, bene erit.** **Sī adfuerit, bene erit.**
Conditions contrary to fact			Both clauses Subjunctive; Imperfect or Pluperfect tense
	Present: *If he were here, it would be well (now).*		**Sī adesset, bene esset.**
	Past: *If he had been here, it would have been well.*		**Sī adfuisset, bene fuisset.**
Conditions of remote future possibility			Both clauses Subjunctive; Present tense
	Future: *If he should be here, it would be well (in the future).*		**Sī adsit, bene sit.**

2. In conditions of fact referring to the future, the English frequently uses a *false* present in the *if*-clause, where Latin more correctly requires a future or future perfect.

171

3. In Latin, **sī** with the future indicative expresses action which continues *during* the time of the main verb; **sī** with the future perfect indicative expresses action *before* the time of the main verb.

4. In conditions contrary to fact, when reference is to *present* time (If he were here *now, but he is not*), the imperfect subjunctive is used; when reference is to the *past* (If you had been here *yesterday, but you were not*), the pluperfect subjunctive is used.

5. Negative conditions are introduced by **nisi** or **sī nōn. Nisi** is used to negative the *if*-clause; **sī nōn,** to negative one word in it.

Nisi haec fēceris, accūsāberis.	*Unless you do (will have done) these things,* you will be blamed.
Sī vir nōn pauper esset, ad urbem Rōmam īret.	*If the man were not poor,* he would go to the city of Rome.

6. After **nisi** and **sī, quis** means anyone, **quid** anything.

Sī quis reverterit, hoc eī dā.	*If anyone returns,* give this to him.
Sī quid habuissem, tibi dedissem.	*If I had had anything,* I would have given it to you.

▶ PRACTICE PATTERNS

A. Translate into English:

1. Sī aderit, vincet. 2. Nisi quid vīs, abī. 3. Sī quis venit, abeō. 4. Sī hoc facit, bene est. 5. Sī pūgnāvisset, vīcisset. 6. Sī procurrit, persecūtī sumus. 7. Sī quid habēbō, tibi laetus dabō. 8. Sī haec nōn vīdisset, nōn crēdidisset. 9. Sī obsidēs mittant, Rōmānī pācem faciant. 10. Sī Jāsōn hīc adesset, comitēs nōn timērent.

B. Translate into Latin:

1. If he fights, he conquers. 2. If he fights, he will conquer. 3. If he fought, he conquered. 4. If anyone comes, he will be seen. 5. If he should fight, he would conquer. 6. Unless he wants something, he does not come. 7. If I had anything, I would give it to you. 8. Unless you do these things, you will be seized. 9. If he were to do (should do) this, I would be grateful. 10. If Jason had not been helped by the king's daughter, he would not have escaped.

SECTION 2 Impersonal Passive

▶ DISCUSSION

1. In both English and Latin, only transitive verbs may be used in the passive with a personal subject:

Mē vocat.	He is calling me.
Ab eō vocar.	I am called by him.

2. An intransitive verb in Latin, when used in the passive, must take an impersonal subject:

Ad castra perventum erat. The camp had been reached.
(Literally: It had been arrived at the camp.)

3. The impersonal passive construction in Latin is used with two kinds of verbs.

It is used with intransitive verbs which require no direct object:

Ācriter pūgnātum est. There was fierce fighting.
(Literally: It was fought fiercely.)

Respōnsum est. The reply was made.
(Literally: It was replied.)

Ad forum concurritur. There is a rush for the Forum.
(Literally: It is rushed to the Forum.)

It is also used with dative-governing intransitive verbs:

Mulieribus ac līberīs parcitur. The women and children are spared.
(Literally: It is spared to the women and children.)

Eīs nōn persuādēbitur. They will not be persuaded.
(Literally: It will not be persuaded to them.)

4. If an intransitive verb is used with the passive periphrastic, it must be used impersonally in the third person singular.

Vōbīs pūgnandum est. You must fight.
(Literally: It must be fought to you.)

Dīcit hostibus resistendum esse. He says that the enemy must be resisted.
(Literally: He says that it must be resisted to the enemy.)

▶ PRACTICE PATTERNS

A. Translate into English:

1. Nēmō eī crēdit. 2. In silvam ītur. 3. Puerō nocitum est. 4. Nōbīs veniendum est. 5. Eī ā nūllō crēditur. 6. Dīcit tibi currendum esse. 7. Diū et ācriter pūgnātum est. 8. Mihi ab eō nōn persuādēbitur. 9. Illī prīncipī crēdī nōn potest. 10. Omnibus mīlitibus imperātum est.

B. Translate into Latin:

1. We must run. 2. A reply had been made. 3. They say that we must run. 4. The river was soon reached. 5. You will be believed by all. 6. The man will not be persuaded. 7. The prisoners are being pardoned. 8. He learns that a

173

battle has taken place. 9. He learns that a battle must take place. 10. The announcement was made that the prisoners were being pardoned.

WORDS TO MASTER

arbor, –oris, *f.,* tree (*arboreal*)

dēripiō, –ere, –ripuī, –reptus, snatch away, tear away

ējiciō, –ere, –jēcī, –jectus, cast out, drive out (*eject*)

intervallum, –ī, *n.,* interval, space, distance

īnsequor, –ī, īnsecūtus sum, *dep.,* follow up, pursue

persequor, –ī, persecūtus sum, *dep.,* follow up, pursue, attack (*persecute*)

praestō, –stāre, –stitī, –stitus, *irreg.,* stand before, excel, surpass

pretium, –ī, *n.,* price, cost

prīdiē, *adv.,* on the day before

prōcurrō, –ere, –currī, –cursūrus, run forward, charge

rāmus, –ī, *m.,* branch, bough (*ramus*)

refulgeō, –ere, –fulsī, —, flash back, gleam, glitter (*refulgent*)

sepeliō, –īre, –īvī, –pultus, bury

sepultūra, –ae, *f.,* burial (*sepulture*)

subdūcō, –ere, –dūxī, –ductus, lead up, lead away, withdraw, draw up (ships)

turris, –is, *f.,* tower (*turret*)

BUILDING WORD POWER

If you come across an English word with the syllable –*gen*– as part of its make-up, you may be pretty sure it is derived from **gīgnere, genitum,** *to produce, beget.* Its original form was **genere.** The noun **genus, generis,** meaning *birth, descent, origin* came to mean also *race, kind,* and *species.* The key words derived from **genus,** which itself came into English meaning *class* or *kind,* are: *gene, genera, general, generate, generic, generous, genuine, ingenuous, ingenuity, gender, indigenous, benign, malign.*

Genius, –ī, was a noun meaning the guardian spirit of a man or a place. Today in English it means great inventive ability and mental capacity, and a person who has such ability and capacity is called a *genius. Genial,* meaning *cordial* and *amiable,* and *congenial,* having the same tastes and temperaments, are derived from **genius. Ingenium** meant *inborn quality.* From this Latin word we have our word *ingenious,* meaning *clever.* Do not confuse this English word with *ingenuous,* of noble birth and therefore candid, sincere. Check the dictionary for the origin of *engine* and (cotton) *gin.*

The words *gentle, genteel, gentile* came from another Latin noun, **gēns, gentis,** *tribe* or *clan.* If one belonged to the tribe, he was well born, therefore a *gentle*man and *genteel. Gentile* to the Jew meant one not of Jewish faith; to the Christian it meant one not a Jew.

174

Explain: *genial* climate; *progenitor* of the race; law of *primogeniture;* *regeneration* of a starfish; electrical *generator.*

SENTENCE PATTERNS

A. Translate into English:

1. Prīdiē sociīs ad mare relictīs, quī praesidiō nāvī essent, ipse cum Mēdēā in silvās sē contulit.
2. Sī locus ipse et nātūrā et arte nōn mūnīrētur, vellus auferre difficile nōn esset.
3. Nōn dubitābant quīn aliqua calamitās accidisset.
4. Sī vellus ex arbore dēripuerit, ad nāvem fugiet.
5. Dum proficīscī parant, lūmen mīrum in modum inter silvās refulgēns cōnspēxērunt.
6. Cum nāvis ingentī esset māgnitūdine, celeriter prōgredī nōn poterat.
7. Sī fugientēs persecūtus esset, fīlium perspēxisset.
8. Prōcurrere incipiēbant ut rāmum ex arbore dēriperent.
9. Intervallō brevī nāvem īnsecūtus est sed, fīliō interfectō, domum revertit ut corpus mortuum ad sepultūram daret.
10. Sī virtūte omnibus praestet, fēminam fortem nōn ējiciat.

B. Translate into Latin:

1. If they should snatch away the branch, they would be able to use it.
2. They would have despaired of their safety if they had not seen the glittering fleece.
3. If he saw the body of his son, he would not pursue the ship.
4. If Jason brings back the fleece, the kingdom will be given back to him.
5. If they will have waited a brief interval of time, they will see the fleece clearly.

Living Mythology:
Medea in Flight

When King Aeetes learned that Jason had accomplished the proposed tasks, he was very angry. He realized that Medea must have helped Jason. Aware of her danger, she made plans to escape. In the middle of the night, she slipped out of the palace with her brother Absyrtus. As quickly as possible she made her way to the place where the *Argo* had been beached, and, throwing herself at Jason's feet, she begged his help. As soon as he learned the cause of her coming, he promised that when he had

175

obtained the fleece he would take her away with him on the *Argo*.

The next day Jason, leaving his companions on the shore to defend the ship if necessary, hastened with Medea into the forest where, she had informed him, the fleece was concealed. Together they walked for a few miles, and then suddenly they saw the Golden Fleece suspended from a tree. Now that they had found it, how were they to take it away? Not only was the fleece protected by nature and by skill, but even by a terrible dragon who guarded the tree from which their long-sought prize was suspended.

More of Medea's Magic

Mēdēa quae, ut suprā dēmōnstrāvimus, magicae artis summam scientiam habēbat, rāmum quem ex arbore proximā dēripuerat venēnō infēcit. Hōc factō, ad locum appropinquāvit et dracōnem quī faucibus apertīs ējus adventum exspectābat venēnō sparsit. Deinde, dum dracō somnō oppressus dormit, Jāsōn vellus aureum ex arbore dēripuit, et cum Mēdēā quam celerrimē ad nāvem fūgit.

Jason, Medea, and the Golden Fleece.

Dum autem ea geruntur, Argonautae, quī ad mare relictī erant, animō anxiō reditum Jāsonis exspectābant. Cum jam ad occāsum sōlis frūstrā exspectāvissent, dē ējus salūte dēspērāre coepērunt. Nōn dubitābant quīn aliquī cāsus accidisset. Dum proficīscī parant ut ducī auxilium ferrent, lūmen quoddam subitō cōnspēxērunt mīrum in modum inter silvās refulgēns. Ad locum statim cucurrērunt. Quō cum vēnissent, Jāsonī et Mēdēae advenientibus occurrērunt, et vellus aureum lūminis ējus causam esse cōgnōvērunt. Omnī timōre sublātō, māgnō cum gaudiō ducem suum excēpērunt.

The Pursuit and the Escape

Hīs rēbus gestīs, omnēs sine morā nāvem rūrsus cōnscendērunt et prīmā vigiliā solvērunt. At rēx Aeētēs māximā cum īrā nāvem longam quam celerrimē dēdūcī jūssit et fugientēs īnsecūtus est. Mēdēa frātrem suum Absyrtum interficere cōnstituit; exīstimābat Aeētam, cum corpus fīlī vīdisset, nōn longius prōsecūtūrum esse. Omnia ēvēnērunt ut (as) Mēdēa spērāverat. Aeētēs nihil sibi prōfutūrum esse arbitrātus, domum revertit ut fīlī corpus ad sepultūram daret.

Tandem Jāsōn post multa perīcula in eundem locum pervēnit unde ōlim profectus erat. Peliae rēgī vellere aureō dēmōnstrātō, postulāvit ut rēgnum sibi trāderētur. Peliās enim pollicitus erat, sī Jāsōn vellus referret, sē rēgnum eī trāditūrum esse. Peliās ita locūtus est: "Nōn dubium est quīn suprēmus diēs mihi appropinquet. Rogō ut paulisper (for a short time) mihi rēgnum relinquās." Hāc ōrātiōne adductus, Jāsōn respondit sē id factūrum esse quod ille rogāvisset.

'Tis not everyone who can afford to go to Corinth.
—Plutarch, A.D. 46–120

Unit XXII

CONVERSATION

MĒDĒA: Vidētis patrem vestrum aetāte jam esse cōnfectum, neque ad labōrem rēgnandī perferendum satis valēre. Vultis eum rūrsus juvenem fierī?

FIRST DAUGHTER OF THE KING: Num hoc fierī potest?

SECOND DAUGHTER: Quis umquam ē sene (*old man*) juvenis factus est?

MĒDĒA: Mē summam scientiam artis magicae habēre scītis.

FIRST: Pater noster est dīgnus quī rūrsus juvenis fīat.

SECOND: Nōbīs dēmōnstrā quō modō haec rēs fierī possit.

MĒDĒA: Arietem aetāte jam cōnfectum interficiam et membra ējus in vāse aeneō pōnam. In aquam quāsdam herbās conjiciam. Dum aqua effervēscit (*boils*), cantum magicum canam.

SECOND: Putāsne arietem quem interfectūra sīs per agrōs rūrsus cursūrum esse?

FIRST: Quis est quī haec crēdere possit?

MĒDĒA: Vidēbitis quantum valeat ars magica.

SECOND: Cōnsilium quod Mēdēa dederit nōn ōmittendum esse putō.

MĒDĒA: Vōs patris membra in vās conjicite; ego herbās magicās praebēbō. Nōlīte dubitāre quīn hoc eī māximē prōfutūrum sit.

SECTION 1 Relative Characteristic Clauses

▶ DISCUSSION

1. A relative characteristic clause describes the general character of the antecedent.

2. It is used regularly after general, indefinite, negative, and interrogative antecedents.

Nēmo est quī hoc probet.	There is *no one who approves this.*
Quis est quī omnia sciat?	*Who* is there *who knows all things?*
Sunt quī hoc crēdant.	There are *those (some) who believe this.*
Is est quī hoc faciat.	*He* is *the man to do this.*

3. It is used regularly after the following: **dīgnus,** *worthy;* **indīgnus,** *unworthy;* **aptus,** *fit;* **idōneus,** *suitable;* **ūnus,** *one;* **sōlus,** *only.*

Vir dīgnus est quī cōnsul fīat.	The man is *worthy to be made consul.*
Sōlus est quī hoc facere possit.	He is *the only one who can do this.*

▶ PRACTICE PATTERNS

A. Translate into English:

1. Sunt quī haec dīcant. 2. Quis est quī haec crēdat? 3. Nūllī sunt quī eum audiant. 4. Nihil est quod virum moveat. 5. Multī sunt quī captīvōs adjuvent. 6. Quid est quod dē hīs rēbus nēsciat?

B. Translate into Latin:

1. There was no one who knew these men. 2. Who is there who excels in all things? 3. He is the only one who says these things. 4. What is there which he has not undertaken? 5. He was unworthy to be in command of the legion. 6. There are some who do not like to remain in Rome during the summer.

SECTION 2 Subordinate Clauses in Indirect Discourse

▶ DISCUSSION

1. The verbs of adjective and adverbial subordinate clauses in an indirect statement, an indirect question, or an indirect command are in the subjunctive mood.

2. The tense of the verb in the subordinate clause is determined by the rule for sequence of tenses.

If the verb in the main clause is *primary*, the present or perfect subjunctive is used in the subordinate clause. The *present* subjunctive is used to represent either the present or the future indicative of direct speech. The *perfect* subjunctive is used to represent either the perfect or the future perfect indicative of the direct speech.

> **Rāmus, quem *perspiciunt*, intrā silvās refulget.**
> **Dīcit rāmum, quem *perspiciant*, intrā silvās refulgēre.**
> He says that the branch, which *they see*, is gleaming within the woods.

> **Rāmus, quem *perspēxērunt*, intrā silvās refulget.**
> **Dīcit rāmum, quem *perspēxerint*, intrā silvās refulgēre.**
> He says that the branch, which *they saw*, is gleaming within the woods.

If the tense of the verb in the main clause is *secondary*, the imperfect or pluperfect subjunctive is used in the subordinate clause. The *imperfect* subjunctive is used to represent the present, imperfect, or future tenses of the indicative in the direct speech. The *pluperfect* subjunctive is used to represent the perfect, pluperfect, or future perfect tenses of the indicative of the direct speech.

Rogāvit ubi rāmus, quem *perspicerent*, esset.	He asked where was the branch which *they saw*.
Imperāvit comitibus, quī rāmum *perspēxissent*, ut ad nāvem properārent.	He ordered his comrades, who *had seen* the branch, to hasten to the ship.

3. Even when there is no verb of saying, thinking, asking, command-

ing, and the like in the main clause, the subjunctive is used in clauses in which indirect discourse or command is implied.

Jāsōn ā rēge rēgnum, *quod pollici-* **tus esset, postulāvit.**	Jason demanded of the king the kingdom *which (as he reminded him) he had promised.*

4. A subordinate clause in indirect discourse which is merely explanatory takes the indicative.

Quod patrem suum timēbat, **putā-** **bat sē cum Jāsone nāve ēvādere** **posse.**	*Because she feared her father,* she thought she could escape with Jason by boat.

Notice that the *quod*-clause is not part of the indirect statement.

▶ PRACTICE PATTERNS

A. Account for the tense and mood of the verb in each of the subordinate clauses in these sentences. Translate the sentences.

1. Jūssit eōs quī adessent sē sequī. 2. Dīcit eōs priusquam vellus vīderint prōcurrisse. 3. Rogābit cūr fūgerītis simul atque rāmum vīderītis. 4. Imperāvit mīlitibus quī adessent ut castra mūnīrent. 5. Rogāverat quō fūgissētis simul atque rāmum vīdissētis.

B. Translate into Latin:

1. He says that the men whom he leads are brave. 2. He thought that the town which he had captured was small. 3. They announce that they will tear away the branch when Jason is present. 4. He had asked why they had not sent the weapons which they had promised. 5. Medea understood that she would be in great danger as soon as she returned.

SECTION 3 Defective Verbs

▶ DISCUSSION

1. Defective verbs are those of which only some forms are found. They are used mainly in the perfect and in forms derived from the perfect.

coepī, coepisse, coeptus	*I have begun, I began*
meminī, meminisse	*I remember*
ōdī, ōdisse, ōsūrus	*I hate*

2. *Coepī* has perfect meaning; *meminī* and *ōdī* have present meaning.

3. The present, imperfect, and future tenses of *coepī* are supplied by

incipiō, begin. The pluperfects and future perfects of *meminī* and *ōdī* have the meanings of imperfects and futures.

▶ PRACTICE PATTERNS

A. Write in Latin a synopsis, first person, plural, indicative mood, of: coepī, meminī, ōdī. Translate each form.

B. Write in Latin:

1. he hates	we shall remember	you (pl.) had begun
2. they began	you (sing.) hated	they hate the enemy
3. we remember	I remember this	they began to fight

WORDS TO MASTER

adhūc, *adv.,* hitherto, up to this time, thus far

āēr, āeris, *m.,* air

āmentia, –ae, *f.,* madness, frenzy, folly

coepī, –isse, coeptus, *defective,* began, started

doleō, –ēre, –uī, dolitūrus, feel pain, suffer, grieve

ērēctus, –a, –um, *adj.,* upright (*erect*)

furor, –ōris, *m.,* madness, frenzy, fury (*furor*)

impellō, –ere, –pulī, –pulsus, drive on, instigate (*impel*)

jūdicō (1), decide, judge, think (*adjudicate*)

meminī, –isse, *defective,* remember, recollect (*memento, reminiscent*)

occāsiō, –ōnis, *f.,* opportunity (*occasion*)

ōdī, –isse, ōsūrus, *defective,* hate; **odium, –ī,** *n.,* hatred (*odious*)

ōmittō, –ere, –mīsī, –missus, let go by, disregard (*omit*)

quasi, *conj.,* as if, as it were

valdē, *adv.,* very much, greatly

vehō, –ere, vēxī, vectus, carry, bear, convey (*vehicle*)

BUILDING WORD POWER

Many derivatives in ordinary use came into English from the root word *movēre, mōtum, to move,* and its frequentative, *mūtāre, mūtātum, to move away, alter, change.* They are easily recognized by the syllables *mo–, mov–, mot–, mut–. Movēre* was joined to the prefixes: *a–, com–, dē–, dis–, ē–, per–, prae–, prō–, re–, sum–,* and *trāns–.* From which of these compounds are the following English words derived: *commotion, emotion, demotion, promotion, remote? Mūtāre* formed compound verbs with *com–, dē–, ē–, per–, sum–, trans–. Commute, permutation,* and *transmute* are the important derivatives from these compounds.

Explain the meanings of the italicized words: *immutable* decrees; unworthy *motives; momentous* occasion; *mobilize* the troops; *transmu-*

181

tation of metals; *mutual* agreement; *mobile* unit; rapid *locomotion;* patriotic *motif; commute* from home to the city; *remote* possibility; *permutation* of numbers; *emotional* stability. Do you know that our word *mob* comes from **mōbile vulgus,** the movable common people? And that *moment* and *movement* are doublets from **movēmentum?**

SENTENCE PATTERNS

A. Translate into English:

1. Quis est quī crēdat Mēdēam Jāsonem tam valdē ōdisse?
2. Sunt quī arbitrentur Jāsonem fuisse dīgniōrem odiō quam Mēdēam.
3. Nōnne dīxērunt fēminam malam, quae fīliōs suōs necāret, furōre atque āmentiā impellī?
4. Sōla est quae hoc facere possit.
5. Sī quis eam vestem induat, corpus ējus quasi īgne cremētur.
6. Jūdicāvitne nōn ōmittendam esse tantam occāsiōnem?
7. Itaque per āēra vecta est in Sōlis currū, quem dracōnēs ālīs īnstructī dūcēbant.
8. Num populus doluit quod nāvis, quae adhūc in lītore ērēcta steterat, virum īnfēlīcem oppressit?
9. Nūllī sunt quī meminērint aspectum mulieris barbarae.
10. Vīs venēnī tālis erat ut corpus ējus coepit quasi īgne dolōre afficī.

B. Translate into Latin:

1. There was no one who grieved about the death of Jason.
2. What is it that he hated so strongly?
3. They judged that the woman had been driven on by rage and madness.
4. There are those who remember the evil deeds of the woman.
5. She began to think that so great an opportunity ought not to be disregarded.

Living Mythology:
Medea's Revenge

When Medea learned these things she was exceedingly vexed, and, led on by the desire for royal power, decided to bring about the death of the aged King Pelias by trickery. Acting on her decision, she visited the daughters of the king and asked them if they did not wish their father to become young again. Since they doubted that such a transformation could be effected, she told them she would show them how it could be done.

She killed a ram now feeble with age and placed his limbs, together with certain magic herbs, in a bronze caldron. As the water boiled up, she sang a magic song. After a short time the ram jumped out of the caldron and ran through the fields with renewed vigor.

Greatly impressed, the daughters of Pelias thought that the advice Medea had given them ought not be disregarded. They killed their father and threw his members into the bronze vessel, but Medea did not give them the same herbs which she herself had used in restoring youth to the ram. After they had waited a long time, they realized that they had been tricked and that their father had really perished.

Medea had hoped that after the death of Pelias her husband would receive the kingdom, but when the citizens learned how Pelias had died, they were horrified at such a great crime and drove Jason and Medea from the kingdom.

Gift to a Rival

Cum Jāsōn et Mēdēa ē Thessaliā expulsī essent, ad urbem Corinthum iērunt, cūjus urbis rēgnum Creōn quīdam tum obtinēbat. Erat Creontī fīlia ūna, nōmine Glaucē; quam ubi vīdit, Jāsōn cōnstituit Mēdēam uxōrem repudiāre (*reject*) eō cōnsiliō ut Glaucēn in mātrimōnium dūceret. At Mēdēa cum intellegeret quae ille in animō habēret, īrā valdē commōta jūre jūrandō (*with an oath*) cōnfīrmāvit sē tantam injūriam ultūram esse (*would avenge*).

Hoc igitur cōnsilium cēpit. Vestem parāvit summā arte contextam (*woven*) et variīs colōribus tīnctam (*dyed*). Hanc mortiferō quōdam venēnō īnfēcit, cūjus vīs tālis erat ut, sī quis eam vestem induisset, corpus ējus quasi īgne cremārētur. Hōc factō, vestem ad Glaucēn mīsit. Illa autem, nihil malī suspicāns, dōnum libenter (*with pleasure*) accēpit, et vestem novam, mōre fēminārum, statim induit.

Vix vestem induerat Glaucē, cum dolōrem gravem per omnia membra sēnsit, et paulō post summō cruciātū (*torture*) affecta, ē vītā discessit. Hīs rēbus gestīs, Mēdēa furōre et āmentiā impulsa, fīliōs suōs necāvit. Tum cum scīret māgnum sibi futūrum esse perīculum sī Corinthī manēret, ex eā regiōne fugere cōnstituit.

Hōc cōnstitūtō, Sōlem ōrāvit ut in tantō perīculō auxilium sibi praebēret. Sōl autem ējus precibus commōtus, currum mīsit, cui erant jūnctī dracōnēs ālīs īnstructī. Mēdēa, nōn ōmittendam esse tantam occāsiōnem arbitrāta, currum ascendit, itaque per āēra vecta incolumis ad urbem Athēnās pervēnit.

Medea escaping to Athens.

Jāsōn ipse post breve tempus mīrō modō interfectus est. Nam
accidit vel cāsū vel cōnsiliō deōrum, ut sub umbrā nāvis suae,
quae in lītus subducta erat, ōlim dormīret. At nāvis, quae adhūc
ērēcta steterat, in eam partem ubi Jāsōn jacēbat subitō dēlāpsa
(*slipped*) virum īnfēlīcem oppressit.

Living Mythology:
Quiz

A. Select the correct answer to the following statements:

1. The Golden Fleece was the skin of: a ram, bull, deer.
2. Jason was the son of: Pelias, Aeson, Iolcus.
3. When Jason came of age he claimed: the ram, the boat, the kingdom.
4. Pelias tried to get rid of Jason by sending him: to prison; on an expedition; around the world.
5. The name of Jason's new boat was: the Golden Fleece, the Argo, the Cosmonaut.
6. Five of the heroes who sailed on the expedition were: Orpheus, Castor, Hercules, Pollux, Phrixus, Helle, Theseus.
7. Phineus' food was seized by: the Argonauts; the Harpies; animals.
8. The Symplegades were: wild tribes; clashing rocks; pirates.
9. The King of Colchis was: Aeetes, Zetes, Nephele.

Trajan's Column in Rome, A.D. 113.

A-1

Trajan's Column (detail). This high relief
depicts incidents from the Dacian War.

A-2

Hadrian's Wall in northern Britain. Built to protect Roman Britain from Picts and Scots, the wall was constructed circa A.D. 122—128.

Arch of Triumph of Caracalla, at Volubilis, Morocco.

Relief. This detail shows grape pressing.

Roman arena. This arena is in Nîmes, France.

Mills and oven at Pompeii.

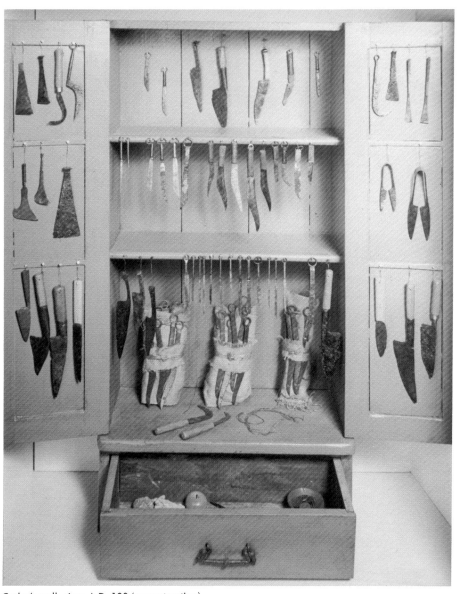

Cutler's stall, circa A.D. 100 (reconstruction).

Roman dining room, circa A.D. 100 (reconstruction).

Roman kitchen, circa A.D. 100 (reconstruction).

Roman temple ruins, second century A.D. These stand in Baalbek, Lebanon, known to the ancients as Heliopolis ("Sun City").

10. The woman who helped Jason was: Atalanta, Medea, Helle.

B. Answer the following questions briefly:

1. What conditions did the king lay on Jason before he could take the Golden Fleece?
2. What happened to Pelias on the return of Jason with Medea?
3. Why is the name Medea used to describe a proud, angry, and outraged wife?
4. What does *naut* mean? Argonaut? Astronaut? Cosmonaut?

PART III

Julius Caesar

Life of Julius Caesar

Few men in the history of the world have had more to do with the making of modern civilization than Julius Caesar. A skilled writer, an outstanding orator, a military genius, a towering political leader, he obtained supreme power in the Roman Republic and became the first master of the Western world. What his contemporaries thought of him has been expressed by one of the characters in Shakespeare's immortal *Julius Caesar:*

> He doth bestride the narrow world
> Like a Colossus, and we petty men
> Walk under his huge legs, and peep about
> To find ourselves dishonorable graves.

The brief sketch of Caesar's life given here is intended to be an introduction to wider reading.

Gaius Julius Caesar was born of a patrician family one hundred years before the birth of Christ (100 B.C.) on the twelfth day of the Roman month which was later to be called July in his honor. At that time Marius, Caesar's uncle by marriage, the conqueror of the Cimbri and the Teutones, held the consulship for the sixth time. Young Julius was educated by a tutor, as were most Roman boys of noble birth, and he studied the subjects commonly taught — Greek, Latin, grammar, composition, public speaking, and philosophy.

As he grew to manhood, he became intensely interested in politics. There were in Rome two important parties: the nobility, or **optimātēs,** led by Sulla, and the democratic party, or **populārēs,** of which Marius was the head. Although born an aristocrat, Caesar decided to join the democratic party. He did more than that. He married Cornelia, the daughter of Cinna, one of the outstanding leaders in the democratic party. In so doing, he defied Sulla, then master of Rome, and, though threatened with death, refused to give up his wife. For several months the young rebel was forced to change his hideouts in the Sabine hills for fear of discovery. Once he was caught, but he bought his escape from Sulla's soldiers with a bribe of two talents. Eventually Sulla, under pressure from the youth's friends, granted a pardon, but not without uttering a prophetic warning: "In this young Caesar I see many a Marius." Caesar kept his Cornelia, and she became the mother of their daughter, Julia.

Rome, however, was not a safe place for Caesar, and he traveled East, where, during three years of service in the army, he gained military experience that was to prove of great value many years later. For saving the life of a comrade in battle, he received from the state a civic crown, his first of many laurels. He was then only a little over twenty years old.

Upon Sulla's death in 78 B.C., Caesar returned to Rome, where he distinguished himself by prosecuting two provincial governors on charges of extortion and corruption. Deciding to perfect himself in oratory, in 76 B.C. he went to Rhodes, where he studied under the famous rhetorician Apollonius Molo.

During one of his voyages across the sea, Caesar was captured by pirates and taken to their hideout. His ransom was fixed at twenty talents ($20,000), but the captive laughingly insisted that such a low sum was no indication of his true worth. To the satisfaction of both parties, the amount was raised to fifty talents. His friends collected and paid the ransom money, and he was freed. When he reached the mainland, he hired a fleet and returned to the island to fulfill his threat of crucifying the pirates. At the time of this exploit Caesar was twenty-four years of age.

EARLY POLITICAL SUCCESSES

When Caesar was thirty-one years old, he entered upon the prescribed order of public offices leading to the consulship. He was successively elected **quaestor, aedile, pontifex maximus,** and **praetor,** and as **prōpraetor** governed Spain. During his journey to Spain, one of his companions mockingly asked him whether there would be any struggle for power in the wretched Alpine village they were then passing. Caesar answered seriously: "For my part, I would rather be the first man among these fellows than the second man in Rome."

It is said that once, after reading part of the history of Alexander, he sat a long while in thought and at last burst into tears. His friends were surprised and asked him the reason for such a display of emotion. "Do you think," said he, "I have not just cause to weep when I consider that Alexander at my age had conquered so many nations, and I have all this time done nothing that is memorable?"

During his propraetorship in Spain, Caesar gained valuable military experience and accumulated enough money to satisfy all his financial obligations. Before his term of office had expired, he left Spain and returned to Rome in 60 B.C., fully determined to secure for himself the highest political reward that Rome could give him — the consulship.

THE FIRST TRIUMVIRATE

While Caesar had been making his rapid political advancement, two other men had risen to positions of prominence at Rome. Gnaeus Pompey and Marcus

Crassus had been consuls in 70 B.C. Pompey had later won military fame and the support of an army in the war against Mithridates, and in 64 B.C. he had subdued Syria, including Phoenicia and Palestine. In 62 B.C. he had returned to Rome. Crassus was the richest man in Rome during this period.

Caesar knew that he could not hope to gain the support of a hostile Senate without the friendship of both of these men. He persuaded Pompey and Crassus, who had ceased to be friends during their consulship, to forget their differences. Caesar, Pompey, and Crassus then entered into a secret "gentlemen's agreement," known in history as the First Triumvirate. Each promised to further the political interests of the other two. The bond was further strengthened in 59 B.C. by the marriage of Pompey to Caesar's daughter, Julia.

Caesar, as spearhead of the triumvirate, was elected consul for 59 B.C. Despite opposition from the other consul, Bibulus, Caesar pushed through the measures that Pompey and Crassus sought. Realizing that Caesar had the full support of the people, Bibulus withdrew in disgust to the quiet of his home. The wags of Rome referred to the consulship of 59 B.C. as that of Julius and Caesar! It was during the year of his consulship, nine years after the death of Cornelia, that Caesar married Calpurnia, daughter of Calpurnius Piso.

Supported by his two allies and by an unprecedented action of the popular assembly, Caesar gained the proconsulship, or governorship, of the Province (the southeastern part of Gaul), together with Cisalpine Gaul and Illyricum, for a period of five years, instead of the usual period of one year. This was later extended for another five years, so that his governorship lasted until 49 B.C. You will read in his own words of Caesar's activities in a military and judicial capacity during these years.

THE ROAD TO DICTATORSHIP

During the latter part of his proconsulship, the powerful triumvirate gradually fell apart. Crassus was killed in battle. Julia, daughter of Caesar and wife of Pompey, died. Pompey and Caesar became more and more distrustful of one another. Finally civil war broke out between Caesar and Pompey. The victory of Caesar over Pompey at Pharsalia and the murder of Pompey in Egypt left Caesar the master of the entire Roman world.

For the victories he had won, Caesar celebrated five different triumphs, each attended with magnificent games and spectacles. He was voted the title of **imperātor** by the Senate and later on was made **dictātor** for life. He was already tribune of the people, **tribūnus,** and **pontifex māximus** for life. Both parties now endorsed him as leader.

CAESAR, THE STATESMAN

Caesar realized more than anyone else perhaps that the days of the Republic were of the past. The common people of Rome were no longer the sturdy stock of olden days; a landless, jobless mob had grown up in and around Rome. The Senate could no longer impose order. Rule by one man seemed to him the kind of government that would best fit the needs of the time.

188

Having been made dictator, he undertook to reorganize the Roman state. He made the Senate a more nearly representative body and appointed most of its members. Distinguished provincials were eligible for membership. Personal worth and public service, not privilege and family, were the qualifications for public office. No meeting of the Senate was called except with his consent. No laws were passed by the Senate without his approval. He nominated most of the magistrates and controlled the election of others. He extended Roman citizenship to the provincials and developed a plan for provincial government that would cure agelong abuses.

He undertook a series of reforms and improvements, many of which were completed by his successors and still affect our lives today. He introduced the Egyptian solar calendar, which we now use in revised form; appointed a commission to codify Roman laws, so numerous and contradictory that they had often hindered justice; settled eighty thousand landless Italians on small farms on the site of Carthage; set a limit to the free doles of grain that only demoralized those who received them; enacted laws to prevent gross luxury on the one hand and to curb hoarding on the other; protected the provincials against dishonest tax collectors; prohibited bribery in the courts; equalized the burden of taxation; and generally tried to purify a society which had become very corrupt.

Caesar initiated the construction of many public works. He aided in founding libraries in Rome and in the larger towns. He planned a vast system of roads for the whole empire. He intended to initiate a project to drain the Pomptine marshes, which, when drained, would have added thousands of acres of arable land to Italy. This project would have provided a large number of small farms for the landless and homeless crowds, in Rome and in other Italian cities, who clamored for free food and free entertainment. However, his assassins gave Caesar only a year to carry out these and other plans.

After the Civil War, Caesar had treated his defeated opponents with the greatest clemency. Yet there were many patriotic men in Rome who were not convinced that the days of the Republic were gone forever. They believed that if Caesar were removed, the old Republic could be restored.

Among these patriots were Brutus and Cassius. They led the group of Senators who on the Ides (15th) of March, 44 B.C., cut short what might have been the greatest chapter in Caesar's life. The assassins gathered around Caesar under pretext of asking him a favor, but at a given signal they drew their daggers from the folds of their togas. Caesar offered what opposition he could, but when he saw his friend Brutus ready to strike, he cried out: **"Et tū, Brūte!"** Then only did one of the noblest Romans resign himself to his fate. At the base of the statue of Pompey, in the hall that had been built by Pompey, he fell with twenty-three wounds in his body. Caesar was dead at the age of fifty-eight. It was a day and an hour that the world has never forgotten.

The aftermath of this Roman tragedy was another triumvirate, another civil war, the overthrow of the Republican forces under Brutus, and the establishment of an avowed imperial government, headed by Caesar's adopted son,

Augustus, first Emperor of Rome. Augustus and succeeding Roman emperors tried to develop some of Julius Caesar's great plans, but two thousand long years have been too short a time in which to make some of his dreams for the betterment of mankind come true.

CAESAR, THE MAN OF LETTERS

Caesar was always very much interested in literature. His own writings included poetry and works on grammar, astronomy, and history. All but the history, contained in the *Gallic War* and the *Civil War*, have been lost. The Latin in these works is clear, vigorous, precise and straightforward, and among the best models of Latin prose that we have. Even in his own day Roman critics regarded his language and style as most elegant. Cicero, the greatest master of Latin prose, compared Caesar's historical works to beautiful and unadorned statues.

Froude, the historian, says: "No military narrative has approached the excellence of the history of the war in Gaul. Nothing is written that could be dispensed with; nothing important is left untold; while the incidents themselves are set off by delicate and just observations on human character."

The story of the Gallic War is told by Caesar in seven parts which are called books but which in length are more like chapters. An eighth book was added later by one of his officers, Aulus Hirtius, in order to complete the account for 51–50 B.C., but in reality the story was over with the surrender of Vercingetorix in 52 B.C. Some authorities think that Caesar wrote one book at the end of each campaign, but it is now agreed that he wrote all seven books at one time, after the capture of Alesia and before the end of the year 52 B.C. These so-called notebooks, **Commentāriī,** about the Gallic War and the Civil War have been read by generation after generation of school children and scholars, as well as by military leaders and generals. They contain an account of thrilling events seen and described by the man who was himself taking the leading role in the historical drama he describes.

It is not merely a history of warfare that Caesar has given us. He has written stirring tales of personal heroism, of characters noble or base, and of peoples, of places, of customs strange and unique. It is an account of the early inhabitants of Western Europe and is one of the earliest sources of information regarding that part of the world.

CAESAR, THE GREAT COMMANDER

Caesar is rated as Rome's greatest general and one of the greatest military commanders of all time. Much of his success was due to thoroughness in military organization, an unusual ability to control men, and a quick and keen comprehension of situations that enabled him to make a decision quickly and act promptly upon that decision.

The Roman forces, as developed by Caesar, surpassed those of all other nations. He worked them with the precision of a machine. Ordinary combat soldiers were trained as engineers, architects, and mechanics of utmost skill. In a few hours they could erect an impregnable camp. They built a bridge across the Arar in a day, bridged the Rhine in a week, and constructed a fleet in a month.

Caesar's soldiers had the highest admiration and affection for their leader and the utmost confidence in his ability to lead them. He took good care of their ordinary needs in food, clothing, shelter, and arms. He never exposed them to needless hardship or danger. More than once he turned what seemed inevitable defeat into complete victory by rushing into the fight, assuming direct command, and inciting his soldiers to renewed courage by his own reckless bravery. He knew the names of all his centurions and of many of his soldiers. He always recognized with ready praise acts of outstanding bravery.

The rapidity of Caesar's military movements and the suddenness of his appearance when he was supposed to be many miles away was most disconcerting to his foes. Within two weeks after he had learned in Rome of the plan of the Helvetians to march through the Roman province, he, with the army he had collected in the interim, stood on the banks of the Rhone ready to prevent their passage. Within a few hours he rushed his forces to the rescue of Quintus Cicero's camp, which had been attacked in the dead of winter. If the occasion required, he traveled night and day without stopping except to change horses. Once he covered almost a hundred miles in twenty-four hours.

CAESAR'S PERSONAL APPEARANCE

The historian Froude wrote: "In person Caesar was tall and slight. His features were more refined than was usual in Roman faces; the forehead was wide and high, the nose large and thin, the lips full, the eyes dark gray like an eagle's, the neck extremely thick and sinewy. His complexion was pale. His beard and mustache were kept carefully shaved. His hair was short and naturally scanty, falling off toward the end of life and leaving him partially bald."

Julius Caesar.

His baldness troubled him greatly. His biographer, Suetonius, says that of all the honors voted him by the Senate and the people, there was none which he received or made use of more gladly than the privilege of wearing a laurel wreath at all times.

His head appears on many coins and there are three or four marble busts. The expression on his face is keen, thoughtful, and sometimes stern.

Warfare at the Time of Caesar

Caesar's army was the indispensable instrument and associate of his fortunes. In his campaigns he relied upon his heavily armed infantry, consisting mainly of Roman citizens from seventeen to forty-six years of age who had enlisted or had been called to military service. Caesar enlisted also a great many provincials in his Gallic army, to whom he afterward gave citizenship as a reward for loyal service.

The term of service, according to the oath of allegiance, **sacrāmentum,** was twenty years. The pay, **stīpendium,** was 225 **dēnāriī,** about $45 a year, or 12½¢ a day. Out of this pay was deducted the cost of food, consisting mainly of wheat or barley, and of military equipment. At the end of twenty years of service, the soldier could retire as a veteran, **veterānus.** He was entitled to a pension and received a reward of money or land or both. Besides his pay, the soldier received a share in the booty.

ORGANIZATION OF CAESAR'S ARMY

1. *The legion.* The principal division of the infantry was the legion. Its full strength was 6000 men, but in Caesar's time there were approximately 3600 men in a legion. The legion consisted of ten cohorts, **cohortēs;** each cohort of three maniples, **manipulī;** and each maniple of two centuries, **ōrdinēs.** Thus as a member of a legion, the soldier belonged to several different groups.

The Roman legions were all numbered. Caesar, at the height of his command, had the seventh through the fifteenth inclusive, and also the first, thus making a total of ten legions under him.

2. *Cavalry.* The Roman army usually had a certain quota of native cavalry, **equitātus, equitēs,** but Caesar's cavalry was made up of mercenaries from his allies, Gauls, Germans, or Spaniards. They were divided into squadrons, **ālae;** troops, **turmae;** and squads, **decuriae.**

3. *Artillery.* Caesar had no regular artillery corps in his army. The engineers, **fabrī,** in siege operations used powerful machines called **tormenta.** There were three types, the **catapulta,** the **ballista,** and the **scorpiō.** The **catapulta** was used for shooting large arrows or darts in an almost horizontal direction. The **ballista** threw large stones through the air at a curve of about forty-five degrees. A small **ballista** was called an **onager.** The **scorpiō** was similar to, but lighter than, the **catapulta** and was used for shooting a single heavy arrow.

Other engines used in siege operations were the battering ram, **ariēs,** and the tower, **turris.** The **turris** was frequently set up at a distance from the town and moved forward to the wall on rollers. The **agger** was an embankment or terrace constructed to furnish an approach to the wall of a camp or of a town. A movable trellis or shed, called a **vīnea,** protected soldiers working near or under a wall. The **pluteus** was a screen behind which the soldiers could carry on siege operations. The **testūdō** was a protective formation made by shields overlapped above the heads of the soldiers.

4. *Auxiliaries.* The auxiliaries were recruited from allied states and included archers, **sagittāriī**; slingers, **funditōrēs**; and soldiers of light armor, **mīlitēs levis armātūrae.** In battle the auxiliaries were stationed with the cavalry on the wings. Their chief use was to confuse the enemy by hurling sling shots and by shooting arrows into their ranks.

5. *Other military personnel.* The engineers, **fabrī**; standard bearers, **aquiliferī** and **sīgniferī**; scouts, **explōrātōrēs**; and spies, **speculātōrēs**, were of minor rank. The prefects, **praefectī,** were in charge of the **ālae** of the cavalry and auxiliary forces, and decurions, **decuriōnēs,** were in charge of the squads. Re-enlisted veterans, **ēvocātī,** received extra pay, were exempt from routine camp duties, and rode horses on the march. In emergencies they were *called out* by the general and formed a select troop, or were distributed in the legions to build up the morale of the troops.

6. *Noncombatants.* The noncombatants were the servants, **calōnēs,** who performed menial camp duties; the drivers and muleteers, **muliōnēs,** who had charge of the heavy baggage, **impedīmenta;** and the traders, **mercātōrēs.**

OFFICERS OF CAESAR'S ARMY

1. The commander-in-chief, **dux,** was the highest officer of the army. After he had won an important victory, he was called **imperātor.** Caesar was a **dux bellī** until his victory over the Helvetians, after which he received the title **imperātor.**

2. The staff officers, **lēgātī,** had no definite command as they have today. They performed whatever duty the commander assigned. In the absence of the general, they held his authority and were regularly in charge of the winter-quarters. Sometimes they were assigned to conduct special expeditions or to be commanders of the legions in battle. They acted also as an advisory body. They were men of senatorial rank. The most prominent **lēgātī** under Caesar were: Titus Labienus, Publius Crassus, and Quintus Cicero, brother of the famous orator.

3. The quartermaster, **quaestor,** was next in rank. He was elected by the people at Rome and was assigned to a province by lot to be associated with the governor. In connection with the army, his duty was to provide for the food, pay, clothing, and equipment of the soldiers. Caesar sometimes placed his **quaestor** in charge of a legion.

4. Each legion had six military tribunes, **tribūnī mīlitum.** They were generally young men of equestrian rank, appointed for personal or political reasons. They were often put in command of the line of march and of the camp and performed various services under the command of the **quaestor.**

5. There were sixty centurions, **centuriōnēs,** to a legion. They were promoted from the ranks by the commander-in-chief because of good service and were men of humbler birth than the lieutenants or tribunes. They were divided into ten classes of six each. The highest centurion, **prīmipīlus,** led the first maniple of the first cohort.

STANDARDS AND MUSICAL INSTRUMENTS

Each Roman legion, cohort, and calvary division had its standard. That of the legion was a bronze or silver eagle, **aquila** (the ancient symbol of Jupiter), held aloft at the top of a pole. This image, represented with wings outspread as though about to fly, was about the size of a dove. The standard was carried by the eagle bearer, **aquilifer**, under the personal supervision of the chief centurion, **prīmipīlus**, of the legion. In camp the eagle was carefully guarded in a shrine, **sacellum**. The loss of the eagle, or of any standard, was regarded as the deepest disgrace.

Cohort standards, **sīgna**, were of various designs, sometimes displaying the figure of an animal or of an open hand. Below was indicated the number of the cohort. The bearer of the **sīgnum** was called **sīgnifer**. His service was very important, because without their standards the cohorts might be easily thrown into confusion. The standard bearer received the order for his division. The phrase **sīgna īnferre** meant to advance; **sīgna referre**, to retreat; **sīgna convertere**, to face about.

The cavalry and infantry auxiliaries had a special standard, **vēxillum**. This was a small white or red banner on a horizontal bar upheld by a staff. The display of a large, red vexillum at headquarters, **praetōrium**, was a signal to get ready for immediate action.

The musical instruments were wind instruments, horns and trumpets, to sound the various signals. The **cornū**, a curved horn made of the horn of an animal, had a deep, loud sound and called the troops to form for battle. The **tuba, a** long, straight trumpet with a sharp, shrill sound like a fife, gave the signals in battle. The **būcina**, a curved bugle, was sounded for reveille, the noon rest, and formations preliminary to battle. The **lituus**, a curved trumpet, was the signal instrument of the cavalry.

CAESAR'S ARMY ON THE MARCH

Under normal conditions the army marched in three divisions. The vanguard, **prīmum agmen**, of cavalry and infantry auxiliaries came first. The legions followed in order, each accompanied by its own baggage train. At the rear was a strong rear guard, **novissimum agmen**. This name was given because the new recruits usually marched in the rear. The entire arrangement was flexible. In case of danger of attack, the majority of the legions were placed ahead of the combined baggage train of the whole army, while the remaining legions followed the baggage and acted as a rear guard.

Since most of the afternoon was given to camp construction, the troops did most of their marching in the morning, beginning at sunrise and sometimes before. The average day's march was about fifteen miles, though forced marches, **māgna itinera**, might be as much as twenty-five miles or more. Caesar's troops on one occasion marched almost one hundred miles in a twenty-four hour period.

194

CAESAR'S CAMP

A Roman army even on the march never spent a night without building a fortified camp, **castra mūnīta.** A Roman general seldom went into battle without such a camp to retire to for rest at night or as protection in case of defeat. A surprise attack at night was impossible.

A special detachment of cavalry and engineers was sent ahead to choose a place suitable for a camp, **locus castrīs idōneus.** If possible, they chose a place on a sloping hillside, with an abundance of wood, water, and forage nearby. Location near a dense wood was avoided for fear of a concealed enemy.

As soon as the main army arrived, legionaries were detailed to construct the fortifications. They carried the tools in their packs. These fortifications consisted of a wide, deep trench, **fossa,** and a rampart, **agger,** formed of the dirt thrown to the inner side of the trench. This rampart would be about five feet high and wide enough on the top for the defenders of the camp to stand comfortably. A line of stakes, **pālī,** were put along the outer edge of this wall, **vallum.** These palisades were about four feet high, low enough for them to fight over it, high enough for them to hide behind it. The amount of labor required in this fortification was very great, but it could be finished in a few hours because of the efficient army organization and endurance of the Roman soldiers.

The camp was usually oblong or square in shape. It was laid out in blocks with two principal streets crossing at right angles and other streets parallel to them. There were four gates at the ends of the main streets. These gates were strongly fortified and so constructed that an enemy seeking to enter would expose his unprotected side. Every division of the army had its assigned quarters and could find them at once. The rampart could be reinforced by towers, redoubts, and other means of defense.

During summer campaigns the soldiers lived in leather-covered tents, ten men to each tent. In winter quarters, **hīberna,** the troops, **cōpiae,** were housed in huts thatched with straw or sod and covered with skins.

The gates were carefully guarded. The guard, a cohort at each gate and sentries on the rampart, was relieved at the end of each watch. The night, from sunset to sunrise was divided into four equal watches, **vigiliae,** of about three hours each. The watchword, **sīgnum,** for the night was written on tablets, **tesserae,** and circulated among the guards. It was changed each night. The musicians sounded a tattoo at nightfall, reveille at dawn, and signals at the end of each watch.

THE ORDER OF BATTLE

The usual arrangement in battle was the triple battle line, **triplex aciēs.** The first line, **aciēs prīma,** consisted of the first four cohorts, arranged from right to left. The first cohort ranked highest. The second line, **aciēs secunda,** consisted of the next three cohorts. The third line, **aciēs tertia,** was formed by the last three cohorts.

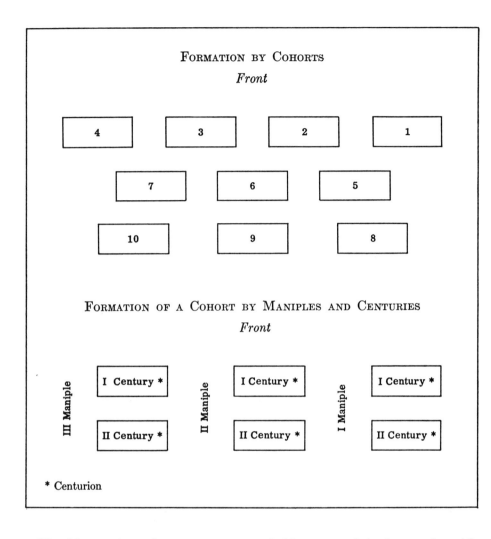

FORMATION BY COHORTS

Front

| 4 | 3 | 2 | 1 |

| 7 | 6 | 5 |

| 10 | 9 | 8 |

FORMATION OF A COHORT BY MANIPLES AND CENTURIES

Front

III Maniple — I Century * / II Century *

II Maniple — I Century * / II Century *

I Maniple — I Century * / II Century *

* Centurion

The 60 men in each century were probably arranged in four ranks with 15 men in each rank. Each soldier stood far enough away from his comrades in order to have plenty of room to use his weapons.

In the first line of cohorts were the tried veterans, and in the first cohort on the extreme right were the finest of these. The first line began the attack. The second line stood ready to relieve the first, while the third line was used to meet any emergency.

THE BATTLE

Great importance was attached to the initial charge, made, if possible, from a gentle hill slope, **ex superiōre locō.** The leader made a brief speech of encouragement, **cohortātiō,** to each legion before the battle. The signal to advance, **sīgna īnferre,** was given. The first line moved forward until within about 125 paces of the enemy. Then on the run, **concursū,** they charged with javelins poised, **pīlīs īnfestīs,** in order to break up the line formation of the enemy and then drew their swords. Each rank in turn advanced and sent its shower of javelins upon the enemy, following that with a sword attack. The battle thus became a series of duels. The first and second lines of cohorts relieved each other, while the third line was held in reserve to be used only in a crisis. The attack of the legions with a volley of javelins followed by hand-to-hand fighting with swords may be likened to a volley of musketry followed by a charge with bayonets.

During the battle the cavalry, which was used for preliminary skirmishing, for guarding the flanks, and for pursuing the enemy, remained on the wings of the battle line. The auxiliaries were also stationed on the wings.

SIEGE OPERATIONS

The Romans excelled in methods of capturing walled towns. The siege assumed one of three forms, according to the strength of the enemy's stronghold: the sudden assault, **oppūgnātiō repentīna,** directly from the march, **ex itinere;** the formal siege, **expūgnātiō;** or the blockade, **obsidiō.**

In the sudden assault, the attackers sought first to drive the defenders from the wall with arrows and sling shots. They would then scale the walls with ladders, **scālae,** or try to break down the gates. They approached the walls or gates in tortoise formation, **testūdō.**

If the stronghold could not be taken by sudden assault, it was necessary to resort to a formal siege. A terrace or mound of earth, stones, and logs, **agger,** in the form of an inclined plane was started just out of reach of the enemy's weapons and gradually prolonged toward the stronghold. The workmen were protected by movable screens, **pluteī,** by sheds like grape arbors, **vīneae,** or by movable sheds, **mūsculī** (little mice), which were somewhat heavier and larger than the **vīneae.** At the lower end of the **agger** were constructed one or more towers, **turrēs ambulātōriae,** from 50 to 180 feet high, which could be moved forward on wheels or rollers up to the town. Such a tower, which was constructed in stories, could carry archers, slingers, legionary soldiers, and artillery in its upper stories and battering rams in the lower stories. When the tower was close to the wall, drawbridges were let down, and the men leaped to the wall and engaged in hand-to-hand fighting. Effective also in the siege were the **tormenta,** already described, and wall hooks, **falcēs mūrālēs,** with which stones could be dislodged from the wall.

In the blockade, an entrenchment, **circumvallātiō,** was drawn entirely around the enemy's stronghold for the purpose of bringing the enemy to terms by means of starvation. These entrenchments were manned by soldiers, ready to meet any attacks of the enemy or to prevent sorties for food or help.

EQUIPMENT OF THE LEGIONARY SOLDIER

1. *Uniform.* The legionary soldier wore a sleeveless tunic, **tunica,** reaching about to the knees and bound around the waist by a belt, **cingulum;** a heavy, woolen mantle or cloak, **sagum,** for wet or cold weather (never worn in action), secured on the right shoulder by a clasp so that the arms were free; heavy hobnailed shoes, **caligae,** held on by leather straps.

The commander-in-chief wore a scarlet cloak, **palūdāmentum,** and the subordinate officers, scarlet tunics. The brilliant color made the officers conspicuous to the soldiers.

2. *Armor.* The legionary soldier wore an iron helmet, **cassis,** or one of leather and brass, **galea,** held in place by a chinpiece; a coat of mail, **lōrīca,** made of leather with metal bands or scales or with chain mail; a shield, **scūtum,** curved to protect the body, made of layers of wood and leather and bound around the edges with a metal rim. The shield measured about four by two and one-half feet.

3. *Weapons.* The Roman legionary used the light spear, **hasta;** the javelin or heavy spear, **pīlum;** and the sword, **gladius.** The shaft of the javelin was about four feet long, made of wood with a head of soft iron about two and a half feet long and tipped with a hard point. After piercing the shield of an enemy, the iron bent, thus making the javelin difficult to extract and useless for hurling back at the foe. The sword, about two feet long, was straight, pointed, and two-edged, and was used largely for thrusting. It was suspended on the right side by a strap, **balteus,** passing over the left shoulder.

4. *Baggage.* The soldier carried, in addition to his armor and weapons, extra clothing, food, and cooking utensils, as well as a saw, hatchet, spade, basket, and one or more stakes for the rampart. These articles were stored in a bundle, **sarcina,** weighing about fifty pounds, which was fastened to a forked stick and carried over the shoulder. With his pack the soldier was said to be encumbered, **impedītus;** without it, unencumbered, **expedītus.**

The heavy baggage, **impedīmenta,** which was hauled by beasts of burden, **jūmenta,** or in carts, **carrī,** consisted of extra supplies of arms, food, clothing, tents, siege artillery, hand mills for grinding, and, in general, equipment and stores for the entire army.

5. *Rations.* Rations, **rēs frūmentāria,** were usually distributed at intervals of fifteen days. They consisted of about half a bushel of wheat (rarely of barley). Every soldier carried a little hand mill with which to grind the grain as needed. Cooking was simple. The flour was mixed with water into a thick paste which was baked. Fruits, vegetables, and fresh meat from the neighboring farms occasionally relieved the monotony of a bread diet.

CAESAR'S NAVY

The Romans had no naval organization in the modern sense. In most of Caesar's campaigns ships were not needed, but they were built and equipped as the occasion demanded. They were manned by soldiers under command of the regular army officers.

Caesar's warships were long, low, and narrow. The war galley, **nāvis longa,** was propelled mainly by oars. It had one or two sails, but the sails were taken down in battle. Instead of rudders, steering paddles were used, one on each side of the stern.

At the prow of the ship was a sharp, metal beak, **rōstrum,** used in ramming the enemy's ship. Light artillery was placed on the deck and sometimes a tower was erected. One method of naval warfare consisted in seizing the hostile ship with a spiked gangplank or drawbridge, **corvus,** by which the legionaries boarded it and began hand-to-hand combat.

Caesar's war galley could carry probably a hundred men. It could be hauled up on the beach by means of rollers and a windlass. Besides the war galleys, there were transports, **nāvēs onerāriae,** to convey men and supplies to necessary points. They were much broader than the galleys and were propelled by sails.

THE WARRIORS OF GAUL

The Gauls about whom Caesar writes and whom he conquered were divided into about sixty tribes. Dissension and intertribal warfare made the whole country ripe for conquest. Physically the Gauls were tall, fair-haired, and of great strength. They wore trousers and many-colored tartan shirts. The chiefs were adorned with rings and bracelets and necklaces of gold. In battle they wore helmets in the shape of some fierce beast's head and surmounted by nodding plumes. They had large and well-built houses and walled towns. Their fields were yellow with grain, their roads suitable for wheeled traffic. They traded with the Greek trading center at Massilia (modern Marseilles), and in their ships they were able to reach and trade with the inhabitants of Britain.

Much of the Gauls' time was spent in warfare. Their weapons were a heavy javelin, or pike, and a long two-edged sword more suitable for slashing than for thrusting. Their defensive armor was a large shield and a metal helmet. In battle they used the mass formation, the **phalanx.** Although the Gallic warriors were taller and far more numerous, and although they fought in familiar territory to preserve their own freedom, they were no match for the well-organized and well-equipped Roman soldiers.

At the start of the battle, the Gallic warrior found himself just another unit in a solid block of human beings, covered above and in front with shields. Unless he was on the edge of the phalanx, he could use no offensive weapon. The first onslaught of a phalanx could be overwhelming, but once its power was resisted, the advantage was with the more open and pliable order of the Roman legion, which could bring up reserves as needed. Bravery and numbers counted for little before the discipline and organization of the Roman army.

Although the infantry was badly trained and ineffective, the Gallic cavalry, composed of nobles, was good. The strength of the Gallic army was in its cavalry. Caesar often made use of the cavalry of friendly Gallic tribes. But the Gallic states did not stand together. Their petty chiefs could not bury their differences and follow a general policy for the common good. As a result they fell one by one before the small but well-disciplined army of Caesar.

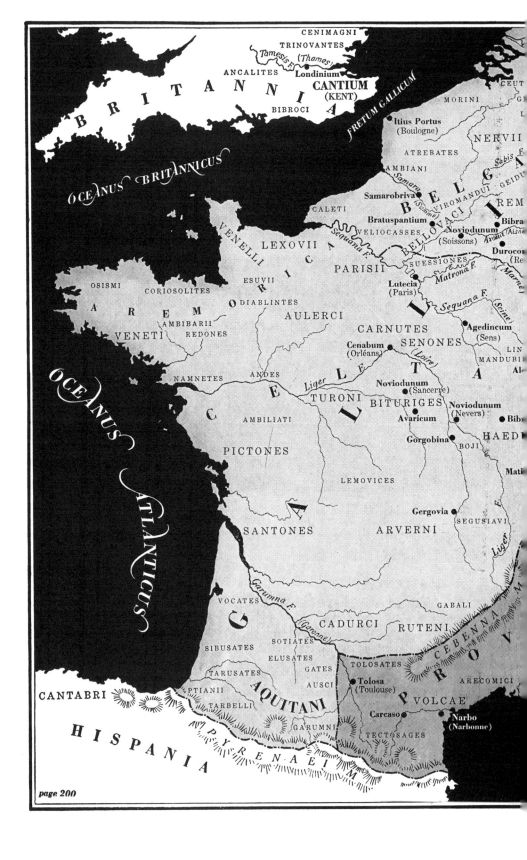

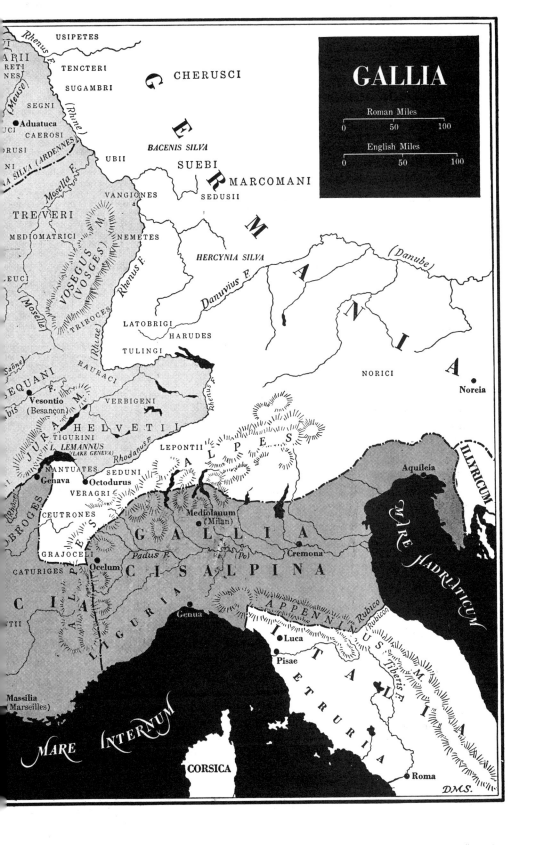

The Gallic War

COMMENTĀRIĪ DĒ BELLŌ GALLICŌ

BOOK ONE

GAUL IN THE TIME OF CAESAR

PREVIEW: In the first chapter Caesar describes the geography of the country and its peoples so that his readers may have an understanding of the background against which his conquests were to be staged. The name *Gallia* was used by the Romans of Caesar's time to include both Cisalpine Gaul (*Gallia Cisalpīna, Gaul on this side of the Alps*) in northern Italy and Transalpine Gaul (*Gallia Trānsalpīna, Gaul across the Alps*), which today is made up of France, Belgium, Holland, Luxembourg, most of Switzerland, and a little of Germany.

The southeastern part of Gaul had been subject to Roman rule for sixty years and organized into a Roman province. It was known as *Prōvincia (the Province)*, and that part of France is today called Provence. Caesar governed this district as proconsul, together with Cisalpine Gaul and Illyricum, a region near the head of the Adriatic Sea.

As generally used by Caesar, however, *Gallia* means Transalpine Gaul, divided, as Caesar tells us, into three parts, the land of the *Belgae* in the northeast, the land of the *Celtae* or *Gallī* in the center, and the land of the *Aquītanī* in the southwest. This was the scene of Caesar's campaigns, lasting through eight seasons (58–51 B.C.).

Ch. 1 Principal Divisions and Peoples of Gaul

Gallia est ¹omnis ²dīvīsa in partēs trēs.
Ūnam partem incolunt Belgae.
Aquītānī aliam partem et Gallī tertiam ³incolunt.
Gallī sē Celtās ⁴appellant.
Rōmānī autem eōs Gallōs appellant.
⁵Hī omnēs ⁶linguā, īnstitūtīs, lēgibus inter sē differunt.

---

1. **omnis**: *on the whole.*
2. **dīvīsa**: a perfect participle of **dīvidō** used as predicate adjective.
3. **incolunt** = **habitant.**
4. **appellant** = **vocant.**
5. **Hī omnēs**: Belgae, Celtae, Aquītānī.
6. **linguā, īnstitūtīs, lēgibus**: ablative of respect.

⁷Garumna flūmen Gallōs ab Aquītānīs dīvidit.

Matrona et Sēquana eōs ā Belgīs ⁸dīvidit.

⁹Hōrum omnium fortissimī sunt Belgae,

quod ā ¹⁰cultū atque ¹¹hūmānitāte Prōvinciae longissimē absunt.

¹²Minimē saepe ¹³ad eōs ¹⁴mercātōrēs adeunt

atque ¹⁵ea, quae ¹⁶ad effēminandōs animōs ¹⁷pertinent, important.

Belgae proximī sunt Germānīs, quī trāns Rhēnum incolunt.

Cum hīs Germānīs Belgae continenter bellum gerunt.

Quā dē causā Helvētiī quoque

reliquōs Gallōs virtūte ¹⁸praecēdunt,

quod ferē cotīdiē cum Germānīs contendunt.

Helvētiī aut suīs fīnibus Germānōs prohibent

aut ipsī in Germānōrum fīnibus bellum gerunt.

FOR COMPREHENSION

● ANSWER IN ENGLISH:

1. What three reasons are given for the Belgians' great courage?
2. Which of these reasons applied also to the Helvetians?
3. What was the natural boundary between the Belgians and the Gauls? between the Aquitanians and the Gauls? between the Germans and the Gauls?
4. Can you find the three divisions of Gaul on the map on pages 200–01 and indicate their boundaries?

● RESPONDĒ LATĪNE:

1. In quot partēs dīvīsa est Gallia omnis?
2. Quōmodo Belgae et Gallī et Aquītānī inter sē differunt?
3. Quōs Matrona et Sēquana flūmina ā Belgīs dīvidunt?
4. Quī hōrum omnium fortissimī sunt?
5. Quā rē Helvētiī reliquōs Gallōs superant?

---

7. **Garumna . . . Matrona et Sēquana:** *The Garonne . . . the Marne and the Seine.*
8. **dīvidit:** the verb is singular because the rivers make one boundary.
9. **Hōrum omnium fortissimī sunt Belgae:** King Albert of Belgium used this sentence in his appeal to the Belgians in 1914 to defend their country against the invasion of the Germans.
10. **cultū:** *civilization* (including manner of life, food, dress, etc.).
11. **hūmānitāte:** *refinement* (of mind and feelings).
12. **Minimē saepe:** *Very seldom.*
13. **ad eōs = ad Belgās.**
14. **mercātōrēs:** Roman merchants from the Province.
15. **ea:** wine and other luxuries.
16. **ad effēminandōs animōs:** *to weaken the character;* gerundive phrase expressing purpose.
17. **pertinent:** *tend.*
18. **praecēdunt = superant.**

1. The Belgians surpassed all the Gauls in courage.
2. The Romans differed from the Gauls in institutions, language, and refinement.

MIGRATION OF THE HELVETIANS

PREVIEW: The Helvetians were a strong and independent people, living in what is now Switzerland, north and east of the Lake of Geneva. They were known to the Romans as the *Helvētiī*. According to Caesar's statistics, the population of their territory amounted to 368,000 persons. Their remote location had given them little contact with Roman civilization, but the Roman soldiers had clashed with these sturdy mountain folk in 107 B.C. and had been defeated by the Tigurini, a subdivision of the Helvetians. Moreover, Caesar had learned that they had the reputation of being among the bravest of the Gauls. They had gained military prowess from their incessant warfare with their neighbors in Germany. Dissatisfied with the narrow and confining territory in which they lived, they decided to migrate westward and seek a new country in the broad and fertile lands of France that lay below them.

Under the leadership of the greatest of their nobles, Orgetorix, the Helvetians formed a three-year plan, which included a general exodus of all their people with no hope of return. They would fight or negotiate their way until they reached less restricted lands and broader horizons. However, Orgetorix let personal ambition replace patriotism. He had planned to use the migration as a means of making himself king of his own tribe and dictator over the whole of Gaul. He at once proceeded to ally with himself similarly ambitious men of two neighboring powerful states, the Sequanians and the Haeduans, whose help he needed to carry out his design. His unpatriotic scheme was discovered. The penalty was death by fire, but he chose suicide instead.

His death, however, did not destroy the plan of departure. Continuing their preparations, they burned their homes, persuaded several neighboring tribes to join them and, on the appointed day, began the trek down the mountains. When news of the proposed migration reached Caesar in Rome, he left the city, and with that lightning speed, blitzkrieg, for which he was later to become famous, he reached the lake, destroyed the bridge across the river Rhine, deployed his one legion along its banks, made defenses, and refused the Helvetians passage into Roman-controlled territory.

Foiled but undeterred, the Helvetians secured permission to march through the country of the Sequanians. They reached and crossed the Saone river into the country of the Haeduans, Rome's allies. In the meantime Caesar had levied and collected five legions and was soon in hot pursuit. Three divisions of the Helvetians had already crossed the river when Caesar surprised and destroyed the fourth one, which had not yet had the opportunity to cross.

Because of the treachery of Dumnorix, a Haeduan ally of Rome, the Roman cavalry was defeated in a skirmish, and the Haeduans did not furnish the

Romans with promised provisions. Caesar was obliged to turn aside to the town of Bibracte for food. This move the Helvetians interpreted as one of fear, and in their turn they became the pursuers. Caesar chose a battleground and defeated the Helvetians in hard-fought battle, with heavy losses on both sides.

At Caesar's command the 110,000 of the original 368,000 Helvetians returned dejectedly to Switzerland to rebuild the homes and replace the crops they had destroyed.

Ch. 2 The Helvetians Decide to Migrate

¹Apud Helvetiōs longē nōbilissimus et dītissimus
fuit Orgetorīx.
Is, ²M. Messālā et M. Pisōne cōnsulibus,
³rēgnī cupiditāte inductus,
⁴conjūrātiōnem nōbilitātis fēcit.
Omnibus cīvibus persuāsit
ut dē fīnibus suīs cum omnibus cōpiīs exīrent.
Dīxit ⁵perfacile esse,
cum virtūte omnibus praecēderent,
tōtius Galliae ⁶imperiō ⁷potīrī.
Facilius eīs persuāsit
quod undique locī nātūrā Helvētiī continentur.
Ūnā ex parte continentur flūmine Rhēnō,
lātissimō atque altissimō,
quī ⁸agrum Helvētium ā Germānīs dīvidit.
Alterā ex parte continentur monte Jūrā altissimō,
quī est inter Sēquanōs et Helvētiōs.
Tertiā ex parte Helvētiī continentur
lacū Lemannō et flūmine Rhodanō
quī ⁹Prōvinciam nostram ab Helvētiīs dīvidit.
¹⁰Hīs rēbus fiēbat,

---

1. **Apud Helvētiōs = In Helvētiā.**
2. **M. Messālā . . . cōnsulibus:** *in the consulship of Marcus Messala and Marcus Piso;* ablative absolute expressing time. The date mentioned here is 61 B.C., three years before Caesar's arrival in Gaul.
3. **rēgnī:** objective genitive. **Orgetorīx rēgnum cupiēbat.**
4. **conjūrātiōnem nōbilitātis:** *a conspiracy of the nobles.* The Helvetians at that time were ruled by chiefs from among the nobles. Under the leadership of Orgetorix, these nobles formed a political ring. Orgetorix hoped that by

leading the migration, he might become king of the Helvetians and eventually of all Gaul.
5. **perfacile = facillimum.**
6. **imperiō:** ablative after **potīrī.**
7. **potīrī:** subjective infinitive, subject of **esse.**
8. **agrum Helvētium = fīnēs Helvētiōrum.**
9. **Prōvinciam nostram = Prōvinciam Rōmānam.**
10. **Hīs rēbus** (ablative of cause) = **Propter hās rēs.**

¹¹ut minus lātē vagārentur
et minus facile fīnitimīs bellum īnferre possent.
Itaque māgnō dolōre afficiēbantur.
¹²Prō multitūdine hominum,
et prō glōriā bellī atque fortitūdinis,
angustōs sē fīnēs habēre arbitrābantur,
quī in longitūdinem mīlia passuum CCXL,
in lātitūdinem CLXXX patēbant.

FOR COMPREHENSION

● ANSWER IN ENGLISH:

1. Where was ancient Helvetia?
2. What was the secret ambition of Orgetorix?
3. What was the principal reason for the general unrest among the Helvetians?
4. What was the natural boundary between the Helvetians and the Roman Province? between the Helvetians and the Sequanians? between the Helvetians and the Germans?
5. In what year did Orgetorix the Helvetian initiate his conspiracy? In what year did Caesar assume the governorship of Gaul?

● RESPONDĒ LATĪNE:

1. Quandō Orgetorīx conjūrātiōnem fēcit?
2. Quibus Orgetorīx persuāsit ut dē fīnibus suīs exīrent?
3. Quae flūmina montēsque Helvētiōs continent?
4. Quantī fīnēs sunt Helvētiōrum?
5. Cūr Helvētiī suōs fīnēs esse angustōs arbitrantur?
6. Quōmodo Helvētiī afficiēbantur?
7. Quālis est Rhēnus flūmen? Quālis est mōns Jūra?

● SCRĪBE LATĪNE:

1. Orgetorix easily persuaded the nobility.
2. The Helvetians were hemmed in by lakes and rivers and mountains.
3. In the consulship of Marcus Messala and Marcus Piso, the Helvetians formed a conspiracy.

Ch. 3 Orgetorix in Control

Helvētiī hīs rēbus adductī
et auctōritāte Orgetorīgis permōtī, cōnstituērunt ea,

---

11. ut . . . vagārentur . . . possent: substantive clause of result, used as subject of impersonal verb fiēbat: *it happened.*

12. Prō: *In proportion to.*

¹quae ad proficīscendum pertinērent, ²comparāre.
³Jūmentōrum et ⁴carrōrum quam māximum numerum coēmērunt.
⁵Sēmentēs quam māximās fēcērunt
    ut in itinere cōpiam frūmentī habērent.
Cum proximīs cīvitātibus pācem et amīcitiam cōnfīrmāvērunt.
Ad eās rēs cōnficiendās
    ⁶biennium satis esse exīstimāvērunt.
In tertium annum profectiōnem ⁷lēge cōnfīrmant.
Ad eās rēs cōnficiendās Orgetorīx dēligitur.
Is ⁸sibi ⁹lēgātiōnem ad cīvitātēs suscēpit.
In eō itinere persuādet Casticō, Sēquanō,
    ut rēgnum in cīvitāte suā occupāret.
Casticī pater rēgnum in Sēquanīs multōs annōs ¹⁰obtinuerat
    et ā senātū populī Rōmānī amīcus appellātus erat.
Itemque Dumnorīgī Haeduō ut idem cōnārētur persuādet.
Dumnorīx erat frāter Dīviciācī,
    et eō tempore prīncipātum in cīvitāte obtinēbat
    ac ¹¹māximē plēbī acceptus erat.
Orgetorīx eī fīliam suam in mātrimōnium dat.
"Perfacile est," inquit, "id perficere,
    quod ego ipse meae cīvitātis ¹²imperium obtentūrus sum.
Nōn est dubium
    quīn tōtīus Galliae ¹³plūrimum Helvētiī possint.
Meīs ¹⁴cōpiīs meōque exercitū ¹⁵rēgna vōbīs conciliābō."
Hāc ōrātiōne adductī,
    inter sē ¹⁶fidem et jūs jūrandum dant.
¹⁷Rēgnō occupātō,
    ¹⁸per trēs potentissimōs populōs
    tōtīus ¹⁹Galliae sēsē potīrī posse spērant.

---

1. **quae ... pertinērent:** *which were needed;* subordinate clause in implied indirect discourse.
2. **comparāre = praeparāre.**
3. **Jūmentōrum:** *yoke animals* (cattle, mules, horses).
4. **carrōrum:** two-wheeled carts, usually drawn by oxen.
5. **Sēmentēs ... fēcērunt:** *(They made sowings.) They sowed grain.*
6. **biennium = duōs annōs.**
7. **lēge cōnfīrmant** (historical present): *fixed by decree.* In both Latin and English the present tense is used to describe a past act vividly.
8. **sibi ... suscēpit:** *took upon himself.*
9. **lēgātiōnem:** *office of envoy.*
10. **obtinuerat = tenuerat, habuerat.**
11. **māximē plēbī acceptus:** *(very much taken to) very popular with the people.*
12. **imperium:** *sovereign power.*
13. **plūrimum ... possint = potentissimī sint.**
14. **cōpiīs:** *resources.*
15. **rēgna ... conciliābō:** *I shall obtain kingdoms for you.*
16. **fidem et jūs jūrandum:** *(a pledge and oath) an oath-bound pledge.*
17. **Rēgnō occupātō = Cum rēgnum occupāvissent.**
18. **per trēs ... populōs = per Helvētiōs et Sēquanōs et Haeduōs.**
19. **Galliae:** genitive instead of ablative with **potīrī.**

- ANSWER IN ENGLISH:

1. What preparations did the Helvetians make for their migration?
2. On what mission did Orgetorix go?
3. Who was Casticus? Dumnorix? Diviciacus?
4. What did Orgetorix urge Casticus and Dumnorix to do?
5. What promise did Orgetorix make to Casticus and Dumnorix?

- RESPONDĒ LATĪNE:

1. Quae Helvētiī coēmērunt?
2. Quō cōnsiliō māgnās sēmentēs fēcērunt?
3. In quem annum profectiōnem cōnfīrmāvērunt?
4. Quibus Orgetorīx persuāsit ut rēgnum occupārent?
5. Cūjus frāter erat Dumnorīx?
6. Quibus rēbus sē imperiō potītūrōs esse spērābant?
7. Cui Orgetorīx fīliam suam in mātrimōnium dedit?

- SCRĪBE LATĪNE:

1. Influenced by the authority of the leader, the Helvetians decide to prepare for their departure.
2. An embassy was sent to the neighboring states for the purpose of encouraging their leading men.
3. They decided to buy as large a number of wagons as possible.

Ch. 4   Orgetorix Is Arrested and Commits Suicide

Ea conjūrātiō Helvētiīs [1]per indicēs ēnūntiāta est.
[2]Mōribus suīs Orgetorīgem [3]ex vinculīs [4]causam dīcere coēgērunt.
Sī Orgetorīx damnārētur,
    poena esset [5]ut īgnī cremārētur.
Diē cōnstitūtā [6]causae dictiōnis
    Orgetorīx ad jūdicium omnem suam [7]familiam,
    ad hominum mīlia decem, undique coēgit.
Omnēs [8]clientēs [9]obaerātōsque suōs,
    quōrum māgnum numerum habēbat, eōdem condūxit.
Per eōs [10]sē ēripuit et causam nōn dīxit.

1. **per indicēs:** *through informers.*
2. **Mōribus suīs:** *In accordance with their custom.*
3. **ex vinculīs:** *chained.*
4. **causam dīcere:** *to plead his case.*
5. **ut ... cremārētur:** substantive clause of result, in apposition with **poena.**
6. **causae dictiōnis:** (*of the pleading of the case*) *to plead his case.*
7. **familiam:** *household* (including dependents and slaves).
8. **clientēs:** *retainers.*
9. **obaerātōs:** *debtors.*
10. **sē ēripuit = effūgit.**

Cum cīvitās ob eam rem incitāta,
    armīs jūs suum [11]exsequī cōnārētur
    et magistrātūs multitūdinem hominum ex agrīs cōgerent,
Orgetorīx mortuus est.
Helvētiī arbitrantur
    Orgetorīgem ipsum [12]sibi mortem cōnscīvisse.

Gallic warriors.

FOR COMPREHENSION

● ANSWER IN ENGLISH:

1. How did the Helvetians learn about the scheme of Orgetorix to seize royal power?
2. What was the legal penalty for such an offense?
3. In what way was the prisoner compelled to stand trial?
4. Was Orgetorix convicted and executed?
5. What is supposed to have been his fate?

● RESPONDĒ LATĪNE:

1. Ā quibus ea rēs Helvētiīs ēnūntiāta est?
2. Quā diē Orgetorīx suam familiam ad jūdicium coēgit?
3. Quōs aliōs Orgetorīx ad jūdicium condūxit?
4. Quid cīvitās facere cōnāta est?
5. Quandō Orgetorīx mortuus est?

---

11. exsequī = cōnfīrmāre, cōnstituere.
12. sibi mortem cōnscīvisse = sē interfēcisse.

- SCRĪBE LATĪNE:
1. Orgetorix led to the trial all his clients and debtors.
2. The Helvetians thought that the unfortunate man killed himself.
3. The state tried to enforce the law, but Orgetorix saved himself.

Ch. 5 Point of No Return

Post Orgetorīgis mortem [1]nihilō minus Helvētiī
id quod cōnstituerant facere cōnātī sunt
et ē fīnibus suīs exīre parāvērunt.
[2]Ubi jam sē ad profectiōnem [3]parātōs esse arbitrātī sunt,
  [4]oppida sua omnia, numerō ad duodecim,
  [5]vīcōs ad quadringentōs,
  reliqua prīvāta aedificia [6]incendunt.
Frūmentum omne, praeter quod sēcum portātūrī erant, [6]combūrunt.
Haec fēcērunt ut domum reditiōnis spem tollerent,
  et parātiōrēs ad omnia perīcula subeunda essent.
[7]Trium mēnsium [8]molita cibāria
  sibi quemque domō efferre jubent.
Persuādent [9]Rauracīs et Tulingīs et Latobrīgīs, fīnitimīs,
  ut, oppidīs suīs vīcīsque exūstīs,
  ūnā cum eīs proficīscantur.
[10]Bōjōs, quī Rhēnum trānsierant Nōrējamque oppūgnāverant,
  ad sē recipiunt atque sociōs sibi [11]ascīscunt.

FOR COMPREHENSION

- ANSWER IN ENGLISH:
1. Did the death of Orgetorix have any effect upon the Helvetian migration?
2. What drastic measures did the Helvetians take to strengthen their determination not to return home?
3. How long did the Helvetians expect to be on the road?

---

1. **nihilō minus:** (by nothing the less) nevertheless.
2. **Ubi jam:** When at last (after two years).
3. **parātōs:** predicate adjective.
4. **oppida:** walled towns or strongholds.
5. **vīcōs:** small unfortified towns or villages.
6. **incendunt:** set fire to; **combūrō = exūrō:** burn up.
7. **Trium mēnsium:** for three months. It has been estimated that a baggage train of over 6,000 wagons and 24,000 yoke

animals would be needed to transport food for the 368,000 emigrants.
8. **molita cibāria:** ground rations.
9. The Rauraci, Tulingi, and Latobrigi were apparently north of the Helvetians, and therefore were exposed to the attacks and the inroads of the Germans; hence, they were ready to join the Helvetians.
10. **Bōjōs:** The name survives in the modern name of Bohemia.
11. **ascīscunt = conjungunt.**

4. What tribes joined the Helvetians in their migration?
5. What is the probable origin of the name Bohemia?

● RESPONDĒ LATĪNE:
1. Quid Helvētiī fēcērunt ubi jam parātī sunt?
2. Quō cōnsiliō domum reditiōnis spem sustulērunt?
3. Quot oppida Helvētiī incendērunt? Quot vīcōs incendērunt?
4. Quanta molita cibāria quisque domō extulit?
5. Quibus Helvētiī persuāsērunt ut cum eīs proficīscerentur?

● SCRĪBE LATĪNE:
1. To remove the hope of returning home, they had set fire to their private dwellings.
2. Each one carried from home sufficient (of) grain for himself.
3. They sent envoys to the Boii and persuaded them to do the same thing.

Ch. 6   The Helvetians Choose Their Route

Erant ¹omnīnō itinera duo,
quibus itineribus domō exīre ²possent.
Ūnum erat per Sēquanōs, ³inter montem Jūram et flūmen Rhodanum.
Hoc iter tam angustum et tam difficile erat
ut vix ⁴singulī carrī perdūcerentur.
⁵Mōns autem altissimus ita impendēbat,
ut ⁶perpaucī eōs facile prohibēre possent.
Alterum iter erat per Prōvinciam nostram.
Hoc iter facilius erat,
quod inter fīnēs Helvētiōrum et ⁷Allobrogum,
quī nūper ab Rōmānīs pācātī erant, Rhodanus fluit.
Id flūmen nōn nūllīs locīs vadō trānsitur.
⁸Extrēmum oppidum Allobrogum
proximumque Helvētiōrum fīnibus Genāva est.

---

1. **omnīnō:** *only*
2. **possent:** subjunctive in characteristic clause.
3. **inter ... Rhodanum:** *on the right bank* of the Rhone.
4. **singulī:** *one at a time.*
5. **Mōns:** The narrowest point of the route is at "Mill-Race Gorge" or Pas de l'Écluse, about 17½ miles below Geneva. The impending cliffs have often served as natural fortifications for a defending army.
6. **perpaucī:** *very few men,* posted on the heights above the road.
7. **Allobrogum:** *of the Allobroges.* The Allobroges were first conquered by Q. Fabius Maximus in 121 B.C. After a revolt in 61 B.C., they were again conquered.
8. **Extrēmum = ūltimum:** the most remote from the viewpoint of Rome.

Ex eō oppidō pōns ad Helvētiōs [9]pertinet.

Helvētiī exīstimābant

sēsē vel Allobrogibus persuāsūrōs esse,

quod nōndum [10]bonō animō in populum Rōmānum vidērentur,

vel vī coāctūrōs esse ut iter sibi darent.

Omnibus rēbus ad profectiōnem comparātīs,

diem [11]dīcunt, quā ad rīpam Rhodanī omnēs conveniant.

Is diēs erat [12]ante diem quīntum Kalendās Aprīlēs,

[13]L. Pīsōne, A. Gabīniō cōnsulibus.

FOR COMPREHENSION

● ANSWER IN ENGLISH:

1. What difficulties faced the Helvetians in the route through the territory of the Sequani?
2. Why was the route through the Roman Province much easier for them? Which did they choose?
3. What were the ways in which it would be possible for the Helvetians to cross the Rhone?
4. Why did the Helvetians think that the Allobroges might be willing to help them?
5. Was Geneva in Helvetian or Roman territory?
6. What was the date set for the start of the migration?

● RESPONDĒ LATĪNE:

1. Quāle erat iter per Sēquanōs? Quāle erat alterum iter?
2. Per quōrum fīnēs erat alterum iter?
3. Quōmodo Rhodanus nōn nūllīs locīs trānsīrī poterat?
4. Quō pōns ex oppidō Genāvā pertinet?
5. Quō cōnsiliō Helvētiī diem dīxērunt?

● SCRĪBE LATĪNE:

1. Let us name a day on which we shall meet at the bank of the Rhone.
2. The bridge which was near the city was useful (for a use) both to the Allobroges and to the Helvetians.
3. The route through the Roman Province was so easy that the Helvetians decided to cross the Rhone.

---

9. pertinet: *reaches across.*
10. bonō animō: *well disposed;* ablative of description.
11. dīcunt = cōnstituunt.
12. ante . . . Aprīlēs. The fifth day before the Kalends would be March 28.

13. L. Pīsōne: Lucius Calpurnius Piso was the father of Calpurnia, whom Caesar had married during the previous year.

Cum Caesarī id nūntiātum esset
Helvētiōs per Prōvinciam nostram iter facere cōnārī
mātūrat ab urbe proficīscī.
[1]Quam māximīs itineribus in [2]Galliam ulteriōrem contendit
   et [3]ad Genāvam pervēnit.
[4]Prōvinciae tōtī quam māximum mīlitum [5]numerum imperat
   (erat omnīnō in Galliā ulteriōre [6]legiō ūna).
Pontem, quī erat ad Genāvam, jubet [7]rescindī.
Ubi dē ējus adventū Helvētiī [8]certiōrēs factī sunt,
   [9]lēgātōs ad eum mittunt, quī dīcerent,
   Helvētiōs habēre in animō
   sine ūllō maleficiō iter per Prōvinciam facere,
   proptereā quod aliud iter [10]habērent nūllum.
Lēgātī rogant, ut [11]ējus voluntāte id sibi facere liceat.
Caesar autem [12]memoriā tenēbat L. Cassium cōnsulem
   occīsum esse exercitumque ējus ab Helvētiīs [13]pulsum esse
   et [14]sub jugum missum.
Hoc igitur concēdendum esse nōn putābat.
Neque hominēs inimīcō animō,
   datā facultāte per Prōvinciam itineris faciendī,
   temperātūrōs esse ab injūriā et maleficiō exīstimābat.
Tamen, ut spatium intercēdere posset,
   [15]dum mīlitēs, quōs imperāverat, convenīrent,
   lēgātīs respondit:
"Diem ad dēlīberandum sūmam. Sī quid vultis,
   ad Īdūs Aprīlēs revertiminī."

---

1. **Quam māximīs itineribus:** (*By the greatest marches possible*) *With the utmost speed.* At this time Caesar was near Rome. Caesar speaks of himself in the third person, but the reader must not forget that the writer was the chief actor in the events he is describing.
2. **Galliam ulteriōrem = Prōvinciam nostram.**
3. **ad:** *in the vicinity of.* If, as Plutarch writes, Caesar arrived at the Rhone on the eighth day after leaving Rome, he must have averaged 90 miles a day as he rode on horseback from Rome to Geneva.
4. **Prōvinciae ... imperat:** *He levied upon the Province.*
5. **numerum:** direct object of **imperat.**
6. **legiō ūna:** destined to be Caesar's favoite, the Tenth Legion.
7. **rescindī = dēlērī.**
8. **certiōrēs factī sunt = cōgnōvērunt:** *they were informed, they learned.*
9. **lēgātōs:** *envoys* (not lieutenants).
10. **habērent:** subjunctive, verb in subordinate clause in indirect discourse.
11. **ējus = Caesaris.**
12. **memoriā tenēbat = meminerat.**
13. The battle here referred to took place in 107 B.C.
14. **sub jugum:** *under the yoke.* Each soldier of the defeated army in token of surrender passed under the "yoke," made by planting two spears in the ground with a third across the top, somewhat like a football goalpost.
15. **dum ... convenīrent:** *until the soldiers should assemble.*

FOR COMPREHENSION

- ANSWER IN ENGLISH:

1. Where was Caesar in 58 B.C. when he learned the plan of the Helvetians?
2. How many legions were there at this time under Caesar's command?
3. What did Caesar do when the report of the migration reached him?
4. Why did he go directly to Geneva?
5. What did the Helvetians do when they heard of Caesar's arrival in the Province?
6. Why did not Caesar refuse the Helvetian envoys' request at once?

- RESPONDĒ LATĪNE:

1. Ubi Caesar certior dē hōc cōnsiliō factus est, quid Prōvinciae imperāvit?
2. Quō cōnsiliō Helvētiī lēgātōs ad Caesarem mīsērunt?
3. Quid hī lēgātī rogāvērunt?
4. Quae Caesar memoriā tenēbat?
5. Quid Caesar lēgātīs Helvētiōrum respondit?

- SCRĪBE LATĪNE:

1. They asked that they be allowed (that it should be allowed to them) to go across the bridge.
2. Caesar remembered that these Gauls had killed a Roman consul and sent his army under the yoke.
3. He said he would take time (a day) for deliberating.

Ch. 8 The Passage of the Helvetians Is Barred

¹Intereā eā ²legiōne, quam sēcum habēbat,
²mīlitibusque, quī ex Prōvinciā convēnerant,
ā lacū Lemannō, quī in flūmen Rhodanum īnfluit,
ad montem Jūram,
quī fīnēs Sēquanōrum ³ab Helvētiīs dīvidit,
mūrum fossamque perdūcit.
Mūrus fossaque in longitūdinem mīlia passuum ⁴XIX fuit
et in altitūdinem pedum sēdecim.
Eō opere perfectō,
praesidia ⁵dispōnit et castella ⁶commūnit,
⁷quō facilius eōs prohibēre posset,

---

1. **Intereā:** *Meanwhile* (while the more distant troops levied on the Province were gathering at the Rhone, and the Helvetians were waiting for Caesar's answer).
2. **legiōne, mīlitibus:** ablative of means.
3. **ab Helvētiīs = ā fīnibus Helvētiōrum.**
4. **XIX = ūndēvīgintī.**

5. **dispōnit:** *he stationed at intervals.*
6. Caesar improved upon the natural defenses. The soldiers, wherever necessary, cut into the river bank to meet the 16-foot requirement in steepness.
7. **quō facilius:** introducing a clause of purpose with a comparative.

sī sē invītō trānsīre cōnārentur.

Ubi ea diēs vēnit, quam cōnstituerat cum lēgātīs,
   et lēgātī ad eum revertērunt, Caesar dīxit:
[8]"Mōre et exemplō populī Rōmānī vōbīs iter dare nōn possum.
Sī vim facere cōnābiminī, vōs prohibēbō."
Helvetiī, [9]eā spē dējectī,
   [10]nāvibus jūnctīs et ratibus complūribus factīs,
   flūmen trānsīre cōnātī sunt.
Aliī vadīs Rhodanī, [11]quā minima altitūdō flūminis erat,
   nōn numquam [12]interdiū,
   saepius [13]noctū perrumpere cōnātī sunt.
Sed [14]operis mūnitiōne et mīlitum tēlīs repulsī
   hōc cōnātū dēstitērunt.

Roman soldiers.

FOR COMPREHENSION

● ANSWER IN ENGLISH:

1. Do you think Caesar ever seriously considered permitting the Helvetians to go through the Province?
2. What did Caesar do during the period between his first and second interviews with the Helvetians?
3. What military preparations did Caesar complete before refusing the request of the Helvetians?

---

8. **Mōre et exemplō:** *In accordance with usage and precedent.*
9. **eā spē dējectī:** (*cast down from this hope*) *disappointed in this hope.*
10. **nāvibus jūnctīs:** *by joining boats* (i.e., by a pontoon bridge). While the main body of the Helvetians tried to cross by pontoon bridges and rafts, some attempted to ford the Rhone at various points.
11. **quā = ubi.**
12. **interdiū:** *in the daytime.*
13. **noctū = nocte.**
14. **operis mūnitiōne = fīrmitūdine mūnitiōnis:** *by the strength of the fortification.*

4. What did the Helvetians try to do when Caesar finally gave his answer?
5. Why were they unsuccessful in their efforts?

● RESPONDĒ LATĪNE:

1. Quō lacus Lemannus īnfluit?
2. Quot mīlia passuum in longitūdinem erat mūrus?
3. Quot pedum in altitūdinem fuit mūrus fossaque?
4. Quō cōnsiliō Caesar praesidia disposuit?
5. Quōmodo flūmen trānsīre Helvētiī cōnātī sunt?
6. Quibus rēbus Helvētiī repulsī sunt?

● SCRĪBE LATĪNE:

1. In the meantime Caesar made many fortresses by which he might more easily repulse the Helvetians.
2. The Helvetians were no longer able to cross the river by means of the bridge.
3. He said that according to the custom of the Roman people he would not give to anyone a route through the Province.

Ch. 9 The Helvetians Find Another Way Out

[1]Relinquēbātur ūna per Sēquanōs via
quā, Sēquanīs invītīs, propter angustiās īre nōn poterant.
Helvētiī, cum [2]suā sponte Sēquanīs persuādēre nōn possent,
    lēgātōs ad Dumnorīgem Haeduum mittunt,
    ut, [3]eō dēprecātōre, ā Sēquanīs impetrārent.
Dumnorīx [4]grātiā et largītiōne apud Sēquanōs plūrimum [5]poterat
    et Helvētiīs erat amīcus, quod ex eā cīvitāte
    Orgetorīgis fīliam in mātrimōnium dūxerat.
Cupiditāte rēgnī adductus [6]novīs rēbus studēbat
    et quam plūrimās cīvitātēs
    [7]suō beneficiō habēre obstrictās volēbat.
Itaque rem suscipit, et ā Sēquanīs impetrat
    ut per fīnēs suōs Helvētiōs īre patiantur.
[8]Obsidēs utī inter sēsē dent, perficit.
Sēquanī obsidēs dant, nē Helvetiōs itinere prohibeant;
    Helvētiī, ut sine maleficiō et injūriā trānseant.

---

1. **Relinquēbātur:** *There remained* (only one road).
2. **suā sponte** = **per sē:** *by their own influence.*
3. **eō** (**Dumnorīx**) **dēprecātōre:** *by his intercession;* ablative absolute.
4. **grātiā:** *because of his popularity.*
5. **poterat** = **valēbat: plūrimum poterat:** *was very influential.*

6. **novīs rēbus** = **novō imperiō:** *for a radical change in government.*
7. **suō beneficiō habēre obstrictās:** *to have under obligations (bound) because of his kindness.*
8. **Obsidēs:** *Hostages.* Often the sons of prominent leaders were liable to the death penalty if a nation broke its contract.

FOR COMPREHENSION

- ANSWER IN ENGLISH:
1. When the Helvetians were prevented from crossing the Rhone, to whom did they next appeal?
2. Was the appeal granted immediately?
3. Why was Dumnorix a good mediator under the circumstances?
4. What were hostages? Why did the Helvetians and the Sequanians exchange hostages?
5. Why did Dumnorix the Haeduan desire a revolution in his own country?

- RESPONDĒ LATĪNE:
1. Cūr Helvētiī per Sēquanōs īre nōn poterant?
2. Quō cōnsiliō Helvētiī lēgātōs ad Dumnorīgem mīsērunt?
3. Quā dē causā Dumnorīx novīs rēbus studēbat?
4. Quid ā Sēquanīs Dumnorīx impetrāvit?
5. Quid Dumnorīx tandem perfēcit?

- SCRĪBE LATĪNE:
1. Since Dumnorix was eager for a revolution, he undertook the affair.
2. He wanted to have as many states as possible under obligations to him on account of his kindness.
3. Although they sent envoys to the Sequanians, they did not obtain their request.

Ch. 10   Caesar Enrolls Fresh Legions

Caesarī [1]renūntiātur [2]Helvētiīs [3]esse in animō
per agrum Sēquanōrum et Haeduōrum
[4]iter in [5]Santonum fīnēs facere.
Santonēs nōn longē ā [6]Tolōsātium fīnibus absunt,
quae cīvitās est in Prōvinciā.
[7]Id sī fieret,
intellegēbat māgnō cum perīculō Prōvinciae futūrum esse,

---

1. **renūntiātur**: *bring back word.* Spies or scouts bring back information.
2. **Helvētiīs**: dative of possession.
3. **(Helvētiīs) esse in animō = (Helvētiōs) habēre in animō**: *that the Helvetians were intending;* infinitive phrase, subject of impersonal verb **renūntiātur.**
4. **iter . . . facere**: infinitive phrase, subject of impersonal verb **esse.**
5. **Santonum**: The Santones were a Celtic tribe living on the Atlantic coast, more than 100 miles from the nearest point of

the Province. If the Helvetians should reach the territory of the Santones, they would be farther from the Province than when they started, yet they might be a greater menace because they would no longer be confined by natural boundaries, nor would they be kept on the defensive by the Germans.
6. **Tolōsātium**: The modern name of Tolosa is Toulouse.
7. **Id**: the migration to the territory of the Santones.

⁸ut hominēs bellicōsōs, populī Rōmānī inimīcōs,
locīs patentibus et māximē frūmentāriīs fīnitimōs habēret.
Ob eās causās eī mūnitiōnī, quam fēcerat,
⁹T. Labiēnum lēgātum praefēcit.
Ipse in Ītaliam māgnīs itineribus contendit.
Ibi ¹⁰duās legiōnēs cōnscrībit.
¹¹Trēs legiōnēs, quae circum ¹²Aquilējam hiemābant,
ex hībernīs ēdūcit.
Cum hīs quīnque legiōnibus ¹³in ūlteriōrem Galliam
per Alpēs contendit.
Ibi ¹⁴Ceutronēs et Grājocelī et Caturīgēs,
locīs superiōribus occupātīs,
itinere exercitum prohibēre cōnantur.
Complūribus hīs ¹⁵proeliīs pulsīs,
in fīnēs Vocontiōrum ūlteriōris prōvinciae
diē septimō pervēnit.
Inde in Allobrogum fīnēs et ab Allobrogibus in Segūsiāvōs
exercitum dūcit.
¹⁶Hī sunt extrā Prōvinciam trāns Rhodanum prīmī.

FOR COMPREHENSION

● ANSWER IN ENGLISH:
1. Where did the Helvetians intend to settle, according to reports received by Caesar?
2. What reason does Caesar give for objecting to this plan?
3. Why did Caesar decide to go to Italy at this critical moment?

---

8. **ut . . . habēret:** substantive clause of result used as subject of **futūrum esse.**
9. **T. Labiēnum lēgātum:** Titus Labienus was one of the ablest and most trusted of Caesar's officers and a capable general in the Gallic Wars, yet he sided against Caesar in the Civil War. The **lēgātus** was an officer appointed by the Senate to serve on the staff of a general carrying on a campaign. Caesar had ten **lēgātī,** whom he employed sometimes as commanders of legions, sometimes as ambassadors or envoys sent to represent him in conferences with the enemy.
10. **duās legiōnēs cōnscrībit:** the Eleventh and the Twelfth. These legions were enrolled by Caesar on his own responsibility. He secured the consent of the Senate three years later.

11. **Trēs legiōnēs:** the Seventh, Eighth, and Ninth.
12. **Aquilējam:** a Roman colony not far from modern Trieste.
13. **in ūlteriōrem Galliam = in Galliam Trānsalpīnam.**
14. **Ceutronēs . . . cōnantur:** Caesar must have been very much annoyed at being held up at this time by these rebellious mountain tribes.
15. **proeliīs:** clashes rather than battles.
16. **Hī sunt extrā Prōvinciam:** Caesar was now in Gallic territory. He left himself open to criticism as he led his troops into foreign fields without an order from the Senate. Nevertheless he was aware that most Romans would ignore this technicality if he scored a smashing victory over the Helvetians.

4. Of what fortifications did Labienus have charge during Caesar's absence?
5. How long did it take Caesar to lead his five legions through the Alps? What delayed him?
6. How would Caesar justify his taking an army into Gallic territory?

● RESPONDĒ LATĪNE:
1. Quid Caesarī renūntiātum est?
2. Quālēs hominēs Caesar Helvētiōs esse putābat?
3. Ubi erant fīnēs Tolōsātium?
4. Quem mūnitiōnī, quam fēcerat, Caesar praefēcit?
5. Quot legiōnēs Caesar in Ītaliā cōnscrīpsit? Quot legiōnēs ex hībernīs ēdūxit?
6. Quō itinere Caesar in ūlteriōrem Galliam hās quīnque legiōnēs dūxit?

● SCRĪBE LATĪNE:
1. Caesar learned that the Helvetians intended (had it in mind) to march through the territory of the Sequani.
2. He placed a lieutenant in command of the legions which had wintered in nearer Gaul.

Ch. 11   Gallic Tribes Appeal to Caesar

Helvētiī jam [1]per angustiās et fīnēs Sēquānōrum
suās cōpiās trādūxerant.
In Haeduōrum fīnēs pervēnerant
eōrumque agrōs [2]populābantur.
Haeduī, cum sē suaque ab eīs dēfendere nōn possent,
lēgātōs ad Caesarem mīsērunt quī auxilium rogārent.
[3]"Omnī tempore," inquiunt lēgātī, [4]"nōs Haeduī
dē populō Rōmānō ita meritī sumus,
ut paene in cōnspectū exercitūs Rōmānī,
nostrī agrī vāstārī nōn dēbuerint,
līberī nostrī in servitūtem abdūcī,
oppida nostra expūgnārī."
Item Allobrogēs,
quī trāns Rhodanum vīcōs possessiōnēsque habēbant,
fugā sē ad Caesarem recipiunt.

---

1. **per angustiās:** Pas de l'Écluse, where wagons could pass only one at a time.
2. **populābantur = vāstābant.**
3. **Omnī tempore = Semper.**
4. **nōs Haeduī . . . meritī sumus:** *we Haeduans (have been so deserving at the hands of the Roman people) have so well*

served *the interests of the Roman people.* More than forty years before, in 121 B.C., the Haeduans had by treaty been recognized as **sociī populī Rōmānī,** allies of the Roman people. Caesar, as a Roman official, was under obligation to protect them.

"Nōbīs," inquiunt, "praeter agrī solum ⁵nihil est reliquum."
⁶Quibus rēbus adductus Caesar
   nōn exspectandum esse sibi statuit
   ⁷dum, omnibus fortūnīs sociōrum cōnsūmptīs,
   in Santonēs Helvētiī pervenīrent.

---

5. nihil . . . reliquum: The plundering Helvetians had destroyed all the buildings and crops of the Allobroges.

6. Quibus rēbus = Hīs rēbus. In Latin a relative pronoun or adjective is frequently used to introduce a sentence, where in English a demonstrative pronoun or adjective would be used.

7. dum . . . pervenīrent: *until . . . (the Helvetians) should reach.*

FOR COMPREHENSION

● ANSWER IN ENGLISH:
1. What had the Helvetians done while Caesar was mobilizing his army?
2. Why was Caesar under obligation to protect the Haeduans?
3. Why did the Allobroges appeal to Caesar for help?
4. Which of these groups seemed to have suffered most severely?
5. What decision did Caesar make?

● RESPONDĒ LATĪNE:
1. Quō Helvētiī cōpiās trādūxerant?
2. Quae Helvētiī faciēbant?
3. Quōs ad Caesarem Haeduī mīsērunt?
4. Quī aliī fugā sē ad Caesarem recēpērunt?
5. Quī Caesarī dēfendendī erant?
6. Quī dēmōnstrāvērunt sibi praeter agrī solum nihil reliquum esse?

● SCRĪBE LATĪNE:
1. The Helvetians sent armies to lay waste the fields.
2. Nothing is left to the Allobroges except the bare ground.
3. The envoys of the Haeduans said that the Roman army ought to protect them from raids.

Ch. 12   Caesar Uses the Blitzkrieg

Flūmen ¹Arar per fīnēs Haeduōrum et Sēquanōrum
in Rhodanum īnfluit tam incrēdibilī lēnitāte
ut oculīs ²in utram partem ³fluat jūdicārī nōn possit.
Id flūmen Helvētiī, ⁴ratibus ac lintribus jūnctīs, trānsībant.

---

1. Arar: *the Saone.*
2. in utram partem: *in which direction.*
3. fluat: subjunctive in indirect question depending on **jūdicārī.**

4. ratibus . . . jūnctis: *rafts and boats joined together* (i.e., a pontoon bridge).

Caesar per explōrātōrēs certior factus est,
   Helvētiōs jam trēs partēs cōpiārum id flūmen trādūxisse,
   atque quārtam ferē partem ⁵citrā flūmen Ararim reliquam esse.
⁶Dē tertiā vigiliā cum ⁷legiōnibus tribus ē castrīs profectus,
   ad eam partem pervēnit quae nōndum flūmen trānsierat.
Eōs ⁸impedītōs et inopīnantēs aggressus,
   māgnam partem eōrum ⁹concīdit.
Reliquī ¹⁰sēsē fugae mandāvērunt
   atque in proximās silvās abdidērunt.
Is ¹¹pāgus appellābātur Tigurīnus;
   nam omnis cīvitās Helvētia in quattuor pāgōs dīvīsa est.
Hic pāgus ūnus, cum domō exīsset,
   ¹²patrum nostrōrum memoriā L. Cassium cōnsulem interfēcerat,
   et ējus exercitum sub jugum mīserat.
Ita sīve cāsū, sīve cōnsiliō deōrum immortālium,
   ea pars cīvitātis Helvētiae,
   quae īnsīgnem calamitātem populō Rōmānō intulerat,
   ¹³prīnceps ¹⁴poenās persolvit.
Quā in rē Caesar nōn sōlum pūblicās,
   sed etiam prīvātās injūriās ultus est.
Nam Tigurīnī L. Pīsōnem lēgātum
   (quī erat avus L. Pīsōnis, socerī Caesaris) interfēcerant
   eōdem proeliō quō Cassium interfēcerant.

FOR COMPREHENSION

- ANSWER IN ENGLISH:
1. What proportion of the Helvetians had not yet crossed the Saone?
2. What injury had the Tigurini done to the Roman people in 107 B.C.?
3. In what way did Caesar avenge public and private wrongs?
4. Why was Caesar's attack upon the Tigurini well planned?
5. Who was Caesar's wife in 58 B.C.?

---

5. **citrā flūmen:** the eastern side of the river Saone.
6. **Dē tertiā vigiliā:** *Just after the third watch.* In military usage the night was divided into four watches of three hours each: **prīmā vigiliā,** commencing at sunset, 6 to 9 P.M.; **secundā vigiliā,** 9 P.M. to 12 midnight; **tertiā vigiliā,** 12 midnight to 3 A.M.; **quārtā vigiliā,** ending at sunrise, 3 to 6 A.M.
7. **legiōnibus tribus:** about 11,000 men, half of Caesar's army.

8. **impedītōs et inopīnantēs:** *hampered and off their guard.*
9. **concīdit = interfēcit, occīdit.**
10. **sēsē fugae mandāvērunt = fūgērunt.**
11. **pāgus:** *district, canton.*
12. **patrum nostrōrum memoriā:** *within the memory of our fathers* (i.e., a generation earlier).
13. **prīnceps = prīma.**
14. **poenās persolvit = poenās dedit:** *paid the penalty.*

1. Quāle flūmen erat Arar?
2. Ā quibus Caesar dē Helvētiīs certior factus est?
3. Quot partēs Helvētiōrum flūmen jam trānsierant?
4. Quot partēs Helvētiōrum illō tempore trānsīre cōnābantur?
5. Quā dē vigiliā Caesar ē castrīs profectus est?
6. Quot in pāgōs dīvīsa est omnis cīvitās Helvētia?
7. Quem alium eōdem proeliō, quō Cassius interfectus erat, Tigurīnī interfēcerant?

● SCRĪBE LATĪNE:
1. We cannot always judge with the eyes in which direction the river is flowing.
2. Did Caesar know how the Helvetians were crossing this river?
3. Caesar had been informed that this was the canton which had sent the Roman army under the yoke.

Summary of Chapters 13–20

After defeating the Tigurini, Caesar bridged the Saone and crossed it in a single day. The alarmed Helvetians then sent envoys under the leadership of Divico, who offered to make peace with the Romans and promised that the Helvetians would settle wherever Caesar wished them to settle. He warned Caesar, however, that if he persisted in war, there would be a repetition of the crushing defeat the Helvetians had once inflicted upon the Romans.

Caesar replied that even if he could forget the old affront, he could not forget their recent hostility in attempting to force a way through the Roman Province and their raids on the Haeduans and the Allobroges. Still he would make peace with them if they would give hostages and pay indemnity to the Haeduans and the Allobroges. Divico replied that the Helvetians were in the habit of receiving hostages, not of giving them, as the Romans themselves could attest. With this response he withdrew from the conference, and the Helvetians continued their march. Caesar pursued them, and his cavalry was defeated in a skirmish.

Meanwhile the Haeduans failed to furnish their promised supply of grain. When Caesar complained to the Haeduan chiefs who were in his camp, he learned that Dumnorix, a popular politician among the Haeduans, was not only responsible for the food failure but was also to blame for the recent defeat of the Roman calvary, since he personally had led the retreat. Although Caesar had overwhelming evidence of the treachery of Dumnorix, he did not order his execution because of political expediency. By way of explanation, he informed Dumnorix that his life had been spared as a gesture of good will toward his brother, Diviciacus, who had tried more than any other Haeduan to promote friendly relations between Rome and his country.

Ch. 21   Plans for a Second Surprise Attack

¹Eōdem diē ab explōrātōribus certior factus est hostēs ²sub monte cōnsēdisse mīlia passuum ab ipsīus castrīs octō; ³quālis esset nātūra montis et quālis ⁴in circuitū ascēnsūs, ⁵quī cōgnōscerent mīsit. Renūntiātum est eum facilem esse.

Dē tertiā vigiliā T. Labiēnum, ⁶lēgātum prō praetōre, cum duābus legiōnibus et eīs ⁷ducibus, quī iter cōgnōverant, summum jugum montis ascendere jubet; ⁸quid suī cōnsilī sit ostendit. Ipse dē quārtā vigiliā eōdem itinere, quō hostēs ierant, ad eōs contendit equitātumque omnem ante sē mittit.

⁹P. Cōnsidius, quī reī mīlitāris peritissimus habēbātur et in exercitū ¹⁰L. Sullae et posteā in ¹¹M. Crassī fuerat, cum explōrātōribus praemittitur.

FOR COMPREHENSION

● ANSWER IN ENGLISH:
1. Where had the Helvetians been imprudent enough to pitch their camp?
2. How did Caesar act in order to take advantage of this opportunity?
3. What orders did he give to Labienus, his most trusted lieutenant?
4. What was the reputation of Considius? How had he gained it?
5. Why does Caesar emphasize this reputation?

● RESPONDĒ LATĪNE:
1. Ubi Helvētiī cōnsēderant?
2. Quālis erat ascēnsus hūjus montis?
3. Quid Caesar Tītum Labiēnum facere jūssit?
4. Quālis Pūblius Cōnsidius habēbātur?
5. In quōrum exercitibus fuerat?

● SCRĪBE LATĪNE:
1. The scouts tried to find out what was the character of the mountain.
2. They reported that the ascent on all sides was easy.
3. About the fourth watch Caesar hastened toward the enemy by the same route which they had taken.

---

1. **Eōdem diē:** *The same day* (that he had held a conference with the Haeduan chieftains).
2. **sub monte:** *at the foot of a hill.*
3. **quālis esset:** indirect question.
4. **in circuitū:** (*in the going around*) *from the other side.*
5. **quī cōgnōscerent:** relative clause of purpose. The antecedent of **quī** is **hominēs** understood, object of **mīsit.**
6. **lēgātum prō praetōre:** lieutenant with power of commander.

7. **ducibus:** *as guides;* in apposition to **eīs.**
8. **quid suī cōnsilī sit:** *what his plan is.*
9. **P. Cōnsidius:** In telling of the qualifications of Publius Considius, a veteran of thirty years' experience, Caesar wishes to justify his choice.
10. **L. Sullae:** Lucius Cornelius Sulla was the conqueror of Mithridates, 88–84 B.C.
11. **M. Crassī:** Marcus Crassus defeated the slaves in the insurrection led by Spartacus, the gladiator, 73–71 B.C.

Ch. 22   The Blunder of a Military Expert

Prīmā lūce, cum summus mōns ā Labiēnō tenērētur, [1]ipse ab hostium castrīs [2]nōn longius mīlle et quīngentīs passibus abesset; neque (ut posteā ex captīvīs comperit), aut [3]ipsīus adventus aut Labiēnī cōgnitus esset, Cōnsidius, [4]equō admissō, ad eum accurrit; dīcit montem, quem ā Labiēnō occupārī voluerit ab hostibus tenērī; id sē ā Gallicīs [5]armīs atque [6]īnsīgnibus cōgnōvisse. Caesar suās cōpiās in proximum collem subdūcit, aciem īnstruit.

Labiēnus, [7]ut erat eī praeceptum ā Caesare, nē proelium committeret nisi [3]ipsīus cōpiae prope hostium castra vīsae essent, ut undique ūnō tempore in hostēs impetus fieret, monte occupātō, nostrōs exspectābat, proeliōque abstinēbat.

Multō dēnique diē per explōrātōrēs Caesar cōgnōvit et montem ā suīs tenērī, et Helvētiōs castra mōvisse, et Cōnsidium, timōre perterritum, quod nōn vīdisset [8]prō vīsō sibi renūntiāvisse. Eō diē, quō cōnsuēverat intervallō, hostēs sequitur, et mīlia passuum tria ab eōrum castrīs castra pōnit.

The Romans battling the Gauls.

1. **ipse** = et Caesar ipse.
2. **nōn longius** = nōn longius quam.
3. **ipsīus:** Caesar's.
4. **equō admissō:** *with his horse at full speed.*

5. **armīs:** The shields and the helmets of the Gauls were different.
6. **īnsīgnibus:** ornaments.
7. **ut:** *as.*
8. **prō vīsō:** *as if seen.*

FOR COMPREHENSION

- ANSWER IN ENGLISH:
1. At daybreak how far away was Caesar from the camp of the enemy?
2. What was Caesar's plan of attack?
3. Who was in command of the two legions who were stationed at the top of the hill?
4. Who was in command of Caesar's cavalry scouts?
5. What possible explanation can there be of Considius' false report? Were field glasses in use in those days?
6. What was Caesar's usual battle formation?
7. In the meantime what was Labienus doing? What had the Helvetians done?

- RESPONDĒ LATĪNE:
1. Ubi erat Caesar prīmā lūce? Labiēnus?
2. Num hostēs aut Caesaris adventum aut Labiēnī cōgnōvērunt?
3. Quā dē causā Cōnsidius dīxit montem ab hostibus tenērī?
4. Quandō Caesar montem ā suīs tenērī cōgnōvit?
5. Quō intervallō Caesar hostēs secūtus est?

- SCRĪBE LATĪNE:
1. Considius said that he had recognized the Gauls by their weapons and the ornaments on their shields.
2. Labienus refrained from battle as he had been instructed.
3. Late in the day Caesar found out that the Helvetians had moved camp.

Ch. 23 Caesar Seeks Supplies; the Helvetians Give Chase

[1]Postrīdiē ējus diēī Caesar, quod omnīnō [2]bīduum [3]supererat, [4]cum exercituī frūmentum mētīrī oportēret, et quod ā [5]Bibracte, oppidō Haeduōrum, nōn amplius [6]mīlibus passuum XVIII aberat, [7]reī frūmentāriae [8]prōspicere cōnstituit. Itaque iter ab Helvētiīs āvertit, ac Bibracte īre contendit.

Ea rēs per fugitīvōs L. Aemilī, decuriōnis equitum Gallōrum, hostibus nūntiātur. Helvētiī, sīve quod Rōmānōs timōre perterritōs discēdere ā sē [9]exīstimārent, sīve quod sē Rōmānōs rē

---

1. **Postrīdiē ējus diēī = Posterō diē:** *(on that day's following day) the next day.*
2. **bīduum:** *two days.* Notice **trīduum:** *three days;* **quadrīduum:** *four days;* but **quīnque diēs:** *five days.*
3. **supererat = super + erat.**
4. **cum ... oportēret:** *(before the time) when it would be necessary.*
5. **Bibracte:** modern Mont Beuvray, some miles west of Autun.
6. **mīlibus:** ablative of comparison.
7. **reī frūmentāriae:** dative with **prōspicere.**
8. **prōspicere = prōvidēre.**
9. **exīstimārent:** subjunctive. Caesar was not sure of the real reason.

frūmentāriā interclūdere posse cōnfīderent, cōnsilium commū-
tāvērunt, atque, [10]itinere conversō, nostrōs [11]ā novissimō agmine
īnsequī ac [12]lacessere coepērunt.

---

10. **itinere conversō:** *reversing their march.*
Their vain confidence led them to return
and give Caesar the chance he had been
waiting for.

11. **ā novissimō agmine:** *from the* (*Ro-mans'*) *rear.*

12. **lacessere = in nostrōs impetum
facere.**

FOR COMPREHENSION

● ANSWER IN ENGLISH:

1. For what reason did Caesar change his course and go toward the town of Bibracte?
2. How did the Helvetians learn of Caesar's changed plans?
3. How did the Helvetians interpret his movement?
4. What change did this make in the plans of the Helvetians?
5. Was there a good reason for the misjudgment of the Helvetians?

● RESPONDĒ LATĪNE:

1. Cūr Caesar ab Helvētiīs iter āvertit? Quō īre contendit?
2. Quī Gallīs cōnsilium mūtātum Caesaris nūntiāvērunt?
3. Cūr Helvētiī cōnsilium suum mūtāvērunt?
4. Quod oppidum nōn amplius mīlibus passuum XVIII aberat?
5. Quandō Helvētiī Rōmānōs lacessere coepērunt?

● SCRĪBE LATĪNE:

1. He thought that he should look out for a supply of grain.
2. The Helvetians changed their route so that they could cut off the Romans from their grain supply.
3. Only two days remained, and he was not more than eighteen miles away from a very large town.

Ch. 24   Preparations for Battle

Postquam Caesar [1]id animum advertit, cōpiās suās Caesar in
proximum collem subdūcit, equitātumque, quī sustinēret hostium
impetum, mīsit. [2]Ipse interim [3]in colle mediō [4]triplicem aciem
īnstrūxit legiōnum quattuor veterānārum (ita utī suprā) et in
summō jugō duās legiōnēs, quās in Galliā citeriōre proximē

---

1. **id animum advertit = id animad-vertit.**
2. **Ipse:** Caesar.
3. **in colle mediō:** *halfway up the hill.*

4. **triplicem aciem:** the famous Roman
battle formation. The first two lines
alternated in fighting; the third line was
reserved for an emergency.

cōnscrīpserat, et omnia ⁵auxilia collocārī jūssit. Ita tōtum montem hominibus complēvit.

Intereā sarcinās in ūnum locum cōnferrī et eum locum ab hīs, quī in superiōre aciē ⁶cōnstiterant, mūnīrī jūssit. Helvētiī cum omnibus suīs carrīs secūtī, impedīmenta in ūnum locum contulērunt. ⁷Ipsī ⁸cōnfertissimā aciē, equitātū nostrō rejectō, ⁹phalange factā, ¹⁰sub prīmam nostram aciem ¹¹successērunt.

5. **auxilia:** lightly armed troops, chiefly slingers and archers.
6. **cōnstiterant** = **īnstructī erant.**
7. **Ipsī:** the Helvetians themselves as opposed to their wagons and baggage.
8. **cōnfertissimā aciē** (ablative of means) = **dēnsissimā aciē.**
9. **phalange factā:** a solid column of warriors with interlocking shields in front and overhead.
10. **sub:** *up toward.* The Helvetians had to advance halfway up the hill, where Caesar had stationed his veteran legions.
11. **successērunt** = **subiērunt:** *went up to* (from a lower position).

FOR COMPREHENSION

● ANSWER IN ENGLISH:

1. Why did Caesar withdraw his army to a hillside?
2. Where did Caesar place his veteran troops? his recently conscripted troops? his auxiliary forces?
3. What formation did Caesar use at the beginning of the battle?
4. What formation did the Helvetians use?
5. Which side was successful in the cavalry skirmish?

● RESPONDĒ LATĪNE:

1. Quō Caesar cōpiās subdūxit? Quō cōnsiliō equitātum mīsit?
2. Quārum legiōnum in colle mediō triplicem aciem Caesar īnstrūxit?
3. Ubi duās novās legiōnēs cōnsistere jūssit?
4. Quō Helvētiī impedīmenta contulērunt?
5. Quō Helvētiī, phalange factā, successērunt?

● SCRĪBE LATĪNE:

1. He ordered the packs of the soldiers to be gathered in one place.
2. The mountain was filled with men in a very compact line.
3. Those in the higher battle line fortified the place where the packs were.

Ch. 25　The Helvetians Retreat but Rally

Caesar prīmum suum equum ex cōnspectū, deinde equōs omnium remōvit, ut, ¹aequātō omnium perīculō, spem fugae tol-

1. **aequātō ... perīculō:** ablative absolute, denoting means. By sending away his horse, Caesar revealed himself as a true leader, since he did not ask his men to do what he himself was unwilling to do.

leret. Deinde cohortātus suōs proelium commīsit. Mīlitēs, [2]pīlīs ē locō superiōre missīs, facile hostium phalangem perfrēgērunt. [3]Eā phalange disjectā, [4]gladiīs dēstrictīs in eōs impetum fēcērunt.

[5]Gallīs erat [6]māgnō impedīmentō [7]ad pūgnam, quod plūra eōrum scūta ūnō ictū pīlōrum [8]trānsfīxa erant et colligāta. Nam cum [9]ferrum sē īnflēxisset, nec pīla [10]ēvellere nec, [11]sinistrā impedītā, satis commodē pūgnāre poterant; ut multī, [12]diū jactātō bracchiō, [13]praeoptārent scūtum manū [14]ēmittere et [15]nūdō corpore pūgnāre. Tandem vulneribus dēfessī Helvētiī [16]pedem referre, et, quod [17]mōns suberat circiter mīlle passuum [18]spatiō, [19]eō sē recipere coepērunt.

[20]Captō monte et succēdentibus nostrīs, Bōjī et Tulingī, quī hominum mīlibus circiter xv agmen hostium claudēbant et [21]novissimō agminī praesidiō erant, nostrōs [22]ab latere apertō circumvenīre coepērunt. Id cōnspicātī Helvētiī, quī in montem sē recēperant, rūrsus proelium redintegrāvērunt.

Rōmānī [23]sīgna conversa bipertītō intulērunt; prīma et secunda

2. **pīlīs:** The **pīlum** was the characteristic weapon of the Roman legionary. It was a heavy spear, about ten pounds in weight, with a thick wooden shaft, four and one-half feet long, and a projecting iron point measuring about two feet. These could be hurled 60–75 feet. Since in this battle they were hurled downward, they must have struck the Helvetian line with tremendous force.

3. **Eā phalange disjectā:** The volley of **pīla** wounded and killed many of the enemy. Once there were openings in the phalanx, the Helvetians suffered heavy losses. Most of them were too close together to use their long swords. The Romans, on the other hand, dashed here and there to thrust with their short swords.

4. **gladiīs dēstrictīs:** hand-to-hand fighting.

5. **Gallīs = Helvetiīs.**

6. **māgnō impedīmentō:** dative of purpose. **Gallīs erat māgnō impedīmentō = Gallī māgnopere impediēbantur.**

7. **ad pūgnam = in pūgnandō.**

8. **trānsfīxa ... colligāta:** A single javelin could pierce and pin together two overlapping shields.

9. **ferrum:** The iron shaft of the javelin was made of soft iron.

10. **ēvellere = extrahere.**

11. **sinistrā impedītā:** ablative absolute. The shield was held in the left hand.

12. **diū jactātō bracchiō:** ablative absolute.

13. **praeoptārent = māllent:** *preferred.*

14. **ēmittere = ējicere.**

15. **nūdō corpore:** *with the body unprotected* (by a shield).

16. **pedem referre:** (*to draw back the foot*) *to yield.*

17. **mōns suberat = mōns prope erat:** The hill was north of their first position.

18. **spatiō:** ablative of degree of difference.

19. **eō = ad eum montem:** *there.*

20. **Captō:** *reached* (not *captured*). The Helvetians had reached the mountain, and the Romans were going up to attack them.

21. **novissimō ... erant:** *were serving as a rear guard.* The Boii and Tulingi had served as an advance guard. When the line of march was reversed, they became the rear guard.

22. **ab latere apertō:** *on the exposed flank.* This was the right flank since a soldier gripped the strap of a shield with his left hand.

23. **sīgna ... intulērunt:** (*bore their reversed ensigns on the enemy*) *faced about and charged in two directions.* The phrase **sīgna conversa** refers only to the movement of the third line, while **intulērunt** denotes the action of the entire army.

aciēs, ut Helvētiīs [24]victīs ac submōtīs resisterent; [25]tertia aciēs
ut venientēs Bōjōs et Tulingōs sustinēret.

---

24. victīs ac submōtīs: *those who had been beaten and driven back.*

25. tertia: The third line faced about and

received the attack of the oncoming
(**venientēs**) Boii and Tulingi.

FOR COMPREHENSION

● ANSWER IN ENGLISH:

1. What act of Caesar's before the battle put him and his officers on the same footing as the common soldiers and boosted their morale?
2. What two weapons of offense were used by the Roman legionary soldiers?
3. Which side had the advantage of position during the first part of this battle?
4. Why was the Helvetian phalanx ineffective against the Roman attack?
5. Why did many of the Helvetians throw down their shields?
6. What effect did the arrival of reinforcements have upon the Helvetians?
7. How did Caesar meet the attack of the Boii and the Tulingi?

● RESPONDĒ LATĪNE:

1. Cūr Caesar equōs omnium remōvit?
2. Quī scūtum manū ēmittere praeoptāvērunt?
3. Quandō Helvētiī pedem referre coepērunt?
4. Cui agminī erant praesidiō Bōjī et Tulingī?
5. Quō cōnsiliō Rōmānī sīgna convertērunt?

● SCRĪBE LATĪNE:

1. Their shields and javelins were an impediment to the weary Gauls.
2. After the Helvetian phalanx had been scattered, the Romans attacked the men with drawn swords.
3. The enemy began to retreat to the mountain which was about a mile away.

Ch. 26   The Romans Pursue the Survivors

Ita [1]ancipitī proeliō diū atque ācriter [2]pūgnātum est. Diūtius
cum sustinēre nostrōrum impetūs nōn possent, [3]alterī, ut coepe-
rant, in montem sē recēpērunt, alterī ad impedīmenta et carrōs
suōs [4]sē contulērunt. Nam hoc tōtō proeliō, [5]cum ab hōrā septimā
ad vesperum pūgnātum sit, [6]āversum hostem vidēre nēmō
potuit.

---

1. ancipitī = ambō (*both*) **+ caput**(*head*): *on two fronts.*

2. pūgnātum est = pūgnāvērunt.

3. alterī ... alterī: the Helvetians ... the Boii.

4. sē contulērunt: *they retreated.* They did not flee but retired in good order.

5. cum = quamquam: *although.*

6. āversum (*turned away*) **hostem = tergum hostis.**

Ad multam noctem etiam ad impedīmenta pūgnātum est, proptereā quod prō vallō carrōs objēcerant, et [7]ē locō superiōre in nostrōs venientēs tēla conjiciēbant et nōn nūllī [8]inter carrōs rotāsque [9]matarās ac trāgulās subjiciēbant nostrōsque vulnerābant. Cum diū pūgnātum esset, [10]impedimentīs castrīsque nostrī potītī sunt. Ibi Orgetorīgis fīlia atque ūnus ē fīliīs captus est.

Ex eō proeliō circiter hominum mīlia cxxx superfuērunt, Hī [11]eā tōtā nocte continenter [12]iērunt. [13]In fīnēs Lingonum diē quārtō pervēnērunt, cum et propter vulnera mīlitum et propter sepultūram [14]occīsōrum nostrī, trīduum morātī, [15]eōs sequi nōn potuissent.

Caesar ad Lingonēs [16]litterās nūntiōsque mīsit atque eōs monuit, [17]nē eōs frūmentō nēve aliā rē juvārent. Sī eōs jūvissent, sē Lingonēs [18]eōdem locō, quō Helvētiōs habēret, habitūrum esse. Ipse, [19]trīduō intermissō, cum omnibus cōpiīs eōs sequī coepit.

A Gaul defending his home.

FOR COMPREHENSION

● ANSWER IN ENGLISH:

1. On what two fronts were the Romans compelled to fight?
2. To what place did the Helvetians withdraw? the Boii and Tulingi?
3. At what time did the battle begin? When did the main battle end?
4. Where was there fighting until late at night?

7. **ē locō superiōre:** from the top of the rampart of carts.
8. **inter carrōs ... subjiciēbant:** They kept throwing their missiles from beneath their carts and from behind solid wooden wheels.
9. **matarās ac trāgulās:** Gallic spears and darts.
10. **impedīmentīs castrīsque:** ablative with **potior.**
11. **eā tōtā nocte = per tōtam noctem.**
12. **iērunt = fūgērunt.**
13. **In fīnēs Lingonum:** more than fifty miles north of the battlefield.
14. **occīsōrum:** *of those who had been slain.*
15. **eōs = Helvētiōs.**
16. **litterās nūntiōsque:** *letters and messages* (as warnings).
17. **nē ... juvārent:** (saying) *that they should not aid.*
18. **eōdem locō:** *in the same place* (as enemies).
19. **trīduō intermissō = post trēs diēs.**

5. How many men, women, and children survived the battle and the capture of the camp? Where did they go?
6. What message did Caesar send to the Lingones?
7. Why did Caesar not pursue the Helvetians at once?

● RESPONDĒ LATĪNE:
1. Quid Helvētiī fēcērunt cum diūtius Rōmānōrum impetūs sustinēre nōn possent?
2. Quid hōc tōtō proeliō nēmō vidēre potuit?
3. Ubi ad multam noctem pūgnātum est?
4. Quī in castrīs hostium captī sunt?
5. Quō Helvētiī diē quārtō pervēnērunt?
6. Quam ob rem Rōmānī eōs sequī nōn poterant?
7. Quandō Caesar fugitīvōs sequī coepit?

● SCRĪBE LATĪNE:
1. Some fled to the mountain; others retreated to the baggage and carts.
2. After they had fought for many hours, the Romans gained possession of the camp.
3. Caesar warned the Lingones not to aid the Helvetians with grain or anything else.

Ch. 27 Unconditional Surrender

Helvētiī, omnium rērum inopiā adductī, lēgātōs dē dēditiōne ad eum mīsērunt. Lēgātī, cum eum in itinere [1]convēnissent, sē ad pedēs Caesaris prōjēcērunt et suppliciter locūtī, flentēs pācem petīvērunt. Caesar [2]eōs in eō locō quō tum [3]essent suum adventum exspectāre jūssit. Paruērunt.

[4]Eō postquam Caesar pervēnit, obsidēs, arma, servōs, quī ad eōs [5]perfūgissent, poposcit. Dum [6]ea conquīruntur et cōnferuntur, circiter hominum mīlia vi ējus pāgī, quī Verbigenus appellātur, [7]prīmā nocte ē castrīs Helvētiōrum ēgressī sunt et ad Rhēnum fīnēsque Germānōrum contendērunt, quod timēbant, [8]nē armīs trāditīs, suppliciō afficerentur, et in tantā multitūdine captīvōrum suam fugam [9]aut occultārī aut omnīnō īgnōrārī posse exīstimābant.

1. **convēnissent:** *met;* usually intransitive verb, but here transitive.
2. **eōs** = Helvētiōs (not the envoys).
3. **essent:** subjunctive in dependent clause in implied indirect discourse.
4. **Eō** = In eum locum.
5. **perfūgissent:** *who* (he alleged) *had fled;* subjunctive in dependent clause in implied indirect discourse.
6. **ea** = obsidēs, arma, servī.
7. **prīmā nocte** = prīmā parte noctis.
8. **nē . . . afficerentur:** *lest they should be visited with punishment.*
9. **aut occultārī aut . . . īgnōrārī posse:** *could either be concealed* (if Caesar tried to find them) *or remain unnoticed.*

FOR COMPREHENSION

- ANSWER IN ENGLISH:
1. Was Caesar's threat to the Lingones effective?
2. What caused the Helvetians, who still outnumbered the Romans, to surrender?
3. What did Caesar demand in addition to hostages?
4. What did six thousand Verbigeni decide to do?
5. Is any act of war permissible after terms of surrender have been accepted by leaders of both sides?
6. What two possible reasons does Caesar suggest for this action of the Verbigeni?

- RESPONDĒ LATĪNE:
1. Cūr Helvētiī lēgātōs dē dēditiōne ad Caesarem mīsērunt?
2. Quid Caesar Helvētiōs facere jūssit?
3. Quandō Verbigenī ē castrīs Helvētiōrum ēgressī sunt?
4. Quō Verbigenī contendērunt?
5. Cūr fugam suam aut occultārī aut īgnōrārī posse exīstimābant?

- SCRĪBE LATĪNE:
1. When the envoys met Caesar, they threw themselves at his feet.
2. Caesar demanded the slaves who had fled to them.
3. The Verbigeni, fearing that they would be captives, left camp early in the night.

Ch. 28 Disastrous Ending of the Helvetian Migration

¹Quod ubi ²resciit, hīs ³quōrum per fīnēs ierant, imperāvit, utī conquīrerent et redūcerent, sī ⁴sibi ⁵pūrgātī esse vellent. ⁶Reductōs ⁷in hostium numerō habuit. Reliquōs omnēs (obsidibus, armīs, ⁸perfugīs trāditīs), in dēditiōnem accēpit.

Helvētiōs, Tulingōs, Latobrīgōs in fīnēs suōs unde erant profectī, ⁹revertī jūssit; et quod, omnibus frūgibus āmissīs, domī nihil erat ¹⁰quō famem tolerārent, Allobrogibus imperāvit ut eīs frūmentī cōpiam ¹¹facerent. ¹²Ipsōs oppida vīcōsque, quōs incenderant, restituere jūssit.

---

1. **Quod = Id**: the fact that 6,000 Verbigeni had tried to escape.
2. **resciit = cōgnōvit, repperit.**
3. **quōrum**: the antecedent is **hīs**, dative with **imperāvit.**
4. **sibi**: (*with reference to him*) *in his eyes;* dative of reference.
5. **pūrgātī** (used as an adjective) = **sine culpā.**
6. **Reductōs = Eōs reductōs**: *those led back.*

7. **in hostium numerō habuit**: He either massacred them all or sold them as slaves.
8. **perfugīs**: *runaway slaves.*
9. **revertī = redīre.**
10. **quō . . . tolerārent**: relative clause of purpose.
11. **facerent = darent.**
12. **Ipsōs**: Helvetians and their allies.

Id [13]eā māximē ratiōne fēcit, quod nōluit eum locum, unde Helvētiī discesserant, vacāre, nē propter [14]bonitātem agrōrum, Germānī, quī trāns Rhēnum incolunt, ē suīs fīnibus in Helvētiōrum fīnēs trānsīrent, et fīnitimī Galliae Prōvinciae Allobrogibusque essent.

Haeduī petīvērunt ut [15]Bōjōs in fīnibus suīs collocārent, quod [16]ēgregiā virtūte erant cōgnitī. Id Caesar concessit. Haeduī Bōjīs agrōs dedērunt, et eōs posteā [17]in parem condiciōnem jūris libertātisque, atque ipsī erant, recēpērunt.

FOR COMPREHENSION

● ANSWER IN ENGLISH:
1. How did Caesar capture at least some of the Verbigeni who had tried to escape?
2. Do you think his treatment of the captured runaways cruel and unnecessary?
3. What disposition did Caesar make of the Helvetians?
4. What tasks awaited the Helvetians on their return home?
5. Who actually supplied the grain to keep the Helvetians alive during the winter?
6. What was Caesar's real reason for ordering the Helvetians to rebuild their homeland?

● RESPONDĒ LATĪNE:
1. Quae Helvētiī Caesarī trādidērunt?
2. Quō Caesar Helvētiōs īre jūssit?
3. Quid Caesar Helvētiōs restituere jūssit?
4. Quid Caesar Allobrogibus ut facerent imperāvit?
5. Quid Caesar timēbat nē Germānī facerent?
6. Ubi Caesar Bōjōs collocāvit?

● SCRĪBE LATĪNE:
1. The Haedui asked Caesar that they might give land to the Boii, a people of outstanding courage.
2. He feared that the Germans, who lived across the Rhine, might seize the territories of the Helvetians.
3. Caesar persuaded the Allobroges to give the Helvetians food.

---

13. **eā ... ratiōne = eā dē causā**: explained by the following **quod**-clause.
14. **bonitātem = fertilitātem.**
15. **Bōjōs ... collocārent**: The Haedui were anxious for this addition to their strength because they were oppressed by the

Sequani. The Boii were a wandering tribe from Central Europe who had no home of their own.
16. **ēgregiā virtūte**: ablative of description.
17. **in parem ... ipsī erant**: *into a like condition ... with themselves.*

Ch. 29 Dead or Missing: 250,000

In castrīs Helvētiōrum ¹tabulae repertae sunt, litterīs Graecīs ²cōnfectae, et ad Caesarem relātae. In hīs tabulīs ³nōminātim ⁴ratiō cōnfecta erat, ⁵quī numerus eōrum domō exīsset, ⁶quī arma ferre possent, et item sēparātim quot ⁷puerī, senēs mulierēsque.

⁸Quārum omnium ⁹rērum summa erat ¹⁰capitum: Helvētiōrum mīlia CCLXIII, Tulingōrum mīlia XXXVI, Latobrīgōrum XIV, Rauracōrum XXIII, Bōjōrum XXXII. Ex hīs, quī arma ferre possent, ad mīlia XCII. Summa omnium fuērunt ad mīlia CCCLXVIII. ¹¹Eōrum quī domum rediērunt, cēnsū habitō, ut Caesar imperāverat, repertus est numerus mīlium C et X.

FOR COMPREHENSION

- ANSWER IN ENGEISH:
1. In what language were the Helvetians' records kept?
2. What alphabet did the Helvetians use?
3. What was the total number of Helvetians (including all the men, women, and children) at the beginning of the migration? How many allies did they have?
4. According to the records, what percentage of the entire body of emigrants were fighting men?
5. About what percentage of those who began the migration returned to their homes at the end of the summer?

- RESPONDĒ LATĪNE:
1. Quid in castrīs Helvētiōrum Caesar repperit?
2. Quālibus litterīs tabulae Helvētiōrum cōnfectae sunt?
3. Quālis ratiō in tabulīs cōnfecta erat?
4. Quanta erat summa omnium quī domō exiērunt?
5. Cēnsū habitō, quantus erat numerus eōrum quī domum rediērunt?

- SCRĪBE LATĪNE:
1. The sum total of the enemy who left home was 368,000; of these, 110,000 returned home. The number of fighting men was 92,000.
2. All who went forth from their territories did not return home.

---

1. **tabulae:** *lists.*
2. **cōnfectae:** *written.*
3. **nōminātim:** *item by item.*
4. **ratiō:** *an account.*
5. **quī ... exīsset:** indirect question.
6. **quī ... possent:** relative characteristic clause.
7. **puerī** = puerī et puellae.
8. **Quārum** = Hārum.
9. **rērum:** *of these items.*
10. **capitum** = Helvētiōrum. In English we use *head* for livestock, not for persons.
11. **Eōrum:** dependent upon cēnsū.

WAR WITH ARIOVISTUS, A GERMAN KING

PREVIEW: The campaign against the Helvetians came to an end early in July. There was ample time for a second campaign, and reason and justification for it were easily and soon found. A hundred thousand Germans, under the leadership of their king, Ariovistus, had crossed the Rhine and settled in Gaul at the time when Caesar was fighting to end the Helvetian migration.

Ariovistus had been summoned previously by one Gallic tribe to assist it in a dispute with a rival Gallic tribe over the collection of certain taxes. The German king came as a mercenary soldier, but he remained as a tyrant. The Gauls turned to Caesar for help. He decided to take steps to check Ariovistus. When Caesar invited Ariovistus to a conference to talk over the situation, the German king arrogantly declined.

Caesar sent three demands to the German leader: that he lead no more men across the Rhine into Gaul; that he return all hostages; that he do no further injury to the Haeduans or their allies. In reply Ariovistus bluntly advised Caesar to mind his own business; that he would do as he pleased with the Haeduans whom he had conquered in war; that no one ever fought with him and his men without getting the worst of it; that he was ready to fight whenever Caesar felt so inclined. Caesar decided that the time for action had come.

At Vesontio, however, Caesar's army panicked. His men had received exaggerated reports about the prowess and savagery of the Germans. Caesar rose to the occasion; his speech restored the morale of the troops and fired them to new determination. They advanced courageously. Two conferences requested by Ariovistus ended treacherously. Ariovistus avoided a general fight but tried to storm Caesar's smaller camp. Then Caesar attacked the German camp directly. Hard fighting ensued with heavy losses on both sides, but military alertness and the arrival of reserve forces turned the tide of battle in favor of the Romans. The Germans fled. Ariovistus barely escaped across the Rhine river in a small boat.

Ch. 30 Congratulations Are in Order

Bellō Helvētiōrum cōnfectō, tōtīus ferē Galliae lēgātī, prīncipēs cīvitātum, ad Caesarem [1]grātulātum convēnērunt. Dīxērunt:

"Intellegimus, tametsī prō veteribus Helvētiōrum [2]injūriīs [3]populī Rōmānī ab hīs poenās bellō repetierīs, tamen eam rem nōn minus [4]ex ūsū terrae Galliae quam populī Rōmānī accidisse, proptereā quod eō cōnsiliō, flōrentibus rēbus, domōs suās Hel-

---

1. **grātulātum**: the supine, expressing purpose.
2. **injūriīs**: with two genitives, **Helvētiōrum** and **populī**.
3. **populī Rōmānī**: *against the Roman people;* objective genitive.
4. **ex ūsū**: *to the advantage.*

vētiī relīquērunt, utī tōtī Galliae bellum īnferrent imperiōque potīrentur, locumque domiciliō ⁵ex māgnā cōpiā dēligerent, quem ex omnī Galliā opportūnissimum ac frūctuōsissimum jūdicāvissent, reliquāsque cīvitātēs stīpendiāriās habērent."

Petīvērunt, utī sibi concilium tōtīus Galliae in diem certam indīcere idque Caesaris voluntāte facere licēret. Dīxērunt sēsē habēre quāsdem rēs, quās ab eō petere vellent. Eā rē permissā, diem conciliō cōnstituērunt et ⁶jūre jūrandō, ⁷nē quis ēnūntiāret, ⁸nisi quibus commūnī cōnsiliō mandātum esset, inter sē sānxērunt.

FOR COMPREHENSION

• ANSWER IN ENGLISH:

1. Why did the leading men of almost all the Gallic nations come to Caesar after the completion of the Helvetian War?
2. Why had the Helvetians migrated?
3. Why did the Gallic chiefs wish to call a council of all Celtic Gauls?
4. What was their reason for wishing to keep this meeting secret?
5. To what did they bind themselves by oath?

• RESPONDĒ LATĪNE:

1. Quā dē causā prīncipēs cīvitātum ad Caesarem convēnērunt?
2. Quō cōnsiliō Helvētiī, flōrentissimīs rēbus, domōs suās relīquerant?
3. Quid ā Caesare Gallī petīvērunt?
4. Quam ob rem jūre jūrandō inter sē sānxērunt?
5. Quī diem conciliō cōnstituērunt?

• SCRĪBE LATĪNE:

1. We fear that those things which we are about to say will be announced throughout the states of Gaul.
2. They said the Helvetians wanted to have the remaining states as tributaries.

Ch. 31 A Plea for Help

Eō conciliō dīmissō, ¹īdem prīncipēs cīvitātum, quī ante fuerant, ad Caesarem revertērunt petīvēruntque, ut sibi sēcrētō, in occultō, dē suā omniumque salūte cum eō agere licēret.

---

1. īdem = eīdem, iīdem.

Eā rē impetrātā, sēsē omnēs flentēs [2]Caesarī ad pedēs prōjēcērunt et dīxērunt: "Nōn minus id contendimus et labōrāmus,
nē ea, quae dīxerīmus, ēnuntientur, quam utī ea, quae velīmus,
impetrēmus, proptereā quod, sī ēnūntiātum erit, summum in cruciātum nōs ventūrōs esse vidēmus."

Posteā prō hīs prīncipibus Dīviciācus Haeduus locūtus est:
"Galliae tōtīus factiōnēs sunt duae; hārum alterius prīncipātum
tenent Haeduī, alterius Arvernī. Hī dē potestāte inter sē multōs
annōs contendērunt. Tandem Arvernī Sēquanīque Germānōs arcessīvērunt. Hōrum prīmō circiter mīlia quīndecim Rhēnum
trānsiērunt; posteā trāductī sunt plūrēs; nunc sunt [3]in Galliā
centum et vīgintī mīlia Germānōrum.

"Cum hīs Germānīs Haeduī eōrumque clientēs semel atque
iterum armīs contendērunt; māgnam calamitātem accēpērunt et
omnem nōbilitātem, omnem senātum, omnem equitātum āmī-
sērunt.

"Sed [4]pējus victōribus Sēquanīs quam Haeduīs victīs accidit,
proptereā quod Ariovistus, rēx Germānōrum, in eōrum fīnibus
cōnsēdit tertiamque partem agrī Sēquanī occupāvit, et nunc dē
alterā parte tertiā Sēquanōs dēcēdere jubet. Ariovistus autem,
homō barbarus et īrācundus, superbē et crūdēliter imperat; nōn
possunt ējus imperia diūtius sustinērī. Tū vel auctōritāte tuā
atque exercitūs, vel recentī victōriā, vel nōmine populī Rōmānī,
dēterrēre potes, nē mājor multitūdō Germānōrum Rhēnum trādū-
cātur, Galliamque omnem ab Ariovistī injūriā potes dēfendere."

FOR COMPREHENSION

- ANSWER IN ENGLISH:
1. Who was the spokesman of the Gauls in their second conference with Caesar?
2. What two factions were there in Gaul at this time?
3. What was the cause of the contention between the two factions?
4. Who called in the Germans as mercenaries?
5. To which of the two factions did the spokesman of the Gauls belong?

- RESPONDĒ LATĪNE:
1. Quī sēsē omnēs flentēs Caesarī ad pedēs prōjēcērunt?
2. Cūr summum in cruciātum sē ventūrōs esse putābant?

---

2. **Caesarī ad pedēs:** *at Caesar's feet;*
dative of reference.
3. **in Galliā:** Alsace, where Caesar and
Ariovistus contended.

4. **pējus:** *a worse thing.*

3. Quī illō tempore prīncipātum Galliae tenēbant?
4. Quae factiō Germānōs arcessīvit?

● SCRĪBE LATĪNE:
1. If the affair is made known, they will suffer torture.
2. For many years they have contended among themselves for the leadership.
3. It came to pass that two states summoned the Germans.

Summary of Chapter 32

Caesar noticed that while Diviciacus was speaking, the Sequanians stood with heads bowed looking sadly at the ground. When he inquired the reason for their attitude, he learned that the Sequanians were in such fear of the cruelty of Ariovistus and so completely at the mercy of this German chief who had taken possession of their towns, that they did not dare complain or ask for help.

Ch. 33   Caesar Concerned About Ariovistus' Power

Hīs rēbus cōgnitīs, Caesar Gallōrum animōs verbīs cōnfirmāvit, pollicitusque est [1]sibi eam rem cūrae futūram; māgnam sē [2]habēre spem, et beneficiō suō et auctōritāte adductum, Ariovistum fīnem injūriīs factūrum. Hāc ōrātiōne habitā, concilium dīmīsit.

Et [3]secundum ea, multae rēs eum hortābantur, [4]quā rē sibi eam rem cōgitandam et suscipiendam putāret; in prīmīs quod Haeduōs, frātrēs cōnsanguineōsque [5]saepenumerō ā senātū appellātōs, in servitūte atque in diciōne vidēbat Germānōrum tenērī, eōrumque obsidēs esse apud Ariovistum ac Sēquanōs intellegēbat; quod in tantō imperiō populī Rōmānī turpissimum sibi et reī pūblicae esse arbitrābātur.

Paulātim autem [6]Germānōs cōnsuēscere Rhēnum trānsīre, et in Galliam māgnam eōrum multitūdinem venīre, populō Rōmānō perīculōsum vidēbat; neque sibi hominēs ferōs ac barbarōs temperātūrōs exīstimābat, quīn, cum omnem Galliam occupāvissent, [7]ut ante Cimbrī Teutonīque fēcissent, in Prōvinciam exīrent, atque inde in Ītaliam contenderent; praesertim cum Sēquanōs ā prōvinciā nostrā [8]Rhodanus dīvideret; quibus rēbus quam mātūr-

---

1. **sibi ... cūrae:** *that this matter (should be for a care to him) should have his attention;* **sibi:** dative of reference; **cūrae:** dative of purpose.
2. **habēre spem = spērāre.**
3. **secundum:** *(following) besides;* prep. with acc.

4. **quā rē ... putāret:** *(why he should think) to think.*
5. **saepenumerō:** *oftentimes.*
6. **Germānōs cōnsuēscere:** *for the Germans to become accustomed to.*
7. **ut:** *as.*
8. **Rhodanus:** *the Rhone.*

rimē occurrendum putābat. Ipse autem Ariovistus tantōs sibi spīritūs, tantam arrogantiam sūmpserat ut ferendus nōn vidērētur.

The Roman and German armies about to clash.

FOR COMPREHENSION

- ANSWER IN ENGLISH:
1. Why did Caesar hope to influence Ariovistus?
2. What two very good reasons did Caesar have for taking up the cause of the Gauls against the Germans?
3. What great honor had the Roman Senate conferred upon the Haeduans?
4. Why had the Haeduans been forced to give hostages both to the Germans and to the Sequanians?
5. Why did Ariovistus himself seem insufferable to Caesar?

- RESPONDĒ LATĪNE:
1. Quid Caesar Gallīs pollicitus est?
2. Quā dē causā sibi eam rem cōgitandam (esse) putābat?
3. Sī Germānī cōnsuēscerent Rhēnum trānsīre, cui populō perīculōsī essent?
4. Quō antīquīs temporibus Cimbrī Teutonīque contenderant?
5. Quod flūmen Sēquanōs ā Prōvinciā Rōmānā dīvīsit?

- SCRĪBE LATĪNE:
1. "It will be my concern," he said, "to defend you."
2. Little by little a large number of Germans were coming into Gaul.
3. When they had seized all Gaul, they would go into the Province and then would hasten into Italy.

Ch. 34 Ariovistus Rebuffs Caesar

Quam ob rem Caesar ad Ariovistum lēgātōs mittere cōnstituit, quī ab eō postulārent, ut aliquem locum [1]medium utrīusque colloquiō dēligeret. Dīxit sēsē velle dē rē pūblicā et [2]summīs utrīusque rēbus cum eō [3]agere.

Eī lēgātiōnī Ariovistus respondit:

[4]"Sī quid mihi ā Caesare opus esset, ad eum vēnissem. Sī quid ille mē vult, illum ad mē venīre oportet. Praetereā, neque sine exercitū in eās partēs Galliae, quās Caesar possidet, venīre audeō, neque exercitum sine māgnō commeātū atque mōlīmentō [5]in ūnum locum contrahere possum.

"Mihi autem mīrum vidētur, [6]quid [7]in meā Galliā, quam bellō vīcī, aut [8]Caesarī aut omnīnō populō Rōmānō [9]negōtī sit."

FOR COMPREHENSION

- ANSWER IN ENGLISH:
1. Was Caesar's suggestion that the leaders meet halfway between the two camps a just one?
2. What were the reasons given by Ariovistus for refusing to meet Caesar?
3. Was it necessary for Ariovistus to bring his army with him?
4. Why did Ariovistus object to bringing his army together in one place?
5. On what grounds did Ariovistus use the expression "my" Gaul?

- RESPONDĒ LATĪNE:
1. Quam ob rem Caesar ad Ariovistum lēgātōs mīsit?
2. Quō modo eī lēgātiōnī Ariovistus respondit?
3. Quibus dē causīs Caesar cum Ariovistō agere volēbat?
4. In quās partēs Galliae Ariovistus venīre nōn audēbat?
5. Quid Ariovistō mīrum vidēbātur?

- SCRĪBE LATĪNE:
1. I do not know what business either Caesar or the Roman people have in my (part of) Gaul.
2. If Caesar wishes anything from me, let him come to me.
3. I cannot bring together an army without great trouble.

---

1. **medium utrīusque:** (*midway of each*) *midway between the two.*
2. **summīs utrīusque rēbus:** *affairs of the utmost importance to both.*
3. **agere:** *to discuss.*
4. **Sī . . . esset:** *If I had needed anything from Caesar.*
5. **in ūnum locum contrahere:** Ariovistus' army seems to have been scattered in various parts of the Sequanian territory which he had occupied.
6. **quid . . . Caesarī . . . negōtī sit:** *what business Caesar has.*
7. **in meā Galliā:** *in my (part of) Gaul.*
8. **Caesarī . . . populō Rōmānō:** dative of possession.
9. **negōtī:** genitive of the whole with **quid.**

240

Ch. 35 Caesar Sends His Ultimatum to Ariovistus

Hīs respōnsīs ad Caesarem relātīs, iterum ad eum Caesar lēgātōs cum ¹hīs mandātīs mittit:

"Quoniam, ²tantō meō populīque Rōmānī beneficiō affectus, cum in ³cōnsulātū meō rēx atque amīcus ā senātū appellātus est, (Ariovistus) hanc mihi populōque Rōmānō grātiam refert, ut, in colloquium venīre invītātus, gravētur, neque dē ⁴commūnī rē dīcendum sibi et cōgnōscendum putet, haec sunt, quae ab eō postulō.

"Prīmum, (postulō) nē (Ariovistus) quam multitūdinem hominum amplius trāns Rhēnum in Galliam trādūcat.

"Deinde, obsidēs, quōs habet ab Haeduīs, reddat, Sēquanīsque permittat, ut (obsidēs), quōs hī habent, voluntāte ējus reddere illīs liceat; nēve Haeduōs injūriā lacessat, nēve hīs sociīsque eōrum bellum īnferat.

"Sī id ita fēcerit, mihi populōque Rōmānō perpetua grātia atque amīcitia cum eō erit. Sī nōn impetrābō, quoniam, M. Messālā, M. Pīsōne cōnsulibus, senātus cēnsuit, utī, quīcumque Galliam prōvinciam obtinēret, ⁵quod ⁶commodō reī pūblicae facere posset, Haeduōs cēterōsque amīcōs populī Rōmānī dēfenderet, Haeduōrum injūriās nōn neglegam."

FOR COMPREHENSION

- ANSWER IN ENGLISH:
1. Of what act of kindness does Caesar remind Ariovistus?
2. How does Ariovistus now repay this kindness?
3. What five demands did Caesar make in his ultimatum to Ariovistus?
4. What will be Ariovistus' reward if he complies with Caesar's demands?
5. What veiled threat does Caesar make to Ariovistus?

- RESPONDĒ LATĪNE:
1. Ā quibus Ariovistus in cōnsulātū Caesaris rēx et amīcus appellātus est?
2. Quō modo Ariovistus Caesarī populōque Rōmānō grātiam refert?
3. Quid Ariovistus, in colloquium venīre invītātus, fēcit?
4. Quī obsidēs Ariovistō reddendī sunt?
5. Cūr Haeduī Caesarī dēfendendī sunt?

---

1. **hīs mandātīs:** *these instructions* (i.e., this message to the envoys, which was to be presented orally).
2. **tantō . . . affectus:** *although treated with so great kindness by myself and the Roman people.*
3. **cōnsulātū meō:** in the previous year, 59 B.C.
4. **commūnī rē:** *a matter of mutual interest.*
5. **quod:** *so far as.*
6. **commodō reī pūblicae:** *consistently with the public interest.*

1. This reply having been reported to Caesar, he decided to send envoys again.
2. The German king hesitates to come to a conference.
3. He ought to be willing to speak about matters of common interest.

Ch. 36   German Defiance

Ad haec Ariovistus respondit: "Jūs est bellī ut victōrēs victīs ¹quem ad modum ²velint imperent. Item populus Rōmānus victīs nōn ³ad alterius praescrīptum, sed ad suum arbitrium imperāre cōnsuēvit. Sī ego populō Rōmānō nōn praescrībō quem ad modum suō jūre ūtātur, nōn oportet mē ā populō Rōmānō in meō jūre impedīrī. Haeduī mihi, quoniam bellī fortūnam temptāvērunt et armīs congressī ac superātī sunt, ⁴stīpendiāriī factī sunt.

"Māgnam Caesar injūriam facit, ⁵quī suō adventū vectīgālia mihi minōra faciat. Haeduīs obsidēs nōn reddam. Neque hīs neque eōrum sociīs ⁶injūriā bellum īnferam, ⁷sī in eō manēbunt quod convenit stīpendiumque quotannīs pendent. Sī id nōn fēcerint, ⁸longē eīs ⁹frāternum nōmen populī Rōmānī aberit.

¹⁰"Quod mihi Caesar dēnūntiat sē Haeduōrum injūriās nōn neglectūrum, nēmō mēcum sine suā ¹¹perniciē contendit. Cum volet, ¹²congrediātur! Intelleget quid invictī Germānī, exercitātissimī in armīs, quī inter annōs quattuordecim ¹³tēctum nōn subiērunt, virtūte ¹⁴possint."

FOR COMPREHENSION

● ANSWER IN ENGLISH:
1. What did Ariovistus mean by "the right of war"?
2. How have the Haeduans become tributaries to Ariovistus?
3. When had the Haeduans ceased to pay the tribute demanded by Ariovistus?
4. Under what conditions does Ariovistus say that he will refrain from war against the Haeduans?
5. How did Ariovistus answer Caesar's threat that he would not overlook the wrongs of the Haeduans?

---

1. **quem ad modum:** *as.*
2. **velint:** subjunctive by attraction.
3. **ad:** *according to.*
4. **stīpendiāriī:** *tributary.*
5. **quī:** *since*
6. **injūriā:** *unjustly.*
7. **sī . . . manēbunt:** *if they will abide by that.*
8. **longē:** *far away* (of no use to them).

9. **frāternum = frātrum:** *the title of brothers.*
10. **Quod:** *As to the fact that.*
11. **perniciē:** *destruction.*
12. **congrediātur:** *let him come on;* volitive subjunctive.
13. **tēctum:** not under a roof, i.e., constantly at war.
14. **possint:** *can (do).*

● RESPONDĒ LATĪNE:
1. Quem ad modum Ariovistus dīcit populum Rōmānum victīs imperāre cōnsuēscere?
2. Quā dē causā Haeduī stīpendiāriī factī sunt?
3. Cui Caesar māgnam injūriam suō adventū fēcerat?
4. Quis dīxit: "Nēmō mēcum sine suā perniciē contendit"?
5. Inter quot annōs Germānī tēctum nōn subierant?

● SCRĪBE LATĪNE:
1. The conquerors rule the conquered as they wish.
2. Ariovistus said that he would not return the hostages.
3. Ariovistus will not make war on the Haeduans if they pay the yearly tribute.

Summary of Chapter 37

Meanwhile, more complaints came in against the Germans. The Haeduans said that the Harudes were ravaging their land; and the Treveri reported that another German tribe, the Suebi, had encamped on the east bank of the Rhine and were ready to cross into Gaul. Caesar decided to act at once. Arranging for a supply of grain, he set out immediately toward Ariovistus.

Ch. 38   Race for the Stronghold of Vesontio

[1]Cum triduī viam prōcessisset, Caesarī nūntiātum est Ariovistum cum suīs omnibus cōpiīs [2]ad occupandum [3]Vesontiōnem, [4]quod est oppidum māximum Sēquanōrum, contendere, triduīque viam ā suīs fīnibus prōcessisse. Hūc Caesar māgnīs nocturnīs diurnīsque itineribus contendit et, occupātō oppidō, ibi praesidium collocat.

Summary of Remainder of Chapter 38

Caesar thought that he should be especially on guard to prevent the occupation of Vesontio by Ariovistus, especially because there was in that town a very large supply of war materials. It was the most important stronghold of the Sequani, and it was so protected by the nature of the terrain that it presented a fine opportunity for a military operation. The river Dubis encircled almost the whole town. Where the river stopped there was a mountain of great height. The base of the mountain reached the bank of the river on either side. An encompassing wall turned this mountain into a fortress and connected it with the town.

---

1. **Cum . . . prōcessisset: cum**-circumstantial clause.
2. **ad occupandum Vesontiōnem: ad** with the gerundive expressing purpose.
3. **Vesontiōnem:** irregularly masculine;

Besancon, one of the strongest natural fortresses in France.
4. **quod:** neuter, attracted to the gender of the predicate noun **oppidum.**

FOR COMPREHENSION

- ANSWER IN ENGLISH:

1. What important news was brought to Caesar about Ariovistus?
2. Why was Vesontio (Besançon) such a good stronghold?
3. Why did Caesar think it important to take possession of Vesontio?
4. Why was it easier in Caesar's day to defend a town so fortified than it would be in modern times?

- RESPONDĒ LATĪNE:

1. Quō Ariovistus contendēbat?
2. Quam longē prōcesserat?
3. Quō modo Vesontiō oppidum ā nātūrā mūniēbatur?
4. Quid flūmen Dūbis paene cingēbat?
5. Quid Caesar, occupātō oppidō, ibi collocāvit?

- SCRĪBE LATĪNE:

1. Both Caesar and Ariovistus were desirous of seizing the largest town of the Sequani.
2. Ariovistus had already advanced a three days' journey from his own borders.
3. This town was so fortified by the river and the mountain that it could be easily defended.

Summary of Chapter 39

While Caesar delayed at Vesontio for a few days, the Roman army became demoralized as a result of the wild tales about the huge size, incredible bravery, and unusual military skill of the Germans. These rumors were spread by some of the Roman soldiers, the Gauls, and the merchants.

They said that often when they met the Germans they could not endure looking at them, such was the sight of their faces and glaring eyes. Suddenly such terror took possession of the entire army that it upset in an extraordinary degree the minds and spirits of all.

The military tribunes and cavalry officers were the first to panic. They were for the most part mere adventurers belonging to aristocratic families at Rome. Most of them had received their commissions through personal friendship or for political reasons, and therefore had little experience in military practice. Hidden in their tents, they either complained about their fate or bewailed the common danger. Generally, throughout the camp, wills were being signed and sealed.

Because of their talk and fear, gradually even those who had much experience in military life, the soldiers and the centurions, were becoming alarmed. They did not wish to be considered cowards, but they feared the narrow passes and the vast forests that lay between them and Ariovistus, also that a sufficient supply of grain could not be furnished. Some even reported to Caesar that when he ordered the soldiers to break camp and advance, they would not obey the word of command nor take up the standards.

Ch. 40 Magic with Words

Haec [1]cum animadvertisset, convocātō cōnsiliō, [2]omniumque
ōrdinum ad id cōnsilium adhibitīs centuriōnibus, vehementer eōs
incūsāvit: prīmum, [3]quod aut quam in partem aut quō [4]cōnsiliō
dūcerentur, [5]sibi quaerendum aut cōgitandum putārent.

Caesar addresses his centurions.

Calling an assembly of officers, Caesar delivered a masterful speech and
forestalled the threatening mutiny. Their fathers under Gaius Marius had defeated the Cimbri and Teutons. Their sons would not be less worthy. These
same Germans had been defeated repeatedly by the Helvetians, yet the Helvetians were not a match for the Roman army. What did they fear?

"Itaque, quod in [6]longiōrem diem [7]collātūrus fuī, repraesentābō;
et hāc nocte dē quārtā vigiliā castra movēbō, ut quam prīmum
intellegere possim, utrum apud mīlitēs pudor atque officium, an
timor, [8]plūs valeat. Quod sī praetereā nēmō sequētur, tamen ego
cum sōlā decimā legiōne ībō, dē quā nōn dubitō, mihique ea
[9]praetōria cohors erit."

Huic legiōnī Caesar et [10]indulserat praecipuē et propter virtūtem cōnfīdēbat māximē.

---

1. **cum animadvertisset: cum**-circum-
   stantial.
2. **omniumque ōrdinum ... centuriōnibus:** The centurions, of whom there
   were sixty in each legion, were of different
   rank. Ordinarily only those of the first
   class were invited to a council of war.
3. **quod ... putārent:** the reason in the
   mind of Caesar the general, not of
   Caesar the writer.

4. **cōnsiliō:** ablative of cause.
5. **sibi quaerendum (esse):** passive periphrastic.
6. **longiōrem:** *more distant.*
7. **collātūrus fuī:** *I was about to put off.*
8. **plūs valeat:** *has the stronger influence;*
   indirect question.
9. **praetōria cohors:** *bodyguard.*
10. **indulserat:** *had favored.*

245

FOR COMPREHENSION

- ANSWER IN ENGLISH:
1. What did Caesar do when he observed the evidences of panic?
2. To what historical event did Caesar refer in the council to prove that the Romans were not inferior to the Germans?
3. Why would Caesar's statement that these same Germans had been repeatedly defeated by the Helvetians tend to restore confidence?
4. What effect did Caesar's selection of the Tenth Legion as a bodyguard have on the others?
5. In your opinion was Caesar's method of preventing a mutiny in his army more effective than if he had resorted to army disciplinary methods?

- RESPONDĒ LATĪNE:
1. Quōs Caesar vehementer incūsāvit?
2. Quī memoriā patrum eōrum Cimbrōs et Teutōnēs superāverant?
3. Quī eōsdem Germānōs saepe repulserant?
4. Quī Rōmānō exercituī parēs esse nōn poterant?
5. Quā dē causā hāc nocte Caesar castra movēbit?

- SCRĪBE LATĪNE:
1. Caesar said that Ariovistus had conquered the Gauls more by cunning than by valor.
2. He knew in what direction and for what purpose he was leading his army.
3. If no one will follow him, he will set out with the Tenth Legion alone.

Summary of Chapters 41–43

Caesar's eloquence transformed the spirits of his soldiers and their officers. The Tenth Legion thanked Caesar and said they were very ready to take the field. The other legions expressed a similar willingness to follow their general. Morale having been restored to his army, Caesar left a detachment to guard Vesontio. Marching without interruption for seven days, he arrived at a point in the Rhine valley east of the Vosges where his scouts informed him that Ariovistus was encamped with his troops twenty-four miles to the north.

Ariovistus sent word that he would now agree to a conference, but he insisted that both sides come to the interview with an escort of cavalry only. Caesar saw through the pretense and resorted to a clever ruse himself. He knew that the German cavalry was superior to the Gallic cavalry attached to his own army. He had the Gauls dismount, and to their horses he assigned regular soldiers of the Tenth Legion. Thus he was sure of a safe escort.

At the meeting Caesar briefly reviewed the terms of his ultimatum. He ordered Ariovistus to bring no more Germans across the Rhine, to return the Gallic hostages, and to stop plundering the Haeduans.

Ariovistus ad [1]postulāta Caesaris pauca respondit; dē suīs virtūtibus multa praedicāvit:

"Trānsiī Rhēnum nōn meā sponte, sed rogātus et arcessītus ā Gallīs. Nōn sine māgnā spē māgnīsque praemiīs domum propinquōsque relīquī. Sēdēs habeō in Galliā ab [2]ipsīs concessās, [3]obsidēs ipsōrum voluntāte datōs. Stīpendium capiō [4]jūre bellī, quod victōrēs [5]victīs impōnere cōnsuēvērunt.

"Nōn [6]ego Gallīs, sed Gallī mihi bellum intulērunt. Omnēs Galliae cīvitātēs ad mē oppūgnandum vēnērunt ac contrā mē castra [7]habuērunt. Eae omnēs cōpiae ā mē ūnō [8]proeliō pulsae ac superātae sunt. Sī (Gallī) iterum experīrī volunt, iterum parātus sum dēcertāre. Sī pāce ūtī volunt, inīquum est dē stīpendiō [9]recūsāre, quod suā voluntāte adhūc pependērunt.

"Ego [10]prius in Galliam vēnī quam populus Rōmānus. Numquam ante hoc tempus exercitus populī Rōmānī Galliae prōvinciae fīnibus ēgressus est. [11]Quid tibi vīs? Cūr in meās possessiōnēs venīs? Prōvincia mea est [12]haec Gallia, sicut illa (Gallia) [13]vestra (prōvincia est). [14]Ut mihi concēdī nōn oporteat, sī in vestrōs fīnēs impetum faciam, sīc item vōs estis inīquī, quod mē in meō jūre interpellātis.

"Nisi dēcēdēs atque exercitum dēdūcēs ex hīs regiōnibus, tē nōn prō amīcō, sed prō hoste habēbō. Quod sī tē interfēcerō, multīs nōbilibus prīncipibusque populī Rōmānī grātum faciam (id ab ipsīs per eōrum nūntiōs comperī) quōrum omnium grātiam atque amīcitiam [15]tuā morte emere poterō.

"Quod sī discesseris et [16]līberam possessiōnem [17]Galliae mihi trādideris, māgnō tē praemiō [18]remūnerābor, et quaecumque bella gerī volēs, sine ūllō [19]tuō labōre et perīculō cōnficiam."

---

1. **postulāta:** *demands.*
2. **ipsīs:** the Gauls.
3. **obsidēs** = et obsidēs.
4. **jūre:** *in accordance with the rights.*
5. **victīs:** *the vanquished.*
6. **ego:** subject of **intulī** from **intulērunt.**
7. **habuērunt:** *set up.*
8. **proeliō:** ablative of means; translate with *in.*
9. **recūsāre:** subjective infinitive.
10. **prius . . . quam:** *before.*
11. **Quid tibi vīs?:** *What do you mean?*
12. **haec:** *this part of.*
13. **vestra:** refers to the Romans.

14. **Ut . . . oporteat:** *As no concession ought to be made to me.*
15. **tuā morte:** Caesar's death. It is not impossible that Ariovistus had been in communication with Caesar's enemies. Caesar may have included this passage as a warning to those at Rome that he knew of their designs on his life.
16. **līberam:** *without interference.*
17. **Galliae:** Celtic Gaul.
18. **remūnerābor:** Ariovistus' bribe.
19. **tuō:** *on your part.* Ariovistus will fight Caesar's battles for him, if he will withdraw.

FOR COMPREHENSION

- ANSWER IN ENGLISH:
1. What reason did Ariovistus give for having crossed the Rhine?
2. Why were the Gauls obliged to pay tribute to Ariovistus?
3. How did Ariovistus justify bringing Germans into Gaul?
4. What ultimatum did Ariovistus lay down to Caesar?
5. What bribe did Ariovistus offer Caesar?

- RESPONDĒ LATĪNE:
1. Cūr Ariovistus Rhēnum trānsierat?
2. Quōrum auctōritāte sēdēs in Galliā habēbat?
3. Quae cīvitātēs ad Ariovistum oppūgnandum vēnerant?
4. Quī populus prīmus in Galliam vēnit? Germānī aut Rōmānī?
5. Cūr Ariovistus Caesarī praemium dabit?

- SCRĪBE LATĪNE:
1. Unless you depart with your army from Gaul, I shall not consider you a friend.
2. If I should kill you, I would be able to buy by your death the favor and friendship of many.
3. If you had departed and handed over the free possession of Gaul to me, I would have repaid you with a very large reward.

Ch. 45   Caesar Refuses to Make Any Concessions

Multa ā Caesare [1]in eam sententiam dicta sunt, quārē negōtiō dēsistere nōn posset:

"Neque mea neque populī Rōmānī cōnsuētūdō patitur, [2]ut optimē meritōs sociōs dēseram; [3]neque jūdicō, Galliam potius [4]esse tuam quam populī Rōmānī. Bellō superātī sunt [5]Arvernī et Rutēnī ā Quīntō Fabiō Māximō, [6]quibus populus Rōmānus [7]īgnōvit; neque (eōs) in prōvinciam redēgit, neque (eīs) stīpendium imposuit.

"Quod sī [8]antīquissimum quodque tempus spectārī oportet, populī Rōmānī jūstissimum est in Galliā imperium. Sī jūdicium senātūs [9]observārī oportet, lībera dēbet esse Gallia, quam, bellō [10]victam, [11]suīs lēgibus ūtī voluit."

---

1. **in eam sententiam:** (to this purport) to show; explained by **quārē . . . posset.**
2. **ut . . . dēseram:** to desert.
3. **neque:** and not.
4. **esse tuam:** to be yours.
5. **Arvernī et Rutēnī:** conquered in 121 B.C., at the same time as the Allobroges.
6. **quibus:** dative with **īgnōvit.**
7. **īgnōvit:** These people were too distant from Rome to be effectively controlled; hence the Romans had with good reason pardoned them.
8. **antīquissimum quodque tempus:** (each earliest time) priority of time.
9. **observārī:** to be regarded.
10. **victam:** although it had been conquered
11. **suīs:** its own, referring to Gaul.

248

Bronze sculpture of Hercules and Antaeus.

Terra-cotta vase, circa 560 B.C. This shows Hercules and the Nemean lion.

B-2

Terra-cotta. Hercules sails to the
Garden of the Hesperides
in a pot coracle.

Terra-cotta. Hercules,
Hermes, and Cerberus.

Bronze chimaera.

Attic amphora. This detail shows Odysseus (Ulysses) and the Sirens.

Odysseus escaping under the ram.

Roman relief, first century B.C. The relief shows the construction of the ship *Argo*, under the supervision of Athena.

Proto-Attic amphora, circa 660 B.C. This detail shows the blinding of Polyphemus by Odysseus and his men.

Achilles and Ajax playing dice.

Terra-cotta vase, early fifth century B.C. Achilles is dragging Hector's body past the tomb of Patroclus.

Ajax and Hector in combat.

Hercules killing Nessos.

B-8

FOR COMPREHENSION

- ANSWER IN ENGLISH:
1. What was Caesar's purpose in replying at length to Ariovistus' ultimatum?
2. What reason did Caesar give in refuting the claim that Gaul belonged to Ariovistus rather than to the Roman people?
3. How had the Romans treated the Arverni and the Ruteni when they had been conquered in war by Quintus Fabius Maxim   ?
4. Why was the supremacy of the Roman people in Gaul most just, according to Caesar?
5. What had the Roman Senate decreed after Gaul had been conquered in war?

- RESPONDĒ LATĪNE:
1. Cūr Caesar Ariovistō multa eō tempore dīxit?
2. Ā quō Arvernī et Rutēnī superātī erant?
3. Quibus populus Rōmānus īgnōverat?
4. Quam ob rem populī Rōmānī jūstissimum in Galliā imperium erat?
5. Quā dē causā Gallī ā Rōmānīs victī suīs lēgibus ūtī poterant?

- SCRĪBE LATĪNE:
1. Caesar said that the Roman people had not reduced these states into a Roman province.
2. If the people used their own laws, they could be free.
3. Caesar could not abandon their most worthy allies.

Summary of Chapters 46–51

While Caesar was still speaking, the interview was interrupted by an attack made by Ariovistus' horsemen on Caesar's mounted escort. Caesar ordered his men not to return the attack; for he did not wish to give the enemy grounds for saying that he had taken advantage of their good faith.

Two days later Ariovistus asked for a renewal of the interview. Seeing no need for a second personal conference, Caesar sent to represent him two provincials, Valerius Procillus and Marcus Mettius. Both men, Caesar thought, could give no occasion of offense. Nevertheless, the moment Ariovistus caught sight of them in his camp, he shouted: "What are you coming here for? to spy?" Before they could answer, he had them seized and thrown into chains.

On the same day Ariovistus attempted to cut Caesar off from his base of supplies. He moved his camp to the foot of a hill six miles from Caesar's camp. On the next day he led his troops past Caesar's camp. For five consecutive days Caesar led out his troops and kept his line in front of his camp in order to give the Germans a chance to fight. Ariovistus kept his army in camp but fought daily cavalry battles.

In order to reopen the road, Caesar selected a site for a smaller camp about two miles from his main camp. He left two legions there and returned to the larger camp. On the following day he drew up his troops according to his usual practice, but still Ariovistus would not fight. Then he learned that the German women had prophesied that the Germans could not win if they should fight before the new moon.

On the next day Caesar drew up a triple line of battle and advanced right up to the German camp. Thus challenged, Ariovistus led forth his troops and arranged them in battle line by tribes.

Ch. 52   A Desperate Encounter

Caesar [1]singulīs legiōnibus singulōs lēgātōs et [2]quaestōrem praefēcit, utī eōs [3]testēs suae [4]quisque virtūtis habēret. Ipse [5]ā dextrō cornū, quod [6]eam partem [7]minimē fīrmam hostium esse animadverterat, proelium commīsit.

[8]Ita nostrī ācriter in hostēs, sīgnō datō, impetum fēcērunt, [9]itaque hostēs repente celeriterque prōcurrērunt, ut [10]spatium [11]pīla in hostēs conjiciendī nōn darētur. [12]Rejectīs pīlīs, [13]comminus gladiīs pūgnātum est.

At Germānī, celeriter [14]ex cōnsuētūdine suā phalange factā, impetūs gladiōrum excēpērunt. Repertī sunt complūrēs nostrī, [15]quī in phalangem īnsilīrent et scūta manibus revellerent et dēsuper vulnerārent.

Cum hostium aciēs ā sinistrō cornū pulsa atque in fugam conjecta esset, ā dextrō cornū vehementer multitūdine suōrum nostram aciem premēbant. Id [16]cum animadvertisset [17]Pūblius Crassus adulēscēns, quī equitātuī praeerat, quod [18]expedītior erat quam eī, quī inter aciem versābantur, tertiam aciem [19]labōrantibus nostrīs subsidiō mīsit.

---

1. **singulīs:** Caesar had six legions. Apparently over each of the five legions he placed a lieutenant, and over the sixth a **quaestor.**
2. **quaestōrem:** The **quaestor** was primarily charged with the provisions and pay of the army, but occasionally he was given military command, as here.
3. **testēs:** *as witnesses;* in apposition to **eōs.**
4. **quisque:** subject of **habēret.**
5. **ā dextrō cornū:** *on the right wing.*
6. **eam partem . . . hostium:** the German left wing.
7. **minimē fīrmam:** *the weakest.*
8. **Ita:** modifies **ācriter.**
9. **itaque** = **et ita.**
10. **spatium** = **tempus.**
11. **pīla:** object of **conjiciendī.**

12. **Rejectīs** = **Abjectīs.**
13. **comminus** = **com- + manus:** *(hand to hand) at close quarters.*
14. **ex:** *according to.*
15. **quī . . . īnsilīrent,** etc.: relative characteristic clause.
16. **cum animadvertisset: cum**-circumstantial.
17. **Pūblius Crassus adulēscēns:** the younger son of Marcus Crassus, the triumvir.
18. **expedītior:** *more free;* so that he had an opportunity to look about and see where help was more needed. The cavalry which Crassus commanded was not fighting.
19. **labōrantibus nostrīs subsidiō:** *as an aid to our men who were hard pressed;* double dative.

FOR COMPREHENSION

- ANSWER IN ENGLISH:
1. How many lieutenants did Caesar have at this time?
2. What purpose did Caesar have in placing a lieutenant-commander in charge of each legion for the duration of the battle?
3. Where did Caesar take his position? Why there?
4. What did some of the Roman soldiers do when confronted with the German phalanx?
5. What act of Crassus probably saved the Roman left wing?
6. Why did the Romans usually hold the third line in reserve?

- RESPONDĒ LATĪNE:
1. Quōs Caesar singulīs legiōnibus praefēcit?
2. Unde Caesar ipse proelium commīsit?
3. Cūr spatium pīla in hostēs conjiciendī nōn dabātur?
4. Quī in phalangem īnsiluērunt et scūta manibus Germānōrum revulsērunt?
5. Quō cōnsiliō Pūblius Crassus tertiam aciem mīsit?

- SCRĪBE LATĪNE:
1. When the signal was given, the Romans ran forward so quickly that they could not hurl the javelins against the enemy.
2. Although the enemy's line on the left wing was quickly put to flight, they vigorously attacked our line on the right wing.
3. When Publius Crassus noticed this, he quickly sent the cavalry to help those who were in distress.

Ch. 53 Caesar Victorious; Ariovistus Escapes

Ita proelium restitūtum est, atque omnēs hostēs terga vertērunt neque [1]prius fugere dēstitērunt, quam ad flūmen Rhēnum, mīlia passuum ex eō locō circiter quīndecim, pervēnērunt. Ibi perpaucī aut, vīribus cōnfīsī, trānāre contendērunt aut, lintribus inventīs, sibi salūtem repperērunt. In hīs fuit Ariovistus, quī, nāviculam dēligātam ad rīpam nactus, [2]eā profūgit; reliquōs omnēs cōnsecūtī equitēs nostrī interfēcērunt.

[3]Duae fuērunt Ariovistī uxōrēs, ūna Suēba [4]nātiōne, quam domō sēcum dūxerat, altera Nōrica, rēgis Vocciōnis soror, quam in Galliā dūxerat, ā frātre missam; utraque in eā fugā periit. Duae fīliae fuērunt; hārum altera occīsa, altera capta est.

---

1. **prius . . . quam:** *until.*
2. **eā:** (*by this*) *in it;* ablative of means; refers to **nāviculum.**

3. **Duae . . . uxōrēs:** Tacitus says that the German nobility practised polygamy.
4. **nātiōne:** *by birth;* ablative of respect.

C. Valerius Procillus, ⁵cum ā cūstōdibus in fugā, trīnīs catēnīs vīnctus, traherētur, ⁶in ipsum Caesarem, ⁷hostēs equitātū īnsequentem incidit. ⁸Quae quidem rēs Caesarī nōn minōrem quam ipsa victōria voluptātem attulit, quod hominem honestissimum prōvinciae Galliae, suum familiārem et hospitem, ēreptum ē manibus hostium, ⁹sibi restitūtum vidēbat, ¹⁰neque ¹¹ējus calamitāte dē tantā voluptāte et grātulātiōne ¹²quidquam fortūna dēminuerat. Hic, ¹³sē praesente, dē sē ¹⁴ter sortibus cōnsultum dīcēbat, utrum ignī statim necārētur an in aliud tempus reservārētur; sortium beneficiō sē esse incolumem. Item M. Mettius repertus et ¹⁵ad eum reductus est.

FOR COMPREHENSION

- ANSWER IN ENGLISH:
1. What caused the tide of battle to turn in favor of the Romans?
2. Is there reason to believe that there were heavy losses on both sides? Why?
3. What happened to Ariovistus? his wives? his daughters?
4. In what way did some of the Germans escape across the Rhine?
5. What became of Caesar's messengers whom Ariovistus held as prisoners?
6. To what extent do you think the victory of the Romans was due to Caesar's good generalship?

- RESPONDĒ LATĪNE:
1. Cum Crassus tertiam aciem Rōmānīs subsidiō mīsisset, quid hostēs fēcērunt?
2. Quam longē ex eō locō erat flūmen Rhēnus?
3. Quid accidit uxōribus et fīliābus Ariovistī?
4. Quō modō Ariovistus profūgit?
5. Quibus temporibus Procillus in ipsum Caesarem incidit?

- SCRĪBE LATĪNE:
1. The enemy did not cease to flee until they reached the river about fifteen miles from the place of battle.
2. Procillus said that the lots had been consulted three times in his own presence.
3. Very few tried to swim across the river; some escaped by boats which had been found; a large number were killed by the Romans.

---

5. **cum . . . traherētur:** cum-circumstantial.
6. **in:** with **Caesarem incidit,** *fell in with Caesar himself.*
7. **hostēs:** object of **īnsequentem.**
8. **Quae . . . rēs** = Et ea rēs: *and this circumstance;* explained by **quod . . . vidēbat, neque . . . dēminuerat.**
9. **sibi:** to Caesar.

10. **neque** = et . . . nōn.
11. **ējus calamitāte:** *(by his misfortune) by misfortune* (to Procillus).
12. **quidquam:** *in the least degree.*
13. **sē praesente:** *in his presence;* ablative absolute.
14. **ter sortibus cōnsultum:** *three times the lots were consulted.*
15. **ad eum:** to Caesar.

Ch. 54 Caesar Goes to North Italy

Hōc proeliō trāns Rhēnum nūntiātō, [1]Suēbī, quī ad rīpās Rhēnī vēnerant, domum revertī coepērunt. [2]Eōs ubi, [3]quī [4]proximī Rhēnum incolunt, perterritōs esse sēnsērunt, īnsecūtī māgnum ex eīs numerum occīdērunt.

Caesar, ūnā aestāte duōbus māximīs bellīs cōnfectīs, mātūrius paulō, quam [5]tempus annī postulābat, in hīberna in Sēquanōs exercitum dēdūxit. Hībernīs Labiēnum praeposuit. Ipse in citeriōrem Galliam [6]ad conventūs agendōs profectus est.

FOR COMPREHENSION

- ANSWER IN ENGLISH:
1. What had the Suebi apparently planned to do if Ariovistus should defeat Caesar?
2. What German tribe was an enemy of the Suebi?
3. Where did Caesar establish his winter quarters?
4. Who was left in command of the winter camp?
5. What civil duties did Caesar now take up?

- RESPONDĒ LATĪNE:
1. Quō Suēbī vēnerant? Hōc proeliō nūntiātō, quid fēcērunt?
2. Quae gēns Germāna proxima Rhēnum incolēbat?
3. Quot bella ūnā aestāte Caesar cōnfēcerat?
4. Quō exercitus in hīberna dēductus est?
5. Quibus Caesar Labiēnum praeposuit?
6. Quō Caesar ipse profectus est?

- SCRĪBE LATĪNE:
1. When this battle was reported across the Rhine, the Suebi began to return home.
2. Caesar finished two great wars in one summer; then he led his army into winter quarters. Labienus was placed in charge of the winter quarters.

---

1. **Suēbī:** a most warlike German tribe which was already encamped on the east bank of the Rhine.
2. **Eōs = Suēbōs:** subject of **perterritōs esse.**
3. **quī = eī quī:** the Ubii.
4. **proximī Rhēnum:** *next to the Rhine.*

Proximus is sometimes followed by the accusative of a place name.
5. **tempus annī:** The battle was fought about September 14.
6. **ad conventūs agendōs:** *to hold the courts.* A governor of a province was supreme judge in the provincial courts.

BOOK TWO

(Sight translation)

DEFEAT OF THE BELGIAN LEAGUE

PREVIEW: Caesar's success in defeating Ariovistus and driving the Germans back over the Rhine led to his establishing theoretically a protectorate over central Gaul. He kept his army throughout the winter at Vesontio in the territory of the Sequanians. This action was deeply resented by the Gauls. It was the first time a Roman army had wintered outside the Province.

The Belgian tribes lived along the English Channel and the North Sea in the territory that is now Belgium and Holland. They were particularly disturbed and feared they would be attacked next. They therefore formed a defensive league to resist the Romans. In this act of the Belgians, Caesar saw justification for waging an offensive war against tribes still nominally at peace with the Romans and an answer to the criticisms of his enemies at Rome, who were already questioning his motives.

Caesar added two new legions to his army, and early in the summer of 57 B.C. he proceeded to northern Gaul. He defeated and made friends with the Remi,

Roman cavalrymen.

who agreed to help him. Following the battle of Axona (Aisne) and the breakup of the Belgian League, Caesar attacked successively each tribe in its own territory: (1) at Bibrax, the allied town of the Remi which had been attacked by the Belgians; (2) at Noviodunum against the Suessiones; (3) at Bratuspantium against the Bellovaci; (4) at Samarobriva against the Ambiani; (5) at the Sambre River against the Nervii; (6) at the Meuse River against the Aduatuci.

Caesar's account closes with a favorable report from Crassus (to whom several tribes on the Atlantic coast had surrendered), the return of Caesar to Italy, and the decree of a period of thanksgiving at Rome.

It is interesting to note that Caesar's campaign in the summer of 57 B.C. covered the territory which became famous during World War I and World War II. The battles of the Meuse-Argonne and the Somme were waged by American troops through the same territory which Caesar traversed with his legions.

Ch. 1 The Belgians Form a League Against the Romans

Cum esset Caesar in citeriōre Galliā, crēbrī rūmōrēs ad eum afferēbantur, litterīsque item Labiēnī certior fīēbat, omnēs Belgās contrā populum Rōmānum conjūrāre obsidēsque inter sē dare.

[1]Conjūrandī hae erant causae: prīmum, Belgae verēbantur, nē, omnī pācātā [2]Galliā, ad eōs exercitus Rōmānus addūcerētur; deinde, ab [3]nōn nūllīs Gallīs [4]sollicitābantur. Multī ex hīs Gallīs populī Rōmānī exercitum hiemāre atque inveterāscere in Galliā [5]molestē ferēbant. Aliī mōbilitāte et levitāte animī [6]novīs imperiīs studēbant. Nōn nūllī etiam dē potentiōribus, quī [7]ad condūcendōs hominēs [8]facultātēs habēbant et [9]vulgō rēgna in Galliā occupābant, minus facile eam rem imperiō nostrō sē [10]cōnsequī posse exīstimāvērunt.

FOR COMPREHENSION

- ANSWER IN ENGLISH:
1. What news reached Caesar at various times in Cisalpine Gaul during the winter 58–57 B.C.?
2. What move did the Belgians fear that Caesar would make during the summer of 57 B.C.?
3. Who increased this fear in the hearts of the Belgians?
4. What three types of Celtic Gauls are represented as opposed to the presence of Romans on Gallic territory?
5. Why did the would-be usurpers of royal power fear the presence of the Romans in Gaul?

---

1. **Conjūrandī = Conjūrātiōnis.**
2. **Galliā:** Celtic Gaul.
3. **nōn nūllīs = complūribus.**
4. **sollicitābantur = excitābantur.**
5. **molestē ferēbant:** *they were annoyed.*
6. **novīs imperiīs:** *revolution.*

7. **ad condūcendōs hominēs:** *(for men being hired) to hire men.*
8. **facultātēs = pecūniam, opēs.**
9. **vulgō = saepe.**
10. **cōnsequī = perficere.**

Ch. 2 Caesar Invades Belgium

Hīs nūntiīs litterīsque commōtus Caesar duās legiōnēs in citeriōre Galliā novās cōnscrīpsit, et initā aestāte Quīntum Pedium lēgātum mīsit quī in ūlteriōrem Galliam eōs dēdūceret.

Ipse, cum prīmum pābulī cōpia esse inciperet, ad exercitum vēnit. ¹Dat negōtium Senonibus reliquīsque Gallīs, quī fīnitimī Belgīs erant, utī ea, quae apud eōs gerantur, cōgnōscant sēque dē hīs rēbus certiōrem faciant.

Hī cōnstanter omnēs nūntiāvērunt ²manūs cōgī et exercitum in ūnum locum condūcī. Tum vērō ³dubitandum esse nōn exīstimāvit quīn ad eōs proficīscerētur. Rē frūmentāriā comparātā, castra movet ⁴diēbusque circiter quīndecim ad fīnēs Belgārum pervenit.

---

1. **Dat negōtium** = Imperat.
2. **manūs** = cōpiās.

3. **dubitandum esse nōn exīstimāvit** = dubitāre sē nōn dēbēre exīstimāvit.
4. **diēbus:** ablative of time within which.

FOR COMPREHENSION

● ANSWER IN ENGLISH:
1. What was Caesar's reaction to the messages about the plans of the Belgians?
2. Who led the two newly enrolled legions into farther Gaul?
3. When did Caesar join his army?
4. What duty did Caesar assign the Senones and other Celtic Gauls on the Belgian border?
5. What decision did Caesar make after he received reports from these Gauls?

Ch. 3 The Remi Surrender to Caesar

¹Eō ²dē imprōvīsō celeriusque omnī opīniōne vēnit. ³Rēmī, quī proximī Galliae ex Belgīs sunt, ad eum ⁴lēgātōs, Iccium et Andecumborium, prīmōs cīvitātis, mīsērunt, quī dīcerent Rēmōs ⁵sē suaque omnia ⁶in fidem atque in potestātem populī Rōmānī permittere.

"Nōs Rēmī," inquiunt lēgātī, "cum Belgīs reliquīs nōn cōnsēnsimus neque contrā populum Rōmānum conjūrāvimus. Parātī sumus et obsidēs dare et frūmentō cēterīsque rēbus Rōmānōs juvāre.

---

1. **Eō** (adverb) = Ad eum locum.
2. **dē imprōvīsō** = contrā exspectātiōnem.
3. **Rēmī:** The modern city Rheims preserves their name.

4. **lēgātōs:** *envoys.*
5. **sē . . . permittere** = sē . . . dēdere.
6. **in fidem:** *under the protection.*

"Reliquī omnēs Belgae in armīs sunt. Germānī, quī cis Rhēnum incolunt, sēsē cum hīs conjūnxērunt. Tantus est eōrum omnium furor, ut nē Suessiōnēs quidem dēterrēre potuerimus, quīn cum hīs cōnsentiant. Hī Suessiōnēs sunt frātrēs cōnsanguineīque nostrī. Eōdem jūre et eīsdem lēgibus ūtuntur atque ūnum imperium nōbīscum habent."

FOR COMPREHENSION

- ANSWER IN ENGLISH:
1. Why did Caesar invade the territory of the Remi first?
2. What caused the Remi to abandon the Belgian league and cast their lot with Caesar and the Romans?
3. What help did the Remi promise to give Caesar?
4. What information did the Remi give Caesar?
5. Who were the Suessiones?

Summary of Chapters 4–19

From the Remi Caesar obtained much invaluable information regarding the strength of the Belgian tribes. The leading tribes in the conspiracy were the Suessiones, the Bellovaci, the Nervii, and several Germanic tribes who dwelt in the eastern part of Belgium. Together they could muster a combined force of 200,000 men and thus outnumber Caesar four to one. Galba, king of the Suessiones, was commander-in-chief.

The testudo.

Caesar knew that the Belgians, although they had numbers, did not have organization. He planned to divide and conquer them. He ordered his allies the Haeduans to invade and plunder the lands of the Bellovaci, hoping to draw the latter away from the coalition and force them to defend their own lands. When the Belgians ran out of supplies, they decided to break up the coalition and return to their own territories. During the night the Bellovaci started out in such disorder that it was comparatively easy for Caesar's troops to follow and slaughter them.

In a forced march Caesar reached Noviodunum, the chief stronghold of the

Suessiones. These people were so impressed with the Roman preparations for a siege that they surrendered without further resistance. Caesar immediately marched westward to Bratuspantium, the chief town of the Bellovaci. They also surrendered without a struggle and gave hostages.

There remained one unconquered Belgian tribe, the most courageous of them all, the Nervii. They lived in the forests and the marshes of the northeast. Deserters informed the Nervii that the Roman legions were widely separated on the march by baggage trains and that the first could be easily attacked and defeated before the others arrived. In the meantime Caesar changed his arrangements and placed six legions at the head of the column and the baggage at the rear. The Nervii, seeing the baggage, attacked what they thought was only one legion which was engaged in building a camp just opposite a wooded hill where the Nervii were encamped. The sudden appearance of the enemy in their midst was a complete surprise to the unarmed Romans. Then began the most desperate of all Caesar's battles in Gaul.

Ch. 20   The Romans Are Caught Off Guard

[1]Caesarī omnia ūnō tempore erant agenda. [2]Vēxillum erat prōpōnendum, quod erat īnsīgne, cum ad arma concurrī oportēret. [3]Sīgnum tubā dandum. Mīlitēs ab opere [4]revocandī. [5]Quī paulō longius aggeris petendī causā prōcesserant, [6]arcessendī. Aciēs [7]īnstruenda. Mīlitēs [8]cohortandī. Sīgnum [9]dandum. [10]Quārum rērum māgnam partem temporis brevitās et incursus hostium impediēbat.

Hīs [11]difficultātibus duae rēs erant [12]subsidiō: prīmum, scientia atque ūsus mīlitum, quī superiōribus proeliīs exercitātī, quid fierī [13]oportēret, nōn minus commodē ipsī [14]sibi praescrībere, quam ab aliīs docērī poterant; deinde, [15]quod ab opere singulīsque legiōnibus singulōs lēgātōs Caesar discēdere, [16]nisi mūnītīs castrīs, vetuerat. [17]Hī propter propinquitātem et celeritātem hostium nihil jam Caesaris imperium exspectābant, sed per sē, quae [18]vidēbantur, administrābant.

---

1. **Caesarī . . . agenda** = necesse erat **Caesarem omnia ūnō tempore agere.**
2. **Vēxillum:** a red flag placed in front of the general's tent before the battle.
3. **Sīgnum . . . dandum:** supply **erat.**
4. **revocandī:** supply **erant.**
5. **Quī** = **Eī quī.**
6. **arcessendī:** supply **erant.**
7. **īnstruenda:** supply **erat.**
8. **cohortandī:** supply **erant.**
9. **dandum:** supply **erat.**
10. **Quārum** = **Eārum.**
11. **difficultātibus:** dative of reference.
12. **subsidiō** = **auxiliō.**
13. **oportēret** = **dēbēret.**
14. **sibi praescrībere** = **sē docēre.**
15. **quod:** *the fact that.*
16. **nisi mūnītīs castrīs** = priusquam **castra mūnīrentur.**
17. **Hī** = **Lēgātī.**
18. **vidēbantur:** *seemed best.*

258

FOR COMPREHENSION

● ANSWER IN ENGLISH:
1. What seven things does Caesar say had to be done at the same time?
2. What was the signal that had to be given immediately?
3. What two factors were a help to the Roman soldiers in this emergency?
4. Why do you think the Romans were so easily caught off guard?
5. Why did the officers act on their own without orders from Caesar?

Summary of Chapter 21

Caesar, having given the necessary directions, dashed into the midst of the lines to encourage his men. By chance he came upon the Tenth Legion and stopped long enough to remind them of their former valor and to exhort them to sustain the attack of the enemy bravely. Since the enemy were not more than a spear's throw away, he gave the signal for commencing battle. So sudden had been the enemy's onslaught that the Romans were forced to rush into the fight without waiting to put on their helmets or uncover their shields. Rather than waste time looking for their particular divisions, they rallied about any standard they could find.

Ch. 22   Difficulties in Forming a Battle Line

Exercitus īnstrūctus est magis [1]ut locī nātūra [2]dējectusque collis et necessitās temporis quam [1]ut reī mīlitāris ratiō atque ōrdō postulābat. Dīversae legiōnēs aliae aliā in parte hostibus resistēbant. Saepibus dēnsissimīs interjectīs, [1]ut ante dēmōnstrāvimus, prōspectus impediēbātur. Certa subsidia collocārī nōn poterant. Neque quid in quāque parte opus esset, prōvidērī poterat. Neque ab ūnō omnia imperia administrārī poterant. Itaque [3]in tantā rērum inīquitāte [4]ēventūs variī fortūnae quoque sequēbantur.

---

1. ut: *as;* with the indicative.
2. dējectus = dēclīvitās.

3. in . . . inīquitāte: *with such adverse conditions.*
4. ēventūs = exitūs.

FOR COMPREHENSION

● ANSWER IN ENGLISH:
1. Why were the Roman lines irregular and interrupted in this battle?
2. Where did the different legions resist the enemy?
3. Why was the view impeded?
4. Why could not one person control the army as a whole or send up reinforcements as needed?
5. What was the result of such unfavorable conditions?

Summary of Chapters 23–26

The Ninth and Tenth Legions were stationed on the left wing. They routed the Atrebates and pursued them across the river. The Eighth and Eleventh Legions, which were in the center, forced the Viromandui down the hill to the bank of the river Sambre. These movements left the front and left sides of the camp exposed to the attack of the main force of the enemy. While one division of the Nervii began to move around to attack the Seventh and Twelfth Legions on their right flank, another division started for the top of the hill where the camp stood.

The sight of the enemy swarming in at the western and southern gates caused panic in the Roman camp. The camp servants, cavalry, slingers, and Numidian archers fled in all directions. Caesar, after encouraging the Tenth Legion, hurried to the Twelfth, which was bearing the brunt of the attack. He seized a shield from one of the recruits and rushed into the front line of the battle. Calling the centurions by name and encouraging the soldiers, he ordered them to open up their ranks, so that they could use their swords more freely. Each one tried to do his best in the presence of Caesar, and the attack of the enemy was somewhat slowed down.

At Caesar's orders the Seventh Legion lined up with its back to the Twelfth, while the cohorts at the ends of the line faced outward; thus the Romans were facing the enemy on every side. In the meantime the two legions which had been left to guard the baggage appeared over the brow of the hill. The Ninth and Tenth Legions had seized the enemy's camp across the river. Labienus ordered the Tenth to recross the river, climb the hill, and attack the Nervii from the rear.

Ch. 27 The Tenth Legion Turns the Tide of Battle

Decimae legiōnis [1]adventū māgna rērum commūtātiō est facta. Nostrī, etiam quī vulneribus cōnfectī prōcubuerant, scūtīs innīxī proelium redintegrābant. Cālōnēs, hostēs perterritōs cōnspicātī, etiam [2]inermēs eīs armātīs occurrēbant. Equitēs vērō, ut [3]turpitūdinem fugae virtūte dēlērent, omnibus in locīs pūgnandō [4]sē legiōnāriīs mīlitibus praeferēbant.

At hostēs etiam in extrēmā spē salūtis summam virtūtem [5]praestitērunt. Cum prīmī eōrum cecidissent, proximī jacentibus īnsistēbant atque ex eōrum corporibus pūgnābant. Hīs dējectīs et coacervātīs [6]cadāveribus, eī quī supererant, ut ex tumulō, tēla in nostrōs conjiciēbant et pīla intercepta remittēbant. Tantae virtūtis hominēs jūdicārī nōn dēbet, nēquīquam ausōs esse trāns-

---

1. adventū = cum ... eō pervēnisset.
2. inermēs = sine armīs.
3. turpitūdinem = īgnōminiam, dēdecus.
4. sē ... praeferēbant = legiōnāriōs mīlitēs superābant.
5. praestitērunt = ostendērunt.
6. cadāveribus = corporibus mortuīs.

īre lātissimum flūmen, ascendere altissimās rīpās, subīre inīquissimum locum. ⁷Ea facilia ex difficillimīs animī māgnitūdō ⁸redēgerat.

---

7. **Ea**: object of **redēgerat**. 8. **redēgerat = fēcerat**.

FOR COMPREHENSION

● ANSWER IN ENGLISH

1. Whose arrival on the right wing turned the tide of battle against the Nervii?
2. Who unexpectedly joined in the battle on the Roman side?
3. How did the Nervii show their desperate courage?
4. Do you think that the javelins picked up by the Nervii and hurled back against the Romans could have been effective as weapons?
5. What factor, according to Caesar, made difficult things easy?

Summary of Chapters 28–32

When the noncombatants of the Nervii, who had hidden in the swamps, learned that their army had been completely defeated, they surrendered. Only 3 out of 600 senators had survived and only 500 out of 60,000 men who were able to bear arms. Caesar permitted the survivors to return to their homes. The Aduatuci, allies of the Nervii, had not arrived in time for the battle. Learning of the defeat of the Nervii, they decided to return home. Caesar followed and laid siege to their stronghold on the Meuse.

The diminutive stature of the Romans aroused the contempt of the natives, and the Aduatuci mocked them when they saw the Romans building an enormous tower some distance from the city's walls. However, the moment they saw the tower, designed to run on rollers, moving toward the walls, they were completely overawed and at once sent envoys to offer submission. At the command of Caesar, the Aduatuci tossed their weapons from the wall into the trench below, secretly keeping back about one third of their weapons and concealing them in the town. During the night they violated their pledge and secretly attacked the Romans.

Ch. 33 The Treachery and Defeat of the Aduatuci

¹Sub vesperum Caesar portās claudī mīlitēsque ex oppidō exīre jūssit, nē quam noctū oppidānī ā mīlitibus injūriam acciperent. Illī partim cum eīs armīs, quae clam retinuerant et celāverant, partim scūtīs ²ex cortice factīs aut vīminibus intextīs, quae subitō, ut temporis exiguitās postulābat, pellibus indūxerant, tertiā vi-

---

1. **Sub**: *Toward.* 2. **ex ... intextīs**: *made of bark or interwoven twigs.*

giliā, quā minimē arduus ad nostrās mūnitiōnēs ascēnsus vidēbātur, omnibus cōpiīs repente ex oppidō ēruptiōnem fēcērunt.

Celeriter, ut anteā Caesar imperāverat, ³īgnibus sīgnificātiōne factā, ex proximīs castellīs ⁴eō concursum est, et ab hostibus ita ācriter pūgnātum est, ut ā virīs fortibus in extrēmā spē salūtis inīquō locō, contrā eōs, quī ex vallō turribusque tēla jacerent, pūgnārī dēbuit, praesertim cum in ⁵ūnā virtūte omnis spēs salūtis cōnsisteret. Occīsīs ⁶ad hominum mīlibus quattuor, reliquī in oppidum rejectī sunt.

Postrīdiē ējus diēī refrāctīs portīs, cum jam dēfenderet nēmō, ⁷sectiōnem ējus oppidī ūniversam Caesar vēndidit. Ab eīs, quī ēmerant, capitum numerus ad eum relātus est mīlium quīnquāgintā trium.

---

3. **īgnibus:** *fire signals.*
4. **eō concursum est:** (*it was hurried to that place*) *men hurried to that place.*
5. **ūnā:** *alone.*
6. **ad:** *about.*
7. **sectiōnem . . . vēndidit:** *sold all the booty in one lot.*

FOR COMPREHENSION

● ANSWER IN ENGLISH
1. What orders did Caesar give toward night?
2. What happened during the night?
3. How had Caesar prepared for possible treachery?
4. How did Caesar punish the Aduatuci?
5. Why did he not give the Aduatuci the same terms as he had given the Nervii?

Summary of Chapter 34

Immediately after the battle with the Nervii, Caesar had sent the Seventh Legion, under the command of Publius Crassus, to subjugate the maritime tribes in western Gaul. At the same time as the Aduatuci were sold into slavery, word came to Caesar from Crassus that all the maritime states had been subjugated to the rule of the Roman people.

Ch. 35 All Gaul Is Subdued

Hīs rēbus gestīs, Gallia omnis est pācāta. Tanta opīniō hūjus bellī ad barbarōs perlāta est, utī lēgātī ab eīs nātiōnibus, quae trāns Rhēnum ¹incolerent, ad Caesarem mitterentur, quī ²sē

---

1. **incolerent:** subjunctive by attraction. 2. **sē:** feminine.

obsidēs datūrās, imperāta factūrās pollicērentur. Quās lēgātiōnēs Caesar, quod in Ītaliam Īllyricumque properābat, initā proximā aestāte ad sē revertī jūssit.

Ipse, in Carnutēs, Andēs, Turonōs, ³quaeque cīvitātēs propinquae hīs locīs erant, ubi bellum gesserat, legiōnēs in hīberna dēdūxit, et in Ītaliam profectus est.

⁴Ob eāsque rēs, ⁵ex ⁶litterīs Caesaris, diērum quīndecim ⁷supplicātiō dēcrēta est, quod ante id tempus accidit ⁸nūllī.

Two Gauls chained to a trophy of their surrendered arms.

FOR COMPREHENSION

● ANSWER IN ENGLISH:

1. When the news about this war was brought to tribes that lived across the Rhine, what did they do?
2. What promises did the envoys make to Caesar?
3. Why did Caesar order the envoys to return at the beginning of next summer?
4. Where did Caesar station his "army of occupation" for the winter of 57–56 B.C.?
5. What unprecedented recognition did Caesar receive at Rome for his victories in Celtic Gaul and Belgium?

---

3. **quaeque cīvitātēs = et in eās cīvitātēs quae.**

4. **Ob eāsque rēs:** *And on account of these things.*

5. **ex:** *after receipt of.*

6. **litterīs:** *dispatches* (to the Roman Senate).

7. **supplicātiō:** solemn thanksgiving.

8. **nūllī = nēminī.**

BOOK THREE

GALBA SECURES THE PASS THROUGH THE ALPS

PREVIEW: During the winter of 57–56 B.C. Caesar, who realized the advantage of controlling the pass (now known as the Great St. Bernard Pass) across the Alps into Gaul, sent a legion under the command of Servius Galba to subdue the mountain tribes along the route. Eventually Galba accomplished his mission, but not without difficulties.

Ch. 1 Galba Is Sent to the Alps

¹Cum in Ītaliam proficīscerētur Caesar, Servium Galbam cum legiōne duodecimā et parte equitātūs in Nantuātēs, Veragrōs Sedūnōsque mīsit, quī ā fīnibus Allobrogum et lacū Lemannō et flūmine Rhodanō ²ad summās Alpēs pertinent. Causa mittendī fuit, quod iter per Alpēs, ³quō māgnō cum perīculō ⁴māgnīsque cum portōriīs mercātōrēs īre cōnsuēverant, patefierī volēbat. ⁵Huic permīsit, sī ⁶opus esse arbitrārētur, utī in hīs locīs legiōnem hiemandī causā collocāret.

Galba, secundīs aliquot proeliīs factīs castellīsque complūribus ⁷eōrum expūgnātīs, missīs ad eum undique lēgātīs obsidibusque datīs et pāce factā, cōnstituit cohortēs duās in Nantuātibus collocāre et ipse, cum reliquīs ējus legiōnis cohortibus, in vīcō Veragrōrum, quī appellātur Octodūrus, hiemāre; quī vīcus positus in valle, ⁸nōn māgnā adjectā plānitiē, altissimīs montibus undique continētur. ⁹Cum ¹⁰hīc in duās partēs flūmine dīviderētur, alteram partem ējus vīcī Gallīs concessit, alteram ¹¹vacuam ab hīs relictam, cohortibus ad hiemandum attribuit. ¹²Eum locum vāllō fossāque mūnīvit.

---

1. **Cum . . . proficīscerētur:** Caesar was setting out for that part of Italy north of the Rubicon known as Cisalpine Gaul.
2. **ad summās Alpēs = ad summam partem Alpium.**
3. **quō:** supply **itinere.**
4. **māgnīsque cum portōriīs:** *and with* (the payment of) *heavy tolls* (levied by the mountaineers, especially on the Roman merchants).

5. **Huic = Galba.**
6. **opus esse = necesse esse.**
7. **eōrum:** of the three tribes which inhabited the Alps.
8. **nōn māgnā = parva.**
9. **Cum:** causal.
10. **hīc:** supply **vīcus.**
11. **vacuam ab hīs = sine incolīs.**
12. **Eum locum:** the west side of the river Dranse.

FOR COMPREHENSION

- ANSWER IN ENGLISH:
1. Why did Caesar send Galba to the Alps?
2. How large a force did Galba take with him?
3. Where did Galba, after defeating the Alpine tribes, station two cohorts?
4. Why was it important for the Romans to control the pass?
5. How did Galba turn his part of the town of Octodurus into a camp?

- RESPONDĒ LATĪNE:
1. Cum quibus cōpiīs Caesar Galbam in Alpēs mīsit?
2. Quae causa mittendī fuit?
3. In quō locō Galba duās cohortēs collocāre cōnstituit?
4. Cum quot cohortibus Galba ipse hiemāre cōnstituit?
5. Quōmodo alteram partem Octodūrī mūnīvit?

- SCRĪBE LATĪNE:
1. Roman merchants were accustomed to go into Gaul by a road through the Alps.
2. This village was situated in a valley hemmed in on all sides by very high mountains.
3. Caesar ordered Galba to pass the winter in the Alps with the Twelfth Legion.

Ch. 2   The Seduni and Veragri Stage a Rebellion

Cum diēs hībernōrum complūrēs trānsīssent, frūmentumque [1]eō comportārī jūssisset, subitō per explōrātōrēs certior factus est, ex eā parte vīcī, quam Gallīs concesserat, omnēs noctū discessisse, montēsque, quī impendērent, ā māximā multitūdine Sedūnōrum et Veragrōrum tenērī.

Id aliquot dē causīs acciderat, ut subitō Gallī bellī renovandī legiōnisque opprimendae cōnsilium caperent: prīmum, quod legiōnem, neque eam plēnissimam, [2]dētrāctīs cohortibus duābus et [3]complūribus [4]singillātim, quī commeātūs petendī causā missī erant, absentibus, propter paucitātem dēspiciēbant; [5]tum etiam, quod propter inīquitātem locī, [6]cum ipsī ex montibus in vallem dēcurrerent et tēla conjicerent, nē prīmum quidem impetum suum posse sustinērī exīstimābant. Accēdēbat, quod suōs ab sē līberōs

---

1. eō = in hīberna.
2. dētrāctīs = dēductīs.
3. complūribus: supply mīlitibus.
4. singillātim: *in small detachments.*

5. tum = deinde: parallel with prīmum, line 12.
6. cum ... dēcurrerent: *when they should run down.*

7abstrāctōs obsidum nōmine dolēbant, et Rōmānōs nōn sōlum itinerum causā, sed etiam perpetuae possessiōnis 8culmina Alpium occupāre cōnārī et ea loca fīnitimae prōvinciae 9adjungere 10sibi persuāsum habēbant.

7. abstrāctōs = abductōs.
8. culmina Alpium = summās Alpēs.
9. adjungere: annex.

10. sibi persuāsam habēbant: (they had persuaded themselves) they were convinced.

FOR COMPREHENSION

● ANSWER IN ENGLISH:
1. Why was the legion quartered in Octodurus not a very full one?
2. What were the reasons for the rebellion of the Seduni and Veragri so soon after giving hostages and making peace with the Romans?
3. Why did the Gauls show so little respect for Galba's army?
4. What other advantage did the Gauls think they had over the Roman garrison?
5. Were the Gauls correct in their suspicion that the Romans desired to annex their territory?

● RESPONDĒ LATĪNE:
1. Quam ob rem Gallī exercitum Galbae dēspiciēbant?
2. Quō cōnsiliō complūrēs singillātim missī erant?
3. Quandō Gallī nē prīmum quidem impetum suum posse sustinērī exīstimābant\
4. Quid Gallī dolēbant?
5. Quid Gallī sibi persuāsum habēbant?

● SCRĪBE LATĪNE:
1. He was informed by scouts that the Gauls had departed from the village at night and were holding the mountains overhanging the valley.
2. Why did they think that the Romans could not sustain even their first attack?
3. They did not know why the Romans were trying to annex these neighboring places to the Roman Province.

Ch. 3 Galba Calls a Council of War

Hīs nūntiīs 1acceptīs, Galba, cum neque opus hībernōrum mūnī· tiōnēsque plēnē essent perfectae, neque dē frūmentō reliquōque commeātū satis esset prōvīsum, quod, dēditiōne factā obsidibusque acceptīs, nihil dē bellō timendum exīstimāverat, 2cōnsiliō celeriter convocātō, sententiās exquīrere coepit.

1. acceptīs = audītīs.
2. cōnsiliō . . . convocātō: The tribunes, the six centurions of the first cohort, and

perhaps the cavalry prefects were called to the council of war.

Quō in cōnsiliō, ³cum tantum repentīnī ⁴perīculī ⁵praeter opīniōnem accidisset ac jam omnia ferē superiōra loca multitūdine
armātōrum complēta cōnspicerentur, ⁶neque subsidiō venīrī neque
commeātūs supportārī, interclūsīs itineribus, possent, prope jam
dēspērātā salūte ⁷nōn nūllae hūjus modī sententiae dīcēbantur, ⁸ut,
impedīmentīs relictīs ēruptiōne factā, eīsdem itineribus, quibus eō
⁹pervēnissent, ad salūtem contenderent. Mājōrī tamen partī placuit, hōc reservātō ad extrēmum cōnsiliō, interim reī ēventum
experīrī et castra dēfendere.

FOR COMPREHENSION

● ANSWER IN ENGLISH:
1. Had Galba been somewhat remiss in performing his duties as commanding officer?
2. What were the three things which made the position of the Romans perilous?
3. What were the two proposals which were made in the council of war which Galba called?
4. What was the opinion which was expressed by the majority of Galba's officers?
5. What did the council decide to do if the worst came to the worst?

● RESPONDĒ LATĪNE:
1. Quae Galba nōn satis parāverat?
2. Cūr Galba nihil dē bellō timendum esse exīstimāvit?
3. Quōrum Galba sententiās exquīrere coepit?
4. Quid minōrī partī placuit?
5. Quid tamen mājōrī partī placuit?

● SCRĪBE LATĪNE:
1. They asked why grain and other supplies had not been sufficiently provided.
2. The majority (The greater part) decided to await the outcome of the situation and to defend the camp.
3. Some thought that they should hasten to safety by the same roads by which they had reached this place.

---

3. **cum:** causal; with **accidisset, cōn-spicerentur,** and **possent.**
4. **perīculī:** partitive genitive with **tantum.**
5. **praeter opīniōnem = contrā exspec-tātiōnem.**
6. **neque subsidiō venīrī (posset):** *and no one could come to their assistance;* **venīrī** is used here impersonally. Both Caesar and the other legions were very far away.

7. **nōn nūllae:** (*not none*) *several;* **nōn nūllae . . . sententiae = aliquot opī-niōnēs.**
8. **ut . . . contenderent:** substantive clause in apposition to **sententiae.**
9. **pervēnissent:** subjunctive by attraction, i.e., it depends on a verb in another clause, in this case, **contenderent.**

Ch. 4 The Roman Garrison Is Hard Pressed by the Gauls

¹Brevī spatiō interjectō, vix ut ²eīs rēbus, quās ³cōnstituissent, collocandīs atque administrandīs tempus darētur, hostēs ⁴ex omnibus partibus sīgnō datō, ⁵dēcurrere, lapidēs gaesaque in vāllum ⁵conjicere. Nostrī prīmō ⁶integrīs vīribus fortiter ⁷repūgnāre neque ūllum frūstrā tēlum ex locō superiōre ⁸mittere, et quaecumque pars castrōrum nūdāta dēfēnsōribus premī vidēbātur, eō occurrere et auxilium ferre; sed hōc superārī, quod ⁹diūturnitāte pūgnae hostēs dēfessī proeliō excēdēbant, aliī ¹⁰integrīs vīribus succēdēbant. Quārum rērum ā nostrīs propter paucitātem fierī nihil poterat, ac nōn modo dēfessō ex pūgnā excēdendī, sed nē sauciō quidem ējus locī, ubi ¹¹cōnstiterat, relinquendī ac suī recipiendī ¹²facultās dabātur.

FOR COMPREHENSION

- ANSWER IN ENGLISH:
1. What happened shortly after the council had broken up?
2. Were the Romans ready for the attack?
3. What missiles did the Gauls use?
4. What advantage did the Romans have at the opening of the attack?
5. What system did Galba's enemies have of relieving their wounded men as the fight went on?

- RESPONDĒ LATĪNE:
1. Quō Gallī lapidēs et gaesa conjiciēbant?
2. Unde Rōmānī tēla dējiciēbant?
3. Cūr hostēs diūturnitāte pūgnae dēfessī excēdere poterant?
4. Quam ob rem hārum rērum ā Rōmānīs fierī nihil poterat?
5. Quae facultās Rōmānīs dēfessīs aut sauciīs nōn dabātur?

- SCRĪBE LATĪNE:
1. While their strength was fresh, the Romans bravely resisted the enemy.
2. Opportunity was not given to the wearied Romans to leave the battle and regain their strength.

---

1. **Brevī spatiō interjectō** = Post breve tempus.
2. **eīs ... administrandīs:** rare dative of the gerundive to express purpose; ad with the gerundive is regularly used.
3. **cōnstituissent:** subjunctive by attraction (see footnote 9, p. 267), depending on **darētur.**
4. **ex omnibus partibus** = undique.
5. **dēcurrere, conjicere:** historical infinitives.
6. **integrīs vīribus:** *while their strength was fresh.*
7. **repūgnāre** = resistere.
8. **mittere** = dējicere.
9. **diūturnitāte** = propter diūturnitātem.
10. **integrīs vīribus:** ablative of description.
11. **cōnstiterat** = stābat.
12. **facultās** = opportūnitās.

3. On account of the small number of men, the Romans were able to do none of these things.

Ch. 5 The Desperate Romans Decide to Make a Sortie

[1]Cum jam amplius hōrīs sex continenter [1]pūgnārētur ac nōn sōlum vīrēs, sed etiam tēla nostrōs [1]dēficerent, atque hostēs ācrius [1]īnstārent languidiōribusque nostrīs vāllum scindere et fossās complēre [1]coepissent, rēsque [1]esset jam ad extrēmum perducta cāsum, Pūblius Sextius Baculus, [2]prīmī pīlī centuriō, quem Nervicō proeliō complūribus cōnfectum vulneribus dīximus, et item Gājus Volusēnus, [3]tribūnus mīlitum, vir et cōnsilī māgnī et virtūtis, ad Galbam accurrunt atque ūnam esse spem salūtis docent, sī, ēruptiōne factā, [4]extrēmum auxilium experīrentur.

Itaque, convocātīs centuriōnibus, celeriter mīlitēs [5]certiōrēs facit, paulisper intermitterent proelium ac [6]tantummodo tēla missa exciperent sēque ex labōre reficerent; [7]post, datō sīgnō, ex castrīs ērumperent atque omnem spem salūtis in virtūte pōnerent.

FOR COMPREHENSION

- ANSWER IN ENGLISH:
1. About how long did the attack on the Roman camp last?
2. Why was the situation very critical for the Romans?
3. What military rank did Baculus hold? On what previous occasion had he been mentioned?
4. What advice did Baculus and Volusenus give Galba?
5. What five orders did Galba issue to the soldiers?

- RESPONDĒ LATĪNE:
1. Quid hostēs facere coepērunt cum vīrēs et tēla Rōmānōs dēficerent?
2. Quid Caesar dē Baculō dīxerat?
3. Quālis fuit Volusēnus?
4. Quid Baculus et Volusēnus Galbam docuērunt?
5. Quid, datō sīgnō, Galba mīlitibus suīs imperāvit?

1. **Cum:** introduces five verbs in the subjunctive.
2. **prīmī pīlī centuriō:** the first centurion of the first maniple and therefore of the legion. This first centurion, although originally promoted from the ranks, was next to the tribune in authority.
3. **tribūnus mīlitum:** a superior officer of the legion but not, as a rule, chosen from the ranks.

4. **extrēmum auxilium:** *a last resource.*
5. **certiōrēs facit:** here equivalent to a verb of commanding and followed by the subjunctive.
6. **tantummodo . . . exciperent:** *they should merely receive* (on their shields) *the weapons sent* (by the enemy).
7. **post = posteā.**

1. The enemy were pressing on our men more fiercely and had begun to tear down the rampart and fill the ditch.
2. We know why Baculus and Volusenus were men of great discretion and bravery.
3. The centurions commanded the soldiers to make a sortie and try their last resource.

Ch. 6   The Gauls Are Defeated

¹Quod jūssī sunt, faciunt, ac ²subitō, ³omnibus portīs ēruptiōne factā, neque cōgnōscendī, quid fieret, neque ⁴suī colligendī hostibus facultātem relinquunt. Ita, commūtātā fortūnā, eōs, quī in spem ⁵potiundōrum castrōrum vēnerant, undique ⁶circumventōs interficiunt et ex hominum mīlibus amplius xxx, quem numerum barbarōrum ad castra vēnisse ⁷cōnstābat, plūs tertiā parte interfectā, reliquōs perterritōs in fugam conjiciunt ac nē in locīs quidem superiōribus cōnsistere patiuntur. Sīc, omnibus hostium ⁸cōpiīs fūsīs armīsque exūtīs, sē intrā mūnītiōnēs suās recipiunt.

Quō proeliō factō, quod saepius fortūnam temptāre Galba nōlēbat, atque aliō sē in hīberna cōnsiliō vēnisse meminerat, aliīs occurrisse rēbus vīderat, māximē frūmentī commeātūsque inopiā permōtus, posterō diē, omnibus ējus vīcī aedificiīs incēnsīs, in prōvinciam revertī contendit, ac, ⁹nūllō hoste prohibente aut iter dēmorante, incolumem legiōnem in Nantuātēs, inde in Allobrogēs perdūxit, ibique hiemāvit.

FOR COMPREHENSION

● ANSWER IN ENGLISH:
1. What did the Romans hope to accomplish in making a sortie from their hard-pressed camp?
2. How many Gauls does Caesar say Galba was obliged to fight?
3. Why did the enemy throw away their arms?
4. What was Galba's original purpose in coming to the Alps?
5. Why did Galba decide to lead his troops into the territory of the Nantuates?

---

1. **Quod = Id quod.**
2. **subitō = repente.**
3. **omnibus portīs = per omnēs portās.**
4. **suī colligendī**: *of gathering themselves together;* **suī**, singular in form but plural in meaning.
5. **potiundōrum = potiendōrum.**
6. **circumventōs interficiunt = circumveniunt et interficiunt; circumventōs** agrees with **eōs,** object of **interficiunt.**

7. **cōnstābat**: *it was certain;* impersonal with the infinitive phrase **quem . . . vēnisse** as subject.
8. **cōpiīs . . . exūtīs**: *the troops having been utterly routed and deprived of arms;* **armīs,** ablative of separation.
9. **nūllō**: ablative absolute with **prohibente** and **dēmorante.**

1. Ēruptiōne factā, quam facultātem Rōmānī hostibus relīquērunt?
2. Quot barbarōs interfectōs esse Galba dīcit?
3. Cūr Galba in Prōvinciam revertī contendit?
4. Quō Galba legiōnem perdūxit?
5. Ubi Galba hiemāvit?

● SCRĪBE LATĪNE:

1. The Gauls had come in the hope of taking possession of the Roman camp, but they were surrounded on all sides and killed.
2. Galba was unwilling to tempt fortune too often, and he was alarmed by the lack of grain and supplies.
3. After all the houses of the village had been burned, he led his legion unharmed into the Province.

NAVAL VICTORY OVER THE VENETI

PREVIEW: It was the rebellion among the maritime states between the Loire and the Seine that called for Caesar's generalship in the summer of 56 B.C. When Caesar demanded supplies of the seacoast states, they revolted and arrested the Roman envoys sent among them. The Veneti, a powerful naval state, led the revolt. Caesar began an extensive campaign against them. He sent Labienus to the Rhine river to prevent uprisings of the Belgians or the Germans; Sabinus he sent to the land of the Venelli; Crassus was ordered to Aquitania in the south. Caesar himself gathered a fleet under the command of Decimus Brutus and attacked the Veneti, strongest seacoast state of the league.

The tides of the ocean and the height of the ships of the Veneti were new experiences for the Romans, but eventually they proved themselves superior to the Veneti and won the first naval battle to be fought on the Atlantic Ocean. In the meantime Sabinus had won a decisive victory over the Venelli in the north, and Crassus had brought about the submission of the Aquitanians. However, Caesar failed to conquer the tribes of the Morini and Menapii whose swampy and forest-covered lands were impenetrable, even for Caesar's troops. Caesar himself, as in the two previous years, returned to his province in northern Italy.

Summary of Chapters 7–13

Meanwhile Publius Crassus with the Seventh Legion was wintering among the Andes near the Atlantic Ocean. The fiercest of the maritime tribes and the most skillful seamen were the Veneti, who lived in western Britanny and carried on an extensive trade with Britain. They had pretended to submit to the authority of Crassus and gave him hostages; but when envoys were sent to them to secure supplies, the envoys were treacherously detained. Other tribes followed their example, and an uprising of the maritime states resulted. They demanded a return of the Gallic hostages in exchange for the Roman envoys whom they had seized.

As soon as Caesar learned of this revolt, he made plans to build and equip a fleet of war galleys and to secure experienced oarsmen from the Province. His plan was to launch a land and sea attack upon the rebellious tribes in the early spring of 56 B.C.

As early as possible in the spring of 56 B.C. Caesar sent troops into various districts of Gaul to check any incipient revolts. He then led his army into the country of the Veneti. The towns of the Veneti were situated on headlands which were cut off from the mainland at high tide, while at low tide ships were grounded. As soon as the capture of a town by the Romans seemed inevitable, the inhabitants gathered together their belongings and fled by boat to another town. There the same maneuvers were repeated. Since storms and the lack of good harbors prevented the mobilization of the Roman fleet, the Veneti kept the Romans at bay for most of the summer.

The ships of the Veneti were made with high prows and flat keels and were constructed of heavy oak beams, fastened with iron bolts. The sails were made of skins instead of cloth, and their anchors were held by iron chains instead of ropes. They were therefore better adapted than Roman vessels to withstand a storm or to fight in shallow water. They were superior to Roman ships in everything but speed.

Ch. 14   The Romans Use a Clever Device

Complūribus expūgnātīs oppidīs, Caesar, ubi intellēxit frūstrā tantum labōrem sūmī neque hostium fugam, captīs oppidīs, reprimī [1]neque eīs nocērī posse, statuit exspectandam classem. Quae ubi [2]convēnit ac prīmum ab hostibus vīsa est, circiter CCXX nāvēs eōrum, parātissimae atque omnī genere armōrum ōrnātissimae, profectae [3]ex portū nostrīs adversae cōnstitērunt; [4]neque satis Brūtō, quī classī praeerat, vel tribūnīs mīlitum centuriōnibusque, quibus singulae nāvēs erant attribūtae, cōnstābat, quid agerent aut quam ratiōnem pūgnae īnsisterent. Rōstrō enim nocērī nōn posse cōgnōverant; turribus autem excitātīs, tamen hās altitūdō puppium ex barbarīs nāvibus superābat, ut neque ex īnferiōre locō satis commodē [5]tēla adigī possent et missa ā Gallīs gravius acciderent.

Ūna erat māgnō ūsuī rēs praeparāta ā nostrīs, falcēs praeacūtae īnsertae affīxaeque longuriīs, [6]nōn absimilī fōrmā mūrālium falcium. Hīs [7]cum fūnēs, [8]quī antemnās ad mālōs dēstinābant, com-

---

1. **neque eīs nocērī posse:** (*and that it could not be harmed them*) *and that no harm could be done to them.*
2. **convēnit:** *arrived.*
3. **ex portū:** the mouth of the Auray.
4. **neque satis . . . cōnstābat:** *nor was it quite clear* (to Brutus, etc.).

5. **tēla adigī possent:** *weapons could be hurled.*
6. **nōn . . . falcium:** *of a form not unlike* (that of) *wall hooks.*
7. **cum:** *whenever.*
8. **quī . . . dēstinābant:** *which bound the sailyards to the masts.*

prehēnsī adductīque erant, nāvigiō rēmīs incitātō, praerumpē-
bantur. Quibus abscīsīs, antemnae necessāriō concidēbant; ut,
cum omnis Gallicīs nāvibus spēs in vēlīs armāmentīsque cōnsisteret, hīs ēreptīs, omnis [9]ūsus nāvium ūnō tempore ēriperētur.
Reliquum erat certāmen positum in virtūte, quā nostrī mīlitēs
facile superābant, atque [10]eō magis, quod [11]in cōnspectū Caesaris

A Roman warship (*right*) attacking a Gallic warship.

atque omnis exercitūs rēs gerēbātur, ut nūllum paulō fortius
factum latēre posset; omnēs enim collēs ac loca superiōra, unde
erat propinquus dēspectus in mare, ab exercitū tenēbantur.

FOR COMPREHENSION

● ANSWER IN ENGLISH:

1. Did Caesar succeed in capturing the towns or the inhabitants of the towns of the Veneti? Why?
2. About how many ships were in the Roman fleet?
3. What four handicaps did the Romans have in this sea fight?
4. What clever device did the Romans under Brutus use in this naval battle?
5. Who were in the grandstand seats for this sea contest?

---

9. **ūsus:** *control.* The ships of the Veneti had no oars.
10. **eō ... quod:** *the more so because.*
11. **in cōnspectū Caesaris:** *in sight of*

Caesar. Caesar and the army were watching the sea fight from the heights of St. Gildas.

1. Quid tandem Caesar statuit?
2. Quis classī praeerat?
3. Quibus singulae nāvēs erant attribūtae?
4. Quandō omnis ūsus nāvium ēripiēbātur?
5. Ā quibus omnēs collēs ac loca superiōra tenēbantur?

● SCRĪBE LATĪNE:
1. It wasn't quite clear to the Romans what they were to do.
2. Sharp hooks fixed to long poles were a great use to our men.
3. When the ropes were broken, all control of the ships was removed at the same time; for the ships of the Veneti had no oars.

Ch. 15   The Romans Win a Decisive Naval Victory

Dējectīs, ut dīximus, antemnīs, [1]cum [2]singulās bīnae ac ternae nāvēs circumsteterant, mīlitēs summā vī trānscendere in hostium nāvēs contendēbant. [3]Quod postquam barbarī fierī animadvertērunt, expūgnātīs complūribus nāvibus, cum [4]eī reī nūllum reperīrētur auxilium, fugā salūtem petere contendērunt.

Ac jam conversīs [5]in eam partem nāvibus, quō ventus ferēbat, tanta subitō [6]malacia ac tranquillitās exstitit, ut sē ex locō movēre nōn possent. Quae quidem rēs ad negōtium cōnficiendum māximē fuit opportūna; nam [7]singulās nostrī cōnsectātī expūgnāvērunt, [8]ut perpaucae ex omnī numerō noctis interventū ad terram pervēnerint, [9]cum ab hōrā ferē quārtā ūsque ad sōlis occāsum pūgnārētur.

FOR COMPREHENSION

● ANSWER IN ENGLISH:
1. Why could the Romans now board the ships of the enemy?
2. What caused the enemy to try to abandon their ships?
3. What prevented the enemy from doing so?
4. About how many ships did the Romans capture in this naval battle?
5. How long did the battle last?

---

1. **cum:** *whenever.*
2. **singulās:** Two or three Roman ships at a time would surround one of the enemy's ships.
3. **Quod = Hoc.**
4. **eī reī:** *for this situation.*
5. **in ... ferēbat:** *in the direction in which the wind was blowing.*

6. **malacia ac tranquillitās:** *a dead calm;* the verb **exstitit** is singular because the two subjects express a single idea.
7. **singulās:** *one after another.*
8. **ut ... pervēnerint:** result clause.
9. **cum . . . pūgnārētur:** cum-causal clause.

- RESPONDĒ LATĪNE:
1. Quandō mīlitēs Rōmānī trānscendere hostium nāvēs contendēbant?
2. Cūr hostēs fugere cōnātī sunt?
3. Quot hostium nāvēs ad terram pervēnērunt?
4. Quae rēs ad negōtium cōnficiendum fuit opportūna?
5. Quam diū pūgnātum est?

- SCRĪBE LATĪNE:
1. Whenever the Roman ships surrounded a ship of the enemy, the soldiers tried to climb aboard the enemy's ship.
2. After the enemy notices that this is being done, they hasten to seek safety in flight.
3. They fought from the fourth hour until sundown.

Ch. 16   End of the Coast Rebellion

Quō proeliō bellum Venetōrum tōtīusque ōrae maritimae cōnfectum est. Nam [1]cum omnis juventūs, omnēs etiam [2]graviōris aetātis, in quibus [3]aliquid cōnsilī aut dīgnitātis fuit, eō convēnerant, [1]tum [4]nāvium quod ubīque fuerat, in locum coēgerant; quibus āmissīs, reliquī neque quō sē reciperent, neque [5]quem ad modum oppida dēfenderent, habēbant. Itaque sē suaque omnia Caesarī dēdidērunt.

In quōs [6]eō gravius Caesar vindicandum (esse) statuit, [7]quō dīligentius in reliquum tempus ā barbarīs [8]jūs lēgātōrum cōnservārētur. Itaque, omnī senātū necātō, reliquōs [9]sub corōna vēndidit.

FOR COMPREHENSION

- ANSWER IN ENGLISH:
1. Who of the maritime tribes had assembled for this desperate battle?
2. Where had all the ships of these tribes been gathered?
3. Why did Caesar punish the Veneti so severely?

1. **cum . . . tum:** *not only . . . but also.*
2. **graviōris aetātis:** *of more advanced age.*
3. **aliquid . . . dīgnitātis:** *any judgment or prestige;* **cōnsilī** and **dīgnitātis** are partitive genitives with **aliquid.**
4. **nāvium . . . fuerat:** (*whatever of ships had been anywhere*) *all their ships;* **nāvium** is a partitive genitive with **quod.**
5. **quem . . . dēfenderent:** *any way to defend their towns.*
6. **eō gravius vindicandum (esse):** (*the more severely it ought to be punished*) *the*
more severe punishment ought to be inflicted;* **vindicandum = pūniendum.**
7. **quō . . . cōnservārētur:** *purpose clause with a comparative.*
8. **jūs lēgātōrum:** *the right of envoys.* Strictly speaking, the officers who had been sent by Crassus to these tribes were not envoys.
9. **sub corōna vēndidit:** (*sold under the crown*) *sold as slaves.* The reference is to the custom of crowning slaves with wreaths when offering them for sale.

4. Whom did Caesar put to death? Whom did he sell as slaves?
5. Was there any justification for Caesar's barbarous treatment of these tribes?

● RESPONDĒ LATĪNE:
1. Quot Venetī in hunc locum convēnerant?
2. Quot nāvēs Venetī coēgerant?
3. Cūr Caesar in Venetōs gravius pūniendum esse statuit?
4. Quōmodo in senātōrēs Venetōrum vindicātum est?
5. Quōmodo reliquī Venetī pūnītī sunt?

● SCRĪBE LATĪNE:
1. What war was finished with this naval battle?
2. Not only all the men who could fight had been gathered together in this one place, but also all their ships.
3. Caesar punished them severely in order to preserve the rights of envoys more carefully.

Summary of Chapters 17–29

Sabinus meanwhile had invaded the country of the Venelli north of the Veneti. Here he encamped and by clever strategy lured the enemy into an unfavorable position. Then by a sudden attack he defeated them. As a result the Venelli and all the rest of the revolting maritime tribes laid down their arms.

Publius Crassus' campaign in Aquitania was conducted in the face of the most frustrating obstacles. By fierce fighting he captured the chief town of the Sotiates, the modern Sos. The neighboring tribes then combined against Crassus and even summoned aid from Spain. Crassus, however, defeated their combined forces and received in surrender the greater part of the Aquitanian states.

After the defeat of the Veneti, Caesar personally conducted a campaign against the Morini and Menapii in the northern part of Belgium. When Caesar reached their territory, the Morini and the Menapii retreated into their forests. With the coming of the rainy season, Caesar contented himself with the capture of some of their cattle and with the burning of their buildings. He quartered his troops for the winter among the Aulerci and the Lexovii.

BOOK FOUR

(Sight translation)

WAR AGAINST THE GERMANS

Summary of Chapters 1–19

A new menace to the peace of Gaul appeared on the northeastern frontier at the close of Caesar's third year in that territory. Two German tribes, the Usipetes and Tencteri, comprising over 400,000 men, women, and children, had been driven from their lands by a more powerful German tribe, the Suebi. These people, the Suebi, were the inhabitants of what is now the central part of Germany.

The Suebi kept a standing army of 200,000, at least half of whom engaged in warfare beyond their borders for the period of one year while the other half remained at home and supported those who had gone to war. The following year the two groups exchanged occupations. Private ownership of land was not permitted. Most of their time was devoted to hunting. They dressed in the skins of animals, and, although their climate was very cold, they bathed in the rivers. This manner of living made them men of great size and of extraordinary physical stamina.

The Suebi tolerated traders only to sell their booty taken in war. They imported practically nothing. Like the Belgians, they were teetotalers, believing that the use of wine would render them physically unfit. They rode bareback, and their horses were trained to stand still while their riders dismounted and fought on foot.

The Usipetes and the Tencteri were held in check for a time by the Menapii on the right bank of the river Rhine. However, they finally succeeded in crossing the river. Overcoming and dispossessing the Menapii in a surprise attack, they then occupied their homes and lived on the stores of the Menapii for the rest of the winter.

Caesar, fearing that other German tribes would also cross the river Rhine and that the fickle Gauls would unite with them, decided to drive out the Germans. When their envoys came to him for land in Gaul on which they could settle, he refused their request and ordered them to leave the country. They pleaded for a delay and gained a truce; later they treacherously attacked Caesar's cavalry, which was no match for the Germans. The latter leaped to the ground, stabbed the horses of the Romans from beneath, killed seventy-four of Caesar's men, and put the rest to an ignominious rout. Among the Roman casualties were two members of the Aquitanian nobility, Piso and his brother, who died valiantly in their vain attempt to save each other. After this attack the Germans sent a large delegation of their leading men to apologize for their conduct in violating the truce. Caesar had them arrested and then, advancing against the almost leaderless troops of Germans, annihilated them. Women and children were ruthlessly slaughtered by the Roman cavalry. The few Germans who escaped the massacre plunged into the swift current of the Rhine and perished.

Caesar then decided to invade Germany. Within ten days, thanks to the efficiency of his trained corps of engineers, he bridged the Rhine with a roadway on a trestle of wooden piles. Caesar then led his army across into Germany. During his eighteen days in Germany several tribes submitted to him, but he was unable to conquer the Sugambri or the Suebi, both of which tribes had taken refuge in the vast forests. Accordingly, after terrifying the Germans and ravaging their fields, he returned to Gaul and destroyed the bridge behind him.

FIRST INVASION OF BRITAIN

PREVIEW: The Romans knew almost nothing about Britain or its inhabitants until Caesar's two invasions of the island in 55 and 54 B.C. He gave as reasons for these invasions that the Britons had given aid to the Gauls in their recent wars and that he wished to learn personally about the people and their land. As he did not penetrate farther than the Thames River, his observations were necessarily limited and many of his statements inaccurate. Actually long before this time the island had become famous for its tin. For many years merchants had been coming from Phoenicia to barter their wares for it.

Like the Gauls, the inhabitants of Britain were Celts. In battles they used a special kind of chariot drawn by trained horses. Druidism flourished here more than in Gaul.

Britain was not romanized in Caesar's time. A century later the Romans came again to the island, and in A.D. 85 it became a Roman province, remaining so for nearly four hundred years.

A British war chariot.

Ch. 20   Caesar Decides to Invade Britain

¹Exiguā parte aestātis reliquā, Caesar, ²etsī in hīs locīs, quod omnis Gallia ad septentriōnēs vergit, ³mātūrae sunt hiemēs, tamen ⁴in Britanniam proficīscī contendit, quod, omnibus ferē Gallicīs bellīs, hostibus nostrīs inde subministrāta auxilia intellegēbat; et sī tempus annī ad bellum gerendum dēficeret, tamen māgnō ⁵sibi ūsuī ⁶fore arbitrābātur. sī modo īnsulam adīsset, genus hominum perspēxisset, loca, portūs, aditūs cōgnōvisset. Haec omnia ferē Gallīs erant incōgnita. ⁷Neque enim temere, praeter mercātōrēs, ⁸illō adit quisquam, ⁹neque eīs ipsīs quicquam praeter ōram maritimam atque eās regiōnēs, quae sunt contrā ¹⁰Galliās, nōtum est.

Itaque vocātīs ad sē undique mercātōribus, neque quanta esset īnsulae māgnitūdō, neque quae aut quantae nātiōnēs incolerent,

---

1. **Exiguā . . . reliquā:** ablative absolute. It was now near the end of July.
2. **etsī:** *in spite of the fact that.*
3. **mātūrae:** *early.*
4. **in Britanniam . . . contendit:** The recorded history of England begins with Caesar's account of this expedition.
5. **sibi ūsuī:** double dative.

6. **fore = futūrum esse:** *that it would be.*
7. **Neque enim . . . quisquam:** (*For neither anyone*) *For no one.*
8. **illō:** (*thither*) *there;* adv.
9. **neque eīs ipsīs quicquam:** with **nōtum est,** *nor even to them is anything known.*
10. **Galliās:** referring to the divisions of Gaul, i.e., **Belgae, Celtae, Aquitānī.**

neque quem ūsum bellī habērent aut quibus īnstitūtīs ūterentur, neque quī essent ad mājōrem nāvium multitūdinem idōneī portūs, reperīre poterat.

FOR COMPREHENSION

● ANSWER IN ENGLISH:
1. What reasons does Caesar give for invading Britain at this time?
2. What did the Romans know about Britain at this time?
3. From whom did Caesar seek information about Britain?
4. What facts about Britain did Caesar want to know in particular?
5. Was he successful in obtaining this information?

Ch. 21   Caesar Sends Volusenus and Commius to Britain

Ad haec cōgnōscenda, ¹priusquam perīculum faceret, idōneum esse arbitrātus Gājum Volusēnum cum nāvī longā praemittit. ²Huic mandat, ut, explōrātīs omnibus rēbus, ad sē quam prīmum revertātur.

Ipse cum omnibus cōpiīs in Morinōs proficīscitur, quod inde erat brevissimus in Britanniam trājectus. Hūc nāvēs undique ex fīnitimīs regiōnibus et, ³quam superiōre aestāte ad Veneticum bellum effēcerat classem, jubet convenīre.

Interim cōnsiliō ējus cōgnitō et per mercātōrēs perlātō ad Britannōs, ā complūribus ējus īnsulae cīvitātibus ad eum lēgātī veniunt, quī ⁴polliceantur obsidēs dare atque imperiō populī Rōmānī obtemperāre. Quibus audītīs, līberāliter pollicitus hortātusque, ut in eā sententiā permanērent, ⁵eōs domum remittit et cum eīs ūnā Commium, quem ipse, Atrebātibus superātīs, rēgem ⁶ibi cōnstituerat, cūjus et virtūtem et cōnsilium probābat et quem sibi fidēlem esse arbitrābātur, cūjusque auctōritās in hīs regiōnibus ⁷māgnī habēbātur, mittit. Huic imperat, quās possit, ⁸adeat cīvitātēs hortēturque, ut populī Rōmānī fidem sequantur, ⁹sēque celeriter eō ventūrum nūntiet.

Volusēnus, perspectīs regiōnibus omnibus, ¹⁰quantum eī facultātis darī potuit, quī nāvī ēgredī ac sē barbarīs committere nōn

---

1. **priusquam ... faceret:** *before he himself* (with the army) *should take the risk.*
2. **Huic mandat:** *He instructed him.*
3. **quam ... classem** = **eam classem quam.**
4. **polliceantur:** relative purpose clause.
5. **eōs** = **lēgātōs Britannōs.**
6. **ibi** = **in Atrebātibus.**

7. **māgnī habēbātur:** (*was considered of great* [value]) *was held in high esteem;* **māgnī:** genitive of description.
8. **adeat:** supply **ut.**
9. **sē** = **Caesarem.**
10. **quantum ... facultātis:** *as far as opportunity;* **facultātis:** partitive genitive.

audēret, quīntō diē ad Caesarem revertitur, [11]quaeque ibi per-spēxisset, renūntiat.

FOR COMPREHENSION

● ANSWER IN ENGLISH:
1. What was Caesar's purpose in sending Volusenus to Britain?
2. How long a time was Volusenus absent?
3. What preparation for the invasion did Caesar make during this time?
4. Why did Caesar send Commius to Britain?
5. What was Caesar's opinion of Volusenus and of Commius?
6. Why should Commius have influence in Britain?

Ch. 22   Many Morini Surrender; the Fleet Assembles

[1]Dum in hīs locīs Caesar nāvium parandārum causā morātur, ex māgnā parte Morinōrum ad eum lēgātī vēnērunt, quī sē [2]dē superiōris temporis cōnsiliō excūsārent, quod hominēs barbarī et [3]nostrae cōnsuētūdinis imperītī, bellum populō Rōmānō fēcissent, sēque ea, quae imperāvisset, factūrōs pollicērentur.

Hoc sibi Caesar [4]satis opportūnē accidisse arbitrātus, quod neque post tergum hostem relinquere volēbat, neque bellī gerendī propter annī tempus facultātem habēbat, neque hās tantulārum rērum occupātiōnēs [5]Britanniae antepōnendās jūdicābat, māgnum eīs numerum obsidum imperat. Quibus adductīs, eōs in fidem recēpit.

Nāvibus circiter LXXX onerāriīs coāctīs contrāctīsque, quot satis esse ad duās trānsportandās legiōnēs exīstimābat, [6]quod praetereā nāvium longārum habēbat, quaestōrī, lēgātīs prae-fectīsque distribuit. [7]Hūc accēdēbant XVIII onerāriae nāvēs, quae ex eō locō [8]ā mīlibus passuum VIII ventō tenēbantur, [9]quōminus in eundem portum venīre possent. Hās equitibus distribuit.

Reliquum [10]exercitum Q. Titūriō Sabīnō et L. Aurunculējō

Cottae lēgātīs in Menapiōs atque in eōs pāgōs Morinōrum, ā quibus ad eum lēgātī nōn vēnerant, dūcendum dedit. P. Sulpicium Rūfum lēgātum cum eō praesidiō, quod satis esse arbitrābātur, portum tenēre jūssit.

FOR COMPREHENSION

● ANSWER IN ENGLISH:

1. Why did Caesar demand hostages from the Morini who had apologized to him?
2. In what way did this submission of the Morini assist Caesar's plans?
3. How many transports did Caesar have? How many legions were to be transported?
4. How many legions did Caesar choose for this expedition? Why did he choose them?
5. What instructions did Caesar give to Sabinus and Cotta?
6. Why did Caesar leave a strong garrison at the point of embarkation? Whom did he leave in command?

Ch. 23   Caesar Arrives off the Coast of Dover

Hīs cōnstitūtīs rēbus, [1]nactus idōneam ad nāvigandum tempestātem, [2]tertiā ferē vigiliā solvit equitēsque in ūlteriōrem portum prōgredī et nāvēs cōnscendere et sē sequī jūssit. [3]Ā quibus cum paulō tardius esset administrātum, ipse [4]hōrā diēī circiter quārtā cum prīmīs nāvibus Britanniam attigit, atque ibi in omnibus collibus expositās hostium cōpiās armātās cōnspēxit.

Cūjus locī haec erat nātūra, atque ita montibus angustē mare continēbātur, utī ex locīs superiōribus in lītus tēlum adigī posset. Hunc ad ēgrediendum nēquāquam idōneum locum arbitrātus, [5]dum reliquae nāvēs eō convenīrent, ad hōram nōnam in ancorīs exspectāvit.

Interim lēgātīs tribūnīsque mīlitum convocātīs, et quae ex Volusēnō cōgnōvisset, et quae fierī vellet, ostendit, monuitque [6](ut reī mīlitāris ratiō, māximēque ut maritimae rēs postulārent) ut,

---

1. nactus ... tempestātem: *finding suitable weather.*
2. tertiā ... vigiliā: just after midnight on August 26, 55 B.C.
3. Ā ... administrātum: *Although his orders were carried out a little more slowly by them* (the cavalry).
4. hōrā ... quārtā: about ten A.M.
5. dum ... convenīrent: *until the ships should assemble.*
6. ut reī ... postulārent: *as the science of warfare and especially as naval tactics demanded.*

281

[7]cum celerem atque īnstabilem mōtum habērent, ad nūtum et ad tempus omnēs rēs ab eīs administrārentur. Hīs dīmissīs, et ventum et [8]aestum ūnō tempore nactus secundum, datō sīgnō et [9]sublātīs ancorīs, circiter mīlia passuum septem [10]ab eō locō prōgressus, [11]apertō ac plānō lītore nāvēs cōnstituit.

---

7. cum ... habērent: *since they have a swift and unsteady motion.*
8. aestum: *the current* (of the channel).
9. sublātīs ancorīs: *(anchors having been lifted) weighing anchor.*

10. ab eō locō: near Dover.
11. apertō ... lītore: northeast of Dover.

FOR COMPREHENSION

● ANSWER IN ENGLISH:

1. How long did it take Caesar to cross the channel?
2. Why did Caesar land at Dover?
3. How long did Caesar wait for the eighteen boats which were carrying the cavalry?
4. Where were the forces of the enemy drawn up when Caesar arrived?
5. What was the reason for Caesar's calling together the lieutenants and the tribunes?
6. How far did he sail, and where did he prepare to land?

Ch. 24 Caesar Encounters Difficulties in Landing

At barbarī, cōnsiliō Rōmānōrum cōgnitō, praemissō equitātū et essedāriīs, [1]quō plērumque genere in proeliīs ūtī cōnsuēvērunt, reliquīs cōpiīs subsecūtī, nostrōs [2]nāvibus ēgredī prohibēbant.

Erat ob hās causās summa difficultās, quod nāvēs propter māgnitūdinem [3]nisi in altō cōnstituī nōn poterant, [4]mīlitibus autem, īgnōtīs locīs, [5]impedītīs manibus, māgnō et gravī onere armōrum oppressīs, simul et dē nāvibus dēsiliendum et in fluctibus cōnsistendum et cum hostibus erat pūgnandum, cum illī aut ex āridō aut paulum in aquam prōgressī, omnibus membrīs expedītīs, [6]nōtissimīs locīs, audācter tēla conjicerent et equōs īnsuēfactōs incitārent.

---

1. quō ... genere: *a kind* (of fighting) *which.* This refers to the custom of fighting in chariots.
2. nāvibus ēgredī: *from landing.*
3. nisi in altō: *except in deep water.*
4. mīlitibus: modified by **oppressīs;** da-
tive of agent. It was necessary for the soldiers to leap, to stand, and to fight.
5. impedītīs manibus: *with their hands hampered* (by their swords and javelins); ablative absolute.
6. nōtissimīs locīs: *in very familiar places.*

Quibus rēbus nostrī perterritī, atque hūjus omnīnō ⁷generis
pūgnae imperītī, nōn eādem alacritāte ac studiō, ⁸quō in pedestri-
bus ⁹ūtī proeliīs cōnsuēverant, ūtēbantur.

7. **generis:** genitive with **imperītī.**
8. **quō:** When the antecedents are of different genders, the relative agrees with
the nearest antecedent.
9. **ūtī:** *to display.*

FOR COMPREHENSION

● ANSWER IN ENGLISH:
1. What did the Britons do when they saw the Roman fleet advancing up the
coast?
2. What disadvantages did the Romans have to contend with in getting ashore?
3. What advantages did the Britons have on this occasion?
4. What effect did this unequal situation have on the Roman soldiers?
5. How does Caesar indirectly praise his men?

Ch. 25   A Standard Bearer Encourages His Comrades

A Roman standard bearer.

¹Quod ubi Caesar animadvertit, nāvēs longās,
quārum et speciēs erat barbarīs inūsitātior et
mōtus ²ad ūsum expedītior, paulum removērī ab
onerāriīs nāvibus et rēmīs incitārī et ad latus apertum hostium cōnstituī, atque inde fundīs, sagittīs,
tormentīs hostēs propellī ac submovērī jūssit;
³quae rēs māgnō ūsuī nostrīs fuit. Nam, et nāvium
figūrā et rēmōrum mōtū et inūsitātō genere tor-
mentōrum permōtī, barbarī cōnstitērunt, ac paulum modo pedem rettulērunt.

Atque nostrīs mīlitibus ⁴cūnctantibus, māximē
propter altitūdinem maris, ⁵quī decimae legiōnis
aquilam ferēbat, obtestātus deōs ut ea rēs legiōnī
fēlīciter ēvenīret, "Dēsilīte," inquit, "commīli-
tōnēs, nisi vultis aquilam hostibus ⁶prōdere. Ego
certē meum reī pūblicae atque imperātōrī officium
praestiterō."

Hoc cum vōce māgnā dīxisset, ⁷sē ex nāvī prōjēcit atque in hostēs aquilam ferre coepit. Tum

1. **Quod:** *This* (i.e., the way in which the
Roman soldiers were handicapped).
2. **ad ūsum expedītior:** *easier to manage.*
3. **quae rēs = haec rēs:** *this* (move)

4. **cūnctantibus = dubitantibus.**
5. **quī = is quī:** *the one who.*
6. **prōdere = trādere.**
7. **sē . . . prōjēcit = dēsiluit.**

nostrī, cohortātī inter sē, nē[8] tantum dēdecus admitterētur, ūniversī ex nāvī dēsiluērunt. Hōs item [9]ex proximīs nāvibus cum
cōnspēxissent, subsecūtī hostibus appropinquāvērunt.

8. **tantum dēdecus:** To lose its ensign, the
eagle, was the greatest disgrace which
could happen to a legion.

9. **ex proximīs nāvibus:** (the men) *from
the nearest ships.*

FOR COMPREHENSION

- ANSWER IN ENGLISH:
1. What naval maneuver was carried out by Caesar?
2. Why did the Roman warships alarm the Britons?
3. What were the tormenta? Where were they stationed?
4. Why did the Roman soldiers still hesitate to land?
5. What was said and done by the standard bearer of the Tenth Legion?
6. What was the effect of the standard bearer's example on the Romans on the
   other ships?

Ch. 26   The Romans Rout the Britons

Pūgnātum est ab utrīsque ācriter. Nostrī tamen, quod neque
ōrdinēs servāre neque fīrmiter īnsistere neque sīgna subsequī
poterant, atque [1]alius aliā ex nāvī, quibuscumque sīgnīs occur-
rerat, sē aggregābat, māgnopere perturbābantur; hostēs vērō,
nōtīs omnibus vadīs, ubi ex lītore [2]aliquōs singulārēs ex nāvī
ēgredientēs cōnspēxerant, incitātīs equīs impedītōs adoriēbantur,
plūrēs paucōs circumsistēbant, aliī [3]ab latere apertō in ūniversōs
tēla conjiciēbant.

Quod cum animadvertisset Caesar, [4]scaphās longārum nāvium,
item [5]speculātōria nāvigia, mīlitibus complērī jussit et, quōs
labōrantēs cōnspēxerat, hīs subsidia submittēbat. Nostrī, [6]simul
in āridō cōnstitērunt, suīs omnibus cōnsecūtīs in hostēs impetum
fēcērunt atque eōs in fugam dedērunt; neque [7]longius prōsequī
potuērunt, [8]quod equitēs cursum tenēre atque īnsulam capere nōn
potuerant. Hoc ūnum ad prīstinam fortūnam Caesarī dēfuit.

1. **alius . . . nāvī:** *one from one ship, another from another.*
2. **aliquōs singulārēs:** *any by themselves.*
3. **ab latere apertō:** *on the exposed side*
(i.e., the right side).
4. **scaphās:** *small boats* (about the size of
a rowboat. These were carried on the
larger ships.).

5. **speculātōria nāvigia:** *scout boats* (accompanying the warships).
6. **simul** = simul atque.
7. **longius:** *very far.*
8. **quod   equitēs . . .   nōn   potuerant:**
They had not yet left the continent.

FOR COMPREHENSION

● ANSWER IN ENGLISH:

1. What were the three chief difficulties which faced the Romans in reaching the beach?
2. What action on Caesar's part made it possible for his men to gain the shore?
3. How did the small boats and the scout boats prove to be more serviceable than the large warships?
4. Where was Caesar's cavalry at this time?
5. What prevented the Romans from pursuing the Britons very far?

Ch. 27   The Britons Sue for Peace

Hostēs proeliō superātī, simul atque sē ex fugā recēpērunt, statim ad Caesarem lēgātōs dē pāce mīsērunt; obsidēs sē datūrōs, [1]quaeque imperāvisset, esse factūrōs pollicitī sunt. Ūnā cum hīs lēgātīs Commius Atrebās vēnit, quem suprā dēmōnstrāveram ā Caesare in Britanniam praemissum. [2]Hunc illī ē nāvī ēgressum, cum ad eōs [3]ōrātōris modō Caesaris mandāta dēferret, comprehenderant atque in vincula conjēcerant; [4]tum, [5]proeliō factō, remīsērunt. In petendā pāce [6]ējus reī culpam in [7]multitūdinem contulērunt et, propter imprūdentiam [8]ut īgnōscerētur, petīvērunt.

Caesar questus, quod, cum [9]ultrō in continentem lēgātīs missīs pācem ab sē petīvissent, bellum sine causā intulissent, īgnōscere sē imprūdentiae dīxit obsidēsque imperāvit; quōrum illī partem statim dedērunt, partem ex longinquiōribus locīs [10]arcessītam paucīs diēbus sēsē datūrōs dīxērunt. Intereā suōs remigrāre in agrōs jussērunt, prīncipēsque undique convenīre et sē cīvitātēsque suās Caesarī commendāre coepērunt.

FOR COMPREHENSION

● ANSWER IN ENGLISH:

1. How did the Britons acknowledge their defeat?
2. What principle of international law had the Britons violated?

---

1. quaeque = et ea quae.
2. Hunc . . . ēgressum: (*Him having gone out from the ship*) *As soon as he had disembarked.*
3. ōrātōris modō = lēgātī officiō: *as an envoy.*
4. tum: here equivalent to **nunc.**
5. proeliō factō = **post proelium.**

6. ējus reī = ējus factī.
7. multitūdinem = vulgus.
8. ut īgnōscerētur: (*that it be pardoned them*) *that he pardon them.*
9. ultrō = suā sponte.
10. arcessītam = cum (or quae) arcessīta esset.

3. What excuse did the Britons give Caesar for mistreating Commius?
4. Were the rabble really responsible for the arrest of Commius?
5. What two demands did Caesar make?

Ch. 28 Storms Drive Roman Transports Back to Gaul

His rebus pace cōnfīrmātā, [1]post diem quārtum quam est in Britanniam ventum, nāvēs XVIII, dē quibus suprā dēmōnstrātum est, quae equitēs sustulerant, ex superiōre portū lēnī ventō solvērunt. Quae cum appropinquārent Britanniae et ex castrīs vidērentur, tanta tempestās subitō coorta est, ut nūlla eārum cursum tenēre posset, sed aliae [2]eōdem, unde erant profectae, referrentur, aliae ad īnferiōrem partem īnsulae, quae est [3]propius sōlis occāsum, māgnō suō cum perīculō dējicerentur; [4]quae [5]tamen ancorīs jactīs cum flūctibus complērentur, necessāriō [6]adversā nocte [7]in altum prōvectae continentem petīvērunt.

1. **post diem quārtum (post) quam . . .**
   ventum = quārtō diē, postquam
   Caesar . . . vēnit.
2. **eōdem = ad eundem locum.**
3. **propius sōlis occāsum:** *near the west.*
4. **quae:** *since.*
5. **tamen . . . jactīs:** *in spite of the fact that they had cast anchor.*
6. **adversā nocte:** *(in the face of the night) with the night against them.*
7. **in altum prōvectae:** *(carried forward into the deep) they put out to sea.*

FOR COMPREHENSION

● ANSWER IN ENGLISH
1. What was the cause of the cavalry's delay in leaving port?
2. When did the transport containing the cavalry finally set sail?
3. Where were the eighteen transports when the storm from the northeast struck them?
4. Why were some ships driven by the wind in one direction and others in another?
5. What danger threatened the ships which were driven to the southwest part of the island?

Ch. 29 The Roman Fleet Is Wrecked by a Storm

Eādem nocte accidit, ut esset lūna plēna, [1]quī diēs maritimōs [2]aestūs māximōs in Ōceanō efficere cōnsuēvit, nostrīsque id erat incōgnitum. Ita ūnō tempore et longās nāvēs, quibus Caesar exer-

1. **quī diēs:** *a time which.*
2. **aestūs māximōs:** *very high tides.* Caesar refers to the spring tides which occur at

the time of the full moon. Sometimes they rise as high as twenty-five feet.

citum trānsportandum cūrāverat, quāsque in āridum subdūxerat, aestus complēbat et onerāriās, quae ad ancorās erant dēligātae, tempestās afflīctābat, neque ūlla nostrīs facultās aut administrandī aut auxiliandī dabātur. Complūribus nāvibus frāctīs, reliquae cum essent, fūnibus, ancorīs reliquīsque armāmentīs āmissīs, ad nāvigandum inūtilēs, māgna, [3]id quod necesse erat accidere, tōtīus exercitūs perturbātiō facta est. [4]Neque enim nāvēs erant aliae, quibus reportārī possent, et omnia deerant, quae ad reficiendās nāvēs erant ūsuī, et quod omnibus cōnstābat, [5]hiemārī in Galliā oportēre, frūmentum in hīs locīs [6]in hiemem prōvīsum nōn erat.

---

3. **id ... accidere:** *(that which was necessary to happen) as was inevitable.*
4. **Neque ... aliae:** *no other.*

5. **hiemārī ... oportēre:** *(that it must be wintered) that the winter would have to be spent.*
6. **in hiemem:** *for the winter.*

FOR COMPREHENSION

● ANSWER IN ENGLISH:
1. Why had not Caesar foreseen the danger from the high tide?
2. What happened to the Roman warships on the night of the full moon?
3. What happened to the transports?
4. Why did the whole Roman army become alarmed?
5. Why had Caesar not provided for a grain supply in Britain?

Ch. 30   The Britons Plan a Rebellion

Quibus rēbus cōgnitīs, [1]prīncipēs Britanniae, quī post proelium ad Caesarem convēnerant, inter sē collocūtī, cum et equitēs et nāvēs et frūmentum Rōmānīs deesse intellegerent, et paucitātem mīlitum ex castrōrum exiguitāte cōgnōscerent, quae [2]hōc erant etiam angustiōra, quod sine impedīmentīs Caesar legiōnēs trānsportāverat, optimum [3]factū esse dūxērunt, rebelliōne factā, frūmentō commeātūque nostrōs prohibēre et [4]rem in hiemem prōdūcere, quod [5]hīs superātīs aut reditū interclūsīs, nēminem posteā bellī īnferendī causā in Britanniam trānsitūrum cōnfīdēbant. Itaque, rūrsus conjūrātiōne factā, paulātim ex castrīs discēdere et [6]suōs clam ex agrīs dēdūcere coepērunt.

---

1. **prīncipēs ... dūxērunt:** dūxērunt = putāvērunt, exīstimāvērunt.
2. **hōc ... quod:** *for this reason because.*
3. **factū:** ablative of the supine to denote specification.
4. **rem = bellum.**

5. **hīs superātīs:** *if these were conquered.*
6. **suōs clam ex agrīs dēdūcere:** *to secretly withdraw their men from the fields* (i.e., the chiefs began to reorganize their disbanded army).

FOR COMPREHENSION

- ANSWER IN ENGLISH:
1. What three circumstances influenced the chiefs of the Britons to organize a rebellion?
2. How did the Britons hope to defeat the Romans?
3. What result did they hope to accomplish?
4. Why was Caesar's camp smaller than usual?
5. What did the chiefs do as a first move? as a second move? as a third move?

Ch. 31 Caesar Anticipates Trouble

At Caesar, etsī nōndum eōrum cōnsilia cōgnōverat, tamen et [1]ex ēventū nāvium suārum et ex eō, quod obsidēs dare intermīserant, [2]fore id, quod accidit, suspicābātur. Itaque ad omnēs cāsūs subsidia comparābat. Nam et frūmentum ex agrīs cotīdiē in castra cōnferēbat et, [3]quae gravissimē afflīctae erant nāvēs, eārum māteriā atque aere ad reliquās reficiendās ūtēbātur et, [4]quae ad eās rēs erant ūsuī, ex continentī comparārī jubēbat. Itaque, cum summō studiō ā mīlitibus [5]administrārētur, [6]XII nāvibus āmissīs, [7]reliquīs ut nāvigārī satis commodē posset, effēcit.

---

1. **ex ēventū:** *from the disaster;* **ex eō, quod:** *from the fact that.*
2. **fore = futūrum esse; fore . . . accidit:** *that that would happen which actually did happen.*
3. **quae . . . nāvēs = eārum nāvium quae.**
4. **quae = ea quae.**
5. **administrārētur:** *the work was carried on.*
6. **XII . . . āmissīs:** *although twelve ships were lost.*
7. **reliquīs:** ablative of means.

FOR COMPREHENSION

- ANSWER IN ENGLISH:
1. What two facts led Caesar to suspect the Britons' new plans?
2. How did Caesar prepare to handle the new emergencies?
3. What material did Caesar use to repair the least damaged ships in his fleet?
4. What materials other than timber and bronze were needed for repairs?
5. How many seaworthy ships did Caesar now have? How many had left Boulogne?

Ch. 32 The Seventh Legion Is Attacked

Dum ea geruntur, legiōne ex cōnsuētūdine ūnā [1]frūmentātum missā, quae appellābātur septima, neque ūllā ad id tempus bellī

---

1. **frūmentātum:** *to forage;* supine expressing purpose.

suspīciōne interpositā, ²cum pars hominum in agrīs remanēret, pars etiam in castra ventitāret, eī, quī prō portīs castrōrum in statiōne erant, Caesarī nūntiāvērunt, pulverem mājōrem, ³quam cōnsuētūdō ferret, in eā parte vidērī, quam in partem legiō iter fēcisset. Caesar id quod erat suspicātus, ⁴aliquid novī ā barbarīs initum cōnsilī, cohortēs, quae in statiōnibus erant, sēcum in eam partem proficīscī, ex reliquīs duās in statiōnem cohortēs succēdere, reliquās armārī et cōnfestim sēsē subsequī jūssit.

Cum paulō longius ā castrīs prōcessisset, suōs ab hostibus premī atque aegrē sustinēre et, cōnfertā legiōne, ex omnibus partibus tēla conjicī animadvertit. Nam quod, ⁵omnī ex reliquīs partibus dēmessō frūmentō, pars ūna erat reliqua, suspicātī hostēs, hūc nostrōs esse ventūrōs, noctū in silvīs dēlituerant; tum dispersōs, dēpositīs armīs in metendō occupātōs subitō adortī, paucīs interfectīs reliquōs, ⁶incertīs ōrdinibus, perturbāverant, simul equitātū atque essedīs circumdederant.

FOR COMPREHENSION

- ANSWER IN ENGLISH:
1. What suspicious fact did Caesar's sentries report to him?
2. Why was Caesar ready for immediate action?
3. What three orders did he issue immediately?
4. What did Caesar notice after he had advanced a little distance from the camp?
5. Where was it that the enemy had hidden themselves during the preceding night?
6. Which legions did Caesar have with him in Britain?

Summary of Chapter 33

Caesar describes the technique of chariot fighting as practised by the Britons. First the charioteers ride in all directions hurling weapons. The terrifying horses and clatter of the wheels disturb the ranks of the enemy very much. When they have weaved their way among their own cavalry, they leap to the ground and fight on foot. Meanwhile the drivers gradually withdraw from the battle in order that their warriors may have a quick means of retreat if hard pressed by the enemy. The chariot fighters display the speed of cavalry combined with the

---

2. **cum**: *since.*
3. **quam ... ferret**: *(than custom brought) than usual.*
4. **aliquid ... initum (esse) cōnsilī**: *that some new plan had been entered upon.*

5. **omnī ... frūmentō**: *after all the grain had been cut in the other sections.*
6. **incertīs ōrdinibus**: *their ranks in disorder;* ablative absolute.

firmness of infantry. Daily practice and training enables them to check their horses at a gallop down a steep declivity, turn them, run along the pole of the chariot, perch on the yoke, and get back into the chariot car in a flash.

Ch. 34   Caesar Rescues the Seventh Legion

[1]Quibus [2]rēbus [3]perturbātis nostrīs, [4]novitāte pūgnae, tempore opportūnissimō Caesar auxilium tulit; namque ējus adventū cōnstitērunt, nostrī sē ex timōre recēpērunt. Quō factō, ad lacessendum hostem et ad committendum proelium aliēnum esse tempus arbitrātus, suō sē locō continuit et, [5]brevī tempore intermissō, in castra legiōnēs redūxit.

Dum haec geruntur, nostrīs omnibus occupātīs, quī erant in agrīs reliquī, discessērunt. Secūtae sunt continuōs complūrēs diēs tempestātēs, [6]quae et nostrōs in castrīs continērent et hostem ā pūgnā prohibērent.

Interim barbarī nūntiōs in omnēs partēs dīmīsērunt paucitātemque nostrōrum mīlitum suīs [7]praedicāvērunt et, quanta praedae faciendae atque [8]in perpetuum suī līberandī facultās darētur, sī Rōmānōs castrīs expulissent, dēmōnstrāvērunt. [9]Hīs rēbus celeriter māgnā multitūdine peditātūs equitātūsque coāctā, ad castra vēnērunt.

FOR COMPREHENSION

● ANSWER IN ENGLISH:

1. What effect did Caesar's arrival have on the attacking Britons? on the Seventh Legion?
2. Why did not Caesar engage in battle at once with the Britons?
3. Why were the native Britons at work in the fields up to the time of the attack on the soldiers of the Seventh Legion? Why did they go away after the battle?

---

1. **Quibus ... pūgnae:** *To our men disturbed by these tactics because of the novelty of the battle.*
2. **rēbus:** ablative of means.
3. **perturbātīs nostrīs:** dative with **tulit.**
4. **novitāte:** ablative of cause.
5. **brevī   tempore   intermissō** = **post breve tempus.**

6. **quae = tālēs ut:** introducing a relative characteristic clause expressing result.
7. **praedicāvērunt:** *announced;* not to be confused with **praedīcō:** *foretell.*
8. **in perpetuum:** *forever.*
9. **Hīs rēbus:** *By these statements.*

4. What effect had the continued bad weather on the two armies?
5. What did the Britons hope to accomplish by sending out messengers in all directions?

Ch. 35   Caesar Defeats and Routs the Britons

Caesar, etsī [1]idem, quod superiōribus diēbus acciderat, fore vidēbat, [2]ut, sī essent hostēs pulsī, celeritāte perīculum [3]effugerent, tamen nactus equitēs circiter xxx, quōs Commius Atrebās, [4]dē quō ante dictum est, sēcum trānsportāverat, legiōnēs in aciē prō castrīs cōnstituit. Commissō proeliō, [5]diūtius nostrōrum mīlitum impetum hostēs ferre nōn potuērunt ac terga vertērunt. Quōs nostrī [6]tantō spatiō secūtī, [7]quantum cursū et vīribus efficere potuērunt, complūrēs ex eīs occīdērunt; deinde, omnibus longē lātēque aedificiīs incēnsīs, sē in castra recēpērunt.

1. **idem:** subject of **fore.**
2. **ut . . . effugerent:** substantive clause in apposition to **idem.**
3. **effugerent:** *they would escape from.*
4. **dē quō ante dictum est:** (*about whom it has been said before*) *who has been mentioned before.*

5. **diūtius:** *very long.*
6. **tantō spatiō = tantum spatium:** *for as great a distance.*
7. **quantum . . . potuērunt:** *as their speed and strength would allow.*

FOR COMPREHENSION

● ANSWER IN ENGLISH:

1. Why did Caesar think a decisive battle unlikely?
2. How many cavalrymen did Caesar have? Where did he obtain them?
3. What was the result of the battle?
4. How far did the Romans pursue the fleeing Britons?
5. What did these Romans do before returning to their own camp?

Ch. 36   Caesar Returns to the Continent

Eōdem diē lēgātī ab hostibus missī, ad Caesarem dē pāce vēnērunt. [1]Hīs Caesar numerum obsidum, quem ante imperāverat, duplicāvit, eōsque in continentem addūcī jūssit, quod,

1. **Hīs:** (In answer) *to these;* dative of reference.

²propinquā diē aequinoctī, ³īnfīrmīs nāvibus ⁴hiemī nāvigātiōnem subjiciendam nōn exīstimābat.

Ipse, idōneam tempestātem nactus, paulō post mediam noctem nāvēs solvit; quae omnēs incolumēs ad continentem pervēnērunt; sed ex eīs onerāriae duae eōsdem portūs, ⁵quōs reliquae, capere nōn potuērunt, et paulō īnfrā dēlātae sunt.

FOR COMPREHENSION

● ANSWER IN ENGLISH:
1. Why did Caesar double the number of hostages that he had previously demanded?
2. Why did Caesar not wait for these hostages to be delivered?
3. At what hour did Caesar sail from Britain?
4. What time of the year was it? Why did he sail at once?
5. What percentage of the ships reached Gaul?

Summary of Chapters 37–38

The three hundred men who had disembarked from their transports were hurrying toward camp when the Morini surrounded them and ordered them to lay down their arms if they did not want to be killed. The Romans resisted, and the din brought about 6,000 more natives to the scene. As soon as Caesar learned the plight of his men, he ordered the entire cavalry to the scene of action,

---

2. **propinquā diē aequinoctī:** *as the time of the equinox was near.*
3. **īnfīrmīs nāvibus:** *with his ships in a disabled condition.*

4. **hiemī:** dative.
5. **quōs reliquae:** supply **capere potuērunt.**

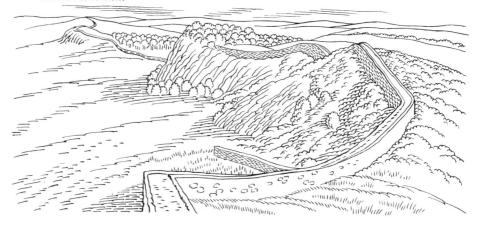

A Roman wall in Britain, built by the Emperor Hadrian in A.D. 120.

but it was more than four hours before relief came to the little group of men valiantly defending themselves. As soon as the cavalry came in sight, the enemy fled, and the cavalry pursued and massacred them in great numbers.

On the next day Caesar sent the Seventh and Tenth Legions under the command of Labienus to punish the rebellious Morini. They quickly surrendered, for the swamps which they had used as hiding places the previous year were now dry. Meanwhile Sabinus and Cotta, who had been sent against the more remote Menapii, returned. They had not succeeded in their mission because the enemy had concealed themselves in inaccessible forests. Nevertheless, the Romans had managed to devastate their fields, cut down their crops, and burn their buildings. Caesar quartered all the legions among the Belgae for the winter. Only two of the British tribes sent hostages there; the others failed to do so. Upon receipt of Caesar's dispatches, the Senate decreed a thanksgiving of twenty days for these achievements.

BOOK FIVE

SECOND INVASION OF BRITAIN

Preview: On this second expedition Caesar remained in Britain for about ten weeks. After a series of engagements marked by heavy losses on both sides, Caesar captured the stronghold of Cassivelaunus, the British leader, and all organized resistance came to an end. The description which Caesar gives in this book of the Britons and of the natural resources and geography of their island is the first accurate information about Britain of which we have any record. It is therefore of utmost historical importance.

Summary of Chapters 1–11

Caesar's first invasion of Britain had taught him that if he hoped to subjugate the Britons he must have more men and more suitable ships. Before going into winter quarters in the fall of 55 b.c., he arranged for the building of a large fleet. In order to expedite loading and beaching, all the ships were to be lower and flatter than those he had used on the first trip. They were to be equipped with oars as well as sails.

He then went to Illyricum and punished the Pirustae, who were menacing the Province. After holding court in Cisalpine Gaul and Illyricum, he returned to Gaul, inspected the fleet, praised the troops and the officers in charge of the work, and then led a force against the Treveri, among whom an anti-Roman spirit had been developing. He quelled the revolt and obliged them by hostages to keep the peace.

Caesar now returned to Portus Itius, modern Boulogne, where the fleet was ready to sail. In order to avoid uprisings in his absence, he decided to take to Britain with him some of the leading Gallic chieftains of whose loyalty he was in doubt. Among these was Dumnorix, the ambitious and crafty Haeduan, who protested violently but in vain. Dumnorix then tried to organize a revolt of the other Gallic chieftains. This was reported to Caesar. While the latter was occupied with the embarkation of the fleet, Dumnorix escaped, but he was captured and killed while resisting arrest. His last words were: "I am a free man and belong to a free state."

Caesar, leaving Labienus with three legions in Gaul, embarked for Britain with 5 legions and 2,000 cavalry in more than 800 ships. After some difficulty with the tide he landed without opposition. The Britains, frightened by the number of ships, had fled from the seacoast. He left his fleet at anchor, moved inland, seized one of the forest strongholds, and on the following day advanced against the enemy.

Just as he was in sight of the enemy, Caesar received the news that a great storm had shattered forty ships and seriously damaged others. Soldiers labored day and night for ten days repairing the fleet, which they beached. Caesar then continued his pursuit of the Britons, who had gathered in great numbers under the leadership of Cassivellaunus.

Ch. 12   The Inhabitants of Britain

Britanniae pars interior ab eīs incolitur, quōs [1]nātōs in īnsulā ipsā dīcunt; maritima pars ab eīs, quī praedae ac bellī īnferendī causā ex Belgiō trānsiērunt (quī omnēs ferē eīs nōminibus cīvitātum appellantur, [2]quibus ortī ex cīvitātibus eō pervēnērunt), et, bellō illātō, ibi permānsērunt atque agrōs colere coepērunt. Hominum est īnfīnīta multitūdō, crēberrimaque aedificia ferē Gallicīs cōnsimilia, pecorum māgnus numerus. Ūtuntur aut aere aut [3]nummō aureō aut tāleīs ferreīs ad certum pondus exāminātīs prō nummō.

Nāscitur ibi [4]plumbum album in mediterrāneīs regiōnibus, in maritimīs ferrum, sed ējus exigua est cōpia; aere ūtuntur importātō. Māteria cūjusque generis, ut in Galliā, est praeter [5]fāgum atque abietem. [6]Leporem et gallīnam et ānserem gustāre fās

---

1. **nātōs . . . ipsā:** *originated on the island itself.*
2. **quibus . . . pervēnērunt:** *as those in which they originated and from which they migrated.*
3. **nummō . . . exāminātīs:** *gold coin or iron bars tested for a fixed weight.*

4. **plumbum album:** *white lead* (i.e., tin).
5. **fāgum . . . abietem:** Caesar was mistaken; birch and fir are native trees.
6. **Leporem . . . ānserem:** *hare, chicken, goose.*

nōn putant; haec tamen alunt [7]animī voluptātisque causā. Loca
sunt temperātiōra quam in Galliā, [8]remissiōribus frīgoribus.

---

7. animī ... causā: *for pastime and pleas-*
ure.

8. remissiōribus frīgoribus: *the cold being*
less severe.

FOR COMPREHENSION

● ANSWER IN ENGLISH:
1. What did the Britons who lived in the interior claim as to their origin?
2. What was the origin, according to Caesar, of the Britons who lived near the
   coast?
3. What kind of money did some of the Britons use?
4. What else besides coined money was sometimes used in trade?
5. What metals were found in Britain?
6. What animal and birds did the Britons think it wrong to eat?

● RESPONDĒ LATĪNE:
1. Ā quibus maritima pars Britanniae incolēbātur?
2. Quālī nummō Britannī ūtēbantur?
3. Ubi plumbum album et ferrum nāscēbantur?
4. Quae arborēs in Britanniā ā Caesare nōn vīsae sunt?
5. Quae avēs Britannī nōn gustābant?

● SCRĪBE LATĪNE:
1. The inhabitants themselves say that they originated on the island.
2. The seacoast was inhabited by those who had crossed from Belgium for the
   sake of booty and of waging war.
3. Caesar found the same kind of lumber as was found in Gaul, except the beech
   and the fir tree.

Ch. 13   The Geography of Britain

Īnsula [1]nātūrā [2]triquetra, cūjus ūnum latus est contrā Galliam.
Hūjus lateris alter angulus, quī est ad Cantium, quō ferē omnēs
ex Galliā nāvēs appelluntur, [3]ad orientem sōlem, īnferior [4]ad
merīdiem spectat. Hoc latus pertinet circiter mīlia passuum D.

Alterum vergit ad Hispāniam atque [5]occidentem sōlem; quā
ex parte est Hibernia, [6]dīmidiō minor (ut exīstimātur) quam
Britannia, sed [7]parī spatiō trānsmissūs atque ex Galliā est in Bri-

---

1. nātūrā: *in shape.*
2. triquetra: *triangular.*
3. ad ... sōlem: *toward the east.*
4. ad merīdiem: *toward the south.*
5. occidentem sōlem: *the west.*

6. dīmidiō minor: (*less by a half*) *half as*
large.
7. parī ... Britanniam: *with a distance*
across equal to that from Gaul to Britain.

tanniam. In hōc mediō cursū est īnsula, quae appellātur Mona; complūrēs praetereā minōrēs subjectae īnsulae exīstimantur; dē quibus īnsulīs nōn nūllī scrīpsērunt, diēs continuōs xxx [8]sub brūmā esse noctem. Nōs nihil dē eō percontātiōnibus reperiēbāmus, nisi [9]certīs ex aquā mēnsūrīs breviōrēs esse quam in continentī noctēs vidēbāmus. Hūjus est longitūdō lateris, [10]ut fert illōrum opīniō, DCC mīlium.

Tertium est contrā septentriōnēs; cui partī nūlla est objecta terra, sed ējus angulus lateris māximē ad Germāniam spectat. Hoc mīlia passuum DCCC in longitūdinem esse exīstimātur. Ita omnis īnsula est in circuitū vīciēs centum mīlium passuum.

---

8. sub brūmā: *about the winter solstice.*
9. certīs ... mēnsūrīs: *by careful measurements with the water clock.*

10. ut ... opīniō: *according to their opinion.*

FOR COMPREHENSION

● ANSWER IN ENGLISH:

1. What are the relative positions of Gaul, Spain, Britain, and Germany according to Caesar's description?
2. How does the size of Ireland compare with that of Britain?
3. How long was night in Britain, according to some sources, during the winter?
4. What scientific device did Caesar use to determine the length of the day?
5. What did they say was the length of the circuit of the whole island?

● RESPONDĒ LATĪNE:

1. Quot latera Britannia habet?
2. Quō prīmum latus spectat?
3. Quam longē hoc latus pertinet?
4. Quanta est longitūdō secundī lateris?
5. Quam longē tertium latus pertinet?

● SCRĪBE LATĪNE:

1. One side of the island looks toward Gaul; the second side stretches south toward Spain; the third side extends toward Germany.
2. They say that they have continuous night there for thirty days.
3. Do you know why Caesar wrote that the length of that side was 700 miles?

Ch. 14   The Customs of the Britons

[1]Ex hīs omnibus longē sunt [2]hūmānissimī, quī Cantium incolunt, quae regiō est maritima omnis, neque multum ā Gallicā

---

1. Ex hīs: *Of these* (i.e., of the Britons).

2. hūmānissimī: *the most civilized.*

differunt cōnsuētūdine. ³Interiōrēs plērīque frūmenta nōn serunt, sed lacte et carne vīvunt pellibusque sunt vestītī.

Omnēs vērō ⁴sē Britannī vitrō īnficiunt, quod ⁵caeruleum efficit colōrem, atque ⁶hōc ⁷horridiōrēs sunt in pūgnā aspectū; ⁸capil-lōque sunt prōmissō.

FOR COMPREHENSION

- ANSWER IN ENGLISH:
1. Which Britons most resembled the Gauls in customs?
2. What did the inland tribes eat and wear?
3. From what plant did the Britons obtain blue dye?
4. Why was the appearance of the Britons wild and horrifying?

- RESPONDĒ LATĪNE:
1. Quī ex hīs omnibus longē sunt hūmānissimī?
2. Quibus rēbus Britannī interiōrēs vīvunt?
3. Quibus rēbus vestītī sunt?
4. Quālem colōrem vitrum efficit?
5. Quālī capillō Britannī sunt?

- SCRĪBE LATĪNE:
1. Why did Caesar think that the inhabitants who lived near the seacoast were most like the Gauls in customs?
2. The inland tribes live on meat and milk and use the skins of animals for clothing.
3. They dye their bodies with woad, and with their long hair they have a horrifying appearance.

Summary of Chapters 15–23

On their march the Romans were attacked by the enemy charioteers and cavalry, whom they beat off and drove into the forests and hills. However, the Romans were handicapped by their heavy armor and by their lack of familiarity with the British method of fighting. Later, when Caesar sent a detachment to forage, the British swooped down upon them. The Romans counterattacked, and, supported by their legions, repulsed the enemy attack.

Caesar then led his army to the Thames. Cassivellaunus, the British leader, gave up hope of open battle and confined himself to guerilla tactics. Meanwhile

---

3. **Interiōrēs plērīque:** *Those living in the interior, for the most part.*
4. **sē ... īnficiunt:** *stain themselves with woad.* Woad is a plant from which a blue dye can be produced.
5. **caeruleum ... colōrem:** *a bluish color.*

6. **hōc:** *on this account.*
7. **horridiōrēs ... aspectū:** *rather wild-looking.*
8. **capillō sunt prōmissō:** *(are with hair let go) they let their hair grow long;* **capillō prōmissō:** ablative of description.

the Trinobantes and several other tribes surrendered to Caesar and sent hostages and grain. Cassivellaunus, moved by numerous setbacks, the devastation of his country, and in particular the defection of his allies, surrendered. Caesar returned to Gaul with his army and prisoners. Not a single ship carrying troops was lost.

ATTACKS ON CAESAR'S WINTER CAMPS

Summary of Chapters 24–43

Because of the scarcity of grain, upon his return to the continent Caesar divided his army into six divisions for the winter and scattered them throughout northern Gaul. The Gauls thought this a favorable time to revolt. They began the uprising by killing Tasgetius, whom Caesar had placed over the Carnutes. Their next move was directed against the garrison of Sabinus and Cotta at Aduatuca. Ambiorix and Catuvolcus, the leaders of the Eburones, finding it impossible to take the Roman camp by force, resorted to guile. They persuaded the Romans that there was a general uprising in northern Gaul against all the Roman garrisons. The Romans believed the story and set out to join Cicero (the brother of Cicero the great orator), in command of the nearest camp. While marching through a narrow pass they were suddenly attacked, and the fifteen cohorts were cut to pieces by the superior numbers of the Gauls.

Ambiorix, elated by his success, hastened westward and easily persuaded the Aduatuci and the Nervii to join him in an attack on Cicero's camp. Here the Gauls adopted Roman methods of siege. On the seventh day, by hurling red hot balls of clay, the Gauls succeeded in setting fire to the thatched roofs of the huts in the Roman camp.

Ch. 44 Pullo and Vorenus

Erant in eā legiōne fortissimī virī, centuriōnēs, quī jam [1]prīmīs ōrdinibus appropinquārent, T. Pullō et L. Vorēnus. Hī perpetuās inter sē contrōversiās habēbant uter alterī anteferrētur, [2]omnibusque annīs [3]dē locō summīs [4]simultātibus contendēbant.

Ex hīs Pullō, cum ācerrimē ad mūnītiōnēs pūgnārētur, [5]"Quid dubitās," inquit, "Vorēne? aut [6]quem locum tuae probandae virtūtis exspectās? Hīc diēs dē nostrīs contrōversiīs jūdicābit."

Haec cum dīxisset, prōcēdit extrā mūnītiōnēs, quaeque pars hostium cōnfertissima est vīsa, in eam irrumpit.

---

1. **prīmīs ōrdinibus:** *the first rank* (i.e., the position of first centurion).
2. **omnibus annīs:** *year in and year out.*
3. **dē locō:** *for promotion.*

4. **simultātibus = contentiōnibus.**
5. **Quid = Cūr.**
6. **quem locum:** *what better opportunity.*

Nē Vorēnus quidem sēsē tum vāllō continet, sed omnium veritus exīstimātiōnem subsequitur.

Mediocrī [7]spatiō relictō, Pullō pīlum in hostēs immittit atque ūnum ex multitūdine prōcurrentem trājicit; [8]quō percussō et exanimātō, [9]hunc scūtīs prōtegunt hostēs, in [10]illum ūniversī tēla conjiciunt neque dant prōgrediendī facultātem. Trānsfīgitur scūtum [11]Pullōnī et verūtum in balteō dēfīgitur. Āvertit hic cāsus vāgīnam et gladium ēdūcere [12]cōnantī dextram [13]morātur manum, impedītumque hostēs circumsistunt. [14]Succurrit [15]inimīcus illī Vorēnus et [16]labōrantī subvenit.

Ad hunc sē cōnfestim ā Pullōne omnis multitūdō convertit; [17]illum verūtō trānsfīxum arbitrantur. Gladiō comminus rem gerit Vorēnus atque, ūnō interfectō, reliquōs paulum prōpellit; dum cupidius īnstat, [18]in locum dējectus īnferiōrem concidit. Huic rūrsus circumventō subsidium fert Pullō, atque ambō incolumēs, complūribus interfectīs, summā cum laude sēsē intrā mūnītiōnēs recipiunt.

Sīc fortūna in [19]contentiōne et certāmine utrumque versāvit ut alter alterī inimīcus auxiliō salūtīque esset, neque dījūdicārī posset uter utrī virtūte [20]anteferendus vidērētur.

FOR COMPREHENSION

- ANSWER IN ENGLISH:
1. When and where did the incident related in this chapter occur?
2. Which of the two centurions encountered the enemy first?
3. What caused Vorenus to attack the enemy?
4. What hindered Pullo from drawing his sword?
5. How did Pullo repay Vorenus for saving his life?
6. Did this contest between Pullo and Vorenus decide which of the two was the better man?

- RESPONDĒ LATĪNE:
1. Quī erant Pullō et Vorēnus?
2. Quae erat inter sē contrōversia?
3. Cūr Vorēnus Pullōnem subsecūtus est?

7. **spatiō**: between Pullo and the enemy.
8. **quō**: the wounded Gaul.
9. **hunc**: the wounded Gaul.
10. **illum** = **Pullōnem**.
11. **Pullōnī**: dative of reference.
12. **cōnantī**: modifies **Pullōnī** understood.
13. **morātur** = **impedit**.
14. **Succurrit** = **Auxilium fert.**

15. **inimīcus**: *his rival.*
16. **labōrantī**: modifies **eī** (**Pullōnī**) understood.
17. **illum** = **Pullōnem**.
18. **in ... īnferiōrem**: *stumbling into a hole.*
19. **contentiōne** = **contrōversiā**.
20. **anteferendus** = **antepōnendus**.

4. Cum hostēs Pullōnem circumsisterent, quis illī succurrit?

5. Quandō Pullō Vorēnō succurrit?

● SCRĪBE LATĪNE:

1. When he had said this, he advanced outside the fortification and charged the enemy.

2. The enemy covered the wounded man with their shields so that they might keep Pullo from advancing.

3. It was impossible to decide which of the two proved braver than the other.

Summary of Chapters 45–47

Every day Cicero tried to send messages of his plight to Caesar; but his messengers were all caught and tortured to death. Finally a friendly native Gaul, carrying the message concealed in the shaft of his lance, delivered the message. Caesar immediately advanced with two legions to relieve Cicero. Meanwhile the Treveri, elated by their victory over the Roman forces led by Sabinus and Cotta, made an attack on the camp of Labienus in the country of the Remi.

Ch. 48   The Dart in the Tower

Caesar [1]māgnīs itineribus in Nerviōrum fīnēs vēnit. Ibi ex captīvīs cōgnōscit, quae [2]apud Cicerōnem gerantur, quantōque in perīculō rēs sit. Tum cuidam ex equitibus Gallīs māgnīs praemiīs persuādet utī ad Cicerōnem epistulam dēferat.

Hanc [3]Graecīs cōnscrīptam litterīs mittit, nē, interceptā epistulā, nostra ab hostibus cōnsilia cōgnōscantur. Sī [4]adīre nōn [5]possit, [6]monet ut trāgulam cum epistulā ad [7]āmentum dēligātā intrā mūnītiōnēs castrōrum abjiciat. In litterīs scrībit sē cum legiōnibus profectum celeriter [8]affore; hortātur, ut prīstinam virtūtem retineat. Gallus perīculum veritus, ut erat praeceptum, trāgulam mittit.

[9]Haec cāsū ad turrim adhaesit, neque ā nostrīs bīduō animadversa, tertiō diē ā quōdam mīlite cōnspicitur, dēmpta ad Cicerōnem dēfertur. Ille [10]perlēctam in conventū mīlitum [11]recitat māximāque omnēs laetitiā afficit. Tum [12]fūmī incendiōrum procul vidēbantur; quae rēs omnem dubitātiōnem adventūs legiōnum expulit.

---

1. **māgnīs itineribus:** *forced marches.* The usual day's march was 12–15 miles; a forced march, 25–30 miles.
2. **apud Cicerōnem** = **in Cicerōnis castrīs.**
3. **Graecīs . . . litterīs:** probably Latin written in Greek letters.
4. **adīre:** *to reach.*

5. **possit:** supply **nūntius** as subject.
6. **monet:** supply **Caesar** as subject.
7. **āmentum:** *the thong* (of the javelin).
8. **affore** = **affutūrum esse,** from **adsum.**
9. **Haec:** the dart.
10. **perlēctam:** supply **epistulam.**
11. **recitat:** He read it aloud.
12. **fūmī:** villages were burned in passing.

Roman soldiers driving captured men and beasts to market.

FOR COMPREHENSION

● ANSWER IN ENGLISH:

1. Who attempted to carry a letter from Caesar to Cicero?
2. What alphabet did Caesar use in writing this letter? Why?
3. What instructions did Caesar give his messenger?
4. How long did the message remain unnoticed? Where?
5. Why was the sight of smoke in the distance taken as proof of Caesar's approach?

● RESPONDĒ LATĪNE:

1. Quō modō Caesar in Nerviōrum fīnēs vēnit?
2. Quid Caesar equitī Gallō persuāsit?
3. Quō cōnsiliō epistula Graecīs litterīs cōnscrīpta est?
4. Quid Caesar in epistulā scrīpsit?
5. Quam diū epistula ad turrim adhaesit?
6. Quis ad Cicerōnem epistulam dēfert?

● SCRĪBE LATĪNE:

1. He learned from the prisoners what was going on in Cicero's camp.
2. The letter was written with Greek letters so that, if the letter were intercepted, the enemy would not find out his plans.
3. He urged Cicero that he keep up his former bravery.

Summary of Chapters 49–58

When the enemy heard that Caesar was coming, they abandoned the siege and set out to meet him. Caesar was warned of this by a message from Cicero. As Cicero and his legion were now safe, Caesar selected a camp on a hilltop and fortified it. Since the Romans were outnumbered six to one, he kept his men in camp. Day by day the enemy grew bolder; finally they came up the hill to Caesar's camp and began to tear down the rampart. Suddenly the Romans charged through the gates. The enemy fled precipitously down the hill, leaving the ground strewn with numberless dead.

Shortly after this event Indutiomarus with a band of Nervii and Eburones attacked the camp of Labienus in the territory of the Remi. Indutiomarus was lured by a pretense of fear to the gates of the Roman camp; he was then slain by the cavalry of Labienus, who had ordered them not to strike a blow at any one until Indutiomarus was killed. After the death of this leader, Caesar says that he "found Gaul a little more peaceful."

BOOK SIX

(Sight translation)

CAESAR ONCE AGAIN BRIDGES THE RHINE

Summary of Chapters 1–10

During the winter of 54–53 B.C. Caesar, fearing a more serious revolt in Gaul, raised two legions in Cisalpine Gaul, one of which replaced the Fourteenth, which had been annihilated at Aduatuca. He also obtained one legion from Pompey; this brought his number of legions up to ten. Before the winter was over, Caesar had quelled a second uprising among the Nervii. He then convoked a general assembly of the Gallic chiefs. Because the Senones, Carnutes, and Treveri failed to send representatives to this assembly, Caesar first marched upon the Senones and Carnutes, who at once surrendered and gave hostages. He next directed his army against the Treveri and Eburones; but first he defeated their allies, the Menapii, whom he forced into submission. In the meantime Labienus, with the help of reinforcements sent to him by Caesar, defeated the Treveri.

Before invading the country of the Eburones, Caesar again built a bridge across the Rhine, a little to the north of the place where he had built his first bridge. He crossed over into Germany, partly to punish the Suebi for sending help to the Treveri and partly to deprive Ambiorix of an asylum. The Suebi, however, retired to an immense forest in the remotest part of their country as soon as they learned of the approach of the Roman army.

HABITS AND CUSTOMS OF THE GAULS AND THE GERMANS

PREVIEW: Because the campaigns of the year 53 B.C. are of less importance and interest, Caesar interrupts his narrative to tell the readers of the customs of the Gauls and the Germans.

Summary of Chapters 11–12

In Gaul the tribes were divided into two factions. The leaders of these factions had the highest authority, and all questions of importance were submitted to them. At Caesar's arrival in Gaul the leaders of one faction were the Haeduans, and of the other, the Sequani; but his arrival changed the situation. The influence of the Haeduans was increased, while the Sequani lost their primacy to the Remi, who stood high in Caesar's favor.

Ch. 13   The People of Gaul and Their Druids

In omnī Galliā eōrum hominum, quī ¹aliquō sunt numerō atque honōre genera sunt duo. Nam ²plēbēs ³paene servōrum habētur locō, quae nihil audet per sē, nūllī adhibētur cōnsiliō. Plērīque, cum aut ⁴aere aliēnō aut māgnitūdine tribūtōrum aut injūriā potentiōrum premuntur, ⁵sēsē in servitūtem dicant nōbilibus, ⁶quibus in hōs eadem omnia sunt jūra, quae ⁶dominīs in servōs.

Sed dē hīs duōbus generibus alterum est ⁷druidum, alterum equitum. Illī rēbus dīvīnīs intersunt, sacrificia pūblica ac prīvāta prōcūrant, ⁸religiōnēs interpretantur; ad eōs māgnus adulēscentium numerus disciplīnae causā concurrit, māgnōque hī sunt apud eōs honōre. Nam ferē dē omnibus contrōversiīs pūblicīs prīvātīsque cōnstituunt; et sī quod est facinus admissum, sī caedēs facta, sī dē hērēditāte, dē fīnibus contrōversia est, īdem dēcernunt, praemia poenāsque cōnstituunt; sī quī aut prīvātus aut populus eōrum ⁹dēcrētō nōn stetit, sacrificiīs interdīcunt.

Haec poena apud eōs est gravissima. Quibus ita est interdictum, hī numerō impiōrum ac scelerātōrum habentur, hīs omnēs dēcēdunt, aditum eōrum sermōnemque dēfugiunt, nē quid ex contāgiōne incommodī accipiant, neque eīs petentibus jūs redditur neque honor ūllus commūnicātur.

Hīs autem omnibus druidibus praeest ūnus, quī summam inter eōs habet auctōritātem. Hōc mortuō aut, sī quī ex reliquīs excellit dīgnitāte, succēdit, aut, sī sunt plūrēs parēs, suffrāgiō druidum, nōn numquam etiam armīs, dē prīncipātū contendunt.

Hī certō annī tempore in fīnibus Carnutum, quae regiō tōtīus

---

1. **aliquō ... numerō**: *of some account;* ablative of description.
2. **plēbēs**: nom. sing.
3. **paene ... locō**: *are treated almost like slaves.*
4. **aere aliēnō**: *by debt.*
5. **sēsē ... dicant**: *attach themselves as bondsmen;* notice **dicant**, not **dīcant**.
6. **quibus, dominīs**: datives of possession.
7. **druidum**: (that of) *the druids.*
8. **religiōnēs**: *religious matters.*
9. **dēcrētō**: *decision.*

Galliae media habētur, [10]cōnsīdunt in locō cōnsecrātō. Hūc omnēs undique, quī contrōversiās habent, conveniunt eōrumque dēcrētīs jūdiciīsque pārent.

[11]Disciplīna in Britanniā reperta atque inde in Galliam trānslāta esse exīstimātur, et nunc, quī dīligentius [12]eam rem cōgnōscere volunt, plērumque [13]illō discendī causā proficīscuntur.

---

10. **cōnsīdunt:** *hold a meeting.* Their meetings were held in oak groves; the oak and the mistletoe were sacred to them.
11. **Disciplīna:** the system of the druids.
12. **eam rem:** *the system.*
13. **illō:** to Britain. There was a school for druids on the isle of Anglesey.

FOR COMPREHENSION

- ANSWER IN ENGLISH:
1. How many important social classes were there in Gaul at the time of Caesar?
2. What were the functions and the powers of the druids?
3. How was a new chief druid elected?
4. Where did the druids meet annually?
5. What business did the druids transact at their usual meetings?
6. Where did druidism have its origin, according to Caesar?

Ch. 14 The Educational System of the Druids

Druidēs [1]ā bellō abesse cōnsuēvērunt neque tribūta [2]ūnā cum reliquīs pendunt; [3]mīlitiae vacātiōnem omniumque rērum habent immūnitātem. Tantīs excitātī praemiīs et suā sponte multī [4]in disciplīnam conveniunt et ā parentibus propinquīsque mittuntur.

Māgnum ibi numerum [5]versuum ēdiscere dīcuntur. Itaque annōs nōn nūllī xx in disciplīnā permanent. Neque fās esse exīstimant [6]ea litterīs mandāre, cum in reliquīs ferē rēbus, pūblicīs prīvātīsque [7]ratiōnibus, Graecīs litterīs ūtantur. Id [8]mihi duābus dē causīs īnstituisse videntur, quod neque [9]in vulgus disciplīnam efferrī velint, neque eōs, quī discunt, litterīs cōnfīsōs minus memoriae studēre; quod ferē plērīsque accidit, ut praesidiō litterārum dīligentiam in discendō ac memoriam remittant.

---

1. **ā bellō abesse:** *to be exempt from war.*
2. **ūnā ... pendunt:** *pay at the same rate as the rest.*
3. **mīlitiae vacātiōnem:** *exemption from military service.*
4. **in disciplīnam:** *for instruction.*
5. **versuum:** *lines.* The metrical form was probably adopted to facilitate meaning.
6. **ea:** *these matters* (i.e., their teachings).
7. **ratiōnibus:** *records; documents.*
8. **mihi:** Caesar here speaks of himself in the first person, which he rarely does in the Gallic War.
9. **in ... efferrī:** *to be made public.*

In prīmīs ¹⁰hoc volunt persuādēre, nōn interīre animās, sed ab aliīs post mortem trānsīre ad aliōs, atque hōc māximē ad virtūtem ¹¹excitārī putant, metū mortis neglēctō. Multa praetereā dē sīderibus atque eōrum mōtū, dē mundī ac ¹²terrārum māgnitūdine, dē rērum nātūrā, dē deōrum immortālium vī ac potestāte disputant et ¹³juventūtī trādunt.

---

10. hoc . . . persuādēre: *to inculcate this belief.*
11. excitārī: *men are spurred on;* impersonal.
12. terrārum = orbis terrārum: *the earth.*
13. juventūtī: *to the young students*

FOR COMPREHENSION

● ANSWER IN ENGLISH:
1. What two important exemptions did the druids have?
2. How did these exemptions affect the young Gauls and their friends?
3. How were the young druids taught?
4. What two explanations of this method does Caesar mention?
5. What did the druids believe happened after death?
6. What effect did this belief have on the Gauls?

Ch. 15   The Warrior Knights and Their Retainers

Alterum genus est equitum. Hī, ¹cum est ²ūsus atque aliquod bellum ³incidit (⁴quod ferē ante Caesaris adventum quotannīs accidere solēbat, utī aut ipsī injūriās īnferrent aut ⁵illātās prōpulsārent), omnēs in bellō versantur, atque eōrum ⁶ut quisque est genere cōpiīsque amplissimus, ita plūrimōs circum sē ⁷ambactōs clientēsque habet. ⁸Hanc ūnam grātiam potentiamque ⁹nōvērunt.

FOR COMPREHENSION

● ANSWER IN ENGLISH:
1. What was the chief occupation of the knights?
2. Why was there no unemployment among the knights before Caesar's arrival?
3. What system of the Middle Ages was similar to that of the knights?
4. What Gallic noble, relying on the number of his retainers, defied the courts?
5. What determined the standing or rank of a Gallic knight?

---

1. cum: *whenever.*
2. ūsus: *need.*
3. incidit: *breaks out.*
4. quod: *and this.*
5. illātās: (injuries) *inflicted* (by others).

6. ut: *as.*
7. ambactōs: *retainers;* a Gallic word.
8. Hanc: referring to the number of retainers one had.
9. nōvērunt: *they recognize.*

Ch. 16　The Superstitions of the Gauls

[1]Nātiō est omnis Gallōrum [2]admodum dēdita [3]religiōnibus, atque ob eam causam quī sunt affectī graviōribus morbīs, quīque in proeliīs perīculīsque versantur, aut [4]prō victimīs hominēs immolant aut [5]sē immolātūrōs vovent, [6]administrīsque ad ea sacrificia druidibus ūtuntur, quod, prō vītā hominis nisi hominis vīta reddātur, nōn posse deōrum immortālium [7]nūmen plācārī arbitrantur; [8]pūblicēque ējusdem generis [9]habent īnstitūta sacrificia.

Aliī [10]immānī māgnitūdine [11]simulācra habent, quōrum contexta vīminibus membra vīvīs hominibus complent; [12]quibus succēnsīs, circumventī flammā exanimantur hominēs.

Supplicia eōrum, quī in fūrtō aut latrōciniō aut [13]aliquā noxiā sint comprehēnsī, grātiōra dīs immortālibus esse arbitrantur; sed cum ējus generis cōpia dēficit, etiam ad innocentium supplicia dēscendunt.

---

1. **Nātiō . . . omnis:** *The nation as a whole.*
2. **admodum = māximē.**
3. **religiōnibus:** *religious rites.*
4. **prō:** *as*
5. **sē:** subject of **immolātūrōs (esse).**
6. **administrīs:** (as) *officiating priests;* ablative in agreement with **druidibus.**
7. **nūmen:** *majesty.*
8. **pūblicē:** *(for the state) on behalf of the state.*
9. **habent īnstitūta:** *had established sacrifices;* has the force of pluperfect tense.
10. **immānī māgnitūdine:** ablative of description.
11. **simulācra = effigiēs:** wickerwork images in human form.
12. **quibus = et eīs (simulācrīs).**
13. **aliquā = aliā aliquā:** *some other.*

FOR COMPREHENSION

- ANSWER IN ENGLISH:
1. What common interest was shared by all Gauls?
2. By what means did the Gauls try to escape death in case of sickness or war?
3. How did a man in danger of losing his life try to appease the gods?
4. Whom did the Gauls frequently offer up for sacrifice?
5. What men did the Gauls think were victims more pleasing to the gods?

Ch. 17　The Divinities of the Gauls

Deōrum māximē Mercurium colunt; hūjus sunt plūrima simulācra; hunc omnium inventōrem artium [1]ferunt, hunc [2]viārum atque itinerum ducem, hunc ad quaestūs pecūniae mercātūrāsque

---

1. **ferunt:** *they say.*
2. **viārum atque itinerum:** Mercury is the guide for roads because he points out the road, and for journeys because he accompanies the traveler on his way.

habēre vim māximam arbitrantur. Post hunc Apollinem et Mārtem et Jovem et Minervam. Dē hīs eandem ferē, quam reliquae
gentēs, habent opīniōnem: Apollinem morbōs dēpellere, Minervam [3]operum atque artificiōrum initia trādere, Jovem imperium
caelestium tenēre, Mārtem bella regere. Huic, cum proeliō dīmi-
cāre cōnstituērunt, ea, quae bellō cēperint, plērumque dēvovent;
cum superāvērunt, animālia capta immolant, reliquās rēs in
ūnum locum cōnferunt. Multīs in cīvitātibus hārum rērum ex-
strūctōs cumulōs locīs cōnsecrātīs [4]cōnspicārī licet; neque saepe
accidit, ut [5]neglēctā quispiam religiōne aut [6]capta [7]apud sē occul-
tāre aut [8]posita tollere audēret, gravissimumque eī reī supplicium
cum cruciātū cōnstitūtum est.

---

3. operum . . . initia: *the elements of arts
and of crafts.*
4. cōnspicārī licet: *one may see.*
5. neglēctā: *disregarding.*
6. capta: *(things which had been taken)
plunder.*

7. apud sē: *at his home.*
8. posita tollere: *to take away what had
been deposited.*

FOR COMPREHENSION

● ANSWER IN ENGLISH:
1. What god was the object of very special worship among the Gauls?
2. What was the function of Apollo? Minerva? Jupiter? Mars?
3. Who gave these Gallic gods their Roman names?
4. What did the Gauls do with animals captured in war? What did they do
   with other booty?
5. How was the observance of this practice rigorously enforced?

Ch. 18   The Strange Beliefs and Customs of the Gauls

Gallī sē omnēs ab [1]Dīte patre [2]prōgnātōs praedicant idque ab
druidibus prōditum dīcunt. Ob eam causam [3]spatia omnis temporis nōn numerō diērum, sed noctium fīniunt; diēs nātālēs et
mēnsium et annōrum initia sīc observant, [4]ut noctem diēs subsequātur.
   In reliquīs vītae īnstitūtīs [5]hōc ferē ab reliquīs differunt, quod

---

1. Dīte: Dis, or Pluto, was the Roman god of
the lower world and therefore associated
with darkness and night.
2. prōgnātōs (esse): *sprang from.*
3. spatia omnis temporis: *the periods of
all time.*
4. ut . . . subsequātur: *that day follows*

night. The twenty-four-hour day was
reckoned from sundown to sundown. Our
use of the words *fortnight* (fourteen
nights) and *Twelfth night* are survivals
of this manner of measuring time.
5. hōc . . . differunt: *they differ from other
peoples chiefly in this respect.*

suōs ⁶līberōs, nisi cum ⁷adolēvērunt, ut mūnus mīlitiae sustinēre possint, palam ad sē adīre nōn patiuntur, fīliumque ⁸puerīlī aetāte in pūblicō in cōnspectū patris assistere ⁹turpe dūcunt.

---

6. līberōs: *sons* (not children).
7. adolēvērunt: *have grown up.*

8. puerīlī aetāte: *while in the age of child-hood.*
9. turpe dūcunt: *consider it disgraceful.*

FOR COMPREHENSION

● ANSWER IN ENGLISH:
1. From what god did the Gauls claim to be descended?
2. From whom was this belief handed down?
3. How did the Gauls reckon time?
4. How were birthdays and the first days of the month and the year observed?
5. What was considered a disrespectful act on the part of a young Gallic boy?

Ch. 19 Marriage Rights and Funeral Customs of the Gauls

¹Virī, quantās pecūniās ab uxōribus ²dōtis nōmine accēpērunt, tantās ex suīs bonīs, ³aestimātiōne factā, ⁴cum dōtibus commūnicant. Hūjus omnis pecūniae ⁵conjūnctim ratiō habētur frūctūsque servantur; uter eōrum vītā superāvit, ad eum pars utrīusque cum ⁶frūctibus superiōrum temporum pervenit.

Virī in uxōrēs, sīcutī ⁷in līberōs, vītae necisque habent potestātem; et cum pater familiae illūstriōre locō nātus dēcessit, ējus propinquī conveniunt et, dē morte sī rēs in suspīciōnem vēnit, dē uxōribus ⁸in servīlem modum quaestiōnem habent et, ⁹sī compertum est, īgnī atque omnibus tormentīs excruciātās interficiunt.

¹⁰Fūnera sunt ¹¹prō cultū Gallōrum māgnifica et sūmptuōsa; omniaque, quae vīvīs ¹²cordī fuisse arbitrantur, in īgnem īnferunt, etiam animālia; ac paulō ¹³suprā hanc memoriam servī et clientēs, quōs ab eīs dīlēctōs esse cōnstābat, ¹⁴jūstīs fūnebribus cōnfectīs, ūnā cremābantur.

---

1. Virī: *Husbands.*
2. dōtis nōmine: *as a dowry.*
3. aestimātiōne factā: *after an evaluation has been made.*
4. cum dōtibus commūnicant: *add to the dowry.*
5. conjūnctim ratiō: *joint account.*
6. frūctibus: *income.*
7. in: *over.*
8. in servīlem modum: *as is done in the case of slaves.*

9. sī compertum: *if* (their guilt) *has been proved.*
10. Fūnera: *Funeral ceremonies; obsequies.*
11. prō cultū: *taking into account the civilization.*
12. cordī fuisse: *were dear.*
13. suprā . . . memoriam: *before this* (our) *time.*
14. jūstīs . . . cōnfectīs: *on the conclusion of the conventional funeral rites.*

FOR COMPREHENSION

● ANSWER IN ENGLISH:

1. What authority did the Gauls have over their wives and children?
2. How do you know from the text that polygamy must have been practised among the Gauls?
3. What property agreement was there between wife and husband?
4. What happened to the wives of a Gallic husband who had died under suspicious circumstances?
5. Did the Gauls in the time of Caesar bury their dead or did they cremate them?

Ch. 20   Censorship of News Concerning the State

¹Quae cīvitātēs ²commodius suam rem pūblicam administrāre exīstimantur, ³habent lēgibus sānctum, sī ⁴quis quid dē rē pūblicā ā fīnitimīs rūmōre ac fāmā accēperit, utī ad magistrātum dēferat ⁵nēve cum ⁶quō aliō commūnicet, ⁷quod saepe hominēs temerāriōs atque imperītōs falsīs rūmōribus terrērī et ad facinus impellī et dē summīs rēbus cōnsilium capere cōgnitum est. Magistrātūs, ⁸quae vīsa sunt, occultant, quaeque esse ex ūsū jūdicāvērunt, multitūdinī prōdunt. Dē rē pūblicā nisi per concilium loquī nōn concēditur.

FOR COMPREHENSION

● ANSWER IN ENGLISH:

1. What legal measures did some Gallic states take to check the spread of unfounded rumors?
2. What was an individual required to do if he learned information about public affairs?
3. What might be the results if imprudent and inexperienced persons heard untrue reports concerning the public welfare?
4. What kind of information did the officers conceal?
5. Where only were the citizens in these states permitted to talk about public affairs?

---

1. **Quae cīvitātēs** = **Eae cīvitātēs quae.**
2. **commodius:** *rather well.*
3. **habent . . . sānctum:** *have it established by law.*
4. **quis quid:** indefinite pronouns following **sī.**
5. **nēve:** *and not.*
6. **quō:** *anyone.*
7. **quod . . . cōgnitum est:** *because it has been found.*
8. **quae vīsa sunt:** *what seems advisable.*

Ch. 21 German Religion and Way of Life

Germānī multum ¹ab hāc cōnsuētūdine differunt. Nam neque ²druidēs habent, ³quī rēbus dīvīnīs praesint, neque sacrificiīs student. Deōrum numerō eōs sōlōs dūcunt, quōs cernunt et quōrum apertē opibus juvantur, Sōlem et Vulcānum et Lūnam; reliquōs ⁴nē fāmā quidem accēpērunt.

Vīta omnis in vēnātiōnibus atque ⁵in studiīs reī mīlitāris ⁶cōnsistit; ⁷ā parvīs labōrī ac dūritiae student.

---

1. **ab hāc cōnsuētūdine:** *from this custom* (of the Gauls).
2. **druidēs:** The Germans did not have druids, but they had priests and priestesses who offered sacrifice and interpreted omens for them.
3. **quī ... praesint:** relative purpose clause.
4. **nē ... accēpērunt:** *they had not even heard of.*
5. **in ... mīlitāris:** *in warlike pursuits.*
6. **cōnsistit = cōnsūmitur.**
7. **ā parvīs = ā puerīs:** *from boyhood.*

FOR COMPREHENSION

● ANSWER IN ENGLISH:

1. In what two respects did the Germans differ from the Gauls in religious matters?
2. Whom alone did the Germans consider gods?
3. What three gods did the Germans worship?
4. In what two pursuits did the Germans pass their days?
5. To what were they accustomed from childhood?

Ch. 22 German Communism

Agrī cultūrae nōn student, mājorque pars eōrum vīctūs in lacte, cāseō, carne cōnsistit. ¹Neque quisquam agrī ²modum certum aut fīnēs habet propriōs; sed magistrātūs ac prīncipēs ³in annōs singulōs gentibus cōgnātiōnibusque hominum, ⁴quīque ūnā coiērunt, ⁵quantum et quō locō vīsum est agrī, attribuunt, atque annō post ⁶aliō trānsīre cōgunt.

Ējus reī multās afferunt causās: nē, assiduā cōnsuētūdine captī, studium bellī gerendī ⁷agrī cultūrā commūtent; nē lātōs fīnēs pa-

---

1. **Neque quisquam:** *And no one.*
2. **modum certum:** *a definite amount.*
3. **in annōs singulōs:** *each and every year.*
4. **quīque = eīsque quī:** *and to those who have joined together.*
5. **quantum ... agrī:** *as much land as*
6. *seems proper and in whatever place (as seems proper).*
6. **aliō = alium in locum:** *to another place.*
7. **agrī cultūrā:** *for agriculture.*

rāre studeant, potentiōrēs atque humiliōrēs possessiōnibus ex-
pellant; nē [8]accūrātius ad frīgora atque aestūs vītandōs aedificent;
nē qua oriātur pecūniae cupiditās, quā ex rē factiōnēs dissēnsiō-
nēsque nāscuntur; ut animī aequitāte plēbem contineant, cum suās
quisque opēs [9]cum potentissimīs aequārī videat.

---

8. accūrātius: *with too great pains.*
9. cum potentissimīs = cum opibus
potentissimōrum.

FOR COMPREHENSION

● ANSWER IN ENGLISH:

1. According to Caesar, what foods made up the major portion of the Germans' diet?
2. Who controlled the distribution of land among the Germans?
3. To what extent did the Germans occupy themselves with agriculture?
4. How much land was distributed to each group?
5. What five reasons does Caesar say the Germans had in mind in forbidding
private ownership of land?

Ch. 23 German Military and Civil Customs

Cīvitātibus māxima laus est quam lātissimē circum sē, vāstātīs
fīnibus, sōlitūdinēs habēre. Hoc [1]proprium virtūtis exīstimant,
expulsōs agrīs fīnitimōs [2]cēdere, neque quemquam prope sē au-
dēre [3]cōnsistere; simul hōc sē fore tūtiōrēs arbitrantur, repentīnae
incursiōnis timōre sublātō.

Cum bellum cīvitās aut illātum dēfendit aut īnfert, magistrātūs,
quī eī bellō praesint et vītae necisque habeant potestātem, dē-
liguntur. In pāce nūllus est commūnis magistrātus, sed prīncipēs
regiōnum atque pāgōrum inter suōs [4]jūs dīcunt contrōversiāsque
minuunt.

[5]Latrōcinia nūllam habent īnfāmiam, quae extrā fīnēs cūjusque
cīvitātis fīunt, atque ea juventūtis exercendae ac dēsidiae minu-
endae causā fierī praedicant. Atque ubi quis ex prīncipibus in
conciliō dīxit sē ducem fore, [6]quī sequī velint, [7]profiteantur, cōnsur-
gunt eī, quī et causam et hominem probant, suumque auxilium

---

1. proprium: *characteristic.*
2. cēdere: *to withdraw; to yield*
3. cōnsistere: *to settle.*
4. jūs dīcunt: *pronounce justice.*

5. Latrōcinia: *Acts of brigandage.*
6. quī: *any who.*
7. profiteantur: *they should volunteer.*

pollicentur, atque ā multitūdine collaudantur; quī ex hīs secūtī nōn sunt, in dēsertōrum ac prōditōrum numerō dūcuntur, [8]omniumque hīs rērum posteā fidēs dērogātur.

[9]Hospitem violāre fās nōn putant; [10]quī quācumque dē causā ad eōs vēnērunt, ab injūriā prohibent, sānctōsque habent, hīsque omnium domūs patent vīctusque commūnicātur.

FOR COMPREHENSION

- ANSWER IN ENGLISH:
1. Why did the Germans like to have waste land around their territory?
2. What power did the magistrates have in time of war?
3. What was the German attitude toward robbery?
4. How was a German treated who refused to take part in a robbery after having promised to do so?
5. How did the Germans treat strangers or guests who happened to be in their territory?

Ch. 24 The Gauls Accustomed to Defeat from the Germans

Ac fuit anteā tempus cum Germānōs Gallī virtūte superārent, ūltrō bella īnferrent, propter hominum multitūdinem agrīque inopiam trāns Rhēnum colōniās mitterent. Itaque [1]ea, quae fertilissima Germāniae sunt, loca circum Hercyniam silvam, quam [2]Eratosthenī et quibusdam Graecīs fāmā nōtam esse videō, quam [3]illī Orcyniam appellant, Volcae Tectosagēs occupāvērunt atque ibi cōnsēdērunt; quae gēns ad hoc tempus hīs sēdibus sēsē continet summamque habet jūstitiae et bellicae [4]laudis opīniōnem.

Nunc, quod in eādem inopiā, egestāte, [5]patientiā, quā ante, Germānī permanent, eōdem vīctū et [6]cultū corporis ūtuntur, Gallīs autem prōvinciārum propinquitās et [7]trānsmarīnārum rē-

---

Terra-cotta, 500 B.C.
These winged horses
are from Tarquinia.

Detail of mosaic showing dancers entertaining.

rum nōtitia [8]multa ad cōpiam atque ūsūs largītur, paulātim assuē-
factī superārī multīsque victī proeliīs, nē sē quidem [9]ipsī cum
[10]illīs virtūte comparant.

---

8. **multa . . . largītur:** (*supplies many
things as regards wealth and necessities*)
*supplies them lavishly with luxuries and
necessities.*

9. **ipsī: Gallī.**
10. **illīs: Germānīs.**

FOR COMPREHENSION

● ANSWER IN ENGLISH:
1. Who had been the braver and more aggressive, the Germans or the Gauls?
2. Were there any Gallic tribes living in Germany in Caesar's day?
3. How had the nearness of the Gauls to the Roman Province affected the
   civilization of the Gauls?
4. To what Greek writer was the Hercynian forest known before Caesar's day?
5. What changes does Caesar say the Germans had made in their manner of life
   within recent years?

Ch. 25 The Hercynian Forest

Hūjus Hercyniae silvae, quae suprā dēmōnstrāta est, [1]lātitūdō
VIIII diērum iter [2]expedītō patet; nōn enim aliter fīnīrī potest,
neque mēnsūrās itinerum nōvērunt. Oritur ab Helvētiōrum et
Nemetum et Rauracōrum fīnibus, [3]rēctāque flūminis Dānuvī regiōne pertinet ad fīnēs Dācōrum et Anartium; hinc [4]sē flectit
sinistrōrsus, [5]dīversīs ā flūmine regiōnibus, multārumque gentium
fīnēs propter māgnitūdinem attingit; neque quisquam est [6]hūjus
Germāniae, quī sē aut adīsse [7]ad initium ējus silvae [8]dīcat, [9]cum
diērum iter LX prōcesserit, aut, quō ex locō oriātur, [10]accēperit;
multaque in eā genera ferārum nāscī cōnstat, [11]quae reliquīs in
locīs vīsa nōn sint; ex quibus quae māximē differant ā cēterīs et
[12]memoriae prōdenda videantur, haec sunt.

---

1. **lātitūdō:** from north to south.
2. **expedītō:** (for anyone) *traveling
   light;* dative of reference.
3. **rēctāque . . . regiōne:** *and in a direction parallel to the river Danube.*
4. **sē flectit sinistrōrsus:** *bends* (itself) *to
   the left* (of the Danube).
5. **dīversīs . . . regiōnibus:** *in a direction
   away from the river.*
6. **hūjus Germāniae:** *of this part of Germany* (i.e., of western Germany).

7. **ad initium:** to the eastern end of the
   forest.
8. **dīcat:** *claims.*
9. **cum:** *although.*
10. **accēperit** = audīverit.
11. **quae . . . vīsa nōn sint:** relative charac-
    teristic clause.
12. **memoriae prōdenda:** *worthy of record-
    ing.*

● ANSWER IN ENGLISH:

1. What was the German method of measuring distances?
2. What was the approximate width of the Hercynian forest?
3. Who were the Daci and where did they live?
4. With what part of Germany only was Caesar personally acquainted?
5. What kinds of animals were said to exist in this forest?

Ch. 26   The One-horned Reindeer

Est ¹bōs cervī figūrā, ²cūjus ā mediā fronte inter aurēs ³ūnum cornū exsistit, ⁴excelsius magisque dērēctum hīs, quae nōbīs nōta sunt, cornibus; ⁵ab ējus summō ⁶sīcut palmae rāmīque lātē diffunduntur. Eadem est fēminae ⁷marisque nātūra, eadem fōrma māgnitūdōque cornuum.

---

1. **bōs:** used here as a general term applicable to any large animal.
2. **cūjus ... fronte:** *from the middle of whose forehead.* Caesar was misinformed, of course.
3. **ūnum cornū:** Caesar's informer may have seen a reindeer after he had shed one of his antlers. The reindeer sheds its antlers every year.

4. **excelsius ... dērēctum:** *higher and straighter.*
5. **ab ējus summō:** *at the tip.*
6. **sīcut palmae rāmīque:** *like palms* (of the hand) *and branches* (of a tree).
7. **marisque:** *and of the male.* The nominative case is **mās.**

● ANSWER IN ENGLISH:

1. In what respect is Caesar's description of the reindeer inaccurate?
2. In what respect is his description accurate?
3. Did Caesar use a Latin word for reindeer? for antler?
4. From what two Latin words is antler derived? Check your answer with the dictionary.
5. Did Caesar himself ever see a reindeer such as he describes?

Ch. 27   The Stiff-legged European Elk

Sunt item, quae appellantur ¹alcēs. Hārum est cōnsimilis ²caprīs figūra et ³varietās pellium, sed māgnitūdine paulō antecēdunt

---

1. **alcēs:** *elks* (the European elk which is akin to the American moose).
2. **caprīs = caprārum figūrae** (dative).

3. **varietās pellium:** *mottled coloring of the hide.*

⁴mutilaeque sunt cornibus et ⁵crūra sine nōdīs articulīsque habent, neque quiētis causā prōcumbunt, neque, sī quō afflīctae cāsū concidērunt, ērigere sēsē ac sublevāre possunt. Hīs sunt arborēs ⁶prō cubīlibus; ad eās ⁷sē applicant atque ita paulum modo reclīnātae quiētem capiunt. Quārum ex vēstīgiīs cum est animadversum ā vēnātōribus, quō sē recipere cōnsuēverint, omnēs eō locō aut ab rādīcibus subruunt aut accīdunt arborēs, tantum ut summa speciēs eārum stantium relinquātur. ⁸Hūc cum sē cōnsuētūdine reclīnāvērunt, īnfīrmās arborēs pondere afflīgunt atque ūnā ipsae concidunt.

---

4. mutilaeque . . . cornibus: (*and they are broken in their horns*) *and their horns appear broken.*
5. crūra sine nōdīs articulīsque: *legs without knots and joints.*

6. prō cubīlibus: *for beds.*
7. sē applicant: *lean.*
8. Hūc = Ad eās arborēs.

FOR COMPREHENSION

● ANSWER IN ENGLISH:
1. What does Caesar say about the size of the elk?
2. What sort of legs did these elks have, according to Caesar?
3. How were these animals easily captured, according to Caesar?
4. Do you think that Caesar ever saw one of these elks?
5. Did men of the Middle Ages know much about natural science?

Ch. 28   The Wild Ox

Tertium ¹est genus eōrum, quī ²ūrī appellantur. Hī sunt māgnitūdine paulō īnfrā elephantōs, speciē et colōre et figūrā taurī. Māgna vīs eōrum est et māgna vēlōcitās, neque hominī neque ferae, quam cōnspexērunt, parcunt.

Hōs ³studiōsē foveīs captōs interficiunt; hōc ⁴sē labōre dūrant adulēscentēs atque hōc genere vēnātiōnis exercent, et quī plūrimōs ex hīs interfēcērunt, relātīs in pūblicum cornibus, ⁵quae sint testimōniō, māgnam ferunt laudem. Sed assuēscere ad hominēs et mānsuēfierī ⁶nē parvulī quidem exceptī possunt. Amplitūdō

---

1. est: *consists.*
2. ūrī: *aurochs* (a species of wild ox or buffalo now extinct).
3. studiōsē . . . captōs: *painstakingly trapped in pits.*
4. sē labōre dūrant: *harden themselves by this sort of labor.*

5. quae . . . testimōniō: *to serve as evidence;* relative purpose clause.
6. nē . . . exceptī: *not even if caught very young.*

cornuum et figūra et speciēs multum ā nostrōrum boum cornibus differt. ⁷Haec studiōsē conquīsīta ⁸ab labrīs argentō circumclūdunt atque in amplissimīs epulīs prō ⁹pōculīs ūtuntur.

---

7. Haec: supply **cornua.**
8. ab labrīs: *at the rims.*
9. pōculīs: *as drinking cups.* Compare a

similar use of drinking horns in the Middle Ages.

FOR COMPREHENSION

- ANSWER IN ENGLISH:
1. What were the characteristics of the wild ox?
2. How did the Germans hunt the wild ox?
3. Why did the Germans hunt the wild ox?
4. What use did they make of the horns?
5. Was the wild ox easy to tame?

CAESAR RETURNS TO GAUL AND PURSUES AMBIORIX

Summary of Chapters 29–37

Since Caesar considered it most unwise to follow the Germans into the forests, he returned to Gaul, destroying only that part of the bridge touching German soil. The Gallic end he let stand, strongly guarded, as a reminder and threat to the Germans. Partitioning his army into four divisions, he made every effort to capture Ambiorix, chief of the Eburones, who was still at large. Cicero was left at Aduatuca with one legion to guard the baggage. The Sugambri, a German tribe, attacked Cicero's camp during Caesar's absence.

Ch. 38 Baculus the Centurion Saves the Roman Camp

Erat aeger in praesidiō relictus P. Sextius Baculus, ¹quī prīmum pīlum apud Caesarem dūxerat, cūjus mentiōnem superiōribus proeliīs fēcimus, ac diem jam quīntum ²cibō caruerat. Hic, diffīsus suae atque omnium salūtī, inermis ex tabernāculō prōdit; videt imminēre hostēs atque in summō rem esse discrīmine; capit arma

---

1. quī . . . dūxerat: Baculus was the chief centurion (**prīmipīlus**) of the first cohort and therefore of the legion.

2. cibō caruerat: *had been without food.*

316

ā proximīs atque in portā cōnsistit. Cōnsequuntur hunc centuriōnēs ējus cohortis, quae in statiōne erat; paulisper ūnā proelium sustinent. [3]Relinquit animus Sextium, gravibus acceptīs vulneribus; aegrē [4]per manūs tractus servātur. [5]Hōc spatiō interpositō, reliquī sēsē cōnfīrmant tantum ut in mūnītiōnibus cōnsistere audeant speciemque dēfēnsōrum praebeant.

A Roman centurion.

FOR COMPREHENSION

- ANSWER IN ENGLISH:
1. What was Baculus' rank in the army?
2. Had Caesar ever mentioned him previously?
3. Where did the present incident take place?
4. In what physical condition was Baculus at the time of the attack?
5. What was the result of Baculus' brave act?

Summary of Chapters 39–44

Unable to capture Ambiorix, who with a few companions had eluded all pursuit and had escaped into the forest of Ardennes, Caesar ravaged the country of the Eburones and left it in ruins. He then called an assembly of the Gallic chiefs at Rheims and instigated an investigation to determine the cause of the revolt among the Senones and Carnutes. The blame was fixed on Acco, a chief of the Senones, and he was flogged to death according to Roman custom. After establishing his troops in winter quarters among the Lingones and the Senones, Caesar went to northern Italy (Cisalpine Gaul) for the winter of 53-52 B.C.

---

3. **Relinquit ... Sextium:** *Sextius fainted.*
4. **per ... tractus:** *by being passed along from hand to hand.*

5. **Hōc ... interpositō:** The time gained by the brave deed of Baculus saved the camp.

BOOK SEVEN

THE GREAT STRUGGLE FOR THE INDEPENDENCE OF GAUL

PREVIEW: In Book VII we are to read the most dramatic part of Caesar's narrative. Here we meet a worthy rival of Caesar in Vercingetorix, who leads the last — and all but successful — attempt to drive Caesar out of Gaul and throw off the Roman yoke. If the leaders of the Gallic tribes had not been so fickle and unstable in crises, and if they had not been so selfish in their personal ambitions, it is conceivable that Caesar's story might have ended differently.

The climax of the titanic struggle for Gaul took place at Alesia. The siege of Alesia was not only Caesar's greatest single contest, but because of its results for Europe and the entire civilized world, it may be ranked among the most significant battles of all history.

Summary of Chapters 1–3

During the winter rumors reached the Gauls that Caesar was being detained in northern Italy by the political unrest in Rome. In a secret meeting the Gallic chiefs decided that the hour for them to strike for freedom had come. They planned a general revolt and hoped to prevent Caesar from joining his army. The Carnutes began the uprising by a massacre of all the Roman citizens at Cenabum (Orléans). The news was broadcast by shouting from field to field. So effective was this Gallic method of sending information that by night the Arverni at Gergovia, one-hundred-sixty miles from Cenabum, had received the news of the massacre at daybreak.

Ch. 4   Vercingetorix Elected Commander-in-Chief

Similī ratiōne [1]ibi Vercingetorīx, Celtillī fīlius, Arvernus, summae potentiae adulēscēns, cūjus pater prīncipātum [2]tōtīus Galliae obtinuerat, et ob eam causam quod rēgnum appetēbat ā cīvitāte erat interfectus, convocātīs suīs clientibus facile incendit. Cōgnitō ējus cōnsiliō, [3]ad arma concurritur. Prohibētur ā Gobannitiōne, patruō suō, reliquīsque prīncipibus, quī hanc temptandam

---

1. ibi: *in the country of the Arverni.*
2. tōtīus Galliae: Celtic Gaul is meant.

3. ad arma concurritur: *they rush to arms;* impersonal.

fortūnam nōn exīstimābant; expellitur ex oppidō [4]Gergoviā; nōn dēsistit tamen atque in agrīs habet [5]dīlēctum egentium ac perditōrum.

Hāc coāctā manū, [6]quōscumque adit ex cīvitāte ad suam sententiam perdūcit; hortātur ut commūnis lībertātis causā arma capiant; māgnīsque coāctīs cōpiīs [7]adversāriōs suōs, ā quibus paulō ante erat ējectus, expellit ex cīvitāte. Rēx ab suīs appellātur. Dīmittit [8]quōque versus lēgātiōnēs; [9]obtestātur ut in fidē maneant.

Celeriter sibi Senonēs, Parīsiōs, Pictonēs, Cadūrcōs, Turonōs, Aulercōs, Lemovīcēs, Andōs reliquōsque omnēs quī, Ōceanum attingunt, adjungit; omnium cōnsēnsū ad eum dēfertur imperium. Quā oblātā potestāte, omnibus hīs [10]cīvitātibus obsidēs imperat; certum numerum mīlitum ad sē celeriter addūcī jubet; [11]armōrum quantum quaeque cīvitās domī, [12]quodque ante tempus efficiat, cōnstituit; in prīmīs equitātuī studet. Summae dīligentiae summam imperī sevēritātem addit; māgnitūdine supplicī dubitantēs cōgit. Nam, [13]mājōre commissō dēlīctō, īgnī atque omnibus tormentīs necat; leviōre dē causā [14]auribus dēsectīs, aut singulīs effossīs oculīs, domum remittit, [15]ut sint reliquīs documentō et māgnitūdine poenae perterreant aliōs.

FOR COMPREHENSION

- ANSWER IN ENGLISH:
1. Who at first opposed Vercingetorix' plans?
2. What class of Gauls first rallied to Vercingetorix?
3. In what important respect does Vercingetorix differ from all the Gallic leaders of the six preceding years?
4. What were some of the military measures adopted by Vercingetorix?
5. What were some of his more severe disciplinary measures?
6. From what tribes do modern Paris, Tours, and Sens derive their names?

4. **Gergoviā**: the chief town of the Arverni.
5. **dīlēctum . . . perditōrum**: *a levy of needy and desperate men.*
6. **quōscumque**: *whomsoever.*
7. **adversāriōs**: *political opponents.*
8. **quōque versus** (adverb) = **in omnēs partēs.**
9. **obtestātur** = **implōrat.**
10. **cīvitātibus**: dative with **imperat.**
11. **armōrum . . . cōnstituit**: *he fixed the quota of arms which each state was to furnish and the date of delivery.*

12. **quodque** = **et quod; quod** is the interrogative with **tempus.**
13. **mājōre commissō dēlīctō**: *if a greater offense is committed.*
14. **auribus . . . remittit**: *he would cut off their ears or gouge out an eye and send them home.*
15. **ut . . . documentō**: *to be a warning to the rest;* **documentō**: dative of purpose.

● RESPONDĒ LATĪNE:

1. Cūr Vercingetorīgis pater interfectus erat?
2. Quis Vercingetorīx ab suīs cōpiīs appellātus est?
3. Quae potestās Vercingetorīgī ā cīvitātibus fīnitimīs oblāta est?
4. Quibus Vercingetorīx obsidēs imperāvit?
5. Quōmodo Vercingetorīx dubitantēs coēgit?

● SCRĪBE LATĪNE:

1. The father of Vercingetorix had been sentenced to death because he desired to be king.
2. When the leader had raised a large force, he drove out those who had driven him out of the state.
3. Having won all his countrymen to his views, he urged them to take arms for their common liberty.

Summary of Chapters 5–49

It was still winter but Caesar knew he must act immediately if he wished to save his army. With a small escort he plowed his way through the deep snow in the Cevennes, and by rapid marching day and night joined his army at Agedincum before Vercingetorix could mobilize his huge Gallic forces. The Gauls had not expected this daring move and soon were on the defensive again. Vercingetorix urged the Gauls not to meet the Romans in open battle but to starve them out by following a "scorched earth" policy.

Though harassed in the rear by Vercingetorix, Caesar laid siege to Avaricum. In spite of the stubborn defense of the Gauls, Avaricum was finally taken. The Romans, maddened by the slaughter of their countrymen at Cenabum and by their long deprivation of food, spared none of the inhabitants, not even the women and children. Vercingetorix kept his leadership and the confidence of his followers by pointing out that the disaster of Avaricum was the result of their failure to follow his advice. He had never sanctioned the defense of Avaricum.

Caesar, after settling a dispute among the Haeduans, now divided his army. He sent four legions north under Labienus to attack the Parisii and Senones, while he himself led six legions south against Gergovia, Vercingetorix' own city. Vercingetorix learned of Caesar's plan and tried to prevent him from crossing the river Elaver (Allier) by cutting down the bridges. However, Caesar outwitted him and followed him toward Gergovia, which he besieged. During the siege Caesar heard that ten thousand of the Haeduans were planning to desert the Romans and transfer their allegiance to the enemy. Caesar left the siege to his officers to go to the Haeduans and win them back. Vercingetorix took advantage of Caesar's absence and attacked the Roman camp. Caesar returned just in time to save his camp, but when the Romans later attacked the town, they were badly defeated. During the battle the Haeduans were sent to help the besieged Romans, but they were mistaken for the enemy on account of their arms and equipment.

Ch. 50 Petronius Gives His Life for His Men

L. Fabius centuriō, [1]quīque ūnā mūrum ascenderant, circumventī atque interfectī mūrō praecipitābantur. M. Petrōnius,
[2]ējusdem legiōnis centuriō, cum portās excīdere cōnātus esset, ā
multitūdine oppressus ac sibi dēspērāns, multīs jam vulneribus
acceptīs, manipulāribus suīs, quī illum secūtī erant, "Quoniam,"
inquit, "mē ūnā vōbīscum servāre nōn possum, vestrae quidem
[3]certē [4]vītae prōspiciam, quōs cupiditāte glōriae adductus in
perīculum dēdūxī. Vōs, datā facultāte, [5]vōbīs cōnsulite."

Simul in mediōs hostēs irrūpit duōbusque interfectīs reliquōs
ā portā paulum submōvit. Cōnantibus auxiliārī suīs, "Frūstrā,"
inquit, [6]"meae vītae subvenīre cōnāminī, quem jam sanguis
vīrēsque dēficiunt. Proinde abīte, dum est facultās, vōsque ad
legiōnem recipite."

Ita pūgnāns post paulum concidit [7]ac suīs salūtī fuit.

FOR COMPREHENSION

● ANSWER IN ENGLISH:
1. In what legion was Petronius a centurion?
2. Where was Petronius fighting at this time?
3. What did Petronius urge his men to do?
4. Who tried to help Petronius? Did Petronius accept this offer?
5. What was the result of Petronius' self-sacrifice?

● RESPONDĒ LATĪNE:
1. Quī mūrō praecipitābantur?
2. Quis erat ējusdem legiōnis centūriō?
3. Cūr M. Petrōnius sibi dēspērābat?
4. Quōmodo M. Petrōnius hostēs ā portā paulum summōvit?
5. Quid M. Petrōnius suīs dīxit?

● SCRĪBE LATĪNE:
1. Marcus Petronius, a centurion of the Eighth Legion, was overwhelmed with
numbers when he tried to cut down the gates.
2. He charged into the middle of the enemy, killed two, and pushed the others
a little way from the gate.
3. In vain you try to save me; my blood and my strength are failing. Get out
while there is a chance, and go back to the legion.

---

1. quīque = et eī quī.
2. ējusdem legiōnis = legiōnis octāvae.
3. certē: *at least.*
4. vītae: dative singular with prōspiciam.
5. vōbīs cōnsulite: *look out for yourselves.*

6. meae vītae subvenīre = meam vītam servāre.
7. ac ... fuit: *but he saved his comrades.* He kept the enemy at bay while his men escaped.

321

Summary of Chapters 51–67

Pressure from every direction dislodged the Romans, who were forced to flee down the hill with the Gauls in hot pursuit. At the foot of the hill stood the Tenth and the Thirteenth legions, which succeeded in covering their retreat and in checking the pursuing Gauls. Caesar had met his first serious defeat.

On the day following the disaster at Gergovia, Caesar paraded his soldiers and reprimanded them for disobeying orders; nevertheless, he encouraged them to further effort. He then marched away into the country of the Haeduans, only to find that they too had joined the rebellion. At Noviodunum, one of their cities, they possessed themselves of his hostages and of a large part of his treasury and destroyed his reserve supplies of grain. Caesar, however, was able to cross the swollen Loire and obtain necessary supplies. In the meantime Labienus with his four legions had defeated the Parisii at Lutecia (Paris) and then marched southward to rejoin Caesar.

All Gaul now rallied around the standard of Vercingetorix except the Remi, the Lingones, and the Treveri, who still remained neutral. Vercingetorix planned to cut off Caesar's supplies, even if it meant that his countrymen had to destroy their own crops and burn their own buildings. He levied additional troops and sent a secret embassy to win over the Allobroges.

At this critical moment Caesar, who was in desperate need of reinforcements, obtained cavalry and lightly armed infantry from German tribes across the Rhine. While on the march toward the country of the Sequani, he was suddenly attacked in force by the cavalry of Vercingetorix. While the battle was raging between the two cavalry forces, the German calvary suddenly dashed down the hill and won their first victory for Caesar. The enemy fled in disorder to their stronghold at Alesia.

Ch. 68 Vercingetorix Retreats to Alesia

Fugātō omnī equitātū Vercingetorīx cōpiās suās, [1]ut prō castrīs collocāverat, redūxit prōtinusque Alesiam, quod est oppidum Mandubiōrum, iter facere coepit, celeriterque impedī-menta ex castrīs ēdūcī et sē subsequī jūssit.

Caesar impedīmentīs in proximum collem ductīs, duābus legiōnibus praesidiō relictīs, secūtus hostēs quantum diēī tempus [2]est passum, circiter III mīlibus ex novissimō agmine interfectīs, [3]alterō diē [4]ad Alesiam castra fēcit. [5]Perspectō urbis sitū perter-ritīsque hostibus, quod [6]equitātū, quā māximē parte exercitūs cōnfīdēbant, erant pulsī, cohortātus ad labōrem mīlitēs Alesiam circumvāllāre īnstituit.

---

1. ut = postquam.
2. est passum: *permitted;* perfect tense of patior.
3. alterō diē = posterō diē.

4. ad = prope.
5. Perspectō . . . sitū: *After surveying the position of the city.*
6. equitātū: ablative of respect.

FOR COMPREHENSION

- ANSWER IN ENGLISH:

1. Toward what town did Vercingetorix retreat after his unsuccessful attack on the Romans?
2. How far did the Roman cavalry pursue the retreating Gauls?
3. When did Caesar reach Alesia?
4. Where had Caesar left the baggage and equipment of the Roman forces?
5. What loss was especially discouraging to the Gauls?

- RESPONDĒ LATĪNE:

1. Quō Vercingetorīx, fugātō omnī equitātū, iter facere coepit?
2. Quae imperātor Gallōrum ex castrīs ēdūcī jūssit?
3. Quot legiōnēs Caesar praesidiō impedīmentīs reliquit?
4. Quam longē Caesar hostēs secūtus est?
5. Cūr Gallī eō tempore māgnopere perterritī sunt?

- SCRĪBE LATĪNE:

1. After all the cavalry of the Gauls had been put to flight, Vercingetorix led his troops directly toward Alesia, a town of the Mandubii.
2. The Gauls were terrified because that branch of the army in which they had most confidence had been defeated by the Romans.
3. Having urged the soldiers to the work, he decided to surround Alesia with a wall.

Ch. 69 Caesar Blockades Alesia

Ipsum erat oppidum [1]in colle summō admodum [2]ēditō locō, ut nisi obsidiōne expūgnārī nōn posse vidērētur. [3]Cūjus collis rādīcēs [4]duo duābus ex partibus flūmina subluēbant.

Ante oppidum [5]plānitiēs circiter mīlia passuum III in longitūdinem patēbat; reliquīs ex omnibus partibus collēs, mediocrī interjectō spatiō, [6]parī altitūdinis fastīgiō oppidum cingēbant.

[7]Sub mūrō, [8]quae pars collis ad orientem sōlem spectābat, hunc omnem locum cōpiae Gallōrum complēverant, fossamque et [9]māceriam in altitūdinem VI pedum praedūxerant.

Ējus mūnītiōnis, quae ab Rōmānīs īnstituēbātur, circuitus XI mīlia passuum [10]tenēbat. Castra opportūnīs locīs erant posita ibi castellaque XXIII facta; quibus in castellīs interdiū [11]sta-

---

1. **in colle summō:** the modern Mont Auxois.
2. **ēditō locō:** *in an elevated position.*
3. **Cūjus** = **Ējus.**
4. **duo ... flūmina:** the Ose and the Oserain.
5. **plānitiēs:** the plain of Les Laumes
6. **parī ... fastīgiō:** *of equal height*
7. **Sub mūrō (oppidī):** *Below the wall (of the town).*
8. **quae pars:** logically in apposition to **hunc omnem locum.**
9. **māceriam:** *a wall of loose stones.*
10. **tenēbat** = **patēbat.**
11. **statiōnēs** = **praesidia.**

tiōnēs pōnēbantur, nē qua subitō ēruptiō fieret; haec eadem noctū [12]excubitōribus ac fīrmīs praesidiīs tenēbantur.

FOR COMPREHENSION

● ANSWER IN ENGLISH:

1. Where was Alesia situated? How was Alesia fortified by nature?
2. Where did Vercingetorix establish the camp of the Gauls?
3. How had the Gauls fortified this camp?
4. How long a line of encircling camps and redoubts did Caesar plan to construct?
5. How many camps and how many redoubts were included in this line of fortifications?
6. Was Caesar's method of attack to be a siege or a blockade?

● RESPONDĒ LATĪNE:

1. Ubi oppidum Alesia positum est?
2. Quae duo flūmina ējus collis rādīcēs subluēbant?
3. Quam longē plānitiēs ante oppidum patēbat?
4. Ubi cōpiae Gallōrum cōnsēderant?
5. Quam longē circuitus mūnītiōnis Rōmānae patēbat?

● SCRĪBE LATĪNE:

1. The Gauls had constructed a ditch and wall of loose stone six feet high.
2. The fortification which the Romans had constructed stretched around for eleven miles.
3. Garrisons were stationed in the redoubts during the day in order to guard against sudden sallies.

Summary of Chapters 70–87

After the cavalry battle that ended with the rout of the Gauls amid great slaughter, Vercingetorix summoned forces from all Gaul, apportioned his scanty supplies, and prepared for a siege. When Caesar learned from deserters that Vercingetorix had summoned an army of relief, he constructed an inner and an outer line of siege works. The purpose of the inner line was to keep Vercingetorix confined in Alesia; the outer line would defend his own army from attack by a relieving army. When his fortifications were complete, he gathered as much grain and fodder as he could in anticipation of the coming struggle.

Meanwhile the Gallic tribes were answering the appeal of Vercingetorix for help. About 250,000 strong were marching to the relief of their countrymen. By this time more than six weeks had passed, and the besieged Gauls were facing starvation. At last the army of relief began to arrive. The hopes of Vercingetorix'

---

12. excubitōribus: *by men sleeping out* (i.e., by bivouacs).

men were revived, and they staked their all in an attack on the Roman fortifications. There followed a day of desperate cavalry fighting, and after a one-day intermission, a night attack by the army of relief.

The Gauls, unable to break through the Roman lines, finally stopped trying. The next move was an attack on Caesar's camp at Mont Réa, where two Roman legions were stationed. When Caesar learned that his men at Mont Réa were too exhausted to resist the enemy, he sent Labienus to their relief. Then Caesar himself, after exhorting his troops and reminding them of how much depended upon their bravery in that day and hour, followed with four cohorts and a division of the cavalry.

Ch. 88   The Gauls Meet with Total Defeat

Ējus adventū ex ¹colōre vestītūs cōgnitō, quō ²īnsīgnī in proeliīs ūtī cōnsuēverat, turmīsque equitum et cohortibus vīsīs, quās sē sequī jūsserat (ut dē locīs superiōribus haec dēclīvia et dēvexa cernēbantur) hostēs proelium committunt. Utrimque clāmōre sublātō, excipit rūrsus ex vāllō atque omnibus mūnītiōnibus clāmor. Nostrī ³ōmissīs pīlīs gladiīs rem gerunt.

Repente post ⁴tergum equitātus cernitur; cohortēs aliae appropinquant. Hostēs terga vertunt; fugientibus equitēs occurrunt. Fit māgna caedēs. Sedulius, dux et prīnceps Lemovīcum, occīditur; Vercassivellaunus Arvernus vīvus in fugā comprehenditur; sīgna mīlitāria LXXIIII ad Caesarem referuntur; paucī ex ⁵tantō numerō sē incolumēs in castra recipiunt.

⁶Cōnspicātī ex oppidō caedem et fugam suōrum, dēspērātā salūte, cōpiās ā mūnītiōnibus ⁷redūcunt.

Fit prōtinus, hāc rē audītā, ⁸ex castrīs Gallōrum fuga. Quod nisi ⁹crēbrīs subsidiīs ac tōtīus diēī labōre mīlitēs essent dēfessī, omnēs hostium cōpiae ¹⁰dēlērī potuissent. Dē mediā nocte missus equitātus novissimum agmen cōnsequitur; māgnus numerus capitur atque interficitur, reliquī ex fugā in cīvitātēs discēdunt.

---

1. **colōre vestītūs:** Caesar wore the general's crimson cloak so that he might be easily recognized by the soldiers.
2. **īnsīgnī:** as a mark of identity.
3. **ōmissīs pīlīs:** The Roman legionaries were charging up hill so that pikes could not be hurled to advantage.
4. **tergum:** supply **hostium.**
5. **tantō numerō:** 60,000 picked men.
6. **Cōnspicātī ex oppidō = Eī, quī in oppidō sunt, cōnspicātī.**

7. **redūcunt:** The subject understood refers to the besieged Gauls.
8. **ex castrīs Gallōrum:** from the camp of the relief army.
9. **crēbrīs subsidiīs:** *by frequent supporting movements.*
10. **dēlērī potuissent:** could have been destroyed; **essent, potuissent:** contrary to fact, condition, and conclusion.

FOR COMPREHENSION

● ANSWER IN ENGLISH:

1. Why did the Roman general wear a red cloak in battle?
2. What did the Gauls try to do before Caesar could arrive?
3. Why did the Romans throw aside their javelins?
4. What effect did the defeat of the Gallic relief army have on the inhabitants of the besieged Alesia?
5. Why weren't all the troops of the enemy wiped out?

● RESPONDĒ LATĪNE:

1. Quā ex rē adventus Caesaris cōgnitus est?
2. Quō modō mīlitēs Rōmānī rem gerēbant?
3. Quandō hostēs terga vertērunt?
4. Quot sīgna mīlitaria ad Caesarem relāta sunt?
5. Quō Gallī quī neque captī neque interfectī erant discessērunt?

● SCRĪBE LATĪNE:

1. When the Gauls saw the troops of cavalry which Caesar had ordered to follow him, they decided to begin battle at once.
2. The Romans were so wearied from the labor of the whole day that they could not wipe out all the troops of the enemy.
3. The inhabitants of the town withdrew their troops from the fortifications and began to flee to neighboring territories.

Ch. 89 Vercingetorix Surrenders

Posterō diē Vercingetorīx, conciliō convocātō, id bellum sē suscēpisse [1]nōn suārum necessitātum, sed commūnis lībertātis causā dēmōnstrat, et [2]quoniam sit fortūnae cēdendum, [3]ad utramque rem sē [4]illīs offerre, seu morte suā Rōmānīs satisfacere seu vīvum trādere velint. Mittuntur dē hīs rēbus ad Caesarem lēgātī. Jubet arma trādī, prīncipēs prōdūcī. Ipse in mūnītiōne prō castrīs cōnsēdit; eō ducēs prōdūcuntur. [5]Vercingetorīx dēditur; arma prōjiciuntur. Reservātīs [6]Haeduīs atque Arvernīs, [7]sī per eōs cīvitātēs recuperāre posset, ex reliquīs captīvīs tōtī exercituī [8]capita singula praedae nōmine distribuit.

---

1. **nōn suārum necessitātum (causā):** *not for his own personal interests.*
2. **quoniam ... cēdendum:** *since one must submit to fate.*
3. **ad utramque rem:** *for either alternative.*
4. **illīs:** to the members of the Gallic council.
5. **Vercingetorīx:** After his surrender to Caesar, Vercingetorix was sent to Rome, where he was kept in the Mamertine

prison for six years; he was then brought forth to grace Caesar's triumph and later executed.
6. **Haeduīs atque Arvernīs:** It was good military and political policy to try to win the friendship of these powerful states, especially because of their proximity to the Province.
7. **sī ... posset:** *in the hope that he might in this way win back these states.*
8. **capita singula:** *a prisoner apiece.*

FOR COMPREHENSION

- ANSWER IN ENGLISH:
1. What offer did Vercingetorix make to the chieftains of the besieged Gallic army?
2. What motive does Vercingetorix say had led him to enter the war against the Romans?
3. What were Caesar's terms of surrender?
4. Where was Vercingetorix surrendered to Caesar?
5. What disposition did Caesar make of the prisoners of war?
6. Why did Caesar make an exception in favor of the Haeduans and the Arvernians?
7. Was Vercingetorix "the noblest Gaul of them all"? Do you know from your reading who was called "the noblest Roman of them all"?

Vercingetorix.

- RESPONDĒ LATĪNE:
1. Quā dē causā Vercingetorīx id bellum suscēperat?
2. Quās ad duās rēs Vercingetorīx sē Gallīs obtulit?
3. Quī dē hīs rēbus ad Caesarem missī sunt?
4. Quae Caesar Gallōs facere jūssit?
5. Quō Vercingetorīx et aliī ducēs prōductī sunt?
6. Quibus reliquōs captīvōs distribuērunt?

- SCRĪBE LATĪNE:
1. The next day Vercingetorix explained why he had undertaken this war.
2. Vercingetorix was surrendered to Caesar sitting in front of the camp.
3. The bravest Gaul of them all had not undertaken the war for the sake of his own interests but for the liberty of all.

Ch. 90   Thanksgiving of Twenty Days at Rome

Hīs rēbus cōnfectīs, in Haeduōs proficīscitur; cīvitātem recipit. Eō lēgātī ab Arvernīs missī, quae imperāret, sē factūrōs pollicentur. Imperat māgnum numerum obsidum. Legiōnēs in hīberna mittit. Captīvōrum circiter xx mīlia Haeduīs Arvernīsque reddit.

T. Labiēnum duābus cum legiōnibus et equitātū in Sēquanōs proficīscī jubet; huic M. Semprōnium Rutilum attribuit.

327

C. Fabium lēgātum et Lūcium Minucium Basilum cum legiōnibus duābus [1]in Rēmīs collocat, nē quam ā fīnitimīs Bellovacīs calamitātem accipiant.

C. Antistium Rēgīnum in Ambivaretōs, T. Sextium in Biturīgēs, C. Canīnium Rebilum in Rutēnōs cum singulīs legiōnibus mittit. Q. Tullium Cicerōnem et P. Sulpicium Cabillōnī et Matiscōne in Haeduīs ad Ararim reī frūmentāriae causā collocat. Ipse Bibracte hiemāre cōnstituit.

Hīs rēbus ex Caesaris litterīs cōgnitīs, Rōmae [2]diērum vīgintī supplicātiō redditur.

FOR COMPREHENSION

● ANSWER IN ENGLISH:

1. Why did Caesar after the conquest of the Gauls at Alesia go to the territory of the Haeduans?
2. Did he succeed in his attempt to win back the Haeduans?
3. What was Caesar's motive for stationing troops among the Remi for the winter of 52–51 B.C.?
4. How was Caesar's victory celebrated at Rome?
5. When did Caesar himself celebrate his victories? Who graced his triumph?
6. What were some of the most important effects of Caesar's subjugation of Gaul?

● RESPONDĒ LATĪNE:

1. Quō Caesar bellō cōnfectō profectus est?
2. Quid lēgātī ab Arvernīs missī pollicitī sunt?
3. Quot captīvōs Caesar Haeduīs Arvernīsque reddidit?
4. Ubi Caesar hiemāvit?
5. Quot diērum supplicātiō Rōmae dēcrēta est?

● SCRĪBE LATĪNE:

1. When all these affairs were completed, Caesar marched into the territory of the Haeduans in order to regain that state.
2. He ordered the Arverni to send him a large number of hostages.
3. A festival of thanksgiving was proclaimed at Rome as soon as Caesar's victory was learned from his letters.

---

1. **in Rēmīs:** Caesar protected the Remi because they had remained loyal to him during the rebellion of almost all the states of Gaul.

2. **diērum vīgintī supplicātiō:** The length of this celebration might well have been increased if the Romans had realized the full significance of Caesar's victory, which broke the resistance of the Gauls. The history of all Europe and of America was vitally affected by what Caesar's leadership and Roman courage accomplished on the slopes of Mont Réa.

RESULTS OF CAESAR'S CONQUEST OF GAUL

The Gauls were a brave people and loved their native land; but the conquest of Gaul by Caesar was an event of supreme importance for the future history of Rome and for the development of Western civilization. Italy was freed for centuries from the fear of invasion by descendants of the barbaric Gallic tribes who, in 390 B.C., had penetrated into Italy and captured and burned Rome. Because the advance of the German tribes was checked at the Rhine, Italy was likewise relieved of the German menace, and the civilization of Western Europe became Roman, and not Teutonic.

Gaul rapidly became romanized. The Gauls learned the language of their conquerors, and Latin, though in changed form, became the language of that part of Europe. Roman colonies were founded; cities were connected by Roman roads; Roman literature, art, architecture, and law developed and flourished. Gaul became more Roman than Rome itself. The Roman government and civilization were at the time the most advanced in the world. When Rome's decline began, it was Gaul that kept alight the torch of civilization and preserved the Roman contribution to world progress.

The Civil War

COMMENTĀRIĪ DĒ BELLŌ CĪVĪLĪ

(Sight translation)

PREVIEW: In the autumn of 50 B.C. Caesar with a small military force was at Ravenna, a city near the boundary of Italy and Cisalpine Gaul. There he was awaiting the expiration of his command in 49 B.C. The Senate had refused his request to run for the consulship *in absentia* and ordered him to disband his Gallic army at once or be considered an outlaw. Two courses of action lay before him. Either he could yield and return to Rome, where as a private citizen he would be liable to impeachment, or he could boldly defy the Senate. He chose the latter course.

To cross the Rubicon, a small river which formed the boundary between Caesar's province and Italy, and appear under arms in forbidden territory would be a revolutionary act. Uttering the immortal words *Jacta alea est* (*The die is cast*), he led his one legion across the river and headed for Rome, either to death or victory. Thus began the Civil War between Caesar and the senatorial party under the leadership of Pompey, once his closest associate but now his bitterest enemy.

City after city and town after town yielded without a struggle to Caesar in his whirlwind drive to prevent Pompey's sailing from Brundisium in southern Italy to Epirus in Greece. Unsuccessful in this attempt, Caesar rushed to Spain where he defeated strong Pompeian forces. Then he returned to Rome to prepare for the pursuit of Pompey. Although Pompey's army was twice the size of Caesar's, Pompey was decisively defeated in August of 48 B.C. on the battle field of Pharsalus in Thessaly. He then fled to Egypt, where he was treacherously murdered by order of the young king, Ptolemy.

THE BATTLE OF PHARSALUS

Summary of Chapters 84–85

When Caesar had arranged for his food supply and had encouraged his soldiers, he led his army out of camp and drew up his lines some distance from the camp of Pompey. On subsequent days he pushed his line up to the foot of the hills held by the army of Pompey. Pompey, who had his camp on the hill, remained stationary. Finally, as Caesar broke camp, it was noticed that Pompey's line had advanced somewhat farther from the rampart, so that it seemed possible for a battle to be fought in a place which was not too unfavorable. Caesar addressed his men: "Let us be prepared in heart for a conflict; we shall not easily find such an opportunity hereafter." Then he led out his lightly armed troops.

Ch. 86   Pompey Is Confident of Victory

Pompējus quoque, ut posteā cōgnitum est, suōrum omnium [1]hortātū statuerat proeliō dēcertāre. Namque etiam in cōnsiliō superiōribus diēbus dīxerat, priusquam concurrent aciēs, fore utī exercitus Caesaris pellerētur. Id cum essent plērīque admīrātī, "Sciō mē," inquit, "paene incrēdibilem rem pollicērī; sed [2]ratiōnem cōnsilī meī accipite, quō fīrmiōre animō in proelium prōdeātis.

"Persuāsī equitibus nostrīs (idque mihi sē factūrōs cōnfirmāvērunt), ut, [3]cum propius sit accessum, [4]dextrum Caesaris cornū ab latere apertō aggrederentur, et, circumventā ā tergō aciē, prius [5]perturbātum exercitum pellerent, quam ā nōbīs tēlum in hostem jacerētur. Ita sine perīculō legiōnum et paene sine vulnere bellum cōnficiēmus. Id autem difficile nōn est, cum tantum equitātū [6]valeāmus."

Simul dēnūntiāvit ut essent animō parātī in posterum diem et, quoniam fieret dīmicandī potestās, [7]ut saepe rogitāvissent, [8]nē suam neu [9]reliquōrum opīniōnem fallerent.

1. **hortātū:** *encouragement.*
2. **ratiōnem:** *explanation.*
3. **cum ... accessum:** *when the lines have drawn nearer.*
4. **dextrum ... aggrederentur:** Caesar's right wing was exposed, while his left wing was protected by a rivulet.
5. **perturbātum:** *into confusion.*
6. **valeāmus:** Pompey had seven times as great a cavalry force as had Caesar.
7. **ut:** *as.*
8. **nē ... fallerent:** *and not disappoint his own expectation or that of the others.*
9. **reliquōrum:** the senators and other important civilians who were with Pompey.

Ch. 87   Labienus Expresses Contempt for Caesar's Army

Hunc [1]Labiēnus [2]excēpit et, cum Caesaris cōpiās dēspiceret, Pompējī cōnsilium summīs laudibus efferret, "Nōlī," inquit, "exīstimāre, Pompējī, hunc esse exercitum, quī Galliam Germāniamque dēvīcerit. Omnibus interfuī proeliīs neque temere incōgnitam rem prōnūntiō. Perexigua pars illīus exercitūs superest;

1. **Labienus:** Labienus had gone over to the other side to Pompey and had shown himself an implacable enemy of Caesar. Under the direction of Caesar, he had been an efficient officer, but he did not measure up to the expectations of his new general.
2. **excēpit:** *followed* (i.e., in speaking).

māgna pars dēperiit (quod accidere tot proeliīs fuit necesse), multōs autumnī pestilentia in Italiā cōnsūmpsit, multī domum discessērunt, multī sunt relictī ³in continentī.

"An nōn ⁴audīstis, ex eīs, quī per causam ⁵valētūdinis remānsērunt, ⁶cohortēs esse Brundisī factās? Hae cōpiae, quās vidētis, ex dīlēctibus ⁷hōrum annōrum in citeriōre Galliā sunt refectae, et plērīque sunt ex colōniīs Trānspadānīs. Ac tamen, quod fuit rōboris, duōbus proeliīs Dyrrachīnīs interiit."

Haec cum dīxisset, jūrāvit sē nisi victōrem in castra nōn reversūrum, reliquōsque, ut idem facerent, hortātus est. Hoc laudāns, Pompējus idem jūrāvit; nec vērō ex reliquīs fuit quisquam, ⁸quī jūrāre dubitāret. Haec tum facta sunt in cōnsiliō, māgnāque spē et laetitiā omnium discessum est; ac jam animō victōriam praecipiēbant, quod dē rē tantā et ā tam perītō imperātōre nihil frūstrā cōnfīrmārī vidēbātur.

Summary of Chapters 88–102

When Caesar came near Pompey's camp, he carefully observed Pompey's line of battle and adjusted his own accordingly. Pompey had 45,000 men, Caesar 22,000. Between the two armies there was only enough space to charge. Caesar briefly addressed his soldiers and then gave the signal to attack. With heroic words Cratinus, a veteran known for his bravery, led the charge. Caesar's veterans hurled themselves on the foe. At first Caesar's cavalry was defeated, but his fourth line routed Pompey's cavalry and attacked Pompey's left wing in the rear. When Caesar's third line entered the action, Pompey's infantry gave way, and Pompey fled to his camp. Caesar took possession of Pompey's camp, where he found many evidences of luxury. Pompey fled from his camp to the sea, where he boarded a grain ship. Caesar completed his victory and took many captives. Of the Pompeian army some 15,000 seem to have been killed; more than 24,000 surrendered; many others took refuge in neighboring states. Caesar preserved all those who had surrendered and commended them to his soldiers, urging that none of them should be injured or deprived of their property.

Caesar determined to put aside all other business and follow Pompey, who, having been refused admittance at Antioch, decided to give up the idea of visiting Syria and sailed to Pelusium, an Egyptian city on the Mediterranean.

---

3. **in continentī:** in Italy.
4. **audīstis = audīvistis.**
5. **valētūdinis:** (under the pretext) *of sickness.*
6. **cohortēs . . . factās:** *cohorts at Brundisium have been made up.*

7. **hōrum annōrum:** years of the Civil War.
8. **quī . . . dubitāret:** relative characteristic clause.

Ch. 103   Pompey Seeks Safety in Egypt

Ibi cāsū rēx erat Ptolemaeus, puer aetāte, māgnis cōpiīs cum
sorōre Cleopātrā bellum gerēns, quam paucīs ante mēnsibus per
suōs propinquōs atque amīcōs rēgnō expulerat; castraque Cleo-
pātrae nōn longō spatiō ab ējus castrīs ¹distābant. Ad eum
Pompējus mīsit, ut, prō ²hospitiō atque amīcitiā patris, Alex-
andrīā reciperētur atque illīus opibus in calamitāte tegerētur.

Sed quī ab eō missī erant, cōnfectō lēgātiōnis officiō, līberius
cum mīlitibus rēgis colloquī coepērunt eōsque hortārī, ut suum
officium Pompējō ³praestārent nēve ējus fortūnam dēspicerent.
In hōc erant numerō complūrēs Pompējī mīlitēs, quōs ex ējus
exercitū acceptōs in Syriā Gabīnius Alexandrīam trādūxerat
bellōque cōnfectō apud Ptolemaeum, patrem puerī, relīquerat.

---

1. **distābant:** *was distant.*
2. **hospitiō:** *hospitality.*

3. **praestārent:** *perform.*

Ch. 104   Death by Treachery

Hīs cōgnitīs rēbus amīcī rēgis, quī propter aetātem ējus in
¹cūrātiōne erant rēgnī, sīve timōre adductī, ut posteā praedicā-
bant, sollicitātō exercitū rēgiō, nē Pompējus Alexandrīam
Aegyptumque occupāret, sīve dēspectā ējus fortūnā, ut plērumque in calamitāte ex amīcīs inimīcī exsistunt, hīs quī erant ab eō
missī ²palam līberāliter respondērunt eumque ad rēgem venīre
jussērunt; ipsī clam cōnsiliō initō Achillam, praefectum rēgium,
singulārī hominem audāciā, et L. Septimium, tribūnum mīlitum,
ad interficiendum Pompējum mīsērunt.

Ab hīs līberāliter ipse appellātus et quādam ³nōtitiā Septimī
⁴prōductus, quod bellō praedōnum apud eum ⁵ōrdinem dūxerat,
nāviculam parvulam cōnscendit cum paucīs suīs; ibi ab Achillā
et Septimiō interficitur. Item L. Lentulus comprehenditur ab
rēge et interficitur.

---

1. **cūrātiōne:** *charge.*
2. **palam:** *in public;* contrasted with **clam.**
3. **nōtitiā:** *acquaintance* (with).

4. **prōductus:** *led on.*
5. **ōrdinem:** *a division.*

PART IV

Survey of Latin Literature

From the third century before Christ until our own day Latin literature has been written and read. In this survey of our Latin literary heritage you will find excerpts from the work of the best-known writers in this language. These selections are not arranged according to difficulty; they are presented in chronological order, but they may be read in whatever order seems best for ease in comprehension or for pleasure and enjoyment.

Since they are representative of many fields of prose and poetry, they offer a wide variety of subject matter. Through their reading you will be able to understand to some extent the influence of Latin literature upon world literature and to appreciate how the culture of the Romans has contributed in an uninterrupted flow to Western civilization.

In order that we may be able to place an author and his work in the proper period, it will be well to keep in mind this brief chronological outline of Latin literature.

I	Early Period	3rd century B.C.–80 B.C.
II	Golden Age	80 B.C.–A.D. 14
	A. Age of Cicero	80 B.C.–43 B.C.
	B. Augustan Period	43 B.C.–A.D. 14
III	Silver Age	A.D. 14–A.D. 138
IV	Patristic Period	late 2nd–5th century A.D.
V	Medieval Period	6th–14th century A.D.
VI	Modern Period	about 15th century A.D.–the present

THE EARLY PERIOD
3rd CENTURY B.C. TO 80 B.C.

As a result of their conquests the Romans came into contact with Greek civilization in the third century before Christ. Greek culture had reached its highest development in the fifth and fourth centuries B.C. The Romans were

334

deeply impressed by the masterpieces in literature and art which they found, and they set to work at once to imitate both. Using the Greek literary forms, meters, subjects, and ideas, the Romans composed epics, dramas, satires, and speeches. The greatest accomplishments of this period which still survive are the comedies of Plautus and Terence, based on Greek plays. These plays in Latin may still be read with enjoyment, especially those of Plautus, whose works were of a more popular nature. Their plots have been used very effectively by later dramatists, such as Shakespeare, whose *Comedy of Errors* is based on Plautus' *Menaechmi*.

Plautus: The Beginning of Roman Comedy

Comedy in ancient Roman times had its beginning when a poor boy of Umbria in Italy came to the city of Rome to make his fortune. His name was Titus Maccius Plautus. When he was born no one knows, but at his death in 184 B.C. he was the most popular literary figure in Rome. At first he worked as a stage

A Roman actor studying his masks.

hand; later, while occupied in menial services in a bakery, he began to write plays. His twenty-one plays were based on the Greek originals of Menander and other talented Athenian writers, but the vigor, humor, and general spirit of these comedies are essentially Roman.

Plautus' business is to make people laugh, and this he does by using plots that reflect the seamy side of life. His middle- and lower-class characters, although bearing Greek names, wearing Greek costumes, and acting against a typical Greek stage setting, represent types quite familiar in the Roman society of his day. Even after the comedies of Plautus ceased eventually to be acted in Rome, they continued to be models for comedy through later centuries.

The following selections are passages taken from Plautus' comedy *Aulularia* (*The Pot of Gold*). The greed of the miser Euclio over the loss of his gold is quite similar to that expressed in Shylock's lament for his lost daughter and ducats in Shakespeare's *Merchant of Venice*. France's great comedy writer Molière modeled his immortal miser, Harpagon, on the character of Euclio.

THE POT OF GOLD

ARGUMENT OF THE PLAY

Euclio, senex avārus, vix sibi crēdēns, domī suae dēfossam (*buried*) aulam (*pot*) aurī invenit. Latrōnum (*of robbers*) ob timōrem rūrsus aulam auri abdit. Lyconīdēs, adulēscēns dīves, Euclionis fīliam clam amat, sed Megadōrus senex, ā sorōre suā adductus, uxōrem dūcere statuit et Euclionis fīliam sibi postulat. Dūrus Euclio Megadōrō fīliam suam prōmittit, sed dē aulā aurī timēns, ē domiciliō eam fert et in silvā proximā abdit. Interim servus Lyconīdis locum, ubi Euclio aulam aurī abdidit, invenit, et aulam raptam clam aufert. Propter damnum (*loss*) aurī, Euclio est āmēns (*beside himself*).

Megadōrus senex, ā Lyconīde persuāsus, fīliam Euclionis in mātrimōnium dūcere jam nōn vult. Tum servus Lyconīdis aulam aurī ad Lyconīdem, dominum suum, fert et per eam sibi lībertā- tem postulat. Dominus autem aulam aurī ad Euclionem, quī per dolum eam āmīserat, portat. Euclio laetissimus aurum accipit et Lyconīdī fīliam dat. Posteā omnēs fēlīciter vīvunt.

PROLOGUE

[*The* LAR FAMILIARIS, *who watched over the safety of the household, is represented as telling the story of the pot of gold which has been buried by his old master, the grandfather of his present master,* EUCLIO, *who is an old miser. The god is pleased with* EUCLIO'S *good daughter because every day she pays him due honor. Accordingly, the* LAR FAMILIARIS *makes known to* EUCLIO *the hiding place of the gold in order that the daughter may have a suitable marriage dowry.*]

LĀR FAMILIĀRIS: Nē quis mīrētur quī sim, paucīs (*in a few words*)
   loquar.
Ego sum Lār familiāris ex hāc familiā
unde exeuntem mē aspēxistis. Hanc domum
jam multōs annōs est cum possideō (*I have possessed*) et colō
patrī avōque jam hūjus quī nunc hīc vīvit,
sed avus hūjus aurī aulam clam in mediō focō
dēfodit (*buried*), implōrāns mē ut id servārem sibi.

Is quoniam moritur [ita avidō ingeniō (*disposition*) fuit],
numquam indicāre id fīliō voluit suō.
Huic fīlia ūna est. Ea mihi cotīdiē
aut tūre (*with incense*) aut vīnō aut aliquī (*with something*) semper
    supplicat,
dat mihi corōnās. Ējus honōris grātiā
fēcī thēsaurum (*treasure*) ut hīc reperīret Eucliō
quō illam facilius nūptum (*bride*), sī vellet, daret.
Sed hic senex jam clāmat intus (*within*) ut solet.
Anum (*old woman*) forās (*out-of-doors*) ējicit, nē sit cōnscia (*aware*).
Crēdō aurum aspicere vult, nē surreptum (*stolen*) sit. [*Exit*
    LAR FAMILIARIS.]

THE MISER'S LAMENT

[*Enter* EUCLIO, *the miser, running wildly back and forth.*]
EUCLIŌ: Periī! Interiī! Occīdī! Quō curram? Quō nōn curram?
Tenē! Tenē! Quem? Quis? Nēsciō! Nihil videō! Caecus eō;
atque equidem quō eam aut ubi sim aut quī sim nēsciō. [*He turns
to the audience.*] Obsecrō vōs ego, date mihi auxilium, ōrō!
obtēstor! Hominem dēmōnstrāte quī meum aurum abstulit.
[*The audience laughs.*] Quid dīcitis? Quid est? Quid rīdētis?
[*Angrily*] Nōvī omnēs, sciō fūrēs esse hīc complūrēs, quī vestītū
et crētā occultant sēsē atque sedent quasi sint frūgī (*honest*).
[*To a spectator*] Quid ais (*say*) tū? Tibi crēdere certum est, nam
esse bonum ex vultū cōgnōscō. Hem! (*Ha!*) Nēmō habet hōrum?
Occīdistī! Dīc, igitur, quis habet? Nēscīs? Heu! (*Alas!*) mē
miserē periī! Hic diēs mihi famem et pauperiem (*poverty*) obtulit.
Miserrimus sum omnium in terrā. Nam quid mihi vītā opus est
quī tantum aurī perdidī, quod tam dīligenter cūstōdīvī! Patī nōn
possum! [*Weeps violently.*]

Quintus Ennius: The Father of Latin Poetry

Quintus Ennius was born in Calabria in 239 B.C. Brought to Rome by Cato
in 204 B.C., he became the friend of some of the most eminent men of his time.
Although he was not the earliest Latin poet, his work was so superior to that
of his predecessors in the field that he is usually called the father of Latin
poetry. His outstanding work was the *Annales*, an eighteen-book epic history
of Rome, written in dactylic hexameter, a form which he introduced into Latin
poetry. From the *Annales* we have only about six hundred lines, found as quotations in the works of many Latin authors, particularly Cicero. We also have
quotations from twenty-two of his tragedies.
    The quotations given here are from the *Annales*. The first one is a tribute to

Fabius Maximus, who had been elected Roman dictator in the Second Punic War. He followed a successful policy of delay, but his Roman colleagues were impatient at what seemed to them a "do-nothing" policy. Accordingly, they dubbed him "Cunctator" (*"the Delayer"*) and replaced him by men who were politicians and amateurs in the art of war. The result was the disastrous defeat of the Romans by Hannibal's forces at Cannae in August of 216 B.C.

TO QUINTUS FABIUS MAXIMUS CUNCTATOR

Ūnus homō nōbīs cūnctandō restituit rem (*the state*).
Nōn rūmōrēs pōnēbat ante salūtem;
Ergō postque magisque virī nunc glōria clāret.

The speaker of the words of the following fragment is Pyrrhus, the Greek general who invaded Italy in 280 B.C. In his reply to the Roman envoys he refused to accept a ransom for his Roman prisoners of war but surrendered them gratis instead. It was for such generous deeds on his part that the Romans esteemed him more highly than the usual enemy.

VICTORY RATHER THAN GOLD

Nec mī aurum poscō, nec mī pretium dēderitis;
nōn cauponantēs (*trading*) bellum sed belligerantēs (*waging war*),
ferrō, nōn aurō, vītam cernāmus utrīque.
Vōsne velit an mē rēgnāre, era (*mistress*) quidve ferat Fors,
virtūte experiāmur. Et hoc simul accipe dīctum:
quōrum virtūtī bellī fortūna pepercit,
eōrundem lībertātī mē parcere certum est.
Dōnō, dūcite, dōque volentibus cum māgnīs dīs.

Cato: The Father of Latin Prose

"Delenda est Carthago!" (*"Carthage must be destroyed!"*) is the most famous and oft-repeated remark of Marcus Porcius Cato (Cato Major). Born in Tusculum, 234 B.C., he enjoyed eighty-five years of remarkable activity and influence in the military and civic life of Rome. He was convinced that the salvation and prosperity of Rome depended upon the destruction of Carthage and the return to the simple virtues that characterized Rome's early days. He was vehemently opposed to the introduction of Greek culture and luxury at Rome.

Cato Major may be regarded as the real father of Latin prose literature. In both history and oratory he was the worthy forerunner of many celebrated Roman successors. The son of a farmer, he kept his interest in things agricultural even after he had made a reputation for himself as a soldier, statesman, orator, and author. His *De Agri Cultura*, from which the following selection is taken, contains random notes on housekeeping and farm management. An interesting account of Cato's life is found in Plutarch's *Lives*.

DUTIES OF THE FARM OVERSEER

Pater familiās (*the head of a household*) ubi ad villam vēnit, ubi Larem familiārem salūtāvit, fundum (*estate*) eōdem diē, sī potest, circumeat; sī nōn eō diē, at postrīdiē. Ubi cōgnōvit quō modō fundus cultus sit, operaque quae facta īnfectaque (*not done*) sint, postrīdiē ējus diēī vīlicum (*overseer*) vocet, roget quid operis sit factum, quid restet.

Haec erunt vīlicī officia. Disciplīnā bonā ūtātur. Feriae (*festivals*) serventur. Aliēnō manum abstineat, sua servet dīligenter. Lītibus (*disputes*) familia supersedeat (*refrain*); opere bene eōs exerceat; facilius malō et aliēnō (*meddling*) prohibēbit. Vīlicus nē sit ambulātor (*gadabout*), sobrius (*sober*) sit semper, nē quō ad cēnam eat. Ea, quae dominus imperāverit, fiant.

Nē cēnseat sē plūs scīre quam dominum. Amīcōs dominī, eōs habeat sibi amīcōs. Sine dominī jūssū, crēdat nēminī. Sēmen (*seed*), vīnum, oleum mūtum (*as a loan*) det nēminī. Duās aut trēs familiās habeat, unde ūtilia roget (*may borrow*) et quibus det. Opus rūsticum omne cūret ut sciat facere, et id faciat saepe. Prīmus māne surgat (*let him rise*), postrēmus dormiat.

THE GOLDEN AGE

80 B.C. TO A.D. 14

This period of Latin literature is called *golden* because during this century Roman writers produced the outstanding literary classics which made Latin literature one of the world's greatest. A classic is a literary or artistic work of the highest excellence, in matter as well as in form. There were so many literary classics produced during the Golden Age that our study will be facilitated if we subdivide this era into two parts, the Age of Cicero and the Augustan Period.

THE AGE OF CICERO (80 B.C.–43 B.C.)

It seems proper that this period of almost forty years should be called the Age of Cicero because during this time he was the most prominent orator and writer in Rome. It was a period of great unrest, of civil wars and dictators, of military might against civil right, of great material prosperity and poverty, of much culture and extravagant display, of moral and religious decadence. In Rome itself the struggles between Marius and Sulla and between Pompey and Caesar clearly foreshadowed the end of the Republic. Yet in spite of these disturbing influences, wealth increased and interest in literature and art was widespread. Varro, Cicero, Caesar, Nepos, Lucretius, Sallust, Catullus, and Syrus produced the works of their genius which, each in its own way, affected Western culture and literature. Since the entire third part of this textbook is devoted to Julius Caesar, no further treatment of his writing is presented in this survey.

Varro: Author of over Five Hundred Books

Marcus Terentius Varro (116–27 B.C.) had the reputation of being the most learned Roman of his time. A writer of tireless industry and vast learning, he produced more than five hundred books on practically every subject of Roman literature and learning. Fate has not been kind to most of them, however. Only the *De Re Rustica* in three books, a small part of the *De Lingua Latina*, and a few fragments of his many other works survive.

His *De Re Rustica*, a treatise on agriculture, is much more learned than Cato's work on the same subject, but the language is plain and unadorned; it is written more as a technical dissertation than as a work of art. In a fragment from one of his other works, Varro represents himself as a Roman Rip Van Winkle who has fallen asleep at the age of ten and awakened at sixty to regard with incredulous wonder the vast changes that have occurred at Rome.

In the passage given here from *De Re Rustica*, written when he was over eighty years of age, Varro once again seems to be soliloquizing in his self-assigned role of Rip Van Winkle.

CHANGING ATTITUDES TOWARD AGRICULTURE

Virī māgnī nostrī mājōrēs nōn sine causā praepōnēbant rūsticōs Rōmānōs urbānīs. Ut rūrī enim quī in villā vīvunt īgnāviōrēs (*lazier*) sunt, quam quī in agrō versantur (*are employed*) in aliquō opere faciendō, sīc quī in oppidō sedērent, quam quī rūra colerent īgnāviōrēs putābant.

Hīs temporibus intrā mūrum ferē omnēs patrēs familiae repsērunt (*have crept*), relictīs falce et arātrō (*plow*), et manūs movēre maluērunt in theātrō ac circō quam in segetibus (*grainfields*) et vīnētīs (*vineyards*). Frūmentum quod volumus ex Āfricā et Sardiniā portātur, et nāvibus vīnum ex īnsulā Coā et Chiā fertur.

Itaque in quā terrā pastōrēs, quī condidērunt urbem, cultūram agrī prōgeniem (*offspring*) suam docuērunt, ibi contrā prōgeniēs eōrum propter avāritiam contrā lēgēs ex segetibus fēcit prāta (*meadows*), īgnōrantēs nōn idem esse agrī cultūram et pāstiōnem (*grazing*). Alius enim pāstor et arātor (*plowman*) est, etiam sī possunt in agrō pāscī (*to be pastured*) gregēs.

Cicero: The Greatest Roman Orator

In the life of Marcus Tullius Cicero, born in 106 B.C., we have the story of a *novus homo*, i.e., the son of parents of the middle or equestrian class, a man without important family connections who became the greatest of Roman orators, the most honored of Roman statesmen, and the most perfect of Latin stylists. During his boyhood Marius and Sulla, notorious dictators, plunged the state into its first Civil War. He lived through the Social War and saw citizenship granted to the Italian communities.

Cicero was on friendly terms with the greatest statesmen and military leaders that Rome ever produced: Pompey, Caesar, and Augustus. Fearlessly he attacked such disreputable grafters as Verres, Catiline, Clodius, and Antony. No stranger to the ups and downs of political life, he suffered banishment for a year and a half. He served the dying Republic with honor; he sided with Pompey against Caesar, by whom he was later pardoned; he attacked the unscrupulous Antony after Caesar's assassination; and finally he was himself assassinated in 43 B.C. by Antony's orders.

Cicero may have failed to save the dying Roman Republic, but he did succeed in producing immortal Latin prose by means of which the learning and culture of Greece and Rome were transmitted to the Middle Ages and modern times. His speeches have served as models for the greatest orators for twenty centuries.

The following passage is taken from one of Cicero's philosophical works, the *De Officiis* or *On Moral Duties*. In it Cicero recounts the story of ten captive Roman nobles who were sent to Rome by Hannibal to arrange for an exchange of prisoners. The nobles took an oath that they would return to Hannibal if they did not succeed in their mission. One of the ten who went out returned immediately to the camp as if he had forgotten something; rationalizing that he had kept his word to return, he then left the camp for good. Cicero condemns this act as a clever evasion of the spirit of a sworn promise.

HONOR THE RULE OF CONDUCT, NOT EXPEDIENCY

Sed, ut laudandus est Rēgulus in cōnservandō jūre jūrandō, sīc decem illī, quōs post Cannēnsem (*of Cannae*) pūgnam jūrātōs (*under oath*) ad senātum mīsit Hannibal sē in castra reditūrōs esse ea, quōrum erant potītī Poenī, nisi dē redimendīs captīvīs impetrāvissent, sī nōn redīrent, vituperandī sunt (*censured*).

Dē quibus nōn omnēs auctōrēs fābulam nārrant eōdem modō; nam Polybius, bonus auctor in prīmīs, ex decem nōbilissimīs, quī tum erant missī, novem revertisse dīcit, rē ā senātū nōn impetrātā; ūnum ex decem, quī paulō postquam erat ēgressus ē castrīs, redīsset, quasi aliquid esset oblītus, Rōmae remānsīsse; reditū enim in castra līberātum sē esse jūre jūrandō interpretābātur (*rationalized*) nōn rēctē; fraus (*deceit*) enim astringit (*aggravates*), nōn dissolvit perjūrium. Itaque dēcrēvit senātus ut ille veterātor (*sly rascal*) et callidus (*shrewd fellow*) vīnctus ad Hannibal dūcerētur.

Sed illud (*the following*) est māximum (*the most important point*). Octō hominum mīlia tenēbat Hannibal, nōn quōs in aciē cēpisset, aut quī perīculō mortis fūgissent, sed quī relīctī in castrīs fuissent ā Paulō et ā Varrōne cōnsulibus. Eōs senātus cēnsuit nōn redimendōs esse, cum id parvā pecūniā fierī posset, ut esset īnsitum (*impressed upon*) mīlitibus nostrīs aut vincere aut morī. Quā quidem rē audītā, frāctum esse animum Hannibalis scrībit īdem [*Polybius*], quod senātus populusque Rōmānus, rēbus afflīctīs (*in time of disaster*), tam excelsō animō fuisset. Sīc honestātis comparātiōne (*consideration*) ea, quae videntur ūtilia, vincuntur (*are outweighed*).

Nepos: A Writer of Biographies

Cornelius Nepos (100–25 B.C.) was born in Cisalpine Gaul, the same district in northern Italy from which came Vergil, Catiline, and Livy. At an early age he moved to Rome, where later he became the friend of various well-known Roman writers like Cicero, Atticus, and Catullus, and devoted his time to literature rather than politics.

Although most of his writings have been lost, some of the biographies contained in his *De Viris Illustribus* have survived. The biographies which are extant are of notable leaders, mostly Greek. Besides the Greek biographies, we have lives of Datames the Persian and two Carthaginians, Hamilcar Barca and Hannibal. There are also extant the biographies of Cato and Atticus: Cato, the strong, stern patriot; and Atticus, the cultured cosmopolitan.

The following selections are incidents taken from Nepos' *Hannibal*. The Latin has been adapted.

HANNIBAL RENEWS WAR WITH THE ROMANS

Cum Rōmānī Poenōs superāvissent (202 B.C.) et pācem fēcissent, lēgātī Carthāginiēnsēs Rōmam vēnērunt, quī senātuī dē pāce factā grātiās agerent et rogārent ut obsidēs Poenōrum redderentur. Rōmānī sē id factūrōs esse respondērunt.

Paulō post Hannibal rēx Poenōrum factus est, et tantam cūram adhibēbat ut nōn modo pecūnia Rōmānīs quotannīs darētur, sed etiam multum in aerāriō (*treasury*) superesset (*remained*). Id cum Rōmānī cōgnōvissent, timēbant nē Hannibal paucīs annīs bellum renovāre posset. Itaque lēgātōs Carthāginem mīsērunt.

Hōs lēgātōs Hannibal exīstimābat ad sē poscendum missōs

esse. Hāc dē causā nāvem ascendit et ad rēgem Antiochum fūgit (196 B.C.). Huic persuāsit ut bellum cum Rōmānīs susciperet.

Antiochus vērō, bellō cum Rōmānīs susceptō, cōnsilia multa Hannibalis accipere nōlēbat. Ex quō accidit ut, cum in Graeciam trānsīsset, Thermopylīs (*at Thermopylae*) superārētur et in Asiam sē reciperet. Ex illō proeliō, cum Hannibal vidēret rēgem pulsum esse, ad Crētam īnsulam fūgit, ut ibi dē salūte suā cōnsilium caperet.

HANNIBAL OUTWITS THE CRETANS

Vīdit autem vir omnium callidissimus (*shrewdest*) in māgnō sē fore (futūrum esse) perīculō propter avāritiam Crētēnsium (*of the Cretans*); māgnam enim sēcum pecūniam portābat, dē quā sciēbat exīsse fāmam. Itaque cēpit tāle cōnsilium.

Amphorās (*large jars*) complūrēs complēvit plumbō, summās (*tops*) operuit (*covered up*) aurō et argentō. Hās, praesentibus prīncipibus, dēposuit in templō Diānae, simulāns sē suās fortūnās illōrum fideī crēdere. Hīs dēceptīs, statuās quās sēcum portābat omnī suā pecūniā complēvit eāsque in vēstibulō domī abjēcit. Crētēnsēs templum māgnā cūrā cūstōdīvērunt, nē ille, īnscientibus eīs, tolleret sua sēcumque dūceret.

Lucretius: A Roman Poet Who Taught Philosophy

Very little is known about the life of this rather mysterious person, born in the first century B.C. and named Titus Lucretius Carus. He is the author of a long poem, *De Rerum Natura*, in which he explains with great intensity of feeling the philosophy of Epicurus and the physical theories borrowed by Epicurus from Democritus. This poem of over 7,000 lines, written in dactylic hexameter, treats of the nature of the pagan gods, the origin of the earth, the heavenly bodies, life, and man and his progress from savagery to civilization.

According to the atomic theory of Democritus, the whole universe is composed of atoms of different shapes and a boundless void in which they move. These atoms are indestructible, and their union or separation is what causes growth or decay, birth or death. Many of the surprisingly modern views which Lucretius expresses were the scientific notions of that time. He used them to fulfill the mission which he thought was his: to free men from superstition and the fear of death.

Lucretius was a far better poet than scientist or philosopher. Note in the selection given here the echo of Lucretius' thought in the lines from Gray's "Elegy Written in a Country Churchyard."

DEATH: THE END OF LIFE'S PLEASURES

"Jam jam (*Soon*) nōn domus accipiet tē laeta, neque uxor
optima nec dulcēs occurrent oscula nātī (*children*)
praeripere (*to snatch*) et tacitā pectus dulcēdine (*with sweetness*)
    tangent.
Nōn poteris factīs flōrentibus (*with flourishing achievements*) esse,
    tuīsque
praesidium. Miserō (with *tibi*, line 6) miserē," ājunt (*they say*),
    "omnia adēmit
ūna diēs īnfēsta tibi tot praemia vītae."
Illud in hīs rēbus nōn addunt, "nec tibi eārum
jam dēsīderium rērum super īnsīdet (*settle upon*) ūnā (rē)."
Quod bene sī videant animō dictīsque sequantur
dissolvant animī māgnō sē angōre metūque.

ELEGY WRITTEN IN A COUNTRY CHURCHYARD

For them no more the blazing hearth shall burn,
Or busy housewife ply her evening care:
No children run to lisp their sire's return,
Or climb his knees the envied kiss to share.

Sallust: The First Real Historian

Gaius Sallustius Crispus was born at Amiternum in the Sabine territory in 86 B.C. Of his early life little is known. A partisan of Caesar and the Democratic Party (*Populares*), he held the usual offices which brought him to the plebeian tribuneship in 52 B.C. Although expelled from the Senate on account of his bad reputation, he was later reinstated by Caesar, to whom he had attached himself in the Civil War. After making the usual fortune from his propraetorship in Numidia, Africa, he retired to his luxurious villa near Rome, where he spent his time in writing.

His most ambitious work, of which only fragments have survived, was the *Historiae* in five books, covering the period of almost twelve years from the death of Sulla, 78–67 B.C. He is known to us primarily for his two skillful political pamphlets, the *Conspiracy of Catiline* and the *Jugurthine War*. On account of his *Historiae*, later Romans ranked him as the greatest Roman historian before Livy. He is, however, inaccurate, sometimes deliberately so; and his straining for rhetorical effect leads him to exaggeration, if not actual fiction.

The selection given here from the preface of the *Conspiracy of Catiline* is intended to show that the principal cause for the deterioration of the Roman people was the wealth accumulated when Rome's conquests put an end to the honest and patriotic poverty of the old days.

344

WEALTH ACCUMULATES AND MEN DECAY

Sed ubi labōre atque jūstitiā rēs pūblica crēvit, māgnī rēgēs bellō superātī sunt, nātiōnēs ferae et populī ingentēs vī victī sunt, Carthāgō, aemula (*rival*) imperī Rōmānī, interiit, cūncta maria terraeque patēbant, mūtāre fortūna et mīscēre omnia coepit. Jam eīs, quī labōrēs, perīcula, dubiās et asperās rēs facile tolerāverant, ōtium atque dīvitiae onerī miseriaeque fuērunt.

Igitur prīmō pecūniae, deinde imperī cupīdō crēvit; ea quasi māteriēs (*cause*) omnium malōrum fuērunt. Namque avāritia fidem, probitātem, cēterāsque artēs bonās subvertit (*destroyed*); prō hīs, superbiam, crūdēlitātem, deōs neglegere, omnia vēnālia (*for sale*) habēre docuit.

Ambitiō multōs mortālēs falsōs fierī subēgit (*drove*), aliud clausum in pectore, aliud in linguā promptum (*ready*) habēre, amīcitiās inimīcitiāsque nōn ex rē (*real worth*) sed ex commodō aestimāre, et bonum vultum magis quam ingenium (*character*) bonum habēre.

Avāritia studium pecūniae habet, quam nēmō sapiēns cupīvit. Avāritia corpus animumque virīlem effēminat (*weakens*); semper īnfīnīta et īnsatiābilis, neque cōpiā neque inopiā minuitur.

Catullus: The First Great Lyric Poet of Rome

By far the greatest lyric poet of Rome was Gaius Valerius Catullus, a native of Transalpine Gaul who lived from about 84 to 54 B.C. Early in life he went to Rome to complete his education. There he became a leader among the literary and gilded youth of the corrupt capital. A number of his most delightful lyrics are addressed to Clodia, a handsome but unprincipled woman with whom he was in love.

Catullus did not confine himself to the writing of lyric poetry. He tried his pen at other types of verse. The earliest important group of Latin elegies that has survived came from his genius and industry. He was not much more than thirty when he died, but he left behind him 116 poems of 2 to 408 lines. These poems are said to be unsurpassed as expressions of personal emotion.

The following poem on his villa at Sirmio was written about 56 B.C. The villa of Catullus was at the southern end of Lake Garda in the modern town of Sermione. He had just returned to Sirmio after a year's absence in Bithynia.

O LOVELY SIRMIO

Paene īnsulārum (Paenīnsulārum), Sirmiō, īnsulārumque ocelle (*jewel*), quāscumque in līquentibus stāgnīs (*pools*)

marīque vāstō fert uterque Neptūnus,
quam tē libenter quamque laetus invīsō (*I visit*),
vix mī ipse crēdēns Thȳniam atque Bīthȳnōs
līquisse (relīquisse) campōs et vidēre tē in tūtō.
Ō quid solūtīs est beātius cūrīs,
cum mēns onus repōnit, ac peregrīnō (*foreign*)
labōre fessī vēnimus larem (*household god; home*) ad nostrum
dēsīderātōque acquiēscimus (*rest*) lectō (*couch*)?
Hoc est quod ūnum est prō labōribus tantīs.
Salvē, O venusta (*lovely*) Sirmiō, erō (*in your master*) gaudē!
Gaudēte vōsque, Ō Lȳdiae lacūs undae!
Rīdēte, quidquid est domī cachinnōrum (*of laughter*)!

The only brother of Catullus had died in the faraway Troad in Asia Minor,
and Catullus stopped at his tomb while on his trip to Bithynia.

FRĀTER, AVĒ ATQUE VALĒ

Multās per gentēs et multa per aequora (*seas*) vectus
    adveniō hās miserās, frāter, ad īnferiās (*funeral rites*)
ut tē postrēmō dōnārem mūnere mortis
    et mūtam nēquīquam (*in vain*) alloquerer (*speak to*) cinerem.
Quandoquidem (*Since*) fortūna mihi (*from me*) tē abstulit ipsum,
    heu (*alas*) miser indīgnē (*prematurely*) adempte mihi!
Nunc tamen intereā haec (*these offerings*), prīscō (*ancient*) quae
        mōre parentum
    trādita sunt tristī mūnere ad īnferiās,
accipe frāternō multum manantia (*overflowing*) flētū,
    atque in perpetuum, frāter, avē atque valē!

Tennyson used this last phrase as the title for a poem inspired by a visit to
the country home of Catullus in Sirmio:

AVE ATQUE VALE

There beneath the Roman ruin where the purple flowers grow,
Came that 'Ave atque Vale' of the poet's hopeless woe,
Tenderest of Roman poets nineteen hundred years ago,
'Frater, Ave atque Vale' — as we wandered to and fro,
Gazing at the Lydian laughter of the Garda lake below,
Sweet Catullus' all-but-island, olive-silvery Sirmio.

Publilius Syrus: A Clever Entertainer Who Wrote Proverbs

Publilius Syrus, a freedman who came from Syria, was a composer of mimes, dramatic sketches usually portraying some scene of everyday life. Syrus is remembered, however, not because he was a clever entertainer or for the plots of his mimes, but as the author of a large number of proverbs, hundreds of which have come down to us. One of the most famous of these wise sayings is: "Jūdex damnātur cum nocēns absolvitur." ("*A rogue acquitted is a judge condemned.*")

Many of the following proverbs are well worth remembering.

PROVERBS

1. Ubi lībertās cecidit, nēmō lībere loquī audet.
2. Bona opīniō hominum tūtior pecūniā est.
3. Multōs timēre dēbet quem multī timent.
4. Stultum est querī (*to complain*) dē adversīs (*misfortunes*) ubi culpa est tua.
5. Aut amat aut ōdit mulier; nil est tertium.
6. Ferās, nōn culpās, quod mūtārī nōn potest.
7. Dēlīberandō saepe perit occāsiō.
8. Audendō virtūs crēscit, tardandō timor.
9. Diū parandum est bellum, ut vincās celerius.
10. Sine dolōre est vulnus quod ferendum est cum victōriā.
11. Stultī timent fortūnam, sapientēs ferunt.
12. Homō semper aliud, Fortūna aliud cōgitat.
13. Mulier, cum sōla cōgitat, male cōgitat.
14. Ibi semper est victōria ubi concordia est.
15. Inopī (*to the needy*) beneficium bis dat quī dat celeriter.

THE AUGUSTAN PERIOD (43 B.C.–A.D. 14)

Although Augustus did not become Emperor until 27 B.C., we shall consider the Augustan Period as comprising those years from the death of Cicero to the death of Augustus. It was during these years that the Golden Age reached its mighty climax.

Not through his own works but through his patronage did the Emperor Augustus make his name memorable in Latin literature. He appointed Maecenas, a close friend and constant adviser, his unofficial minister of state. In spite of his fine literary taste Maecenas produced no works of value himself; however, he made possible the classics of Vergil and Horace, which gave glory to the Emperor and added lustre to the empire. Under Augustus, the great prose writer Livy produced his *History of Rome*, and Ovid, a great poet, his *Metamorphoses*.

Vergil: The Greatest of Roman Poets

For almost two thousand years Publius Vergilius Maro has been revered as the greatest of Roman poets. He was born October 15, 70 B.C. at Andes, a village near Mantua in north Italy, then called Cisalpine Gaul. His father was a farmer, and the boy was educated at Cremona, Milan, and later at Rome. He then probably lived on his father's farm until 42 B.C.

In that year his estate was allotted to a returned soldier from the Civil War. Fortunately, through the influence of friends it was restored to him by Octavian. His gratitude is expressed in the first of the pastoral poems called *Eclogues*, or *Bucolics*, all ten of which were published about 38 B.C.

Maecenas, the minister of Augustus and great patron of literature, now urged Vergil to write the *Georgics*, treatises which describe and glorify agriculture in all its branches. This work was especially pleasing to Augustus, for he was anxious to foster the agricultural spirit among the veterans of the civil wars, who possessed the best of Italy's fertile soil.

Augustus then suggested that Vergil should attempt a national epic. The last eleven years of Vergil's life — from 30 to 19 B.C. — were devoted to the composition of his greatest work, the *Aeneid*, an epic poem in twelve books. The subject is the fall of Troy and the adventures of Aeneas, but the poem anticipates constantly the great destiny of Rome as the conqueror and governor of the world. After working on his masterpiece for ten years, Vergil suddenly became ill. Not satisfied with the perfection of his work, he left orders before he died that it should be burned. Happily Augustus prevented these orders from being carried out.

Vergil was highly regarded among his contemporaries and immediate successors. His poems were soon used as textbooks in the schools and have been used as such ever since. In the Middle Ages he was considered the outstanding poet of antiquity, the least pagan of the pagan authors. The fourth Eclogue was interpreted as foretelling the coming of Christ. A practice developed of opening his works at random and taking the advice of the first sentence that one read. He was even credited with being a scientist with magic powers, and it became the fashion to attribute to him all kinds of marvelous deeds.

After the Renaissance, Vergil was again valued for his real merits. His fame can be judged by the frequent quotations from authors who have been inspired by him. The Italian Dante and the English Milton seem most like him in spirit as well as in the mastery of the epic. Perhaps Tennyson has been able to interpret and appreciate Vergil better than any other critic. In the last stanza of the poem *To Vergil*, composed at the request of the Mantuans for the nineteenth centenary of Vergil's death, Tennyson writes:

> Wielder of the stateliest measure
> Ever moulded by the lips of man.

In 1930, two thousand years after the birth of Vergil, scholars from all civilized nations made a pilgrimage to Italy to pay honor to the great poet of Mantua. His position as a poet of all time and of all the world is unquestioned.

In the following selection from the *Aeneid*, Aeneas tells Dido, queen of Carthage, how the Trojans discovered the wooden horse of the Greeks.

THE WOODEN HORSE

Est in cōnspectū Tenedos, nōtissima fāmā
īnsula; dīves opum Priamī dum rēgna manēbant,
nunc tantum sinus et statiō male fīda (*treacherous*) carīnīs.
Hūc sē prōvectī dēsertō in lītore condunt.
Nōs abiisse ratī et ventō petiisse Mycēnās.
Ergō omnis longō solvit sē Teucria lūctū (*mourning*):
panduntur portae; juvat īre et Dōrica castra
dēsertōsque vidēre locōs lītusque relictum.
Pars stupet innūptae (*unmarried*) dōnum exitiāle (*deadly*)
Minervae,
et mōlem mīrantur equī; prīmusque Thymoetēs
dūcī intrā mūrōs hortātur et arce locārī.
Scinditur incertum studia in contrāria vulgus.

Prīmus ibi ante omnēs, māgnā comitante (*accompanying*)
catervā,
Lāocoōn ārdēns summā dēcurrit ab arce,
et procul: "Ō miserī, quae tanta īnsānia, cīvēs?
Crēditis āvectōs hostēs? Aut ūlla putātis
dōna carēre dolīs Danaum? Sīc nōtus Ulixēs?
Aut hōc inclūsī līgnō occultantur Achīvī,
aut aliquis latet error; equō nē crēdite, Teucrī.
Quidquid id est, timeō Danaōs et dōna ferentēs."

Horace: Rome's Most Perfect Lyric Poet

Quintus Horatius Flaccus was a freedman's son, born on a little farm at Venusia, December 8, 65 B.C. His father, ambitious for his son, sent him to the best schools in Rome and later to Athens to study philosophy. In several places Horace speaks with affection and appreciation for his father and the sacrifices he made. In 44 B.C., after the murder of Julius Caesar, Horace joined Brutus in the Civil War that ensued. He returned to Rome after the disastrous battle of Philippi. Having lost his farm, he became a clerk of the quaestors but gave as much time as he could to writing poetry.

At Rome Vergil recognized Horace's talent and introduced him to Maecenas, his friend and patron. Maecenas admitted Horace to his literary circle, where he made valuable contacts with the best-known writers of his age. A few years later Maecenas presented Horace with an estate among the Sabine hills. There he spent his remaining years producing the Epodes, Satires, Epistles, and especially the Odes, those lyric poems on which his fame chiefly rests. He died November 27, 8 B.C., only a few weeks after the death of Maecenas, and he was buried near his friend's tomb on the Esquiline.

Horace has been a favorite poet in every age and in every country. He speaks for the cultivated Roman of his day, yet with an understanding of all the levels of society. No man can consider himself liberally educated who has not read the polished and powerful poetry of Horace.

In the following Ode, Horace expresses justifiable pride in what he has accomplished and predicts lasting fame for his work. Literature to this day is evidence that his own prophecy of immortality has come true.

A MONUMENT MORE LASTING THAN BRONZE

Exēgī monumentum aere perennius
rēgālīque sitū (*structure*) pȳramidum altius,
quod nōn imber edāx, nōn Aquilō impotēns (*furious*)
possit dīruere (*destroy*) aut innumerābilis
annōrum seriēs et fuga temporum (*of the ages*).
Nōn omnis (*entirely*) moriar, multaque (*and great*) pars meī
vītābit Libitīnam; usque ego posterā
crēscam laude recēns (*ever young*), dum (*as long as*) Capitōlium
scandet cum tacitā virgine pontifex.
Dīcar (*I shall be famed*), quā violēns obstrepit (*roars*) Aufidus
et quā pauper aquae (*in water*) Daunus agrestium (*rustic*)
rēgnāvit populōrum, ex humilī (*from lowly birth*) potēns
prīnceps (*first*) Aeolium carmen (*verse*) ad Ītalōs
dēdūxisse (*to have adapted*) modōs. Sūme superbiam
quaesītam meritīs et mihi Delphicā
laurō cinge volēns, Melpomenē, comam (*hair*).

Livy: A Model for Later Historians

The only great prose writer of the Augustan Period is Livy. Titus Livy was born at Patavium (Padua) in 59 B.C. and died in his native place in A.D. 17. Of his life little is known. About 30 B.C. he moved to Rome, where he lived the greater part of his time until his death. He was on intimate terms with the Emperor Augustus, although he took no part in political affairs. He devoted his time and his talents exclusively to literature.

Several minor works on philosophy and rhetoric written by Livy are mentioned by ancient writers, but his great work is his exhaustive history of Rome from the coming of Aeneas to his own day. At the time of his death he had written 142 books and had brought the history down to the year 9 B.C. Of this vast work only 35 books are extant.

As a historian Livy is interested in the human element rather than in dates and political events. His fine command of language and his keen sense of the dramatic make his work one of the most readable histories ever produced. His history served as a model for later Roman writers and for more than one historian in recent times. It has been well said that Livy accomplished in prose what Vergil had done in the *Aeneid;* thus his history may be called the prose epic of Rome.

The selection given here is a description of a battle in the Second Punic War in which the Romans suffered one of their greatest disasters.

DISASTER AT LAKE TRASIMENE

Jam Hannibal pervēnerat ad loca nāta (*fitted by nature*) īnsidiīs, ubi Lacus Trasumennus est prope montēs Cortonēnsēs. Via perangusta (*very narrow*) tantum (*only*) interest; deinde paulō lātior patet campus; inde collēs surgunt. Ibi castra in apertō locō posuit, ut ibi ipse cum Āfrīs modo (*only*) Hispānīsque mīlitibus cōnsīderet. Baleārēs cēterāsque levēs armātūrās cōpiās post montēs circumdūxit. Equitēs ad ipsum aditum saltūs (*pass*) occultāvit ut, cum Rōmānī campum intrāvissent, equitātū et lacū et montibus clauderentur.

Flāminius, cum (*although*) prīdiē sōlis occāsū ad lacum pervēnisset, inexplōrātō (*without reconnoitering*) posterō diē prīmā lūce per aditum in lātiōrem campum agmen dūxit. Ibi aciem īnstruere coepit, ut impetum faceret in hostēs, quōs ex adversō (*straight ahead*) cōnspēxit; īnsidiae ab tergō ac super caput nōn vīsae sunt. Hannibal, ubi Rōmānōs lacū ac montibus ac equitātū suō clausōs habuit, sīgnum oppūgnandī simul omnibus dedit. Haec rēs eō magis (*the more*) subita et imprōvīsa (*unforeseen*) fuit, quod nebula, orta ex lacū, in campō cōnsīderat.

Flāminius, clāmōre ortō, sē undique circumventum esse sēnsit. Tamen audācter perturbātōs ōrdinēs īnstruit, ut (*as*) tempus locusque patiēbantur, et, quācumque (*wherever*) adīre audīrīque poterat, suōs stāre ac pūgnāre jūssit. Erat in tantā nebulā mājor ūsus aurium (*ears*) quam oculōrum. Aliī fugientēs vī pūgnantium retinēbantur; aliī redeuntēs in pūgnam āvertēbantur fugientium agmine.

Trēs ferē hōrās pūgnātum est, et ubīque atrōciter. Circum cōnsulem, tamen, ācrior īnfēstiorque pūgna erat. Subitō eques — Ducāriō nōmen erat — "Hic est," inquit, "quī legiōnēs cecīdit, agrōsque et urbem vāstāvit!" Subditīs calcāribus (*applying spurs*) equō, per hostium turbam impetum fēcit; cōnsulem lanceā (*with a spear*) trānsfīxit.

Haec est nōbilis (*well known*) ad Trasumennum pūgna atque memorābilis inter paucās māgnās populī Rōmānī calamitātēs. Quīndecim mīlia Rōmānōrum in aciē caesa sunt, in quibus fuit cōnsul Flāminius et omnēs ferē ējus praefectī (*commanders of the cavalry*). Decem mīlia, fugā sparsa per omnem Etrūriam, dīversīs itineribus Rōmam petīvērunt. Duo mīlia quīngentī (2,500) hostium in aciē, multī posteā ex vulneribus periērunt.

Ovid: The Author of *Metamorphoses*

The greatest of the Latin elegists, Publius Ovidius Naso (43 B.C.–A.D. 17), belonged to an equestrian family. He was educated at Rome and Athens and traveled extensively in the East. His father had destined him for the study of law, but Ovid's talents lay elsewhere. When scarcely more than a boy, he began to write and publish poetry and soon became a member of the highest literary and social circles in Rome.

Ovid's love elegies earned the poet recognition as the most brilliant and interesting of the Latin elegists. They are remarkable for their vivid imagery, variety, flashes of humor, and exquisite finish. On the other hand they are utterly lacking in genuine feeling and seriousness of purpose.

In A.D. 8 for some unexplained reason the Emperor Augustus banished Ovid to a little town on the Black Sea near the mouth of the Danube. In vain his loyal wife worked at Rome in his behalf; in vain he sent frequent appeals to those in power to allow him to return to Rome. The permission was never granted, and he died in exile in A.D. 17.

One of Ovid's works, the *Fasti* (*Calendar of Roman Festivals*), contributes much to our knowledge of Roman religion, life, and ancient customs. His greatest and best-known work, however, is the *Metamorphoses* (*Magic Changes*). It gives us in story form the myths about miraculous transformations of men, animals, and inanimate objects into different forms. This work was immediately popular and has remained popular ever since, a mine of ancient legend for artists and writers. A wealth of ancient mythological allusion in modern literature finds its chief source in Ovid's *Metamorphoses*. The popular musical *My Fair Lady* is based on George Bernard Shaw's play *Pygmalion*, in which an English professor transforms an uneducated girl into a fine lady and then falls in love with her. Shaw took the title for his play from the Greek myth about the sculptor Pygmalion who carved an ivory statue of a maiden which the goddess Aphrodite brought to life.

The following selection is about Echo and Narcissus. Because of Echo's idle chatter the goddess Juno condemned her never to talk again except to repeat what was said to her. "You will always have the last word," Juno said, "but no power to speak first." This was most unfortunate because Echo loved Narcissus and could not speak to him. She could only echo his words. He turned away in disgust, and she wasted away to a voice that can be heard only in a cave or similar hollow place.

LADY ECHO

Forte puer (Narcissus), comitum sēductus (*separated*) ab agmine fīdō,
dīxerat, "Ecquis (*anyone*) adest?" et "adest" respōnderat Ēchō.
Hīc stupet, atque aciem partēs dīmittit in omnēs;
vōce, "Venī!" māgnā clāmat. Vocat illa vocantem.
Respicit, et rūrsus nūllō vidente, "Quid," inquit,
"mē fugis?" et totidem quot dīxit, verba recēpit.
Perstat, et alternae dēceptus imāgine vōcis,
"Hūc coeāmus (*Let us meet*)," ait, nūllīque libentius umquam
respōnsūra sonō, "Coeāmus," rettulit Ēchō.

The following echo poem was written by Capellanus in *Do You Speak Latin?*
Read these lines orally in Latin before translating.

"Fuerōne beātus sī persevērābō in bonīs litter*īs?*"   "*Eris.*"
"Quid, sī uxōrem dū*xerō?*"   "*Sērō.*"
"Nōn mē dēlectant sermōnēs tuī disyll*abī.*"   "*Abī.*"
"Fācundior essēs (*you would be*), opīnor, sī longius ab*essem?*"
   "*Essem.*"
"Coepī prior, sed videō nōn posse vītārī, quīn posterior dē*sinās.*"
   "*Sinās.*"
"Sī mē volēs abīre, dī*citō.*"   "*Ītō!*"

THE SILVER AGE
A.D. 14 TO A.D. 138

With the death of Augustus, the Golden Age of Latin literature came to an end. While the literary Latin of the Golden Age was an artificial language, it was developed by the great masters from the pure Latin of Rome, from the common language of everyday life.

On the other hand, the literary Latin of the Silver Age was not developed from the popular speech but from the literary Latin of the Golden Age. The Silver Age did produce some writers of genuine ability — such as Martial, Pliny, Tacitus, and Juvenal — but the tendency in literature was to become more and more artificial while the popular speech withdrew further and further from the literary Latin of its own or previous times. We must also remember that the tyrants of that period had a blighting effect on writers and writing.

Phaedrus: A Slave Who Became a Fabulist

Phaedrus was a Greek, and probably, like Aesop, his famous Greek predecessor, was once a slave. It is believed that he was born about 15 B.C., came to Rome as a boy, and was eventually set free by Augustus or his successor, Tiberius, perhaps as a reward for his literary attainments.

Phaedrus was the first Latin poet to imitate Aesop's fables of talking beasts, birds, and trees. His first two books seem to have been published during the reign of Tiberius (A.D. 14–37); three books were added later at different times. They are all written in iambic verse, and they always have a moral.

When the political satire behind some of his fables was interpreted as a slur against Sejanus, the corrupt and powerful prime minister of Tiberius, Phaedrus was punished with some severity. No further details of the poet's life are known.

The fables of Phaedrus came into great favor in the Middle Ages and were widely read. Because they are interesting to young people and are written in the simple classical Latin of the early Augustan Period, they frequently appear in textbooks. La Fontaine, the French fabulist, is the best known of Phaedrus' later imitators.

THE WOLF AND THE LAMB

Ad rīvum eundem lupus et āgnus vēnerant,
sitī compulsī. Superior stābat lupus,
longēque īnferior āgnus. Tum fauce (*appetite*) improbā
latrō incitātus jurgiī (*quarrel*) causam intulit.
"Cūr," inquit, "turbulentam (*muddy*) fēcistī mihi
aquam bibentī?" Lāniger (*lamb*) contrā timēns:
"Quī possum, quaesō, facere quod quereris, lupe?
Ā tē dēcurrit ad meōs haustūs (*drinkings*) liquor."
Repulsus ille vēritātis vīribus,

"Ante hōs sex mēnsēs male," ait, "dīxistī mihi."
Respondit āgnus: "Equidem nātus nōn eram."
"Pater, hercle (*by Hercules*), tuus ibi," inquit, "maledīxit mihi,"
atque ita correptum lacerat injūstā nece.
Haec propter illōs scrīpta est hominēs fābula
quī fictīs (*trumped-up*) causīs innocentēs opprimunt.

Seneca: The Philosopher

Lucius Annaeus Seneca, called the Younger, or the Philosopher, to distinguish him from his well-known father, was born at Corduba (Cordova),
Spain, about the year 4 B.C. Educated at Rome, he became a brilliant student
of philosophy and rhetoric. At about the age of thirty-five he held the quaestor-
ship and thus became a member of the Senate.

His eloquence aroused the jealousy of Emperor Caligula. On a trumped-up
charge of misconduct, Seneca was condemned to banishment and spent eight
unhappy years on the island of Corsica. In A.D. 49 Agrippina secured the return
of the exile in order that he might serve as tutor to her son Nero. The master
won the affection and esteem of his pupil.

When Nero later became Emperor, Seneca had so much power and responsibility that he practically controlled the empire. His influence, however, was
short-lived. Upon the elevation of the vicious Tigellinus to power, Seneca retired from public life. Three years later (A.D. 65) he was accused of conspiracy
and forced to take his own life.

As a man of letters and as a moral philosopher Seneca exerted a profound
influence through succeeding ages. The following selection from one of his letters
is of unusual interest because of the extraordinary and humane attitude which
Seneca reveals with regard to slavery, an attitude without parallel in ancient
Roman literature.

ON MASTER AND SLAVE

Libenter ex eīs quī ā tē veniunt cōgnōvī familiāriter tē cum
servīs tuīs vīvere. Hoc prūdentiam tuam, hoc ērudītiōnem decet.
"Servī sunt," dīcunt. Immō (*on the contrary*) hominēs (sunt).
"Servī sunt." Immō comitēs. "Servī sunt." Immō humilēs amīcī.
"Servī sunt." Immō cōnservī (*fellow slaves*), sī cōgitāveris fortū-
nam servōs atque līberōs similiter regere.

Itaque rīdeō istōs, quī turpe (esse) exīstimant cum servō cenāre
(*to dine*). Quārē, nisi quia superbissima cōnsuētūdō cenantī
dominō stantium servōrum turbam circumdedit?

Alia crūdēlia, inhūmāna praetereō, quod nē tamquam hominibus quidem, sed tamquam jūmentīs abūtimur. Vīs tū cōgitāre

355

(*just remember*) istum quem servum tuum vocās, ex eīsdem sēminibus ortum esse, eōdem fruī caelō, aequē spīrāre, aequē vīvere, aequē morī! tam tū illum vidēre ingenuum potes quam ille tē servum.

Nōlō dē ūsū servōrum disputāre, in quōs superbissimī, crūdēlissimī, contumēliōsissimī sumus. Haec moneō: sīc cum īnferiōre vīvās, quemadmodum (*as*) tēcum superiōrem velīs vīvere. "At ego," inquis, "nūllum habeō dominum." Fortasse habēbis. Nēscīs, quā aetāte Hecuba servīre coeperit, quā Croesus, quā Dāreī (*of Darius*) māter, quā Platōn, quā Diogenēs?

Vīve cum servō clēmenter. In sermōnem illum admitte et in cōnsilium. Saepe bona māteria cessat sine artifice (*artist*); temptā et experiēre. "Servus est." Sed fortasse līber animō. "Servus est." Hoc illī nocēbit? Ostende, quis nōn sit; alius avāritiae servit; alius ambitiōnī; omnēs timōrī. Nūlla servitūs turpior est quam voluntāria.

Petronius: Novelist and Poet

Gaius Petronius Arbiter lived in the first century of the Christian era. As director of palace amusements during the reign of the infamous Emperor Nero (A.D. 54–68), he led a riotous and luxurious life. Tigellinus, Nero's praetorian prefect, having grown jealous of Petronius, trumped up a charge of treason against him. The frivolous Petronius then decided to kill himself in a leisurely fashion. He caused himself to bleed to death slowly so that it would appear his death came from natural causes.

The *Satyricon*, a novel in prose interspersed with verse, is regarded as Petronius' masterpiece. It may be classified as a very realistic account of the adventures of a certain rascal, by name Encolpius, who wanders among the seaports and towns of southern Italy. The best-known character in the work is Trimalchio, an ex-slave, a self-made man, and a multi-millionaire from a town in Magna Graecia. In the selection that follows, Encolpius and his boon companions are dining at Trimalchio's villa. The guests exchange stories, and one of them tells of a werewolf, a man who is supposed to be able to change at will from a man into a wolf and back again into a man.

THE WEREWOLF

Cum adhūc servīrem (*was a slave*), habitābāmus in vīcō parvō. Forte ad quendam amīcum īre cupiēbam. Nactus ego occāsiōnem persuādeō mīlitī, dominī hospitī, ut mēcum ad quīntum mīliārium (*milestone*) veniat. Mihi vidēbātur mīles fortis. Profectī sumus circā gallīcinium (*cock crow*). Lūna lūcēbat tamquam merīdiē.

Vēnimus extrā vīcum prope monumenta (*tombstones*). Mīles meus coepit ad monumenta accēdere. Sedeō ego et cantō. Deinde ut respēxī ad comitem, ille omnēs vestēs in viā posuit. Mihi anima in nāsō est (*my heart is in my mouth*); stābam tamquam mortuus. Ille subitō lupus factus est. Nōlīte mē jocārī (*joke*) putāre. Sed, ut coeperam dīcere, postquam lupus factus est, ululāre (*howl*) coepit et in silvās fūgit.

Ego prīmum nesciēbam ubi essem; deinde accessī ut vestēs ējus tollerem. Illī autem lapideī (*stone*) factī sunt. Quis morī timōre potuit nisi ego? Gladium tamen strīnxī (*drew*) et in tōtā viā umbrās cecīdī dōnec ad villam amīcī meī pervenīrem.

Ut intrāvī, paene animam ēbullīvī (*breathed out*); sūdor (*per-spiration*) mihi per ōs volābat, oculī mortuī (*glazed*), vix umquam refectus sum. Amīcus meus mīrārī coepit cūr tam sērō ambulārem et "Sī ante," inquit, "vēnissēs profectō nōs adjūvissēs; lupus enim villam intrāvit et omnia pecora dēvorāvit. Servus noster lanceā collum ējus trājēcit."

Haec ut audīvī, operīre oculōs amplius nōn potuī, sed lūce clārā domum fūgī, et postquam vēnī in illum locum in quō lapideī vestēs erant factī, nihil invēnī nisi sanguinem. Ut vērō domum vēnī, jacēbat mīles meus in lectō (*bed*) tamquam bōs, et collum illīus medicus (*doctor*) cūrābat. Tum intellēxī illum versipellem (*werewolf*) esse, nec posteā cum illō pānem gustāre potuī, nōn sī mē occīdissēs.

Quintilian: A Great Roman Writer and Teacher

Marcus Fabius Quintilianus was born in Spain about A.D. 35. After his education at Rome under the best teachers of the time, he returned to Spain. In A.D. 68 the Emperor Galba called Quintilian to Rome, where he became a teacher of rhetoric and received a salary from the imperial treasury. After teaching for twenty years, he gave up his school and devoted himself to the composition of his great work, the *Institutio Oratoria* (*Introduction to Public Speaking*), which became a very important general treatise on education. Some idea of his enlightened and sane views on education may be obtained from the following passage adapted from the *Institutio Oratoria*.

RELATIONSHIP BETWEEN TEACHER AND PUPIL

Ante omnia lūdī magister parentis animum ergā discipulōs suōs habeat (*let . . . have*) et operam det ut intret in eōrum locum ā quibus līberī eī trāditī sunt. Ipse nē habeat vitia nēve (*nor*) ferat. Nē austēritās (*severity*) ējus trīstis, nē dissolūta (*lax*) sit comitās (*affability*), nē inde odium hinc contemptus (*contempt*) oriātur.

Plūrimus eī dē rēbus honestīs et bonīs sermō sit. Saepe discipulōs moneat, rārō castīget (*chastise*). Minimē sit īrācundus; sī, tamen, errāverint discipulī, nē neglegat errōrēs. Sī discipulī interrogant, libenter respondeat; sī tacent, ipse multa dē rēbus eīs quās docuit, roget.

Bonōs discipulōs laudet; in laudibus tamen māxima semper cūra sit nē aut malīgnus (*niggardly*) aut effūsus (*extravagant*) videātur. Discipulī enim, sī semper laudās, mox labōribus sunt dēfessī; sī numquam, omnia neglegunt. Ubi ea ēmendat (*correct*) quae discipulī nōn satis bene aut dīxērunt aut scrīpsērunt, nē sit acerbus nēve contumēliōsus (*insulting*). Magistrī nōn numquam (*sometimes*) ā studiīs discipulōs āvertunt cum acerbē eōs castīgent. Multa bona quoque magister cotīdiē dīcat quae, ubi audīverint, discipulī memoriā tenēbunt. Nam ut (*as*) magistrōrum officium est docēre, sīc discipulōrum praebēre sē dociles.

Martial: The Master of the Epigram

An epigram is a literary form consisting of two parts; the first introduces the subject; the second gives the real point, often with an unexpected turn. The master writer of epigrams in first-century Rome was Marcus Valerius Martialis. He was born in Spain about A.D. 40, received an excellent education, and came to Rome about the year 64.

Seneca, Lucan, and Quintilian, his countrymen, introduced him to the leading men of Roman society, but after the execution of Seneca and Lucan, he found it hard even to eke out a living. About the year 100 he returned to Spain where a Spanish lady gave him a country estate. There he died after four years of unhappiness because of his longing for the vitality and variety of ever-changing Rome.

Martial wrote fourteen books of epigrams. Not the trite mythologies of other poets, but life in all its seamiest phases was his theme. In the epigrams we see reflected with almost photographic accuracy the characters, the places, and the events that passed in review on the stage of cosmopolitan Rome. His descriptions are concise, clear, and accurate. Although he was no great poet and lacked lofty inspiration as well as depth of character, he won great fame in his own day and in all succeeding ages; for at his best he is unsurpassed in his chosen field of epigram.

I DON'T LIKE YOU

Nōn amō tē, Sabidī, nec possum dīcere quārē;
Hoc tantum possum dīcere: nōn amō tē.

TOMORROW AND TOMORROW AND TOMORROW

Crās tē victūrum, crās dīcis, Postume (*Procrastinator*), semper.
Dīc mihi, crās istud, Postume, quandō venit?
Quam longē crās istud, ubi est? Aut unde petendum?
Numquid apud Parthōs Armeniōsque latet?
Jam crās istud habet Priamī vel Nestoris annōs.
Crās istud quantī, dīc mihi, posset emī?
Crās vīvēs? Hodiē jam vīvere, Postume, sērum est;
Ille sapit quisquis (*whoever*), Postume, vīxit herī.

WHOSE BOOKLET?

Quem recitās meus est, Ō Fīdentīne, libellus;
Sed male cum recitās, incipit esse tuus.

DESCRIPTION OF A FRIEND

Difficilis, facilis, jūcundus, acerbus es īdem.
Nec tēcum possum vīvere nec sine tē.

Tacitus: Rome's Greatest Historian

Nothing is known of the birth or ancestry of Publius Cornelius Tacitus, without question the most impressive of Roman historians. He lived from about A.D. 55 to 117. His thorough education, honorable public career, and marriage to the daughter of Agricola, the governor of Britain in the second half of the first century, are sufficient evidence that he came from a good family.

Tacitus wrote the *Agricola*, a biography of his father-in-law, which contains a valuable description of Britain and the history of the island at that time, and the *Germania*, a study of the origin, abode, and customs of the people of Germany. His two greatest historical works were the *Historiae* and the *Annales*. The *Historiae*, published first, covered the period from A.D. 69, the year of the four emperors, to the death of Domitian in the year 96. The *Annales*, his masterpiece, covered the period from the death of Augustus in A.D. 14 to that of Nero in 68. Only a portion of the *Historiae* and the *Annales* is preserved.

Tacitus' style is concise, powerful, and sustained, rich in poetic words and phrases. He gradually developed a unique and peculiar diction, far removed from the spoken language and therefore artificial. He strove with all the literary power at his command to depict Roman life under the Caesars of the first century, toward whom he was filled with suppressed bitterness.

For some time the works of Tacitus were not regarded with favor. Late in the third century Emperor Tacitus, a supposed relation of the author, required every library to have a copy. Since these were manuscripts in the true sense of the word, written by hand, the Emperor specified that ten should be produced in a year. After the sixth century the works of Tacitus were ignored until their rediscovery by the Italian humanists. From the sixteenth century on, his writings have had great influence upon European writers.

In the following selection, which is taken from the *Agricola*, Calgacus, one of Britain's bravest leaders, urges his followers to make a desperate attempt to repel the attack of the Romans.

BRITONS WILL NEVER BE SLAVES

Jam super trīgintā mīlia armātōrum aspiciēbantur, et adhūc conveniēbant omnis juventūs et senectūs, cum Calgacus, Britannōrum dux fortissimus, in hunc modum locūtus est:

"Quotiēs causās bellī et necessitātem nostram cōnsīderō, māgna mihi fidēs est hunc diem et cōnsēnsumque vestrum initium lībertātis tōtīus Britanniae futūrum esse. Nōbīs nūlla servitūs fuit; sunt nūllae ūltrā terrae nōs, tamen nē mare quidem secūrum est, imminente nōbīs classe Rōmānā. Ita proelium atque arma, quae fortibus honesta (*honors*) offerēbant, eadem etiam īgnāvīs tūtissima sunt.

"Priōrēs pūgnae, quibus adversus Rōmānōs variā fortūnā ā nōbīs pūgnātum est, spem ac subsidium in nostrīs manibus relinquēbant, quia nōs, nōbilissimī tōtīus Britanniae, et in ipsīs penetrālibus (*heart*) terrae habitantēs, nec servientium lītora aspicientēs, oculōs nostrōs quoque ā servitūte tūtōs habēbāmus. Nōs, terrārum ac lībertātis extrēmōs, recessus (*remote position*) ipse in hunc diem dēfendit.

"Nunc terminus ipse Britanniae patet. Atque omne īgnōtum prō māgnificō (*the marvelous*) est. Sed nūlla est jam ūltrā nōs gēns nihil nisi flūctūs et saxa, et īnfēstiōrēs Rōmānī, quōrum superbiam (*domination*) frūstrā per obsequium (*submission*) effūgeris. Latrōnēs orbis, quibus dēfuērunt terrae cūncta vāstantibus, jam mare explōrant. Sī dīvēs hostis est, avārī sunt; sī pauper, dominātiōnem dēsīderant; quibus nōn Oriēns, nōn Occidēns satis est. Sōlī omnium hominum opēs atque inopiam parī cupiditāte concupīscunt. Latrōcinium, caedem, rapīnam (*plunder*) imperium appellant; atque ubi sōlitūdinem faciunt, pācem appellant."

Juvenal: The Best-known Latin Satirist

There is much obscurity about Juvenal's life and career. His full name is given in some manuscripts as Decimus Junius Juvenalis. Born at Aquinum about A.D. 60, he evidently received a good education. He served in the army, held public office, and seems to have been an orator for some years. He came to Rome about the year 90. His satires were written between the years 100 and 127, and he died about 135. Of one thing we are certain: he was the last classical Latin poet of importance and the best known of the satirists.

A satire is a literary work in which follies, vices, stupidities, abuses, and the like are held up to ridicule and contempt. The target of Juvenal's sixteen satires was contemporary Roman society, which he makes out as very vile but equally interesting. He makes the evils as hateful as he can but suggests no remedies. Juvenal draws a very different picture of Roman society from that presented by the urbane and tolerant Pliny. We must remember, however, that Pliny was a wealthy and successful statesman while Juvenal for the greater part of his life was a poor and unsuccessful man, often at his wits' end to obtain the necessities of life.

One of the most interesting satires is the third, in which the streets of the city are described. This satire is imitated by Samuel Johnson (1709–1784) in his *London*, which has been justly called one of the finest modern imitations of an ancient poem. The tenth satire has been imitated, quoted, and referred to by many writers through the ages, but the best imitation is also by Johnson in his *Vanity of Human Wishes*.

The verses quoted here are from the closing passage of the tenth satire. Juvenal, in a lofty utterance of human wisdom, tells us what are the proper objects of prayer.

A PATH TO PEACE

Ōrandum est ut sit mēns sāna in corpore sānō.
Fortem posce animum, mortis terrōre carentem (*free from*),
quī spatium vītae extrēmum inter mūnera (*blessings*) pōnat
nātūrae, quī ferre queat (*can*) quōscumque (*any whatsoever*)
    labōrēs,
nēsciat īrāscī, cupiat nihil et potiōrēs (*better than*)
Herculis aerumnās (*troubles*) crēdat saevōsque labōrēs
et Venere (*than love*) et cēnīs et plūmā (*downy couches*) Sardana-
    pallī.
Mōnstro quod ipse tibī possīs dare. Sēmita certē
tranquillae per virtūtem patet ūnica vītae.

Pliny: The Ideal Letter Writer

Pliny the Younger was born in A.D. 61 at Novum Comum in northern Italy. His name was Gaius Plinius Caecilius Secundus, which he took in accordance with the will of his uncle, Pliny the Elder, who had adopted him. Pliny the Elder was a prominent writer of natural history. His nephew followed the senatorial career and held the offices of quaestor, tribune, praetor, and consul. Like Cicero, whom he consciously tried to imitate, he was a patriotic and honest man. He died about the year 113.

Pliny is best remembered for the nine or ten volumes of letters which he wrote and which he later prepared for publication. He is the commentator of his age, writing on a variety of subjects, including events in the lives of prominent men he had known, important trials held at Rome, and the eruption of Vesuvius, which he had witnessed in the year 79.

In one of his letters, Pliny relates the charming story of a close friendship between a boy and a dolphin.

THE BOY AND THE DOLPHIN

Est in Āfricā colōnia, nōmine Hippō, marī proxima atque nāvigābilī stāgnō (*lagoon*). Ex hōc in modum flūminis aestuārium (*estuary*) fluit, quod ut aestus aut repressit (*ebbs*) aut impulit (*flows*), nunc īnfertur marī, nunc redditur stāgnō. Omnis hīc aetās studiō piscandī (*of fishing*), nāvigandī, atque etiam natandī tenētur, māximē puerī, quōs ōtium lūdusque dēlectant. Glōria et virtūs puerōs ad aquās altissimās incitant. Victor est ille quī longissimē et lītus et simul natantēs sēcum relīquit.

Hōc certāmine puer quīdam audācior cēterīs in ulteriōra natābat. Delphīnus illī occurrit, et incipiēbat nunc praecēdere puerum, nunc sequī, nunc circumīre, et postrēmō subīre, dēpōnere, iterum subīre, trepidantemque ferre prīmum in altum; mox flectit ad lītus et eum reddit comitibus.

Serpit (*spreads slowly*) per colōniam fāma; concurrunt omnēs, ipsum puerum tamquam mīrāculum (*prodigy*) aspiciunt, interrogant, audiunt, nārrant. Posterō diē obsident lītus, et prōspectant mare. Natant puerī, prīmus puer est inter hōs, sed cautius. Delphīnus rūrsus ad tempus advenit, rūrsus ad puerum appropinquat. Fūgit ille cum cēterīs. Delphīnus, quasi eōs invītet et revocet, exsilit, mergitur, variōsque orbēs et figūrās in aquā facit.

Hōc posterō diē, hōc tertiō, hōc plūribus fēcit, dōnec hominēs, semper prope mare habitantēs, caperet timendī pudor. Accēdunt et lūdunt et appellant et tangunt delphīnum. Crēscit audācia experīmentō. Puer, quī prīmus expertus est, cum delphīnō nantī natat, īnsilit tergō, fertur referturque. Delphīnus agnōscī sē et amārī putat, puerum amat ipse; neuter timet, neuter timētur; hūjus cōnfidentia, mānsuētūdō (*tameness*) illīus augētur. Aliī puerī dextrā laevāque simul natant, hortantēs monentēsque.

Mīrābile dictū, natat ūnā cum prīmō delphīnus alius, sed tantum spectātor et comes. Nihil enim simile prīmō aut faciēbat aut patiēbātur, sed alterum dūcēbat et redūcēbat ut puerum cēterī puerī. Vidētur incrēdibile, tam vērum tamen quam prior pars fābulae, sed dīcitur delphīnum gestātōrem (*bearer*) collūsōremque (*playmate*) puerōrum, in terram quoque sē extrahere solitum, arēnīsque siccātum (*having dried himself*), ubi incaluisset (*had become warm*), in mare revolvī.

Cōnstat Octāvium Avītum, lēgātum prōcōnsulis, religiōne prāvā (*religious superstition*) in lītus ēductō delphīnō superfūdisse (*poured over*) unguentum, cūjus novitātem odōremque in altum eum refūgisse, nec nisi post multōs diēs vīsum esse, languidum et maestum (*gloomy*); mox redditīs vīribus priōrem lascīviam (*playfulness*) et solita officia repetīsse.

Cōnfluēbant omnēs ad spectāculum magistrātūs, quōrum adventū et brevī morā modica rēs pūblica (*public treasury*) novīs sūmptibus (*expenses*) atterēbātur (*was ruined*). Postrēmō, locus ipse quiētem suam sēcrētumque perdēbat; delphīnus incolīs occultē interficiendus erat.

Suetonius: Biographer of the Great

The last important writer of the Silver Age and of the reign of Hadrian was Gaius Suetonius Tranquillus. He was born in approximately A.D. 70. After practicing in the law courts, he acted for a time as private secretary to Emperor Hadrian, and later he devoted himself to historical study. Of his later life nothing is known, but he probably devoted himself to his literary labors. As his works were numerous, we may assume that he lived to an advanced age.

His most important surviving work is the *Lives of the Caesars*, a series of biographies of Julius Caesar, Augustus, and the ten emperors who succeeded the latter. His works are a strange mixture of careful historical research and scandalous gossip. They are valuable as sources of information rather than as literary productions. However, they are entitled to some praise even from a literary point of view since their author avoided the affectations of style fashionable at that period.

APPRECIATION OF CAESAR, THE GENERAL

Armōrum perītissimus, labōris ūltrā fidem patiēns erat. In agmine nōn numquam (*sometimes*) equō, saepius pedibus anteībat (*he went before*), capite dētēctō (*uncovered*). Longissimās viās incrēdibilī celeritāte cōnfēcit expedītus. Flūmina nandō (*by swimming*) trānsiit vel innīxus īnflātīs utribus (*skins*), ut saepe nūntiōs dē sē praevēnerit (*arrived before*).

In obeundīs hostibus, dubium est utrum (*whether*) cautior (*more cautious*) an audācior. Exercitum neque per īnsidiōsa (*open to ambush*) itinera dūxit umquam nisi speculātus (*having examined*) locōrum sitūs, neque in Britanniam trānsvēxit (*transported*) priusquam per sē portūs et nāvigātiōnem et accessum (*approach*) ad īnsulam explōrāvit. At idem, obsessiōne (*blockading*) castrōrum in Germāniā nūntiātā, per statiōnēs hostium Gallicō habitū penetrāvit ad suōs.

Ā Brundisiō Dyrrachium inter oppositās classēs hieme sē trājēcit, et cum cōpiās quās subsequī jūsserat frūstrā saepe arcessīvisset, ipse clam noctū parvum nāvigium sōlus obvolūtō (*muffled up*) capite cōnscendit, neque aut quis esset ante dētēxit aut gubernātōrem cēdere adversae tempestātī passus est, quam paene obrutus est (*overwhelmed*) flūctibus.

Mīlitēs trāctābat (*treated*) parī sevēritāte atque indulgentiā. Dēlīcta neque observābat omnia neque prō modō exsequēbātur (*followed up*), sed dēsertōrēs ac sēditiōsōs ācerrimē solēbat pūnīre, cēterīs veniam dabat. Quam fortiter dīmicāverint mīlitēs, hoc est indicium: adversō semel apud Dyrrachium proeliō factō, poenam in sē ūltrō poposcērunt, ut cōnsolandōs eōs magis imperātor quam pūniendōs esse habuerit.

Cēterīs proeliīs immēnsās hostium cōpiās, multīs partibus ipsī pauciōrēs, facile superāvērunt. Dēnique ūna sextae legiōnis cohors, cui commissum erat castellum quoddam, quattuor Pompējī legiōnēs per aliquot hōrās sustinuit, paene omnēs trānsfīxī multitūdine sagittārum, quārum centum trīgintā mīlia intrā vallum posteā reperta sunt.

Gellius: The Author of *Attic Nights*

Of the life of Aulus Gellius we know very little. He was probably a Roman by birth or came to that city very early in life. He lived in the second century and spent some time at Athens in study. During this time he kept a notebook in which he jotted down anything of interest which he read in books or heard in conversation.

From the material thus gathered he compiled his only work, the *Noctes Atticae* (*Attic Nights*), which may be likened to a scrapbook of unrelated extracts from various authors on language, literature, law, philosophy, and natural science. Its chief importance is the light it throws on questions of grammar, history, and ancient customs. Of special value are the fragments it contains from many earlier works that are now lost. The *Attic Nights* is not great literature; the interest in the work is mainly for its content.

THE BOY WHO COULD KEEP A CONFIDENCE

Mōs anteā senātōribus Rōmae fuit in Cūriam cum praetextātīs fīliīs (*sons under age*) intrāre. Tum, cum in senātū rēs mājor cōnsultāta eaque in diem posterum prōlāta est (*postponed*) placuit nē quis (eam rem) ēnūntiāret priusquam dēcrēta esset. Māter Papīrī puerī, quī cum patre suō in Cūriā fuerat, rogābat fīlium quid in senātū patrēs ēgissent. Puer respondit id dīcī nōn licēre. Māter fit audiendī cupidior; sēcrētum reī et silentium puerī animum ējus excitāvērunt; quaesīvit igitur vehementer.

Tum puer, mātre urgente, mendācī (*of a lie*) cōnsilium cēpit. Āctum esse in senātū dīxit, utrum vidērētur ūtilius exque rē pūblicā ūnus vir ut duās uxōrēs habēret, an ut ūna (*fēmina*) duōbus virīs nūpta esset. Hoc illa ubi audīvit, domō trepidāns (*panic-stricken*) ēgressa est et ad cēterās mātrōnās properāvit.

Pervēnit ad senātum postrīdiē mātrōnārum multitūdō. Lacrimantēs ōrant ut ūna potius duōbus nūpta fieret quam ut ūnī virō duae. Senātōrēs, ingredientēs in Cūriam, postulātum (*demand*) mulierum mīrābantur. Puer Papīrius in mediam Cūriam prōgressus, quid ipse mātrī dīxisset, nārrāvit. Senātus fidem atque ingenium puerī laudāvit, sed cōnsultum fēcit, nē posthāc (*thereafter*) puerī cum patribus in Cūriam intrārent, praeter Papīrium, quem posteā Praetextātum appellābant ob tacendī loquendīque prūdentiam.

Apuleius: The First Novelist

Lucius Apuleius, who was born about A.D. 125, was the son of one of the principal officials of Madaura, in Numidia. He was educated at Carthage and then went to Athens to study philosophy. About A.D. 150, he seems to have gone to Rome and to have been a successful lawyer there. He later returned to Africa, where he married a wealthy widow, settled in Carthage, and lectured in various African cities. The date and the place of his death are not known.

His chief work is the *Metamorphoses*, now better known as *The Golden Ass*. It has the distinction of being the first novel and the only complete Roman novel extant. The work is taken from a Greek original in which the hero, traveling in Thessaly, is transformed for a time into an ass, retaining, however, his human mind and sensibilities. Into this story of strange adventures Apuleius inserted many entertaining tales, such as the story of Cupid and Psyche, narrated by an old woman to console a kidnapped bride.

At the command of an oracle, Psyche, the very beautiful and the youngest daughter of a king, had been abandoned on a barren mountain, where she was to be married to a dreadful creature. In reality, the beast was Cupid, who then

365

had Psyche carried off to a magnificent palace, where he visited her only at night. Naturally, Psyche wished to see her husband, but Cupid sternly warned her that to gaze upon him would mean his unhappiness and her misfortune. When Psyche's jealous sisters visited her and learned that she had never actually seen her husband, they took advantage of her curiosity and persuaded her to light a lamp that night and spy upon her husband as he slept. Hesitantly she did so but was so overcome by his beauty that she allowed a drop of hot oil to fall from her lamp onto his sleeping form. Thus awakened, Cupid arose and vanished angrily into the night. His mother, Venus, who was very jealous of Psyche's great beauty, then caused the wretched girl to undergo many hardships and trials in an effort to win back her husband. In the end, however, Jupiter, the father of the gods, consented to Cupid's marriage to Psyche, Venus saw Cupid and Psyche reunited, and the lovers were formally married in the presence of the entire court of Olympic heaven.

THE STORY OF PSYCHE

Erant in quādam urbe rēx et rēgīna. Hī trēs fīliās, fōrmā cōnspicuās, habuērunt; sed mājōrēs quidem nātū, quamvīs grātissimā speciē, idōneē tamen celebrārī posse laudibus hūmānīs crēdēbantur; at vērō puellae juniōris tam praecipua, tam praeclāra pulchritūdō nec exprimī ac nē satis quidem laudārī sermōnis hūmānī penūriā (*lack*) poterat.

Multī dēnique cīvēs et advenae convēnerant quī ēgregiam puellam vidērent et eam sīcut deam Venerem ipsam colerent. Jamque per proximās urbēs et fīnitimās regiōnēs patriae fāma dīlāta est vel deam, quae ē marī orta erat in mediīs mortālibus habitāre, vel certē alteram Venerem ē terrā ortam esse.

Jam multī mortālēs quī in ūltimīs terrīs habitābant longīs itineribus terrā marīque factīs pervēnerant quī fōrmam hūjus puellae quae erat tam similis deae cōnspicerent. Paphum nēmō, Cnidum nēmō ac nē ipsa quidem Cythera ad cōnspectum deae Veneris nāvigābant; sacra dēseruntur, templa dēfōrmantur, pulvīnāria (*image-couches*) praetereuntur, caerimōniae negleguntur; incorōnāta simulācra et ārae viduae frīgidō cinere foedātae sunt (*are disgraced*).

Hī honōrēs dīvīnī ad puellam mortālem trānslātī animum vērae Veneris vehementer incendunt. Ad sē vocāvit fīlium suum Cupīdinem et dīxit: "Hanc puellam ab homine aliquō īnfimī generis amārī pateris cui ipsa Fortūna neque dīgnitātem neque pecūniam dedit quod volō nēminem per orbem tōtum terrārum miseriōrem quam eam puellam invenīrī."

Sīc Psȳchē honōrēs ūniversōrum sed nūllum suae fōrmae praemium accēpit. Frūstrā spectābātur ab omnibus, laudābātur ā multitūdine, nam nōn quisquam, nōn rēx, nē humilis homō quidem eam in mātrimōnium dūcere voluit. Duae sorōrēs mājōrēs nātū ējus jam marītōs bonōs rēgēs nactae erant.

THE LATE LATIN PERIOD
LATE 2nd TO 5th CENTURY A.D.

The Late Latin Period in the history of Latin literature is usually referred to as the Patristic Period because most of the literature worthy of the name was written by Christian leaders known as the Fathers (*Patres*). Among these were Tertullian, Cyprian, Jerome, and Augustine. These men had been well educated in, and were fond of, the Latin classics. Many of them had been teachers or lawyers in schools and courts around the Roman empire before their conversion to Christianity. In dealing with the educated class, they used classical Latin style, but since their message was for all people, it was necessary for them to use many of the idioms of the Vulgar Latin that the ordinary people understood. Jerome, for instance, used Ciceronian Latin in his letters; but in his most important work, the Latin edition of the Bible called the Vulgate, he used the language of the common people, the *vulgus*.

Eutropius: A Fourth-Century Historian

Little is known for certain of the life of Eutropius. Only once in his work does he mention himself. This occurs in the account of the invasion of Persia by the Emperor Julian, A.D. 363, "In which expedition I also took part."

The only work of Eutropius which is extant is the *Breviarium ab Urbe Condita*, a brief history of Rome from the founding of the city until the death of the Emperor Jovian in A.D. 364, in the second year of his reign. Eutropius dedicated the work to Jovian's successor, the Emperor Valens. The subject matter was abridged from Livy, Suetonius, and later writers.

The work is short but well balanced, showing good judgment and impartiality. The author's style is simple and direct, and the diction is very good for the age in which it was written. There are some errors, mostly in the matter of dates. The *Breviarium* was used by Jerome and later by writers of the Middle Ages, but it has no independent value as a historical work.

THE ROMAN EMPEROR VESPASIAN

Vespasiānus Vitelliō successit, factus apud Palaestīnam imperātor. Obscūrē quidem nātus est, sed optimīs imperātōribus comparandus est; prīvātā vītā fuit illustris. Ā Claudiō in Germāniam et deinde in Britanniam missus est; trīciēs et bis (*thirty-two times*) cum hoste contendit, et duās validissimās gentēs, vīgintī oppida, īnsulam Vectam (*Isle of Wight*), Britanniae proximam, imperiō Rōmānō adjēcit.

Rōmae sē in imperiō moderātissimē gessit. Pecūniae paulō avidior fuit, sed ita ut eam nūllī injūstē auferret; cum pecūniam māgnā cum dīligentiā colligeret, tamen māgnā cum alacritāte eam largiēbātur, praecipuē pauperibus; nūllus prīnceps quī ante eum vīxit līberālior fuit. Tālis fuit lēnitās ējus ut illōs, quī etiam majestātis (*of treason*) contrā sē reōs (*guilty*) fuissent, nōn facile pūnīret, ūltrā exsilī poenam.

Sub hōc prīncipe, Jūdaea imperiō Rōmānō accessit (*was added*) et Hierosolyma (*Jerusalem*) quoque, quae fuit urbs nōbilissima Palaestīnae. Achājam, Lyciam, Rhodum, Byzantium, Samum, quae līberae ante hoc tempus fuerant; et item Thrāciam, Ciliciam, Commāgēnen (*Commagene*), quae sub rēgibus amīcīs ēgerant, in prōvinciārum fōrmam redēgit.

Offēnsārum et inimīcitiārum memor nōn fuit. Hic cum Titō fīliō dē Hierosolymīs triumphāvit. Per haec (*deeds*) cum senātuī et populō, postrēmō cūnctīs gentibus amābilis ac jūcundus esset, mortuus est in villā propriā, circā Sabīnōs, annum aetātis agēns (*being*) sexāgēsimum nōnum, imperī nōnum et diem septimum, atque inter deōs relātus (*enrolled*) est.

THE ROMAN EMPEROR TITUS

Titus fīlius successit, quī et ipse Vespasiānus est dictus. Vir erat omnium virtūtum genere mīrābilis adeō ut amor et dēliciae (*delight*) hūmānī generis dīcerētur. Fācundissimus (*most eloquent*), bellicōsissimus, moderātissimus (erat). Causās Latīnē ēgit: poēmata et tragoediās Graecē composuit. In oppūgnātiōne Hierosolymōrum (*of Jerusalem*), sub patre mīlitāns, duodecim prōpūgnātōrēs (*defenders*) duodecim sagittārum ictibus cōnfīxit.

Rōmae tantae cīvīlitātis in imperiō fuit, ut nūllum omnīnō pūnīret. Convictōs adversum sē conjūrātiōnis ita dīmīserit ut in eādem familiāritāte quā anteā habuerit. Facilitātis tantae fuit ut, cum nūllī quidquam negāret et ab amīcīs reprehenderētur, responderit nūllum trīstem dēbēre ab imperātōre discēdere. Praetereā, cum quādam diē in cēnā recordātus fuisset nihil sē illō diē cuiquam praestitisse, dīxit: "Amīcī, hodiē diem perdidī." Hīc Rōmae amphitheātrum aedificāvit, et quīnque mīlia ferārum in dēdicātiōne ējus occīdit.

Cum morbō perīret, tantus dolor eō mortuō pūblicus erat ut omnēs tamquam in propriā dolērent orbitāte (*bereavement*).

Jerome: Biographer and Translator

One of the scholars of this period was Eusebius Hieronymus, known to us as Jerome. He was born in Dalmatia about 348, and died in Bethlehem in 420. He was educated in Rome by the celebrated scholar Donatus and other learned men.

Jerome had a remarkable knowledge of Latin, Greek, and Hebrew. After long years of travel and study, especially in the East, he returned to Rome, where he lived from 382 to 385. He made the close acquaintance of the Pope, Damasus, under whose patronage he translated the Bible into Latin: the Old Testament from the Hebrew, and the New Testament from the Greek. This translation is known as the Latin Vulgate.

Jerome also translated into Latin the writings of many learned men, and he enriched the state of learning in the western world by the original products of his own pen. The biographies that he wrote show that he had all the qualities necessary for a great storyteller. His letters, of which one hundred and fifty-four are extant, compare favorably with the correspondence of Cicero, of whose works he was an ardent admirer.

The following selection is taken from Jerome's biography of the monk Malchus.

A NARROW ESCAPE

Dum timēmus et vēstīgiīs per arēnās nōs prōditōs esse intelligimus offertur ad dextram nostram spēlunca longē sub terram penetrāns. Igitur timentēs venēnāta (*poisonous*) animālia (nam solent vīperae, serpentēs, et scorpiōnēs, cēteraque hūjus modī, fervōrem sōlis fugientia, umbrās petere) intrāvimus quidem spēluncam; sed statim in ipsō introītū (*entrance*) sinistrae nōs foveae (*pit*) crēdidimus, nēquāquam ūltrā prōgredientēs nē dum mortem fugimus occurrerēmus in mortem.

Quid putās fuisse nōbīs animī, quid terrōris, cum ante spēluncam nec longē stārent dominus et servus, et vēstīgiō sīgnō jam ad umbrās pervēnissent? Ō multō gravior exspectāta quam illāta mors! Rūrsus cum labōre et timōre lingua balbutit (*stuttered*); et quasi clāmante dominō loquī nōn audeō. Mittit servum ut nōs dē spēluncā trahat; ipse camelōs (*camels*) tenet; et ēvāgīnātō (*unsheathed*) gladiō nostrum exspectat adventum.

Intereā tribus paene vel quattuor cubitīs (*cubits*) ingressō servō, nōbīs ex occultō tergum videntibus (nam oculōrum istīus modī nātūra est ut post sōlem umbrās intrantibus caeca sint

omnia), vōx per spēluncam sonat: "Exīte, furcīferī (rascals);
exīte moritūrī; quid stātis? quid morāminī? Exīte, dominus vocat,
patienter exspectat."

Adhūc loquēbātur, et ecce per tenebrās aspicimus leōnem cor-
ripuisse hominem et, faucibus strangulātīs, illum cruentum
(bloody) intrō trahere. Quid tunc terrōris nōbīs, quid gaudī fuit!
Spectābāmus, dominō nēsciente, hostem nostrum perīre!

Augustine: An Outstanding Author in World Literature

One of the most outstanding men in the history of world literature was
Aurelius Augustinus of Hippo, North Africa. He was born at Tagaste, a small
town of Numidia, not far from Hippo, in A.D. 354. His father, Patricius, was a
pagan; his mother, Monica, a Christian. When Augustine was twelve years old,
he attended a grammar school at Madaura. He tells us he liked Latin but found
Greek difficult.

At sixteen Augustine returned to Tagaste. His father died about this time,
and a wealthy man of the town paid Augustine's expenses to study at Carthage.
Here he applied himself diligently to the study of rhetoric, and here he read the
best of the Latin authors, Cicero, Vergil, and Varro.

For nine years he conducted schools of rhetoric and grammar at Carthage
and Tagaste. During this period he became an adherent of a sect known as the
Manichaeans. Then, in 383, he set out for Rome and there opened a school of
rhetoric, which was not a financial success. Fortunately he was appointed to a
school in Milan, where he was a brilliant scholastic success and where he made
the acquaintance of the bishop, Ambrose. As a result of the bishop's sermons,
Augustine turned from Manichaeism to Christianity.

After his mother's death in Ostia, Augustine returned to Africa, where he was
ordained a priest. Later he became Bishop of Hippo. From 395 until his death
in 430, he wrote voluminously. There are one hundred and eighteen separate
titles to his credit. His best known works are *Confessiones* and *De Civitate Dei*.
The following excerpt has been adapted from the first book of the *Confessiones*.

A BOY WHO LIKED LATIN BUT NOT GREEK

Quae sit causa cūr Graecās litterās ōderim, quibus puerulus
(little boy) imbuēbar, nē nunc quidem mihi satis (fully) explōrātus
est. Adamāveram (I loved) enim Latīnās, nōn quās prīmī magistrī,
sed quās docent quī grammaticī (teachers of literature) vocantur.
Nam illās prīmās (litterās), ubi legere et scrībere et numerāre
(counting) discitur, nōn minus onerōsās (burdensome) poenālēsque
(and irksome) habēbam quam omnēs Graecās.

Peccābam (I was wrong) puer (as a boy), cum inānia ūtiliōribus
praepōnēbam. Jam vērō "ūnum et ūnum (sunt) duo, duo et duo

quattuor" odiōsa (*hateful*) cantiō (*chanting*) mihi erat; et dulcissimum spectāculum erat equus līgneus plēnus armātōrum, et Trōjae incendium atque ipsīus umbra (*ghost*) Creusae.

Cūr ergō Graecam etiam grammaticam (*literature*) ōderam quae tālia (*such tales*) cantābat? Nam et (*also*) Homerus erat perītus tālēs fābulās ad texendās (*spinning*). Mihi tamen amārus (*bitter*) erat puerō. Crēdō etiam Graecīs puerīs Vergilium ita esse, cum eum (*Vergil*) sīc discere cōgantur, ut ego illum (*Homer*). Nam difficultās discendae linguae peregrīnae (*foreign*) quasi felle (*gall*) aspergēbat (*sprinkled*) omnēs suāvitātēs (*charms*) Graecās fābulōsārum nārrātiōnum.

THE MEDIEVAL PERIOD
FROM THE 6th TO THE 14th CENTURIES

During this period Latin was the international language of Europe. It was the living language of the Christian Church and of medieval scholars. Latin writing was vital and varied. Religious treatises, histories, romances, anecdotes, dramas, and sacred and secular poetry were produced, sometimes in very excellent classical Latin, at other times in Latin modified by the changes that had slipped into the language because of natural growth and development in customs and ideas.

During the first three centuries of the Medieval Period, vulgar Latin was undergoing such changes that it could hardly be recognized as Latin at all. Declensional endings were lost, prepositions were used more frequently, auxiliary verbs were introduced, and the rules of classical Latin writing were radically changed. The Romance languages, varying with the locality, had begun.

Isidore of Seville: Scholar of the Seventh Century

Isidore of Seville (560–636) was a famous and influential scholar who, at an early age, distinguished himself for his learning. His interest in the classics led him to gather into digests or encyclopedias various historical and scientific works. The most important of these is *Etymologiae sive Origines* (*Etymologies or Beginnings*), a work of encyclopedic nature that became the most widely used school book in medieval times and exerted a powerful influence on other writers of the period.

In *Etymologiae*, Isidore starts the treatment of each subject etymologically; that is, he explains the true meaning and origin of the matter under discussion and then proceeds to give as much related historical, descriptive, and anecdotal information as was known at the time. He frequently enriches his work by quoting from the classical writers, and his Latin style is essentially classical.

Vitrum (*glass*) dictum est quod lūx trānslūcet (*shines through*). In aliā enim māteriā quidquid in parte interiōre continētur absconditur; in vitrō vērō liquidum vel speciēs quālis est intus tālis extrā dēclārātur, et quōdam modō clausus patet.

Vitrī orīgō haec fuit. In illā parte Syriae, quae Phoenīcē (*Phoenicia*) vocātur, fīnitima Jūdaeae, circā radīcēs montis Carmelī (*Carmel*) palus est, ex quā nāscitur Bēlus flūmen, quīnque mīlia passuum in mare fluēns jūxtā Ptolomaidem (*Egypt*), cūjus arēnae flūctibus torrentis pūrgantur.

Hīc fāma est: frāctā nāve mercātōrum nitrī (*of niter, natural soda*), hominēs sparsim (*here and there*) in lītore cibum parābant. Cum essent nūllī lapidēs ad vāsa sustinenda, glēbīs (*lumps*) nitrī ūsī sunt. Hīs accēnsīs et arēnā lītoris permīxtīs, trānslūcentēs rīvī novī liquidī flūxērunt.

Mox homō nōn fuit contentus mīxtūrā nitrī et arēnae; aliās mīxtūrās cōnātus est. Nam ubi mīxtūra cum līgnīs levibus aridīsque coquitur (*is heated*), adjectō cyprō (*copper*), continuīsque fornācibus (*kilns*), massae (*lumps*) fiunt. Posteā mīxtūra calida (*hot*) in vāsīs funditur quae in officīnīs (*workshops*) locāta sunt; deinde alia figūra flātū (*by blowing*) fingitur, alia tornō (*wheel*) teritur (*is smoothed*), alia argentī modō caelātur (*is engraved*).

Dīcitur autem quendam artificem (*craftsman*), Tiberiō Caesare rēgnante, invēnisse vitrī temperāmentum (*tempering*) ut flēxibile et ductile fierī posset. Cum ille admissus esset ad Caesarem, huic phialem (*drinking-vessel*) dedit, quam Caesar īrātus in solō prōjēcit. Artifex autem sustulit dē solō phialem quae sē complicāverat (*had folded = had been dented*) tamquam vās aeneum; deinde mārculum (*small hammer*) prōtulit et phialem corrēxit (*straightened*).

Hōc factō, Caesar artificī dīxit: "Num quid alius scit hanc conditūram (*making*) vitrōrum?" Postquam ille jūrāns negāvit alterum hoc scīre, jūssit illum Caesar dēcollārī (*beheaded*), nē cum hoc cōgnitum fieret, aurum prō lutō (*mud*) habērētur et pretium omnium metallōrum dēminuerētur; et rēctē, quia sī vāsa vitrea nōn frangerentur, meliōra essent quam aurum et argentum.

Einhard: Biographer of Charlemagne

Einhard (c. 770–840) was born of noble parentage in the eastern part of the realm of the Franks. He began his education at the monastery school of Fulda. In 796 he was transferred from Fulda to the palace school of Charlemagne, which was then under the guidance of the famous English scholar, Alcuin. Einhard soon rose in the emperor's service and enjoyed his friendship and favor. After the death of Charlemagne in 814, Einhard served the new emperor as tutor, adviser, and diplomat. In 830, weary of the factions and intrigues about him, he retired to Mulinheim, where he died in 840.

His *Vita Caroli Magni* is his most important work and reveals an intimate knowledge of the emperor. As a model for his Latin style, he chose Suetonius' *De Vitis Caesarum.* In the following selection he gives us in simple and direct language an interesting picture of the emperor as a student.

CHARLEMAGNE THE STUDENT

Erat ēloquentiā cōpiōsus (*fluent*) poteratque quidquid vellet clārissimē exprimere. Nec patriō (*native*) sermōne contentus, etiam peregrīnīs linguīs discendīs operam dedit; in quibus Latīnam ita didicit ut aequē illā ac patriā linguā ūtī sit solitus, Graecam vērō melius intellegere quam loquī poterat.

Artēs līberālēs quam māximē coluit, eārumque doctōrēs (*teachers*) plūrimum venerātus est, atque illīs māgnōs honōrēs dedit. In discendā grammaticā (*grammar*) Petrum Pīsānum senem (*elderly*) audīvit, sed in cēterīs disciplīnīs Alcoinum (*Alcuin*) dē Britanniā Saxonicī generis hominem, virum doctissimum, praeceptōrem (*teacher*) habuit, apud quem et rhētoricae et dialecticae (*logic*), et praecipuē astronomiae discendae plūrimum et temporis et labōris impertīvit (*spent*). Discēbat artem computandī et applicātiōne dīligentī sīderum (*stars*) cursum spectābat.

Temptābat et scrībere tabulāsque et cōdicillōs (*small note paper*) ad hoc (*for this reason*) in lectō (*bed*) sub cervīcālibus (*pillows*) circumferre solēbat, ut, cum vacuum tempus esset, manum litterīs effigiendīs (*forming*) assuēsceret, sed parum successit labor sērō inceptus.

Ekkehart of Aura: Author of a Universal History

Little is known of Ekkehart except that he lived from the end of the eleventh century to the middle of the twelfth and that he devoted his life to the compilation of a universal history of mankind from the time of Moses to the end of the eleventh century. As history, his work has little value because he made no careful distinction between fact and fiction. As a popular book, however, his work was an immense success because his narratives were interesting and his anecdotes, amusing. His style of Latin is medieval; his sentences are simple; his word order approaches that of English; and his syntax shows considerable change from that of Cicero's time.

Caesar itaque, bellīs cīvīlibus tōtō orbe compositīs, Rōmam rediēns agere īnsolentius (*insolently*) coepit contrā cōnsuētūdinem Rōmānae lībertātis. Cum ergō honōrēs ex suā voluntāte praestāret quī anteā ferēbantur ā populō, nec senātuī ad sē venientī assurgeret (*rise*), aliaque rēgia et paene tyrannica faceret, conjūrātum est in eum ā ducentīs et sexāgintā vel amplius senātōribus equitibus Rōmānīs. Praecipuī inter conjūrātōs fuērunt duo Brūtī, ex genere illīus Brūtī quī prīmus cōnsul fuerat Rōmae rēgēsque expulerat, et Gnaeus Cassius et Servīlius Casca.

Quādam igitur diē senātū in cūriā congregātō, cum Caesar advēnisset, vīgintī tribus cultrīs (*knives*) senātōriīs cōnfossus est (*was stabbed*), moxque auctōrēs caedis, strictīs (*having been drawn*) pūgiōnibus (*short daggers*), in Capitōlium sēcessērunt. Turbātō populō, diū dēlīberātum est utrum Capitōlium cum auctōribus caedis oportēret incendī. Corpus ējus raptum populus, dolōre stimulātus, in forō fragmentīs tribūnālium ac subselliōrum cremāvit.

Eādem vērō nocte quae caedem ējus praecessit, Calpurnia, uxor ējus, vīdit in somniō (*dream*) eum cōnfossum vulneribus in sinū (*lap*) suō jacēre; ōrāvitque eum nē māne adīret in senātum; sed hic, auspiciōrum (*prophecy*) verba saepe negligēns, contempsit somnium, reī autem probāvit ēventus.

Ante paucōs quoque diēs bove ex mōre mactātā (*sacrificed*), cor in extīs (*entrails*) nōn est repertum. Quod cum Spūrinna haruspex (*soothsayer*) prōnūntiāsset eī ad vītae perīculum pertinēre, Caesar memor cōnstantiae ait: "Mīrāris sī bōs nōn cor habet." Sed mox vītae ējus fīnis fuit.

Īdem Spūrinna ante paucōs ferē annōs eīdem Caesarī dīxerat cavendās eī esse Īdūs Mārtiās. Quō diē vīsō, ait Spūrinnae Caesar, "Īdūs Mārtī vēnērunt." Ille respondit: "Sed nōndum trānsiērunt."

Eōdem diē Caesar cōnfossus est. Erat vir quō nūllus umquam magis bellīs ēnituit (*was distinguished*). Ējus ductū ūndeciēs (*eleven times*) centum nōnāgintā (*ninety*) duo mīlia hominum caesa sunt; nam quantum bellīs cīvīlibus vīcit annotāre (*note down*) nōluit.

Sīgnīs collātīs, quīnquāgiēs (*fifty times*) dīmicāvit, Mārcum Mārcellum sōlus superātus, quī trīgintā noviēs (*thirty-nine times*) in proeliō pūgnāverat. Praetereā, nūllus celerius scrīpsit, nēmō vēlōcius lēgit, et quaternās (*four at a time*) etiam epistulās simul dictāvit. Tantae fuit bonitātis ut quōs armīs subēgerat clēmentiā magis vīcerit. Eōdem tempore Rōmae trēs simul ortī sōlēs paulātim in eundem orbem coiērunt (*came together*). Inter cētera quoque portenta, quae tōtō orbe facta sunt, bōs in suburbānō (*estate*) Rōmae ad arantem locūtus est frūstrā sē urgērī, nōn enim frūmenta, sed hominēs brevī tempore dēfutūrōs esse.

Aelfric: Author of Medieval Latin Textbooks

Little of importance is known about Aelfric (c. 955–1020), except that he was the author of a Latin *Grammar* and an elementary Latin reader, *Colloquium*. Because of these books, he was sometimes called "the Grammarian" by the boys at the English monastery school where he taught. The Latin conversation given here has been adapted from his *Colloquium*.

A MEDIEVAL LESSON

PUER: Nōs puerī tē rogāmus, magister, ut nōs doceās Latīnē loquī rēctē, quia idiōtae (*uneducated persons*) et corruptē (*incorrectly*) loquimur.

MAGISTER: Quid vultis loquī?

PUER: Quid loquī volumus, nisi ōrātiōnem bonam et ūtilem?

MAGISTER: Interrogō tē, quid mihi loquēris? Dīc mihi quā sīs arte (*trade*).

PUER: Ego cupiō fierī magister, et linguam Latīnam bene discere cupiō. Meī sociī nōn eādem arte sunt: aliī sunt vēnātōrēs (*hunters*); aliī mercātōrēs; aliī pastōrēs; aliī arātōrēs (*plowmen*); aliī piscātōrēs (*fishermen*); aliī pistōrēs (*bakers*).

MAGISTER: Tū, vēnātor, scīsne tū aliquid?

VĒNĀTOR: Ūnam artem ūtilem sciō. Vēnātor rēgis sum. Rētia (*nets*) mea in locō opportūnō et idōneō intrā silvam pōnō; tum canēs meōs incitō ut animālia per campum et silvam persequantur. Ita animālia in meīs rētibus paene cotīdiē capiō.

MAGISTER: Quid herī cēpistī?

VĒNĀTOR: Duōs cervōs et ūnum aprum (*boar*) cēpī.

MAGISTER: Quō modō tū, arātor, opus tuum exercēs?

ARĀTOR: Cotīdiē prīmā lūce exeō et bovēs (*oxen*) jungō et ad agrum agō. Nōn est tam acris hiems ut dominī meī timōre domī manēre audeam, sed cotīdiē in agrīs labōrō.

MAGISTER: Māgnus quidem et ūtilis est tuus labor. Quam artem scīs tū, piscātor?

PISCĀTOR:	Ego sum piscātor. Cibum et vestēs et pecūniam nancīscor.
MAGISTER:	Quō modō piscēs capis?
PISCĀTOR:	Nāvem ascendō et in flūmine mea rētia pōnō. Postquam rētia piscibus complēta sunt, ē flūmine ea extrahō et piscēs in urbe vēndō.
MAGISTER:	Quis eōs emit?
PISCĀTOR:	Tot cīvēs eōs emunt ut mox cōpia mea piscium cōnsūmātur.
MAGISTER:	Quid dīcēs tū, mercātor?
MERCĀTOR:	Ego nāvem ascendō cum rēbus meīs et ad regiōnēs, quae trāns mare sunt, nāvigō, ubi rēs meās vēndō. Tum aliās rēs, quae hōc in locō invenīrī nōn possunt, comparō et hūc addūcō ut eās cōnsūmātis. Perīcula patior. Audācem esse mercātōrem oportet, quī mare nāvigat.
MAGISTER:	Quid dīcis tū, pistor? Quā es tū arte?
PISTOR:	Potestis quidem per aliquod spatium temporis sine meā arte vīvere, sed nōn diū nec bene; nam sine meā arte omnis mēnsa vacua esse vidētur. Nihil ūtilius aut melius quam panis ūsquam (*anywhere*) invenīrī potest. Sī pānis dēficit, vīrēs hominum etiam dēficiunt.
MAGISTER:	Nunc interrogō vōs cūr tam dīligenter studeātis.
PUER:	Quod nōlumus esse sīcut brūta animālia quae nihil sciunt nisi herbam et aquam.
MAGISTER:	Et vultis vōs?
PUER:	Volumus esse sapientēs.
MAGISTER:	Ō puerī, vōs omnēs hortor ut cotīdiē bene labōrētis et dīligenter studeātis ut virī bonī fīātis. Valēte.
PUERĪ:	Valē et tū, magister.

Petrus Alphonsus: A Storyteller of the Twelfth Century

Petrus Alphonsus, a native of Aragon, lived in the early part of the twelfth century. He collected from Arab fables many tales which were intended to illustrate the advice a father would give his son. Some of these tales are found in other collections of stories such as the *Gesta Romanorum*.

You will enjoy reading the humorous dialogue given here. The servant certainly tried to break the bad news gently.

Julius Caesar.

Mount Vesuvius erupting, March 1944.

Dominus quīdam dē forō laetus veniēbat. Servus, Maymundus, contrā dominum suum exīvit. Quem cum vidēret, dominus timuit nē aliquōs malōs rūmōrēs, ut mōs ējus erat, dīceret.

DOMINUS: Cavē nē dīcās mihi rūmōrēs malōs.

SERVUS: Nōn dīcam rūmōrēs malōs sed canis nostra parvula Bispella mortua est.

DOMINUS: Quōmodo mortua est?

SERVUS: Mūlus noster perterritus est, et dum fugit sub pedibus suīs canem oppressit.

DOMINUS: Quid āctum est dē mūlō?

SERVUS: In puteum (*well*) cecidit et mortuus est.

DOMINUS: Quōmodo perterritus est mūlus?

SERVUS: Fīlius tuus cecidit dē sōlāriō (*balcony*) et mortuus est, et inde territus est mūlus.

DOMINUS: Quid agit puerī māter?

SERVUS: Māgnō dolōre mortua est.

DOMINUS: Quis cūstōdit domum?

SERVUS: Nēmō, quoniam in cinerem (*ashes*) versa est et omnia quae in eā erant.

DOMINUS: Quōmodo combūsta est?

SERVUS: Eādem nocte quā domina mortua est, ancilla (*handmaid*) oblīta est candēlam in cubiculō (*bedroom*) et ita combūsta est domus tōta.

DOMINUS: Ubi est ancilla?

SERVUS: Ipsa volēbat īgnem exstinguere et cecidit trabs super ējus caput et mortua est.

DOMINUS: Tū vērō quōmodo ēvāsistī, cum tam piger (*lazy*) sīs?

SERVUS: Cum vidērem ancillam dēfūnctam (*dead*), effūgī.

Geoffrey of Monmouth: A Chronicler of the Arthurian Legend

Geoffrey of Monmouth lived in the first half of the twelfth century. He wrote a *History of the Kings of Britain,* which is of little historical value and which might have been forgotten were it not for its legends about King Arthur and his knights. This section of his work has served as a source book for many famous writers on the legendary deeds and exploits of King Arthur.

One of the most frequently read of the adventures of the famous Arthur is given here.

King Arthur about to kill the giant.

KING ARTHUR, THE GIANT KILLER

Ōlim rēgī Arturō nūntiātum est gigantem ingentis māgnitūdinis ex Hispāniā pervēnisse et Helenam, neptem (*niece*) ducis Hoelī, ēripuisse et in cacūmen (*summit*) montis cum illā fūgisse. Rēx etiam certior factus est mīlitēs, gigantem persecūtōs, nihil contrā eum valuisse; nam sīve (*whether*) in marī sīve (*or*) in terrā eum sequēbantur, ille aut eōrum nāvēs ingentibus saxīs mersit aut variōrum generum tēlīs eōs interfēcit. Plūrēs capiēbat quōs dēvorābat.

Noctū igitur rēx Arturus cum duōbus servīs ex castrīs clam profectus est. Ut (*as*) prope montem vēnērunt, quandam anum (*old woman*) flentem aspēxērunt. Quae ubi servum vīdit quem rēx praemīserat statim in hunc modum locūta est: "Ō īnfēlīx homō, quid tē hunc ad locum tulit? Mōnstrum horribile tē hāc nocte cōnsūmet, sī hīc manēbis. Aderit enim ille gigās quī neptem ducis (quam modo hīc sepelīvī) interfēcit et mē, ējus nūtrīcem (*nurse*), in hōc monte retinet. Fuge, amīce mī, fuge, nē tē quoque terribilī caede dīlaniet (*tear to pieces*)." At ille eam amīcīs verbīs sēdāvit (*calmed*) et ad Arturum revertit et omnia, quae invēnerat, dēmōnstrāvit.

Arturus autem, cāsum dolēns puellae, gigantī occurrere et eum aggredī sōlus statuit. Servīs autem imperāvit ut, sī necessitās accideret, sibi auxilium ferrent. Dīrēxērunt inde iter ad cacūmen montis, rēge praecēdente. Aderat prope īgnem, quī in monte erat, ille inhūmānus gigās, speciē quidem horribilī. Ōs ējus illitum (*smeared*) erat sanguine recentī vīgintī porcōrum, quōs partim (*partly*) dēvorāverat.

Ubi gigās illōs ex imprōvīsō (*unexpectedly*) aspēxit, clāvam (*club*) statim sūmpsit, quam duo juvenēs vix ā terrā levāre poterant. Rēx gladiō dēstrictō (*drawn*) illum aggressus est et in frontem vulnus grave sed nōn lētāle (*deadly*) intulit. Ille cum esset caecātus (*blinded*) sanguine, quī in oculōs flūxerat, tamen impetum in rēgem iterum fēcit et eum genua humī flectere coēgit. Sed hic summā vī tantum vulnus intulit ut gigās in terram concideret sicut concidit māgna quercus (*oak*), quae tempestāte frācta est.

Rēx rīsit et praecēpit ut caput gigantis ab corpore caederētur et ad castra dēferrētur ut spectāculum omnibus fieret.

Odo of Cerinton: Author of Animal Parables

The two important facts that we know of Odo of Cerinton, or Sherrington, are that he was the teacher of the celebrated scholar, John of Salisbury (c. 1115–1180), and that he wrote a *Book of Parables*. The parables are animal stories with morals, based partly on the *Romulus* version of the fables of Phaedrus and partly on the beast epics which were popular all over Europe during the Middle Ages.

THE DANCING KING

In conciliō quōdam bestiārum tam bene saltāverat (*had danced*) simia (*monkey*) ut paene cūnctīs suffrāgiīs rēx creārētur. Quod eum stultissimum esse cōgnōvisset vulpēs (*fox*), callidē (*slyly*) simiam ā cēterīs animālibus sēvocāvit (*called aside*) et hīs verbīs temptāvit: "Rēgnum," inquit, "cum tibi suffrāgiīs obtingeret (*fell to your lot*), nōn celābō tē, quod scīre dēbēs."

"Quid est?" interrogāvit simia. "Māgnus thēsaurus (*treasure*)," respondit illa, "in sēcrētō quōdam silvae locō abditus, ā patre dē vītā dēcēdente mihi est indicātus, quī jūre rēgnī ad tē jam vidētur pertinēre."

"Laudō," inquit simia, "officiōsam (*dutiful*) tuam abstinentiam (*restraint*); cūrā, igitur, ut clam perveniāmus ad illum locum."

Itaque cum reliqua animālia discessissent, clandestīnīs (*secret*) viīs vulpēs novum rēgem abdūcēbat et, cum diū per tōtam silvam errāvissent, tandem dēnsa dēmōnstrāns virgulta (*thicket*), "Hīc," inquit, "dīcēbat pater abditum esse thēsaurum."

Jam cupidē illūc penetrābat simia, sed subitō in venātōris laqueōs (*snares*) incidit. Frūstrā cum implōrāvisset amīcī auxilium, sērō sēnsit cōnsilium et temperantiam rēgī magis necessārium esse quam artem saltandī. Vulpēs autem, convocātīs bestiīs omnibus, trepidantem in laqueīs ostendēns simiam, "Habētis jam," inquit, "saltantem vestrum rēgem."

A WOLF TRICKED BY A FOX

Lupus obviāns (*meeting*) vulpī dīxit: "Amīce, unde venis?" et respondit vulpēs: "Dē quōdam vīvāriō (*fish-pond*), ubi optimōs piscēs cēpī et sufficienter comēdī (*have eaten*)." Quaesīvit lupus: "Quō modō cēpisti?" et ait vulpēs: "Caudam (*tail*) in aquam posuī et ibi diū tenuī. Et piscēs crēdentēs caudam esse edibilem vel mortuam, caudae adhaesērunt. Trāxī celeriter eōs ad terram et comedī."

Et ait lupus: "Ego sīc piscēs capere poterō?" Ait vulpēs: "Optimē poteris, quia es fortior quam ego." Statim lupus ad vīvārium properāvit et caudam in aquam posuit et diū tenuit dōnec erat congelāta (*frozen*) propter frīgus. Post longam moram voluit caudam extrahere crēdēns multitūdinem piscium eī adhaerēre. Sed nōn potuit propter glaciem (*ice*) quae caudam tenēbat. Dētentus est ibi usque māne.

Tum vēnērunt hominēs et lupum ferē usque ad mortem verberāvērunt (*beat*). Et ubi vix ēvāsit et caudam āmīsit, maledīxit vulpī quī sibi piscēs prōmīserat, sed verbera (*lashings*) et vulnera et ferē mortem parāverat.

THE LADY MOUSE AND HER WOOING

Ōlim mūs (*mouse*) mātrimōnium contrahere et marītum (*husband*) accipere fortissimum voluit. Et cōgitāvit quis esset validissimus. Tandem vidēbātur Ventus fortissimus esse quod prōsternit cedrōs (*cedar trees*), turrēs, domōs. Mīsit nūntiōs Ventō quī rogārent ut hic esset marītus.

Dīxit Ventus: "Quāre vult mē in mātrimōniō habēre?" Dīxērunt nūntiī: "Quod inter omnēs creātūrās es fortissimus."

Respondit Ventus: "Immō, castrum Narbōnēnse (*of Narbo*) fortius est mē, quod jam plūs quam mīlle annōs stetit adversum mē et numquam potuī id prōsternere."

Reversī sunt nūntiī et retulērunt respōnsum.

Dīxit mūs: "Quod fortior est Turris, volō Turrim esse marītum."

Indicāvērunt haec Turrī et dīxit Turris: "Certē mūrēs sunt fortiōrēs me, quod tōtā diē perforant (*penetrate*) et frangunt et faciunt viam per mē."

Et ita, habitō conciliō, sīc dēcrētum est: "Mūs mūrem in mātrimōniō habēre dēbuit."

Jacques de Vitry: A Collector of Anecdotes

Jacques de Vitry was a well-known lecturer in France in the early part of the thirteenth century. His effectiveness before an audience can be traced in part to his successful use of *exempla*, or anecdotes, in making his point. Late in his life, he put together and published a collection of *exempla* for the use of other lecturers. These anecdotes, drawn from many European and Mediterranean sources, are important today for the light they shed on the study of comparative literature and the cultural history of the Middle Ages.

THE PROFESSOR WHO REFUSED TO BE SILENCED

Audīvī rēgem Franciae valdē commōtum esse et īrātum contrā praeclārum (*famous*) magistrum Petrum Baalardum (*Abelard*), quī Parīsius (*at Paris*) legēbat (*was lecturing*), et prohibuit nē Petrus posteā legeret in terrā suā. Magister autem altam arborem prope cīvītātem ascendit, et eō omnēs scholārēs eum secūtī sunt, audientēs sub arbore magistrī suī lectiōnēs (*lessons*). Cum autem rēx quādem diē dē palātiō (*palace*) suō vidēret multitūdinem scholārium sub arbore sedentium, quaesīvit quid hoc esset. Et dictum est eī hōs esse scholārēs quī magistrum Petrum audiēbant.

Ille vērō valdē īrātus jūssit magistrum ad sē venīre et dīxit eī: "Quō modō tam audāx fuistī ut contrā prohibitiōnem meam in terrā meā lēgerīs?" Cui ille: "Domine, nōn lēgī post prohibitiōnem vestram in terrā tuā, vērum tamen lēgī in āere."

Tum rēx prohibuit eum et in terrā suā et in āere suō docēre. At ille intrāvit in nāviculam et dē nāviculā scholārēs suōs docēbat. Cum rēx quōdem diē vidēret scholārēs in rīpā flūminis sedentēs, quaesīvit quid hoc esset, et dictum est eī magistrum Petrum in locō illō scholam regere.

Māgnā cum indīgnātiōne commōtus, rēx jūssit Petrum ad sē vocārī et eī dīxit: "Nōnne prohibueram legere et tē in terrā meā et in āere?" Illō respondente: "Nec in terrā tuā nec in āere tuō lēgī, sed in aquā tuā," rēx rīdēns et in mānsuētūdinem (*meekness*) īram convertēns, ait: "Vīcistī mē; posteā, ubicumque (*wherever*) volueris, tam in terrā meā quam in āere vel in aquā legere licet."

381

Roger Bacon: A Famous Medieval Scientist

Roger Bacon (1214–1294) was the most famous scientific investigator of the Middle Ages. Bacon studied at Oxford and spent some years at the University of Paris. He specialized in languages, mathematics, and science of a more or less experimental nature.

It is interesting to read in the following excerpt from *De Secretis Operibus* his predictions of inventions and devices which have been made in modern times.

THIRTEENTH-CENTURY SCIENTIFIC PREDICTIONS

Nārrābō igitur nunc prīmō opera artis et nātūrae mīranda, ut posteā causās et modum eōrum assīgnem (*I may explain*); in quibus nihil magicum est, ut videātur quod omnis magica potestās sit īnferior hīs operibus et indīgna (*worthless*).

Nam īnstrūmenta nāvigandī possunt fierī ut nāvēs māximae ferantur, ūnō homine regente, mājōrī vēlōcitāte quam sī plēnae essent hominibus. Item currūs possunt fierī ut sine animālī moveantur cum impetū inaestimābilī (*incalculable*). Item possunt fierī īnstrūmenta volandī ut homō sedeat in mediō īnstrūmentō et alae artificiāliter (*skillfully*) factae āera verberent (*beat*) modō avis volantis. Item īnstrūmentum, parvā māgnitūdine, ad ēlevandum et dēprimendum (*lowering*) pondera quasi īnfīnīta, quō nihil ūtilius est.

Potest etiam facile fierī īnstrūmentum quō ūnus homō traheret ad sē mīlle hominēs contrā eōrum voluntātem. Possunt etiam īnstrūmenta fierī ambulandī in marī vel flūminibus sine perīculō. Nam Alexander Māgnus hīs ūsus est ut sēcrēta maris vidēret. Haec autem facta sunt antīquitus et nostrīs temporibus facta sunt, ut certum est; nisi sit īnstrūmentum volandī, quod nōn vīdī nec hominem quī vīdisset cōgnōvī. Et īnfīnīta quasi tālia fierī possunt; ut pontēs super flūmina sine columnā, et māchinātiōnēs (*machinery*) et ingenia inaudīta (*unheard of devices*).

Anonymous: Songs of the Wandering Students

Student life in the Middle Ages was different in many ways from that of modern times. Groups of young men often wandered from one university to another, living a merry and irresponsible life. Their songs ranged from serious verses to drinking songs. The most important collection of such songs is known as the *Carmina Burana* (from the abbey of Benedictbeuern), and the wandering students themselves were known as the Goliards, a name which was derived from that of their mythical patron saint "Bishop Golias."

The two songs given here are taken from a medieval manuscript. Notice that the meter is trochaic and that some of the lines rhyme. In classical poetry the quantity of the syllable was important, but in this verse the rules of quantity are not observed.

ENJOY LIFE WHILE YOU MAY

Gaudeāmus igitur,
Juvenēs dum sumus;
Post jūcundam juventūtem,
Post molestam senectūtem
Nōs habēbit humus!

Vīta nostra brevis est,
Brevī fīniētur,
Venit mors vēlōciter
Rapit nōs atrōciter,
Nēminī parcētur.

Ubi sunt, quī ante nōs
In mundō fuēre?
Vādite ad superōs,
Trānsite ad īnferōs,
Ubi jam fuēre.

Vīvat acadēmia,
Vīvant professōrēs,
Vīvat membrum quodlibet,
Vīvant membra quaelibet,
Semper sint in flōre!

THIS VAIN WORLD

Iste mundus
Furibundus
Falsa praestat gaudia,
Quae dēfluunt
Et dēcurrunt
Ceu (*like*) campī līlia.

Rēs mundāna
Vīta vāna
Vēra tollit praemia;
Nam impellit
Et submergit
Animās in Tartarā.

Anonymous: *Gesta Romanorum*

This collection of stories in Latin is of unknown authorship. As there is usually a moral added to each story, it may have been compiled by some monk of the thirteenth century for purposes of preaching. The title *Gesta Romanorum* (*Deeds of the Romans*) is quite misleading although the names of Roman emperors are frequently used as principal characters in various tales. It is very probable that some of these stories may have been brought back from the East by returning crusaders.

The tales of the *Gesta Romanorum* were frequently used by later writers, such as Chaucer and Shakespeare. Given here are the story of the three coffers, used so effectively by Shakespeare in *The Merchant of Venice*, and a story with a Roman emperor as hero.

ALL THAT GLITTERS IS NOT GOLD

Quīdam imperātor, nōmine Honōrius, ūnum fīlium habuit quem multum amāvit. Fāma ējus imperātōris per orbem terrārum volābat quod in omnibus bonus erat et jūstus. Tamen contrā ūnum rēgem bellum gerēbat et eum vincēbat. Rēx iste tandem cōgitābat: "Ūnam fīliam habeō et adversārius meus ūnum fīlium. Sī fīliam meam cum fīliō imperātōris in mātrimōniō jungam, pācem perpetuam obtinēbō." Nūntiōs igitur ad Honōrium mīsit quī imperātōrī persuādērent ut fīlius ējus fīliam rēgis in mātrimōnium dūceret.

Imperātor, habitō conciliō, indūtiās (*truce*) ūnīus annī fēcit. Rēx igitur nāvem parāvit quā fīlia sua per mare in rēgnum imperātōris trānsīret. At dum nāvis in altō marī nāvigat, tempestās māxima orta est. Postquam perīcula multa terrā marīque passa est, puella cum sociīs suīs ad terram imperātōris pervēnit.

Imperātor cum eam vīdisset ait (*said*): "Cārissima fīlia, sit bene tibi nunc et semper. Sed tibi dīcō, fīlia, antequam fīlium meum prō marītō tuō (*your husband*) habēbis, tē probābō in ūnum āctum." Statim trēs cophinōs (*caskets*) clausōs ante puellam pōnī jūssit. Prīmus erat dē aurō pūrissimō lapidibus pretiōsīs ōrnātus. In illō haec verba scrīpta sunt: "Quī mē aperuerit, in mē inveniet quod meruit." Et tōtus cophinus erat plēnus ossibus (*bones*) mortuōrum.

Secundus erat dē argentō pūrissimō, plēnus gemmīs ex omnī parte. In eō haec verba scrīpta sunt: "Quī mē ēlēgerit, in mē inveniet quod nātūra dedit." Ille cophinus erat plēnus terrae.

Tertius cophinus erat dē plumbō (*lead*), et haec verba habuit: "Potius ēligō hīc esse quam in thesaurō rēgis permanēre." In illō cophinō erant trēs anulī (*rings*) pretiōsī.

Tum imperātor puellae dīxit: "Cārissima, hīc sunt trēs cophinī. Ēlige (*choose*) quemcumque volueris; et sī bene ēlēgeris, fīlium meum in mātrimōnium obtinēbis." Puella trēs cophinōs spectāvit.

Cum prīmum cophinum tetigisset et verba lēgisset, cōgitābat: "Illum ēligere nōlō." Deinde secundum cophinum manibus suīs tenuit et scrīptūram lēgit. Iterum cōgitābat: "Illum ēligere nōlō." Tum ad tertium cophinum ambulāvit et verba lēgit. Et altā vōce clāmābat, "Istum cophinum ēligō."

Imperātor cum hoc audīvisset, "Ō bona puella," inquit, "prūdenter ēlēgistī. In istō cophinō sunt trēs anulī meī pretiōsī, ūnus prō mē, secundus prō fīliō, tertium prō tē in sīgnum spōnsālis (*of betrothal*)." Puellam cum fīliō suō in mātrimōniō jūnxit, et diū fēlīciterque posteā vīxērunt.

JUST JUDGMENT

Illō tempore imperātor Theodosius in cīvitāte Rōmānā rēgnābat, sed quamquam prūdēns erat, lūmen oculōrum āmīserat. Campānam (*bell*) igitur in palātiō pendī jūssit. Quīqumque aliquam causam trāctāre (*present*) vellet, illum fūnem campānae manibus trahere jūssit. Quō factō, jūdex ad locum cōnstitūtum vēnit et illī jūstitiam fēcit.

Forte autem serpēns nīdum (*nest*) suum propinquum fūnī campānae fēcerat et pullōs (*young ones*) prōdūxerat. Quōdam diē cum pullī ambulāre poterant, serpēns cum pullīs ē nīdō exiit. Dum absunt, būfō (*toad*) nīdum serpentis intrāvit atque sibi occupāvit. Cum hoc vīdisset, serpēns fūnem campānae caudā suā trāxit. Jūdex cum sonum campānae audīvisset, dēscendit, sed nēminem vidēns in palātium rediit.

Tum serpēns fūnem campānae iterum trāxit, ac sī dīceret (*as if to say*): "Dēscende celeriter, jūdex, et mihi jūstitiam fac; būfō audāx nīdum meum occupāvit." Jūdex quam celerrimē dēscendēns serpentum fūnem trahere vīdit et būfōnem nīdum ējus occupāre. Statim ad imperātōrem rediit et illī haec nārrāvit.

Imperātor īrātus eī "Dēscende," inquit, "et nōn modo būfōnem expelle, sed etiam eum occīde ut serpēns nīdum suum habeat." Hōc factō, serpēns iterum nīdum suum possēdit.

Posteā, cum imperātor Theodosius quōdam diē in lectō (*bed*) jacēret, serpēns cubiculum (*bedroom*) intrāvit portāns in ōre lapidem parvum. Cum eam vīdissent, servī trepidantēs clāmābant. Imperātor autem "Nōlīte eam impedīre! Crēdō enim illam mihi maleficium nōn factūram esse."

Tum serpēns super lectum imperātōris ascendit. Deinde cum ad oculōs imperātōris pervēnisset, lapidem super oculōs ējus posuit et statim discessit. Cum autem lapis oculōs imperātōris tetigisset, vīsum (*sight*) recēpit. Imperātor quam diū vīxit lapidem cōnservāvit et in pāce vītam fīnīvit.

THE MODERN PERIOD
LATE 14th CENTURY TO THE PRESENT

Petrarch's appreciation of Cicero as the supreme master of Latin prose, his passion for collecting original manuscripts and inscriptions in Latin, and his recognition of the value of studying the Greek classics in the original made him the leader and the inspiration of Renaissance scholars. The latter despised Medieval Latin and turned to the works of the ancient classicists for models and for inspiration.

It was an artificial movement with disastrous results, for Latin ceased to be the spontaneous, living, growing language it had been during the Middle Ages. However, Latin continued to live as the language of the Roman Catholic Church, and until the middle of the nineteenth century it was for all classical scholars a second mother tongue and an invaluable means of communication.

Petrarch: The First Modern Man

Petrarch, a native of Italy, was born in Arezzo in 1304 and died at Arqua in 1374. He was a student of law and letters, a churchman and a courtier, poet laureate and scholar. Although he lived in the fourteenth century, he is generally credited with initiating the later revival of learning in Europe and is sometimes referred to as "the first modern man." He was not only a great Italian poet but also an ardent admirer of the Latin classics and collector of ancient manuscripts. The following fable of the rustic and the donkey, entitled *On Traducers and Calumniators*, was taken from one of his letters.

PLEASE EVERYBODY, PLEASE NOBODY

Senex quīdam, quī asinum vēndere voluit, cum fīliō eum ad urbem dūcēbat. Mox occurrērunt eīs virginēs, quae dōna ad templum Minervae portābant. Māxima nātū (*The eldest*) ex hīs dīxit: "Num quid potest stultius illīs, quī pedibus iter faciunt, nec asinō vehuntur?" Hoc ubi audīvit senex, fīlium asinum cōnscendere jūssit, et ipse pedibus alacriter iter faciēbat. Nōn longē ab eō

locō aliquī senēs (*old men*) colloquium inter sē habēbant. Tum
ūnus, "Eheu (*Alas*)," inquit, "Quantum tempora mūtantur! Ubi
nunc est ille senectūtis proprius honor?" Pudōre fīlius victus
patrem ascendere coēgit.

Via secundum flūmen dūcēbat in quō duae fēminae vestēs lavā-
bant. Hae, ubi viātōrēs vīdērunt, ūnā vōce crūdēlitātem patris,
fīlīque difficilem labōrem plōrāvērunt (*deplored*). Senex igitur quī
omnibus placēre volēbat, puerum post sē sedēre jūssit. Nec
tamen ea rēs bene ēvēnit, cum alius viātor eīs occurreret. "Facilius potestis," inquit, "asinum vehere quam vōs miserum animal."

Tum senex, quī nē id quidem ineptum (*silly*) putābat, postquam
crūra (*legs*) asinī fūnibus (*ropes*) ad māgnum contum (*pole*) vīnx-
erat, novum onus cum māximō labōre in suōs fīlīque umerōs
sublevāvit. At asinus, cui haec minimē placēbant, dum ponte
flūmen trānseunt, subitō vincula rumpit et in aquam incidit. Tum
pater dīxit: "Nihil quod ab omnibus probētur fierī potest; repetā-
mus prīstinum mōrem nostrum."

Nihil amplius dīcam; nec necesse est; rudis fābula, sed bona.

Erasmus: A Great European Scholar

Erasmus, the most eminent scholar of western Europe during the fifteenth
century, was Dutch by birth (?1466), but all his adult life was spent in close
relationship with German, English, Italian, and Swiss scholars and scholarship.
He had various learned works published, among them books on grammar and
related subjects, editions of several Latin authors, and the first edition of the
Greek Testament. His *Praise of Folly* is one of the most remarkable of satires.
The *Colloquia* (*Dialogues*) have been frequently translated into English. The
dialogue was a favorite method of teaching.

A TRICKY CUSTOMER

Quīdam stābat ad jānuam frūctuāriae (*fruit dealer*), fēminae
vehementer obēsae (*stout*), oculīs intentīs in aliquōs fīcōs (*figs*).
Illa cum vidēret hominem, ex mōre quaesīvit sī quid vellet.
"Vīs," rogāvit, "fīcōs? Sunt optimī." Cum ille annuisset (*nodded*),
rogāvit quot lībrās (*pounds*) vellet. "Vīs," inquit, "quīnque lībrās?" Ille annuit. Fīcōs effūdit (*she poured*) in gremium (*lap*).

Dum illa repōnit lancēs (*scales*) ille cum fīcīs sē subdūxit, nōn
cursū sed placidē. Cum acceptūra pecūniam prōdīsset, vīdit ēmp-

tōrem (*buyer*) abīre. Īnsequitur mājōre vōce quam cursū. Ille dissimulāns pergit quō coepit īre; tandem multīs ad fēminae vōcem concurrentibus restitit. Ibi in populī corōnā (*circle*) agitur causa; ēmptor negābat sē ēmīsse, sed sē quod ūltrō datum esse accēpisse. Omnēs rīsērunt.

ANOTHER TRICKY CUSTOMER

Cum quīdam Maccus vēnisset in urbem quae dīcitur Leydis (*Leyden*), ac vellet innōtēscere (*to become known*) jocō (*joke*), ingressus est officīnam (*shop*) calceārī (*shoemaker*); eum salūtat. Calceārius Maccum rogat num vellet ocreās (*leggings*). Annuente Maccō, quaerit ocreās aptās tībiīs (*legs*) illīus; inventās prōtulit et, ut solent, indūcit illī. "Quam bene," inquit Maccus, "congrueret (*match*) hīs ocreīs pār (*pair*) calceōrum duplicātīs soleīs (*soles*)." Rogātus an et calceōs vellet, annuit. Repertī sunt et additī pedibus. Maccus laudābat ocreās, laudābat calceōs.

Calceārius tacitē gaudēbat, spērāns pretium aequius, cum ēmptōrī (*buyer*) māgnopere placēret merx (*merchandise*). Hīc Maccus: "Dīc mihi," inquit, "bonā fidē, numquamne ūsū accidit tibi ut, quem sīc ocreīs et calceīs ad cursum armāvissēs, quem ad modum nunc armāvistī, abierit, nōn numerātō (*having paid*) pretiō?" "Numquam," ait ille. "Atquī sī forte," inquit, "veniat ūsū, quid tū tum facerēs?" "Cōnsequerer," inquit calceārius, "fugientem." Tum Maccus, "Sēriōne (*In seriousness*) ista dīcis, an jocō?" "Sēriō," inquit alter, "loquor; et sēriō facerem." "Experiar," ait Maccus. "Ēn (*Behold*) prō calceīs praecurrō (*run ahead*), tū cursū (*race*) sequere."

Simulque cum dictō conjēcit sē in pedēs. Calceārius ē vēstīgiō cōnsecūtus est quantum poterat, clāmāns: "Tenēte fūrem, tenēte fūrem!" Ad hanc vōcem cum cīvēs undique cucurrissent ex domibus, hōc dolō cohibuit (*checked*) illōs Maccus nē quis manum injiceret; rīdēns ac vultū placidō: "Nē quis," inquit, "morētur cursum nostrum; certāmen est dē cūpā (*keg*) cervisiae (*beer*)." Itaque jam omnēs praebuērunt sēsē certāminis spectātōrēs. Suspicābantur autem calceārium dolō clāmōrem eum fingere, ut hāc occāsiōne anteverteret (*get ahead of*). Tandem calceārius cursū victus, sūdāns (*perspiring*) et anhēlus (*gasping*) domum rediit. Maccus tulit praemium. Ubi satis rīsum est (*they had laughed*), quīdam ē jūdicibus vocāvit Maccum ad cēnam, et numerāvit calceāriō pretium.

Pietro Bembo: A Contemporary of Columbus

Pietro Bembo (1470–1547), a Florentine by birth, was the son of a Venetian nobleman and a member of a scholarly family. After completing his education in Latin and Greek at Messina and Padua, he joined his father at the court of Ferrara. From Ferrara he proceeded to Urbino and became a brilliant figure in the cultured society of the court. He later lived in Rome, where he was considered the outstanding scholar of his time and the leading master of Ciceronian prose style. His excellent verse was modeled on the best elegiac types of the classical period, such as those of Catullus, Tibullus, and Ovid.

After Columbus discovered America in 1492, Bembo wrote an account of the discovery, from which the following selection is taken.

COLUMBUS DISCOVERS THE NEW WORLD

Sententia Columbī, quam quidem septem annōs rejēcerant, ab rēge et rēgīnā Hispāniae, novā spē incitātīs, ad extrēmum probāta est, itaque tribus cum nāvibus Columbus ad īnsulās, quās Canāriās appellant, profectus est. Ab eīs īnsulās, trēs et trīgintā tōtōs diēs, occidentem secūtus sōlem, sex numerō reperit. Hārum sunt duae ingentis māgnitūdinis; hīs in īnsulīs lusciniae (*nightingales*) Novembrī mēnse canunt.

Hominēs nūdī, ingeniō mītī, lintribus ex ūnō līgnō factīs ūtuntur. Animālium quadrupedum (*four-footed*) genera habent perpauca; ex hīs canēs pusillōs (*very small*), quī mūtī etiam sunt nec lātrant (*bark*); avēs vērō plūrimās habent, nostrīs tum (*some*) grandiōrēs, tum etiam minōrēs, et avēs parvae inveniuntur, quae singulae, suō cum nīdō (*nest*), vīcēsimam quārtam unciae (*ounce*) partem nōn superant; psittacōrum (*parrots*) māgnam cōpiam habent, fōrmā et colōre variam.

Fibrās (*fibers*) similēs vellerī sponte nāscentēs ex nemoribus (*groves*) atque montibus colligunt; sed eās cum volunt candidiōrēs (*whiter*) meliōrēsque fierī, eās ipsī pūrgant, atque apud domōs suās serunt (*spin*). Aurum, quod in flūminum arēnīs legunt, habent; ferrum nōn habent.

Thomas More: The King's Good Servant

Thomas More was born in London in 1477. He received a thorough education in religion, the classics, and the law. His legal career took him to Parliament, where he attracted the attention of King Henry VIII. In 1532 he was made Lord Chancellor. A short time later, unable to accept the opinions of the King regarding marriage and the supremacy of the Pope, he resigned his office. He abandoned honors and dignities with more readiness than most men embrace them. Refusing to take the oath of royal supremacy, he was condemned to death for high treason. On July 6, 1535, he paid with his life for his convictions.

The following excerpt is taken from More's famous work *Utopia*, a social satire. In the first book he drew a picture of the corruption of English life at the beginning of the sixteenth century. In the second book we are shown an ideal society. Here tyranny and luxury have been abolished, private property is unknown, and manual labor is looked upon as the sole profitable occupation.

THE UTOPIANS SCORN GOLD AND SILVER

Itaque ingressī sunt lēgātī trēs cum comitibus centum, omnēs vestītū versicolōrī (*changeable colors*), plērīque sericō (*silk*), lēgātī ipsī, nam domī nōbilēs erant, amictū aureō (*cloth of gold*), māgnīs torquibus (*necklaces*) et inauribus (*earrings*) aureīs, ad haec anulīs aureīs in manibus, monilibus īnsuper appēnsīs in pileō, quae margarītīs (*pearls*) ac gemmīs fulgēbant; omnibus postrēmō rēbus ōrnātī quae apud Utopiēnsēs aut servōrum supplicia, aut īnfāmium dēdecora aut puerōrum nūgāmenta (*trifles*) fuērunt.

Itaque operae pretium (*worthwhile*) erat vidēre quōmodo cristās (*plumes*) ērēxerint, ubi suum ōrnāmentum cum Utopiēnsium vestītū (nam in viīs sēsē populus effūderat) contulērunt. Contrā, nōn minus erat voluptātis cōnsīderāre quam longē sua eōs spēs exspectātiōque fefellerat, et quam longē ab eā exīstimātiōne aberant, quam sē cōnsecūtūrōs esse putāverant. Nam Utopiēnsium oculīs omnium, exceptīs perpaucīs, quī aliās gentēs aliquā idōneā dē causā vīsitāverant, tōtus ille splendor apparātūs (*of apparel*) turpis vidēbātur; et īnfimum quemque prō dominīs reverenter (*reverently*) salūtantēs. Lēgātōs ipsōs, ex aureārum ūsū catēnārum prō servīs habitōs, sine ūllō honōre praeteriērunt.

Puerī, quī gemmās ac margarītās adjēcerant, ubi in lēgātōrum pileīs eās affīxās cōnspēxērunt, mātrem appellāvērunt: "Ēn (*Look*), māter, quam māgnus nebulō (*good-for-nothing*) margarītīs adhūc et gemmīs ūtitur, ac sī esset puerulus (*little boy*)!" At parēns graviter "Tacē," inquit, "fīlī; est, opīnor (*I think*), ūnus ē mōriōnibus (*fools*) lēgātōrum."

George Buchanan: A Scottish Classicist

George Buchanan was born in Stirlingshire, Scotland, in 1506, and lived until 1582. At the age of fourteen, he was sent to study at the University of Paris, where he was trained in the composition of Latin verse. After ten years he returned to Scotland and studied at the University of St. Andrews. He later returned to Paris, where he spent about ten years, and then began his lifelong devotion to the study of the classical authors.

In 1562 Buchanan wrote two *Epithalamia* (nuptial songs or poems) for Mary, Queen of Scots. He afterward turned against Mary and defamed her in works which later evidence proved were libelous.

One of his works, the *Rerum Scoticarum Historia*, was regarded by his contemporaries as superior to the histories of Caesar, Livy, and Sallust. Even Samuel Johnson, the celebrated English critic of the eighteenth century, considered Buchanan "a very fine poet — the only man of genius his country ever produced."

The following selection is taken from the *Rerum Scoticarum Historia*.

MACBETH

Ad fāmam Milcolumbī (*Malcolm's*) exercitūs māgnī in Scotiā (*Scotland*) mōtūs factī sunt (*occurred*); māgnae multitūdinēs cotīdiē ad novum rēgem concurrērunt. Macbethus, prope dēsertus ab omnibus, cum in tam repentīnā dēfectiōne (*defection*) nihil melius occurreret, in arcem Dūnsinanam sē inclūsit, missīs in Aebudās et Hiberniam amīcīs ut pecūniā illīc mīlitēs condūcerent. Milcolumbus, cōnsiliō ējus audītō, rēctā (*directly*) ad eum exercitum dūxit, populō, quācumque ībat, bene precante ac faustīs (*favorable*) acclāmātiōnibus eum prōsequente.

Hōc velut omine victōriae laetī mīlitēs frondēs (*leaves*) virentēs galeīs omnēs apposuērunt, triumphantiumque magis quam ad pūgnam prōgredientium speciē agmen incēdēbat. Eā perterritus hostium fidūciā (*courage*), Macbethus cōnfestim in fugam sē dedit; mīlitēs ējus, ā dūce dēsertī, Milcolumbō sē dēdidērunt. Macduffus tyrannum fugientem assecūtus caput rēgis occīsī ad suōs rettulit.

Multa hīc fābulōsē quīdam nostrōrum fingunt; sed quia theātrīs aut fābulīs sunt aptiōra quam historiae ea omittō. Macbethus septendecim (*seventeen*) annōs Scotiae praefuit. Decem prīmīs optimī rēgis officiō est fūnctus; septem suprēmīs annīs crūdēlitātem saevissimōrum tyrannōrum facile aequāvit.

Luigi Galvani: The Theory of Animal Electricity

In 1790, when George Washington was President of the United States, Luigi Galvani (1737–1798), a lecturer in anatomy in the University of Bologna, wrote an account of his experiments with frogs' legs which had "danced" when touched by chance with a magnetized scalpel. He repeated the experiment hundreds of times and then, wondering if lightning would have the same effect, during a thunderstorm he hung a pair of frogs' legs from a brass hook fastened to an iron pole outdoors. Even after the storm the legs kept twitching. He then proposed the now discarded theory that the muscles moved because of the "animal electricity" within the frog.

It remained for another Italian scientist, Alessandro Volta, the physicist, to explain this phenomenon. He showed that it was a matter of arranging two different metals so that they were separated by a conducting fluid. In Galvani's experiment the brass of the hook and the iron of the pole were the two different metals; the salt water in the legs served as the conductor.

GALVANI'S EXPERIMENT

Operae pretium factūrum mē esse exīstimāvī, sī brevem et accūrātam inventōrum historiam afferrem eō ōrdine et ratiōne quā mihi illa partim cāsus et fortūna obtulit, partim industria et dīligentia dētēxit: nōn tantum nē plūs mihi quam fortūnae aut plūs fortūnae quam mihi tribuātur, sed ut vel eīs, quī hanc ipsam experiendī viam inīre voluissent, facem praeferrēmus aliquam, vel saltem (*at least*) honestō doctōrum hominum dēsīderiō satisfacerēmus, quī solent rērum, quae novitātem in sē recondunt aliquam, orīgine ipsā prīncipiōque dēlectārī . . .

Rānam (*frog*) dissecuī (*dissected*) atque praeparāvī, eamque in mēnsā, omnia mihi alia prōpōnēns, in quā erat māchina ēlectrica, collocāvī ab ējus conductōre penitus (*deep inside*) sējūnctam (*separated*) atque haud (*not*) brevī spatiō dissitam (*spread*). Dum scalpellī cuspidem (*point*) ūnus ex eīs, quī mihi operam dabant, crūrālibus hūjus rānae internīs nervīs cāsū vel leviter admovēret, continuō omnēs artuum mūsculī (*muscles*) ita contrahī vīsī sunt ut in vehementiōrēs incidisse tonicās convulsiōnēs vidērentur. Eōrum vērō alter, quī nōbīs ēlectricitātem tentantibus praestō (*at hand*) erat, animadvertere sibi vīsus est rem contingere dum ex conductōre māchinae scintilla extorquerētur.

W. K. C. Guthrie: Public Orator at Cambridge University

In 1946 General Dwight D. Eisenhower received an honorary degree from Cambridge University, England, in recognition of his leadership of the Allied forces at the end of World War II. For this occasion, W. K. C. Guthrie, a noted classical scholar and historian, composed the following citation in Latin, which he delivered at the public ceremonies.

IN HONOR OF AN AMERICAN GENERAL[1]

Quī igitur ōlim sīcut alter [2]Aenēās āere saeptus (*enveloped*) vēnit et amictus (*clothed*) nebulīs (*clouds*), nē quis audēret "veniendī poscere causās," illum nunc apertīs plausibus studēmus ōrnāre. Ampliōrem intereā apud suōs gradum assecūtus est, [3]Summī Concilī Mīlitāris Praeses (*Chief*) creātus. Īgnōscet autem nōbīs, ut opīnor, sī laureā (*laurel*) nostrā hodiē corōnāre mālumus Cōpiārum Foederātārum Imperātōrem Suprēmum, lībertātis prōpūgnātōrem, cūjus cōnsiliō ductūque tyrannōrum dominātiōnem, quae complūribus Eurōpae cīvitātibus lībertātem adēmerat (*had taken away*), nostram etiam in discrīmen extrēmum addūxerat, exstīnximus atque dēlēvimus.

Nōtum est omnibus quantum victōriae condūxerit concordia et cōnspīrātiō (*union*) admīrābilis inter cōnsiliōrum ductōrēs (*strategists*) hūjus labōribus facta. Erat nīmīrum (*undoubtedly*) in eō tam mītis sapientia, tanta simul gravitās, hūmānitās, urbānitās ut nihil aliud jam cūrārent cēterī, quam prō salūte omnium voluntāte commūnī labōrāre. Tālem inter Americānōrum cīvitātem potentem et nōs ipsōs concordiam cum in pācis tempora extendere permāgnī referat, in animō semper habendum est quod ipse (ut nūper lēgī) dīxit: sociōrum concordiam nōn semel et in perpetuum conciliārī posse, vērum assiduā (*persistent*) omnium vigilantiā in diēs recreandam et cōnfīrmandam esse. Hanc rēgulam secūtus vīcit, utinam eādem ūsī pācem omnibus et prōsperitātem redintegrāre possīmus!

Dūcō ad vōs cīvem Americānum praeclārum (*distinguished*), populī Britannicī amīcum, Dwight David Eisenhower.

---

1. From *Advanced Latin Tests* by Sidney Morris. Reprinted by permission of the publishers, George C. Harrap & Co., Ltd.
2. Aeneas, son of a Trojan prince and Venus, goddess of love, fought with great valor in the Trojan War. Guthrie's reference is to a passage in Vergil's *Aeneid*, in which Venus rendered Aeneas and his companions invisible on their way to Carthage in order to protect them from harm and delays.

At Venus obscūrō gradientēs āere saepsit,
et multō nebulae circum dea fūdit amictū,
cernere nē quis eōs neu quis contingere posset
mōlīrīve moram aut veniendī poscere causās.
— *Aeneid*, Book I, lines 411–14.

3. Eisenhower had first served as Commander of the European Theater of Operations.

Pronunciation of Latin

Syllabication

1. A syllable is the smallest pronounceable unit. It consists of a vowel or a diphthong with or without one or more consonants. Hence a Latin word has as many syllables as it has vowels or diphthongs or both. There are no silent letters in Latin: **sa/lū/tā/ris, pae/ne.**

2. Whenever possible a Latin syllable begins with a consonant. A single consonant between two vowels goes with the second: **rē/gī/na.** A prefix generally remains as a whole: **ad/est (ad + est).**

3. If two or more consonants occur between vowels, the first consonant is joined with the preceding vowel: **hos/tis, obs/cū/ra.**

4. Double consonants, as **tt** or **ss**, are always separated: **mit/tō, mis/sus.**

5. The letter **x** is treated as a double consonant, but is pronounced with the preceding vowel: **dūx/ī, rēx/it.**

6. Whenever a mute, **p, b, t, d, c, g,** is followed by a liquid, **l** or **r**, both the mute and the liquid are pronounced in the following syllable: **sa/crum, cas/tra, pū/bli/cus.**

Quantity of Syllables

1. A syllable is *long by nature* if it contains a long vowel or a diphthong: **mā/ter, a/māns, cau/sa.**

2. A syllable is *long by position* if it contains a short vowel followed immediately by two or more consonants, or by **x**. The vowel retains its short sound. A mute followed by a liquid does not make a syllable long.

3. A syllable is short if it contains a short vowel, followed by a vowel or a single consonant: **vi/a, pe/des.**

Accent or Stress

1. Accent is the emphasis given to a syllable by stress, pitch, or both.

2. In Latin the last syllable of a word, the ultima, is never stressed.

3. The first syllable of a word of two syllables is always stressed, whether the vowel is long or short: **vi′/a, vī′/ta.**

4. In a word of more than two syllables the second-to-last syllable, the penult (**paene,** *almost* + **ūltima,** *last*), if long, is stressed: **nā/tū′/ra, in/jūs′/tus;**

if the penult is short, the third-last syllable, the antepenult, is stressed: **īn'su/la, pe'/di/tēs. Ante** means *before.*

Dactylic Hexameter

You will appreciate Latin poetry more if you read it, preferably aloud, while observing the rhythm in which it is written. Rhythm in English and Latin is different. In English it depends upon accent or stress; in Latin, on the quantity of syllables.

You have already been using macrons to mark long vowels in Latin. They are an aid to correct pronunciation. A syllable is long if it contains a long vowel or a diphthong, or if it contains a short vowel followed by two or more consonants, or by a double consonant, such as **x.**

A foot is a combination of syllables. Poetic feet are named according to the stress and the number of syllables in a particular foot. In this lesson we shall concentrate on dactylic hexameter. A line of poetry is called dactylic hexameter if it contains six dactylic feet or their equivalent. In English a dactyl consists of an accented or stressed syllable followed by two unaccented syllables. In Latin a dactyl contains one long and two short syllables ($-\smile\smile$); its equivalent is called a spondee, which contains two long syllables ($--$). A spondee in English consists of two equally accented syllables.

The dactylic hexameter was used by Homer in the *Iliad* and the *Odyssey.* The poet Ennius was the first Latin poet who used this meter. Lucretius, Vergil, Horace, Ovid, and many other Latin poets also wrote Latin poems in dactylic hexameter. It is the traditional meter for epic poetry.

To practice reading dactylic hexameter in English, use the opening lines of Longfellow's *Evangeline:*

> This' is the for'est prime'val. The mur'muring pines' and the hem'locks,
> Bear'ded with moss', and in gar'ments green', indistinct' in the twi'light,
> Stand' like Dru'ids of eld', with voi'ces sad' and prophet'ic,
> Stand' like har'pers hoar', with beards' that rest' on their bos'oms.

When a word in Latin poetry ends in a vowel, diphthong, or **m,** and the following word begins with a vowel or **h,** the first vowel or diphthong is regularly elided. Elision is not a total omission, but rather a light and quick half-pronunciation, somewhat like a grace note in music.

Vergil's *Aeneid* begins with the following lines. When you read these lines orally, the words should be kept distinct, and no break should be made between the separate feet unless there is a pause in sense.

> Arma vi|rumque ca|nō, Trō|jae quī | prīmus ab | ōrīs
> Ītali|am fā|tō profu|gus Lā|vīnaque | vēnit
> lītora | multum il|le et ter|rīs jac|tātus et | altō

395

vī supe|rum sae|vae memo|rem Jū|nōnis ob | īram,
_́ ⌣ ⌣|_́ _|_́ ⌣ ⌣|_́ _|_́ ⌣ ⌣ |_́ _

multa quo|que‿et bel|lō pas|sus, dum | conderet | urbem
_́ ⌣ ⌣|_́ _|_́ _|_́ _ | _́ ⌣ ⌣|_́ _

īnfer|retque de|ōs Lati|ō; genus | unde La|tīnum
_́ _|_́ ⌣ ⌣|_́ ⌣ ⌣|_́ ⌣ ⌣ | _́ ⌣ ⌣|_́ _

Albā|nīque pa|trēs at|que‿altae | moenia | Rōmae.
_́ _|_́ ⌣ ⌣|_́ _|_́ _ | _́ ⌣ ⌣|_́ _

In marking the scansion, the sign (⁻) is used below the line to indicate a long syllable, and the sign (˘) is used for a short syllable. The feet are separated by a perpendicular line; the metrical accent is shown by (′) below the first syllable of each foot; and elision is indicated by (⌢) connecting the elided vowel with the vowel following.

How the Romans Expressed Time

Years: A Roman year was reckoned from the traditional date of the founding of Rome by Romulus. It was indicated by A.U.C. meaning **ab urbe conditā** or **annō urbis conditae.** The city was founded in 753 B.C. according to our reckoning.

$$70 \text{ A.D.} = 753 + 70 + 1 \text{ (inclusive reckoning)}$$
$$= 824 \text{ A.U.C.}$$
$$70 \text{ B.C.} = 753 - 70 + 1$$
$$= 684 \text{ A.U.C.}$$

A particular year was usually designated by the names of the two consuls who were in office. The names with **cōnsulibus** form an ablative absolute phrase.

M. Messālā M. Pīsōne cōnsulibus *in the consulship of Marcus Messala and Marcus Piso*

Months: Names of the Roman months were originally adjectives with **mēnsis,** *month,* expressed or understood.

Jānuārius	Aprīlis	Jūlius (Quīntīlis)	Octōber
Februārius	Māius	Augustus (Sextīlis)	November
Mārtius	Jūnius	September	December

The first month of the Roman year was originally **Mārtius,** the month of plowing and planting, so that the fifth month was **Quīntīlis,** the sixth **Sextīlis,** etc. The tenth month was **December,** followed by **Jānuārius** and **Februārius.** From the time of Augustus, the fifth and sixth months became **Jūlius** and **Augustus,** named after Julius and Augustus Caesar.

Before Julius Caesar's time, the Roman calendar was based on the lunar month, i.e., the interval between one new moon and the next. All months had twenty-nine days except March, May, July, and October, which had thirty-one days, and February, which had twenty-eight days. Since the calendar year of three hundred and fifty-five days was shorter than the solar year of three hundred sixty-five and one-fourth days, a month of varying length was inserted after February 23 every other year and was called **mēnsis intercalāris.**

Julius Caesar corrected the calendar by lengthening the year 46 B.C. to fifteen months and by introducing a new calendar on January 1, 45 B.C. This new Julian calendar contained three hundred sixty-five and one-fourth days, so arranged that every fourth year an extra full day was to be added to February. This calendar was used in Europe till the latter part of the sixteenth century, when the even more accurate Gregorian calendar was adopted. The Julian calendar, however, was used in Russia until 1918, and in Greece until 1923.

Days: Only three days of the month had names of their own:

1. The *Calends* (**Kalendae, Kal.**), the first day of each month.
2. The *Nones* (**Nōnae, Nōn.**), the fifth day of most months, but in "March, July, October, May, the Nones fall on the seventh day."
3. The *Ides* (**Īdūs, Īd.**), the thirteenth day of most months, but in "March, July, October, May, the Ides fall on the fifteenth day."

When used as dates, the Calends, Nones, and Ides were indicated by the ablative of time:

Kalendīs Aprīlibus	*on the April Kalends* (April 1)
Nōnīs Octōbribus	*on the October Nones* (October 7)
Īdibus Mārtiīs	*on the Ides of March* (March 15)

The day immediately preceding the Calends, Nones, or Ides was designated idiomatically by **prīdiē,** followed by the accusative:

prīdiē Kalendās Jūliās (June 29)
prīdiē Nōnās Mārtiās (March 6)
prīdiē Īdūs Aprīlēs (April 12)

Other dates were reckoned backward from these three key dates, just as we say "ten days before Christmas," "nine days before Christmas," etc. In counting the number of days, however, the Romans included both the day they started from and the day they were counting to. This is called *inclusive reckoning.* For example, our March 28 was reckoned backwards from April 1, counting April 1 as the first day in the series, March 31 as the second, etc. Thus:

April 1	Mar. 31	Mar. 30	Mar. 29	Mar. 28
I	II	III	IV	V

Accordingly March 28 is expressed in Latin as: **a. d. V. Kal. Apr. (ante diem quīntum Kalendās Aprīlēs**). Notice that all words following **ante** are in the accusative.

Hours: The day between sunrise (**sōlis ortus**) and sunset (**sōlis occāsus**) was divided into twelve portions called **hōrae.** The length of each **hōra** varied with the season of the year and the latitude. It was always one-twelfth of the time from sunrise to sunset (**ab ortō usque ad occidentem sōlem**). If there was daylight from 6 A.M. to 6 P.M. the following would be true:

At 6 A.M. (daybreak) = **prīmā lūce**   At noon = **merīdiē**
From 6 A.M. to 7 A.M. = **prīmā hōrā**   From noon to 1 P.M. = **septima hōrā**
From 9 A.M. to 10 A.M. = **quārtā hōrā**   From 1 P.M. to 2 P.M. = **octāvā hōrā**

Vigiliae: The night was divided equally into four **vigiliae,** *watches,* the length of which varied with the season of the year and the latitude. The four watches of the night would be as follows:

At 6 P.M. = **prīmā nocte**   At midnight = **mediā nocte**
From 6 P.M. to 9 P.M. = **prīmā vigiliā**   From midnight to 3 A.M. = **tertiā vigiliā**
From 9 P.M. to midnight = **secundā vigiliā**   From 3 A.M. to 6 A.M. = **quārtā vigiliā**

Building Word Power

Latin words may be root words, derivatives, or compounds.

A *root word* may be defined as the simplest or earliest form of a word in the Latin language from which other words have been formed by derivation or by composition, as **portāre,** *to carry.* A *root* is the simplest element to which a word can be reduced. It is generally a monosyllable and contains the fundamental idea of the word, as **port–** *carry.*

Derivatives are formed from the stems of nouns, adjectives, verbs, or adverbs by the addition of prefixes and suffixes, as **trānsportāre,** *to carry across.* A *stem* is that part of a word to which inflectional endings (indicators) are attached, as **portā–.** A *prefix* is a syllable, or syllables, placed at the beginning of a word. It gives a particular shade of meaning to the root, as **trānsportāre,** *to carry across.* A *suffix* is a syllable, or syllables, attached to the end of a word. It may modify not only the meaning but also the part of speech, as **portābilis,** *able to be carried.* For lists of prefixes and suffixes, see Appendix of Book I.

Compounds are formed by adding together two or more stems or words, as **agricultūra (agri– + cultūra),** *agriculture.*

Latin-English Roots and Stems

Root or Stem	General Meaning	English Derivatives
ac–, acr–, acu–	*sharp*	acetic, acrid, acute
ag–, act–	*do, drive, impel*	agile, act
agr–	*field*	agriculture
ali–	*other, another*	alias, alibi, alien
alter–	*other, change*	alter, alternate

Root or Stem	General Meaning	English Derivatives
am–, amic–, –imic–, amat–	*love, friendly*	amour, amicable, inimical, amateur
anim–	*mind, soul, spirit*	animate, animosity
annu–, –enni–	*year*	annual, perennial
aqu–	*water*	aquatic, aquamarine
arm–	*arms, weapons*	arms, army, armada, armature
aud–, audit–	*hear*	audible, auditorium
aug–, auct–	*augment, increase*	augment, auction
–bel, bell–	*war*	rebel, belligerent
ben–, bene–	*well, good*	benign, benefactor
brev–, –brev–	*short, brief*	brevity, abbreviate
cad, cas–, –cid–	*fall, happen*	cadaver, casual, accident
caed–, –cid–, –cis–	*cut down, kill*	homicide, incision
cap–, –cip–, capt–, –cept	*take, seize*	capable, recipient, captive, accept
capit–, –capit–, –cipit–	*head*	capital, decapitate, precipitate
ced–, –ced–, –cess	*go, yield*	cede, intercede, recess
cent–	*hundred*	cent, centennial, centenarian
claus–, –clud–, –clus–, clos–	*close, shut*	clause, include, seclusion, closet
cogn–, –cogn–	*know, be acquainted*	cognition, recognize
cor–, –cord, cord–	*heart*	core, record, cordate
corp–, –corp–	*body*	corpus, corpulent, incorporate
creat–, –creat–	*create*	creator, recreation
cred–, –cred–, credit–	*believe, trust*	creed, credible, incredulous, credit
culp–, –culp–	*fault, blame*	culpable, exculpate
cur–, –cur–	*care, care for*	cure, accurate
–cur, curr–, curs–	*run, course*	concur, current, cursive
da–, dat–, –dit	*give*	date, dative, edit
dec–	*ten*	decade, decennial
di–, diurn–, –duum	*day*	diary, diurnal, triduum
–dic–, dicat–	*proclaim, dedicate*	abdicate, indication
–dic–, dict–	*say, speak, word*	edict, diction, dictum
dign–, –dign–	*worthy*	dignity, indignant
doc–, –doct–	*teach, prove*	docile, indoctrinate
du–	*two*	dual, duplicate
–duc–, –duct–	*lead*	induce, abduct
(a)equ–, –iqu–	*equal*	equal, equity, iniquity
esse–, ent–, futur–	*being*	essence, entity, futurity
fac–, –fact–, –fic–, –fect–, –fy	*do, make*	facile, manufacture, efficient, effect, magnify

Root or Stem	General Meaning	English Derivatives
fid–, –fid–	*belief, trust, faith*	fidelity, confide
fin–	*end, limit*	finite, final
firm–, –firm	*firm, strong*	firm, confirm, infirm
form–, –form	*form, shape*	form, stelliform
fort–, –fort	*strong*	fortitude, comfort
gener– (genus)	*class, birth, kind*	generate, genus
grat–, –grat–	*pleasing*	gratitude, ingratiate
grav–	*weight, heavy*	grave, gravity, gravitate
–jac–, jact–, –ject	*throw*	ejaculate, jactation, object
jud–	*judge*	judiciary
junct–, –jug–	*join*	junction, conjugation
jur–, –jurat–	*swear*	jury, adjuration
labor–, –labor–	*work*	labor, laboratory, elaborate
leg–	*law*	legal, legitimate
leg–, –lig–, –lect	*choose, collect, read*	legion, legend, eligible, intellect
legat–, –legat–	*send as envoy*	legate, delegate, relegate
lev–, –leve–	*light, rise*	levity, lever, alleviate
lig–, ligat–	*bind*	ligament, ligature
lingu–, –lingu–	*tongue*	lingual, bilingual
lit–	*letter*	literature
loc–, –locat–	*place*	local, locate, bilocate
luc–, –luc–	*light, shine*	lucid, translucent
lud–, –lud–, –lus–	*school, play, mock*	ludicrous, delude, elusive
magn–	*large*	magnify
major–	*larger*	major, majority
maxim–	*largest*	maxim, maximum
mal–	*bad*	malefactor
pejor–	*worse*	pejorative
pessim–	*worst*	pessimist
man–, manu–, –mand, mandat–	*hand*	manage, manufacture, command, mandate
mar–	*sea*	marine
matr–	*mother*	matrimony
medi–, –medi–	*middle*	median, intermediate
ment–, –ment	*mind*	mental, comment
min–	*less*	minus, minister
–mit–, miss–	*send*	admit, mission
mon–, –mon, –monit–	*warn, advise*	monitor, summon, admonition
mont–, –mont–, –mount	*mountain*	montane, tramontane, amount
mor–	*custom*	moral, morose

400

Root or Stem	General Meaning	English Derivatives
mov–, mob–, mot–	*move*	move, mobile, motion
multi–	*many*	multitude, multiply
nav–	*ship*	nave, navy, navigate
nomen, –nomen, nomin–	*name*	nomenclature, cognomen, nominate
nov–	*new*	novice, novelty
–nunc–, –nounce	*message*	pronunciation, announce
ocul–	*eye*	ocular, inoculate
omni–	*all*	omnibus, omniscient
ora–, ori–, os–	*mouth*	oration, orifice, oscillate
ordin–	*order*	ordinary
par, –par–	*equal*	par, parity, compare
–para–	*get ready*	prepare, apparatus
patr–, –patr–	*father*	patrimony, repatriate
ped–, –ped–	*foot*	pedal, impede, expedite
–pel–, puls–, –puls–	*drive, strike, beat*	repel, pulse, repulse
pen–	*punishment*	penal, penance
pet–, –pet–	*seek, fly toward*	petition, appetite
–pon–, –posit–	*place, set*	deponent, apposition
port–, –port	*carry*	portable, export
pot–, poss–	*power*	potent, posse, possible
prim–	*first*	prime, primary
–prim–, –press–	*press*	imprimatur, depression
–put–, –putat–	*think, clean, clear up*	compute, amputation
–quir–, –quis–	*inquire, ask*	inquire, inquisitive
reg–, –rig–, –rect–, rect–	*rule, straight, right*	regal, corrigible, correct, rectitude
rid–, –rid–, –ris–	*laugh*	ridicule, deride, derision
rog–, –rog–	*ask, propose a law*	rogation, abrogate
sacr–	*sacred, holy*	sacred, sacrifice
sanct–	*holy*	sanctity, sanctuary
scrib–, –scrib–, –script–	*write*	scribe, describe, inscription
sed–, –sid–, sess–	*sit, seat*	sediment, residence, session
sent–, –sent, sens–	*feel, perceive, think*	sentient, resent, sense
simil–, –simil–	*like, similar*	similar, assimilate
sol–, –sol–	*alone*	sole, desolate
spec–, –spic–, –spect	*see, look closely*	specimen, conspicuous, inspect
spir–, –spir–	*breathe*	spiracle, inspire
sta–, stat–, –sist, –stitu–	*stand*	stable, status, consist, constitution

Root or Stem	General Meaning	English Derivatives
ten–, –tin–, –tent, –tain	*hold*	tenant, continue, content, contain
tend–, tens–, tent–	*stretch*	tend, tension, tent
tot–	*total*	total
tract–, –tract	*draw*	tractor, extract
uni–	*one*	unite, uniform
urb–	*city*	urban, urbane
vac–	*empty*	vacant, vacuole
veh–, –vect–	*carry*	vehicle, convection
–ven–, –vent, vent–	*come*	convene, advent, venture
ver–	*true*	veracity, verify
vert–, –vert, vers–, –vers–	*turn*	vertigo, invert, verse, reverse
via–, –via–	*way*	viaduct, deviate, devious
vid–, –vid–, vis–, –vis–	*see*	video, evidence, vision, invisible
vinc–, vict–, –vict	*conquer*	vincible, victor, convict
viv–, –viv–, vict–, vit–	*live, food, life*	vivify, revive, victuals, vital
voc–, –vocat–	*call, voice*	vocal, vocation, advocate

Latin Forms

Declension of Nouns

FIRST DECLENSION

SINGULAR	PLURAL
Nom. puella, *a girl*	puellae, *the girls*
Gen. puellae, *of a girl* or *a girl's*	puellārum, *of the girls* or *the girls'*
Dat. puellae, *to* or *for a girl*	puellīs, *to* or *for the girls*
Acc. puellam, *a girl*	puellās, *the girls*
Abl. puellā, *from, by,* or *with a girl*	puellīs, *from, by,* or *with the girls*

1. In form the vocative case is always the same as the nominative case.

2. Nouns of the first declension are feminine, except nouns denoting males, which are masculine.

3. The dative and ablative plural of **fīlia** is **fīliābus**, and of **dea, deābus**.

SECOND DECLENSION

SINGULAR

Nom.	servus	ager	vir	fīlius	oppidum
Gen.	servī	agrī	virī	fīlī	oppidī
Dat.	servō	agrō	virō	fīliō	oppidō
Acc.	servum	agrum	virum	fīlium	oppidum
Abl.	servō	agrō	virō	fīliō	oppidō

PLURAL

Nom.	servī	agrī	virī	fīliī	oppida
Gen.	servōrum	agrōrum	virōrum	fīliōrum	oppidōrum
Dat.	servīs	agrīs	virīs	fīliīs	oppidīs
Acc.	servōs	agrōs	virōs	fīliōs	oppida
Abl.	servīs	agrīs	virīs	fīliīs	oppidīs

1. Second declension nouns in −us, −er, or −ir are masculine; those in −um are neuter.

2. **Fīlius,** proper names in −ius, and nouns in −ium usually have −ī (not −iī) in the genitive singular, with the accent on the penult.

3. The vocative singular of nouns in −us is −e; **fīlius** and proper names in −ius have −ī: **serve, fīlī, Cornēlī.**

THIRD DECLENSION
Masculine and Feminine Consonant Stems

SINGULAR

Nom.	honor, *m.*	pater, *m.*	regiō, *f.*	rēx, *m.*	prīnceps, *m.*	cīvitās, *f.*	pēs, *m.*
Gen.	honōris	patris	regiōnis	rēgis	prīncipis	cīvitātis	pedis
Dat.	honōrī	patrī	regiōnī	rēgī	prīncipī	cīvitātī	pedī
Acc.	honōrem	patrem	regiōnem	rēgem	prīncipem	cīvitātem	pedem
Abl.	honōre	patre	regiōne	rēge	prīncipe	cīvitāte	pede

PLURAL

Nom.	honōrēs	patrēs	regiōnēs	rēgēs	prīncipēs	cīvitātēs	pedēs
Gen.	honōrum	patrum	regiōnum	rēgum	prīncipum	cīvitātum	pedum
Dat.	honōribus	patribus	regiōnibus	rēgibus	prīncipibus	cīvitātibus	pedibus
Acc.	honōrēs	patrēs	regiōnēs	rēgēs	prīncipēs	cīvitātēs	pedēs
Abl.	honōribus	patribus	regiōnibus	rēgibus	prīncipibus	cīvitātibus	pedibus

Some masculine and feminine nouns of the third declension end in −s in the nominative. If the stem of a noun ends in −c or −g, the nominative will end in −x, as **reg−** + s = **rēx; duc−** + s = **dux.** Nouns with stems ending in −tr have the nominative ending in −ter, as **pater** from **patr−.** A final −t or −d of the stem is dropped before −s, as **ped−** + s = **pēs.** Short −i in the stem of more than one syllable changes to short −e in the nominative, as **prīncip−** + s = **prīnceps.** Nouns with stems ending in −din and −gin end in −ō in the nominative, as **virgō, virginis** and **multitūdō, multitūdinis.**

Neuter Consonant Stems

SINGULAR

Nom.	flūmen	corpus	genus	caput	iter
Gen.	flūminis	corporis	generīs	capitis	itineris
Dat.	flūminī	corporī	generī	capitī	itinerī
Acc.	flūmen	corpus	genus	caput	iter
Abl.	flūmine	corpore	genere	capite	itinere

PLURAL

Nom.	flūmina	corpora	genera	capita	itinera
Gen.	flūminum	corporum	generum	capitum	itinerum
Dat.	flūminibus	corporibus	generibus	capitibus	itineribus
Acc.	flūmina	corpora	genera	capita	itinera
Abl.	flūminibus	corporibus	generibus	capitibus	itineribus

i-*Stems*

Masculine and Feminine   *Neuter*

SINGULAR

Nom.	cīvis, *mf.*	caedēs, *f.*	urbs, *f.*	nox, *f.*	cohors, *f.*	mare
Gen.	cīvis	caedis	urbis	noctis	cohortis	maris
Dat.	cīvī	caedī	urbī	noctī	cohortī	marī
Acc.	cīvem	caedem	urbem	noctem	cohortem	mare
Abl.	cīve	caede	urbe	nocte	cohorte	marī

PLURAL

Nom.	cīvēs	caedēs	urbēs	noctēs	cohortēs	maria
Gen.	cīvium	caedium	urbium	noctium	cohortium	marium
Dat.	cīvibus	caedibus	urbibus	noctibus	cohortibus	maribus
Acc.	cīvēs (–īs)	caedēs (–īs)	urbēs (–īs)	noctēs (–īs)	cohortēs (–īs)	maria
Abl.	cīvibus	caedibus	urbibus	noctibus	cohortibus	maribus

1. Masculine and feminine i-stem nouns fall into three classes:

   a. Nouns ending in –is or –es and having the same number of syllables in the genitive as the nominative.

   b. Monosyllables in –s or –x whose base ends in a double consonant.

   c. Nouns ending in –ns or –rs.

2. Neuter nouns ending in –e, –al, –ar are i-stems.

3. **Turris** and some proper names in –is have –im in the accusative singular as **turrim, Tiberim.**

FOURTH DECLENSION   FIFTH DECLENSION

SINGULAR

	M.	F.	N.	M.	F.
Nom.	impetus	domus	cornū	diēs	rēs
Gen.	impetūs	domūs (domī, *loc.*)	cornūs	diēī	reī
Dat.	impetuī	domuī, domō	cornū	diēī	reī
Acc.	impetum	domum	cornū	diem	rem
Abl.	impetū	domō	cornū	diē	rē

404

	M.	F.	N.	M.	F.
Nom.	impetūs	domūs	cornua	diēs	rēs
Gen.	impetuum	domuum, domōrum	cornuum	diērum	rērum
Dat.	impetibus	domibus	cornibus	diēbus	rēbus
Acc.	impetūs	domūs, domōs	cornua	diēs	rēs
Abl.	impetibus	domibus	cornibus	diēbus	rēbus

Most fourth declension nouns in −us are masculine; **manus** and **domus** are feminine; a few in −u are neuter. Fifth declension nouns are feminine, except **diēs**, which is sometimes masculine in the singular, always in the plural.

Irregular Nouns
SINGULAR

Nom.	vīs, *f.*	nēmō, *mf.*	deus, *m.*	bōs, *mf.*	Juppiter, *m.*
Gen.	—	(nūllīus)	deī	bovis	Jovis
Dat.	—	nēminī	deō	bovī	Jovī
Acc.	vim	nēminem	deum	bovem	Jovem
Abl.	vī	(nūllō)	deō	bove	Jove

PLURAL

Nom.	vīrēs	—	deī, diī, dī	bovēs	—
Gen.	vīrium	—	deōrum, deum	bovum, boum	—
Dat.	vīribus	—	deīs, diīs, dīs	bōbus, būbus	—
Acc.	vīrēs	—	deōs	bovēs	—
Abl.	vīribus	—	deīs, diīs, dīs	bōbus, būbus	—

Declension of Adjectives
FIRST AND SECOND DECLENSIONS

	SINGULAR			PLURAL		
	M.	F.	N.	M.	F.	N.
Nom.	bonus	bona	bonum	bonī	bonae	bona
Gen.	bonī	bonae	bonī	bonōrum	bonārum	bonōrum
Dat.	bonō	bonae	bonō	bonīs	bonīs	bonīs
Acc.	bonum	bonam	bonum	bonōs	bonās	bona
Abl.	bonō	bonā	bonō	bonīs	bonīs	bonīs
Nom.	miser	misera	miserum	miserī	miserae	misera
Gen.	miserī	miserae	miserī	miserōrum	miserārum	miserōrum
Dat.	miserō	miserae	miserō	miserīs	miserīs	miserīs
Acc.	miserum	miseram	miserum	miserōs	miserās	misera
Abl.	miserō	miserā	miserō	miserīs	miserīs	miserīs
Nom.	pulcher	pulchra	pulchrum	pulchrī	pulchrae	pulchra
Gen.	pulchrī	pulchrae	pulchrī	pulchrōrum	pulchrārum	pulchrōrum
Dat.	pulchrō	pulchrae	pulchrō	pulchrīs	pulchrīs	pulchrīs
Acc.	pulchrum	pulchram	pulchrum	pulchrōs	pulchrās	pulchra
Abl.	pulchrō	pulchrā	pulchrō	pulchrīs	pulchrīs	pulchrīs

ADJECTIVES OF SPECIAL DECLENSION

The following adjectives have a genitive singular termination in –īus, a dative singular termination in –ī, and their other forms like **bonus, miser,** and **pulcher.**

alius, alia, aliud, *other, another*
alter, altera, alterum, *the other*
uter, utra, utrum, *which (of two)?*
uterque, utraque, utrumque, *each of two, both*
neuter, neutra, neutrum, *neither (of two)*

ūnus, ūna, ūnum, *one, alone*
ūllus, ūlla, ūllum, *any*
nūllus, nūlla, nūllum, *none*
sōlus, sōla, sōlum, *only, single, alone*
tōtus, tōta, tōtum, *the whole, entire, all*

SINGULAR

	M.	F.	N.	M.	F.	N.	M.	F.	N.
Nom.	ūnus	ūna	ūnum	alter	altera	alterum	uter	utra	utrum
Gen.		ūnīus			alterius			utrīus	
Dat.		ūnī			alterī			utrī	
Acc.	ūnum	ūnam	ūnum	alterum	alteram	alterum	utrum	utram	utrum
Abl.	ūnō	ūnā	ūnō	alterō	alterā	alterō	utrō	utrā	utrō

1. The plurals are those of **bonus, miser,** and **pulcher.**
2. **Alius** has **aliud** in the nominative and accusative singular neuter.
3. **Alter** has **alterius** in the genitive singular which is frequently used for the genitive of **alius.**

NUMERICAL ADJECTIVES

	M.	F.	N.	M.&F.	N.	N.
Nom.	duo	duae	duo	trēs	tria	mīlia
Gen.	duōrum	duārum	duōrum	trium		mīlium
Dat.	duōbus	duābus	duōbus	tribus		mīlibus
Acc.	duōs, duo	duās	duo	trēs	tria	mīlia
Abl.	duōbus	duābus	duōbus	tribus		mīlibus

In the singular **mīlle,** *thousand,* is an indeclinable adjective. In the plural **mīlia** is a neuter noun followed by the genitive of the noun denoting the persons or things that are numbered.

Arabic	*Roman Numerals*	*Cardinal*	*Ordinal*
1	I	ūnus, –a, –um	prīmus, –a, –um
2	II	duo, duae, duo	secundus, alter
3	III	trēs, tria	tertius
4	IIII or IV	quattuor	quārtus
5	V	quīnque	quīntus
6	VI	sex	sextus
7	VII	septem	septimus
8	VIII	octō	octāvus
9	VIIII or IX	novem	nōnus
10	X	decem	decimus

406

11	XI	ūndecim	ūndecimus
12	XII	duodecim	duodecimus
13	XIII	tredecim	tertius decimus
14	XIIII or XIV	quattuordecim	quārtus decimus
15	XV	quīndecim	quīntus decimus
16	XVI	sēdecim	sextus decimus
17	XVII	septendecim	septimus decimus
18	XVIII	duodēvīgintī	duodēvīcēsimus
19	XVIIII or XIX	ūndēvīgintī	ūndēvīcēsimus
20	XX	vīgintī	vīcēsimus
21	XXI	ūnus et vīgintī, vīgintī ūnus	vīcēsimus prīmus
28	XXVIII	duodētrīgintā	duodētrīcēsimus
29	XXIX	ūndētrīgintā	ūndētrīcēsimus
30	XXX	trīgintā	trīcēsimus
40	XXXX or XL	quadrāgintā	quadrāgēsimus
50	L	quīnquāgintā	quīnquāgēsimus
60	LX	sexāgintā	sexāgēsimus
70	LXX	septuāgintā	septuāgēsimus
80	LXXX	octōgintā	octōgēsimus
90	LXXXX or XC	nōnāgintā	nōnāgēsimus
100	C	centum	centēsimus
101	CI	centum (et) ūnus	centēsimus (et) prīmus
200	CC	ducentī, –ae, –a	ducentēsimus
300	CCC	trecentī, –ae, –a	trecentēsimus
400	CCCC	quadringentī	quadringentēsimus
500	D	quīngentī	quīngentēsimus
600	DC	sescentī	sescentēsimus
700	DCC	septingentī	septingentēsimus
800	DCCC	octingentī	octingentēsimus
900	DCCCC	nōngentī	nōngentēsimus
1,000	M	mīlle	mīllēsimus
2,000	MM	duo mīlia	bis mīllēsimus

THIRD DECLENSION

	Two Terminations		*Three Terminations*			*One Termination*	
	M.&F.	N.	M.	F.	N.	M.&F.	N.
				SINGULAR			
Nom.	brevis	breve	ācer	ācris	ācre	potēns	
Gen.	brevis			ācris		potentis	
Dat.	brevī			ācrī		potentī	
Acc.	brevem	breve	ācrem	ācrem	ācre	potentem	potēns
Abl.	brevī			ācrī		potentī	
				PLURAL			
Nom.	brevēs	brevia	ācrēs	ācrēs	ācria	potentēs	potentia
Gen.	brevium			ācrium		potentium	
Dat.	brevibus			ācribus		potentibus	
Acc.	brevēs (–īs)	brevia	ācrēs (–īs)		ācria	potentēs	potentia
Abl.	brevibus			ācribus		potentibus	

407

PRESENT ACTIVE PARTICIPLE

	SINGULAR		PLURAL	
	M.&F.	N.	M.&F.	N.
Nom.	vocāns		vocantēs	vocantia
Gen.	vocantis		vocantium	
Dat.	vocantī		vocantibus	
Acc.	vocantem	vocāns	vocantēs	vocantia
Abl.	vocante (–ī)		vocantibus	

When the present participle is used as an adjective, the ablative indicator is –ī.

REGULAR COMPARISON OF ADJECTIVES

Positive	Comparative	Superlative
clārus, –a, –um	clārior, clārius	clārissimus, –a, –um
fortis, –e	fortior, fortius	fortissimus, –a, –um
audāx (audācis)	audācior, audācius	audācissimus, –a, –um
potēns (potentis)	potentior, potentius	potentissimus, –a, –um
līber, –era, –erum	līberior, līberius	līberrimus, –a, –um
ācer, ācris, ācre	ācrior, ācrius	ācerrimus, –a, –um
similis, –e	similior, similius	simillimus, –a, –um

IRREGULAR COMPARISON OF ADJECTIVES

bonus, –a, –um	melior, melius	optimus, –a, –um
malus, –a, –um	pējor, pējus	pessimus, –a, –um
māgnus, –a, –um	mājor, mājus	māximus, –a, –um
parvus, –a, –um	minor, minus	minimus, –a, –um
multus, –a, –um	——, plūs	plūrimus, –a, –um
multī, –ae, –a	plūrēs, plūra	plūrimī, –ae, –a

The positive degree of the following adjectives, with the exception of **idōneus**, is rare or not in common use. The last five are prepositions or adverbs.

idōneus, –a, –um	magis idōneus	māximē idōneus
exterus, –a, –um	exterior, –ius	extrēmus, –a, –um
īnferus, –a, –um	īnferior, –ius	īnfimus, or īmus, –a, –um
posterus, –a, –um	posterior, –ius	postrēmus, or postumus, –a, –um
superus, –a, –um	superior, –ius	suprēmus, or summus, –a, –um
(cis, citrā)	citerior, –ius	citimus, –a, –um
(in, intrā)	interior, –ius	intimus, –a, –um
(prae, prō)	prior, prius	prīmus, –a, –um
(prope)	propior, –ius	proximus, –a, –um
(ūltrā)	ūlterior, –ius	ūltimus, –a, –um

408

DECLENSION OF COMPARATIVE ADJECTIVES

	M.&F.	N.	M.&F.	N.
SINGULAR				
Nom.	clārior	clārius	—	plūs
Gen.	clāriōris		—	plūris
Dat.	clāriōrī		—	—
Acc.	clāriōrem	clārius	—	plūs
Abl.	clāriōre		—	plūre
PLURAL				
Nom.	clāriōrēs	clāriōra	plūrēs	plūra
Gen.	clāriōrum		plūrium	
Dat.	clāriōribus		plūribus	
Acc.	clāriōrēs (-īs)	clāriōra	plūrēs (-īs)	plūra
Abl.	clāriōribus		plūribus	

In the singular **plūs** is used as a neuter noun and has no masculine or feminine forms.

Adverbs

REGULAR COMPARISON

Positive	Comparative	Superlative
clārē	clārius	clārissimē
līberē	līberius	līberrimē
fortiter	fortius	fortissimē
celeriter	celerius	celerrimē
similiter	similius	simillimē

IRREGULAR COMPARISON

Positive	Comparative	Superlative
bene	melius	optimē
male	pējus	pessimē
māgnopere	magis	māximē
multum	plūs	plūrimum
parum	minus	minimē

Declension of Pronouns

PERSONAL

	First Person		Second Person	
	SINGULAR	PLURAL	SINGULAR	PLURAL
Nom.	ego	nōs	tū	vōs
Gen.	meī	nostrum, nostrī	tuī	vestrum, vestrī
Dat.	mihi	nōbīs	tibi	vōbīs
Acc.	mē	nōs	tē	vōs
Abl.	mē	nōbīs	tē	vōbīs

There is no personal pronoun of the third person. Its place is taken either by a demonstrative pronoun (usually **is,** *he;* **ea,** *she;* **id,** *it*) or, if the antecedent is the subject of the sentence or clause, by a reflexive pronoun.

REFLEXIVE

| | First Person | | Second Person | | Third Person | |
	SINGULAR	PLURAL	SINGULAR	PLURAL	SINGULAR	PLURAL
Nom.	—	—	—	—	—	—
Gen.	meī	nostrī	tuī	vestrī	suī	suī
Dat.	mihi	nōbīs	tibi	vōbīs	sibi	sibi
Acc.	mē	nōs	tē	vōs	sē, sēsē	sē, sēsē
Abl.	mē	nōbīs	tē	vōbīs	sē, sēsē	sē, sēsē

POSSESSIVE

Referring to Singular Antecedent

First Person   **meus, –a, –um,** *my, mine*
Second Person **tuus, –a, –um,** *your, yours*
Third Person   **suus, –a, –um,** *his, her, hers, its* (reflexive)
                ējus (gen. sing. of **is**) *his, her, hers, its* (not reflexive)

Referring to Plural Antecedent

First Person   **noster, –tra, –trum**   *our, ours*
Second Person **vester, –tra, –trum**   *your, yours*
Third Person   **suus, –a, –um**   *their, theirs* (reflexive)
                eōrum, eārum, eōrum (gen. pl. of **is**) *their, theirs* (not reflexive)

The vocative masculine singular of **meus** is **mī. Meus, tuus, suus, noster, vester** are used as adjectives, agreeing with the thing possessed.

DEMONSTRATIVE PRONOUNS AND ADJECTIVES

| | SINGULAR | | | PLURAL | | |
	M.	F.	N.	M.	F.	N.
Nom.	hic	haec	hoc	hī	hae	haec
Gen.		hūjus			hōrum	hārum	hōrum
Dat.		huic			hīs		
Acc.	hunc	hanc	hoc	hōs	hās	haec
Abl.	hōc	hāc	hōc		hīs		
Nom.	ille	illa	illud	illī	illae	illa
Gen.		illīus			illōrum	illārum	illōrum
Dat.		illī			illīs		
Acc.	illum	illam	illud	illōs	illās	illa
Abl.	illō	illā	illō		illīs		
Nom.	is	ea	id	eī, iī	eae	ea
Gen.		ējus			eōrum	eārum	eōrum
Dat.		eī			eīs, iīs		
Acc.	eum	eam	id	eōs	eās	ea
Abl.	eō	eā	eō		eīs, iīs		

	SINGULAR			PLURAL		
	M.	F.	N.	M.	F.	N.
Nom.	iste	ista	istud	istī	istae	ista
Gen.		istīus		istōrum	istārum	istōrum
Dat.		istī			istīs	
Acc.	istum	istam	istud	istōs	istās	ista
Abl.	istō	istā	istō		istīs	

	M.	F.	N.	M.	F.	N.
Nom.	īdem	eadem	idem	eīdem, īdem	eaedem	eadem
Gen.		ējusdem		eōrundem	eārundem	eōrundem
Dat.		eīdem			eīsdem, iīsdem	
Acc.	eundem	eandem	idem	eōsdem	eāsdem	eadem
Abl.	eōdem	eādem	eōdem		eīsdem, iīsdem	

INTENSIVE PRONOUN AND ADJECTIVE

	SINGULAR			PLURAL		
	M.	F.	N.	M.	F.	N.
Nom.	ipse	ipsa	ipsum	ipsī	ipsae	ipsa
Gen.		ipsīus		ipsōrum	ipsārum	ipsōrum
Dat.		ipsī			ipsīs	
Acc.	ipsum	ipsam	ipsum	ipsōs	ipsās	ipsa
Abl.	ipsō	ipsā	ipsō		ipsīs	

RELATIVE PRONOUN

	SINGULAR			PLURAL		
	M.	F.	N.	M.	F.	N.
Nom.	quī	quae	quod	quī	quae	quae
Gen.		cūjus		quōrum	quārum	quōrum
Dat.		cui			quibus	
Acc.	quem	quam	quod	quōs	quās	quae
Abl.	quō	quā	quō		quibus	

INTERROGATIVE PRONOUN AND ADJECTIVE

	SINGULAR					PLURAL		
	Pronoun		*Adjective*			*Pronoun and Adjective*		
	M.&F.	N.	M.	F.	N.	M.	F.	N.
Nom.	quis	quid	quī	quae	quod	quī	quae	quae
Gen.	cūjus			cūjus		quōrum	quārum	quōrum
Dat.	cui			cui			quibus	
Acc.	quem	quid	quem	quam	quod	quōs	quās	quae
Abl.	quō		quō	quā	quō		quibus	

411

The interrogative adjective in the singular is the same as the relative pronoun, except that the nominative masculine may be **quis** or **quī**. The plural of the interrogative adjective and pronoun and the relative pronoun is the same.

INDEFINITE PRONOUNS AND ADJECTIVES

Pronouns	*Adjectives*
quis, quid, *anyone, anything*	**quī, quae (qua), quod,** *any*
aliquis, aliquid, *someone*	**aliquī, aliqua, aliquod,** *some*
quisque, quidque, *each one*	**quīque, quaeque, quodque,** *each*
quīdam, quaedam, quiddam, *a certain person or thing*	**quīdam, quaedam, quoddam,** *a certain*

1. Indefinite pronouns are declined in general like the interrogative **quis**.
2. Indefinite adjectives are declined in general like the relative pronoun **quī**.
3. The feminine singular of the indefinite adjective **aliquī** is **aliqua**.
4. In the declension of **quīdam**, **m** becomes **n** before **d**.
5. The indefinite **quis, quid**, is generally used after **sī, nisi, num,** or **nē.**

Regular Verbs

PRINCIPAL PARTS

First Conj.	*Second Conj.*	*Third Conj.*	*Third Conj. (–io)*	*Fourth Conj.*
vocō	**moneō**	**regō**	**capiō**	**audiō**
vocāre	**monēre**	**regere**	**capere**	**audīre**
vocāvī	**monuī**	**rēxī**	**cēpī**	**audīvī**
vocātus	**monitus**	**rēctus**	**captus**	**audītus**

STEMS *

vocā–	monē–	rege–	cape–	audī–
vocāv–	monu–	rēx–	cēp–	audīv–
vocāt–	monit–	rēct–	capt–	audīt–

INDICATIVE MOOD

Active Voice

PRESENT

I call, am calling, do call	*I warn, am warning, do warn*	*I rule, am ruling, do rule*	*I take, am taking, do take*	*I hear, am hearing, do hear*
voc**ō**	mone**ō**	reg**ō**	cap**iō**	aud**iō**
voc**ās**	mon**ēs**	reg**is**	cap**is**	aud**īs**
voc**at**	mon**et**	reg**it**	cap**it**	aud**it**
voc**āmus**	mon**ēmus**	reg**imus**	cap**imus**	aud**īmus**
voc**ātis**	mon**ētis**	reg**itis**	cap**itis**	aud**ītis**
voc**ant**	mon**ent**	reg**unt**	cap**iunt**	aud**iunt**

* In the following paradigms the stem or the part of a stem that is used in a given form appears in lightface type. **The tense indicator and person indicator appear in boldface type.** *Generally, letters that are neither a part of the stem nor a part of the indicators appear in italics.* **In certain forms where such type distinction is impractical, the entire form appears in boldface type.**

412

I was calling, called, used to call	*I was warning, warned, used to warn*	*I was ruling, ruled, used to rule*	*I was taking, took, used to take*	*I was hearing, heard, used to hear*
vocābam	monēbam	regēbam	capiēbam	audiēbam
vocābās	monēbās	regēbās	capiēbās	audiēbās
vocābat	monēbat	regēbat	capiēbat	audiēbat
vocābāmus	monēbāmus	regēbāmus	capiēbāmus	audiēbāmus
vocābātis	monēbātis	regēbātis	capiēbātis	audiēbātis
vocābant	monēbant	regēbant	capiēbant	audiēbant

FUTURE

I shall call	*I shall warn*	*I shall rule*	*I shall take*	*I shall hear*
vocābō	monēbō	regam	capiam	audiam
vocābis	monēbis	regēs	capiēs	audiēs
vocābit	monēbit	reget	capiet	audiet
vocābimus	monēbimus	regēmus	capiēmus	audiēmus
vocābitis	monēbitis	regētis	capiētis	audiētis
vocābunt	monēbunt	regent	capient	audient

PERFECT

I called, have called	*I warned, have warned*	*I ruled, have ruled*	*I took, have taken*	*I heard, have heard*
vocāvī	monuī	rēxī	cēpī	audīvī
vocāvistī	monuistī	rēxistī	cēpistī	audīvistī
vocāvit	monuit	rēxit	cēpit	audīvit
vocāvimus	monuimus	rēximus	cēpimus	audīvimus
vocāvistis	monuistis	rēxistis	cēpistis	audīvistis
vocāvērunt	monuērunt	rēxērunt	cēpērunt	audīvērunt

PLUPERFECT

I had called	*I had warned*	*I had ruled*	*I had taken*	*I had heard*
vocāveram	monueram	rēxeram	cēperam	audīveram
vocāverās	monuerās	rēxerās	cēperās	audīverās
vocāverat	monuerat	rēxerat	cēperat	audīverat
vocāverāmus	monuerāmus	rēxerāmus	cēperāmus	audīverāmus
vocāverātis	monuerātis	rēxerātis	cēperātis	audīverātis
vocāverant	monuerant	rēxerant	cēperant	audīverant

FUTURE PERFECT

I shall have called	*I shall have warned*	*I shall have ruled*	*I shall have taken*	*I shall have heard*
vocāverō	monuerō	rēxerō	cēperō	audīverō
vocāveris	monueris	rēxeris	cēperis	audīveris
vocāverit	monuerit	rēxerit	cēperit	audīverit
vocāverimus	monuerimus	rēxerimus	cēperimus	audīverimus
vocāveritis	monueritis	rēxeritis	cēperitis	audīveritis
vocāverint	monuerint	rēxerint	cēperint	audīverint

Passive Voice

PRESENT

I am called	*I am warned*	*I am ruled*	*I am taken*	*I am heard*
vocor	moneor	regor	capior	audior
vocāris	monēris	regeris	caperis	audīris
vocātur	monētur	regitur	capitur	audītur
vocāmur	monēmur	regimur	capimur	audīmur
vocāminī	monēminī	regiminī	capiminī	audīminī
vocantur	monentur	reguntur	capiuntur	audiuntur

IMPERFECT

I was called	*I was warned*	*I was ruled*	*I was taken*	*I was heard*
vocābar	monēbar	regēbar	capiēbar	audiēbar
vocābāris	monēbāris	regēbāris	capiēbāris	audiēbāris
vocābātur	monēbātur	regēbātur	capiēbātur	audiēbātur
vocābāmur	monēbāmur	regēbāmur	capiēbāmur	audiēbāmur
vocābāminī	monēbāminī	regēbāminī	capiēbāminī	audiēbāminī
vocābantur	monēbantur	regēbantur	capiēbantur	audiēbantur

FUTURE

I shall be called	*I shall be warned*	*I shall be ruled*	*I shall be taken*	*I shall be heard*
vocābor	monēbor	regar	capiar	audiar
vocāberis	monēberis	regēris	capiēris	audiēris
vocābitur	monēbitur	regētur	capiētur	audiētur
vocābimur	monēbimur	regēmur	capiēmur	audiēmur
vocābiminī	monēbiminī	regēminī	capiēminī	audiēminī
vocābuntur	monēbuntur	regentur	capientur	audientur

PERFECT

I was called, have been called		*I was warned, have been warned*		*I was ruled, have been ruled*	
vocātus, −a, −um	sum es est	monitus, −a, −um	sum, etc.	rēctus, −a, −um	sum, etc.
vocātī −ae, −a	sumus estis sunt	monitī, −ae, −a		rēctī, −ae, −a	

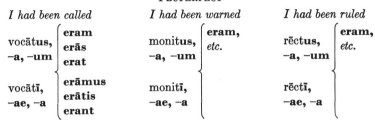

I was taken,
have been taken

captus, { **sum,**
–a, –um *etc.*

captī,
–ae, –a

I was heard,
have been heard

audītus, { **sum,**
–a, –um *etc.*

audītī,
–ae, a

Pluperfect

I had been called

vocātus, { **eram**
–a, –um **erās**
  erat

vocātī, { **erāmus**
–ae, –a **erātis**
  erant

I had been warned

monitus, { **eram,**
–a, –um *etc.*

monitī,
–ae, –a

I had been ruled

rēctus, { **eram,**
–a, –um *etc.*

rēctī,
–ae, –a

I had been taken

captus, { **eram,**
–a, –um *etc.*

captī,
–ae, –a

I had been heard

audītus, { **eram,**
–a, –um *etc.*

audītī,
–ae, –a

Future Perfect

I shall have been
called

vocātus, { **erō**
–a, –um **eris**
  erit

vocātī, { **erimus**
–ae, –a **eritis**
  erunt

I shall have been
warned

monitus, { **erō,**
–a, –um *etc.*

monitī,
–ae, –a

I shall have been
ruled

rēctus, { **erō,**
–a, –um *etc.*

rēctī,
–ae, –a

I shall have been
taken

captus, { **erō,**
–a, –um *etc.*

captī,
–ae, –a

I shall have been
heard

audītus, { **erō,**
–a, –um *etc.*

audītī,
–ae, –a

415

SUBJUNCTIVE MOOD

Active Voice

PRESENT

vocem	moneam	regam	capiam	audiam
vocēs	moneās	regās	capiās	audiās
vocet	moneat	regat	capiat	audiat
vocēmus	moneāmus	regāmus	capiāmus	audiāmus
vocētis	moneātis	regātis	capiātis	audiātis
vocent	moneant	regant	capiant	audiant

IMPERFECT

vocārem	monērem	regerem	caperem	audīrem
vocārēs	monērēs	regerēs	caperēs	audīrēs
vocāret	monēret	regeret	caperet	audīret
vocārēmus	monērēmus	regerēmus	caperēmus	audīrēmus
vocārētis	monērētis	regerētis	caperētis	audīrētis
vocārent	monērent	regerent	caperent	audīrent

PERFECT

vocāverim	monuerim	rēxerim	cēperim	audīverim
vocāverīs	monuerīs	rēxerīs	cēperīs	audīverīs
vocāverit	monuerit	rēxerit	cēperit	audīverit
vocāverīmus	monuerīmus	rēxerīmus	cēperīmus	audīverīmus
vocāverītis	monuerītis	rēxerītis	cēperītis	audīverītis
vocāverint	monuerint	rēxerint	cēperint	audīverint

PLUPERFECT

vocāvissem	monuissem	rēxissem	cēpissem	audīvissem
vocāvissēs	monuissēs	rēxissēs	cēpissēs	audīvissēs
vocāvisset	monuisset	rēxisset	cēpisset	audīvisset
vocāvissēmus	monuissēmus	rēxissēmus	cēpissēmus	audīvissēmus
vocāvissētis	monuissētis	rēxissētis	cēpissētis	audīvissētis
vocāvissent	monuissent	rēxissent	cēpissent	audīvissent

Passive Voice

PRESENT

vocer	monear	regar	capiar	audiar
vocēris	moneāris	regāris	capiāris	audiāris
vocētur	moneātur	regātur	capiātur	audiātur
vocēmur	moneāmur	regāmur	capiāmur	audiāmur
vocēminī	moneāminī	regāminī	capiāminī	audiāminī
vocentur	moneantur	regantur	capiantur	audiantur

vocārer	monērer	regerer	caperer	audīrer
vocārēris	monērēris	regerēris	caperēris	audīrēris
vocārētur	monērētur	regerētur	caperētur	audīrētur
vocārēmur	monērēmur	regerēmur	caperēmur	audīrēmur
vocārēminī	monērēminī	regerēminī	caperēminī	audīrēminī
vocārentur	monērentur	regerentur	caperentur	audīrentur

PERFECT

vocātus, −a, −um	sim sīs sit	monitus, −a, −um	sim, *etc.*	rēctus, −a, −um	sim, *etc.*
vocātī, −ae, −a	sīmus sītis sint	monitī, −ae, −a		rēctī, −ae, −a	

captus, −a, −um	sim, *etc.*	audītus, −a, −um	sim, *etc.*
captī, −ae, −a		audītī, −ae, −a	

PLUPERFECT

vocātus, −a, −um	essem essēs esset	monitus, −a, −um	essem, *etc.*	rēctus, −a, −um	essem, *etc.*
vocātī, −ae, −a	essēmus essētis essent	monitī, −ae, −a		rēctī, −ae, −a	

captus, −a, −um	essem, *etc.*	audītus, −a, −um	essem, *etc.*
captī, −ae, −a		audītī, −ae, −a	

IMPERATIVE MOOD

Active Voice

PRESENT

SING.	vocā, *call*	monē, *warn*	rege, *rule*	cape, *take*	audī, *hear*
PL.	vocāte, *call*	monēte, *warn*	regite, *rule*	capite, *take*	audīte, *hear*

417

INFINITIVES

	Active Voice			Passive Voice		
PRES.	vocāre monēre regere capere audīre	*to*	*call* *warn* *rule* *take* *hear*	vocārī monērī regī capī audīrī	*to be*	*called* *warned* *ruled* *taken* *heard*
PERF.	vocāvisse monuisse rēxisse cēpisse audīvisse	*to have*	*called* *warned* *ruled* *taken* *heard*	vocātus, –a, –um esse monitus, –a, –um esse rēctus, –a, –um esse captus, –a, –um esse audītus, –a, –um esse	*to have been*	*called* *warned* *ruled* *taken* *heard*
FUT.	vocātūrus, –a, –um esse monitūrus, –a, –um esse rēctūrus, –a, –um esse captūrus, –a, –um esse audītūrus, –a, –um esse	*to be about to*	*call* *warn* *rule* *take* *hear*			

The future passive infinitive is seldom used and therefore is not given here.

PARTICIPLES

	Active Voice			Passive Voice		
PRES.	vocāns, –antis monēns, –entis regēns, –entis capiēns, –entis audiēns, –entis	*calling* *warning* *ruling* *taking* *hearing*				
PERF.				vocātus, –a, –um monitus, –a, –um rēctus, –a, –um captus, –a, –um audītus, –a, –um	*having been*	*called* *warned* *ruled* *taken* *heard*
FUT.	vocātūrus, –a, –um monitūrus, –a, –um rēctūrus, –a, –um captūrus, –a, –um audītūrus, –a, –um	*about to*	*call* *warn* *rule* *take* *hear*	vocandus, –a, –um monendus, –a, –um regendus, –a, –um capiendus, –a, –um audiendus, –a, –um	*requir- ing to be*	*called* *warned* *ruled* *taken* *heard*

The future passive participle is also called the gerundive.

418

GERUNDS

Nom.	(vocāre)	(to call)	(monēre)	(regere)	(capere)	(audīre)
Gen.	vocandī	of calling	monendī	rēgendī	capiendī	audiendī
Dat.	vocandō	for calling	monendō	rēgendō	capiendō	audiendō
Acc.	vocandum	calling	monendum	rēgendum	capiendum	audiendum
Abl.	vocandō	by calling	monendō	rēgendō	capiendō	audiendō

The gerund has no nominative. The place of the nominative is filled by the infinitive.

SUPINES

Acc.	vocātum		monitum	rēctum	captum	audītum
Abl.	vocātū		monitū	rēctū	captū	audītū

Deponent Verbs

Deponent verbs have active meanings for passive forms. They are conjugated like the passive of their respective conjugations in the indicative, subjunctive, and imperative.

PRINCIPAL PARTS

First Conj.	Second Conj.	Third Conj.	Third Conj. (–io)	Fourth Conj.
cōnor	vereor	sequor	patior	largior
cōnārī	verērī	sequī	patī	largīrī
cōnātus sum	veritus sum	secūtus sum	passus sum	largītus sum

STEMS

cōnā–	verē–	seque–	pate–	largī–
cōnāt–	verit–	secūt–	pass–	largīt–

INDICATIVE MOOD
PRESENT

I try	I fear	I follow	I suffer	I bestow
cōnor	vereor	sequor	patior	largior
cōnāris	verēris	sequeris	pateris	largīris
cōnātur	verētur	sequitur	patitur	largītur
cōnāmur	verēmur	sequimur	patimur	largīmur
cōnāminī	verēminī	sequiminī	patiminī	largīminī
cōnantur	verentur	sequuntur	patiuntur	largiuntur

IMPERFECT

| cōnābar | verēbar | sequēbar | patiēbar | largiēbar |

FUTURE

| cōnābor | verēbor | sequar | patiar | largiar |

cōnātus sum	veritus sum	secūtus sum	passus sum	largītus sum

cōnātus eram	veritus eram	secūtus eram	passus eram	largītus eram

FUTURE PERFECT

cōnātus erō	veritus erō	secūtus erō	passus erō	largītus erō

SUBJUNCTIVE MOOD

PRESENT

cōner	verear	sequar	patiar	largiar

IMPERFECT

cōnārer	verērer	sequerer	paterer	largīrer

PERFECT

cōnātus sim	veritus sim	secūtus sim	passus sim	largītus sim

PLUPERFECT

cōnātus essem	veritus essem	secūtus essem	passus essem	largītus essem

IMPERATIVE MOOD

PRESENT

SING.	cōnāre	verēre	sequere	patere	largīre
PL.	cōnāminī	verēminī	sequiminī	patiminī	largīminī

INFINITIVES

PRESENT

cōnārī	verērī	sequī	patī	largīrī

PERFECT

cōnātus esse	veritus esse	secūtus esse	passus esse	largītus esse

FUTURE ACTIVE

cōnātūrus esse	veritūrus esse	secūtūrus esse	passūrus esse	largītūrus esse

PARTICIPLES

PRESENT ACTIVE

cōnāns	verēns	sequēns	patiēns	largiēns

FUTURE ACTIVE

cōnātūrus	veritūrus	secūtūrus	passūrus	largītūrus

PERFECT PASSIVE

cōnātus	veritus	secūtus	passus	largītus

FUTURE PASSIVE (GERUNDIVE)

cōnāndus	verendus	sequendus	patiendus	largiendus

420

GERUNDS

| Gen. | cōnand**ī** | verend**ī** | sequend**ī** | pat*iend*ī | larg*iend*ī |

SUPINES

| Acc. | cōnā**tum** | veri**tum** | secū**tum** | pass**um** | largī**tum** |
| Abl. | cōnā**tū** | veri**tū** | secū**tū** | pass**ū** | largī**tū** |

SEMIDEPONENT VERBS

Four verbs which have *active* forms in the tenses of the *present system* become *deponents* in the *perfect system;* they are called *semideponents.* They are:

audeō	**audēre**	**ausus sum,** *dare*
gaudeō	**gaudēre**	**gāvīsus sum,** *rejoice*
soleō	**solēre**	**solitus sum,** *be accustomed*
fīdō	**fīdere**	**fīsus sum,** *trust*

Periphrastic Conjugations

1. When the future active participle is used with the forms of the verb **sum,** it expresses future or intended action and is called the *active periphrastic.*

2. When the future passive participle (gerundive) is used with forms of **sum,** it denotes obligation or necessity and is called the *passive periphrastic.*

Active Periphrastic Conjugation

INDICATIVE		SUBJUNCTIVE
	PRESENT	
vocātūrus **sum**	*I am about to call*	vocātūrus **sim**
	IMPERFECT	
vocātūrus **eram**	*I was about to call*	vocātūrus **essem**
	FUTURE	
vocātūrus **erō**	*I shall be about to call*	—
	PERFECT	
vocātūrus **fuī**	*I have been, was about to call*	vocātūrus **fuerim**
	PLUPERFECT	
vocātūrus **fueram**	*I had been about to call*	vocātūrus **fuissem**
	FUTURE PERFECT	
vocātūrus **fuerō**	*I shall have been about to call*	—

INFINITIVES

| PRES. | vocātūrus **esse** |
| PERF. | vocātūrus **fuisse** |

421

INDICATIVE		SUBJUNCTIVE
	PRESENT	
vocandus sum	*I am to be, must be called*	vocandus sim
	IMPERFECT	
vocandus eram	*I was to be, had to be, called*	vocandus essem
	FUTURE	
vocandus erō	*I shall have to be called*	—
	PERFECT	
vocandus fuī	*I was to be, had to be, called*	vocandus fuerim
	PLUPERFECT	
vocandus fueram	*I had had to be called*	vocandus fuissem
	FUTURE PERFECT	
vocandus fuerō	*I shall have had to be called*	—

Irregular Verbs

Sum, *I am*

PRINCIPAL PARTS: **sum, esse, fuī, futūrus**

INDICATIVE MOOD

PRESENT	IMPERFECT	FUTURE
I am	*I was*	*I shall be*
sum	eram	erō
es	erās	eris
est	erat	erit
sumus	erāmus	erimus
estis	erātis	eritis
sunt	erant	erunt

PERFECT	PLUPERFECT	FUTURE PERFECT
I have been, was	*I had been*	*I shall have been*
fuī	fueram	fuerō
fuistī	fuerās	fueris
fuit	fuerat	fuerit
fuimus	fuerāmus	fuerimus
fuistis	fuerātis	fueritis
fuērunt	fuerant	fuerint

SUBJUNCTIVE MOOD

Present	Imperfect	Perfect	Pluperfect
sim	essem	fuerim	fuissem
sīs	essēs	fuerīs	fuissēs
sit	esset	fuerit	fuisset
sīmus	essēmus	fuerīmus	fuissēmus
sītis	essētis	fuerītis	fuissētis
sint	essent	fuerint	fuissent

IMPERATIVE MOOD

PRES. SING. **es,** *be*
PRES. PL.   **este,** *be*

INFINITIVES

PRES. **esse,** *to be*
PERF. **fuisse,** *to have been*
FUT. **futūrus, –a, –um esse**
   or **fore,** *to be about to*
   (to be going to) be

PARTICIPLE

FUT. **futūrus, –a, –um,**
   about to
   (going to) be

Possum, *I am able, I can*

PRINCIPAL PARTS: **possum, posse, potuī**

INDICATIVE MOOD

Present	Imperfect	Future
I am able, I can	*I was able, I could*	*I shall be able*
possum	poteram	poterō
potes	poterās	poteris
potest	poterat	poterit
possumus	poterāmus	poterimus
potestis	poterātis	poteritis
possunt	poterant	poterunt

Perfect	Pluperfect	Future Perfect
I have been able, I could	*I had been able*	*I shall have been able*
potuī	potueram	potuerō
potuistī	potuerās	potueris
potuit	potuerat	potuerit
potuimus	potuerāmus	potuerimus
potuistis	potuerātis	potueritis
potuērunt	potuerant	potuerint

SUBJUNCTIVE MOOD

Present	Imperfect	Perfect	Pluperfect
possim	possem	potuerim	potuissem
possīs	possēs	potuerīs	potuissēs
possit	posset	potuerit	potuisset
possīmus	possēmus	potuerīmus	potuissēmus
possītis	possētis	potuerītis	potuissētis
possint	possent	potuerint	potuissent

423

INFINITIVES	PARTICIPLE

PRES. posse, *to be able*
PERF. potuisse, *to have been able*

PRES. potēns (adj.), *powerful*

Ferō, *I bear, I bring*

PRINCIPAL PARTS: **ferō, ferre, tulī, lātus**

Active Voice   *Passive Voice*

INDICATIVE MOOD

PRES.	fero	ferimus	feror	ferimur
	fers	fertis	ferris	feriminī
	fert	ferunt	fertur	feruntur

IMPERF.	ferēbam		ferēbar
FUT.	feram		ferar
PERF.	tulī		lātus, –a, –um sum
PLUPERF.	tuleram		lātus, –a, –um eram
FUT. PERF.	tulerō		lātus, –a, –um erō

SUBJUNCTIVE MOOD

PRES.	feram	ferar
IMPERF.	ferrem	ferrer
PERF.	tulerim	lātus, –a, –um sim
PLUPERF.	tulissem	lātus, –a, –um essem

IMPERATIVE MOOD

SING.	fer	—
PL.	ferte	—

INFINITIVES

PRES.	ferre	ferrī
PERF.	tulisse	lātus, –a, –um esse
FUT.	lātūrus, –a, –um esse	—

PARTICIPLES

PRES.	ferēns	—
PERF.	—	lātus, –a, –um
FUT.	lātūrus, –a, –um	ferendus, –a, –um

GERUND
Gen.   ferendī, *etc.*

SUPINE
Acc.   lātum
Abl.   lātū

Eō, *I go*

PRINCIPAL PARTS: **eō, īre, iī (īvī), itūrus**

INDICATIVE MOOD

PRES.		IMPERF.	ībam
eō	īmus	FUT.	ībō
īs	ītis	PERF.	iī (īvī)
it	eunt	PLUPERF.	ieram
		FUT. PERF.	ierō

SUBJUNCTIVE MOOD

PRES.	eam
IMPERF.	īrem
PERF.	ierim
PLUPERF.	īssem

IMPERATIVE MOOD

SING.	ī
PL.	īte

INFINITIVES

PRES.	īre
PERF.	īsse (iisse)
FUT.	itūrus, –a, –um esse

PARTICIPLES

PRES.	iēns, *euntis*
FUT.	itūrus, –a, –um
PERF.	itum (*impers.*)
FUT.	eundus, –a, –um

Fīō, *I am made* (passive of **faciō**)

PRINCIPAL PARTS: **fīō, fierī, factus sum**

INDICATIVE MOOD

PRES.		IMPERF.	fiēbam
fīō	—	FUT.	fīam
—	—	PERF.	factus sum
fit	fīunt	PLUPERF.	factus eram
		FUT. PERF.	factus erō

SUBJUNCTIVE MOOD

PRES.	fīam
IMPERF.	fierem
PERF.	factus sim
PLUPERF.	factus essem

IMPERATIVE MOOD

SING.	fī
PL.	fīte

INFINITIVES

PRES.	fierī
PERF.	factus, –a, –um esse

PARTICIPLES

PERF.	factus, –a, –um
FUT.	faciendus, –a, –um

GERUND

Gen. facie**ndī**, *etc.*

Volō, *be willing;* Nōlō, *be unwilling;* Mālō, *prefer*

PRINCIPAL PARTS

volō, velle, voluī	nōlō, nōlle, nōluī	mālō, mālle, māluī

INDICATIVE MOOD

PRES.	volō	volumus	nōlō	nōlumus	mālō	mālumus
	vīs	vultis	nōn vīs	nōn vultis	māvīs	māvultis
	vult	volunt	nōn vult	nōlunt	māvult	mālunt
IMPERF.	volēbam		nōlēbam		mālēbam	
FUT.	volam		nōlam		mālam	

PERF.	voluī	nōluī	māluī
PLUPERF.	volueram	nōlueram	mālueram
FUT. PERF.	voluerō	nōluerō	māluerō

SUBJUNCTIVE MOOD

PRES.	velim velīmus	nōlim nōlīmus	mālim mālīmus
	velīs velītis	nōlīs nōlītis	mālīs mālītis
	velit velint	nōlit nōlint	mālit mālint
IMPERF.	vellem	nōllem	māllem
PERF.	voluerim	nōluerim	māluerim
PLUPERF.	voluissem	nōluissem	māluissem

IMPERATIVE MOOD

—	nōlī, nōlīte	—

INFINITIVES

PRES.	velle	nōlle	mālle
PERF.	voluisse	nōluisse	māluisse

PARTICIPLES

PRES.	volēns, –entis	nōlēns, –entis	—

Defective Verbs

Verbs which lack certain forms are said to be *defective*. The following verbs are defective in that they have no present system: **coepī**, *I began;* **meminī**. *I remember;* **ōdī**, *I hate.*

INDICATIVE MOOD

PERF.	coepī	meminī	ōdī
PLUPERF.	coeperam	memineram	ōderam
FUT. PERF.	coeperō	meminerō	ōderō

SUBJUNCTIVE MOOD

PERF.	coeperim	meminerim	ōderim
PLUPERF.	coepissem	meminissem	ōdissem

IMPERATIVE MOOD

—	mementō	—
	mementōte	

INFINITIVES

PERF.	coepisse	meminisse	ōdisse
FUT.	coeptūrus, –a, –um esse	—	ōsūrus, –a, –um esse

PARTICIPLES

PERF.	coeptus, –a, –um		ōsus, –a, –um

426

Note that **meminī** and **ōdī**, while perfect in form, have the meanings of the present. The pluperfect and future perfect have the meanings of the imperfect and future, respectively. **Coepī** is used only in the perfect system. For the present system **incipiō** is used.

Impersonal Verbs

1. Impersonal verbs appear in the neuter of the third person singular of each tense and in the infinitive. The most common are **licet,** *it is permitted,* and **oportet,** *it is proper.* For the principal parts, see Vocabulary, pages 488, 494.

2. Some verbs are used impersonally with a special meaning, as:

accēdit, *it is added*	**accidit,** *it happens*	**placet,** *it pleases*
cōnstat, *it is evident*	**praestat,** *it is better*	**vidētur,** *it seems best*

3. Intransitive verbs may be used in the passive impersonally, as:

ītur, *some one goes* (lit., *it is gone*)	**curritur,** *some one runs* (lit., *it is run*)
ventum est, *some one came* (lit., *it was come*)	**pūgnābātur,** *fighting was going on* (lit., *it was being fought*)

Contracted Forms

Perfects in **–āvī** and **–ēvī** (as well as other tenses in the perfect system) are sometimes contracted, losing **–ve–** before **–r,** and **–vi–** before **–s,** as:

amārunt for **amāvērunt; cōnsuērat** for **cōnsuēverat**

Summary of Rules of Syntax

Agreement

A word is said to agree with another when it is required by usage to be in the same gender, number, case, or person. There are four general forms of agreement:

1. The agreement of a noun in apposition or as a predicate noun.
2. The agreement of the adjective with its noun.
3. The agreement of the relative with its antecedent.
4. The agreement of the finite verb with its subject.

1. *Agreement of Nouns*

    a. A noun used to describe another is called an *appositive* and is said to be in *apposition.* An appositive generally agrees with its noun in *gender* and *number,* but it always agrees in *case.*

    Urbem *Rōmam* incendērunt.   They burned the city (of) *Rome.*

b. A *predicate noun* is in the same case as its subject.

Ancus pācis semper *homō* erat.	*Ancus* was always *a man* of peace.
Dīxit *Ancum* pācis semper *hominem* **esse.**	He said that *Ancus* was always *a man* of peace.

2. *Agreement of Adjectives*

a. Adjectives agree in gender, number, and case with the nouns which they modify or to which they refer.

***bonus* imperātor**   a *good* commander

Bonus modifies or restricts the noun **imperātor**.

b. An adjective describing two or more nouns of different gender regularly agrees with the nearest.

vir et cōnsilī *māgnī* et virtūtis   a man of *great* wisdom and courage

c. A *predicate adjective* after a linking verb refers to the subject and agrees with it in gender, number, and case. Forms of the verb **sum** and passive forms of **videō** and **faciō** are the most frequently used of the linking verbs.

Imperātor *bonus* vidētur.   The commander seems *good*.

d. A *predicate adjective* describing two or more nouns of different gender is regularly plural; it is *masculine* when the nouns described are *persons,* and usually *neuter* when the nouns denote *things* or *abstract qualities.*

Pater et māter sunt *bonī*.	Father and mother are *good*.
Oppidum et vīcus sunt *parva*.	The town and the village are *small*.

e. A *predicate adjective* after a complementary infinitive is in the nominative case, agreeing with the subject of the main verb.

Amīcus *fīdus* esse dēbet.   A friend ought to be *faithful*.

f. A *predicate adjective* after an objective infinitive is in the accusative case, agreeing with the subject of the infinitive.

Vir amīcum *fīdum* esse cupit.   A man wishes his friend to be *faithful*.

g. Adjectives are often used as nouns, the masculine to denote *men* or *people in general;* the feminine to denote *women;* and the neuter to denote *things.*

nostrī, *our men*   **Sabīnae,** *the Sabine women*   **bona,** *goods, property*

h. An adjective agreeing with the subject or object is often used to modify the action of the verb, and so it is used in place of an adverb.

***Prīmus* vēnit.**	He was *the first* to come. He came *first*.
Fēminae *laetae* ad lūdōs properāvē-runt.	The women *joyfully* (*joyful*) hurried to the games.

i. A *participle*, as a verbal adjective, follows the rules for the agreement of adjectives.

Nōs *moritūrī* tē salūtāmus!   We, (*who are*) *about to die*, salute you!

428

3. Agreement of Relative Pronouns

a. The *relative pronoun* agrees with its antecedent in *gender, person,* and *number,* but its *case* is determined by its use in its own clause.

Nōs quī sumus cīvēs cīvitātem servā-   We *who* are citizens will save the state.
bimus.

b. If a *relative pronoun* has two or more antecedents, it follows the rules for the agreement of predicate adjectives (p. 428).

Fīlium et fīliam, quōs dīlēxit, āmīsit.   He lost a son and daughter *whom* he loved.

c. The *relative pronoun* often agrees with a predicate noun in its clause instead of with the antecedent.

Alba Longa, quod erat parvum oppi-   Alba Longa, *which* was a small town
dum

d. The *antecedent* of the relative pronoun is sometimes omitted.

    quī legiōnis sīgnum ferēbat   (*he*) *who* carried the standard of the legion

e. The *relative pronoun* is never omitted as it sometimes is in English.

    praemium quod mihi dedērunt   the reward they gave me

f. When the *antecedent* is a singular collective noun, the relative may be plural if individuals are thought of.

Equitātum praemīsit quī vidērent.   He sent *the cavalry* ahead to see.

g. A *relative pronoun* often stands at the beginning of a sentence, serving to connect it with the sentence which precedes.

    Quae cum ita sint   And since *this* is so

4. Agreement of Verbs

a. A *finite verb,* that is, one having personal endings, agrees with its subject in *person* and *number.*

    Caesar respondit.   *Caesar replied.*

b. If the verb contains a participle, the participle agrees with the subject in *gender, number,* and *case.*

    Id nūntiātum est.   *This* was *reported.*
Agrōs vāstātōs esse exīstimābant.   They thought that *the fields* had been *laid waste.*

c. When the subject is a collective noun, the verb may be plural if the individuals are thought of.

    Multitūdō lapidēs conjiciēbant.   *The multitude were hurling* stones.

d. When there are two or more subjects:

    (1) The verb may agree with the nearest subject.

Orgetorīgis fīlia atque ūnus ē fīliīs   The daughter of Orgetorix and *one* of his
captus est.   sons *were captured.*

(2) The verb may be singular if the compound subject is regarded as one idea.

Matrona et Sēquana *dīvidit*   the Marne and the Seine *separate*

(3) The verb is singular when two or more singular subjects are connected by conjunctions meaning *or* or *nor*.

Neque **agrī cultūra** *nec* **ūsus bellī** *inter-*   *Neither* agriculture *nor* the practice of war
mittitur.   *is interrupted.*

     e. When subjects are of different persons, the verb is usually in the *first* person rather than the *second*, and in the *second* rather than the *third*. The first person is also *first* in order.

Si *tū* et *Tullia* valētis, ego et *Cicerō*   If *you* and *Tullia* are well, Cicero and *I*
valēmus.   *are well.*

Noun Syntax

1. *Nominative Case*

     a. The subject of a finite verb (that is, a verb which has person and number) is in the nominative case.

     b. A *predicate noun* is in the nominative case. It is connected with the subject by a linking verb, such as **sum, videor, fīō,** and the like, or by a passive form of a verb meaning *to call, choose, name, elect.*

         Sum *incola* Américae.   I am *an inhabitant* of America.
         Brūtus *cōnsul* creātus est.   Brutus was elected *consul.*

     c. A noun used in *apposition* to the *subject* of a finite verb is in the nominative case.

         Urbs *Rōma* est antīqua.   The city (of) *Rome* is ancient.

2. *Genitive Case*

     a. The genitive case is used to denote *possession* or *close connection:*

         liber *puerī*, *the boy's* book   **tribūnus *populī*,** tribune *of the people*

     b. A genitive naming the whole may depend upon words that express a part of that whole. Instead of the *genitive of the whole* (partitive genitive), the ablative with **ex** or **dē** is regularly used with **quīdam** (*a certain one*) and with cardinal numerals except **mīlia.**

         pars *mīlitum*   part *of the soldiers*
         quīdam *ē mīlitibus*   certain *of the soldiers*
         decem *ē mīlitibus*   ten *of the soldiers*

     c. The genitive of the whole is especially common with the neuter of adjectives and pronouns of quantity and with the adverb **satis,** *enough.*

         nihil *vīnī*   no *wine* (nothing *of wine*)
         plūs *pecūniae*   more *money* (more *of money*)

d. The genitive modified by an adjective may be used to describe a person or thing. This *genitive of description* is used for the most part to express measure, number, and permanent (never temporary) qualities.

> **mūrus *trium pedum***   a wall *of three feet* (in height)
> **homirēs *māgnae virtūtis***   men *of great courage*

(See ablative of description, p. 436.)

e. The *objective genitive* is used to express the receiver or the *object* of the action suggested by the noun on which it depends.

> **cupiditās *pācis***   eagerness *for (of) peace*
> **occāsiō *fugae***   chance *for (of) escape*

Certain adjectives denoting desire, knowledge, memory, fullness, power, skill, sharing, guilt, and their opposites are completed by the *objective genitive*.

> ***jūris* perītus**   skilled *in law*
> ***laudis* avidus**   greedy *for praise*

f. The *subjective genitive* is used to express the doer or the *subject* of the action.

> **adventus *Caesaris***   the arrival *of Caesar*
> **mora *exercitūs***   the delay *of the army*

g. The following words, though translated into English by expressions containing *of*, are adjectives in Latin and agree with their nouns:

extrēmus, *the end of*	**omnis,** *all of*	**ūltimus,** *the last part of*
medius, *the middle of*	**plērīque,** *most of*	**hī omnēs,** *all (of) these*
multus, *much of*	**reliquus,** *the rest of*	**summus mōns,** *the top of the mountain*
multī, *many of*	**summus,** *the top of*	**in colle mediō,** *halfway up the hill*

h. The *genitive* may be used as the logical object of verbs of *remembering* and *forgetting*.

Reminīscere *incommodī* populī Rō-mānī.   Remember (Be mindful of) *the disaster* of the Roman people.

3. *Dative Case*

a. The *indirect object* of a verb is in the dative case. Verbs meaning to *give, tell, show,* and *offer* often have an indirect object and a direct object:

> ***Servō* pecūniam dedit.**   He gave money *to the slave.*

b Many *intransitive verbs* by virtue of their meaning take a dative of indirect object; but the dative is translated into English as if it were the accusative. Such verbs have the following English meanings: *favor, help, injure, please, trust, distrust, command, obey, serve, resist, threaten, envy, pardon, spare, desire, persuade.*

> ***Cīvibus* persuāsit.**   He persuaded *the citizens.*

431

In the passive these verbs become impersonal and retain the dative. The perfect passive participle of such verbs is used only in the neuter.

> **Cīvibus persuāsum est.**   *The citizens* were persuaded.

c. Many *compound verbs* with the prefixes **ad–, ante–, circum–, con–, dē–, in–, inter–, ob–, post–, prae–, prō–, sub–,** and **super–** take the dative of indirect object. Verbs with the prefixes **ante–, in–, ob–, prae–,** and **sub–** are most frequently used.

> **Brūtus nāvibus praeerat.**   Brutus was in command of *the ships.*

d. The *dative of separation* is used with verbs of *taking away*, especially compounds with **ab–, dē–,** or **ex–.** It is usually confined to persons.

> **Mīlitī scūtum dētrāxit.**   He snatched a shield *from the soldier.*

e. The *dative of purpose* is used with certain verbs (most frequently **sum**) to indicate *what something is for, what purpose it serves,* or *what effect it produces.*

> **Hanc pecūniam *praemiō* dedī.**   I gave this money *as a reward (for a reward).*
> **Scūtum *impedīmentō* erit.**   The shield will be a *hindrance (for a hindrance).*

f. The *dative of reference* is used to denote the person or thing with reference to whom a statement is true. It corresponds to the English *so far as someone (something) is concerned, as for, for, to,* and *of.*

> **Praesidium *oppidō* relīquit.**   He left a garrison *for the town.*

g. The *double dative* combines the datives of *purpose* and *reference.*

> **Mīlitēs *hostibus impedīmentō* mīsit.**   He sent the soldiers *as a hindrance to the enemy.*

h. The *dative of agent* is used with the passive periphrastic to denote the agent or person by whom an act ought to be or must be done.

> **Auxilium *ducī* mittendum est.**   Help ought to be sent *by the leader.*

i. The *dative of possession* is used in the predicate with **sum** to indicate the *possessor;* the thing possessed is then in the nominative case as the subject of a form of **sum.** The dative of possession emphasizes the fact of ownership rather than the owner.

> **Sunt *tibi* multī librī.**   *You* have many books. (lit., Many books are *to you*.)

j. The *dative* is used *with adjectives.* The most common are adjectives meaning *near, similar, useful, equal, favorable, suitable, sufficient, friendly,* and their opposites.

> **Proximī sunt *Germānīs*.**   They are nearest *to the Germans.*

4. *Accusative Case*

a. The *direct object* of a transitive verb is in the accusative case.

> **Patriam laudāmus.**   We praise *our native land.*

(1) A verb which requires a direct object is called a *transitive* verb, because the action goes over (**trānseō,** *go over*) from the subject to the object. **Faciō,** *make, do,* is a transitive verb.

(2) A transitive verb may be used in the passive voice. The object then becomes the subject.

ACTIVE. **Nūntiōs mīsit.**   He sent *messengers.*
PASSIVE. **Nūntiī missī sunt.**   *Messengers* were sent.

(3) A verb which does not have a direct object is called an *intransitive* verb. **Currō,** *run,* is an intransitive verb.

(4) Intransitive verbs are not used in the passive voice in English, but in Latin they may be used in the passive impersonally.

Pūgnātum est.   *They fought.* (*It was fought.*)

(5) Some intransitive verbs, when compounded with prefixes, become transitive and may take a direct object. The most common of these prefixes are **ad–, circum–, in–, per–, prae–, sub,** and **trāns–.**

Id *flūmen* **Helvētiī trānsībant.**   The Helvetians were crossing this *river.*

b. Verbs meaning *make, choose, call, consider,* and the like may take *two accusatives.* The second object refers to the same person or thing as the direct object and is called the *predicate acccusative.*

Populus Brūtum *cōnsulem* **creāvit.**   The people elected Brutus *consul.*

The second accusative may be a predicate adjective.

Caesarem *certiōrem* **fēcērunt.**   They informed Caesar (made Caesar *more certain*).

In the passive the second object takes the nominative case.

Brūtus *cōnsul* **creātus est.**   Brutus was elected *consul.*
Caesar *certior* **factus est.**   Caesar was informed (was made *more certain*).

c. Verbs meaning *ask, demand,* or *teach* sometimes take *two accusatives,* one of the person and one of the thing.

Rōmānī multās *gentēs lēgēs* **suās docuērunt.**   The Romans taught many *nations* their own *laws.*

(1) In the passive the accusative of the thing may be retained.

(2) **Petō, poscō, postulō** take **ab,** and **quaerō** takes **ab, dē,** or **ex,** with the ablative of the person.

Pācem *ab Rōmānīs* **petīvērunt.**   They sought peace *from the Romans.*

d. Verbs compounded with **circum–** or **trāns–** often have two accusatives, one the object of the verb, the other of the preposition.

Mīlitēs *pontem* **trādūxit.**   He led *the soldiers* across *the bridge.*

In the passive the object of the prefix is retained.

Mīlitēs *pontem* trāductī sunt.   The soldiers were led across *the bridge.*

e. The *subject of an infinitive* is in the accusative case.

> **Puerum īre necesse est.**   *The boy* must go. (It is necessary that *the boy* go).

f. The *place toward which* or *limit of motion* is regularly expressed by the accusative with **ad** or **in**.

> **In urbem venit.**   He comes *into the city.*

With the names of cities, towns, small islands, **domus,** and a few other place words, the preposition is omitted.

Caesar *Rōmam* profectus est.   Caesar set out *for Rome.*
Domum contendērunt.   They hastened *home.*

Ad may be used with the meaning *in the vicinity of.*

> **Ad Genāvam pervēnit.**   He arrived *in the vicinity of* Geneva.

g. The accusative is used to express *extent of space* and *extent of time* (*duration of time*).

Mīlitēs *decem mīlia passuum* iter fēcērunt.   The soldiers marched *ten miles.*

> **Rēx *decem annōs* rēgnāvit.**   The king reigned (*for*) *ten years.*

h. The following prepositions govern the accusative case:

ad, *to*	**extrā,** *outside*	**prope,** *near*
adversus, *against*	**in,** *into, against*	**propter,** *on account of*
ante, *before*	**īnfrā,** *below*	**secundum,** *next to*
apud, *at, among*	**inter,** *between*	**sub,** *under, toward*
circiter, *about*	**intrā,** *within*	**super,** *over*
circum, *around*	**jūxtā,** *near*	**suprā,** *above*
cis, *this side of*	**ob,** *on account of*	**trāns,** *across*
citrā, *this side of*	**per,** *through*	**ūltrā,** *beyond*
contrā, *against*	**post,** *after*	**versus,** *toward*
ergā, *toward*	**praeter,** *past*	

The prepositions **in** and **sub** govern the accusative when they denote *place toward which* but the ablative when they denote *place where.*

in aquam, *into the water*   **in aquā,** *in the water*

5. *Ablative Case*

a. The *ablative of separation,* used with or without **ab, dē,** or **ex,** emphasizes the state of being apart. With verbs meaning *to free, to lack,* and *to deprive,* prepositions are regularly omitted; however, with words denoting persons, prepositions are regularly used.

Hostēs *ab urbe* prohibuērunt.   They kept the enemy away *from the city.*
Cīvēs *perīculō* līberāvit.   He freed the citizens *from danger.*
Patriam *ab hostibus* līberāvit.   He freed the fatherland *from the enemy.*

b. The *ablative* is used with **ab, dē,** or **ex** to denote the *place from which.*

> **Ex urbe fūgērunt.**   They fled *from the city.*

With names of cities, towns, small islands, **domus,** etc., the preposition is regularly omitted. If used, the preposition means *from the vicinity of.*

Rōmā **fūgērunt.**	They fled *from Rome.*
Ab Rōmā **fūgērunt.**	They fled *from the vicinity of Rome.*

c. The *ablative,* with or without **ab, dē,** or **ex,** is used to denote *source* or *origin.*

Marius humilissimō *genere* **nātus est.**	Marius was born of a very lowly *family.*
Belgae sunt ortī *ā Germānīs.*	The Belgians are descended *from the Germans.*

d. The *ablative* with **dē** or **ex** may be used to denote the *material* of which something is made.

Nāvēs factae sunt *ex rōbore.*	The ships were made *of oak.*

e. The *ablative of personal agent* is used to denote the person by whom an action is done. This ablative requires the *passive voice,* a *person,* and the *preposition* **ā** or **ab.**

Frūmentum *ā servīs* **portābātur.**	The grain was carried *by the slaves.*

f. The *ablative of cause* is used to express the cause, reason, or motive of the action expressed by the verb. It is generally used without a preposition; sometimes it is used with **dē** or **ex.** This ablative is frequently used with verbs and adjectives which express emotion.

Hīs rēbus **labōrābat.**	He was suffering *on account of these conditions.*

Cause is frequently expressed by **propter** or **ob** with the accusative.

Propter **(***Ob***)** *tempestātem* **timēbant.**	They were afraid *on account of the storm.*

A common use of the ablative of cause is **causā** following a genitive.

lībertātis *causā*	*for the sake* of freedom

g. The *ablative of comparison* may be used after comparative adjectives (nominative and accusative only) and after comparative adverbs.

Eōrum vītam suā *salūte* **habēbat cāriōrem.**	He held their life dearer than his own *safety.*
Longius *annō* **remanēbat.**	He remained longer than *a year.*

The Latin also expresses comparison with **quam,** *than,* as in English. The two things compared are then in the same case. **Quam** must be expressed if the first of the two things compared is in the genitive, dative, or ablative.

Erant cupidiōrēs *bellī* **quam** *pācis.*	They were more eager for *war* than for *peace.*

h. The *ablative of degree of difference,* without a preposition, is used with comparatives and words implying comparison to express a measure of difference between persons or things. Words implying comparison are **paulō, multō, post, ante,** etc., which may be regarded as adverbs.

Pede altior quam frāter est.	He is *a foot* taller (taller *by a foot*) than his brother.
tribus annīs ante	*three years* ago (before *by three years*)
multō mājor	*much* larger (larger *by much*)

i. The *ablative of accompaniment* with **cum** is used to denote accompaniment or conflict.

Puer *cum patre* ambulat.	The boy is walking *with his father.*
Graecī *cum Rōmānīs* pūgnāvērunt.	The Greeks fought *with the Romans.*

Cum is sometimes omitted in *military expressions* containing a modifying adjective (other than a numeral).

Omnibus cōpiīs contendērunt.	They hastened *with all their forces.*

j. The *ablative* of abstract nouns is regularly used with the preposition **cum** to express the *manner* of an action. When there is a modifying adjective, **cum** may be omitted.

Puer *cum studiō* labōrat.	The boy is working *with zeal.*
Puer *māgnō (cum) studiō* labōrat.	The boy is working *with great zeal.*

k. The *ablative of description*, without a preposition but always with a modifying adjective, is used to denote some quality of a noun. It is the only ablative that regularly modifies a noun. It is regularly used for temporary qualities, such as personal appearance, but it may also be used for permanent characteristics. (See *genitive of description*, p. 431.)

hominēs *inimīcā faciē*	men *with an unfriendly appearance*
mōns *māgnā altitūdine*	a mountain *of (with) great height*

l. The *ablative of means*, without a preposition, is used to denote the means or instrument of an action — persons as well as things.

Gladiō pūgnābat.	He was fighting *with a sword.*

m. The *ablative* is used with the *deponent verbs* **ūtor, fruor, fungor, potior,** and **vescor.** In English these verbs govern direct objects.

Oppidīs potītī sunt.	They got possession of *the towns.*

Potior occasionally takes the genitive.

Totīus Galliae potīrī cōnātī sunt.	They tried to get possession of *all Gaul.*

n. The *ablative* is used *with adjectives* meaning *worthy of, full of, relying on,* and *contented with.* Such adjectives are **dīgnus, indīgnus, frētus, contentus,** etc. (**Plēnus** generally takes the genitive.)

victōriīs frētī	relying on *their victories*
vir *laude* dīgnus	a man worthy of *praise*

o. The *ablative of specification (respect)*, without a preposition, is used to indicate in what respect the meaning of a verb, noun, or adjective applies. It answers the question: "In what respect?"

Sociōs *virtūte* superābat.	He surpassed his companions *in courage.*

436

The ablative supine (p. 452) is used as an ablative of respect.

optimum *factū*   the best thing *to do*

p. The *ablative absolute* is equivalent to an adverbial clause and is expressed by a noun and a participle, a noun and an adjective, or two nouns in the ablative case. Grammatically it is independent of the rest of the sentence. It may represent clauses of time, cause, concession, condition, etc.

Rēge interfectō . . .	*After he had killed the king* . . . (Time)
Superātīs Belgīs . . .	*Since the Belgians were conquered* . . . (Cause)
Pāce factā . . .	*If peace is made* . . . (Condition)
Caesare vīvō . . .	*During Caesar's lifetime* . . . (Noun and adjective)
Regulō duce . . .	*With Regulus as leader* . . . (Two nouns)

q. The *ablative* is governed by the following *prepositions:*

ā, ab, or **abs,** *from, by*	**ē** or **ex,** *from, out of*	**prō,** *in front of, for*
cum, *with*	**in,** in	**sine,** *without*
dē, *from, concerning*	**prae,** *before*	**sub,** under

(1) The prepositions **in** and **sub** govern the ablative when they denote *place where,* but the accusative when they denote *place toward which.*

sub aquā   *under the water*
sub jugum mittere   *to send under the yoke*

(2) **Cum,** when used with the personal and reflexive pronouns, becomes an enclitic; it may also be used as an enclitic with the relative and interrogative pronouns: **vōbīscum,** *with you;* **sēcum,** *with themselves;* **quibuscum,** *with whom.*

r. The *ablative* is used without a preposition to express *time when* or *within which.*

eō tempore, *at that time*   **paucīs diēbus,** *within a few days*

s. The *ablative* is used with the preposition **in** or **sub** to express *place where (place in which).*

In Ītaliā **manēbat.**   He remained *in Italy.*
Sub monte **pūgnāvērunt.**   They fought *at the foot of the mountain.*

The preposition may be omitted with certain words like **locō, locīs, parte, partibus,** and also in certain fixed expressions like **tōtō orbe terrārum,** *in the whole world.* With names of cities, towns, small islands, **domus,** and a few other place words, *place where* is expressed by the *locative case* without a preposition.

6. *Locative Case*

With names of cities, towns, small islands, **domus,** and a few other place words, *place where* is expressed by the *locative case* without a preposition.

a. In the singular of the first and second declensions, the form of the locative is identical with the genitive.

Alesiae, *at Alesia*   **domī,** *at home*

437

b. In the first and second declension plural, and in the third declension, the locative is formed like the dative or ablative.

Athēnīs   *at Athens*
Carthāginī or **Carthāgine**   *at Carthage*

7. *Vocative Case*

a. The person or thing addressed is in the *vocative* case. The vocative is postpositive, that is, it stands after one or more words in the sentence.

Ad castra venīte, *puerī.*   Come to the camp, *boys.*

b. The form of the vocative is regularly like the nominative except in the second declension.

(1) Nouns and adjectives of this declension ending in –us have a vocative singular in –e.

Amīce cāre!   *O dear friend!*

(2) **Fīlius** and proper names in –ius have a vocative in –ī (not –ie).

Cornēlī, fīlī!   *O Cornelius, (my) son!*

(3) The vocative singular of **deus**, *god*, is **deus;** the vocative masculine singular of **meus**, is **mī.**

Fīlī mī!   *My son!*

Verb Syntax

1. *Moods.* There are three moods in Latin: the indicative, the subjunctive, and the imperative.

a. The *indicative* mood asserts a fact or asks a question. It may be used in principal (independent) and subordinate (dependent) clauses.

b. The *subjunctive* mood represents an act as willed, desired, conditioned, or prospective. It is often translated as the English indicative. It may be used in both principal and subordinate clauses.

c. The *imperative* mood is used to express a command.

2. *Tenses of the Indicative.* The tenses of the indicative are classified in two groups: primary (principal) and secondary (historical). The *primary* tenses are: the present, future, present perfect, and future perfect. The *secondary* tenses are: the imperfect, (historical) perfect, and pluperfect.

a. The *present* tense indicates present time or describes an action as *now* going on.

Bellum nunc gerunt.   *They are* now *waging* war.

438

For the sake of vividness past events are sometimes stated in Latin in the present tense. It is generally best to translate this *historical present* by the English past tense.

> **Rōmam *proficīscuntur*.**   *They depart(ed) for Rome.*

(1) When the historical present is vivid enough to be a *real present*, it is followed by a *primary* tense; when it is *definitely past*, it is followed by a *secondary* tense.

Fīnitimīs *persuādent* ut proficīscantur.   *They persuade(d) the neighbors to set out.*
**Prīncipī *persuādent* ut rēgnum occupāret.*   *They persuade(d) the chief to seize the royal power.*

(2) **Dum,** meaning *while*, is used with the historical present of the indicative to denote an act as *contemporaneous* with that of the main verb.

> **Dum hoc *narrat*, forte audīvī.**   By chance I heard this while *he was telling* it.

b. The *future* tense indicates future time.

> **Ego vōbīscum pācem *faciam*.**   *I shall make* peace with you.

The Latin often employs the future tense where the English, less accurately, uses a *false* present which actually refers to future time.

Cum in oppidō *erit*, eum vidēbō.   When *he is (will be)* in town, I shall see him.

c. The *present perfect* tense indicates an action completed at the present time, corresponding to English present perfect with *has* and *have*.

> **ut suprā *dēmōnstrāvimus***   as *we have shown* above

The following perfects are equivalent to presents: **cōgnōvī,** *I know* (*I have found out*); **nōvī,** *I know* (*I have learned*); **cōnsuēvī,** *I am accustomed* (*I have become accustomed*).

d. The *future perfect* tense indicates an action completed before some future time. This tense is used much more frequently in Latin than in English, which less accurately uses a *false* present.

Helvētiī ībunt ubi eōs tū *volueris*.   The Helvetians will go where *you wish* (*will have wished*) them to be.

e. The *imperfect* tense indicates an action or condition continuing, customary, repeated, or attempted in the past.

> **Mīlitēs in Forō *stābant*.**   The soldiers *were standing* (*used to stand, kept on standing, tried to stand, stood*) in the Forum.

f. The (historical) *perfect*, or simple past, indicates an action completed at some indefinite past time.

> **Equitātum *mīsit*.**   *He sent* the cavalry.

The *perfect* is the tense of *narration*. The *imperfect* is *descriptive;* it gives the background for the action of the perfect.

Etsī mōns iter *impediēbat*, **tamen ad fīnēs Arvernōrum** *pervēnit*.	Although the mountain *stood in the way of* his march, *he arrived* at the territory of the Arverni.

g. The *pluperfect* (past perfect) tense indicates an action completed at or before a certain past time. It corresponds to the English past perfect tense.

Vir *pervēnerat.*	The man *had arrived.*

The following pluperfects are equivalent to imperfects: **cōgnōveram,** *I knew* (*I had found out*); **nōveram,** *I knew* (*I had learned*); **cōnsuēveram,** *I was accustomed* (*I had become accustomed*).

h. The *present* and *imperfect* are frequently used with **jam, jam diū, jam prīdem,** and **jam dūdum** to indicate an action already in progress for a considerable period. The *present* should be translated with a *progressive perfect*, and the *imperfect*, with a *progressive pluperfect*.

Tē jam dūdum *hortor.*	I have long *been urging* you.
Tē jam prīdem *hortābar.*	I had been urging you for a long time.

3. *Tenses of the Subjunctive.* The tense of the subjunctive in a *principal* (*independent*) clause indicates time in relation to the time of the speaker. The *present* tense always refers to future (or indefinite) time; the *imperfect* to either past or present; the *perfect* to either future or past; the *pluperfect* always to past. There are no future or future perfect tenses in the subjunctive.

The tense of the subjunctive in a *subordinate* (*dependent*) clause is determined by the time relationship that exists between the main verb in the principal clause and the dependent verb in the subordinate clause. This time relationship is known as sequence of tenses. (See p. 92.)

4. *Sequence of Tenses.* (See p. 92.)

5. *Subjunctive Used in the Main Verb.* The subjunctive mood in independent sentences expresses the action of the verb not as a fact, but as an idea. These subjunctive clauses are classified as *volitive* (willed), *optative* (wished for), *potential* (possible), *deliberative* (question in which uncertainty is implied).

	Positive	*Negative*
Volitive		
1. Hortatory	**Exeāmus.** *Let us go out.*	**Nē exeāmus.**
2. Jussive	**Exeant.** *Let them go out.*	**Nē exeant.**
Optative	**(Utinam) exeās!** *May you go out!*	**Nē exeās!**
	Utinam adessēs! *Would that you were here!*	**Utinam nē adessēs!**
	Utinam adfuissēs! *Would that you had been here!*	**Utinam nē adfuissēs!**
Potential	**Aliquis exeat.** *Someone may go out.*	**Aliquis nōn exeat.**
Deliberative	**Quid agam?** *What am I to do?*	**Quid nōn agam?**

440

6. *Subordinate Clauses.* The moods used in subordinate clauses are the indicative and the subjunctive. The indicative occurs only in clauses of fact. The subjunctive mood has many idiomatic uses. It is sometimes translated by the English indicative; sometimes by the infinitive; frequently by means of the auxiliaries *may, might, would,* or *should.*

7. *Uses of Subordinate Clauses.* A subordinate clause considered as a unit is used:

a. As a noun (substantive clause), usually as the subject or object of the verb in the principal clause. It may also be used as an appositive.

b. As an adjective (adjective or relative clause)

c. As an adverb (adverbial clause)

8. *General Types of Subordinate Clauses.* Subordinate clauses are united to the principal clause by:

a. Subordinate conjunctions (clauses of purpose, result, temporal, causal, concessive, conditional, comparative, interrogative)

b. Relative pronouns, adjectives, adverbs (relative clauses)

c. Interrogative words (indirect questions)

9. *Clauses Introduced by Subordinate Conjunctions*

a. *Purpose Clauses.* Purpose clauses introduced by **ut** (negative **nē**) are either *adverbial* or *substantive.* Relative purpose clauses introduced by **quī, quae, quod,** or by **quō** with the comparative, are adverbial. All these clauses take the present or imperfect subjunctive.

(1) *Adverbial* and *relative clauses of purpose* state the purpose of the action of the main verb.

Vēnī *ut tē vidērem.*	I came *to see (in order to see) you.*
Currit *nē capiātur.*	He runs *so as not to be taken.*
Legiōnem relīquit *quae urbem dēfenderet.*	He left a legion *to protect the city.*
Legiōnem relīquit *quō facilius hostēs prohibērentur.*	He left a legion *that the enemy might be repelled more easily.*

(2) *Substantive clauses of purpose,* used chiefly as objects of the main verb, may be considered as indirect commands or requests.

Ōrō *tē ut veniās.*	I beg *you to come.*
Imperāvit *tibi nē venīrēs*	He commanded *you not to come.*

(a) **Hortor, rogō, moneō, ōrō, implōrō** take the accusative of the person commanded.

(b) **Imperō, mandō, persuādeō, permittō** take the dative of the person commanded.

(c) **Petō, postulō** take **ā** or **ab** and the ablative of the person commanded.

(d) **Jubeō, vetō, patior** take the accusative of the person and the objective infinitive.

441

(e) **Volō, nōlō, mālō, cupiō, studeō** take the objective infinitive and the accusative of the person if a subject of the infinitive is expressed.

b. *Result Clauses.* Result clauses introduced by **ut** (negative **ut nōn**) are either *adverbial* or *substantive;* those introduced by the relative pronoun **quī, quae, quod** are *adverbial.* Result clauses take the present or imperfect subjunctive. The perfect subjunctive is sometimes used even when the main verb is in secondary sequence.

(1) *Adverbial* and *relative clauses of result* merely state the result of the action of the main verb. The main clause usually contains signal words, such as **tam, ita, sīc, adeō, tantus, tālis.**

Mīlitēs tam fortiter pūgnāvērunt *ut vincī nōn possent.*	The soldiers fought so bravely *that they could not be conquered.*
Tanta tempestās fuit *ut nāvēs dēlēverit.*	So great was the storm *that it destroyed the ships.*
Secūtae sunt tempestātēs, *quae* (= *tālēs ut*) *nostrōs in castrīs continērent.*	Storms followed *which kept our men in camp.*

COMPARISON OF NEGATIVE PURPOSE AND NEGATIVE RESULT CLAUSES

Negative purpose		Negative result
nē quis	*that no one*	**ut nēmō**
nē quid	*that nothing*	**ut nihil**
nē ūllus	*that not any*	**ut nūllus**
nē umquam	*that never*	**ut numquam**

(2) *Substantive clauses of result*, used as nouns, complete what is implied in the main verb. They may be:

(a) Objects of verbs meaning *accomplish* or *bring about*, especially **faciō** and its compounds **efficiō, perficiō,** etc.

Obsidēs ut inter sēsē dent perficit. He brings it about *that they exchange hostages.*

(b) Subjects of impersonal verbs such as **accidit, ēvenit, fit,** etc., meaning *it happens, it comes about*, etc.

Accidit ut incolumēs pervēnīrent. It happened *that they arrived unharmed.*

(c) Predicate nominatives with expressions such as **jūs est,** *it is right;* **mōs est,** *it is the custom.*

Jūs est ut ducem laudēmus. It is right *that we praise the leader.*

c. *Substantive Clauses as Objects of Verbs of Fearing.* These clauses are introduced by **nē,** *that* (affirmative), and **ut,** *that not* (negative), with verbs in the subjunctive mood, usually present or imperfect.

Timeō nē errēs.	I fear *that you are (will be, may be) wrong.*
Timēbam nē errārēs.	I feared *that you were wrong.*

442

Timeō *nē errāverīs*.	I fear *that you were wrong.*
Timēbam *nē errāvissēs*.	I feared *that you had been wrong.*
Vereor *ut effugiāmus*.	I fear *that we shall not escape.*

As a general rule, when a verb of fearing takes the infinitive in English, it also takes the infinitive in Latin.

Timeō *īre*.   I am afraid *to go.*

    d. *Substantive Clauses as Objects of Verbs of Hindering, Preventing,* etc. These clauses are introduced by **quōminus,** *so that not,* followed by the subjunctive. If the main verb is affirmative, the subordinate clause may be introduced by **nē;** if negative, by **quīn,** *that not, but that, without.* The verbs in these clauses are always in the subjunctive mood.

Nōs impedīvērunt *quōminus* (*nē*) *abī-rēmus.*	They hindered us *from going away.*
Tē nōn dēterrent *quōminus* (*quīn*) *abeās.*	They are not deterring you *from going away.*

Prohibeō, *prevent,* is regularly followed by the objective infinitive with the subject in the accusative.

Prohibent *nōs abīre*.   They are preventing *us from going away.*

    e. *Substantive Clauses with Expressions of Doubt.* These clauses have two constructions, in both of which the subjunctive mood is used.

    (1) With negative expressions of doubt the substantive clause is introduced by **quīn,** *but that.*

Nōn dubitō *quīn vērum sit*.   I do not doubt *that it is true.*

    (2) Affirmative expressions of doubt take an indirect question introduced by **num,** *whether;* **an,** *whether, or;* or **sī,** *if.*

Dubitat *num veniant*.   He doubts *whether they will come.*

    f. *Temporal Clauses.* These clauses are adverbial and take the indicative or subjunctive. They are introduced as follows:

    (1) By **postquam,** *after;* **ubi, ut,** *when;* **cum prīmum, ut prīmum, ubi prīmum, simul, simul atque (ac),** *as soon as.* When expressing a single past act, these clauses take the perfect indicative.

Caesar, *postquam id vīdit*, equitātum praemīsit.	*After he had seen this,* Caesar sent forward the cavalry.
Ubi *Caesarem vīdērunt*, lēgātōs ad eum mīsērunt.	*When they saw Caesar,* they sent envoys to him.
Simul atque *illum vīdērunt*, fūgērunt.	*As soon as they saw him,* they fled.

    (2) By **cum,** *when, whenever.*

        (a) Referring to present or future time, **cum** is used with the indicative.

Cum pictūram tuam spectō, tēcum esse videor.	*When I am looking at your picture,* I seem to be with you.

| Tē *cum in urbe eris* vidēbō. | *When you are in the city,* I shall see you. |
| Tē *cum in urbem vēneris,* vidēbō. | *When you come to the city,* I shall see you. |

(b) Referring to definite past time, **cum** is used with the indicative.

| *Cum* in urbem *vēnistī,* tē vīdī. | *At the time when you came* into the city, I saw you. |

(c) Referring to past time and describing the circumstances of the action of the main verb, **cum** is used with the subjunctive, imperfect or pluperfect tense. This use is called **cum-circumstantial.**

| *Cum id facerent,* sonitus terribilis audītus est. | *When they were doing this,* a terrible sound was heard. |
| *Cum id fēcissent,* sonitus terribilis audītus est. | *When they had done this,* a terrible sound was heard. |

(3) By **dum, dōnec, quoad, quam diū,** *as long as, while, until;* **antequam, priusquam,** *before.*

(a) **Dum,** *while,* takes the historical present tense in the indicative to denote continued action in past time.

| *Dum exspectat,* lēgātī vēnērunt. | *While he was waiting,* the envoys came. |

It is preferable to use the present participle instead of **dum** with the present indicative, if the expression is active and the subject of both clauses is the same. (See p. 73.)

(b) **Dum, dōnec, quoad, quam diū,** *as long as,* take the indicative and the same tense as that in the principal clause.

| *Dum in hortō sedēbam,* legēbam. | *While (As long as) I was sitting in the garden,* I read (was reading). |

(c) **Dum, dōnec, quoad,** *until,* take the indicative for actual occurrence and the subjunctive for actions that are anticipated, desired, or intended.

| Hostēs vincere nōn poterāmus *dum auxilium missum est.* | We could not conquer the enemy *until help was sent.* |
| *Dum nāvēs convenīrent,* exspectāvērunt. | They waited *until the ships should assemble.* |

(d) **Antequam, priusquam,** *before,* take the indicative to denote actual facts, and the subjunctive to denote anticipation or expectancy.

Indicative

Antequam abeō, tibi pecūniam dabō.	*Before I go away,* I shall give you the money.
Nōn abībō *antequam tibi pecūniam dederō.*	I shall not go away *before I give you the money.*
Antequam abiī, tibi pecūniam dedī.	*Before I went away,* I gave you the money.

444

Subjunctive

Antequam abīrem, **tibi pecūniam dedī.**   *Before I could go away,* I gave you the money.

    g. *Causal Clauses.* These clauses are adverbial and take the indicative or subjunctive. They are introduced as follows:

       (1) By **quod, quia, quoniam, quandō,** *because, since.* They take the indicative when the reason is stated as a definite fact on the authority of the speaker or writer. They take the subjunctive when the reason is alleged, assumed, or indirectly quoted and not that of the speaker or writer.

    Domī mānsit *quod aeger erat.*   He remained at home *because he was sick.*

Imperātor accūsāvit mīlitēs *quod*   The general blamed the soldiers *because*
fortēs nōn essent.   *(as was said) they were not brave.*

       (2) By **cum,** *since, because,* taking the subjunctive in whatever tense is required by the English.

    Cum fortis sit, **nihil timet.**   *Because he is brave,* he fears nothing.

    Cum fortis esset, **nihil timēbat.**   *Because he was brave,* he feared nothing.

    h. *Concessive Clauses.* These clauses are adverbial and take the indicative or subjunctive. They are introduced as follows:

       (1) By **quamquam,** *although.* **Quamquam** generally introduces a statement of fact and takes the indicative (of any tense required by the meaning).

Quamquam māgnum est perīculum,   *Although the danger is great,* I shall remain
in īnsulā morābor.   on the island.

       (2) By **cum,** *although,* always taking the subjunctive (of any tense required by the meaning).

Cum māgnum sit perīculum, **in īn-**   *Although the danger is great,* I shall remain
sulā morābor.   on the island.

       (3) By **quamvīs,** *although.* **Quamvīs** is used with a clause that represents an act merely as conceived. It is always followed by the subjunctive.

Quamvīs māgnum sit perīculum, **in**   *Although the danger may be great,* I shall
īnsulā morābor.   stay on the island.

       (4) By **etsī,** *although.* **Etsī** takes the indicative or subjunctive like conditional clauses with **sī.** (See following section.)

Etsī hiemēs mātūrae sunt, **in Galliam**   *Although the winters are early,* he hastens
proficīscī contendit.   to set out for Gaul.

    i. *Conditional Clauses.* These clauses are adverbial and take the indicative or subjunctive. The conditional sentence is made up of the *condition* (the subordinate clause) and the *conclusion* (the principal clause). Both the condition and the conclusion are regularly in the same mood, and very frequently in the same tense. The condition is introduced by:

445

sī, *if;* **sī nōn,** *if not;* **nisi,** *unless;* or **sīn,** *but if.* Conditional sentences are of three types.

(1) *Conditions of fact.* The indicative is used in both clauses in the tense required by the meaning.

Sī adest, bene est.	*If he is here,* it is well.
Sī aderat, bene erat.	*If he was here,* it was well.
Sī aderit, bene erit.	*If he will be here,* it will be well.

(2) *Conditions contrary to fact.* The subjunctive is used in both clauses in the imperfect or pluperfect.

Sī adesset, bene esset.	*If he were here,* it would be well (now).
Sī adfuisset, bene fuisset.	*If he had been here,* it would have been well.

(3) *Conditions of remote future possibility.* The subjunctive is used in both clauses, usually in the present tense.

Sī adsit, bene sit.	*If he should be here,* it would be well.

Nisi, *unless,* makes the whole clause negative; **sī nōn,** *if not,* makes negative the single word which follows the **nōn.**

Parva sunt forīs arma *nisi* est cōnsilium domī.	Arms avail (are) little abroad *unless there is wisdom at home.*
Sī *nōn possumus* id facere, moriēmur.	If *we are not able* to do this, we shall die.

j. *Clauses of Comparison.* These clauses are adverbial and are introduced:

(1) By **ut, sīcut, quemadmodum,** *as,* taking the indicative.

ut suprā dēmōnstrāvimus	*as we have shown above*

(2) By **quasi, velut (sī), tamquam (sī),** *as if.* These are really conditional clauses and take the subjunctive.

Velut sī cōram adesset, horrēbant.	They trembled *as if he were there before them.*

10. *Clauses Introduced by Relative Words.* Most of these clauses are introduced by the relative pronoun **quī, quae, quod.** The negative is **nōn.** Relative clauses are primarily adjectives in their use, but in Latin they are often used with the force of an adverb.

a. When the relative clause simply describes, it is an adjective clause and takes the indicative.

Pontem *quī erat ad Genāvam* rescindī jūssit.	He ordered the bridge *that was near Geneva* to be cut down.

b. When the relative clause expresses *purpose* or *result,* it is adverbial. (See pp. 441–42.)

c. *Characteristic* or *descriptive* clauses. These are adjective relative clauses which describe an indefinite antecedent. They take the subjunctive and are used especially after such expressions as **est quī, sunt quī, ūnus quī, sōlus quī, quis est quī, ējus modī, tālis, dīgnus, idōneus,** etc.

Sunt *quī putent.*	There are some *who think.*
Nēmō est *quī nesciat.*	There is nobody *who does not know.*
Indīgnus est *quī imperet.*	He is unworthy *to rule.*

11. *Clauses Introduced by Interrogative Words* (Indirect Questions).

a. Indirect questions are substantive clauses used as the object of verbs of inquiring, saying, knowing, perceiving, showing, etc. They are introduced by the same interrogative words that are used in direct questions. The verb is always subjunctive. The indirect question is one form of *indirect discourse.*

Quaerō *quid faciās.*	I ask *what you are doing.*
Dīc nōbīs *ubi fuerīs.*	Tell us *where you were.*
Mīror *cūr mē accūsēs.*	I wonder *why you accuse me.*
Num quid vellet **rogāvī.**	I asked *whether he wished anything.*

b. *Whether . . . or* in double indirect questions is expressed by:

utrum . . . an	Dīc *utrum* verum *an* falsum sit.	⎫
–ne . . . an	Dīc vērum*ne an* falsum sit.	⎪ Say *whether* it is true *or* false.
–ne	Dīc vērum falsum*ne* sit.	⎬
an	Dīc vērum *an* falsum sit.	⎭

Or not is expressed by **necne** (for **annōn** of the double direct question).

Dīc vērum sit *necne.*	Say whether it is true *or not.*

12. *Subordinate Clauses in Indirect Discourse.* Adjective and adverbial subordinate clauses in indirect discourse have their verbs in the subjunctive mood. The tense of the verb in the subordinate clause is determined by the rule for sequence of tenses.

Dīxit mīlitēs vēnisse.	He said that the soldiers had come.
Dīxit mīlitēs *quōs vīdissēmus* **vēnisse.**	He said that the soldiers *whom we saw* had come.

Subordinate clauses depending upon an indirect statement expressed by a perfect infinitive take secondary sequence, even if the main verb is primary.

Dīcit sē nūntium *quem mīsissēs* **audīvisse.**	He says that he heard the messenger *whom you had sent.*

13. *Imperative Mood.* The imperative states the action of the verb as a *command* or *request.* The imperative has only two tenses, the present and the future. Generally the present imperative is used.

Dīvide et imperā.	*Divide and conquer.*

Negative commands may be expressed by **nōlī** or **nōlīte** with the infinitive.

Nōlī timēre, **puer.**	*Don't fear,* boy.
Nōlīte timēre, **puerī.**	*Don't fear,* boys.

Four verbs drop final –e in the imperative singular: **dīc, dūc, fac, fer.**

14. *Infinitives.* An infinitive is an indeclinable verbal noun. Its form is not limited by person and number, though it is limited by tense and voice. It has several important uses.

    a. *Complementary infinitive.* It is used to complete the meaning of certain verbs, such as **dēbeō, cupiō, possum, volō, nōlō, mālō, parō, properō, contendō,** etc.

        (1) The complementary infinitive has no accusative subject because its subject is the same as the nominative subject of the verb on which it depends.

                Īre **potest.**   He can *go* (is able *to go*).

        (2) A predicate noun or adjective after a complementary infinitive is in the nominative case.

                Hic vir *cōnsul* **esse vult.**   This man wishes to be *consul.*

    b. *Objective infinitive.* With an accusative subject it is used as object of another verb.

                Eōs īre **jūssit.**   He ordered *them to go.*

        (1) The objective infinitive has an accusative subject; the complementary infinitive has not.

        (2) The objective infinitive may be found after the following verbs: **jubeō, cōgō, cupiō, prohibeō, patior,** etc.

    c. *Subjective infinitive.* With or without an accusative subject, it may be the subject of a verb used impersonally. The predicate adjective referring to the subjective infinitive is neuter.

         Legere **est grātum.**   It is pleasant *to read* (*To read* is pleasant).

      Legere bonōs librōs **est grātum.**   It is pleasant *to read good books.*

   Puerum **bonōs librōs** *legere* **oportet.**   *The boy* ought *to read* good books. (It is necessary that *the boy read* good books.)

    d. *Indirect statement.* The infinitive, with accusative subject, is used in indirect statements after verbs of saying, thinking, knowing, and perceiving. The tenses of the infinitive denote time relative to that of the main verb.

        (1) The present infinitive is used to denote action going on at the same time as that of the main verb.

                Dīxit sē *vincere.*   He said that he *was conquering.*

        (2) The perfect infinitive refers to action before that of the main verb.

                Dīxit sē *vīcisse.*   He said that he *had conquered.*

        (3) The future infinitive refers to action that is to take place after the time of the main verb.

                Dīxit sē *vīctūrum esse.*   He said that he *would conquer.*

    Verbs which lack the participial stem supply their missing future infinitive by **fore ut** or **futūrum esse ut** with the subjunctive.

  Spērō *fore ut contingat id* **nōbīs.**   I hope *that this will happen* to us.

15. *Participles.* A participle is a verbal adjective.

    a. Regular transitive verbs have three participles: the present and the future in the active voice, and the perfect in the passive voice.

        (1) The present active participle indicates an act as going on at the same time as the main verb.

Pompam arēnam *intrantem* **videō (vīdī, vidēbō).**	I see (I saw, I shall see) the procession *entering* the arena.

        (2) The perfect passive participle denotes an act completed before the time of the main verb.

Urbēs ab hostibus *captae* **incenduntur (incēnsae sunt, incendentur).**	The cities *captured* by the enemy are being burned (were burned, will be burned).

        (3) The future active participle denotes an act taking place after the time of the main verb.

Moritūrī **tē salūtāmus (salūtāvimus, salūtābimus).**	We, *who are about (going) to die*, salute (saluted, shall salute) you.

    b. A participle, as a verb, governs the same case as the verb to which it belongs.

Eum *epistulam* **scrībentem vīdimus.**	We saw him *writing a letter.*
Eum *mīlitibus persuādentem* **audīvimus.**	We heard him *persuading the soldiers.*

    c. A participle may be used as a simple adjective agreeing with a noun in gender, number, and case.

oppidum captum	*the captured town*
servī fugientēs	*the fleeing slaves*

    d. Participles may be used as predicate adjectives.

Gallia est *dīvīsa.*	Gaul is *divided.*

    e. Participles are frequently used as the equivalent of various kinds of subordinate clauses.

Urbēs ab hostibus *captae* **incēnsae sunt.**	The cities *which had been captured* by the enemy were burned.
Cōpiae victae **erant miserae.**	*After the troops were conquered*, they were unhappy.

    f. A participle is sometimes equivalent to a clause coordinate with the main clause.

Cōpiae *victae* **erant miserae.**	The troops *were conquered* and were unhappy.

    g. Deponent verbs have three participles, all with active meaning; for example: **sequēns,** *following;* **secūtūrus,** *about to follow;* **secūtus,** *having followed.*

    h. *Active Periphrastic Conjugation.* The future active participle is often

449

used with forms of **sum** to denote likelihood or intention; it may be translated *about to, going to, intend to,* etc.

Discessūrus est.	*He is about to leave.*
Discessūra erat.	*She was going to leave.*
Discessūrī fuerant.	*They had intended to leave.*

Indirect questions expressing future time with reference to the main verb require the use of the active periphrastic.

Rogāvit *quid factūrus essem.*   He asked *what I was going to do.*

i. *Ablative Absolute.* An ablative absolute phrase consists of two words in the ablative case.

(1) A noun or pronoun with a perfect passive participle.

Agrīs vāstātīs, hostēs discessērunt.   *After devastating the fields,* the enemy departed.

(2) A noun or pronoun with a present participle.

Imperātōre spectante, fortiter pūgnā- *While the general was watching,* they fought
vērunt. bravely.

(3) A noun or pronoun with a noun, pronoun, or adjective. (**Sum** has no present participle.)

Eō duce, fortiter pūgnāvērunt.   *Under his leadership,* they fought bravely.
Amīcō meō vīvō, Rōmānī nōn superātī   *In the lifetime of my friend,* the Romans
sunt. were not defeated.

The ablative absolute, like other participial phrases, is best translated into English by a subordinate clause (temporal, causal, concessive, conditional) according to the best meaning of the context. It may even be translated as a principal clause.

Hostēs, *agrīs vāstātīs,* **discessērunt.**

When (After, Since, Because, As, Although, If) the fields had been devastated, the enemy departed.

The fields were devastated, and the enemy departed.

j. Many English participial phrases containing a perfect active participle cannot be translated literally into Latin. Methods of translating such phrases are as follows:

(1) If the participle is from a transitive verb, use the ablative absolute.

The enemy, *having devastated the fields,* de-   **Hostēs,** *agrīs vāstātīs,* **discessērunt.**
parted.

(2) If the verb is deponent, the sentence may be translated literally.

The enemy, *having devastated the fields,*   **Hostēs,** *agrōs populātī,* **discessērunt.**
departed.

(3) If the participle is from an intransitive verb and no deponent verb is available, such phrases must be translated into Latin by a clause

with **ubi** (*when*) + the perfect indicative, or **cum** (*when, since*) + the pluperfect subjunctive.

Caesar, *having arrived at the town*, demanded hostages.	Caesar, *ubi ad oppidum pervēnit* (**cum ad oppidum pervēnisset**), **obsidēs postulāvit.**

16. *Gerund.* The gerund is an active verbal noun of the second declension neuter. It is found only in the genitive, dative, accusative, and ablative singular; the infinitive is used instead of the nominative. It corresponds to the English verbal noun in *–ing*.

Nominative: **Vidēre est crēdere.** *Seeing* (*To see*) *is believing* (*to believe*).
Genitive: **cupidus discēdendī,** desirous *of leaving*
        fīnis pūgnandī, end *of fighting*
        videndī causā, for the sake *of seeing*
Dative: **ūtilis bibendō,** useful *for drinking*
Accusative: **ad pūgnandum,** for *fighting* (*to fight*)
Ablative: **morandō,** *by delaying*
        in labōrandō, in *working*

17. *Gerundive.* The gerundive, also called the future passive participle, is a passive verbal adjective. It is declined like adjectives of the first and second declensions. It is used to express the notions of duty, obligation, and necessity. It is totally unlike any usage in English. It always agrees with some noun, expressed or understood.

The meaning of the gerundive phrase is generally expressed in English by an active verbal form ending in *–ing* with an object expressed.

    difficultās *nāvium faciendārum*   the difficulty *of building ships* (*of ships to be built*)

It may be translated as an adjective:

    lēgēs *observandae*   laws *to be kept*

    a. The gerundive in agreement with its noun is to be preferred to the gerund governing a direct object. The direct object takes the case which would be required by the gerund, and the gerundive is placed in agreement.

cupidus *urbis videndae* (not **urbem videndī**)   desirous *of seeing the city*
nāvibus faciendīs (not **nāvēs faciendīs**)   *by making ships*

    b. If the object is a neuter pronoun or a neuter adjective used substantively, the gerund should be used to avoid ambiguity. This avoids confusing the neuter and masculine genders.

        cupidus *hoc faciendī*   desirous *of doing this*
        cupiditās *plūra habendī*   greed *for having more*

    c. The gerund should always be used with intransitive verbs.

        spēs ducī *persuādendī*   the hope *of persuading* the leader

451

d. The gerundive construction is generally used for verbs that govern the ablative case (**ūtor, fruor,** etc.).

> in *fungendō mūnere* in *performing the duty*

e. The genitives **meī, tuī, suī, nostrī, vestrī** are used with gerundives without regard to gender.

> *suī dēfendendī* **causā** for the sake *of defending herself* (*himself, themselves*)

f. The accusative of the gerund and the gerundive is used after the preposition **ad** to express purpose. If the object is expressed, the gerundive construction is used.

ad nāvēs faciendās (not **faciendum**) *for the purpose of building ships*

g. The genitive of the gerund or gerundive with **causā** or **grātiā** expresses purpose. If the object is expressed, the gerundive construction is used.

causā nāvium faciendārum (not **faciendī**) *for the purpose of building ships*

h. *Passive Periphrastic Conjugation.* The gerundive, as a predicate adjective, is used in combination with forms of **sum.** It denotes necessity, obligation, or duty, and is translated *ought* or *must.* Like all predicate adjectives, the gerundive agrees with the subject in gender, number, and case. The person or the agent by whom the act must be done is regularly expressed by the dative of agent. (See p. 136.)

Cōpiae ducī *mittendae sunt.* The leader *has to send* troops.
Dīcit cōpiās ducī *mittendās esse.* He says that the leader *has to send* troops.

i. The passive periphrastic of an intransitive verb may be used only in the impersonal form, with the gerundive in the neuter singular and the verb in the third person singular.

Nōbīs fortiter *pūgnandum est.* We *must fight* bravely. (*It must be fought* bravely by us.)

18. *Supines.* The supine is a verbal noun of the fourth declension. It is formed from the participial stem and is found only in the accusative or ablative singular.

a. The accusative supine in –**um** may be used with verbs of *motion toward* to express purpose. The supine in –**um** may take an object.

Vēnērunt pācem *petītum.* They came *to seek* peace.

b. The ablative supine in –**u** is used with certain adjectives as an ablative of specification or respect. The supine in –**u** never takes an object.

facile factū *easy to do* (*easy in the doing*)
difficile vīsū *hard to see* (*hard in the seeing*)
mīrābile dictū *wonderful to relate* (*wonderful in the relating*)

Glossary of Literary Terms

dactyl: an accented, or stressed, syllable followed by two unaccented syllables, as in *daf'/fo/dil*. See explanation of dactylic hexameter, page 395.

elegy: a lyric poem expressing sorrow or serious reflection on some phase of death. Catullus wrote an elegy in memory of his brother.

epic: a long narrative poem, written in an elevated style, dealing with the deeds of a national or mythical hero. Vergil's *Aeneid* is an epic.

epigram: a short, pointed, often witty saying or poem. Martial is the one surviving example of Roman epigram at its best.

fable: a brief narrative intended to teach a moral lesson, especially one in which animals speak and act as if they were human. Phaedrus wrote fables.

foot: a division in verse consisting of a group of syllables equivalent to a measure in music.

hexameter: a verse of six metrical feet. See explanation of dactylic hexameter, page 395.

lyric: a poem that is personal, melodic, and emotional, such as the ode and the elegy. Catullus and Horace are renowned for their lyrics.

meter: the systematic measurement of the rhythm of poetry in terms of lines or verses.

ode: a lyric poem that is formal in manner, lofty in tone, and dignified in subject or theme. The odes written by Horace are the best in Latin literature.

satire: a work which ridicules or scorns human follies and vices. Juvenal wrote satires.

spondee: a poetic foot of two equally accented syllables, used to vary regular meters, as in *house'/boat'* and *hand'/made'*.

Glossary of Proper Names

English Pronunciation of Names

Latin proper names in English translation should be pronounced as English words. The values of the following consonants should be carefully observed:

1. soft **g** (before **e** and **i**) = *j:* **Verbigenus, Allobrogēs, Latobrīgī**
2. soft **c** (before **e** and **i**) = *s:* **Aulercī**
3. hard **c** (before **a, o, u**) = *k:* **Casticus, Vocontiī, Dīviciācus**
4. **x** = *ks:* **Orgetorīx**
5. **c** and **t** before **io** and **iu** have the sound of *sh;* and the **i** has the sound of *y* in *yes:* **Lūcius**
6. final **s** after **e** has the sound of *z:* **Allobrogēs**
7. **qu** = *kw:* **Aquītānī**

The student should remember to accent the first syllable when the word has but two syllables; in words of more than two syllables, accent the penult (next to the last) if long in Latin; otherwise, accent the antepenult (third last).

A

A., *abbr. for* **Aulus,** Roman praenomen (first name).

Absyrtus, –ī, *m.,* Medea's brother.

Accō, –ōnis, *m.,* leader among the Senones.

Achillās, –ae, *m.,* slayer of Pompey.

Achīvus, –a, –um, *adj.,* Greek.

Admētē, –ēs, *f.,* daughter of Eurystheus, king in Mycenae.

Aduatuca, –ae, *f.,* fortress of the Eburones, near the Meuse.

Aduatucī, –ōrum, *m.pl.,* Belgian tribe.

Aeētēs, –ae, *m.,* king of Colchis, father of Medea.

Aegyptus, –ī, *f.,* Egypt.

Aemilius, –ī, *m.,* Lucius Aemilius, a decurion of the Gallic cavalry.

Aeolia, –ae, *f.,* small island off the coast of Sicily.

Aeolus, –ī, *m.,* ruler of Aeolia and god of the winds.

Aesōn, –onis, *m.,* father of Jason.

Aetna, –ae, *f.,* volcano in Sicily.

Āfer, –fra, –frum, *adj.,* from Africa.

Āfrica, –ae, *f.,* Roman province of Africa.

Agēdincum, –ī, *n.,* chief city of the Senones; now Sens.

Alcinous, –ī, *m.,* king of the Phaeacians, Ulysses' host.

Alcmēna, –ae, *f.,* mother of Hercules.

Alesia, –ae, *f.,* chief city of the Mandubians; now Alise-Sainte-Reine.

Alexandria, –ae, *f.,* capital of Egypt.

Allobrogēs, –um, *m.pl.,* Gallic tribe in the N.E. part of the Province.

Alpēs, –ium, *f.pl.,* mountains separating Cisalpine Gaul from Transalpine Gaul and Germany.

Amāzonēs, –um, *f.pl.,* famous race of women warriors.

Ambarrī, –ōrum, *m.pl.,* Gallic tribe E. of the Arar.

Ambiānī, –ōrum, *m.pl.,* tribe in W. Belgic Gaul.

Ambibariī, –ōrum, *m.pl.,* tribe in N.W. Gaul.

Ambiliatī, –ōrum, *m.pl.,* tribe in central Gaul.

Ambiorīx, –īgis, *m.,* leader of the Eburones.

Ambivaretī, –ōrum, *m.pl.,* tribe in central Gaul.

Ambivaritī, –ōrum, *m.pl.,* Belgian tribe.

Anartēs, –ium, *m.pl.,* tribe in Dacia (Hungary).

Ancalitēs, –um, *m.pl.,* British tribe.

Andecumborius, –ī, *m.,* leader among the Remi.

Andēs, –ium, *m.pl.,* Gallic tribe N. of the Liger (Loire).

Antiochus, –ī, *m.,* king of Syria, protector of Hannibal in exile.

Antistius, –ī, *m* , Gajus Antistius Reginus, a lieutenant of Caesar.

Antōnius, –ī, *m.,* Marcus Antonius, a lieutenant of Caesar; member of the Second Triumvirate; and rival of Octavianus.

Aphrodīte, Greek name for Venus, goddess of Beauty and Love.

Apollō, –inis, *m.,* god of the sun.

Appennīnus, ī, *m.,* the Apennine Mountains in N. Italy.

Appius, –ī, *m.,* Roman praenomen.

Aprīlis, –e, *adj.,* of April.

Aquilēia, –ae, *f.,* city at the head of the Adriatic.

Aquītānī, –ōrum, *m.pl.,* inhabitants of Aquitania.

Aquītānia, –ae, *f.,* one of the three main divisions of Gaul.

Arar, –aris, *m.,* Arar River, tributary of the Rhone; now Saône.

Arcadia, –ae, *f.,* country in Greece.

Arduenna, –ae, *f.,* the Ardennes, a forest-covered range of hills of N.E. Gaul.

Arecomicī, –ōrum, *m.pl.,* division of the Volcae in the Province.

Arelās, –ātis, *f.,* town in S. Gaul, N. of Massilia; now Arles.

Aremoricus, –a, –um, *adj.,* referring to a small group of states in N.W. Gaul.

Argō, –ōnis, *f.,* the Argo, Jason's ship.

Argolicus, –a, –um, *adj.,* of Argolis, a district of Greece.

Argonautae, –ārum, *m.pl.,* Argonauts, the crew of Jason's ship.

Argus, –ī, *m.,* builder of Jason's ship.

Ariovistus, –ī, *m.,* German king, defeated by Caesar.

Arvernī, –ōrum, *m.pl.,* powerful tribe S.W. of the Haeduans.

Asia, –ae, *f.,* Roman province of Asia.

Athēnae, –ārum, *f.pl.,* Athens, a city of Greece.

Atlanticus, with **Ōceanus,** the Atlantic Ocean.

Atlās, –antis, *m.,* legendary giant.

Atrebātēs, –ium, *m.pl.,* Belgian tribe.

Aufidus, –ī, *m.,* river in Apulia in S.E. Italy.

Augēās, –ae, *m.,* king of Elis.

Aulercī, –ōrum, *m.pl.,* tribe in central Gaul.

Aulus, –ī, *m.,* Roman praenomen.

Aurunculējus, –ī, *m.,* Lucius Aurunculeius Cotta, lieutenant of Caesar; killed by the Eburones.

Auscī, –ōrum, *m.pl.,* tribe in E. Aquitania.

Avaricum, –ī, *n.,* largest city of the Bituriges; now Bourges.

Axona, –ae, *f.,* Belgian river; now the Aisne.

B

Bacchus, –ī, *m.,* god of wine.

Bacēnis, –is, *f.,* forest in Germany.

Baculus, –ī, *m.,* Publius Sextius Baculus, one of the bravest of Caesar's centurions.

Baleārēs, –ium, *m.pl.,* natives of the Balearic Islands; famous as slingers.

Basilus, –ī, *m.,* Lucius Minucius Basilus, an officer in Caesar's army.

Batāvī, –ōrum, *m.pl.,* tribe near the mouth of the Rhine.

Belgae, –ārum, *m.pl.,* the Belgians, inhabitants of one of the three main divisions of Gaul.

Belgium, –ī, *n.,* the land of the Belgians.

Bellovacī, –ōrum, *m.pl.,* powerful Belgic tribe.

Bibracte, –is, *n.,* chief town of the Haeduans.

Bibrax, –actis, *f.,* town of the Remi, N. of the Axona.

Bibrocī, –ōrum, *m.pl.,* tribe in S. Britain.

Bīthȳnia, –ae, *f.,* country in northwest Asia Minor.

Biturīgēs, –um, *m.pl.,* tribe in central Gaul.

Bōjī, –ōrum, *m.pl.,* Celtic tribe once widely diffused over central Europe.

Brātuspantium, –ī, *n.,* stronghold of the Bellovaci in S. Belgium.

Britannī, –ōrum, *m.pl.,* the Britons.

Britannia, –ae, *f.,* Britain.

Britannicus, –a, –um, *adj.,* of Britain, British.

Brundisium, –ī, *n.,* ancient seaport in

S.E. Italy on the Adriatic; the principal port of embarkation for Greece; now Brindisi.

Brūtus, -ī, m., Decimus Junius Brutus Albinus, an officer of Caesar in the Gallic and Civil Wars; afterwards a conspirator against him.

C

C., *abbr. for* **Gājus**, Roman praenomen.

Cabūrus, -ī, m., Gaius Valerius Caburus, a Gaul honored with Roman citizenship.

Cācus, -ī, m., legendary giant.

Cadūrcī, -ōrum, m.pl., tribe of Aquitania.

Caerōsī, -ōrum, m.pl., tribe in Belgic Gaul.

Caesar, -aris, m., Gaius Julius Caesar, general, author, statesman.

Calais, Calais, m., one of the Argonauts.

Caletī, -ōrum, m.pl., tribe in S.W. Belgium.

Calypsō, -ūs, f., nymph, ruler of the island Orgygia.

Canīnius, -ī, m., Caninius Rebilus, one of Caesar's officers.

Cantabrī, -ōrum, m.pl., warlike tribe in N. Spain.

Cantium, -ī, n., district in S.E. England; now Kent.

Capitōlium, -ī, n., (1) the Capitol, a temple of Jupiter in Rome; (2) one of the seven hills of Rome.

Carcasō, -ōnis, f., town in the Province; now Carcassonne.

Carnutēs, -um, m.pl., tribe of central Gaul, N. of the Loire.

Carthāgō, -inis, f., city in N. Africa.

Cassius, -ī, m., Lucius Cassius Longinus, a Roman consul, defeated and slain by the Helvetii, 107 B.C.

Cassivellaunus, -ī, m., leader of the British army against Caesar in 54 B.C.

Casticus, -ī, m., prominent Sequanian.

Castor, -oris, m., twin brother of Pollux.

Catamantāloedis, -is, m., leader among the Sequanians before Caesar's time.

Caturīgēs, -um, m.pl., Gallic tribe in E. Provincia.

Catuvolcus, -ī, m., ruler of the Eburones.

Cavillōnum, -ī, n., town of the Haedui.

Cebenna, -ae, f., the Cevennes, a mountain range in S. Gaul.

Celtae, -ārum, f.pl., inhabitants of central Gaul.

Celtillus, -ī, m., Arvernian ruler, father of Vercingetorix.

Cēnabēnsēs, -ium, m.pl., inhabitants of Cenabum.

Cēnabum, -ī, n., chief city of the Carnutes; now Orléans.

Cēnimāgnī, -ōrum, m.pl., British tribe.

Cerberus, -ī, m., three-headed watchdog of the lower world.

Cerēs, -eris, f., goddess of agriculture.

Ceutronēs, -um, m.pl., (1) tribe in E. Provincia; (2) Belgic tribe subject to the Nervii.

Charōn, -ontis, m., ferryman in the lower world.

Charybdis, -is, f., whirlpool between Sicily and Italy in the Straits of Messina.

Cheruscī, -ōrum, m.pl., German tribe N. of the Suebi.

Cicerō, -ōnis, m., Quintus Tullius Cicero, brother of Marcus Tullius Cicero, the orator; Quintus became one of Caesar's lieutenants in Gaul in 55 B.C.

Cimbrī, -ōrum, m.pl., Germanic people that joined with the Teutons in the invasion of Gaul; invaded Italy and were defeated by Marius.

Circē, -ēs, -ae, -ēn, -ē, f., an enchantress.

Cisalpīnus, -a, -um, adj., Cisalpine, on this (the Italian) side of the Alps.

Cleopātra, -ae, f., queen of Egypt, sister of Ptolemy.

Clōdius, -ī, m., Aulus Clodius, a friend of Caesar and of Scipio.

Cn., *abbr. for* **Gnaeus**, Roman praenomen.

Colchis, Colchidis, f., country on E. shore of the Black Sea.

Commius, -ī, m., an Atrebatan whom Caesar made king.

Condrūsī, -ōrum, m.pl., Belgian tribe on E. bank of Mosa (Meuse).

Cōnsidius, -ī, m., Publius Considius, an officer in Caesar's camp.

Corinthus, -ī, f., city of Greece.

Coriosolitēs, –um, *m.pl.,* tribe in N.W. Gaul.

Corsica, –ae, *f.,* island W. of Italy.

Cotta, –ae, *m.,* see **Aurunculējus.**

Crassus, –ī, *m.,* (1) Marcus Licinius Crassus, member of the triumvirate with Caesar and Pompey, consul in 55 B.C.; (2) Publius Licinius Crassus, younger son of the triumvir, officer of Caesar in Gaul.

Crāstinus, –ī, *m.,* brave soldier in Caesar's army.

Cremōna, –ae, *f.,* town in N.E. Italy.

Creōn, –ontis, *m.,* king of Corinth.

Crēta, –ae, *f.,* island S. of Greece.

Croesus, –ī, *m.,* king of Lydia, a country in Asia Minor, famous for his riches.

Cūria, –ae, *f.,* meeting place of the Roman Senate.

Cyclōps, Cyclōpis *m.,* Cyclops, one of a race of one-eyed giants.

Cyzicus, –ī, *f.,* town on the Propontis (Sea of Marmora).

D

D., *abbr. for* **Decimus,** Roman praenomen.

Dācī, –ōrum, *m.pl.,* tribe N. of the Danube.

Danaus, –a, –um, *adj.,* Greek; **Danaī, –ōrum,** *m.pl.,* the Greeks.

Dānuvius, –ī, *m.,* the Danube, a river flowing into the Black Sea.

Dārēus, –ī, *m.,* Darius, a Persian king.

Decimus, –ī, *m.,* Roman praenomen.

Dējanīra, –ae, *f.,* wife of Hercules.

Delphī, –ōrum, *m.,* small town in Phocis in N. Greece famous for its oracle of Apollo.

Delphicus, –a, –um, *adj.,* of Delphi, with reference to Apollo.

Diablintēs, –um, *m.pl.,* tribe in N.W. Gaul.

Dīdō, –ōnis, *f.,* queen of Carthage.

Diogenēs, –is, *m.,* Greek philosopher.

Diomēdēs, –is, *m.,* king of Thrace.

Dīs, Dītis, *m.,* with **pater,** Father Dis, god of the lower world; Pluto.

Dīviciācus, –ī, *m.,* Haeduan chief, loyal to Caesar.

Dīvicō, –ōnis, *m.,* Helvetian chieftain.

Druidēs, –um, *m.pl.,* Druids, a Gallic priesthood.

Dūbis, –is, *m.,* river in Gaul, tributary of the Arar.

Dumnorīx, –īgis, *m.,* prominent Haeduan, brother of Diviciacus.

Dūrocortorum, –ī, *n.,* capital of the Remi; now Rheims.

Dyrrachīnus, –a, –um, *adj.,* of Dyrrachium.

Dyrrachium, –ī, *n.,* ancient town on the west coast of the Adriatic Sea.

E

Eburōnēs, –um, *m.pl.,* Belgian tribe, N. of the Treverans.

Ēlis, –idis, *f.,* district of Greece.

Elaver, –eris, *n..* tributary of the Liger (Loire); now Allier.

Elusātēs, –um, *m.pl.,* tribe in Aquitania.

Ēpīrus, –ī, *f.,* region in N.W. Greece.

Eporēdorīx, –īgis, *m.,* Haeduan leader.

Eratosthenēs, –is, *m.,* famous geographer, mathematician, historian, grammarian.

Ēridanus, –ī, *m..* Greek name of the river Padus (Po) in Italy.

Erymanthus, –ī, *m.,* mountain in Arcadia in the Peloponnesus.

Erythēa, –ae, *f.,* small island in the bay of Cadiz on which the giant Geryon lived.

Esquiliae, –ārum, *f.pl.,* the Esquiline, one of the seven hills of Rome.

Esuviī, –ōrum, *m.pl.,* tribe in N.W. Gaul.

Etrūria, –ae, *f.,* district in N.W. Italy; now Tuscany.

Eunomus, –ī, *m.,* Theban boy whom Hercules killed by chance.

Eurōpa, –ae, *f.,* continent of Europe.

Eurylochus, –ī, *m.,* companion of Ulysses.

Eurystheus, –ī, *m.,* king in Mycenae, who imposed on Hercules his twelve labors.

Eurytiōn, –ōnis, *m.,* giant who guarded Geryon's cattle.

Eurytus, –ī, *m.,* king of Oechalia, father of Iole.

F

Fabius, –ī, *m.,* (1) Quintus Fabius Maximus, opponent of Hannibal in the

Second Punic War; (2) Gaius Fabius, one of Caesar's officers.

Flaminius, –ī, m., Gaius Flaminius, defeated by Hannibal at Lake Trasimene.

Fretum Gallicum, –ī, n., the English Channel.

G

Gabalī, –ōrum, m.pl., tribe in S.W. Gaul.

Gabīnius, –ī, m., consul with Lucius Calpurnius Piso, 58 B.C.

Gājus, Roman praenomen; sometimes in English written Caius.

Galba, –ae, m., Servius Sulpicius Galba, one of Caesar's officers.

Gallia, –ae, f., see page 202 for explanation of parts.

Gallicus, –a, –um, adj., of Gaul, Gallic.

Gallus, –ī, m., a Gaul, an inhabitant of Gaul; pl., the Gauls.

Garumna, –ae, f., river in S.W. Gaul; now the Garonne.

Garumnī, –ōrum, m.pl., tribe in Aquitania.

Gatēs, –ium, m.pl., tribe in Aquitania.

Geidmunī, –ōrum, m.pl., tribe in Belgic Gaul.

Genāva, –ae, f., city of the Allobroges on Lake Lemannus (Geneva).

Genua, –ae, f., city in N.E. Italy.

Gergovia, –ae, f., chief town of the Arverni.

Germānia, –ae, f., land of the Germans.

Germānus, –a, –um, adj., German; **Germānī, –ōrum, m.pl.,** the Germans.

Gēryōn, –ōnis, m., fabulous monster.

Gnaeus, –ī, m., abbr. Cn., Roman praenomen.

Glaucē, –ēs, –ae, –ēn, –ē, f., daughter of Creon, king of Corinth; murdered by Medea.

Gobannitiō, –ōnis, m., uncle of Vercingetorix.

Gorgobina, –ae, f., town in the country of the Haeduans, inhabited by the Boii.

Graecia, –ae, f., Greece.

Graecus, –a, –um, adj., Greek; **Graecī, –ōrum, m.pl.,** the Greeks.

Grajocelī, –ōrum, m.pl., Gallic Alpine tribe.

H

Hades, the home of the dead; the lower world.

Hadriāticum, with **Mare,** the Adriatic Sea.

Haeduus, –a, –um, adj., Haeduan; **Haeduus, –ī, m.,** an Haeduan.

Hannibal, –alis, m., leader of the Carthaginians.

Harpȳia, –ae, f., Harpy, mythical creature, half bird and half woman.

Harūdēs, –um, m.pl., German tribe between the Danube and upper Rhine.

Hecuba, –ae, f., wife of Priam, king of Troy.

Helle, f., sister of Phrixus.

Helvētiī, –ōrum, m.pl., Helvetians, a tribe of Celtic Gaul.

Helvētius, –a, –um, Helvetian, of the Helvetians.

Helviī, –ōrum, m.pl., Gallic people in the Province.

Herculēs, –is, m., hero famous for great strength.

Hercynius, –a, –um, adj., Hercynian; **Hercynia Silva,** forest in S. Germany and Austria.

Hesperidēs, –um, f.pl., daughters of Atlas, keepers of the golden apples.

Hibernia, –ae, f., Ireland.

Hippolytē, –ēs, –ae, –ēn, –ē, f., queen of the Amazons.

Hispānia, –ae, f., Spain.

Homērus, –ī, m., Homer, legendary Greek author of the *Iliad*.

Horātius, –ī, m., (1) Horace, a Roman poet; (2) a Roman family name.

Hȳdra, –ae, f., the Hydra, legendary serpent with many heads.

Hylās, Hylae, m., beautiful youth, one of the Argonauts.

I

Iccius, –ī, m., leader of the Remi.

Īdūs, –uum, f.pl., abbr. Īd., the Ides, the fifteenth day of March, May, July, and October; the thirteenth day of other months.

Īlias, Īliadis, f., the *Iliad*.

Illyricum, –ī, *n.,* Illyricum, Illyria, territory, N.E. of the Adriatic, which formed part of Caesar's province.

Indutiomārus, –ī, *m.,* a Treveran, rival of Cingetorix and hostile to Caesar.

Internum, with **Mare,** the Mediterranean Sea.

Iolāus, –ī, *m.,* Iolaus, constant companion of Hercules.

Īphiclēs, –is, *m.,* brother of Hercules.

Ītalia, –ae, *f.,* Italy.

Ītalī, –ōrum, *m.pl.,* the Italians.

Ithaca, –ae, *f.,* island in the Ionian Sea, home of Ulysses.

Itius, –ī, *m.,* Portus Itius, harbor from which Caesar sailed to Britain; now Boulogne.

J

Jāsōn, –onis, *m.,* Greek hero, leader of the Argonauts.

Jovis, *gen.* of **Juppiter.**

Jūnius, –a, –um, *adj.,* name of a Roman family.

Jūnō, –ōnis, *f.,* queen of the gods.

Juppiter, Jovis, *m.,* Jupiter, king of the gods.

Jūra, –ae, *m.,* Jura, a range of mountains from the Rhine to the Rhone, forming the boundary between the Helvetians and the Sequanians.

K

Kal., *abbr. for* **Kalendae.**

Kalendae, –ārum, *f.pl.,* Calends, the first day of the month.

L

L., *abbr. for* **Lūcius,** Roman praenomen.

Labiēnus, –ī, *m.,* Titus Labienus, the most prominent of Caesar's lieutenants in the Gallic War.

Lacōnia, –ae, *f.,* country of Greece.

Lāocoōn, –ontis, *m.,* priest of Neptune in Troy.

Lār, Laris, *m.,* household god; *usually pl.*

Lārīsa, –ae, *f.,* city in Thessaly.

Latobrīgī, –ōrum, *m.pl.,* Gallic tribe, neighbors of the Helvetians.

Lemannus, –ī, *m.,* with **Lacus,** Lake Geneva.

Lemovīcēs, –um, *m.pl.,* Gallic tribe W. of the Arvernians.

Lentulus, –ī, *m.,* Lucius Lentulus, consul in 49 b.c., a partisan of Pompey.

Lepontiī, –ōrum, *m.pl.,* Alpine tribe.

Lernaeus, –a, –um, *adj.,* of Lerna, a lake and swamp of Greece.

Leucī, –ōrum, *m.pl.,* tribe of E. Gaul.

Levācī, –ōrum, *m.pl.,* Belgic tribe, dependents of the Nervii.

Lexoviī, –ōrum, *m.pl.,* Gallic tribe near the Seine.

Libitīna, –ae, *f.,* goddess of corpses, death.

Lichās, –ae, *m.,* servant of Hercules.

Licinius, *see* **Crassus.**

Liger, –eris, *m.,* river flowing through the heart of Gaul; now the Loire.

Ligurēs, –um, *m.pl.,* Ligurians, inhabitants of Liguria.

Liguria, –ae, *f.,* district where Cisalpine Gaul and the Province meet.

Lingonēs, –um, *m.pl.,* tribe of Celtic Gaul, W. of the Sequanians.

Liscus, –ī, *m.,* chief magistrate of the Haeduans in 58 b.c.

Londinium, –ī, *n.,* London.

Lūcius, –ī, *m.,* Roman praenomen.

Lūna, –ae, *f.,* goddess of the moon.

Lutecia, –ae, *f.,* city on an island in the Seine; now Paris.

Lȳdia, –ae, *f.,* country in Asia Minor.

M

M., *abbr. for* **Marcus,** Roman praenomen.

Mandubiī, –ōrum, *m.pl.,* Gallic tribe N. of the Haeduans.

Mānlius, –ī, Roman praenomen.

Marcomanī, –ōrum, *m.pl.,* Germanic tribe, allies of Ariovistus.

Mārcus, –ī, *m.,* Roman praenomen.

Marius, –ī, *m.,* great Roman general.

Mārs, Martis, *m.,* god of war.

Massilia, –ae, *f.,* coastal town in the Province; now Marseilles.

Matiscō, –ōnis, *f.,* city of the Haeduans on the Arar.

Matrona, –ae, *f.,* river in N. Gaul; now the Marne.

Mēdēa, -ae, *f.*, enchantress, daughter of king Aeetes in Colchis.

Mediolānum, -ī, *n.*, town in N. Cisalpine Gaul; now Milano.

Mediomatricī, -ōrum, *m.pl.*, Gallic people near the Rhine.

Melpomenē, -ēs, *f.*, the muse of tragic and lyric poetry.

Menapiī, -ōrum, *m.pl.*, tribe in N.E. Belgic Gaul.

Mercurius, -ī, *m.*, messenger of the gods.

Messāla, -ae, *m.*, Marcus Valerius Messala, consul 61 B.C.

Metius, -ī, *m.*, Marcus Metius, an envoy of Caesar to Ariovistus.

Minerva, -ae, *f.*, goddess of wisdom and the arts.

Mīnōs, Mīnōis, *m.*, mythical king and lawgiver in Crete.

Minyae, -ārum, *m.pl.*, neighbors of the Thebans.

Mona, -ae, *f.*, the Isle of Man, in the Irish Sea.

Morinī, -ōrum, *m.pl.*, Belgic tribe on seacoast opposite Cantium (Kent).

Mosa, -ae, *f.*, river in Gaul; now the Meuse.

Mosella, -ae, *f.*, tributary of the Rhine; now the Moselle.

Mycēnae, -ārum, *f.pl.*, city in Argolis.

Mȳsia, -ae, *f.*, country in N.W. Asia Minor.

N

Namnetēs, -um, *m.pl.*, Gallic tribe north of the Liger.

Nantuātēs, -um, *m.pl.*, Gallic tribe S.E. of Lake Geneva.

Narbō, -ōnis, *m.*, capital of the Province; now Narbonne.

Nausicaa, -ae, *f.*, daughter of king Alcinous of the land of the Phaeacians.

Nemeaeus, -a, -um, *adj.*, of Nemea, a city in Greece.

Nemetēs, -um, *m.pl.*, Germanic tribe settled W. of the Rhine.

Neptūnus, -ī, *m.*, god of the sea.

Nerviī, -ōrum, *m.pl.*, the most powerful tribe of the Belgae.

Nessus, -ī, *m.*, centaur killed by Hercules.

Nestōr, -oris, *m.*, oldest Greek chieftain in the Trojan War.

Nōrēja, -ae, *f.*, chief city of the Norici; now Neumarkt.

Nōricī, -ōrum, *m.pl.*, German tribe S. of Danube.

Noviodūnum, -ī, *n.*, (1) capital city of the Suessiones on the Axona; now Soissons; (2) town of the Bituriges, S. of Cenabum; now Sancerre; (3) town of the Haeduans on the bank of the Liger (Loire); now Nevers.

Nymphae, -ārum, *f.pl.*, spirits of the streams, woods, seas, etc.

O

Ōceanus, -ī, *m.*, Ocean; Atlantic Ocean.

Ocelum, -ī, *n.*, town of Cisalpine Gaul.

Octodūrus, -ī, *m.*, chief town of the Veragri, a Gallic Alpine tribe.

Oechalia, -ae, *f.*, town in Euboea, an island in the Aegean Sea.

Oeneus, -eī, *m.*, father of Dejanira.

Olympus, -ī, *m.*, famous mountain in Thessaly; home of the gods.

Orcus, -ī, *m.*, infernal regions.

Orcynia, -ae, *f.*, Hercynian forest.

Orgetorīx, -īgis, *m.*, Helvetian nobleman who plotted to seize supreme power.

Orpheus, -ī, *m.*, mythical minstrel of Thrace; husband of Eurydice.

Osismī, -ōrum, *m.pl.*, coastal tribe N. of the Veneti.

P

P., *abbr. for* **Pūblius,** Roman praenomen.

Padus, ī, *m.*, river in Cisalpine Gaul; now the Po.

Paemānī, -ōrum, *m.pl.*, Belgian tribe.

Parīsiī, -ōrum, *m.pl.*, Gallic tribe on Sequana (Seine); name survives in Paris.

Pedius, -ī, *m.*, Quintus Pedius, one of Caesar's officers.

Peliās, -ae, *m.*, uncle of Jason.

Pēlūsium, -ī, *n.*, city in Egypt.

Pēnelopē, -ēs, -ae, -ēn, -ē, *f.*, faithful wife of Ulysses.

Petrōnius, -ī, *m.*, Marcus Petronius, a centurion of the Eighth Legion.

Pharsālus, –ī, *f.,* town in Thessaly near which Pompey was defeated by Caesar.

Phāsis, –idis (*acc.,* **Phāsim**), *m.,* river in Colchis.

Phīneus, –ī, *m.,* king of Salmydessus, tormented by Harpies in punishment for crime.

Pholus, –ī, centaur.

Phrixus, –ī, *m.,* brother of Helle.

Pictonēs, –um, *m.pl.,* tribe in W. Gaul.

Pīrūstae, –ārum, *m.pl.,* tribe in Illyricum.

Pīsae, –ārum, *f.pl.,* town in N. Italy; now Pisa.

Pīsō, –ōnis, *m.,* (1) Marcus Piso, consul in 61 B.C.; (2) Lucius Calpurnius Piso, consul in 58 B.C., father-in-law of Caesar; (3) L. Calpurnius Piso, consul in 112 B.C.

Platō, –ōnis, *m.,* celebrated Greek philosopher.

Plūtō, –ōnis, *m.,* king of the lower world, husband of Proserpina.

Poenī, –ōrum, *m.pl.,* Carthaginians.

Polyphēmus, –ī, *m.,* Cyclops, legendary one-eyed giant, blinded by Ulysses.

Pompējus, –ī, *m.,* Roman general and statesman, rival of Julius Caesar.

Priamus, –ī, *m.,* Priam, king of Troy.

Proserpina, –ae, *f.,* wife of Pluto, daughter of Ceres, queen of the lower world.

Provincia, –ae, *f.,* the Province, in S.E. Gaul.

Ptiāniī, –ōrum, *m.pl.,* small tribe in Aquitania.

Ptolomaeus, –ī, *m.,* Ptolemy, king of Egypt in 49 B.C., brother of Cleopatra.

Pūblius, –ī, *m.,* Roman praenomen.

Pullō, –ōnis, *m.,* brave centurion.

Pȳrēnaeī, with **Montēs,** the Pyrenees mountains, between France and Spain.

Pȳthia, –ae, *f.,* priestess of Apollo.

Q

Q., *abbr. for* **Quīntus,** Roman praenomen.

Quīntus, –ī, *m.,* Roman praenomen.

R

Rauracī, –ōrum, *m.pl.,* Gallic tribe, neighbors and allies of the Helvetii.

Redonēs, –um, *m.pl.,* tribe in N.W. Gaul.

Rēmī, –ōrum, *m.pl.,* tribe in Belgic Gaul; chief city was Durocortorum (Rheims).

Rhēnus, –ī, *m.,* the Rhine, river between Gaul and Germany.

Rhodanus, –ī, *m.,* the Rhone, a river rising in Alps, flowing through Lake Geneva, and reaching Mediterranean; about 500 miles long.

Rōma, –ae, *f.,* Rome.

Rōmānus, –a, –um, *adj.,* Roman; **Rōmānī, –ōrum,** *m.pl.,* the Romans.

Rubicō, –ōnis, *m.,* small river in Italy, boundary between Italy and Cisalpine Gaul.

Rūfus, –ī, *m.,* Roman cognomen.

Rutēnī, –ōrum, *m.pl.,* Gallic tribe, S. of the Arverni.

S

Sabīnus, –ī, *m.,* Quintus Titurius Sabinus, one of Caesar's officers.

Sabis, –is, *m.,* river in Belgic Gaul; now the Sambre.

Salmydēssus, –ī, *m.,* town in Thrace.

Samara, –ae, *f.,* river in W. Belgium; now Somme.

Samarobrīva, –ae, *f.,* town of the Ambiani; now Amiens.

Santonēs, –um, *m.pl.,* coastal Gallic tribe north of the Garumna.

Sardanapallus, –ī, *m.,* effeminate king of Syria.

Sardinia, –ae, *f.,* island in the Mediterranean.

Scylla, –ae, *f.,* rock at the entrance to the straits between Sicily and Italy.

Sedulius, –ī, *m.,* leader of the Lemovices.

Sedūnī, –ōrum, *m.pl.,* Alpine tribe S.E. of Lake Lemannus (Geneva).

Segusiāvī, –ōrum, *m.pl.,* Gallic tribe subject to the Haeduans.

Semprōnius, –ī, *m.,* Marcus Sempronius Rutilus, a Roman cavalry officer.

Senonēs, –um, *m.pl.,* Gallic tribe S. of the Sequana.

Septimius, –ī, *m.,* Lucius Septimius, a military tribune.

Sēquana, –ae, *f.,* principal river of N. Gaul; now the Seine.

Sēquanī, –ōrum, *m.pl.*, Gallic tribe W. of Jura Mts.; chief city, Vesontio.

Servius, –ī, *m.*, Roman praenomen.

Sextius, *see* Baculus.

Sibusātēs, –um, *m.pl.*, tribe in Aquitania.

Sicilia, –ae, *f.*, island of Sicily.

Sīrēnēs, –um, *f.pl.*, the Sirens, birds with faces of women whose songs lured sailors to their destruction.

Sōl, Sōlis, *m.*, god of the sun.

Sōtiātēs, –um, *m.pl.*, tribe in Aquitania.

Stymphālus, –ī, *m.*, lake in Arcadia, abode of birds of prey.

Styx, Stygis, *f.*, river in the infernal regions.

Suēbī, –ōrum, *m.pl.*, the Swabians, powerful German tribe E. of Belgium.

Suessiōnēs, –um, *m.pl.*, tribe of Belgic Gaul.

Sugambrī, –ōrum, *m.pl.*, German tribe E. of Belgium.

Sulla, –ae, *m.*, (1) Lucius Cornelius Sulla, dictator and leader of the nobility against Marius; (2) Publius Cornelius Sulla, nephew of the dictator, one of Caesar's officers.

Sulpicius, –ī, *m.*, Publius Sulpicius Rufus, one of Caesar's officers.

Symplēgadēs, –um, *f.pl.*, the Clashing Rocks, situated, according to legend, at the entrance to the Black Sea.

Syria, –ae, *f.*, country on E. coast of the Mediterranean.

T

T., *abbr. for* Titus, Roman praenomen.

Tamesis, –is, *m.*, the Thames, river in England.

Tarbellī, –ōrum, *m.pl.*, tribe in Aquitania.

Tartarus, –ī, *m.*, the lower world.

Tarusātēs, –um, *m.pl.*, tribe in Aquitania.

Tectosagēs, –um, *m.pl.*, tribal division of the Volcae.

Tĕlemachus, –ī, *m.*, son of Ulysses and Penelope.

Tencterī, –ōrum, *m.pl.*, German tribe that crossed the Rhine with the Usipites.

Tenedos, –ī, *f.*, island in the Aegean Sea near Troy.

Teucrī, –ōrum, *m.pl.*, the Trojans.

Teutonī, –ōrum, *m.pl.*, German tribe. allies of the Cimbri, defeated by Marius.

Thēbae, –ārum, *f.pl.*, Thebes.

Thēbānī, –ōrum, *m.pl.*, Thebans.

Thermōdōn, –ontis, *m.*, river of Pontus, a region near the Black Sea

Thermopylae, –ae, *f.pl.*, pass on the borders of Thessaly.

Thēseus, –ī, *m.*, king of Athens, slayer of the Minotaur.

Thessalia, –ae, *f.*, Thessaly, a section of Greece.

Thrācia, –ae, *f.*, Thrace, region N. of Greece.

Thȳnia, –ae, *f.*, N. part of Bithynia.

Tiberis, –is, *m.*, the Tiber, river on which Rome is situated.

Tigurīnī, –ōrum, *m.pl.*, canton of the Helvetians.

Tiresia (–ās), –ae, *m.*, famous blind soothsayer of Thebes.

Tīryns (*acc.*, Tīryntha), *f.*, Greek town where Hercules was brought up.

Titus, –ī, *m.*, Roman praenomen.

Tolōsa, –ae, *f.*, town in the Province; now Toulouse.

Tolōsātēs, –ium, *m.pl.*, tribe in the Province.

Trānsalpīnus, –a, –um, *adj.*, Transalpine, beyond the Alps.

Trānspadānus, –a, –um, *adj.*, beyond the Padus (Po).

Trasimēnus, –ī, *m.*, lake in Etruria.

Trebōnius, –ī, *m.*, Gaius Trebonius, one of Caesar's officers.

Trēverī, –ōrum, *m.pl.*, Belgic tribe near the Rhine.

Tribocēs, –um, *m.pl.*, German tribe near the Rhine.

Trinobantēs, –um, *m.pl.*, tribe in Britain.

Trōad, district in Asia Minor governed by the Trojans.

Trōja, –ae, *f.*, Troy, city in Asia Minor.

Trōjānus, –a, –um, *adj.*, Trojan.

Tulingī, –ōrum, *m.pl.*, neighbors and allies of the Helvetians.

Turonī, –ōrum, *m.pl.*, Gallic tribe near the Liger (Loire).

U

Ubiī, –ōrum, *m.pl.*, German tribe on the Rhine E. of Belgium.

Ulixēs, –is, *m.*, Ulysses, king of Ithaca, hero of Homer's *Odyssey.*

Usipetēs, –um, *m.pl.*, German tribe that crossed the Rhine with the Tencteri.

V

Vacalus, –ī, *m.*, branch of the Rhine near its mouth.

Valerius, –ī, *m.*, (1) Gaius Valerius Procillus, sent by Caesar as envoy to Ariovistus; (2) Gaius Valerius Flaccus, Roman governor in Gaul; (3) *see* **Cabūrus.**

Vangionēs, –um, *m.pl.*, German tribe, allies with Ariovistus.

Veliocassēs, –um, *m.pl.*, Belgian tribe.

Venellī, –ōrum, *m.pl.*, coastal tribe in N.W. Gaul.

Venetī, –ōrum, *m.pl.*, Venetans, a seafaring coastal tribe in W. Gaul.

Venetia, –ae, *f.*, country of the Venetans.

Veneticus, –a, –um, *adj.*, of the Venetans.

Veragrī, –ōrum, *m.pl.*, Alpine tribe S.E. of Lake Lemannus (Geneva).

Verbigenī, –ōrum, *m.pl.*, canton of the Helvetians.

Vercassivellaunus, –ī, *m.*, Gallic general at Alesia.

Vercingetorīx, –īgis, *m.*, an Arvernian, leader of all Gallic forces against the Romans in 52 B.C.

Vesontiō, –ōnis, *m.*, chief city of the Sequani; now Besançon.

Vespasiānus, –ī, *m.*, Titus Flavius Vespasianus, son and successor of Vespasian.

Vienna, –ae, *f.*, town of the Allobroges; now Vienne.

Viromanduī, –ōrum, *m.pl.*, Belgic tribe near the Somme.

Vocātēs, –um, *m.pl.*, tribe in Aquitania.

Vocontiī, –ōrum, *m.pl.*, Gallic tribe in the Province.

Volcae, –ārum, *m.pl.*, Gallic tribe in the Province.

Volusēnus, –ī, *m.*, Gaius Volusenus Quadratus, a military tribune.

Vorēnus, –ī, *m.*, Lucius Vorenus, a centurion.

Vosegus, –ī, *m.*, the Vosges, range of mountains in E. Gaul.

Vulcānus, –ī, *m.*, Vulcan, son of Jupiter and Juno, god of fire.

Z

Zephyrus, –ī, *m.*, warm west wind, zephyr.

Zētēs, –ae, *m.*, one of the Argonauts.

Vocabulary

Latin-English

Words preceded by an asterisk appear in the required New York State list for Latin Two Years. (It should be noted that this use of the asterisk is quite different from its use in the general vocabulary of Book One of this series.)

The future active participle is usually given as the fourth principal part of words that are wholly, or generally, intransitive.

All proper names are listed separately in the Glossary of Proper Names on pages 454–63.

*ā, ab, abs, *prep* + *abl.*, from, away from, out of, on, by; **ab utrōque latere,** on both sides.

abdō, –ere, –didī, –ditus, put away, conceal, hide.

abdūcō, –ere, –dūxī, –ductus, lead away, withdraw, take off.

*abeō, –īre, –iī (–īvī), –itūrus, go away, depart.

abiēs, –ietis, *f.*, fir tree, spruce.

abjiciō, –ere, –jēcī, –jectus, throw away, throw down, hurl, cast.

abluō, –ere, –luī, –lūtus, wash off, wash, cleanse.

aboleō, –ēre, –ēvī, –itus, blot out, destroy.

abōminātiō, –ōnis, *f.*, abomination.

abripiō, –ere, –uī, –reptus, catch up, seize, carry off, snatch away.

abscīdō, –ere, –cīdī, –cīsus, cut away, cut off.

abscindō, –ere, –scidī, –scissus, tear away, tear off, tear.

abscondō, –ere, –condī, –conditum, lose sight of, conceal.

absimilis, –e, *adj.*, unlike.

abstineō, –ēre, –uī, abstentus, abstain, restrain, keep away, refrain.

abstrahō, –ere, –trāxī, –tractus, draw away from, drag away.

*absum, –esse, āfuī, āfutūrus, be away, be absent, be distant.

abundō, –āre, –āvī, –ātūrus, overflow.

abūtor, –ī, –ūsus sum, waste, squander, abuse.

abyssus, –ī, *m.*, abyss.

ac, *see* **atque.**

*accēdō, –ere, –cessī, –cessūrus, go to, approach, move toward.

acceptus, –a, –um, *adj.*, acceptable, dear.

*accidō, –ere, –cidī, ––, fall to, happen; **accidit,** it happens.

accīdō, –ere, –cīdī, –cīsus, cut into.

*accipiō, –ere, –cēpī, –ceptus, take to oneself, receive, accept.

accumbō, –ere, –uī, ––, recline at, lie down.

accūrātus, –a, –um, *adj.*, careful, exact.

accurrō, –ere, –currī (–cucurrī), –cursūrus, run to, come up.

accūsātor, –ōris, *m.*, accuser, informer.

accūsō, –āre, –āvī, –ātus, blame, accuse.

*ācer, ācris, ācre, *adj.*, sharp, keen, active, fierce.

acerbē, *adv.*, bitterly, harshly.

acerbus, –a, –um, *adj.*, bitter.

*aciēs, –ēī, *f.*, edge, line of battle, battle line.

ācriter, *adv.*, sharply, fiercely.

āctiō, –ōnis, *f.*, action, doing.

āctus, –ūs, *m.*, driving, moving, act.

acūmen, –inis, *n.*, sharp point, sharpness of understanding.

acūtus, –a, –um, *adj.*, sharp, sharpened, pointed, acute.

ad, *prep* + *acc.*, to, toward, near, about, for the purpose of, at, about.

adamō, –āre, –āvī, –ātus, fall in love with, covet.

addō, –ere, –didī, –ditus, give to, add.

addūcō, –ere, –dūxī, –ductus, lead to, influence, induce.

adeō, *adv.*, to such a degree, so.

adeō, –īre, –iī (–īvī), –itūrus, go to, visit.

adhaereō, –ēre, –haesī, —, stick to, adhere.

adhaerēscō, –ere, –haesī, —, cling to, stick to, adhere.

adhibeō, –ēre, –uī, –itus, apply, hold to, employ, show.

adhortor, –ārī, –ātus sum, encourage, exhort, urge.

adhūc, *adv.*, thus far, hitherto, to this time, still.

adigō, –ere, –ēgī, –āctus, drive to, push up, cast, hurl.

adimō, –ere, –ēmī, –ēmptus, take to oneself, take away, take off, cut off.

adipēs, –ium, *adj.*, *pl.*, corpulent.

adipīscor, –ī, adeptus sum, arrive at, secure, obtain, win.

aditus, –ūs, *m.*, approach, access, entrance; *pl.*, landing places.

adjiciō, –ere, –jēcī, –jectus, throw, pile up, add, join to.

adjūdicō, –āre, –āvī, –ātus, adjudge.

adjungō, –ere, –jūnxī, –jūnctus, join to, annex, unite with.

adjuvō, –āre, –jūvī, –jūtus, help, aid, assist, support.

administrō, –āre, –āvī, –ātus, render assistance, manage, administer, govern.

admīrābilis, –e, *adj.*, admirable, astonishing.

admīror, –ārī, –ātus sum, wonder at, marvel at, admire.

admittō, –ere, –mīsī, –missus, let go, admit, be guilty of.

admoneō, –ēre, –uī, –itus, advise, admonish, warn.

admonitus, –ūs, *m.*, warning, advice.

admoveō, –ēre, –mōvī, –mōtus, move to, bring to.

adolēscō, –ere, –olēvī, –ultus, grow up.

adorior, –īrī, –ortus sum, rise against, attack, assault.

adōrō, –āre, –avī, –ātus, pray to, worship.

adsum, –esse, –fuī, –futūrus, be present, be near, be at hand.

adulēscēns, –entis, *m.*, youth, young man.

adulēscentia, –ae, *f.*, youth.

advena, –ae, *mf.*, one who has come, a stranger, foreigner.

adveniō, –īre, –vēnī, –ventūrus, come to, arrive.

adventus, –ūs, *m.*, arrival, advent, coming.

adversārius, –a, –um, *adj.*, opposed; *noun, m.*, enemy, adversary.

adversus (adversum), *prep* + *acc.*, opposite to, against.

adversus, –a, –um, *adj.*, turned towards, facing, opposed, toward: **rēs adversae,** misfortune.

advertō, –ere, –vertī, –versus, turn to, direct, turn.

aedificium, –ī, *n.*, building, dwelling, house.

aedificō, –āre, –āvī, –ātus, build.

aedīlis, –is, *m.*, aedile (commissioner of buildings, trade, health, and games).

aeger, –gra, –grum, *adj.*, sick, ill.

aegrē, *adv.*, with difficulty.

aemulātiō, –ōnis, *f.*, rivalry, emulation.

aemulor, –ārī, –ātus sum, rival, emulate.

aēneus, –a, –um, *adj.*, of copper, bronze.

aequē, *adv.*, in like manner, equally.

aequinoctium, –ī, *n.*, equinox.

aequitās, –tātis, *f.*, fairness, equity, justice.

aequō, –āre, –āvī, –ātus, make level, equal.

aequor, –ōris, *m.*, sea.

aequus, –a, –um, *adj.*, level, equal, fair.

āēr, –āeris, *m.*, air.

aes, aeris, *n.*, copper, bronze, money; **aes aliēnum** (another's money), debt.

aestās, –tātis, *f.*, summer.

aestimātiō, –ōnis, *f.*, valuation.

aestimō, –āre, –āvī, –ātus, estimate, value in money.

aestus, –ūs, *m.*, heat, tide.

aetās, –tātis, *f.*, age, time of life.

aeternus, –a, –um, *adj.*, everlasting, perpetual, eternal.

afferō, –ferre, attulī, allātus, bring to, carry to, offer, report.

afficiō, –ere, –fēcī, –fectus, do something to, affect, afflict.

affīgō, –ere, –fīxī, –fīxus, fasten to.

afflīctō, –āre, –āvī, –ātus, shatter, damage.

afflīgō, –ere, –flīxī, –flīctus, dash against, shatter.

affore = **affutūrus esse**, *fut. inf. of* **adsum**.

ager, agrī, *m.*, cultivated land, field, territory; *pl.*, lands, country, the country; **agrī cultūra**, farming, agriculture.

agger, –eris, *m.*, rampart.

aggredior, –gredī, –gressus sum, step up to, approach, attack, fall upon, attempt.

aggregō, –āre, –āvī, –ātus, crowd together, collect, join.

agmen, –inis, *n.*, army on the march, marching column; **agmen claudere**, bring up the rear; **novissimum agmen**, the rear guard; **prīmum agmen**, the vanguard.

āgnōscō, –ere, –nōvī, –nitus, recognize, acknowledge, understand.

agnus, –ī, *m.*, lamb.

agō, –ere, ēgī, āctus, drive, carry on, do, act; **grātiās agere**, give thanks.

agricola, –ae, *m.*, farmer.

āiō, ais, ait, ājunt, *imperf.*, **ājēbam**, *defective*, say.

āla, –ae, *f.*, wing, wing of an army.

alacer, –cris, –cre, *adj.*, eager, brisk, cheerful.

alacritās, –tātis, *f.*, eagerness, alacrity.

ālārius, –a, –um, *adj.*, auxiliaries, allies.

albus, –a, –um, *adj.*, white.

alcēs, –is, *f.*, moose, European elk.

aliēnus, –a, –um, *adj.*, belonging to another, strange, foreign.

aliō, *adv.*, elsewhere, to another place.

aliquamdiū, *adv.*, for some time.

aliquandō, *adv.*, sometime, at last.

aliquī, aliqua, aliquod, *indef. adj.*, some, any, some other.

aliquis, aliquid, *indef. pron.*, someone, something, anyone, anybody, anything; *pl.*, some, any.

aliquot, *adj.*, *indecl.*, some, several.

aliter, *adv.*, in any other way, otherwise, differently; **aliter ac**, otherwise than.

alius, –a, –ud, *gen.*, alterius, *adj.*, another, some, other, different, else; **alius aliud**, one, one thing, one another; **aliī ... aliī**, some ... other; **longē alius atque**, very different from.

alligō, –āre, –āvī, –ātus, bind to, fasten, tie to.

almus, –a, –um, *adj.*, fostering, gracious, propitious.

alō, –ere, –uī, altus, nourish, sustain, increase.

alter, –era, –erum, *gen.*, alterius, *adj.*, one of two, the other, second; **alter ... alter**, the one ... the other.

alternus, –a, –um, *adj.*, one after the other, alternate.

altitūdō, –inis, *f.*, height, depth.

altus, –a, –um, *adj.*, high, lofty, tall, deep; **altum**, –ī, *n.*, the deep, the sea.

ambactus, –ī, *m.*, vassal, dependent.

ambiō, –īre, –iī (–īvī), –itūrus, go around, surround, approach.

ambitiō, –ōnis, *f.*, a going around, desire for favor, ambition.

ambitiōsus, –a, –um, *adj.*, seeking popularity, ambitious.

ambō, –ae, –ō, *adj.*, both.

ambulō, –āre, –āvī, –ātūrus, walk, march, stroll.

āmentia, –ae, *f.*, madness, folly, frenzy.

āmentum, –ī, *n.*, thong, strap for hurling a dart.

amīcitia, –ae, *f.*, friendship.

amīcus, –a, –um, *adj.*, friendly, well disposed.

amīcus, –ī, *m.*, friend.

āmittō, –ere, –mīsī, –missus, send away, let go, lose.

amō, –āre, –āvī, –ātus, love, be fond of, like.

amor, –ōris, *m.*, love, affection.

āmoveō, –ēre, –mōvī, –mōtus, move away, take away, remove.

amphitheātrum, –ī, *n.*, amphitheater.

amphora, –ae, *f.,* narrow-necked jar with two handles.

***amplus, –a, –um,** adj.,* great, large, ample, spacious; **amplius,** *adv.,* more.

an, *conj.,* or.

anceps, –cipitis, *adj.,* two-headed, double; **anceps proelium,** battle on two fronts.

ancilla, –ae, *f.,* maidservant, handmaid.

ancora, –ae, *f.,* anchor.

angelus, –ī, *m.,* angel.

angor, –ōris, *m.,* mental distress, anguish.

angulus, –ī, *m.,* corner.

angustiae, –ārum, *f.pl.,* narrow place, mountain pass, difficulties, narrowness.

angustus, –a, –um, *adj.,* narrow, close, steep.

anima, –ae, *f.,* breath, life, soul.

***animadvertō, –ere, –vertī, –versus,** turn the mind to, notice, punish.

animal, –ālis, *n.,* living being, animal.

animō, –āre, –āvī, –ātus, give life to, animate.

animōsus, –a, –um, *adj.,* full of spirit, courageous.

***animus, –ī,** *m.,* spirit, feeling, mind, courage; **in animō habēre,** intend.

annūntiō, –āre, –āvī, –ātus, declare, announce.

annuō, –ere, –uī, –utūrus, nod to, assent.

***annus, –ī,** *m.,* year.

ānser, –eris, *m.,* goose.

***ante,** *adv./prep.,* before.

anteā, *adv.,* before this, before, formerly.

anteferō, –ferre, –tulī, –lātus, prefer.

antemna, –ae, *f.,* a spar, sail yard.

antepōnō, –ere, –posuī, –positus, put before, value more highly.

***antequam** *or* **ante . . . quam,** *conj.,* before, until, sooner than.

antīquitus, *adv.,* of old, in former times.

antīquus, –a, –um, *adj.,* ancient, old-time, old, former.

anulus, –ī, *m.,* ring.

anxius, –a, –um, *adj.,* anxious, uneasy.

aper, –prī, *m.,* wild boar.

aperiō, –īre, –uī, –tus, uncover, open, show, disclose, reveal.

apertē, *adv.,* openly, clearly.

***apertus, –a, –um,** *adj.,* open, uncovered, exposed, unprotected, clear.

appareō, –ēre, –uī, –itūrus, appear, be plain.

***appellō, –āre, –āvī, –ātus,** address, call, name, call by name.

appellō, –ere, –pulī, –pulsus, bring to, land.

appetō, –ere, –īvī, –ītus, desire, seek, draw near.

applicō, –āre, –āvī, –ātus, fold, join; **sē applicāre ad,** lean against.

appōnō, –ere, –posuī, –positus, place near, set before, serve.

***appropinquō, –āre, –āvī, –ātus,** draw near to, approach.

aptus, –a, –um, *adj.,* fitted, suitable, apt.

***apud,** *prep.* + *acc.,* at, on, with, near, among, in the presence of, at the house of.

***aqua, –ae,** *f.,* water.

***aquila, –ae,** *f.,* eagle.

aquilō, –ōnis, *m.,* north wind, the north.

āra, –ae, *f.,* altar.

arātrum, –ī, *n.,* plow.

arbitrium, –ī, *n.,* judgment, decision, authority.

***arbitror, –ārī, –ātus sum,** think, consider, believe.

***arbor, –oris,** *f.,* tree.

arcessō, –ere, –īvī, –ītus, cause to come, send for, summon.

arcus, –ūs, *m.,* bow, arch.

ārdeō, –ēre, ārsī, ārsūrus, be on fire, burn, blaze, glow with eagerness.

ārdor, –ōris *m.,* fire, ardor.

arduus, –a, –um, *adj.,* high, steep.

arēna, –ae, *f.,* sand, arena.

argentum, –ī, *n.,* silver, money.

arguō, –ere, –uī, –ūtus, make clear, show, prove.

āridus, –a, –um, *adj.,* parched, thirsty.

ariēs, –etis, *m.,* ram, battering-ram.

***arma, –ōrum,** *n.pl.,* implements of war, arms, armor, weapons.

armāmentum, –ī, *n.,* equipment, implements, rigging.

armātūra, –ae, *f.,* armor, equipment; **levis armātūrae peditēs,** light infantry.

armātus, –a, –um, *adj.,* armed, equipped; **armātī, –ōrum,** *m.pl.,* armed men, soldiers.

*armō, –āre, –āvī, –ātus, arm, equip.
arō, –āre, –āvī, –ātus, plow, till.
arripiō, –ere, –uī, –reptus, seize, snatch.
arroganter, adv., arrogantly, presumptuously.
arrogantia, –ae, f., arrogance, insolence, presumption.
ars, artis, f., skill, art.
articulus, –ī, m., joint, knuckle.
artificium, –ī, n., art, trade, trick.
artus, –a, –um, adj., close, dense.
artus, –ūs, m., joint.
arx, arcis, f., citadel, stronghold.
ascendō, –ere, –scendī, –scēnsus, climb up, ascend, scale.
ascēnsus, –ūs, m., ascent, climbing.
ascīscō, –ere, –scīvī, –scītus, take to, add, adopt.
asinus, –ī, m., an ass.
aspectus, –ūs, m., appearance, aspect, sight.
asper, aspera, asperum, adj., rough, harsh, severe.
aspergō, –ere, –spersī, –spersus, sprinkle.
aspiciō, –ere, –spēxī, –spectus, look on, see, behold, regard.
assector, –ārī, –sectātus sum, follow eagerly.
assequor, –ī, –secūtus sum, follow, pursue, overtake.
assuēfaciō, –ere, –fēcī, –factus, accustom, train.
assuēscō, –ere, –suēvī, –suētus, become accustomed.
assūmō, –ere, –sūmpsī, –sūmptus, take to, adopt, assume.
asylum, –ī, n., place of refuge, asylum.
*at, conj., but, yet, but yet.
*atque or ac, conj., and, and also, and even, and in particular, as, than; idem atque and pār atque, the same as; simul atque, as soon as.
*atrium, –ī, n., atrium, forecourt, main hall of a Roman house.
atrōx, –ōcis, adj., fierce, savage, atrocious.
atrōciter, adv., harshly, cruelly.
attendō, –ere, –tendī, –tentus, stretch to, attend to, listen.

attingō, –ere, –tigī, –tāctus, touch upon, touch, reach, adjoin.
attonitus, –a, –um, adj., thunderstruck, astonished.
attribuō, –ere, –uī, –ūtus, assign, allot, put in charge of.
auctor, –ōris, m., authority, originator, producer, advocate.
*auctōritās, –tātis, f., authority, power, influence, weight.
*audācia, –ae, f., daring, boldness, audacity, rashness.
*audācter, adv., boldly, fearlessly.
*audāx, –ācis, adj., daring, bold, audacious.
*audeō, –ēre, ausus sum, semidep., dare, risk, attempt.
*audiō, –īre, –īvī, –ītus, hear, listen to, hear of.
auferō, –ferre, abstulī, ablātus, bear away, carry away, take away, remove.
*augeō, –ēre, auxī, auctus, increase, enlarge, add to, augment.
aula, –ae, f., forecourt, inner court, palace.
aureus, –a, –um, adj., golden, splendid.
aurīga, –ae, m., chariot driver.
auris, –is, f., ear.
aurum, –ī, n., gold.
*aut, conj., or; aut . . . aut, either . . . or, excluding the other.
*autem, conj., postpositive, but, however, on the contrary, moreover.
autumnus, –ī, m., autumn.
auxilior, –ārī, –ātus sum, give aid.
*auxilium, –ī, n., help, aid, relief; pl., auxiliaries, resources.
avāritia, –ae, f., greed, avarice, covetousness.
avārus, –a, –um, adj., greedy, avaricious.
āvehō, –ere, –vēxī, –vectus, carry away; pass., sail off.
aveō, –ēre, —, —, be well; avē, imperative, hail, farewell.
āversus, –a, –um, adj., turned away, in the rear; āversum hostem, retreating enemy.
āvertō, –ere, –vertī, –versus, turn aside, avert, alienate.
avidē, adv., eagerly, greedily.
avidus, –a, –um, adj., eager, desirous, craving, avid, greedy.

avis, –is, *f.*, bird.
āvocō, –āre, –āvī, –ātus, call away.
āvolō, –āre, –āvī, –ātus, fly away, hasten away, rush away.
avus, –ī, *m.*, grandfather.

B

balteus, –ī, *m.*, belt.
*barbarus, –a, –um, *adj.*, foreign, barbarous, uncivilized; barbarī, –ōrum, *m.pl.*, foreigners, barbarians.
beātus, –a, –um, *adj.*, blessed.
bellicōsus, –a, –um, *adj.*, warlike, fierce, bellicose.
bellicus, –a, –um, *adj.*, relating to war, warlike.
bellō, –āre, –āvī, –ātus, wage war, make war, fight.
*bellum, –ī, *n.*, war; bellum gerere, carry on war; bellum īnferre, wage, make war.
*bene, *adv.*, well, ably, successfully
benedīcō, –ere, –dīxī, –dictus, speak well, praise, bless.
beneficentia, –ae, *f.*, kindness, beneficence.
*beneficium, –ī, *n.*, service, kindness; beneficiō obstringere, put under obligation.
benīgnē, *adv.*, kindly, courteously, benignly.
benīgnitās, –tātis, *f.*, favor, courtesy, benignity, generosity.
benīgnus, –a, –um, *adj.*, kind, friendly, generous.
bestia, –ae, *f.*, beast, animal.
bibō, –ere, bibī, —, drink.
biceps, –cipitis, *adj.*, having two heads, two-headed.
biduum, –ī, *n.*, space of two days, two days.
biennium, –ī, *n.*, (period of) two years.
bīnī, –ae, –a, *adj.*, two by two, two at a time.
bipertītō, *adv.*, in two divisions.
bipertītus, –a, –um, *adj.*, divided in two, in two divisions.
*bis, *adv.*, on two occasions, twice, in two ways.
bonitās, –tātis, *f.*, goodness, excellence, fertility (of land).

*bonus, –a, –um, *adj.*, good; bonum, –ī, *n.*, good thing, the good; bona, –ōrum, *n.pl.*, goods, possessions; bonī, –ōrum, *m.pl.*, the good, good men.
bōs, bovis, *gen.pl.*, boum *or* bovum; *dat./abl.pl.*, bōbus *or* būbus, *mf.*, ox, bull, cow; *pl.*, oxen, cattle.
bracchium, –ī, *n.*, forearm, arm.
brevī, *adv.*, in a short time, soon, quickly.
*brevis, –e, *adj.*, short, brief, shallow.
brevitās, –tātis, *f.*, shortness, brevity.
breviter, *adv.*, shortly.
brūma, –ae, *f.*, the winter solstice, winter.
bulla, –ae, *f.*, round swelling, stud, amulet.

C

cacūmen, –inis, *n.*, top, summit.
cadāver, –eris, *n.*, dead body, corpse, cadaver.
cadō, –ere, cecidī, cāsūrus, fall, be slain.
caecus, –a, –um, *adj.*, blind.
*caedēs, –is, *f.*, killing, murder, slaughter.
caedō, –ere, cecīdī, caesus, cut, cut down, cut to pieces, slay.
caelestis, –e, *adj.*, heavenly; caelestēs, –ium, *m.pl.*, the gods.
*caelum, –ī, *n.*, sky, heaven, heavens.
caeruleus, –a, –um, *adj.*, dark blue, sky-blue, dark.
*calamitās, –tātis, *f.*, disaster, loss, defeat, calamity.
calcar, –āris, *n.*, spur.
calceus, –ī, *m.*, shoe.
calix, –icis, *m.*, goblet, drinking vessel.
cālō, –ōnis, *m.*, soldier's servant, camp servant.
calor, –ōris, *m.*, warmth, heat, glow.
calumnior, –ārī, –ātus sum, accuse falsely, calumniate.
calx, calcis, *f.*, heel.
camīnus, –ī, *m.*, forge, fireplace.
*campus, –ī, *m.*, plain, field.
cancer, –eris, *m.*, crab.
candēla, –ae, *f.*, candle.
candor, –ōris, *m.*, whiteness, lustre.
canis, –is, *mf.*, dog, hound.
canō, –ere, cecinī, cantus, sing, prophesy.
cantō, –āre, –āvī, –ātus, sing, play, predict, chant.
cantus, –ūs, *m.*, song, singing, chant.

capillus, –ī, *m.,* hair.

capiō, –ere, cēpī, captus, take, seize; **initium capere,** begin; **cōnsilium capere,** form a plan.

capra, –ae, *f.,* she-goat.

captīvus, –ī, *m.,* captive, prisoner.

caput, –itis, *n.,* head, mouth (of a river); **capitis poena,** capital punishment; **capite dēmissō,** with head bowed down; **duo mīlia capitum,** two thousand souls.

carcer, –eris, *m.,* prison, dungeon.

careō, –ēre, –uī, –itūrus, be without, lack, want.

carīna, –ae, *f.,* keel, ship.

cāritās, –tātis, *f.,* dearness, high price, love.

carmen, –inis, *n.,* song, verse.

carō, carnis, *f.,* flesh, meat.

carpō, –ere, carpsī, carptus, pluck, seize.

carrus, –ī, *m.,* cart, wagon.

cārus, –a, –um, *adj.,* dear, beloved, high-priced.

casa, –ae, *f.,* hut, cottage; *pl.,* barracks.

caseus, –ī, *m.,* cheese.

castellum, –ī, *n.,* little camp, fort, redoubt, fortress, garrison.

castīgō, –āre, –āvī, –ātus, reprove, chastise.

castrum, –ī, *n.,* fort, fortress; *pl.,* camp; **castra movēre,** break camp; **castra pōnere,** pitch camp.

cāsus, –ūs, *m.,* fall, chance, accident.

catēna, –ae, *f.,* chain, fetter.

caterva, –ae, *f.,* crowd.

cauda, –ae, *f.,* tail.

causa, –ae, *f.,* cause, reason, excuse; *abl.,* **causā,** *with preceding gen.,* for the sake of.

cautē, *adv.,* cautiously.

caveō, –ēre, cāvī, cautūrus, be on one's guard, beware.

caverna, –ae, *f.,* hollow place, cavern, cave.

cēdō, –ere, cessī, cessūrus, go away, yield, retreat.

celebrō, –āre, –āvī, –ātus, throng, crowd, celebrate.

celer, –eris, –ere, *adj.,* swift, quick, speedy.

celeritās, –tātis, *f.,* swiftness, speed, celerity.

celeriter, *adv.,* swiftly, quickly.

cēlō, –āre, –āvī, –ātus, hide, keep secret.

cēna, –ae, *f.,* banquet, dinner.

cēnseō, –ēre, cēnsuī, cēnsus, estimate, judge, decree.

cēnsus, –ūs, *m.,* census, registration by censors, enumeration.

centaurus, –ī, *m.,* centaur (half man, half horse).

centum, *adj., indecl.,* one hundred.

centuria, –ae, *f.,* company of 100, century.

centuriō, –ōnis, *m.,* centurion, commander of **centuria.**

cēra, –ae, *f.,* wax.

cernō, –ere, crēvī, crētus, separate, see, discern, perceive.

certāmen, –inis, *n.,* contest, battle.

certē, *adv.,* certainly, surely, at least.

certus, –a, –um, *adj.,* determined, fixed, certain; **certiōrem facere,** inform; **certior fierī,** be informed.

cervus, –ī, *m.,* stag, deer.

cessō, –āre, –āvī, –ātus, be remiss, delay, loiter, cease.

cēterus, –a, –um, *adj.,* other, the other, the rest; *pl.,* the rest, the others; **cēterī, –ōrum,** *m.pl.,* the others, all the rest; **cētera, –ōrum,** *n.pl.,* the rest, everything else.

cibāria, –ōrum, *n.pl.,* provisions, rations.

cibus, –ī, *m.,* food.

cingō, –ere, cīnxī, cīnctus, surround, encircle, gird, wreathe.

cinis, –eris, *m.,* ashes.

circēnsis, –e, *adj.,* pertaining to the circus; *pl.,* circus games.

circinus, –ī, pair of compasses.

circiter, *adv./prep.* + *acc.,* about, near.

circuitus, –ūs, *m.,* circuit, way around.

circum, *adv./prep.* + *acc.,* about, around, round.

circumdō, –dare, –dedī, –datus, place around, surround, encircle.

circumdūcō, –ere, –dūxī, –ductus, lead around, draw around.

circumeō, –īre, –iī (–īvī), –itus, go around, surround.

circumsistō, –ere, –stetī (–stitī), —, stand around, surround, beset.

circumvallō, –āre, –āvī, –ātus, surround with a rampart, blockade.

*circumveniō, –īre, –vēnī, –ventus, come around, go around, surround.

circus, –ī, *m.,* circle.

cis, *prep.* + *acc.,* on this side of.

*citerior, –ōris, *adj.,* on this side, hither, nearer.

citrā, *prep.* + *acc.,* this side of.

cīvīlitās, –tātis, *f.,* politeness, civility.

cīvis, –is, *mf.,* citizen.

cīvitās, –tātis, *f.,* body of citizens, state, nation, citizenship.

clam, *adv.,* secretly.

*clāmō, –āre, –āvī, –ātūrus, call out, cry out, shout.

*clāmor, –ōris, *m.,* outcry, cry, shout, clamor.

clārē, *adv.,* clearly.

clārō, –āre, –āvī, –ātus, make clear, make renowned.

*clārus, –a, –um, *adj.,* clear, bright, distinct, loud.

*classis, –is, *f.,* class, division of the people, fleet.

*claudō, –ere, clausī, clausus, shut, close; **agmen claudere,** bring up the rear.

clāva, –ae, *f.,* club, cudgel.

clēmenter, *adv.,* quietly, mildly.

clēmentia, –ae, *f.,* clemency, mercy, kindness.

cliēns, –entis, *m.,* dependent, follower, client.

coacervō, –āre, –āvī, –ātus, heap up, pile up.

coemō, –ere, –ēmī, –ēmptus, buy up.

coeō, –īre, –iī (–īvī), –itūrus, go together, unite.

*coepī, –isse, coeptus, *defective,* begin, commence.

coerceō, –ere, –uī, –itus, confine, restrain, check.

cōgitātiō, –ōnis, *f.,* thinking, reflection, idea.

cōgitō, –āre, –āvi, –ātus, consider, reflect on, think.

*cōgnōscō, –ere, –gnōvī, –gnitus, become acquainted with, learn, know, recognize.

*cōgō, –ere, –ēgī, –āctus, drive together, gather, force, compel.

*cohors, –hortis, *f.,* cohort (the tenth part of a legion).

*cohortor, –ārī, –ātus sum, encourage, cheer up, urge, exhort.

collaudō, –āre, –āvī, –ātus, praise highly, commend.

colligō, –āre, –āvī, –ātus, bind together.

colligō, –ere, –lēgī, –lēctus, gather together, collect.

*collis, –is, *m.,* hill, height, elevation.

*collocō, –āre, –āvī, –ātus, place together, place, station; **collocātus, –a, –um,** situated.

*colloquium, –ī, *n.,* conference, interview.

colloquor, –ī, –locūtus sum, talk with, confer, hold a conference.

collum, –ī, *n.,* neck.

colō, –ere, –uī, cultus, till, cultivate, inhabit, worship.

colōnia, –ae, *f.,* colony, settlement.

color, –ōris, *m.,* color.

columba, –ae, *f.,* dove, pigeon.

columna, –ae, *f.,* column.

coma, –ae, *f.,* hair.

combūrō, –ere, –bussī, –būstus, burn up, consume, set fire.

comes, –itis, *mf.,* companion, comrade, retainer.

comitor, –ārī, –ātus sum, attend, accompany.

commeātus, –ūs, *m.,* passing to and fro, trip, supplies.

commemorō, –āre, –āvī, –ātus, mention, relate.

commendō, –āre, –āvī, –ātus, intrust, commend, defend.

commentārius, –ī, *m.,* notebook, source book.

commeō, –āre, –āvī, –ātus, go and come, visit, resort to.

comminus, *adv.,* hand to hand.

*committō, –ere, –mīsī, –missus, bring together, entrust, commit; **proelium committere,** begin battle, fight.

commodus, –a, –um, *adj.,* fitting, suitable, convenient; **commodum, -ī,** *n.,* convenience, advantage, profit.

commoror, -ārī, -ātus sum, delay, stay temporarily, remain.

__commoveō,__ -ēre, -mōvī, -mōtus, move thoroughly, startle, alarm, disturb.

commūnicō, -āre, -āvī, -ātus, share with, communicate.

commūniō, -īre, -iī (-īvī), -ītus, strongly fortify, intrench.

__commūnis,__ -e, *adj.,* common, general, public; **commūnī cōnsiliō,** by common consent.

commutātiō, -ōnis, *f.,* change, exchange.

commūtō, -āre, -āvī, -ātus, change, alter, exchange.

__comparō,__ -āre, -āvī, -ātus, prepare, get together.

comparō, -āre, -āvī, -ātus, match, compare.

compellō, -ere, -pulī, -pulsus, drive together, force back, compel.

comperiō, -īre, -perī, -pertus, find out, learn.

complector, -ī, -plexus sum, embrace, encircle, include.

__compleō,__ -ēre, -ēvī, -ētus, fill completely, fill up, complete.

__complūrēs,__ -a, *adj., pl.,* several, many; **complūrēs, -ium,** *m.pl.,* a great many.

compōnō, -ere, -posuī, -positus, put together, compose, include.

__comportō,__ -āre, -āvī, -ātus, bring in, bring together, carry.

comprehendō, -ere, -ī, -hēnsus, seize, grasp at, catch, arrest, understand.

comprimō, -ere, -pressī, -pressus, press together, compress, repress, squeeze.

cōnātus, -ūs, *m.,* attempt, trial.

__concēdō,__ -ere, -cessī, -cessūrus, withdraw, concede, allow, yield, grant.

concidō, -ere, -cidī, —, fall down, collapse.

concīdō, -ere, -cīdī, -cīsus, cut to pieces, kill, destroy.

conciliō, -āre, -āvī, -ātus, win over, conciliate, reconcile, procure.

__concilium,__ -ī, *n.,* meeting, assembly, council.

conclāmō, -āre, -āvī, -ātūrus, shout, cry out.

concupīscō, -ere, -cupīvī, -cupītus, greatly desire, covet.

concurrō, -ere, -currī, -cursūrus, run together, rush, charge, dash together.

concursus, -ūs, *m.,* running together, concourse, meeting, shock.

__condiciō,__ -ōnis, *f.,* condition, agreement, terms.

condō, -ere, -didī, -ditus, put together, form, build, found, conceal.

condūcō, -ere, -dūxī, -ductus, bring together, lead together, collect.

__cōnferō,__ -ferre, -tulī, collātus, bring together, collect, convey; **sē cōnferre,** betake one's self, proceed.

cōnfertus, -a, -um, *adj.,* crowded together, dense, in close array, compact.

cōnfestim, *adv.,* at once, speedily.

__cōnficiō,__ -ere, -fēcī, -fectus, do thoroughly, perform, accomplish, finish, complete.

cōnfīdenter, *adv.,* confidently, boldly.

cōnfīdō, -ere, -fīsus sum, *semidep.,* rely upon, have confidence in, trust firmly, confide.

cōnfīgō, -ere, -fīxī, -fīxus, fasten together, join.

__cōnfirmō,__ -āre, -āvī, -ātus, confirm, strengthen, establish, assure, encourage, enforce.

cōnfiteor, -ērī, cōnfessus sum, confess, admit.

cōnflīgō, -ere, -flīxī, -flīctus, dash together, harass.

cōnflō, -āre, -āvī, -ātus, blow together, produce, cause.

cōnfluō, -ere, -flūxī, -flūxūrus, flow together, assemble.

congaudeō, -ēre, —, —, rejoice with someone.

congredior, -gredī, -gressus sum, come together, meet.

congregō, -āre, -āvī, -ātus, collect into a flock, assemble.

__conjiciō,__ -ere, -jēcī, -jectus, hurl, throw, strike; **conjicere in fugam,** put to flight.

*conjungō, –ere, –jūnxī, –jūnctus, join together, unite.

conjūnx, –jugis, *mf.*, husband, wife.

conjūrātiō, –ōnis, *f.*, conspiracy, plot.

conjūrō, –āre, –āvī, –ātus, swear together, conspire, form a conspiracy.

*cōnor, –ārī, –ātus sum, attempt, try.

conquīrō, –ere, –quaesīvī, –quīsītus, hunt out, bring together, collect.

consanguineus, –a, –um, *adj.*, of the same blood; *noun, mf.*, relative, kinsman.

cōnscendō, –ere, –scendī, –scēnsus, mount, ascend, embark, board a ship, climb aboard.

cōnscientia, –ae, *f.*, consciousness, knowledge, sense of right and wrong.

cōnscīscō, –ere, –scīvī, –scītus, agree on, decree; cōnscīscere sibi mortem, commit suicide.

cōnscius, –a, –um, *adj.*, conscious.

cōnscrībō, –ere, –scrīpsī, –scrīptus, write, enroll.

cōnsector, –ārī, –ātus sum, pursue, overtake.

cōnsēnsus, –ūs, *m.*, consent, agreement.

cōnsentiō, –īre, –sēnsī, –sēnsus, think together, agree, unite.

*cōnsequor, –ī, –secūtus sum, follow up, overtake, accomplish, gain.

*cōnservō, –āre, –āvī, –ātus, preserve, keep, observe, save.

cōnsīderō, –āre, –āvī, –ātus, look at closely, consider, contemplate.

*cōnsīdō, –ere, –sēdī, —, sit down, settle.

*cōnsilium, –ī, *n.*, consultation, counsel, advice, plan, judgment, purpose; cōnsilium capere (inīre, facere), form a plan.

cōnsimilis, –e, *adj.*, very like, exactly like.

*cōnsistō, –ere, –stitī, —, stand, stay, be formed of, consist (in), depend (on).

cōnsolor, –ārī, –ātus sum, speak kindly to, console.

*cōnspectus, –ūs, *m.*, view, sight.

*cōnspiciō, –ere, –spēxī, –spectus, catch sight of, behold; *pass.*, be conspicuous.

cōnspicor, –ārī, –ātus sum, get sight of, see.

cōnstanter, *adv.*, resolutely, uniformly, unanimously.

cōnstantia, –ae, *f.*, firmness, steadfastness, constancy.

*cōnstituō, –ere, –uī, –ūtus, establish, set up, station, determine, decide, constitute.

cōnstō, –āre, –stitī, –stātūrus, stand firm, consist of; *impers.*, cōnstat, it is agreed (well known, certain, evident).

cōnsuēscō, –ere, –suēvī, –suētus, accustom; *perf.*, be accustomed.

cōnsuētūdō, –inis, *f.*, custom, habit, mode of life.

*cōnsul, –ulis, *m.*, consul, the highest magistrate at Rome.

cōnsulātus, –ūs, *m.*, consulship.

cōnsulō, –ere, –uī, –sultus, take counsel, consult.

cōnsultātiō, –ōnis, *f.*, consideration, consultation.

cōnsultō, *adv.*, on purpose, purposely.

cōnsultō, –āre, –āvī, –ātus, deliberate, take counsel.

cōnsultum, –ī, *n.*, decree, decision.

cōnsummō, –āre, –āvī, –ātus, sum up, finish, consummate.

*cōnsūmō, –ere, –sūmpsī, –sūmptus, use up, devour, consume, burn up.

cōnsurgō, –ere, –rēxī, –rēctūrus, arise together, stand up.

contagiō, –ōnis, *f.*, contact.

contegō, –ere, –tēxī, –tēctus, cover, cover over, bury.

*contendō, –ere, –tendī, –tentus, strive, struggle, contend, hasten.

contentiō, –ōnis, *f.*, effort, struggle, contention.

contentus, –a, –um, *adj.*, contented.

contestor, –ārī, –ātus sum, invoke.

contexō, –ere, –uī, –textus, weave, make of wickerwork, join, construct.

continēns, –entis, *adj.*, bordering; *as noun, f.*, the mainland, continent.

continenter, *adv.*, continually.

*contineō, –ēre, –uī, –tentus, hold together, contain, bound, limit, hem in.

contingō, –ere, –tigī, –tāctus, touch, be near, border on, happen.

continuō, *adv.*, immediately, at once.

*continuus, –a, –um, *adj.*, unbroken, continuous, successive.

*contrā, *adv.*, opposite, face to face, on the contrary; *prep.* + *acc.*, opposite, facing, contrary to, against.

contrahō, –ere, –trāxī, –trāctus, draw together, contract, concentrate.

contrārius, –a, –um, *adj.*, opposite, contrary.

contrōversia, –ae, *f.*, debate, controversy, strife.

contumēlia, –ae, *f.*, insult, affront, abuse, contumely.

contumēliōsus, –a, –um, *adj.*, insulting, contumelious.

*conveniō, –īre, –vēnī, –ventūrus, come together, assemble, convene, meet; *impers.*, **convenit,** it is fitting, it is agreed.

conventus, –ūs, *m.*, assembly, meeting; **conventūs agere,** hold court.

conversiō, –ōnis, *f.*, turning around, periodical return.

convertō, –ere, –vertī, –versus, turn about, wheel about, change; **conversa sīgna īnferre,** face about and advance.

convincō, –ere, –vīcī, –victus, prove, convict, conquer.

convīvium, –ī, *n.*, banquet, feast.

*convocō, –āre, –āvī, –ātus, call together, summon, convoke.

coorior, –īrī, –ortus sum, arise, appear.

cooperiō, –īre, –operuī, –opertus, cover entirely, overwhelm.

*cōpia, –ae, *f.*, supply, abundance, plenty; *pl.*, wealth, forces, troops.

cōpiōsus, –a, –um, *adj.*, wealthy, well supplied, copious.

cor, cordis, *n.*, heart.

cōram, *adv.*, before, face to face, personally; *prep.* + *abl.*, in the presence of.

*cornu, –ūs, *n.*, horn, wing of an army.

corōna, –ae, *f.*, garland, chaplet; **sub corōnā vendere,** sell as slaves.

corōnō, –āre, –āvī, –ātus, crown, surround.

*corpus, –oris, *n.*, body.

corripiō, –ere, –uī, –reptus, snatch up, seize, press on.

cortex, –icis, *mf.*, bark of a tree.

cotīdiānus, –a, –um, *adj.*, daily.

cotīdiē, *adv.*, every day, daily.

crās, *adv.*, tomorrow.

creātor, –ōris, *m.*, creator.

creātūra, –ae, *f.*, a thing created, creature, creation.

crēber, –bra, –brum, *adj.*, thick, frequent, abundant.

*crēdō, –ere, –didī, –ditūrus, believe, trust.

cremō, –āre, –āvī, –ātus, burn, consume by fire.

creō, –āre, –āvī, –ātus, bring forth, produce, create; (of officials) elect, choose.

crepitus, –ūs, *m.*, rattling, creaking, noise.

crepundia, –ōrum, *n.pl.*, rattle child's plaything.

crēscō, –ere, crēvī, crētūrus, grow, increase, become great.

crēta, –ae, *f.*, chalk.

crīmen, –inis, *n.*, accusation, charge, crime, offense.

cruciātus, –ūs, *m.*, torture, suffering.

crūdēlis, –e, *adj.*, cruel, ruthless.

crūdēlitās, –tātis, *f.*, cruelty.

crūdēliter, *adv.*, cruelly.

crūs, crūris, *n.*, leg.

crux, crucis, *f.*, cross, gallows.

cubīle, –is, *n.*, bed, resting place.

cubō, –āre, –uī, –itūrus, lie down, recline at table.

culmen, –inis, *n.*, top, summit.

culpa, –ae, *f.*, fault, blame.

culpō, –āre, –āvī, –ātus, blame, disapprove.

cultūra, –ae, *f.*, tilling, cultivation.

cultus, –ūs, *m.*, civilization.

*cum, *prep.* + *abl.*, with, together with.

*cum, *conj.*, *temporal*, when, while, as long as, after, whenever, as often as; *causal*, since, because, as; *concessive*, although; **cum prīmum,** as soon as.

cūnae, –ārum, *f.pl.*, a cradle.

cunctor, –ārī, –ātus sum, delay, hesitate.

cūnctus, –a, –um, *adj.*, all together, all, whole, entire.

cupiditās, –tātis, *f.*, eagerness, desire, ambition.

cupīdō, –inis, *f.*, longing, desire.

*cupidus, –a, –um, *adj.,* eager for, desirous of.

*cupiō, –ere, –īvī, –ītus, long for, desire, want, wish.

*cūr, *interrog. adv.,* why? wherefore? for what reason?; *rel. adv.,* why, wherefore.

*cūra, –ae, *f.,* care, concern, anxiety, worry.

cūrātiō, –ōnis, *f.,* care, management.

*cūrō, –āre, –āvī, –ātus, take care of, provide for, see to.

curriculum, –ī, *n.,* a running, racecourse, chariot.

*currō, –ere, cucurrī, cursūrus, run.

*currus, –ūs, *m.,* chariot, car.

*cursus, –ūs, *m.,* a running, course, advance.

cūstōdia, –ae, *f.,* protection, custody, guard, watch.

cūstōdiō, –īre, –īvī, –ītus, watch, guard.

cūstōs, –ōdis, *mf.,* a guard, watchman, keeper.

D

damnō, –āre, –āvī, –ātus, condemn, sentence.

damnum, –ī, *n.,* loss.

*dē, *prep.* + *abl.,* from, down from, concerning.

*dēbeō, –ēre, –uī, –itus, owe, be in debt, ought, must, should.

dēbitor, –ōris, *m.,* debtor.

dēcēdō, –ere, –cessī, –cessūrus, go away, retire, withdraw, depart, die.

*decem, *adj., indecl.,* ten.

dēcernō, –ere, –crēvī, –crētus, decide, determine, decree.

dēcertō, –āre, –āvī, –ātus, fight to a finish, fight a decisive battle.

dēcidō, –ere, –cidī, —, fall, fall down.

*decimus, –a, –um, *adj.,* tenth.

dēcipiō, –ere, –cēpī, –ceptus, catch, deceive.

dēclārō, –āre, –āvī, –ātus, make clear, declare, announce.

dēclīvis, –e, *adj.,* sloping down, descending.

dēcuriō, –ōnis, *m.,* decurion, a cavalry officer in charge of a **decuria** (ten horsemen).

dēcurrō, –ere, –cucurrī (–currī),

–cursūrus, run down, rush down, hasten.

decus, –oris, *n.,* beauty, grace, glory.

dēdecus, –oris, *n.,* disgrace, dishonor.

dēdicātiō, –ōnis, *f.,* consecration, dedication.

dēditīcius, –a, –um, *adj.,* surrendered, subject; **dēditīciī, –ōrum,** *m.pl.,* prisoners of war, captives.

*dēditiō, –ōnis, *f.,* surrender.

dēditus, –a, –um, *adj.,* devoted.

*dēdō, –ere, –didī, –ditus, give up, surrender, hand over.

*dēdūcō, –ere, –dūxī, –ductus, lead down, lead away, lead, launch.

*dēfendō, –ere, –fendī, –fēnsus, ward off, repel, defend.

dēfensiō, –ōnis, *f.,* defence.

*dēfēnsor, –ōris, *m.,* defender, protector.

dēferō, –ferre, –tulī, –lātus, carry away, bear away, report.

dēfessus, –a, –um, *adj.,* wearied, weary, exhausted.

dēfetīscor, –ī, dēfessus sum, become tired.

dēficiō, –ere, –fēcī, –fectus, fail, be lacking, rebel.

dēfīgō, –ere, –fīxī, –fīxus, drive in.

dēfodiō, –ere, –fōdī, –fossus, bury.

dēfluō, –ere, –flūxī, –flūxūrus, flow down, fall.

dēfugiō, –ere, –fūgī, —, flee from, avoid.

deinde, *adv.,* then, thereafter, next, thence.

dējectus, –ūs, *m.,* slope, declivity.

*dējiciō, –ere, –jēcī, –jectus, throw down, dislodge, rout.

dēlābor, –ī, –lāpsus sum, slip down.

dēlectō, –āre, –āvī, –ātus, delight, charm.

dēlēgō, –āre, –āvī, –ātus, transfer, commit, assign.

dēleō, –ēre, –ēvī, –ētus, wipe out, erase, destroy.

dēlīberō, –āre, –āvī, –ātus, weigh, consider, deliberate.

dēlīctum, –ī, *n.,* defense, crime.

dēligō, –āre, –āvī, –ātus, tie to, fasten.

*dēligō, –ere, –lēgī, –lēctus, choose, pick out, select.

dēlitēscō, –ere, –lituī, —, hide oneself, lie in wait.

dēmēns, –mentis, *adj.,* out of mind, mad, distracted.

dēmetō, –ere, –mēssuī, –messus, reap, cut.

dēminuō, –ere, –uī, –ūtus, lessen, diminish.

dēmittō, –ere, –mīsī, –missus, send down, let fall, drop, depress.

dēmō, –ere, dēmpsī, dēmptus, take down.

*dēmōnstrō, –āre, –āvī, –ātus, point out, explain, demonstrate, show.

dēmoror, –ārī, –ātus sum, delay, hinder.

dēmum, *adv.,* at length, at last, finally.

dēnārius, –ī, *m.,* a Roman silver coin.

dēnegō, –āre, –āvī, –ātus, refuse.

dēnī, –ae, –a, *adj.,* ten each.

dēnique, *adv.,* at length, finally, at last.

*dēns, dentis, *m.,* tooth.

dēnsus, –a, –um, *adj.,* thick, close, dense.

dēnūdo, –āre, –āvī, –ātus, lay bare, uncover.

dēnūntiō, –āre, –āvī, –ātus, announce, give warning.

deorsum, *adv.,* downwards

dēpellō, –ere, –pulī, –pulsus, drive away, dislodge.

dēpereō, –īre, –periī, –peritūrus, perish, be lost.

dēpōnō, –ere, –posuī, –positus, put down, put aside, put away, lay aside.

dēpopulor, –ārī, –ātus sum, ravage, lay waste, waste.

dēprecātor, –ōris, *m.,* intercessor; **eō dēprecātōre,** by his intercession.

dēprimō, –ere, –pressī, –pressus, sink.

dērīdeō, –ēre, –rīsī, –rīsūrus, mock, laugh at, deride.

dēripiō, –ere, –uī, –reptus, snatch away, tear off, tear away.

dērogō, –āre, –āvī, –ātus, withdraw.

dēscendō, –ere, –scendī, –scēnsus, climb down, descend, dismount.

dēsecō, –āre, –uī, –sectus, cut off.

dēserō, –ere, –uī, –sertus, leave, abandon, desert.

dēsertor, –ōris, *m.,* deserter, runaway.

dēsīderium, –ī, *n.,* longing, desire.

dēsīderō, –āre, –āvī, –ātus, long for, desire greatly, want, wish.

dēsidia, –ae, *f.,* indolence, idleness.

dēsīgnō, –āre, –āvī, –ātus, mark out, designate.

dēsiliō, –īre, –uī, –sultus, leap down, dismount.

dēsīnō, –ere, –siī (sīvī), –sitūrus, leave off, cease.

dēsistō, –ere, –stitī, –stitūrus, leave off, desist from, give up, cease.

dēspectus, –ūs, *m.,* downward view.

*dēspērō, –āre, –āvī, –ātūrus, despair of, give up hope of.

dēspiciō, –ere, –spēxī, –spectus, look down upon, despise.

dēspoliō, –āre, –āvī, –ātus, deprive, despoil.

dēstino, –āre, –āvī, –ātus, make fast, bind, assign.

dēstringō, –ere, –strīnxī, –strictus, strip off, scrape, draw (a sword).

dēsum, –esse, –fuī, –futūrus, be wanting, be lacking, fail.

dēsuper, *adv.,* from above.

dētegō, –ere, –tēxī, –tēctus, uncover, expose, reveal.

dētendō, –ere, –tendī, –tēnsus, unstretch, relax, strike (a tent).

dēterior, –ōris, *adj.,* worse, meaner.

dēterreō, –ēre, –uī, –itus, frighten off, prevent, deter.

dētestor, –ārī, –ātus sum, avert by entreaty, hate, detest.

dētrahō, –ere, –trāxī, –trāctus, draw off, rob, remove, disparage, detract.

dētrīmentum, –ī, *n.,* loss, damage, defeat, harm.

*deus, –ī, *m.;* **dea, –ae,** *f.,* god; goddess.

dēveniō, –īre, –vēnī, –ventūrus, come.

dēvexus, –a, –um, *adj.,* sloping; **dēvexa, –ōrum,** *n.pl.,* slopes.

dēvincō, –ere, –vīcī, –victus, conquer, subdue.

dēvorō, –āre, –āvī, –ātus, swallow, devour.

dēvoveō, –ēre, –vōvī, –vōtus, vow, devote, consecrate.

*dexter, –tra, –trum, *adj.,* right; **dextra, –ae,** *f.,* right hand; **ā dextrā,** on the right.

diābolus, –ī, *m.,* devil.

dicĭō, –ōnis, f., sovereignty, lordship.

dicō, –āre, –āvī, –ātus, devote, offer.

*dīcō, –ere, dīxī, –dictus, say, talk, tell, speak; diem dīcere, name a day; causam dīcere, plead a case.

dictĭō, –ōnis, f., a pleading of a case.

dictum, –ī, n., a word, saying, speech.

*diēs, –ēī, mf., day, time; multō diē, late in the day; in diēs, day by day; diem ex diē, from day to day; diem dīcere, name a day; triduum, –ī, n., three days.

differentia, –ae, f., difference, distinction.

differō, –ferre, distulī, dīlātus, spread, scatter, differ, delay.

*difficilis, –e, adj., hard, difficult.

*difficultās, –tātis, f., difficulty, trouble.

diffundō, –ere, diffūdī, –fūsus, pour out, spread out, diffuse, scatter.

*digitus, –ī, m., finger, toe.

dīgnitās, –tātis, f., worth, merit, dignity.

dīgnus, –a, –um, adj., worthy, deserving.

dījūdicō, –āre, –āvī, –ātus, decide, settle.

dīlēctus, –ūs, m., levy, enlistment.

*dīligēns, –entis, adj., industrious, diligent.

dīligenter, adv., carefully, diligently.

*dīligentia, –ae, f., industry, care, diligence.

dīligō, –ere, –lēxī, –lēctus, choose, value, love.

dīmicō, –āre, –āvī, –ātus, fight, contend, struggle.

dīmidius, –a, –um, adj., half.

*dīmittō, –ere, –mīsī, –missus, send apart, dismiss, send off, release, leave.

dīrigō, –ere, –rēxī, –rēctus, direct, steer.

dirimō, –ere, –ēmī, –ēmptus, break up, end.

dīripiō, –ere, –uī, –reptus, plunder, pillage.

*discēdō, –ere, –cessī, –cessūrus, go away, depart, leave behind.

discessus, –ūs, m., departure.

*disciplīna, –ae, f., training, instruction, learning.

discipulus, –ī, m., pupil, follower.

discō, –ere, didicī, —, learn, learn how.

discordia, –ae, f., strife, discord.

discrīmen, –inis, n., crisis, peril, interval.

discutiō, –ere, –cussī, –cussus, shatter, clear away.

disertus, –a, –um, adj., eloquent, expressive.

disjiciō, –ere, –jēcī, –jectus, drive apart, scatter, disperse, throw apart.

dispergō, –ere, –spersī, –spersus, scatter, disperse.

dispōnō, –ere, –posuī, –positus, place here and there, dispose, distribute.

disputō, –āre, –āvī, –ātus, examine, discuss, dispute.

dissiliō, –īre, –siluī, —, leap apart, be torn asunder.

*dissimilis, –e, adj., unlike, dissimilar.

dissimulō, –āre, –āvī, –ātus, make unlike, keep secret.

dissipō, –āre, –āvī, –ātus, strew, scatter, dissipate.

dissolvō, –ere, –solvī, –solūtus, loosen, break up, melt, pay a debt.

distō, –āre, —, —, stand apart, be distant.

distribuō, –ere, –uī, –ūtus, divide, distribute.

disyllabus, –a, –um, adj., dissyllabic.

*diū, adv., long, for a long time; comp., diūtius; superl., diūtissimē; quam diū, as long as; jam diū, a long time ago.

diurnus, –a, –um, adj., of the day, by day, during the day.

diūturnitās, –tātis, f., long duration.

dīversus, –a, –um, adj., opposite, different, diverse.

dīves, –itis, adj., rich, wealthy.

*dīvidō, –ere, –vīsī, –vīsus, separate, divide.

dīvīnus, –a, –um, adj., godlike, divine.

dīvitiae, –ārum, f.pl., riches, wealth.

*dō, dare, dedī, datus, give, grant; poenās dare, suffer punishment; negōtium dare, direct; in fugam dare, put to flight; operam dare, give attention; in mātrimōnium dare, give in marriage.

*doceō, –ēre, –uī, doctus, teach, inform.

docilis, –e, adj., docile

doctrīna, –ae, f., teaching, training, learning.

doctus, –a, –um, adj., learned.

documentum, –ī, n., proof, warning.

doleō, –ēre, –uī, –itūrus, suffer, grieve, feel pain.

*dolor, –ōris, m., pain, grief, resentment.

dolus, –ī, m., deceit, treachery, cunning trick.

*domicilium, –ī, n., habitation, dwelling.

*domina, –ae, f., lady, mistress (of a household).

dominor, –ārī, –ātus sum, be master, rule, domineer.

*dominus, –ī, m., lord, master (of a household).

*domus, –ūs, f., house, dwelling, home; loc., domī, at home; acc., domum, homeward.

dōnec, conj., as long as, while, until.

*dōnō, –āre, –āvī, –ātus, give, present, reward.

*dōnum, –ī, n., gift, present.

*dormiō, –īre, –īvī, –itūrus, sleep.

dracō, –ōnis, m., dragon, serpent.

*dubitātiō, –ōnis, f., doubt, hesitation.

*dubitō, –āre, –āvī, –ātus, doubt, hesitate.

dubius, –a, –um, adj., doubtful; dubium, –ī, n., doubt.

ducentī, –ae, –a, adj., two hundred.

*dūcō, –ere, dūxī, ductus, lead, guide; (of a trench) make; consider; in mātrimōnium dūcere, marry.

dūdum, adv., a while ago, lately; jam dūdum, now for a long time.

dulcēdō, –inis, f., pleasantness, charm, sweetness.

dulcis, –e, adj., sweet.

*dum, conj., while, as long as, until, till.

*duo, –ae, –o, adj., two, both.

duodecim, adj., indecl., twelve.

duodecimus, –a, –um, adj., twelfth.

duodēvīgintī, adj., indecl., eighteen.

duplicō, –āre, –āvī, –ātus, make double, double.

dūrō, –āre, –āvī, –ātus, make hard, become hard.

dūrus, –a, –um, adj., harsh, severe, cruel.

*dux, ducis, m., leader, guide, general.

E

*ē or ex, prep. + abl., out of, from, after, since, according to; ūnā ex parte, on one side.

eā, adv., on that side, there, in that way.

ecce, interj., behold! see! here is (are).

ecclesia, –ae, f., a church, place of assembly.

edāx, edācis, adj., voracious.

ēdīcō, –ere, –dīxī, –dictus, proclaim, appoint.

ēdiscō, –ere, –didicī, —, learn by heart.

ēdō, –ere, ēdidī, ēditus, put forth, state, explain.

edō, ēsse, ēdī, ēsus, eat.

ēdoceō, –ēre, –uī, –doctus, teach carefully, instruct.

*ēdūcō, –dūcere, –dūxī, –dūctus, lead forth, draw up.

effector, –ōris, m., one who produces, causes, originates.

effēminō, –āre, –āvī, –ātus, make womanish, enervate.

efferō, –ferre, extulī, ēlātus, carry out, carry from, extol; pass., be elated.

*efficiō, –ere, –fēcī, –fectus, work out, bring about, effect, construct, accomplish.

effodiō, –ere, –fōdī, –fossus, dig out, gouge out.

effugiō, –ere, –fūgī, —, flee away, escape.

effundō, –ere, –fūdī, –fūsus, pour out, spread, waste.

egēns, –entis, adj., needy.

egeō, –ēre, –uī, —, be in want, need.

egestās, –tātis, f., privation, destitution, want.

*ego, meī, pers. pron., I.

*ēgredior, –ī, –gressus sum, go forth, leave, disembark, leave behind.

ēgregius, –a, –um, adj., eminent, distinguished, excellent, outstanding.

*ējiciō, –ere, –jēcī, –jectus, drive out, cast out, expel; sē ējicere, rush out.

ēlabōrō, –āre, –āvī, –ātus, work out.

elephantus, –ī, m., elephant.

ēlevō, –āre, –āvī, –ātus, lift up, elevate, raise.

ēligō, –ere, –lēgī, lēctus, choose, select.

ēloquium, –ī, n., eloquence.

ēloquor, –ī, –locūtus sum, speak out, speak.

ēmigrō, –āre, –āvī, –ātus, move out, emigrate.

ēmittō, –ere, –mīsī, –missus, send out, send forth, let go, hurl, throw.

emō, –ere, ēmī, ēmptus, take, buy.

ēnārrō, –āre, –āvī, –ātus, narrate, explain.

***enim,** conj., postpositive,* for, indeed, in fact.

***ēnūntiō, –āre, –āvī, –ātus,** report, tell, announce, make known.

***eō, īre, iī (īvī), itūrus,** go, march, advance.

***eō,** adv.,* to that place, thither; **eō magis,** the more.

***eōdem,** adv.,* to the same place.

***epistula, –ae, f.,** letter, epistle.

epulae, –ārum, f.pl., dishes of food, banquet, feast.

epulor, –ārī, –ātus sum, banquet, feast.

***eques, –itis, m.,** horseman, cavalryman; *pl.,* cavalry. The **Equitēs,** Knights, was one of the three orders of Roman society.

equester, –tris, –tre, adj., of cavalry, equestrian, of the Knights.

equidem, adv., truly, indeed, for my part.

***equitātus, –ūs, m.,** cavalry.

equitō, –āre, –āvī, –ātus, ride on horseback.

***equus, –ī, m.,** horse, steed.

ērēctus, –a, –um, adj., upright, erect.

ergā, prcp. + acc., towards.

ergō, adv., therefore, consequently.

ērigō, –ere, –rēxī, –rēctus, erect, raise to a standing position.

ēripiō, –ere, –uī, –reptus, snatch away, rescue; **sē ēripere,** make one's escape.

ērogō, –āre, –āvī, –ātus, ask for and obtain.

errō, –āre, –āvī, –ātus, go astray, wander, be mistaken, err.

error, –ōris, m., error, mistake, wandering.

ērudiō, –īre, –īvī, –ītus, polish, educate, train.

ērudītiō, –ōnis, f., teaching, learning, erudition.

ērumpō, –ere, –rūpī, –ruptus, burst forth, break open, make a sortie, erupt.

ēruptiō, –ōnis, f., sally, sortie, rush, eruption, raid.

essedārius, –ī, m., chariot fighter, charioteer.

essedum, –ī, n., British war chariot.

estō (fut. imperative of **sum**), be, shall be; *pl.,* **estōte.**

***et,** conj.,* and; **et . . . et,** both . . . and; *adv.,* also, too, even.

***etiam,** adv./conj.,* and also, also, still, too, even; **nōn sōlum . . . sed etiam,** not only . . . but also.

***etsī,** conj.,* even if, although.

ēvādō, –ere, –vāsī, –vāsūrus, go forth, get away, escape.

ēvellō, –ere, –vellī, –vulsus, pull out.

ēveniō, –īre, –vēnī, –ventūrus, come out, turn out, happen; *impers.,* **ēvenit,** it happens.

ēventus, –ūs, m., outcome, result, chance, accident.

ēvocō, –āre, –āvī, –ātus, call out, summon, challenge.

ex, see **ē.**

examinō, –āre, –āvī, –ātus, weigh, examine.

exanimō, –āre, –āvī, –ātus, make breathless, kill; *pass.,* be exhausted, be out of breath.

exaudiō, –īre, –īvī, –ītus, hear clearly, discern, hear from afar.

***excēdō, –ere, –cessī, –cessūrus,** go forth, depart, go beyond, exceed, leave behind.

excellō, –ere, –celsī, –celsus, be eminent, excel.

excelsus, –a, –um, adj., high.

excīdō, –ere, –cīdī, –cīsus, cut out, cut down.

***excipiō, –ere, –cēpī, –ceptus,** take out, receive, except, relieve.

excitō, –āre, –āvī, –ātus, arouse, stir up, excite, raise up.

exclāmō, –āre, –āvī, –ātūrus, cry out, shout, exclaim.

exclūdō, –ere, –clūsī, –clūsus, shut out, exclude, hinder.

excūsō, –āre, –āvī, –ātus, excuse.

exemplum, –ī, n., specimen, copy, example, precedent.

***exeō, –īre, –iī (–īvī), –itūrus,** go forth, march out, perish, result.

exerceō, –ēre, –uī, –itus, exercise, train, drill, keep at work.

exercitātiō, –ōnis, *f.*, training, exercise.

exercitō, –āre, –āvī, –ātus, train thoroughly.

exercitus, –ūs, *m.*, army.

exigō, –ere, –ēgī, –āctus, drive out, expel.

exiguitās, –tātis, *f.*, smallness, scantiness, shortness.

exiguus, –a, –um, *adj.*, scanty, small, short.

exīstimātiō, –ōnis, *f.*, opinion, judgment, estimation.

exīstimō, –āre, –āvī, –ātus, think, believe.

exitiālis, –e, *adj.*, destructive, deadly.

exitus, –ūs, *m.*, a going out, a way out, outcome, departure, end, mouth of river, result.

expediō, –īre, –īvī, –ītus, disengage, extricate, set free, be expedient.

expedītus, –a, –um, *adj.*, unencumbered, light-armed, free; **expedītus, –ī,** *m.*, light-armed soldier.

expellō, –ere, –pulī, –pulsus, push out, drive out, expel.

experior, –īrī, –pertus, try, prove, experience.

expiō, –āre, –āvī, –ātus, atone for, expiate.

expleō, –ēre, –plēvī, –plētus, fill out, complete, make good.

explōrātor, –ōris, *m.*, scout, spy.

explōrō, –āre, –āvī, –ātus, find out, spy out, investigate, explore.

expōnō, –ere, –posuī, –positus, set forth, disembark, set ashore, put out, expose, explain.

exprimō, –ere, –pressī, –pressus, press out, force out, express.

expūgnō, –āre, –āvī, –ātus, take by storm, storm, assault.

exquīrō, –ere, –quīsīvī, –quīsītus, search out, inquire into.

exsequor, –ī, –secūtus sum, follow up, perform, execute, enforce.

exsilium, –ī, *n.*, exile, banishment.

exsistō, –ere, –stitī, —, stand forth, rise out, exist, be.

exspectātiō, –ōnis, *f.*, a looking for, expectation.

exspectō, –āre, –āvī, –ātus, look out for, await, expect, wait for, watch.

exspīrō, –āre, –āvī, –ātus, breathe out, expire, die.

exstinguō, –ere, –stīnxī, –stīnctus, quench completely.

exstō, –āre, —, —, stand forth, exist, be extant.

exstruō, –ere, –strūxī, –strūctus, pile up, build, construct.

exsultō, –āre, –āvī, –ātus, spring out, swell, rejoice, exult.

extendō, –ere, –tendī, –tentus, stretch forth, stretch out, extend.

exter *or* **exterus, –a, –um,** *adj.*, outward, outer.

exterior, –ius, *adj.*, outer, exterior.

extollō, –ere, —, —, raise up, exalt.

extorqueō, –ēre, –torsī, –tortus, force from, wrest from.

extrā, *adv./prep.* + *acc.*, outside of.

extrahō, –ere, –trāxī, –trāctus, draw out, drag out.

extrēmus, –a, –um, *adj.*, farthest, last, extreme, outermost.

extrūdō, –ere, –trūsī, –trūsus, thrust out.

exuō, –ere, –uī, –ūtus, draw out, pull off, undress.

exūrō, –ere, –ūssī, –ūstus, burn up, consume.

exuviae, –ārum, *f.pl.*, spoils.

F

fābula, –ae, *f.*, story, play, fable.

fābulōsus, –a, –um, *adj.*, fabled, fabulous.

faciēs, –ēī, *f.*, appearance, face.

facile, *adv.*, easily.

facilis, –e, *adj.*, easy, easy to do, facile.

facilitās, –tātis, *f.*, ease, facility.

facinus, –oris, *n.*, deed, misdeed, crime.

faciō, –ere, –fēcī, factus, do, make, construct; **iter facere,** march, make a journey; **vim facere,** use force; **imperāta facere,** obey commands; **certiōrem facere,** inform.

factiō, –ōnis, *f.*, political party, faction.

*factum, -ī, *n.,* deed, action, fact.
*facultās, -tātis, *f.,* ability, opportunity, faculty, means, power.
fāgus, -ī, *f.,* beech tree, beech.
fallāx, -ācis, *adj.,* deceitful, fallacious, false.
fallō, -ere, fefellī, falsus, deceive, cheat.
falx, falcis, *f.,* sickle, hook.
*fāma, -ae, *f.,* report, rumor, reputation, fame
famēs, -is, *f.,* hunger, famine.
*familia, -ae, *f.,* household, family.
familiāris, -e, *adj.,* of the family or household, familiar.
familiāritās, -tātis, *f.,* familiarity, intimacy, friendship.
familiāriter, *adv.,* familiarly.
fās, —, *n., indecl., only nom. and acc. sing. in use,* right, allowable, divine right or law.
fascinō, -āre, -āvī, -ātus, bewitch, fascinate, envy.
fastigium, -ī, *n.,* top, summit, peak, declivity.
fātālis, -e, *adj.,* fated, fatal, deadly.
fateor, -ērī, fassus sum, admit, confess.
fātum, -ī, *n.,* fate, destiny.
faucēs, -ium, *f.pl.,* jaws, throat, narrow pass.
faveō, -ēre, fāvī, fautūrus, favor, be propitious.
fēcundus, -a, -um, *adj.,* fruitful, rich in.
fēlīcitās, -tātis, *f.,* good luck, felicity.
fēlīciter, *adv.,* luckily, happily.
*fēlīx, -īcis, *adj.,* lucky, happy.
*fēmina, -ae, *f.,* woman, female.
fēminīnus, -a, -um, *adj.,* feminine.
fera, -ae, *f.,* wild beast, animal.
ferē, *adv.,* almost.
fēriae, -ārum, *f.pl.,* holidays.
*ferō, ferre, tulī, lātus, bear, carry, produce, endure; **sīgna ferre,** advance; **lēgem ferre,** pass a law.
ferōx, -ōcis, *adj.,* fierce, savage.
ferreus, -a, -um, *adj.,* made of iron, iron, inflexible.
ferrum, -ī, *n.,* iron, sword.
fertilis, -e, *adj.,* fertile, fruitful.
ferus, -a, -um, *adj.,* wild, rude, savage, fierce.

fervidus, -a, -um, *adj.,* glowing, fervid, seething.
fervor, -ōris, *m.,* boiling heat, fervor.
fessus, -a, -um, *adj.,* weary, tired.
fidēlis, -e, *adj.,* faithful, trustworthy.
fidēliter, *adv.,* faithfully.
*fidēs, -eī, *f.,* trust, belief.
fīdō, -ere, fīsus sum, *semidep.,* trust, confide in.
fīdus, -a, -um, *adj.,* trustworthy, faithful.
figūra, -ae, *f.,* form, shape, figure.
*fīlia, -ae, *f.,* daughter.
*fīlius, -ī, *m.,* son.
fingō, -ere, fīnxī, fīctus, form, fashion, imagine.
*fīniō, -īre, -īvī, -ītus, limit, define, finish, end.
*fīnis, -is, *m.,* end, limit, extent; *pl.,* confines, boundaries, territory, country, border.
*fīnitimus, -a, -um, *adj.,* neighboring, adjoining; **fīnitimī, -ōrum,** *m.pl.,* neighbors.
*fīō, fierī, factus sum (*pass. of* facio), be made, be done, become, happen, take place; **certior fierī,** be informed.
fīrmāmentum, -ī, *n.,* support, the firmament.
fīrmiter, *adv.,* steadily, firmly.
*fīrmus, -a, -um, *adj.,* strong, firm, solid.
flagellum, -ī, *n.,* scourge, whip.
flagitium, -ī, outrage, crime.
flagitō, -āre, -āvī, -ātus, demand.
flamma, -ae, *f.,* flame, fire.
flammō, -āre, -āvī, -ātus, set aflame.
flectō, -ere, flēxī, flexus, bend, turn, persuade, flex.
fleō, -ēre, flēvī, flētus, weep.
flētus, -ūs, *m.,* weeping, tears.
flō, -āre, -āvī, -ātus, blow.
flōrēns, -entis, *adj.,* flourishing, prosperous.
flōreō, -ēre, -uī, —, flourish, be prosperous.
flōs, flōris, *m.,* flower.
flūctus, -ūs, *m.,* flood, wave, surf.
*flūmen, -inis, *n.,* stream, river.
fluō, -ere, flūxī, flūxūrus, flow.

focus, –ī, m., fireplace, hearth.

foedus, –eris, n., treaty, agreement.

forāmen, –inis, n., hole, opening.

fore = futūrum esse, see sum.

foris, –is, f., door; forīs, adv., outdoors, outside; forās, adv., outdoors, forth, out.

*fōrma, –ae, f., form, figure, beauty.

fors, fortis, f., chance, luck, accident.

forte, adv., by chance.

*fortis, –e, adj., strong, brave, valiant.

fortiter, adv., bravely, boldly, courageously.

*fortitūdō, –inis, f., bravery, fortitude, courage, valor.

*fortūna, –ae, f., fortune, luck; personified, the goddess Fortune.

*forum, –ī, n., market place; Forum (Rōmānum), the Forum in Rome.

*fossa, –ae, f., ditch, trench.

fovea, –ae, f., pit, pitfall.

frangō, –ere, frēgī, frāctus, break, shatter, wreck.

*frāter, –tris, m., brother.

frāternus, –a, –um, adj., brotherly.

frequēns, –entis, adj., often, repeated, frequent.

fretum, –ī, n., strait of water.

frētus, –a, –um, adj., relying on.

frīgus, –oris, n., cold, cold weather.

frōns, frontis, f., forehead, front.

frūctuōsus, –a, –um, adj., fruitful, productive.

frūctus, –ūs, m., fruit, profit.

*frūmentārius, –a, –um, adj., grain-producing; rēs frūmentāria, supply of grain.

frūmentor, –ārī, –ātus sum, get grain, forage.

*frūmentum, –ī, n., grain; pl. often, grain crops.

fruor, –ī, frūctus sum, enjoy.

*frūstrā, adv., in vain.

frūx, frūgis, f., fruit; pl., fruits of the earth, produce.

*fuga, –ae, f., flight; in fugam dare, put to flight; sē in fugam dare, flee.

*fugiō, –ere, fūgī, —, run away, flee, escape.

fugitīvus, –a, –um, adj., fugitive.

fugō, –āre, –āvī, –ātus, put to flight, rout.

fulgeō, –ēre, fulsī, —, flash, gleam, glitter, glisten.

fulmen, –inis, n., lightning, thunderbolt.

fūmus, –ī, m., smoke.

funda, –ae, f., sling.

fundō, –āre, –āvī, –ātus, found, establish.

fundō, –ere, fūdī, fūsus, pour, scatter, rout.

fūnebris, –e, adj., funeral; fūnebria, –ium, n.pl., funeral rites.

fungor, –ī, fūnctus sum, perform, function.

fūnis, –is, m., rope, cable.

fūnus, –eris, n., funeral.

fūr, fūris, mf., thief.

furiae, –ārum, f., rage, frenzy.

furibundus, –a, –um, adj., frantic.

furor, –ōris, m., rage, fury, frenzy, madness.

fūrtim, adv., by stealth, secretly.

G

gaesum, –ī, n., heavy Gallic javelin.

galea, –ae, f., helmet.

gallīna, –ae, f., hen.

gaudeō, –ēre, gāvīsus sum, semidep., rejoice, be delighted.

gaudium, –ī, n., joy, gladness.

gemitus, –ūs, m., groaning.

gemma, –ae, f., jewel, gem, precious stone.

generātim, adv., by tribes.

generō, –āre, –āvī, –ātus, beget, produce.

*gēns, gentis, f., clan, gens, tribe, nation, race.

genū, –ūs, n., knee.

*genus, –eris, n., birth, race, kind, class, rank, tribe.

germinō, –āre, –āvī, –ātus, sprout forth, germinate.

*gerō, –ere, gessī, gestus, bear, carry, manage, wear, perform, fill, wage; sē gerere, behave; bellum gerere, wage, carry on, make war; rēs gestae, exploits, deeds.

gigās, –antis, m., giant.

gīgnō, –ere, genuī, genitus, give birth to; pass., be born.

*gladiātor, –ōris, *m.*, swordsman, gladiator.

*gladius, –ī, *m.*, sword.

glāns, glandis, *f.*, acorn, bullet thrown from a sling.

*glōria, –ae, *f.*, glory, fame.

glōrificō, –āre, –āvī, –ātus, glorify.

gradus, –ūs, *m.*, step, pace.

grandis, –e, *adj.*, large, great, grand, advanced in age.

*grātia, –ae, *f.*, favor, gratitude, grace; *pl.*, thanks; **grātiam habēre,** be grateful; **grātiās agere,** give thanks; **grātiā,** *with preceding genitive,* for the sake of.

grātulātiō, –ōnis, *f.*, congratulation, joy.

grātulor, –ārī, –ātus sum, congratulate.

grātum, –ī, *n.*, a kindness, a favor.

*grātus, –a, –um, *adj.*, acceptable, pleasant, grateful; **grātum facere,** do a favor.

*gravis, –e, *adj.*, heavy, serious, grave.

graviter, *adv.*, seriously, gravely; **graviter ferre,** be annoyed.

gravō, –āre, –āvī, –ātus, weigh down, load; *pass.*, make trouble, resist.

grex, gregis, *m.*, herd, flock.

gubernātor, –ōris, *m.*, pilot, helmsman.

gubernō, –āre, –āvī, –ātus, steer, manage.

gustō, –āre, –āvī, –ātus, taste.

H

*habeō, –ēre, –uī, –itus, have, hold, consider; **cēnsum habēre,** take a census; **ōrātiōnem habēre,** make a speech, **in animō habēre,** intend.

*habitō, –āre, –āvī, –ātūrus, dwell, live, inhabit.

habitus, –ūs, *m.*, condition, attire.

haereō, –ēre, **haesī, haesūrus,** stick, adhere, hesitate.

hasta, –ae, *f.*, spear.

haud, *adv.*, not, not at all, by no means.

hauriō, –īre, **hausī, haustus,** drink up, absorb.

haustus, –ūs, *m.*, a drinking, draught.

herba, –ae, *f.*, herb, grass, plant.

herc(u)le (*voc. of* **Herculēs**), by Hercules! assuredly!

hērēditās, –tātis, *f.*, inheritance.

herī, *adv.*, yesterday, lately.

heu, *interj.*, oh! alas!

*hībernus, –a, –um, *adj.* wintry; **hīberna,** –ōrum, *n.pl.*, winter quarters.

*hic, haec, hoc, *gen.*, **hūjus,** *dem. pron./ adj.*, this, the following; he, she, it, the latter.

*hīc, *adv.*, here, at this place.

*hiemō, –āre, –āvī, –ātus, pass the winter.

*hiēms, hiemis, *f.*, winter.

hinc, *adv.*, from this place, hence, next; **hinc . . . hinc,** on this side . . . on that.

*hodiē, *adv.*, this day, today.

*homō, –inis, *m.*, human being, man.

honestās, –tātis, *f.*, honor, reputation, integrity.

honestus, –a, –um, *adj.*, honorable.

*honor (honōs), –ōris, *m.*, honor, dignity.

honōrificus, –a, –um, *adj.*, honorable.

*hōra, –ae, *f.*, hour.

horreō, –ēre, –uī, —, tremble at, shudder at, bristle at.

horribilis, –e, *adj.*, horrible, dreadful, horrifying.

horridus, –a, –um, *adj.*, terrible, fearful, horrifying.

horror, –ōris, *m.*, horror.

hortātus, –ūs, *m.*, encouragement, urging.

*hortor, –ārī, –ātus sum, encourage, exhort, urge.

hortus, –ī, *m.*, garden.

hospes, –itis, *m.*, host, guest.

hospitium, –ī, *n.*, hospitality.

hostīlis, –e, *adj.*, hostile.

*hostis, –is, *m.*, public enemy, foe; *pl.*, the enemy.

hūc, *adv.*, hither, to this place, here.

hūmānitās, –tātis, *f.*, humanity, refinement, culture.

hūmānus, –a, –um, *adj.*, human, civilized.

humilis, –e, *adj.*, low, obscure, humble.

humus, –ī, *f.*, ground; **humī,** on the ground.

I

*ibi, *adv.*, there.

ictus, –ūs, *m.*, blow, stroke.

** īdem, eadem, idem,** *dem. pron./adj.,* the same, also, besides.

ideō, *adv.,* therefore, on that account.

ídōneus, –a, –um, *adj.,* suitable.

ígitur, *conj./adv., postpositive,* then, therefore.

īgnāvus, –a, –um, *adj.,* cowardly, lazy.

ígnis, –is, *m.,* fire; *pl.,* watchfires.

īgnōrō, –āre, –āvī, –ātus, be ignorant of, not know.

īgnōscō, –ere, –nōvī, –nōtus, pardon, forgive, excuse.

ígnōtus, –a, –um, *adj.,* unknown, unacquainted with.

ílle, illa, illud, *dem. pron./adj.,* that, the well-known, the former, he, she, it, they.

illīc, *adv.,* in that place, there.

illūc, *adv.,* to that place, thither, there.

illūminō, –āre, –āvī, –ātus, light up, illuminate.

illustris, –e, *adj.,* prominent, distinguished, illustrious.

imāgō, –inis, *f.,* likeness, image.

imber, –bris, *m.,* rain, shower.

imbuō, –ere, –uī, –ūtus, wet, saturate, soak, stain.

immānis, –e, *adj.,* monstrous, huge.

immēnsus, –a, –um, *adj.,* immeasurable, immense, vast.

immineō, –ēre, —, —, overhang, be near, threaten.

immittō, –ere, –mīsī, –missus, send in, let go, insert.

immō, *adv.,* nay, no indeed, by no means.

immolō, –āre, –āvī, –ātus, sprinkle with sacred meal, sacrifice, immolate.

ímmortālis, –e, *adj.,* immortal, eternal.

immūnitās, –tātis, *f.,* exemption.

impatiēns, –entis, *adj.,* impatient.

ímpedīmentum, –ī, *n.,* hindrance, impediment; *pl.,* heavy baggage.

ímpediō, –īre, –īvī, –ītus, encumber, hinder, impede.

impedītus, –a, –um, encumbered, hindered.

ímpellō, –ere, –pulī, –pulsus, drive on, impel, urge on, instigate.

impendeō, –ēre, —, —, overhang, impend, threaten.

ímperātor, –ōris, *m.,* commander, general, imperator, emperor.

imperītus, –a, –um, *adj.,* unskilled, inexperienced.

ímperium, –ī, *n.,* command, chief command, order, power, authority, government, rule, military authority, the state, empire; **Imperium Rōmānum,** the Roman Empire.

ímperō, –āre, –āvī, –ātus, command, rule, exercise authority, levy, draft.

impetrō, –āre, –āvī, –ātus, obtain by request, accomplish, gain one's end.

ímpetus, –ūs, *m.,* attack, rush, charge, impetus, fury, impetuosity, force.

impius, –a, –um, *adj.,* wicked, impious.

impleō, –ēre, –plēvī, –plētus, fill in, fill up.

implicātus, –a, –um, *adj.,* complex.

implōrō, –āre, –āvī, –ātus, beseech, implore.

impōnō, –ere, –posuī, –positus, place upon, impose upon, levy upon.

importō, –āre, –āvī, –ātus, bring in, import.

improbus, –a, –um, *adj.,* wicked, depraved.

imprōvīsō, *adv.,* unexpectedly, suddenly.

imprōvīsus, –a, –um, *adj.,* unforeseen, unexpected.

imprūdentia, –ae, *f.,* imprudence, ignorance.

impūbēs, –eris, *adj.,* under age, unmarried.

impudēns, –entis, *adj.,* impudently, shamelessly.

impūgnō, –āre, –āvī, –ātus, attack, assail.

ín, *prep.* + *acc.* (*motion toward*), into, to, in, on, upon, against; *prep.* + *abl.* (*place where*), in, on, upon, among.

inānis, –e, *adj.,* empty, vacant, inane.

incēdō, –ere, –cessī, –cessūrus, walk.

incendium, –ī, *n.,* burning, fire.

íncendō, –ere, –cendī, –cēnsus, set fire to, burn, excite, incense.

íncertus, –a, –um, *adj.,* uncertain, doubtful, not sure.

incidō, –ere, –cidī, —, fall in, happen upon, occur, break out.

*incipiō, –ere, –cēpī, –ceptūrus, begin, undertake.

*incitō, –āre, –āvī, –ātus, urge on, incite, spur on.

inclīnātiō, –ōnis, *f.,* leaning, inclination.

inclīnō, –āre, –āvī, –ātus, lean, be inclined.

inclūdō, –ere, –clūsī, –clūsus, shut up, imprison, include, enclose.

incōgnitus, –a, –um, *adj.,* unknown, incognito.

*incola, –ae, *mf.,* inhabitant.

incolō, –ere, –uī, —, live, dwell, inhabit.

*incolumis, –e, *adj.,* unharmed, safe, unhurt.

incommodum, –ī, *n.,* inconvenience, disaster, harm.

incommodus, –a, –um, *adj.,* inconvenient, annoying.

incrēdibilis, –e, *adj.,* unbelievable, incredible.

incursiō, –ōnis, *f.,* invasion, raid, inroad.

incursus, –ūs, *m.,* onrush, assault.

incūsō, –āre, –āvī, –ātus, blame.

inde, *adv.,* thence, from that place, from there, then.

index, –icis, *m.,* informer.

indicium, –ī, *n.,* indication, proof, information.

indicō, –āre, –āvī, –ātus, point out, inform, indicate.

indīcō, –ere, –dīxī, –dictus, declare, convoke, appoint.

indīgnor, –ārī, –ātus sum, deem unworthy, be angry.

indīgnus, –a, –um, *adj.,* unworthy.

indīligens, –entis, *adj.,* negligent, remiss.

indīligenter, *adv.,* negligently, carelessly.

indiscrētē, *adv.,* without distinction, indiscreetly.

indūcō, –ere, –dūxī, –ductus, lead on, induce, influence.

indulgentia, –ae, *f.,* tenderness, indulgence.

indulgeō, –ēre, –dulsī, —, be indulgent to, favor.

induō, –ere, –uī, –ūtus, put on, dress in.

industria, –ae, *f.,* activity, energy.

*ineō, –īre, –iī (–īvī), –itus, go into, begin, enter.

inermis, –e, *adj.,* unarmed, defenseless.

inēvītābilis, –e, *adj.,* unavoidable, inevitable.

infāmia, –ae, *f.,* disgrace, dishonor, infamy.

infāmis, –e, *adj.,* ill-famed, disgraced.

īnfāns, –antis, *adj.,* not speaking; *as noun, mf.,* infant.

*īnfēlīx, –īcis, *adj.,* unfortunate, unhappy.

īnfēnsus, –a, –um, *adj.,* hostile, offensive, dangerous.

inferior, –ius, *adj.,* lower, inferior.

*īnferō, –ferre, –tulī, illātus, bring in, inflict, make; **bellum īnferre,** make, carry on war; **sīgna īnferre,** advance.

īnferus, –a, –um, *adj.,* below, underneath; **īnferī, –ōrum,** *m.pl.,* inhabitants of the underworld, the lower world.

īnfēstus, –a, –um, *adj.,* unsafe, hostile, threatening, dangerous.

īnficiō, –ere, –fēcī, –fectus, taint, dye, stain, poison.

īnfimus *or* **īmus, –a, –um,** *adj.,* lowest, at the bottom.

īnfīnītus, –a, –um, *adj.,* unlimited, infinite.

īnfīrmus, –a, –um, *adj.,* weak, infirm.

īnflammō, –āre, –āvī, –ātus, set on fire, inflame.

īnflectō, –ere, –flēxī, –flexus, bend.

īnflēxibilis, –e, *adj.,* inflexible.

īnflīgō, –ere, –flīxi, –flīctus, dash against, inflict a blow.

īnflō, –āre, –āvī, –ātus, blow into, inflate, inspire.

īnfluō, –ere, –flūxī, –flūxūrus, flow into.

īnfrā, *adv./prep.* + *acc.,* below.

īnfundō, –ere, –fūsī, –fūsus, pour in, pour on.

ingenium, –ī, *n.,* nature, character, disposition, cleverness.

ingēns, –entis, *adj.,* vast, huge, enormous.

ingenuous, –a, –um, *adj.,* native, freeborn, noble.

ingredior, –ī, –gressus sum, advance, step in, enter.

inhūmānus, –a, –um, *adj.,* inhuman.

inimīcitia, –ae, *f.,* enmity.

*inimīcus, –a, –um, *adj.,* unfriendly,

hostile; **inimīcus, –ī,** *m.,* personal enemy.

inīquē, *adv.,* unequally, unjustly, unfairly.

inīquitās, –tātis, *f.,* unevenness, disadvantage, unfairness.

*__iniquus, –a, –um,__ *adj.,* unfair, unjust.

*__initium, –ī,__ *n.,* beginning.

injiciō, –ere, –jēcī, –jectus, throw in, inspire, infuse, inject.

*__injūria, –ae,__ *f.,* wrong, injury, harm.

injūssus, –ūs, *m.,* without orders; *used only in abl.*

injūstē, *adv.,* unjustly.

injūstus, –a, –um, *adj.,* unjust.

innītor, –ī, –nīxus sum, lean upon.

innocēns, –entis, *adj.,* harmless, blameless, innocent.

innocentia, –ae, *f.,* innocence, integrity.

innoxius, –a, –um, *adj.,* harmless, innocent.

innumerābilis, –e, *adj.,* innumerable.

*__inopia, –ae,__ *f.,* want, need, scarcity.

inopīnāns, –antis, *adj.,* not expecting, unawares.

inops, –opis, *adj.,* without means, helpless.

inquam, inquis, inquit, *defective, postpositive,* say.

inquīrō, –ere, –quīsīvī, –quīsītus, seek for, inquire into.

īnsānia, –ae, *f.,* insanity, madness.

īnsatiābilis, –e, *adj.,* insatiable.

īnsciēns, –entis, *adj.,* not knowing, unaware.

*__īnsequor, –ī, –secūtus sum,__ follow up, pursue.

īnserō, –ere, –uī, –sertus, plant, insert.

īnsideō, –ēre, –sēdī, –sessūrus, sit in, sit on.

*__īnsidiae, –ārum,__ *f.pl.,* ambush, treachery.

īnsīdō, –ere, –sēdī, —, settle on, beset, occupy.

īnsīgnis, –e, *adj.,* marked, distinguished, conspicuous; **īnsīgnia, –ōrum,** *n.pl.,* ornaments.

īnsiliō, –īre, –uī, —, leap upon.

īnsinuō, –āre, –āvī, –ātus, push in, penetrate.

īnsistō, –ere, –stitī, —, stand upon, pursue, insist.

īnstabilis, –e, *adj.,* unsteady.

īnstanter, *adv.,* instantly.

*__īnstituō, –ere, –uī, –ūtus,__ draw up, build, construct, establish, institute, decide, train.

īnstitūtum, –ī, *n.,* plan, practice, institution.

īnstō, –stāre, –stitī, –stātūrus, be near at hand, press on.

īnstrūmentum, –ī, *n.,* tool, equipment.

*__īnstruō, –ere, –strūxī, –strūctus,__ build, construct, draw up, equip.

īnsuēfactus, –a, –um, *adj.,* accustomed, well trained.

*__īnsula, –ae,__ *f.,* island.

īnsum, –esse, –fui, —, be in.

īnsuper, *adv.,* over, above.

*__integer, –gra, –grum,__ *adj.,* untouched, unimpaired, whole, entire, fresh, vigorous.

*__intellegō, –ere, –lēxī, –lēctus,__ understand, perceive, comprehend, know.

intendō, –ere, –tendī, –tentus, stretch out, strain, extend, aim, intend.

intentus, –a, –um, *adj.,* attentive, intent.

*__inter,__ *prep. + acc.,* between, among, during; **inter sē,** with each other.

intercēdō, –ere, –cessī, –cessūrus, go between, exist between, intervene.

intercipiō, –ere, –cēpī, –ceptus, cut off, intercept, seize.

interclūdō, –ere, –clūsī, –clūsus, shut off, cut off, intercept, blockade.

interdīcō, –ere, –dīxī, –dictus, forbid, interdict, exclude.

interdiū, *adv.,* in the daytime, by day, during the day.

interdum, *adv.,* sometimes, now and then.

*__intereā,__ *adv.,* in the meantime, meanwhile.

intereō, –īre, –iī, –itūrus, perish, die.

*__interficiō, –ere, –fēcī, –fectus,__ destroy, kill.

*__interim,__ *adv.,* in the meantime, meanwhile.

interior, –ius, *gen.,* **–ōris,** *adj.,* inner, interior.

interjiciō, –ere, –jēcī, –jectus, throw between.

*__intermittō, –ere, –mīsī, –missus,__ send between, interrupt, break, stop, check.

internus, -a, -um, *adj.*, inward, internal.

interpellō, -āre, -āvī, -ātus, break in upon, interfere, interrupt.

interpōnō, -ere, -posuī, -positus, place between, interpose, pledge, allow.

interpretor, -ārī, -ātus sum, explain.

*interrogō, -āre, -āvī, -ātus, ask, question, interrogate.

intersum, -esse, -fuī, —, be between, be present at; *impers.*, interest, it concerns.

*intervallum, -ī, *n.*, interval, space, distance.

interventus, -ūs, *m.*, intervention.

intexō, -ere, -uī, -tum, weave into, weave in.

intimus, -a, -um, *adj.*, inmost.

*intrā, *adv./prep.* + *acc.*, within, inside, during.

intrō, *adv.*, within, inside.

intrō, -āre, -āvī, -ātus, go into, enter.

introeō, -īre, -iī, -itus, go in, come in, enter.

intueor, -ērī, -tuitus sum, look upon, regard.

intus, *adv.*, within, on the inside.

inūsitātus, -a, -um, *adj.*, unusual.

inūtilis, -e, *adj.*, useless, of no use.

*inveniō, -īre, -vēnī, -ventus, come upon, find, discover, invent.

inventor, -ōris, *m.*, originator, inventor.

inveterāscō, -ere, -veterāvī, —, grow old, become established.

invicem, *adv.*, in turn.

invictus, -a, -um *adj.*, unconquerable, invincible.

invideō, -ēre, -vīdī, -vīsūrus, look askance at, envy.

invidia, -ae, *f.*, envy, jealousy.

invīsus, -a, -um, *adj.*, unseen, secret.

invītō, -āre, -āvī, -ātus, invite.

invītus, -a, -um, *adj.*, unwilling, not willing.

*ipse, -a, -um, *gen.*, ipsīus, *intens. pron./adj.*, self, himself, herself, itself, themselves, he, they; *emphatic*, very.

*īra, -ae, *f.*, wrath, rage, anger.

īrācundus, -a, -um, *adj.*, inclined to anger, passionate.

īrāscor, -ī, īrātus sum, grow angry.

īrātus, -a, -um, *adj.*, angry, enraged.

irrītō, -āre, -āvī, -ātus, anger, provoke.

irrītus, -a, -um, *adj.*, baffled, in vain.

irrumpō, -ere, -rūpī, -ruptus, burst into, charge.

*is, ea, id, *gen.*, ējus, *dem. pron./adj.*, that, this, he, she, it.

iste, ista, istud, *gen.*, istīus, *dem. pron./adj.*, that of yours, that, this, he, she, it, such.

*ita, *adv.*, in this way, thus, so.

*itaque, *adv.*, and so, and thus, therefore.

*item, *adv.*, also, likewise.

*iter, itineris, *n.*, journey, route, line of march, road, route, way; **māgnum iter**, forced march; **ex itinere**, on the march; **iter facere**, march.

iterum, *adv.*, again, a second time.

J

jaceō, -ēre, -uī, —, lie, be prostrate.

*jaciō, -ere, jēcī, jactus, throw, cast, hurl.

jactō, -āre, -āvī, -ātus, throw, cast, toss, boast.

*jam, *adv.*, already, now, immediately; **nōn jam**, no longer; **jam prīdem**, long ago, long since. *See* dūdum.

jānua, -ae, *f.*, door, entrance.

*jubeō, -ēre, jūssī, jūssus, order, command.

jūcundus, -a, -um, *adj.*, pleasant, agreeable.

jūdex, -icis, *m.*, judge, juror.

jūdicium, -ī, *n.*, judgment, decision, trial.

*jūdicō, -āre, -āvī, -ātus, judge, decide, think.

*jugum, -ī, *n.*, yoke, ridge.

jūmentum, -ī, *n.*, beast of burden, yoke animal.

*jungō, -ere, jūnxī, jūnctus, join, unite, annex.

*jūrō, -āre, -āvī, -ātus, take oath, swear.

*jūs, jūris, *n.*, right, justice, law.

jūs jūrandum, jūris jūrandī, *n.*, oath.

jūssus, -ūs, *m.*, order, command; *used only in abl. sing.*

jūstitia, -ae, *f.*, justice, uprightness.

jūstus, -a, -um, *adj.*, just, fair.

juvenis, -is, *adj.*, young; *noun, mf.*, youth (young person).

juventūs, –tūtis, ƒ., youth (the prime of life), young men.
juvō, –āre, jūvī, jūtus, help, aid, assist.
jūxtā, adv./prep. + acc., nearby, near.

K

Kalendae, –ārum, ƒ.pl., Calends, the first day of the month; abbrev., Kal.

L

labia, –ae, ƒ., lip.
labium, –ī, n., lip.
labor, –ī, lapsus sum, slip, glide.
*labor, –ōris, m., toil, labor, exertion, distress.
*labōrō, –āre, –āvī, –ātus, labor, toil, suffer.
labrum, –ī, n., lip, edge, rim.
lac, lactis, n., milk.
lacerō, –āre, –āvī, –ātus, tear, mutilate.
lacessō, –ere, –īvī, –ītus, provoke, challenge, assail.
lacrima, –ae, ƒ., tear.
lacus, –ūs, m., lake, pond.
laetitia, –ae, ƒ., joy, gladness.
laetus, –a, –um, adj., joyful, glad, happy.
languidus, –a, –um, adj., weak, faint, exhausted.
laniger, –era, –erum, adj., wool-bearing; laniger, –grī, m., lamb.
lapis, –idis, m., stone.
lār, laris, m., lar, a protecting deity.
largior, –īrī, –ītus sum, give freely, bestow.
largītiō, –ōnis, ƒ., lavish giving, bribery.
lātē, adv., widely, broadly.
lateō, –ēre, –uī, —, lie hid, be concealed.
*lātitūdō, –inis, ƒ., width, breadth, latitude.
latrō, –ōnis, m., robber, brigand.
latrōcinium, –ī, n., robbery, brigandage.
*lātus, –a, –um, adj., broad, wide.
*latus, –eris, n., side, flank of an army; latus apertum, exposed flank; ab latere, on the flank.
laudābilis, –e, adj., praiseworthy, laudable.
*laudō, –āre, –āvī, –ātus, praise, extol.
laurus, –ī, ƒ., laurel.
*laus, laudis, ƒ., praise, renown.

lavō, –āre, lāvī, lautus (lōtus), wash.
lēgātiō, –ōnis, ƒ., embassy, legation, deputation.
*lēgātus, –ī, m., ambassador, envoy, lieutenant-general, second in command.
*legiō, –ōnis, ƒ., legion, largest unit in the Roman army, 3000–6000 soldiers.
legiōnārius, –a, –um, adj., legionary.
lēgitimus, –a, –um, adj., lawful, legal, legitimate.
lēgō, –āre, –āvī, –ātus, appoint legally, commission, bequeath.
*legō, –ere, lēgī, lēctus, gather, pick, choose, read.
lēnis, –e, adj., gentle, mild, soft.
lēnitās, –tātis, ƒ., gentleness, softness, mildness, lenience.
leō, –ōnis, m., lion.
lepus, –oris, m., hare.
*levis, –e, adj., light, slight, trivial.
levitās, –tātis, ƒ., lightness, fickleness, levity.
leviter, adv., lightly.
*lēx, lēgis, ƒ., law, statute, rule.
libellus, –ī, m., booklet.
libenter, adv., willingly, gladly.
*līber, –a, –um, adj., free.
*liber, –brī, m., book.
līberālis, –e, adj., noble, generous, liberal.
*līberī, –ōrum, m.pl., children.
*līberō, –āre, –āvī, –ātus, set free, free, liberate.
*lībertās, –tātis, ƒ., freedom, liberty.
*licet, –ēre, licuit, licitum est, impers., it is allowed, lawful, permitted.
līgnum, –ī, n., wood.
līgneus, –a, –um, adj., wooden.
ligō, –āre, –āvī, –ātus, bind, tie.
līlium, –ī, n., lily.
līmus, –ī, m., mud, mire.
*lingua, –ae, ƒ., tongue, language.
linquō, –ere, līquī, lictus, leave.
linter, –tris, ƒ., small boat, skiff.
liqueō, –ēre, –uī, —, be fluid, liquid, clear.
liquor, –ōris, m., liquid.
*littera, –ae, ƒ., letter (of the alphabet); pl., literature, epistle.
*lītus, –oris, n., beach, shore.
*locō, –āre, –āvī, –ātus, place, put, arrange, locate.

*locus, –ī, *m.*, place, rank, station; *pl.*, loca, –ōrum, *n.*, region, locality.

longaevus, –a, –um, *adj.*, great age, aged.

longē, *adv.*, far, by far.

longinquus, –a, –um, *adj.*, distant, remote, lasting.

longitūdō, –inis, *f.*, length, longitude.

longurius, –ī, *m.*, long pole.

*longus, –a, –um, *adj.*, long, extended, remote, tall.

*loquor, –ī, locūtus sum, speak, talk, say.

lōtus, –ī, *f.*, fruit of the lotus tree.

lūceō, –ēre, lūxī, —, be bright, shine, glitter.

lūdibrium, –ī, *n.*, mockery, plaything.

lūdō, –ere, lūsī, lūsus, play, make sport of.

*lūdus, –ī, *m.*, game, play, school.

lūgeō, –ēre, lūxī, lūctus, grieve, mourn, deplore.

lūmen, –inis, *n.*, light.

lūmināre, –āris, *n.*, that which gives light, a heavenly body, luminary.

lūminōsus, –a, –um, *adj.*, full of light, luminous.

*lūna, –ae, *f.*, the moon.

lupus, –ī, *m.*, wolf.

*lūx, lūcis, *f.*, light, daylight; prīmā lūce *or* ortā lūce, at daybreak.

lūxūriōsus, –a, –um, *adj.*, luxurious, extravagant, dissolute.

M

maceria, –ae, *f.*, wall of loose stone.

māchina, –ae, *f.*, machine.

māchinor, –ārī, –ātus, contrive, invent, scheme.

magicus, –a, –um, *adj.*, magic.

*magis, *adv.*, *comp. of* māgnopere, more, rather; eō magis, all the more.

*magister, –trī, *m.*, master, teacher.

*magistrātus, –ūs, *m.*, magistracy, magistrate.

*māgnitūdō, –inis, *m.*, greatness, size, magnitude.

*māgnopere, *adv.*, very much, greatly, specially.

*māgnus, –a, –um, *adj.*, great, large, loud; māgnī, of great importance.

mājestās, –tātis, *f.*, greatness, grandeur, majesty.

*mājor, –jus, *gen.*, –ōris, *adj.*, *comp. of* māgnus, greater; mājōrēs, –um, *m.pl.*, forefathers, ancestors; mājor nātū, elder.

malacia, –ae, *f.*, calm, dead calm.

male, *adv.*, badly.

maledīcō, –ere, –dīxī, –dictus, speak ill, curse.

maledictum, –ī, *n.*, abusive language, cursing.

maledicus, –a, –um, *adj.*, abusive.

maleficium, –ī, *n.*, evil deed, outrage, crime.

mālō, mālle, māluī, —, prefer.

mālum, –ī, *n.*, apple, fruit.

mālus, –ī, *m.*, mast.

*malus, –a, –um, *adj.*, bad, evil, wicked.

mandātum, –ī, *n.*, order, command, mandate; *pl.*, instructions.

*mandō, –āre, –āvī, –ātus, hand over, entrust, order, command.

mandō, –ere, mandī, mānsus, devour, chew, eat.

mandūcō, –āre, –āvī, –ātus, chew, masticate, devour, eat.

māne, *adv.*, early in the morning.

*maneō, –ēre, mānsī, mānsūrus, remain, stay, abide.

mānēs, –ium, *m.pl.*, souls of the dead, departed spirits.

manifēstus, –a, –um, *adj.*, clear, evident, manifest.

manipulāris, –is, *m.*, soldier of a maniple.

manipulus, –ī, *m.*, company of soldiers, maniple, the third of a cohort.

mānsuēfaciō, –ere, –fēcī, –factus, make tame, tame.

*manus, –ūs, *f.*, hand, band (of men), forces.

*mare, maris, *n.*, sea.

*maritimus, –a, –um, *adj.*, of the sea, maritime, seacoast.

mās, maris, *m.*, male.

māsculīnus, –a, –um, *adj.*, of the male sex, masculine.

māsculus, –a, –um, *adj.*, of the male sex, male.

matara, –ae, *f.*, Celtic javelin, pike, spear.

489

*māter, –tris, *f.,* mother.

*māteria, –ae, *f.,* timber, lumber, material, wood.

mātrimōnium, –ī, *n.,* matrimony, marriage.

mātrona, –ae, *f.,* a married woman, matron.

mātūrē, *adv.,* early.

mātūrō, –āre, –āvī, –ātus, make haste, hasten.

mātūrus, –a, –um, *adj.,* ripe, early, mature.

māxilla, –ae, *f.,* jawbone, jaw.

māximē, *adv., superl. of* **māgnopere,** very greatly, very much, especially.

māximus, –a, –um, *adj., superl. of* **māgnus,** greatest, very large.

medicāmentum, –ī, *n.,* drug, medicine.

mediocris, –e, *adj.,* moderate, ordinary.

mediterrāneus, –a, –um, *adj.,* inland.

*medius, –a, –um, *adj.,* in the middle of, middle; **in colle mediō,** halfway up the hill; **mediā nocte,** midnight.

melior, –ius, *gen.,* **–ōris,** *adj., comp. of* **bonus,** better.

melius, *adv., comp. of* **bene,** better.

membrum, –ī, *n.,* member, limb.

mementō, mementōte, *imperative of* **meminī,** remember.

meminī, –isse, *defective,* remember, recollect.

memor, –oris, *adj.,* mindful.

memorābilis, –e, *adj.,* memorable.

*memoria, –ae, *f.,* memory.

mendācium, –ī, *n.,* lie, falsehood.

mendāx, –ācis, *adj.,* lying, deceitful.

mendicus, –ī, *m.,* beggar.

*mēns, mentis, *f.,* mind, intellect.

*mēnsa, –ae, *f.,* table.

*mēnsis, –is, *m.,* month.

mēnsura, –ae, *f.,* measure.

mentiō, –ōnis, *f.,* mention.

mentior, –īrī, mentītus sum, lie, deceive.

*mercātor, –ōris, *m.,* merchant, trader.

mercātūra, –ae, *f.,* trade; *pl.,* commercial transactions.

mercēs, –ēdis, *f.,* wages, reward.

mereō, –ēre, –uī, meritus, deserve, merit.

mergō, –ere, mersī, mersus, dip, plunge into, sink, immerse, cause to sink.

*merīdiēs, –ēī, *m.,* midday, noon, south.

meritus, –a, –um, *adj.,* worthy.

mētior, –īrī, mēnsus sum, measure out, distribute.

metō, –ere, messuī, messus, reap.

metus, –ūs, *m.,* fear, dread, apprehension.

*meus, –a, –um, *poss. adj.,* my, mine.

*mīles, –itis, *m.,* soldier.

mīlitāris, –e, *adj.,* of a soldier, of war, military; **rēs mīlitāris,** art of war.

mīlitia, –ae, *f.,* military service.

mīlitō, –āre, –āvī, –ātus, be a soldier, make war.

*mīlle, *adj., indecl.,* a thousand; **mīlia, –ium,** *n.pl.,* thousands; **mīlle passūs,** a mile; **mīlia passuum,** miles.

minae, –ārum, *f.pl.,* threats, menaces, perils.

minimē, *adv., superl. of* **parum,** least of all, not at all, no, by no means.

minimus, –a, –um, *adj., superl. of* **parvus,** smallest, least.

ministrō, –āre, –āvī, –ātus, attend to, manage, furnish.

minor, –ārī, –ātus sum, threaten, menace.

minor, –us, *gen.,* **minōris,** *adj., comp. of* **parvus,** smaller, less, lesser.

minuō, –ere, –uī, –ūtus, diminish, reduce.

minus, *adv., comp. of* **parum,** less.

mīrābilis, –e, *adj.,* wonderful.

mīror, –ārī, –ātus sum, wonder at, marvel at, be astonished.

mīrus, –a, –um, *adj.,* wonderful, marvelous, strange.

mīsceō, –ēre, –uī, mīxtus, mix, mingle.

*miser, –era, –erum, *adj.,* wretched, miserable, unfortunate.

miserē, *adv.,* wretchedly.

miseria, –ae, *f.,* distress.

misericordia, –ae, *f.,* pity, compassion, mercy.

misericors, –cordis, *adj.,* merciful, compassionate.

miseror, –ārī, –ātus sum, take pity on, pity.

mītēscō, –ere, —, —, become gentle, grow mild.

mītis, –e, *adj.,* mild, gentle.

*__mittō, –ere, mīsī, missus,__ send, dismiss, hurl.

mōbilitās, –tātis, *f.,* mobility, speed.

moderātor, –ōris, *m.,* manager, ruler, moderator.

moderātus, –a, –um, *adj.,* restrained, moderate.

moderor, –ārī, –ātus sum, check, slow down, moderate.

*__modo,__ *adv.,* only, merely, just now; **nōn modo . . . sed etiam,** not only . . . but also.

*__modus, –ī,__ *m.,* measure, manner, fashion, way; **quem ad modum,** how, just as; **ējus modī,** of such a kind.

moechor, –ārī, –ātus sum, commit adultery.

moenia, –ium, *n.pl.,* (city) walls, fortifications.

mōlēs, –is, *f.,* mass, massive structure.

molestia, –ae, *f.,* trouble, annoyance.

mōlīmentum, –ī, *n.,* trouble.

molō, –ere, –uī, –itus, grind.

monasterium, –ī, *n.,* monastery.

*__moneō, –ēre, –uī, –itus,__ warn, advise.

monīle, –is, *n.,* necklace, collar.

*__mōns, montis,__ *m.,* mountain.

mōnstrō, –āre, –āvī, –ātus, point out, show.

mōnstrum, –ī, *n.,* monster.

monumentum, –ī, *n.,* memorial, monument.

*__mora, –ae,__ *f.,* delay.

morbus, –ī, *m.,* disease, sickness.

mordeō, –ēre, momordī, morsus, bite.

*__morior, –īrī, mortuus sum,__ die.

*__moror, –ārī, –ātus sum,__ delay, linger, stay.

*__mors, mortis,__ *f.,* death.

mortālis, –e, *adj.,* mortal.

mortifer, –fera, –ferum, *adj.,* death-bringing, deadly, fatal.

mortuus, –a, –um, *adj.,* dead.

*__mōs, mōris,__ *m.,* habit, custom.

mōtus, –ūs, *m.,* motion, movement, uprising.

*__moveo, –ēre, mōvī, mōtus,__ move, remove; **castra movēre,** break camp.

*__mox,__ *adv.,* soon, presently, next.

mūgiō, –īre, —, —, bellow (as an ox).

mulier, –eris, *f.,* woman, wife.

multiplicō, –āre, –āvī, –ātus, multiply.

*__multitūdō, –inis__ *f.,* large number, multitude, crowd.

multō, *adv.,* by much, much, far, greatly.

multum, *adv.,* greatly, much; **multum posse** *or* **valēre,** have great power or influence.

*__multus, –a, –um,__ *adj.,* much; *pl.,* many; **multō diē,** late in the day.

mūlus, –ī, *m.,* mule.

mundus, –ī, *m.,* world, universe.

mundus, –a, –um, *adj.,* clean.

*__mūniō, –īre, –īvī, –ītus,__ fortify, protect, guard, construct.

*__mūnītiō, –ōnis,__ *f.,* fortification, defenses.

mūnus, –eris, *n.,* duty, service, gift, spectacle.

mūrālis, –e, *adj.,* of a wall, mural.

*__mūrus, –ī,__ *m.,* wall, rampart.

mutilus, –a, –um, *adj.,* maimed, broken.

mūtō, –āre, –āvī, –ātus, change, exchange.

mūtus, –a, –um, *adj.,* dumb, mute.

mūtuus, –a, –um, *adj.,* mutual, reciprocal.

mystērium, –ī, *n.,* mystery.

N

*__nam,__ *conj.,* for.

namque, *conj.,* for, and in fact.

nancīscor, –ī, nactus (nanctus) sum, obtain, get.

nārrātiō, –ōnis, *f.,* narration, narrative.

*__nārrō, –āre, –āvī, –ātus,__ tell, describe, narrate.

*__nāscor, –ī, nātus sum,__ be born, arise, begin, originate.

nātālis, –e, *adj.,* of birth; **diēs nātālis,** birthday.

*__nātiō, –ōnis,__ *f.,* birth, race, nation, tribe.

natō, –āre, –āvī, –ātus, swim, float.

*__nātūra, –ae,__ *f.,* nature, character.

nātūrālis, –e, *adj.,* natural.

nātus, –a, –um, *adj.,* sprung, born, old.

nātus, –ī, *m.,* son.

nātus, –ūs, *m.,* birth; **minor nātū,**

younger; **minimus nātū**, youngest; **mājor nātū**, elder.

nauta, –ae, f., sailor.

nauticus, –a, –um, adj., nautical, naval.

nāvālis, –e, adj., naval.

nāvicula, –ae, f., small boat, skiff.

nāvigātiō, –ōnis, f., sailing, navigation, voyage.

nāvigium, –ī, n., boat, vessel.

*nāvigō, –āre, –āvī, –ātus, sail.

*nāvis, –is, f., ship; **nāvis longa,** battle-ship, galley; **nāvis onerāria,** transport.

*nē, adv., not; **nē . . . quidem,** not even (emphasizing the word between **nē** and **quidem**).

*nē, conj., that . . . not, lest, not to; after verbs of fearing, that.

*–ne, interrog. particle, enclitic, used in asking questions simply for information; **–ne . . . an** or **–ne . . . nē,** whether . . . or.

*nec, see **neque.**

*necessārius, –a, –um, adj., necessary, urgent.

*necesse, adj., indecl., necessary.

necessitās, –tātis, f., necessity.

necessitūdō, –inis, f., necessity.

necne, conj., or not.

necō, –āre, –āvī, –ātus, kill, destroy.

neglegō, –ere, –lēxī, –lēctus, disregard, neglect.

negligentia, –ae, f., disregard.

negō, –āre –āvī, –ātus, deny, say . . . not, refuse.

negōtiātor, –ōris, m., wholesale dealer.

*negōtium, –ī, n., business, task, difficulty.

*nēmō, (nēminis), mf., no one, nobody; pl. and gen. and abl. sing. not in use; they are replaced by forms from **nūllus.**

nēquāquam, adv., not at all, by no means.

*neque (nec), conj., and not, nor, not, but . . . not; **neque . . . neque,** neither . . . nor.

nēquīquam, adv., in vain, to no purpose.

nervus, –ī, m., sinew, muscle; pl., power, force.

*nescíō, –īre, –iī (–īvī), —, not know, be ignorant; **nescíō quis (quid),** I know not who (what).

*neuter, –tra, –trum, gen. **neutrīus,** adj., neither (of two); **neutrī, –ōrum,** neither side.

nēve (neu), conj., and not, nor, and that . . . not, and lest.

nex, necis, f., violent death, murder, death.

niger, –gra, –grum, adj., black.

*nihil (nīl), n., indecl., nothing; adv., not at all, by no means.

*nisi, conj., if not, unless, except.

nītor, nītī, nīxus or **nīsus,** lean, support, strive.

*nōbilis, –e, adj., noted, noble; **nōbilēs, –ium,** m.pl., nobles, men of rank; **nōbilissimus, –ī,** m., man of highest rank.

*nōbilitās, –tātis, f., nobility, high rank, nobles.

*noceō, –ēre, –uī, —, do harm, injure.

noctū, adv., by night, at night.

nocturnus, –a, –um, adj., occurring at night, nightly.

nōdus, –ī, m., knot, node on the joint of an animal.

*nōlō, nōlle, nōluī, —, not wish, be unwilling; **nōlī, nōlīte,** with infin., do not . . .

*nōmen, –inis, n., name.

nōminātim, adv., by name.

nōminō, –āre, –āvī, –ātus, call, name.

*nōn, adv., not, no; **nōn jam,** no longer.

nōnāgintā, adj., indecl., ninety.

*nōndum, adv., not yet.

*nōnne, interrog. adv., used in questions expecting an affirmative answer.

*nōn nūllus (nōnnūllus), –a, –um, adj., some, several.

nōn numquam (nōnnumquam), adv., sometimes.

*nōnus, –a, –um, adj., ninth.

nōs, pl. of **ego,** we, us.

nōscō, –ere, nōvī, nōtus, know, learn.

*noster, –tra, –trum, adj., our, our own; **nostrī, –ōrum,** m.pl., our men, our side.

nōtitia, –ae, f., acquaintance.

notō, –āre, –āvī, –ātus, brand, reprimand, check.

*nōtus, –a, –um, adj., well known, familiar, known.

*novem, adj., indecl., nine.

novitās, –tātis, f., newness, novelty.

*novus, –a, –um, adj., new, fresh, strange; novissimus, last, at the rear; novissimī, –ōrum, m.pl., those at the rear, the rear; novissimum agmen, the rear.

*nox, noctis, f., night, evening; noctū, at night; prīmā nocte, early in the night; multā nocte, late at night.

nūbēs, –is, f., cloud.

nūbō, –ere, nūpsī, nūptus, be married, marry, wed.

nūdō, –āre, –āvī, –ātus, strip, expose, leave unprotected.

nūdus, –a, –um, adj., unprotected, nude, bare, naked.

*nūllus, –a, –um, gen., nūllīus, adj., not any, none, no; nūllus, –īus, m., no one.

num, interrog. adv., used in questions expecting a negative answer; in indirect questions, whether, if.

nūmen, –inis, n., divine will; divine help.

*numerus, –ī, m., number, quantity.

nummus, –ī, m., (piece of) money, coin.

*numquam, adv., never.

num quis, anyone? any?

*nunc, adv., now, at present.

*nūntiō, –āre, –āvī, –ātus, announce, report, give orders.

*nūntius, –ī, m., messenger, message, news.

nuper, adv., lately, recently.

nūptiae, –ārum, f.pl., wedding, nuptials.

nūtus, –ūs, m., nod, command; ad nūtum, instantly.

nympha, –ae, f., nymph.

O

*ob, prep. + acc., on account of, for.

obaerātus, –a, –um, adj., in debt; obaerātus, –ī, m., debtor.

obeō, –īre, –īvī, –itus, go to meet, attend to, die.

objiciō, –ere, –jēcī, –jectus, throw in one's way, cast, object.

oblinō, –ere, –lēvī, litus, smear over.

oblīvīscor, –ī, –lītus sum, forget, be forgetful, disregard.

obsecrō, –āre, –āvī, –ātus, entreat by what is sacred, implore.

observō, –āre, –āvī, –ātus, watch, observe.

*obses, –idis, mf., hostage, pledge.

*obsideō, –ēre, –sēdī, –sessus, besiege, blockade.

obsidiō, –ōnis, f., siege, blockade.

obsīgnō, –āre, –āvī, –ātus, put a seal to, seal.

obstō, –āre, –stitī, –stātūrus, oppose, resist.

obstringō, –ere, –strīnxī, –strictus, bind, lay under obligation.

obtemperō, –āre, –āvī, –ātūrus, obey.

obtestor, –ārī, –ātus sum, call as a witness against.

*obtineō, –ēre, –uī, –tentus, hold fast, hold, obtain.

occāsiō, –ōnis, f., opportunity, occasion, chance.

*occāsus, –ūs, m., setting; sōlis occāsus, sunset, sundown.

occidēns, –entis, m., the evening, the west, occident.

*occidō, –ere, –cidī, –cāsūrus, fall, perish, go down, set.

*occīdō, –ere, –cīdī, –cīsus, cut down, kill.

occulō, –ere, –uī, –cultus, conceal, hide, cover.

occultō, –āre, –āvī, –ātus, hide, conceal, keep secret.

occupātiō, –ōnis, f., occupation, employment.

*occupō, –āre, –āvī, –ātus, seize, capture, take possession of, occupy.

occurrō, –ere, –currī, –cursūrus, run to meet, meet, find, occur, happen upon.

*Ōceānus, –ī, m., the Ocean, sea.

*octāvus, –a, –um, adj., eighth.

*octō, adj., indecl., eight.

octōgintā, adj., indecl., eighty.

*oculus, –ī, m., eye.

ōdī, ōdisse, ōsūrus, defective, hate.

odium, –ī, n., hate, hatred.

odiōsus, –a, –um, adj., hateful, troublesome.

odor, –ōris, m., smell, fragrance, odor.

offendō, –ere, –fendī, –fēnsus, offend, be offensive.

offerō, –ferre, obtulī, oblātus, bring before, offer, proffer, present.

*__officium,__ –ī, *n.,* service, favor, duty, employment, office.

oleum, –ī, *n.,* olive oil, oil.

*__ōlim,__ *adv.,* once upon a time, formerly, once.

ōmen, –inis, *n.,* omen, portent.

ōmittō, –ere, –mīsī, –missus, let go, give up, dismiss, omit, disregard.

omnīnō, *adv.,* altogether, only; *with negatives,* at all.

*__omnis,__ –e, *adj.,* every, all, whole; **omnēs,** –ium, *m.pl.,* all men, all; **omnia,** –ium, *n.pl.,* all things, everything.

onerārius, –a, –um, *adj.,* suitable for a burden; **nāvis onerāria,** transport ship.

onus, –eris, *n.,* load, burden.

opera, –ae, *f.,* labor, effort, work.

operiō, –īre, –uī, opertus, cover, hide.

opīniō, –ōnis, *f.,* idea, belief, good opinion, conjecture, supposition.

opīnor, –ārī, –ātus sum, believe, think, suppose.

*__oportet, –ēre, –uit,__ *impers.,* it is necessary, fitting; ought.

*__oppidum,__ –ī, *n.,* fortified town, city.

oppōnō, –ere, –posuī, –positus, place opposite, oppose.

opportūnitās, –tātis, *f.,* advantage, opportunity.

*__opportūnus,__ –a, –um, *adj.,* favorable, suitable, opportune.

oppositus, –a, –um, *adj.,* placed opposite, lying in the way.

*__opprimō, –ere, –pressī, –pressus,__ press against, overwhelm, crush, oppress.

oppūgnātiō, –ōnis, *f.,* assault, storming.

*__oppūgnō, –āre, –āvī, –ātus,__ assault, storm, besiege, attack.

(ops), opis, *f.,* power, help, wealth; *pl.,* **opēs,** –um, resources, riches, influence.

optātus, –a, –um, *adj.,* desired, welcome.

optimē, *adv., superl.* of **bene,** best.

optimus, –a, –um, *adj., superl.* of **bonus,** best, very good, excellent.

optō, –āre, –āvī, –ātus, wish, desire.

opus, —, *n.,* necessity, need; *used only*

in nom. and acc.; impers., **opus est,** it is necessary.

*__opus,__ –eris, *n.,* work, labor, works, fortifications.

ōra, –ae, *f.,* coast, shore.

ōrāculum, –ī, *n.,* oracle, prophecy.

*__ōrātiō,__ –ōnis, *f.,* speech, address, oration.

ōrātor, –ōris, *m.,* speaker, orator.

orbis, –is, *m.,* circle, orbit, world; **orbis terrārum,** the world, the whole earth.

*__ōrdō,__ –inis, *m.,* row, series, order.

oriēns, –entis, *m.,* the rising sun, the east, orient.

orīgō, –inis, *f.,* origin, source.

*__orior, –īrī, ortus sum,__ arise, rise, spring from, spring up, begin.

ōrnāmentum, –ī, *n.,* equipment, ornament.

ōrnātus, –a, –um, *adj.,* equipped.

ōrnō, –āre, –āvī, –ātus, furnish, equip, adorn.

*__ōrō, –āre, –āvī, –ātus,__ pray, entreat, plead, beg (for).

ortus, –ūs, *m.,* rising.

ōs, ōris, *n.,* mouth.

ōsculor, –ārī, –ātus sum, kiss.

ōsculum, –ī, *n.,* kiss.

*__ostendō, –ere, –tendī, –tentus,__ show, display.

ostentō, –āre, –āvī, –ātus, show, display.

ōstium, –ī, *n.,* doorway, mouth, entrance, door.

ōtium, –ī, *n.,* leisure.

ovis, –is, *f.,* sheep.

P

pābulum, –ī, *n.,* fodder, forage, food.

pācificus, –a, –um, *adj.,* peace-making.

*__pācō, –āre, –āvī, –ātus,__ pacify, subdue.

*__paene,__ *adv.,* almost.

paenīnsula, –ae, *f.,* peninsula.

paenitentia, –ae, *f.,* repentance, regret.

paenitet, *impers.,* it repents, it grieves.

pāgus, –ī, *m.,* district, canton.

palam, *adv.,* openly, publicly.

pallium, –ī, *n.,* coverlet, cloak.

palma, –ae, *f.,* palm of the hand, hand, palm tree.

pālus, –ī, *m.,* stake, pale.

palūs, –ūdis, *f.,* swamp, marsh.

pandō, –ere, pandī, passus, spread out; **passīs manibus,** with hands out-stretched.

panis, –is, *m.,* bread, loaf.

*****pār, paris,** *adj.,* equal; **pār atque,** same as.

parātus, –a, –um, *adj.,* prepared, ready.

parcō, –ere, pepercī, parsūrus, spare.

parcus, –a, –um, *adj.,* sparing, slight.

parēns, –entis, *mf.,* parent.

*****pāreō, –ēre, –uī, –itus,** obey, submit to.

pariēs, –etis, *m.,* wall (of house).

pariō, –ere, peperī, partus, bear, bring forth, accomplish.

*****parō, –āre, –āvī, –ātus,** prepare, make ready, acquire.

*****pars, partis,** *f.,* part, region, direction, branch, side; *pl.,* party, faction; **pars mājor,** the majority; **ūnā ex parte,** on one side; **in omnēs partēs,** in every direction.

particeps, –cipis, *adj.,* sharing, participating in; *noun, mf.,* participant, sharer.

partim, *adv.,* partly, in part.

parum, *adv.,* little, too little, not enough.

parvulus, –a, –um, *adj.,* very young, trifling.

*****parvus, –a, –um,** *adj.,* small, little.

pāscō, –ere, pāvī, pāstus, feed, pasture, eat.

pāscuum, –ī, *n.,* pasture.

*****passus, –ūs,** *m.,* step, pace; **mīlle passūs,** a mile; **mīlia passuum,** miles.

pāstor, –ōris, *m.,* shepherd.

patefaciō, –ere, –fēcī, –factus, open, disclose.

*****pateō, –ēre, –uī, —,** lie open, stand open, extend, spread.

*****pater, –tris,** *m.,* father; **patrēs, –um,** fathers, forefathers, senators; **patrēs cōnscrīptī,** senators.

patiēns, –entis, *adj.,* enduring, patient.

patientia, –ae, *f.,* endurance, patience.

*****patior, patī, passus sum,** suffer, endure, permit, allow.

*****patria, –ae,** *f.,* fatherland, native land, country.

patrō, –āre, –āvī, –ātus, accomplish.

patruus, –ī, *m.,* uncle on father's side.

paucitās, –tātis, *f.,* small number.

*****paucus, –a, –um,** *adj.,* little; *pl.,* few; **pauca, –ōrum,** *n.pl.,* few (words).

paulātim, *adv.,* little by little, gradually.

paulisper, *adv.,* for a short time, a little while.

*****paulō,** *adv.,* (by) a little.

*****paulum,** *adv.,* a little, somewhat.

pauper, –eris, *adj.,* poor; *noun, m.,* poor man.

pavidus, –a, –um, *adj.,* trembling.

pāvō, –ōnis, *m.,* peacock.

*****pāx, pācis,** *f.,* peace.

peccō, –āre, –āvī, –ātus, err, injure, sin.

peccātum, –ī, *n.,* error, fault, sin.

pectus, –oris, *n.,* breast, chest.

*****pecūnia, –ae,** *f.,* money.

pecus, –oris, *n.,* cattle, herd, flock.

pecus, –udis, *f.,* a head of cattle, cattle, animal.

*****pedes, –itis,** *m.,* foot soldier; *pl.,* **peditēs, –um,** infantry.

peditātus, –ūs, *m.,* infantry.

pējor, pējus, *gen.,* **–ōris,** *adj., comp. of* **malus,** worse.

pellis, –is, *f.,* skin, hide.

*****pellō, –ere, pepulī, pulsus,** strike, drive, drive away, rout.

pendō, –ere, pependī, pēnsus, weigh out, suspend, hang, pay.

penetrō, –āre, –āvī, –ātus, enter, penetrate.

*****per,** *prep.* + *acc.,* through, across, during, by; *in composition with adverbs and adjectives,* very, thoroughly, through.

peragō, –ere, –ēgī, –āctus, finish, complete.

peragrō, –āre, –āvī, –ātus, wander.

perambulō, –āre, –āvī, –ātus, walk through, pass through.

percipiō, –ere, –cēpī, –ceptus, gain, acquire, hear, learn, perceive.

percontātiō, –ōnis, *f.,* inquiry.

percurrō, –ere, –cucurrī (–currī), –cursūrus, run through, run along.

percutiō, –ere, –cussī, –cussus, beat, strike, pierce, shock.

perdiscō, –ere, –didicī, —, learn thoroughly.

perditus, –a, –um, *adj.,* desperate; **perditī, –ōrum,** *m.pl.,* desperate men.

perdō, –ere, –didī, –ditus, destroy, ruin.

perdōnō, –āre, –āvī, –ātus, pardon.

perdūcō, –ere, –dūxī, –ductus, lead through, lead, bring, construct.

peregrīnus, –a, –um, *adj.,* foreign, strange.

perennis, –e, *adj.,* lasting, perennial.

pereō, –īre, –iī (–īvī), –itūrus, go through, be lost, perish, be killed.

perequitō, –āre, –āvī, –ātus, ride through, ride about.

perexiguus, –a, –um, *adj.,* very small.

perfacilis, –e, *adj,* very easy.

perferō, –ferre, –tulī, –lātus, carry through, report, endure, suffer.

*perficiō, –ere, –fēcī, –fectus, do thoroughly, cause, arrange, finish.

perfidus, –a, –um, *adj.,* faithless, treacherous.

perfodiō, –ere, –fōdī, –fossus, dig through.

perfringō, –ere, –frēgī, –frāctus, break through, violate.

perfuga, –ae, *m.,* deserter.

perfugiō, –ere, –fūgī, —, flee for refuge.

perfugium, –ī, *n.,* place of refuge, refuge.

pergō, –ere, –rēxī, –rēctus, go on, proceed, advance.

perhibeō, –ēre, –uī, –itus, propose, say.

perīculōsus, –a, –um, *adj.,* perilous, dangerous.

*perīculum, –ī, *n.,* trial, attempt, danger.

perītus, –a, –um, *adj.,* experienced, skilled.

perlegō, –ere, –lēgī, –lēctus, read through.

perluō, –ere, –luī, –lūtus, wash, bathe.

permaneō, –ēre, –mānsī, –mānsūrus, continue, remain.

permīsceō, –ēre, –uī, –mīxtus, mix, mingle.

permittō, –ere, –mīsī, –missus, let pass, entrust, permit, allow.

*permoveō, –ēre, –mōvī, –mōtus, move deeply, alarm, influence, disturb.

perniciēs, –ēī, *f.,* destruction, disaster.

perpaucī, –ae, –a, *adj.,* very few; *noun, m.pl.,* a very few.

perpetuus, –a, –um, *adj.,* continuous, perpetual; **in perpetuum,** forever.

perrumpō, –ere, –rūpī, –ruptus, break through, force a passage.

persaepe, *adv.,* very often.

perscrībō, –ere, –scrīpsī, –scrīptus, write out in full, report, recount.

*persequor, –ī, –secūtus sum, follow up, pursue, attack, accomplish.

persecūtiō, –ōnis, *f.,* prosecution.

persevērō, –āre, –āvī, –ātus, persevere, be persistent in, persist.

persolvō, –ere, –solvī, –solūtus, pay in full, pay.

*perspiciō, –ere, –spēxī, –spectus, look through, see clearly, learn, perceive.

perstō, –āre, –stitī, –stātūrus, stand firm, remain, persist.

*persuādeō, –ēre, –suāsī, –suāsūrus, persuade, convince, induce.

*perterreō, –ēre, –uī, –itus, frighten thoroughly, terrify.

pertinācia, –ae, *f.,* perseverance, obstinacy, pertinacity.

*pertineō, –ēre, –uī, —, extend through, reach, concern, pertain.

pertrānseō, –īre, –iī (–īvī), –itus, pass through, pass by.

perturbātiō, –ōnis, *f.,* disturbance, commotion, perturbation.

*perturbō, –āre, –āvī, –ātus, disturb, confuse (greatly), perturb.

*perveniō, –īre, –vēnī, –ventūrus, reach, come to, arrive at.

*pēs, pedis, *m.,* foot; **pedibus,** on foot; **pedem referre,** retreat.

pessimē, *adv., superl. of* **male,** worst.

pessimus, –a, –um, *adj., superl. of* **malus,** worst, very bad.

pestilentia, –ae, *f.,* plague, pestilence, fever.

pestis, –is, *f.,* plague.

*petō, –ere, –īvī (–iī), –ītus, seek, go to, demand, ask for, beg for.

phalanx, –angis, *acc.,* **–a** *or* **–em,** *f.,* close formation of troops, phalanx.

pictūra, –ae, *f.,* painting, picture.

pietās, –tātis, *f.,* sense of duty, devotion, piety.

pila, –ae, *f.,* ball, game of ball.

pīl(l)eus, –ī, *m.,* (close-fitting) cap.

pīlum, –ī, *n.,* javelin, pike.

pīlus, -ī, *m.,* a division of a maniple of the three forward ranks of soldiers in line of battle; **prīmī pīlī centūriō** *or* **prīmipīlus,** centurion of the highest rank in a legion.

pinna, -ae, *f.,* feather, wing, battlement.

pīrāta, -ae, *m.,* pirate.

piscis, -is, *m.,* fish.

placeō, -ēre, -uī, -itūrus, please, be agreeable; *impers.,* **placet,** it pleases, it is agreed, it is decided.

placidē, *adv.,* quietly, calmly.

placidus, -a, -um, *adj.,* quiet, gentle, calm.

placō, -āre, -āvī, -ātus, appease, conciliate, pacify.

plāga, ae, *f.,* stroke, blow.

plānitiēs, -ēī, *f.,* level ground, plain.

plānus, -a, -um, *adj.,* level, flat.

plaudō, -ere, plausī, plausus, clap, applaud.

plausus, -ūs, *m.,* applause.

plēbēs, -eī (is), *f.,* common people, plebeians.

***plēbs, plēbis,** *f.,* common people, plebeians.

plēnē, *adv.,* fully, completely.

plēnus, -a, -um, *adj.,* full, filled.

plērumque, *adv.,* generally, for the most part.

plērusque, -aque, -umque, *adj.,* very many, most; **plērīque, -ōrumque,** *m.pl.,* the majority.

pluit, -ere, pluit (plūvit), *impers.,* it rains.

plūma, -ae, *f.,* plume, feather.

plumbum, -ī, *n.,* lead; **plumbum album,** tin.

plūrēs, plūra, *gen.,* **-ium,** *adj., comp. of* **multī,** more, several, many.

plūrimum, *adv., superl. of* **multum,** very much, most, especially.

plūrimus, -a, -um, *adj., superl. of* **multus,** most; *pl.,* very many, most.

plūs, plūris, *adj., comp. of* **multus,** more; **plūs valēre,** have more power.

pōculum, -ī, *n.,* cup, drinking cup.

poēma, -atis, *n.,* poem.

***poena, -ae,** *f.,* fine, punishment, penalty; **poenās dare,** pay the penalty, punish.

***poēta, -ae,** *m.,* poet.

***polliceor, -ērī, -itus sum,** promise, offer.

pōmum, -ī, *n.,* apple, fruit.

pondus, -eris, *n.,* weight, quantity.

***pōnō, -ere, posuī, positus,** place, put.

***pōns, pontis,** *m.,* bridge.

pontus, -ī, *m.,* the open sea, deep.

populāris, -e, *adj.,* of the people, popular.

populor, -ārī, -ātus sum, lay waste, waste, devastate.

***populus, -ī,** *m.,* people, nation, citizens.

porcus, -ī, *m.,* pig.

***porta, -ae,** *f.,* gate, entrance.

portiō, -ōnis, *f.,* part, section, division, portion.

***portō, -āre, -āvī, -ātus,** bear, carry, bring.

portōrium, -ī, *n.,* toll, tax, customs.

***portus, -ūs,** *m.,* harbor, port.

poscō, -ere, poposcī, —, ask, demand, beg.

possessiō, -ōnis, *f.,* possession.

possideō, -ēre, -sēdī, -sessūrus, hold, occupy, possess, own.

***possum, posse, potuī, —,** be able, can.

***post,** *adv.,* afterwards, after; **annō post,** a year later; **paucīs post diēbus,** a few days later.

***post,** *prep.* + *acc.,* after, behind, later.

***posteā,** *adv.,* afterwards.

posterior, -ius, *gen.,* **-ōris,** *adj.,* later, posterior.

***posterus, -a, -um,** *adj.,* next, following; **in posterum,** for the future; **posterī, -ōrum,** *m.pl.,* descendants, posterity.

***postquam,** *conj.,* after, when; *often* **post . . . quam.**

postrēmō, *adv.,* at last, finally.

postrēmus, -a, -um, *adj.,* last, latest; **ad postrēmum,** finally.

***postrīdiē,** *adv.,* on the day after, next day; **postrīdiē ējus diēī,** on the following day.

postulātum, -ī, *n,* demand, claim, request.

***postulō, -āre, -āvī, -ātus,** demand, require.

***potēns, -entis,** *adj.,* powerful, influential.

potentātus, –ūs, *m.,* political power, supremacy.

potentia, –ae, *f.,* might, power, influence.

*****potestās, –tātis,** *f.,* ability, power.

potior, –īrī, –ītus sum, obtain (get, take) possession of, gain.

potis, –e, *adj.,* able, powerful.

potius, *adv.,* rather; **potius quam,** rather than.

pōtus, –ūs, *m.,* a drinking, draught, drink.

prae, *prep.* + *abl.,* before, in front of, in comparison with; *in composition with adjectives and adverbs,* very.

praeacūtus, –a, –um, *adj.,* sharpened to a point, pointed.

praebeō, –ēre, –uī, –itus, hold forth, offer, present, show, provide.

praecaveō, –ēre, –cāvī, –cautus, take precaution, beware.

praecēdō, –ēre, –cessī, –cessūrus, go before, precede, surpass, excel.

praeceps, –itis, *adj.,* headlong, steep, precipitous.

praecipiō, –ere, –cēpī, –ceptus, anticipate, advise, instruct, command.

praecipuē, *adv.,* especially.

praecipuus, –a, –um, *adj.,* particular, especial.

praecō, –ōnis, *m.,* herald, crier.

praeda, –ae, *f.,* booty, plunder.

praedicō, –āre, –āvī, –ātus, boast, proclaim, make known.

praedīcō, –ere, –dīxī, –dictus, say beforehand, warn, predict.

praedūcō, –ere, –dūxī, –ductus, lead forward, construct.

praeeō, –īre, –iī (–īvī), –itūrus, go before, precede.

praefectus, –ī, *m.,* commander; **praefectus equitum,** cavalry prefect.

praeferō, –ferre, –tulī, –lātus, place before, prefer, reveal.

*****praeficiō, –ere, –fēcī, –fectus,** place over, place in command of, in charge of.

*****praemittō, –ere, –mīsī, –missus,** send forward, send in advance.

*****praemium, –ī,** *n.,* reward, recompense, booty.

praeoptō, –āre, –āvī, –ātus, prefer.

praeparō, –āre, –āvī, –ātus, get ready, prepare.

praepōnō, –ere, –posuī, –positus, set over, place in command, prefer.

praerumpō, –ere, –rūpī, –ruptus, break, break off.

praescrībō, –ere, –scrīpsī, –scrīptus, direct, prescribe.

praesēns, –entis, *adj.,* at hand, present.

praesentia, –ae, *f.,* presence, present time.

praesertim, *adv.,* especially, particularly.

*****praesidium, –ī,** *n.,* defense, guard, garrison.

*****praestō, –āre, –stitī, –stitus,** stand before, excel, show, surpass.

*****praesum, –esse, –fuī, —,** have command of, be in command of, in charge of.

*****praeter,** *prep.* + *acc.,* past, beyond, besides, except.

*****praetereā,** *adv.,* besides, moreover, too.

praetereō, –īre, –īvī, –itūrus, pass by, go by, pass over, disregard.

praeterquam, *adv.,* more than, beyond; *after negative,* except; *with* **quod,** apart from the fact that.

praetextātus, –a, –um, *adj.,* wearing the toga praetexta.

praetextus, –a, –um, *adj.,* bordered; **praetexta, –ae,** *f.,* a toga bordered with purple.

*****praetor, –ōris,** *m.,* praetor, one of the chief Roman magistrates.

praetōrius, –a, –um, *adj.,* praetorian, pertaining to a praetor; **praetōria porta,** *f.,* praetorian gate, the front gate of a camp; **praetōrium, –ī,** *n.,* general's tent, headquarters.

praevideō, –ēre, –vīdī, –vīsus, foresee.

prandium, –ī, *n.,* lunch, midday meal.

prātum, –ī, *n.,* meadow.

prehendō, –ere, –hendī, –hēnsus, take, seize, grasp.

*****premō, –ere, pressī, pressus,** press, press hard, oppress, pursue, overwhelm.

*****pretium, –ī,** *n.,* price, value.

prex, precis, *f.,* prayer, entreaty, curse, imprecation.

prīdem, *adv.*, long ago, long since; **jam prīdem,** long ago.

***prīdiē,** *adv.*, the day before.

***prīmō,** *adv.*, at first, first.

***prīmum,** *adv.*, at first, in the first place, for the first time; **cum prīmum (ubi, ut),** as soon as; **quam prīmum,** as soon as possible.

***prīmus, -a, -um,** *adj.*, first, earliest, foremost; **prīmī, -ōrum,** *m.pl.*, the foremost men, chiefs, nobles; **in prīmīs,** especially.

***prīnceps, -ipis,** *adj.*, leading, first, chief; *as noun, m.*, leader, chief, prince.

***prīncipātus, -ūs,** *m.*, supremacy, leadership, principate.

prīncipium, -ī, *n.*, beginning.

***prior, -us,** *gen.*, **priōris,** *adj.*, former, prior; **priōrēs, -um,** *m.pl.*, those in advance.

prīstinus, -a, -um, *adj.*, former, old-time, original, pristine.

prius, *adv.*, before, earlier, rather.

***priusquam,** *conj.*, sooner than, before, until; *often* **prius . . . quam.**

prīvātus, -a, -um, *adj.*, personal, private; *noun, m.*, private citizen.

prīvō, -āre, -āvī, -ātus, deprive, rob, release.

***prō,** *prep.* + *abl.*, in front of, in behalf of, for, in proportion, as.

probitās, -tātis, *f.*, honesty, uprightness.

probō, -āre, -āvī, -ātus, approve, prove.

***prōcēdō, -ere, -cessī, -cessūrus,** go forward, march on, proceed.

procul, *adv.*, at a distance, far, far off.

prōcumbō, -ere, -cubuī, —, sink down, be beaten down, lie down.

prōcūrātiō, -ōnis, *f.*, a caring for, management.

prōcūrātor, -ōris, *m.*, manager, agent, one who collected revenue.

prōcūrō, -āre, -āvī, -ātus, look after, have charge of.

***prōcurrō, -ere, -currī (-cucurrī), -cursūrus,** run *or* rush forward, advance, charge.

procus, -ī, *m.*, suitor, wooer.

prōdeō, -īre, -iī (-īvī), -itūrus, come forth, advance.

prōditor, -ōris, *m.*, traitor.

prōdō, -ere, -didī, -ditus, put forth, hand down, reveal, surrender, betray.

***prōdūcō, -ere, -dūxī, -ductus,** lead forth, bring out, extend.

***proelium, -ī,** *n.*, battle.

profectiō, -ōnis, *f.*, departure, setting out.

prōferō, -ferre, -tulī, -lātus, bring forth, put forth, mention, extend.

prōficiō, -ere, -fēcī, -fectus, effect, accomplish, gain.

***prōficīscor, -ī, -fectus sum,** set out, proceed, march.

profiteor, -ērī, -fessus sum, declare publicly, profess.

profugiō, -ere, -fūgī, —, flee, escape, take refuge.

prōfundus, -a, -um, *adj.*, deep, profound, abysmal.

prōgeniēs, -ēī, *f.*, offspring.

prōgnātus, -a, -um, *adj.*, sprung, descended.

***prōgredior, -ī, -gressus sum,** step forward, advance, make progress, proceed.

***prohibeō, -ēre, -uī, -itus,** hold back, check, prohibit, keep away (from, out), prevent, repulse, hinder.

proinde, *adv.*, hence, and so, therefore.

prōjiciō, -ere, -jēcī, -jectus, throw forward, hurl, throw down, project.

prōmissus, -a, -um, *adj.*, (of hair) hanging down, flowing.

prōmittō, -ere, -mīsī, -missus, put forth, promise.

prōmoveō, -ēre, -mōvī, -mōtus, move forward, push forward, promote.

prōnūntiō, -āre, -āvī, -ātus, announce, declare.

***prope,** *adv.*, near, nearly, almost; *prep.* + *acc.*, near.

prōpellō, -ere, -pulī, -pulsus, drive forward, drive away, impel, propel.

***properō, -āre, -āvī, -ātus,** hasten, hurry.

propinquitās, -tātis, *f.*, nearness, vicinity.

***propinquus, -a, -um,** *adj.*, near, neighboring; *noun, m.*, relative.

propior, -us, *gen.*, **propiōris,** *adj.*, nearer.

propius, *adv./prep.* + *acc.*, nearer.

*prōpōnō, -ere, -posuī, -positus, set forth, place before, propose.

prōpositiō, -ōnis, *f.*, proposition, subject of discourse.

proprius, -a, -um, *adj.*, one's own, characteristic, peculiar.

*propter, *prep.* + *acc.*, on account of, in consequence of.

*proptereā, *adv.*, for this reason, therefore; **proptereā quod,** because.

prōpūgnātor, -ōris, *m.*, defender.

prōpūgnō, -āre, -āvī, -ātus, come forth to fight, fight on the defensive, defend.

prōpulsō, -āre, -āvī, -ātus, drive off, drive back, repel.

prōra, -ae, *f.*, prow.

prōsequor, -ī, -secūtus sum, follow after, follow up, pursue.

prōspectus, -ūs, *m.*, view, sight, prospect.

prōsperitās, -tātis, *f.*, prosperity, good fortune.

prōspiciō, -ere, -spēxī, -spectus, look forward, look, look out for.

prōsternō, -ere, -strāvī, -strātus, throw down in front, cast down, debase, ruin.

prōsum, prodesse, profuī, —, be useful, do good, benefit.

prōtegō, -ere, -tēxī, -tēctus, cover in front, protect.

prōtinus, *adv.*, immediately, at once, directly.

prōvehō, -ere, -vēxī, -vectus, carry forward; *pass.*, ride forward, drive, sail.

prōvideō, -ēre, -vīsī, -vīsus, foresee, provide for, look out for.

*prōvincia, -ae, *f.*, province.

prōvinciālis, -e, *adj.*, provincial, in a province.

proximē, *adv.*, nearest, next, last.

*proximus, -a, -um, *adj.*, nearest, next, last.

prūdentia, -ae, *f.*, foresight, good judgment, prudence, discretion.

pūblicānus, -a, -um, *adj.*, of the public revenue; *noun, m.*, revenue collector.

pūblicē, *adv.*, publicly.

*pūblicus, -a, -um, *adj.*, of the people, public.

pudor, -ōris, *m.*, decency, honor.

*puella, -ae, *f.*, girl.

*puer, -ī, *m.*, boy, child; **ā puerō,** from boyhood.

puerīlis, -e, *adj.*, boyish, childish, puerile.

pueritia, -ae, *f.*, boyhood, childhood.

*pūgna, -ae, *f.*, fight, battle.

pūgnāx, -ācis, *adj.*, fond of fighting, pugnacious.

*pūgnō, -āre, -āvī, -ātūrus, fight, contend, engage in battle; **pūgnātum est,** the battle raged.

*pulcher, -chra, -chrum, *adj.*, beautiful, noble; **pulchritūdo,** *f.*, beauty.

pulsō, -āre, -āvī, -ātus, beat, lash, disturb.

pulvīnus, -ī, *m.*, pillow, cushion.

pulvis, -eris, *m.*, dust, powder.

pūnctum, -ī, *n.*, puncture, point, point of time.

pūniō, -īre, -īvī, -ītus, punish, chastise.

puppis, -is, *f.*, stern of ship.

pūrgō, -āre, -āvī, -ātus, make clean, cleanse, purify, free from blame.

pūrus, -a, -um, *adj.*, clean, pure.

*putō, -āre, -āvī, -ātus, think, consider, believe, judge.

pȳramis, -idis, *f.*, a pyramid.

Q

quā, *adv.*, where.

quadrāginta, *adj., indecl.*, forty.

quadrīgae, -ārum, *f.pl.*, chariot.

quadringentī, -ae, -a, *adj.*, four hundred.

*quaerō, -ere, quaesīvī, quaesītus, look for, seek, desire, inquire.

quaesō, -ere, —, —, beg, beseech.

*quaestor, -ōris, *m.*, quaestor, state treasurer.

quaestus, -ūs, *m.*, getting of money, gain.

quālis, -e, *adj.*, what? what kind of? of what kind? of such a kind, such as, as; **tālis . . . quālis,** such . . . as.

*quam, *adv./conj.*, how? how much?; *with superl.*, as possible; *after comparatives*, than, as; **tam . . . quam,** so . . . as; **quam diū,** as long as; *with expressions of time*, after.

quam ob rem (quamobrem), *interrog./*

rel. phrase, on what account? why? on account of which, why.

quam prīmum, *adv.*, as soon as possible.

quamquam, *conj.*, although.

quamvīs, *conj.*, however much, although.

quandō, *interrog. adv.*, at what time? when?; *indef. adv.*, at any time, ever; *conj.*, when, since; **sī quandō,** whenever.

***quantus, -a, -um,** *adj., interrog.*, how great? how large? how much?; **quantō opere,** how much? *rel., following* **tantus,** (as much) as; *noun,* **quantum,** *with gen. of the whole,* as much as.

quā rē (quārē), *adv.*, for what reason? why? and on this account, therefore.

***quārtus, -a, -um,** *adj.*, fourth.

quasi, *adv./conj.*, as if, as though, as it were.

***quattuor,** *adj., indecl.*, four.

quattuordecim, *adj., indecl.*, fourteen.

***-que,** *conj., enclitic,* and, but.

quem ad modum (quemadmodum), *interrog./rel. phrase,* in what way? how? in whatever way, as, just as.

queror, -ī, questus sum, complain, lament.

***quī, quae, quod,** *gen.* **cūjus,** *interrog. adj.*, which? what? what kind of?

***quī, quae, quod,** *gen.* **cūjus,** *rel. pron.*, who, which, that.

quī, quae (qua), quod, *indef. adj./pron.*, any, anyone, anything; **sī quī,** if anyone.

quia, *conj.*, since, because.

quīcumque, quaecumque, quodcumque, *indef. pron.,* whoever, whatever, whichever.

quid, *see* **quis.**

***quīdam, quaedam, quoddam (quiddam),** *indef. adj./pron.*, certain, a certain one, a certain thing.

***quidem,** *adv.*, indeed, in fact, at least; **nē ... quidem,** not even; *the word emphasized is always placed between* **nē** *and* **quidem.**

quiēs, -ētis, *f.*, rest, quiet, sleep.

quiēscō, -ere, -ēvī, -ētūrus, go to rest, keep quiet, sleep.

quīn, *conj., chiefly after negative expressions of doubting and hindering,* that not, that, but that, without; *often from* with *a present participle;* **quīn etiam,** even, in fact, moreover.

quīndecim, *adj., indecl.*, fifteen.

quīngentī, -ae, -a, *adj.*, five hundred.

quīnquāgintā, *adj., indecl.*, fifty.

***quīnque,** *adj., indecl.*, five.

***quīntus, -a, -um,** *adj.*, fifth.

***quīque, quaeque, quodque,** *indef. adj.*, each, every.

***quis, quid,** *gen.* **cūjus,** *interrog. pron.*, who? what?, *neut.* **quid,** *with gen. of the whole,* **quid cōnsilī,** what plan?

***quis, quid,** *indef. pron., often after* **sī,** **nisi, nē,** *and* **num,** anyone, anything; **sī quis,** if anyone; **nē quis,** that not anyone, that no one.

quispiam, quidpiam, *indef. pron./adj.*, anyone, anything, any.

quisquam, quidquam, *indef. pron./adj.*, anyone, anything, any.

***quisque, quidque,** *indef. pron.*, each one, each thing.

quīvīs, quaevīs, quidvīs, *indef. pron.*, anyone, anything you please; **quīvīs, quaevīs, quodvīs,** *indef. adj.*, any whatever.

***quō,** *adv. and conj., interrog. adv.*, whither? to what place? where?; *rel. adv.*, whither, where, when; *indef. adv., after* **sī** *and* **nē,** to any place, to any point, anywhere; *conj., used after comparative and with subjunctive,* in order that, that.

quoad, *conj.*, as long as, until, till.

***quod,** *conj.*, that, in that; because, inasmuch as; as to the fact that, so far as; **proptereā quod,** because; **quod sī,** but if.

quōminus, *conj.*, so that not, from; *often from* with *a participle.*

quōmodo, *interrog. adv.*, in what manner? in what way? how?

quondam, *adv.*, at some time, formerly, once on a time; *of the future,* someday, hereafter.

quoniam, *conj.*, since, as, because, whereas.

quoque, *adv., postpositive,* also, too.

quot, *adj., indecl.*, how many? **quot ... tot,** as many ... as.

quotannīs, *adv.,* yearly, every year.

quotiēs (quotiēns), *adv.,* as often as, how often; *interrog.,* how often?

quotquot, *adj., indecl.,* however many, as many soever as.

R

rādīx, –īcis, *f.,* root, foot, base.

rādō, –ere, rāsī, rāsus, scrape.

rāmus, –ī, *m.,* branch, bough.

rapidus, –a, –um, *adj.,* swift, rapid.

rapiō, –ere, –uī, raptus, seize and carry off, snatch, hurry, pillage.

rārus, –a, –um, *adj.,* thin, few, rare.

*ratiō, –ōnis, *f.,* reckoning, account, sum, plan, manner, method, reason, means, consideration.

ratis, –is, *f.,* raft.

rebelliō, –ōnis, *f.,* uprising, rebellion.

recēdō, –ere, –cessī, –cessūrus, go back, recede.

*recēns, –entis, *adj.,* fresh, recent, late, new, young.

receptus, –ūs, *m.,* retreat.

*recipiō, –ere, –cēpī, –ceptus, take back, receive, regain, admit; **sē recipere** withdraw, retreat.

recitō, –āre, –āvī, –ātus, read aloud, recite.

reclīnō, –āre, –āvī, –ātus, bend back, lean back.

recordor, –ārī, –ātus sum, recall to mind, recollect.

rēctē, *adv.,* rightly, properly, nobly.

recumbō, –ere, –cubuī, —, recline, lie back.

rēctus, –a, –um, *adj.,* straight.

recūsō, –āre, –āvī, –ātus, refuse, decline.

rēda, –ae, *f.,* wagon.

*reddō, –ere, –didī, –ditus, give back, restore, render, repay, return.

*redeō, –īre, –iī (–īvī), –itūrus, go back, return, be reduced.

redigō, –ere, –ēgī, –āctus, drive back, reduce, render, make.

redimō, –ere, –ēmī, –ēmptus, buy back, ransom.

redintegrō, –āre, –āvī, –ātus, renew, revive.

reditiō, –ōnis, *f.,* a going back, return.

*reditus, –ūs, *m.,* return.

*redūcō, –ere, –dūxī, –ductus, lead back, draw back, bring back, reduce.

referō, –ferre, rettulī, relātus, carry back, bring back, pay back, refer, relate, report; **sē referre,** go back; **pedem referre,** retreat; **grātiam referre,** make return, requite.

reficiō, –ere, –fēcī, –fectus, make over, repair, refresh, renovate, reinforce.

refringō, –ere, –frēgī, –frāctus, break open, break off.

refugiō, –ere, –fūgī, —, fly back, flee, escape, run away from.

refulgeō, –ēre, –fulsī, —, flash back, gleam, shine, glitter.

rēgālis, –e, *adj.,* royal, regal.

rēgia, –ae, *f.,* palace.

*rēgīna, –ae, *f.,* queen.

*regiō, –ōnis, *f.,* direction, region, district.

rēgius, –a, –um, *adj.,* of a king, kingly, regal, royal.

rēgnō, –āre, –āvī, –ātūrus, reign, be king, be supreme, rule.

*rēgnum, –ī, *n.,* kingship, kingdom, realm, reign.

*regō, –ere, rēxī, rēctus, direct, control, rule.

regredior, –ī, –gressus sum, go back, retreat.

rejiciō, –ere, –jēcī, –jectus, throw, hurl back, carry back, drive back, reject.

religiō, –ōnis, *f.,* sense of right, duty, religious scruples, fear of the gods, religion.

*relinquō, –ere, –līquī, –lictus, leave, leave behind, abandon, give up, bequeath.

*reliquus, –a, –um, *adj.,* remaining, the rest; **reliquī, –ōrum,** *m.pl.,* the rest; **reliquum, –ī,** *n.,* remainder, rest; **nihil reliquī,** nothing left.

*remaneō, –ēre, –mānsī, –mānsūrus, stay behind, remain.

remigrō, –āre, –āvī, –ātūrus, move back, return.

remissus, –a, –um, *adj.,* relaxed, mild.

*remittō, –ere, –mīsī, –missus, send back, throw back, remit, relax.

removeō, -ēre, -mōvī, -mōtus, move back, remove.

remūneror, -ārī, -ātus sum, repay, reward, remunerate.

rēmus, -ī, *m.,* oar.

rēnō, -ōnis, *m.,* reindeer skin, deerskin.

renovō, -āre, -āvī, -ātus, renew, restore, revive, renovate, repair.

renūntiō, -āre, -āvī, -ātus, bring back word, report.

reor, rērī, rātus sum, believe, think, suppose, reckon.

repellō, -ere, reppulī, repulsus, drive back, repulse, repel.

repente, *adv.,* suddenly, unexpectedly.

repentīnus, -a, -um, *adj.,* sudden, hasty, unexpected.

reperiō, -īre, repperī (reperī), repertus, find out, discover, learn.

repetō, -ere, -īvī, -ītus, seek again, demand, exact.

repleō, -ēre, -ēvī, -ētus, fill up, supply amply.

repōnō, -ere, -posuī, -positus, put back, put aside, keep, replace, restore, renew.

reportō, -āre, -āvī, -ātus, carry back.

repraesentō, -āre, -āvī, -ātus, do at the present time, do at once.

reprehendō, -ere, -hendī, -hēnsus, seize, catch, blame, reprehend.

reprimō, -ere, -pressī, -pressus, press back, check, prevent, restrain, repress.

reptile, -is, *n.,* reptile.

repudiō, -āre, -āvī, -ātus, put away, divorce, reject, repudiate.

repūgnō, -āre, -āvī, -ātus, be opposed, oppose, resist.

requiēscō, -ere, -quiēvī, -quiētus, rest.

requīrō, -ere, -quīsīvī, -quīsītus, require, miss, feel the want of, inquire after.

rēs, reī, *f.,* thing, object, matter, affair, situation, event; **rēs mīlitāris,** warfare, military science; **rēs novae,** revolution; **quā rē (quārē),** therefore, and for this reason; **rē vērā,** indeed, in truth; **rēs pūblica, reī pūblicae,** *f.,* commonwealth, state, public interest, government.

rescindō, -ere, -scidī, -scissus, cut off, cut down, break up, destroy, annul.

rescīscō, -ere, -scīvī (-sciī), -scītus, learn, find out, discover.

rescrībō, -ere, -scrīpsī, -scrīptus, write again, transfer, promote.

reservō, -āre, -āvī, -ātus, keep back, reserve.

resistō, -ere, -stitī, —, remain, halt, stop, resist, oppose.

respiciō, -ere, -spēxī, -spectus, look back, look back upon, consider, respect.

respondeō, -ēre, -spondī, -spōnsus, answer, reply, respond.

respōnsum, -ī, *n.,* answer, reply.

respuō, -ere, -spuī, —, reject, refuse.

restituō, -ere, -uī, -ūtus, replace, rebuild, restore, revive.

restō, -āre, -stitī, —, stand back, withstand, remain, be left.

resurgō, -ere, -surrēxī, -surrectūrus, rise again.

retineō, -ēre, -uī, -tentus, hold back, retain, detain, preserve, maintain.

retrō, *adv.,* backward, back.

reus, -ī, *m.,* accused person, guilty one.

revellō, -ere, -vellī, -vulsus, pull back, tear away.

reveniō, -īre, -vēnī, -ventūrus, come back, return.

revertō, -ere, -vertī, —, *only in tenses from perfect stem, and* **revertor, -ī, -versūrus sum,** return, go back, revert.

revīvō, -ere, —, -vīctus, live again.

revocō, -āre, -āvī, -ātus, call back, recall, revoke.

rēx, rēgis, *m.,* king, ruler.

rīdeō, -ēre, rīsī, rīsus, laugh at, mock.

rīpa, -ae, *f.,* bank of a river.

rīvus, -ī, *m.,* stream.

rōbur, -oris, *n.,* hard wood, oak, strength.

rogitō, -āre, -āvī, -ātus, ask, inquire eagerly.

rogō, -āre, -āvī, -ātus, ask, question, beg, request.

rōstrum, -ī, *n.,* beak, bill, prow of a ship; *pl.,* **Rōstra,** the Rostra, a platform for speakers in the Forum.

rota, -ae, *f.,* wheel.

rubus, -ī, *m.,* bramble, briar.

rudis, –e, *adj.*, rough, rude.
ruīna, –ae, *f.*, falling, ruin, destruction.
rūmor, –ōris, *m.*, rumor, report.
rūpēs, –is, *f.*, cliff, rock.
*rūrsus, *adv.*, back, again.
rūs, rūris, *n.*, the country, lands, estate; *locative*, rūrī, in the country.
rūsticus, –a, –um, *adj.*, of the country, rural, rustic.

S

saccus, –ī, *m.*, sack, bag, money bag.
sacer, –cra, –crum, *adj.*, consecrated, sacred.
sacerdōs, –dōtis, *mf.*, priest, priestess.
sacrificium, –ī, *n.*, sacrifice.
sacrificō, –āre, –āvī, –ātus, sacrifice.
*saepe, *adv.*, often; saepe numerō, oftentimes, repeatedly.
saepēs, –is, *f.*, hedge.
saevus, –a, –um, *adj.*, raging, fierce, savage, cruel.
*sagitta, –ae, *f.*, arrow.
saltus, –ūs, *m.*, mountain pass, ravine, glade, dale.
*salus, –ūtis, *f.*, health, welfare, safety.
salūtō, –āre, –āvī, –ātus, greet, hail, salute.
Salvē, *imperative of* salvēre (be well), Hail! Good day! Welcome!
*salvus, –a, –um, *adj.*, well, sound, safe.
sanciō, –īre, sānxī, sānctus, render sacred, ratify.
sānctificō, –āre, –āvī, –ātus, sanctify.
sānctus, –a, –um, *adj.*, sacred, solemn.
sanguis, –inis, *m.*, blood, bloodshed.
sānitās, –tātis, *f.*, soundness of mind, good sense.
sānus, –a, –um, *adj.*, sound, healthy, sane.
sapiēns, –entis, *adj.*, wise, discreet; *noun*, *m.*, man of wisdom, sage.
sapienter, *adv.*, wisely.
sapientia, –ae, *f.*, wisdom.
sapiō, –ere, –īvī, —, taste, be sensible, understand.
sarcinae, –ārum, *f.pl.*, baggage, pack that each soldier carried.
*satis, *adj.*, *indecl.*, enough, sufficient, suitable; *adv.*, enough, sufficiently.

satisfaciō, –ere, –fēcī, –factūrus, satisfy, content, placate.
satisfactiō, –ōnis, *f.*, amends, reparation, satisfaction, apology.
saturō, –āre, –āvī, –ātus, satisfy, fill.
saucius, –a, –um, *adj.*, wounded.
saxum, –ī, *n.*, stone, rock.
scandō, –ere, scandī, scānsus, climb, mount.
scapha, –ae, *f.*, light boat, skiff.
scelerātus, –ā, –um, *adj.*, impious, criminal; scelerātus, –ī, *m.*, criminal.
scelerō, –āre, –āvī, –ātus, desecrate, pollute.
scelus, –eris, *n.*, wicked deed, crime, sin.
sceptrum, –ī, *n.*, sceptre, rule, sway.
schola, –ae, *f.*, school.
*scientia, –ae, *f.*, knowledge, science.
scindō, –ere, scidī, scissus, tear, split, rend.
*sciō, –īre, –īvī, –ītus, know, know how, perceive.
*scrībō, –ere, scrīpsī, scrīptus, write, communicate.
sculptilis, –e, *adj.*, carved, sculptured.
scūtātus, –a, –um, *adj.*, armed with a shield.
*scūtum, –ī, *n.*, shield.
sē, sēsē, *see* suī.
sēcēdō, –ere, –cessī, –cessūrus, go apart, withdraw, secede.
sēcernō, –ere, –crēvī, –crētus, separate, distinguish, discern.
sēcrētō, *adv.*, secretly, privately.
sēcrētus, –a, –um, *adj.*, hidden, secret.
sectiō, –ōnis, *f.*, cutting, booty, lot.
secundum, *prep.* + *acc.*, next to, according to.
*secundus, –a, –um, *adj.*, next, propitious, favorable, following, second.
secus, *adv.*, otherwise, not so.
*sed, *conj.*, but, yet, but yet.
sēdecim, *adj.*, *indecl.*, sixteen.
*sedeō, –ēre, –sēdī, sessūrus, sit, be encamped, settle.
sēdēs, –īs, *f.*, seat, chair, throne, habitation.
sēditiōsus, –a, –um, *adj.*, seditious, treasonable.
seges, –etis, *f.*, field of corn, grain, crop.

sēgregō, –āre, –āvī, –ātus, remove, separate.

semel, *adv.,* once.

sēmen, –inis, *n.,* seed.

sēmentis, –is, *f.,* sowing, seeding.

sēminō, –āre, –āvī, –ātus, sow, plant, produce.

sēmita, –ae, *f.,* path.

*semper, *adv.,* always.

*senātor, –ōris, *m.,* senator.

*senātus, –ūs, *m.,* council of elders, senate.

senectūs, –ūtis, *f.,* old age.

senex, –is, *adj.,* old; *noun, m.,* old man.

*sententia, –ae, *f.,* opinion, judgment, saying, sentence; **sententiam dīcere,** express an opinion.

*sentiō, –īre, sēnsī, sēnsus, perceive, feel, think, know.

sēparātim, *adv.,* separately, apart.

sēparō, –āre, –āvī, –ātus, separate, divide.

sepeliō, –īre, –īvī, –pultus, bury.

*septem, *adj., indecl.,* seven.

septentriō, –ōnis, *m.,* the Great Bear or the Little Bear constellation; the north.

*septimus, –a, –um, *adj.,* seventh.

septingentī, –ae, –a, *adj., indecl.,* seven hundred.

sepulcrum, –ī, *n.,* burial place, tomb.

sepultūra, –ae, *f.,* burial, funeral.

*sequor, –ī, secūtus sum, follow, attend, pursue, comply with.

seriēs, *gen. and dat. not found, acc.,* **–em,** *abl.,* **–ē,** *f.,* row, series.

sermō, –ōnis, *m.,* speech, talk, conversation, language, diction.

sērō, *adv.,* late.

serō, –ere, sēvī, satus, sow, plant.

serpēns, –entis, *m.,* serpent, snake.

sērus, –a, –um, *adj.,* late.

serva, –ae, *f.,* (female) slave.

servīlis, –e, *adj.,* of slaves, servile.

serviō, –īre, –īvī, –ītūrus, serve.

servitūs, –ūtis, *f.,* slavery, servitude.

*servō, –āre, –āvī, –ātus, save, preserve, keep, guard.

*servus, –ī, *m.,* slave, servant.

sescentī, –ae, –a, *adj.,* six hundred.

sēsē, *acc. and abl. of* **suī.**

sētius, *adv.,* less.

seu, *see* **sīve.**

sevērē, *adv.,* seriously, gravely, severely.

sevēritās, –tātis, *f.,* gravity, seriousness.

sevērus, –a, –um, *adj.,* serious, grave.

*sex, *adj., indecl.,* six.

sexāgintā, *adj., indecl.,* sixty.

*sextus, –a, –um, *adj.,* sixth.

sexus, –ūs, *m.,* sex.

*sī, *conj.,* if, whether; **quod sī,** but if; **sī quis (quid),** if anyone (anything).

sibi, *see* **suī.**

*sīc, *adv.,* so, in this way, thus; **ut . . . sīc,** as . . . so; **sīc . . . ut,** so . . . that, just as.

sīcut, *adv.,* just as, as, as if, as it were.

sīdus, –eris, *n.,* constellation, star.

sīgnificātiō, –ōnis, *f.,* sign, signal.

sīgnificō, –āre, –āvi, –ātus, show, announce, mean.

sīgnō, –āre, –āvī, –ātus, mark, mark with a seal, indicate, sign.

*sīgnum, –ī, *n.,* mark, sign, military standard, ensign, signal, seal of a letter, statue, figure.

*silentium, –ī, *n.,* silence.

*silva, –ae, *f.,* wood, forest.

*similis, –e, *adj.,* like, resembling, similar.

similiter, *adv.,* similarly.

similitūdō, –inis, *f.,* similarity, resemblance, similitude.

simplex, –plicis, *adj.,* single, simple.

simpliciter, *adv.,* plainly, simply.

*simul, *adv.,* at the same time, at once, together; **simul atque (ac),** as soon as.

simulācrum, –ī, *n.,* likeness, image, statue.

simulātiō, –ōnis, *f.,* pretense, deceit.

simulō, –āre, –āvī, –ātus, make like, imitate, copy, simulate.

simultās, –ātis, *f.,* rivalry, hatred.

sīn, *conj.,* if, however, but if.

*sine, *prep. + abl.,* without.

singillātim, *adv.,* one by one, individually.

singulāris, –e, *adj.,* one by one, single, singular.

*singulī, –ae, –a, *adj.,* one to each, one by one, one at a time, single, individual.

*sinister, –tra, –trum, *adj.,* left, on the left.

sinistra, –ae, *f.,* left (hand); **sub sinistrā,** on the left.

sinistrōrsus, *adv.,* to the left.

sinō, –ere, sīvī, situs, allow, permit.

sinus, –ūs, *m.,* fold, gulf, bay.

sitiō, –īre, —, —, thirst, be thirsty, thirst for.

sitis, –is, *f.,* thirst.

situs, –ūs, *m.,* location, site.

sīve (seu), *conj.,* or if; **sīve (seu) . . . sīve (seu),** if . . . or if, whether . . . or, either . . . or.

socer, –erī, *m.,* father-in-law.

societās, –tātis, *f.,* society, alliance, confederation.

*socius, –ī, *m.,* companion, comrade, ally.

*sōl, sōlis, *m.,* the sun; **sōlis occāsus,** sunset, sundown.

soleō, –ēre, solitus sum, *semidep.,* be wont, be accustomed.

sōlitūdō, –inis, *f.,* wilderness, waste, solitude.

sollicitō, –āre, –āvī, –ātus, stir up, disturb, rouse, solicit, tempt.

*solum, –ī, *n.,* lowest part, bottom, ground, soil.

sōlum, *adv.,* only; **nōn sōlum . . . sed etiam,** not only . . . but also.

*sōlus, –a, –um, *gen.,* **solīus,** *adj.,* alone, only, sole.

*solvō, –ere, solvī, solūtus, loose, pay, release, set free; **nāvem solvere,** set sail.

*somnus, –ī, *m.,* sleep, slumber.

sonitus, –ūs, *m.,* sound, noise, din.

sonō, –āre, –uī, –itus, sound, resound.

sonus, –ī, *m.,* sound, noise.

sordidus, –a, –um, *adj.,* foul, filthy, unclean.

*soror, –ōris, *f.,* sister.

sors, sortis, *f.,* lot, fate, casting of lots.

sortior, –īrī, –ītus sum, cast lots, select by lot.

spargō, –ere, sparsī, sparsus, strew, sprinkle, scatter.

*spatium, –ī, *n.,* space, room, distance.

*speciēs, –ēī, *f.,* aspect, appearance, show, sight; **ad speciem,** for show.

spectāculum, –ī, *n.,* show, spectacle, exhibition, entertainment.

*spectō, –āre, –āvī, –ātus, look at, watch, see, consider, look toward.

speculātōrius, –a, –um, *adj.,* spying, scouting; **speculātōrium nāvigium,** spy boat.

spēlunca, –ae, *f.,* cave.

*spērō, –āre, –āvī, –ātus, hope, expect.

*spēs, speī, *f.,* hope, expectation.

spīritus, –ūs, *m.,* breathing, breath, breath of life, spirit, courage.

spīrō, –āre, –āvī, –ātus, breathe, blow.

splendidus, –a, –um, *adj.,* shining, gleaming.

splendor, –ōris, *m.,* splendor.

spoliō, –āre, –āvī, –ātus, strip, rob, pillage, despoil.

spolium, –ī, *n.,* skin, hide; *pl.,* booty, spoils.

spōnsus, –ī, *m.,* bridegroom, spouse.

sponte, *abl. of obsolete word* **spōns,** of one's own will, of his (her, their) own accord.

stabilis, –e, *adj.,* steady, stable, firm.

stabilitās, –tātis, *f.,* steadiness, stability.

stabulum, –ī, *n.,* stall, stable, standing place.

*statim, *adv.,* immediately, at once.

statiō, –ōnis, *f.,* outpost, picket, guard, garrison.

*statuō, –ere, –uī, –ūtus, set, place, build, resolve, determine, decide.

statūra, –ae, *f.,* height, stature.

stella, –ae, *f.,* star.

sternō, –ere, strāvī, strātus, strew, spread out, devastate.

stimulō, –āre, –āvī, –ātus, spur, stimulate.

stimulus, –ī, *n.,* goad, stimulus.

stīpendiārius, –a, –um, *adj.,* tributary.

stīpendium, –ī, *n.,* tribute, pay, stipend; **stīpendia facere,** serve in the army.

*stō, stāre, stetī, stātūrus, stand, abide by, remain.

strangulō, –āre, –āvī, –ātus, strangle.

strepitus, –ūs, *m.,* noise.

*studeō, –ēre, –uī, —, be eager for, strive for, give attention to, study.

*studium, –ī, *n.,* zeal, eagerness, study.

stultus, –a, –um, *adj.,* foolish.

stupeō, –ēre, –uī, —, be astounded, amazed.

suāviter, *adv.,* sweetly.

*sub, *prep. + acc. (motion toward),* under, towards, close to, until; *prep. + abl.*

(place where), under, beneath, at the foot of, during.

subdūcō, –ere, –dūxī, –ductus, lead up, lead away, carry off, withdraw, draw up (of ships).

subeō, –īre, –iī (–īvī), –itūrus, go under, go up to, ascend, undergo, submit to.

subigō, –ere, –ēgī, –āctus, conquer, subjugate, compel.

*subitō, *adv.*, suddenly.

subitus, –a, –um, *adj.*, sudden, unexpected.

subjectus, –a, –um, *adj.*, lying near, subject to.

subjiciō, –ere, –jēcī, –jectus, throw from beneath, place near, expose, make subject.

sublevō, –āre, –āvī, –ātus, lift up, assist, support, raise, raise up, lighten.

sublimis, –e, *adj.*, raised up, sublime.

subluō, –ere, —, —, wash, flow at the foot of.

submergō, –ere, –mersī, –mersus, plunge under, submerge, sink.

subministrō, –āre, –āvī, –ātus, furnish, provide.

submittō, –ere, –mīsī, –missus, send under, submit.

submoveō, –ēre, –mōvī, –mōtus, move from under, drive back.

subruō, –ere, –uī, –utus, undermine.

subsellium, –ī, *n.*, low bench, seat.

*subsequor, –ī, –secūtus sum, follow up, follow closely.

*subsidium, –ī, *n.*, reserve, resource, assistance, help.

substantia, –ae, *f.*, substance, essence.

subsum, –esse, —, —, be near, be at hand, be in reserve.

subtrahō, –ere, –trāxī, –trāctus, carry off, withdraw, subtract.

subveniō, –īre, –vēnī, –ventus, come to help, relieve, assist.

succēdō, –ere, –cessī, –cessūrus, come up, approach closely, come next, succeed.

succurrō, –ere, –currī, –cursūrus, run toward, run to the help of, aid, succor.

sūcus, –ī, *m.*, juice, sap.

sufferō, –ferre, sustulī, sublātus, endure.

suffrāgium, –ī, *n.*, vote.

*suī, sibi, sē (sēsē), *reflex. pron.*, himself, herself, itself, themselves, him, her, it, them.

*sum, esse, fuī, futūrus, be, exist, consist.

summergō, *see* **submergō.**

sumministrō, *see* **subministrō.**

summittō, *see* **submittō.**

summoveō, *see* **submoveō.**

*summus, –a, –um, *adj.*, *superl. of* **superus,** highest, top of, greatest, most important; **summum, –ī,** *n.*, top, summit, end; **summa, –ae,** *f.*, sum, total; **summa imperī,** supreme command.

*sūmō, –ere, sūmpsī, sūmptus, take on, take, put on, assume, inflict.

sūmptuōsus, –a, –um, *adj.*, costly.

*super, *adv.*, above, moreover; *prep. +* *acc. (motion toward)*, over, above, upon; *prep. + abl. (place where)*, over, upon, in addition to, beyond.

superbia, –ae, *f.*, pride.

superbus, –a, –um, *adj.*, overbearing, proud, haughty.

*superior, –ius, *gen.*, **–ōris,** *adj.*, *comp. of* **superus,** higher, former, previous; *noun, mf.*, superior.

*superō, –āre, –āvī, –ātus, overcome, surpass, defeat.

supersedeō, –ēre, –sēdī, –sessūrus, sit above, preside over, refrain.

superstitiō, –ōnis, *f.*, superstition.

supersum, –esse, –fuī, —, be left, remain, survive.

*superus, –a, –um, *adj.*, above, high, upper.

suppetō, –ere, –īvī, –ītus, be at hand, be available, hold out.

supplex, –icis, *adj.*, kneeling in entreaty, suppliant.

supplicātiō, –ōnis, *f.*, thanksgiving.

supplicium, –ī, *n.*, punishment, torture, death penalty.

supplicō, –āre, –āvī, –ātus, pray humbly, supplicate.

*suprā, *adv.*, above, before, formerly; *prep.* *+ acc.*, above, over, beyond, more than.

suprēmus, –a, –um, *adj.*, *superl. of* **superus,** highest, greatest, supreme.

surgō, –ere, –rēxī, –rēctūrus, lift up, rise, grow.

surripiō, –ere, –ripuī, –reptus, take away secretly, steal, pilfer.

*suscipiō, –ere, –cēpī, –ceptus, undertake, take up, assume, begin.

suspectus, –a, –um, adj., object of suspicion, suspected.

suspendō, –ere, –pendī, –pēnsus, hang up, suspend.

*suspiciō, –ōnis, f., mistrust, suspicion.

suspicor, –ārī, suspicātus sum, mistrust, suspect, surmise.

sustentō, –āre, –āvī, –ātus, endure, hold out.

*sustineō, –ēre, –uī, –tentus, hold up, keep up, sustain, restrain, endure.

*suus, –a, –um, reflex. poss. adj., his, her, its, their; suī, suōrum, m.pl., his or their men, friends, party; sua, suōrum, n.pl., his, her, their property, possessions; sē suaque, themselves and their possessions.

T

taberna, –ae, f., shop, tavern.

tabernāculum, –ī, n., tent, tabernacle.

tabula, –ae, f., board, writing tablet, record, list.

taceō, –ēre, –uī, –itus, be silent.

tacitus, –a, –um, adj., silent.

tālea, –ae, f., block, bar, stick.

tālis, –e, adj., such, of such a kind, the following; tālis . . . quālis, of such kind . . . as, such . . . as.

*tam, adv., so, so much, so very; tam . . . quam, so . . . as, such . . . as.

*tamen, conj., however, nevertheless, notwithstanding, yet, but, still.

tametsī, conj., although, though.

tamquam, adv., as, just as.

tandem, adv., at length, at last, finally.

tangō, –ere, tetigī, tāctus, touch.

tantopere, adv., so earnestly, with so great effort.

tāntulus, –a, –um, adj., so very small, so slight, so trifling.

tantum, adv., so much, only so much, only.

*tantus, –a, –um, adj., so great, so large, such; tantus . . . quantus, so great, so much, only so much . . . as; tantī, of such value, worth so much; tantō, by so much, so much.

tardē, adv., slowly, tardily.

*tardō, –āre, –āvī, –ātus, check, retard, impede, slow down, hinder, delay.

*tardus, –a, –um, adj., slow, sluggish, tardy, late.

taurus, –ī, m., bull.

tegō, –ere, tēxī, tēctus, cover, hide, guard, protect.

*tēlum, –ī, n., dart, spear, weapon.

temerārius, –a, –um, adj., rash, headstrong.

temere, adv., rashly, blindly.

temperantia, –ae, f., temperance, moderation, self control.

temperātus, –a, –um, adj., moderate, temperate, mild.

temperō, –āre, –āvī, –ātus, control oneself, control, regulate, refrain.

*tempestās, –tātis, f., weather, storm, tempest, gale.

*templum, –ī, n., temple, shrine.

*temptō, –āre, –āvī, –ātus, try, attempt, attack, tempt, bribe.

*tempus, –oris, n., time, period, season, occasion; in reliquum tempus, for the future; ad tempus, on time, promptly; omnī tempore, always.

tenebrae, –ārum, f.pl., darkness, gloom.

*teneō, –ēre, –uī, —, hold, grasp, keep in, keep; memoriā tenēre, remember.

ter, adv., three times, thrice.

*tergum, –ī, n., back; ā tergō or post tergum, in the rear, behind; terga vertere, flee.

terminus, –ī, m., boundary, limit, end.

ternī, –ae, –a, adj., three each, three at a time.

*terra, –ae, f., earth, land, territory, country, region, ground.

*terreō, –ēre, –uī, –itus, frighten, alarm, terrify.

terribilis, –e, adj., frightful, terrible.

*terror, –ōris, m., terror, panic, fear, horror, fright.

*tertius, –a, –um, adj., third.

tēstāmentum, –ī, n., will, testament.

tēstimōnium, –ī, *n.,* witness, proof, testimony.

tēstis, –is, *mf.,* witness.

texō, –ere, –uī, textus, weave, construct.

thalamus, –ī, *m.,* bedchamber, couch.

theātrum, –ī, *n.,* theater.

*timeō, –ēre, –uī, —, fear, dread.

timidus, –a, –um, *adj.,* fearful, cowardly, timid.

*timor, –ōris, *m.,* fear, dread, panic.

tinniō, –īre, —, —, tinkle, ring.

*toga, –ae, *f.,* flowing garment of white woolen cloth.

tolerō, –āre, –āvī, –ātus, bear, support, endure, tolerate.

*tollō, –ere, sustulī, sublātus, lift up, raise, carry away, carry off, remove, kill.

tormentum, –ī, *n.,* windlass, military engine, missile, torture.

torrēns, –entis, *m.,* rushing stream, torrent.

*tot, *adj., indecl.,* so many.

totidem, *adj., indecl.,* just as many.

*tōtus, –a, –um, *gen.,* **tōtīus,** *adj.,* the whole, all, entire.

trabs, –is, *f.,* beam, trunk.

*trādō, –ere, –didī, –ditus, hand over, give up, deliver, surrender, betray, transmit, say.

*trādūcō, –ere, –dūxī, –ductus, lead across, transport, win over.

tragoedia, –ae, *f.,* tragedy.

trāgula, –ae, *f.,* dart, javelin.

*trāhō, –ere, trāxī, trāctus, draw, drag.

trājectus, –ūs, *m.,* crossing, passage.

trājiciō, –ere, –jēcī, –jectus, throw across, pierce, transfix, pass over.

trānō, –āre, –āvī, —, swim across, swim over.

tranquillitās, –tātis, *f.,* calm, stillness, tranquillity.

tranquillus, –a, –um, *adj.,* calm, still, tranquil.

*trāns, *prep. + acc.,* across, over, beyond.

trānscendō, –ere, –scendī, —, climb across, board.

*trānseō, –īre, –iī, (–īvī), –itus, go across, cross, pass by, pass over, pass through.

trānsferō, –ferre, –tulī, –lātus, bear across, transport, translate.

trānsfīgō, –ere, –fīxī, –fīxus, pierce through, transfix.

trānsmarīnus, –a, –um, *adj.,* foreign, transmarine.

trānsmissus, –ūs, *m.,* passage, crossing.

*trānsportō, –āre, –āvī, –ātus, carry over, take across.

trecentī, –ae, –a, *adj.,* three hundred.

trepidō, –āre, –āvī, –ātus, be in alarm, be afraid, hurry, tremble, waver.

*trēs, tria, *gen.,* **trium,** *adj.,* three.

*tribūnus, –ī, *m.,* tribune; **tribūnus plēbis,** tribune of the people; **tribūnus mīlitum,** military tribune.

tribuō, –ere, –uī, –ūtus, assign, ascribe, grant, pay, render, attribute.

tribūtum, –ī, *n.,* tax, tribute.

triduum, –ī, *n.,* (space of) three days.

trīgintā, *adj., indecl.,* thirty.

trīnī, –ae, –a, three, threefold, triple.

triplex, –icis, *adj.,* threefold, triple.

triquetrus, –a, –um, *adj.,* three-cornered, triangular.

trīstis, –e, *adj.,* sad, sorrowful.

trīstitia, –ae, *f.,* sadness, dejection.

*tū, tuī, *pers. pron.,* thou, you.

*tuba, –ae, *f.,* trumpet.

tueor, –ērī, tūtus sum, look at, gaze at, protect.

*tum, *adv.,* then, at that time, in those times; **cum . . . tum,** not only . . . but also.

tumultus, –ūs, *m.,* commotion, uprising.

tumulus, –ī, *m.,* mound, hillock.

tunc, *adv.,* then, at that time.

tunica, –ae, *f.,* undergarment, tunic.

turba, –ae, *f.,* commotion, crowd.

turbō, –āre, –āvī, –ātus, throw into confusion.

turbulentus, –a, –um, *adj.,* confused, stormy, restless, turbulent.

turma, –ae, *f.,* troop of thirty horsemen, squadron.

turpis, –e, *adj.,* ugly, unsightly, disgraceful.

turpitūdō, –inis, *f.,* baseness, disgrace, turpitude.

*turris, –is, *f.,* tower.

tūs, tūris, *n.,* incense.

tūtō, *adv.,* safely, securely.

tūtor, –ōris, *m.,* guardian, tutor.
tūtus, –a, –um, *adj.,* safe, secure.
*****tuus, –a, –um,** *poss. adj.,* thy, your, yours.

U

*****ubi,** *interrog. adv./conj.,* where? when? when, where; **ubi prīmum,** as soon as.
ubīque, *adv.,* anywhere, everywhere.
ulcīscor, –ī, ūltus sum, avenge oneself on, punish, avenge.
*****ūllus, –a, –um,** *gen.,* **ūllīus,** *adj.,* any, anyone.
*****ūlterior, –ius,** *gen.,* **–ōris,** *adj.,* farther, beyond, more remote.
ūltimus, –a, –um, *adj.,* farthest, last.
ūltiō, –ōnis, *f.,* an avenging, revenge.
ūltrā, *adv./prep.* + *acc.,* beyond, more than, besides.
ūltrō, *adv.,* besides, moreover, also, voluntarily.
umbra, –ae, *f.,* shade, shadow, ghost.
umerus (humerus), –ī, *m.,* upper arm, shoulder.
umquam, *adv.,* at any time, ever.
*****ūnā,** *adv.,* at the same time, together.
unda, –ae, *f.,* wave.
unde, *adv., rel.,* whence, where; *interrog.,* whence? where? on which side?
ūndecim, *adj., indecl.,* eleven.
ūndēvīgintī, *adj., indecl.,* nineteen.
*****undique,** *adv.,* from all sides, on all sides, everywhere.
unguentum, –ī, *n.,* ointment.
ūnicus, –a, –um, *adj.,* sole, single, only.
ūnigenitus, –ī, *m.,* only begotten son.
ūniversus, –a, –um, *adj.,* all together, all, the whole of, entire, universal.
*****ūnus, –a, –um,** *gen.,* **ūnīus,** *adj.,* one, only one, only, sole; *pl.,* **ūnī,** alone, only; **ad ūnum omnēs,** all to a man.
urbānus, –a, –um, *adj.,* of the city, urban.
*****urbs, urbis,** *f.,* city.
urgeō, –ēre, –ursī, —, press hard; *pass.,* be hard pressed.
ūrus, –ī, *m.,* wild ox.
ūsque, *adv.,* as far as, even; **ūsque ad,** all the way to, as far as, up to, until.
*****ūsus, –ūs,** *m.,* use, practice, employment, advantage, experience; **ūsuī est,** it is useful.

*****ut (utī),** *adv.,* as, just as, as if, how, where; **ut prīmum,** as soon as; *conj., with indic.,* when, as soon as; *with subj.,* that, so that, in order that, though, although.
uter, utra, utrum, *gen.,* **utrīus,** *adj./ pron.,* which (of two), whichever, which, which (of two)? which?
*****uterque, –traque, –trumque,** *gen.,* **utrīusque,** *adj.,* each, both; *noun, m.,* both, each; *pl.* **utrīque,** both sides, both peoples.
*****ūtilis, –e,** *adj.,* useful, helpful, expedient.
utinam, *adv.,* would that! oh that!; *introduces wishes in the subjunctive.*
*****ūtor, –ī, ūsus sum,** make use of, use, exercise, employ.
utrum, *adv.,* whether.
uxor, –ōris, *f.,* wife, consort.

V

vacātiō, –ōnis, *f.,* exemption.
vacō, –āre, –āvī, –ātus, be empty, be vacant, lie waste.
*****vacuus, –a, –um,** *adj.,* empty, vacant, free from.
vādō, –ere, vāsī, vāsūrus, go, advance.
vadum, –ī, *n.,* shallow spot, shoal, ford.
vāgīna, –ae, *f.,* sheath, scabbard.
vagor, –ārī, –ātus sum, wander about, roam about.
valdē, *adv.,* strongly, very much, powerfully, greatly.
*****valeō, –ēre, –uī, –itūrus,** be strong, be able, be well, be powerful, avail, prevail; **multum valēre,** be very powerful, have great influence; **valē, valēte,** *impers.,* farewell, good-by.
valētūdō, –inis, *f.,* state of health, illness.
*****validus, –a, –um,** *adj.,* strong, stout, powerful.
*****vallēs (vallis), –is,** *f.,* valley.
*****vāllum, –ī,** *n.,* rampart, earthworks.
vānus, –a, –um, *adj.,* vain, ostentatious.
varietās, –tātis, *f.,* variety, mottled appearance.
varius, –a, –um, *adj.,* different, various.

vās, vāsis, *n.,* vessel, dish; *pl.,* **vāsa, –ōrum,** receptacle, military equipment.

***vāstō, –āre, –āvī, –ātus,** lay waste, ravage, devastate, destroy.

vāstus, –a, –um, *adj.,* vast, immense.

vātēs, –is, *m.,* prophet, soothsayer, poet, bard.

vāticinātiō, –ōnis, *f.,* prophesying, prophecy.

–ve, *conj., enclitic,* or.

vectīgal, –ālis, *n.,* tax, tribute, revenue.

vehemēns, –entis, *adj.,* violent, impetuous, vehement.

vehementer, *adv.,* vehemently, vigorously, powerfully, strongly, very much.

vehō, –ere, vēxī, vectus, bear, carry, convey; *pass.,* ride, sail.

***vel,** *adv.,* even, actually, indeed; *conj.,* or; **vel . . . vel,** either . . . or.

vellus, –eris, *n.,* fleece.

vēlō, –āre, –āvī, –ātus, veil.

vēlōcitās, –tātis, *f.,* swiftness, rapidity, velocity.

vēlōx, –ōcis, *adj.,* swift.

vēlum, –ī, *n.,* sail, curtain, veil; **vēla ventīs dare,** make sail, sail away.

velut (velutī), *adv.,* just as; **velut sī,** just as if.

vēnātiō, –ōnis, *f.,* hunting.

vēnātor, –ōris, *m.,* hunter.

vēndō, –ere, –didī, –ditus, sell.

venēnum, –ī, *n.,* drug, poison, venom.

veneror, –ārī, –ātus sum, revere, respect, worship, venerate.

venia, –ae, *f.,* favor, pardon, permission.

***veniō, –īre, vēnī, ventūrus,** come.

venter, –tris, *m.,* belly, stomach.

ventitō, –āre, –āvī, –ātus, come often, go often.

***ventus, –ī,** *m.,* wind.

***verbum, –ī,** *n.,* word, saying.

vērē, *adv.,* truly, really.

***vereor, –ērī, –itus sum,** respect, fear, dread, be afraid of.

vergō, –ere, —, —, incline, slope, stretch toward.

vēritās, –tātis, *f.,* truth, truthfulness.

***vērō,** *adv.,* in truth, really, indeed.

versō, –āre, –āvī, –ātus, turn often, keep turning.

versor, –ārī, –ātus sum, move about, dwell, live, be, be employed.

versus, *adv./prep. + acc.,* toward, in the direction of.

versus, –ūs, *m.,* line, row, verse.

***vertō, –ere, vertī, versus,** turn, direct, change; *pass.,* return; **terga vertere,** turn and flee, flee.

***vērum, –ī,** *n.,* truth.

***vērus, –a, –um,** *adj.,* true; **rē vērā,** indeed, in truth.

verūtum, –ī, *n.,* dart.

vescor, –ī, —, eat, feed upon, live on.

***vesper, –erī (–eris),** *m.,* evening.

vesperī, *adv.,* in the evening.

***vester, –tra, –trum,** *poss. adj.,* your, yours.

vestibulum, –ī, *n.,* entrance court, vestibule.

vēstīgium, –ī, *n.,* footstep, footprint, trace, track, vestige.

vestiō, –īre, –īvī, –ītus, clothe.

vestis, –is, *f.,* clothes, clothing, garment, robe.

vestītus, –ūs, *m.,* clothing, apparel.

veterānus, –a, –um, *adj.,* old, veteran; **veterānī, –ōrum,** *m.,* veteran soldiers, veterans.

vetō, –āre, –uī, –itus, forbid.

vetus, –eris, *adj.,* old, former, ancient.

vēxillum, –ī, *n.,* small flag or banner.

vexō, –āre, –āvī, –ātus, harass, molest, annoy.

***via, –ae,** *f.,* road, street, passage, journey, way.

viātor, –ōris, *m.,* wayfarer, traveler, stranger.

vīcēsimus, –a, –um, *adj.,* twentieth.

vīciēs, *adv.,* twenty times.

vicīnus, –a, –um, *adj.,* neighboring.

vicissitūdō, –inis, *f.,* change, alteration, vicissitude.

victima, –ae, *f.,* victim, animal for sacrifice.

***victor, –ōris,** *m.,* conqueror, victor.

***victōria, –ae,** *f.,* victory, success.

vīctus, –ūs, *m.,* mode of life, food, provisions.

***vīcus, –ī,** *m.,* village, hamlet.

vidēlicet, *adv.,* it is clear, namely.

*videō, –ēre, vīdī, vīsus, see, perceive, observe; *pass.*, **videor, –ērī, vīsus sum,** be seen, seem, appear, seem good, seem best.

*vigilia, –ae, *f.*, sleeplessness, watchfulness, night watch, sentinel, guard, watch.

*vigilō, –āre, –āvī, –ātūrus, be awake, keep awake, be alert, watch.

*vīgintī, *adj., indecl.,* twenty.

*villa, –ae, *f.*, country house, farm, villa.

vinciō, –īre, vīnxī, vīnctus, bind, tie around, fetter.

*vincō, –ere, vīcī, victus, conquer, defeat, surpass, exceed, overcome.

vinculum (vinclum), –ī, *n.*, bond, chain, fetter; *pl.*, prison.

vindicō, –āre, –āvī, –ātus, lay legal claim to, avenge, punish, claim for liberty, set free, vindicate.

vīnea, –ae, *f.*, vinea, a movable shed.

vīnētum, –ī, *n.*, vineyard.

vīnum, –ī, *n.*, wine.

violēns, –entis, *adj.*, violent, vehement.

violō, –āre, –āvī, –ātus, treat with violence, violate.

*vir, virī, *m.*, man, husband.

virēns, –entis, *adj.*, green, blooming, youthful.

vīrēs, –ium, *f.pl. of* **vīs,** strength.

virga, –ae, *f.*, twig, switch, rod, magic wand.

virgō, –inis, *f.*, maiden, virgin.

virīlis, –e, *adj.*, manly, virile.

*virtūs, –tūtis, *f.*, manliness, courage, valor, bravery, virtue.

*vīs, acc., vim, abl., vī, *f.*, force, strength, energy, vim; *pl.*, **vīrēs, vīrium.**

vīsiō, –ōnis, *f.*, vision.

vīsitō, –āre, –āvī, –ātus, see often, visit.

*vīta, –ae, *f.*, life; **vītam agere,** live.

vitium, –ī, *n.*, flaw, defect, fault, crime.

vītō, –āre, –āvī, –ātus, shun, avoid.

vitrum, –ī, *n.*, woad (a plant producing a blue dye).

vitulus, –ī, *m.*, young bullock, calf.

vīvō, –ere, vīxī, vīctus, live, be alive.

*vīvus, –a, –um, *adj.*, alive, living, vivacious.

vix, *adv.*, with difficulty, hardly, scarcely.

*vocō, –āre, –āvī, –ātus, call, summon, name.

volātilis, –e, *adj.*, flying, winged.

volō, –āre, –āvī, –ātūrus, fly, rush.

*volō, velle, voluī, —, will, wish, desire, be willing, want.

volucer, –cris, –cre, *adj.*, winged, flying; **volucris, –is,** *f.*, flying creature, bird.

voluntārius, –a, –um, *adj.*, willing, voluntary; **voluntāriī, –ōrum,** *m.pl.*, volunteers.

*voluntās, –tātis, *f.*, will, wish, desire.

voluptās, –tātis, *f.*, pleasure, enjoyment, delight.

volvō, –ere, volvī, volūtus, roll, revolve, turn over.

vorō, –āre, –āvī, –ātus, eat greedily, swallow up, devour.

vortex (vertex), –icis, *m.*, whirl, point on top of a whirl, head, summit, vertex.

voveō, –ēre, vōvī, vōtus, vow, dedicate, consecrate.

*vōx, vōcis, *f.*, voice, utterance, word; **māgna vōx,** loud voice; **clāra vōx,** distinct voice.

vulgō, *adv.*, generally, commonly, everywhere.

vulgus, –ī, *n.*, common people, multitude, crowd.

*vulnerō, –āre, –āvī, –ātus, wound, hurt.

*vulnus, –eris, *n.*, wound.

vultus, –ūs, *m.*, expression, countenance, looks, face.

English-Latin

A

abandon, relinquō, –ere, –līquī, –lictus; dēserō, –ere, –uī, –sertus.

able, be, possum, posse, potuī, —.

about, dē + *abl.;* ad + *acc.; adv. with numerals,* circiter.

about to, *use fut. part.*

above, *adv.,* suprā; **from above,** dēsuper; *prep.,* super + *acc.*

absent, be, absum, –esse, āfuī, āfutūrus.

accept, accipiō, –ere, –cēpī, –ceptus.

accomplish, cōnficiō, –ere, –fēcī, –fectus; perficiō, –ere, –fēcī, –fectus; efficiō, –ere, –fēcī, –fectus.

account, on account of, ob, propter + *acc.*

accustom, cōnsuēscō, –ere, –suēvī, –suētus; *perf.;* **be accustomed;** soleō, –ēre, solitus sum (*semidep.*), be accustomed.

across, trāns + *acc.;* (a bridge) in + *abl.*

admire, (ad)mīror, –ārī, –ātus sum.

advance, prōcēdō, –ere, –cessī, –cessūrus; prōgredior, –ī, –gressus sum.

advise, (ad)moneō, –ēre, –uī, –itus.

affair, rēs, reī, *f.*

afraid of, vereor, –ērī, –itus sum.

after, *adv.,* post, posteā; *prep.,* post + *acc.; conj.,* postquam.

afterward, post, posteā.

again, rūrsus; iterum (**a second time**).

against, in, contrā + *acc.*

aid, *noun,* auxilium, –ī, *n.;* subsidium, –ī, *n.; verb,* (ad)juvō, –āre, –jūvī, –jūtus.

alarm, commoveō, –ēre, –mōvī, –mōtus; permoveō, –ēre, –mōvī, –mōtus.

alive, vīvus, –a, –um.

all, omnis, –e (*pl.*); tōtus, –a, –um (**the whole**); cūnctus, –a, –um (**all together**); ūniversus, –a, –um (**all together**).

allow, patior, –ī, passus sum; permittō, –ere, –mīsī, –missus; concēdō, –ere, –cessī, –cessūrus.

ally, socius, –ī, *m.*

almost, paene; ferē.

alone, sōlus, –a, –um; ūnus, –a, –um.

already, jam.

also, etiam (*with verbs*); quoque (*with nouns and pronouns; postpositive*).

altar, āra, –ae, *f.*

although, quamquam, etsī, cum; *use participle or ablative absolute.*

altogether, omnīnō.

always, semper.

among, inter, apud + *acc.*

ancient, antīquus, –a, –um.

and, et; atque (ac); –que.

anger, īra, –ae, *f.*

angry, īrātus, –a, –um.

animal, animal, –ālis, *n.*

annex, (ad)jungō, –ere, –jūnxī, –jūnctus.

announce, (ē)nūntiō, 1; **announcement,** *use verb.*

another, alius, alia, aliud.

answer, respondeō, –ēre, –spondī, –spōnsus.

any, ūllus, –a, –um (*in negative expressions*); aliquī, –qua, –quod; quī, quae, quod (*after* sī).

anyone, anything, aliquis, –quid; quis, quid (*after* sī).

appearance, aspectus, –ūs, *m.;* speciēs, –ēī, *f.*

apple, pōmum, –ī, *n.*

approach, *noun,* adventus, –ūs, *m.,* aditus –ūs, *m.; verb,* appropinquō, 1 (*with dat.,* or ad + *acc.*); accēdō, –ere, –cessī, –cessūrus (*with* ad + *acc.*); adeō, –īre, –iī (–īvī), –itūrus.

approve, probō, 1.

arise, orior, –īrī, –ortus sum.

arm, armō, 1.

armed, armātus, –a, –um.

arms, arma, –ōrum, *n.pl.*

army, exercitus, –ūs, *m.*

around, circum + *acc.*

arrival, adventus, –ūs, *m.*

arrive, perveniō, –īre, –vēnī, –ventūrus (*with* ad, in + *acc.*).

arrow, sagitta, –ae, *f.*

as, ut; quem ad modum; **as . . . as possible,** quam + *superl. adj./adv.;* **as soon as possible,** quam prīmum; **as soon as,**

simul atque (ac); **as long as,** dum; **as ... as,** tam ... quam; **as great as ...,** tantus ... quantus; **as many as ...,** tot ... quot; **as often as ...,** totiēns ... quotiēns; **such ... as,** tālis ... quālis.

ascend, ascendō, –ere, –scendī, –scēnsus.

ascent, ascēnsus, –ūs, *m.*

ask, rogō, 1; petō, –ere, –īvī, –ītus; quaerō, –ere, –sīvī, –sītus; ōrō, 1.

at, *use abl. of time or place where, or locative;* apud, ad, in + *acc.*

at first, prīmō, prīmum.

at last, tandem.

at once, statim.

atrium, atrium, –ī, *n.*

attack, *noun,* impetus, –ūs, *m.; verb,* oppūgnō, 1; aggredior, –ī, –gressus sum; facere impetum in + *acc.*

authority, auctōritās, –tātis, *f.*

avoid, vītō, 1.

await, exspectō, 1.

away from, ā, ab + *abl.*

B

back, tergum, –ī, *n.*

bad, malus, –a, –um.

baggage, heavy, impedīmenta, –ōrum, *n.pl.*

band (of men), manus, –ūs, *f.*

bank, rīpa, –ae, *f.*

bare, nūdus, –a, –um.

battle, proelium, –ī, *n.;* pūgna, –ae, *f.;* **begin battle,** proelium committō, –ere, –mīsī, –missus.

battle line, aciēs, –ēī, *f.*

be, sum, esse, fuī, futūrus.

be able, possum, posse, potuī, —.

be absent, be away, absum, –esse, āfuī, āfutūrus.

be afraid, timeō, –ēre, –uī, —. *See* **vereor.**

be in command (charge) of, praesum, –esse, –fuī, –futūrus (*with dat.*).

be near (be present), adsum, –esse, –fuī, –futūrus.

be unwilling, nōlō, nōlle, nōluī, —.

be willing, volō, velle, voluī, —.

bear, ferō, ferre, tulī, lātus; portō, 1.

beautiful, pulcher, –chra, –chrum.

because, quod, quia, quoniam, proptereā quod; cum (*with subjunctive*); *use participle or ablative absolute.*

because of, propter, ob + *acc.*

become, be done, be made, fīō, fierī, factus sum.

beech, fāgus, ī, *f.*

before, *adv.,* anteā, ante; *prep.,* ante + *acc.; conj.,* antequam, priusquam.

beg (for), ōrō, 1; petō, –ere, –īvī, –ītus.

begin, incipiō, –ere, –cēpī, –ceptus; *perf. tenses, use* coepī, –isse, coeptus (*defective*); **begin battle,** proelium committō, –ere, –mīsī, –missus.

beginning, initium, –ī, *n.*

behalf, on behalf of, prō + *abl.*

behind, post + *acc.*

believe, crēdō, –ere, –didī, –ditūrus (*with dat.*).

belt, balteus, –ī, *m.*

besides, *adv.,* praetereā; *prep.,* praeter + *acc.*

besiege, obsideō, –ēre, –sēdī, –sessus.

best, optimus, –a, –um.

better, *adj.,* melior, –ius; *adv.,* melius.

between, inter + *acc.*

bind, ligō, 1; vinciō, –īre, vīnxī, vīnctus.

bird, avis, –is, *f.;* volucris, –is, *f.*

blame, accūsō, 1.

blind, caecus, –a, –um.

blood, sanguis, –inis, *m.*

blow, flō, 1.

boar, wild, aper, aprī, *m.*

board (a ship), cōnscendō, –ere, –scendī, –scēnsus.

boat, linter, –tris, *m.;* nāvicula, –ae, *f.;* scapha, –ae, *f.*

body, corpus, –oris, *n.*

bold, audāx, –ācis; **boldly,** audācter.

boldness, audācia, –ae, *f.*

book, liber, –brī, *m.*

booty, praeda, –ae, *f.*

border (of a country), fīnis, –is, *m.*

both, ambō, –ae, –ō; uterque, –traque, –trumque (*each of two*); **both ... and,** et ... et.

bow, arcus, –ūs, *m.*

boy, puer, puerī, *m.*

branch, rāmus, –ī, *m.;* pars, partis, *f.*

brave, fortis, –e; **bravely,** fortiter.

bravery, fortitūdō, –inis, *f.;* virtūs, –tūtis, *f.*

break, frangō, –ere, frēgī, fractus.

break camp, castra moveō, –ēre, mōvī, mōtus.

break through, perrumpō, –ere, –rūpī, –ruptus.

bridge, pōns, pontis, m.

brief, brevis, –e.

bring, ferō, ferre, tulī, lātus; bring aid, auxilium ferre.

bring about, efficiō, –ere, –fēcī, –fectus.

bring back, referō, –ferre, rettulī, –lātus; redūcō, –ere, –dūxī, –ductus.

bring in, bring upon, īnferō, –ferre, –tulī, illātus.

bring together, contrahō, –ere, –trāxī, –trāctus.

broad, lātus, –a, –um.

brother, frāter, –tris, m.

build, aedificō, 1; (ex)struō, –ere, –strūxī, –strūctus; cōnstruō, –ere, –strūxī, –strūctus; faciō, –ere, fēcī, factus.

building, aedificium, –ī, n.

bull, taurus, –ī, m.

burn, incendō, –ere, –cendī, –cēnsus; combūrō, –ere, –bussī, –būstus; cremō, 1.

burst, ērumpō, –ere, –rūpī, –ruptus.

business, negōtium, –ī, n.

but, sed.

buy, emō, –ere, ēmī, ēmptus.

by, abl. without prep.; ā, ab + abl.

C

call, vocō, 1; call by name, appellō, 1; call out, ēvocō, 1; clāmō, 1.

camp, castra, –ōrum, n.pl.; break camp, castra moveō, –ēre, mōvī, mōtus; pitch camp, castra pōnō, –ere, posuī, positus.

can, see be able.

canton, pāgus, –ī, m.

captive, captīvus, –ī, m.

care, cūra, –ae, f.; dīligentia, –ae, f.

care for (take care of), cūrō, 1.

carefully, dīligenter.

carry, portō, 1; ferō, ferre, tulī, lātus; gerō, –ere, gessī, gestus; carry on war, bellum gerere; carry away, tollō, –ere, sustulī, sublātus; carry off, rapiō, –ere, –uī, raptus; auferō, –ferre, abstulī, ablātus; carry back, referō, –ferre, rettulī, relātus; carry from, efferō, –ferre, extulī, ēlātus; carry over, across¦ trānsportō, 1.

cart, carrus, –ī, m.

cattle, bovēs, boum, mf.pl.; pecus, –oris, n.; a single head of, pecus, –udis, f.

cause, causa, –ae, f.

cavalry, equitātus, –ūs, m.; equitēs, –um, m.pl.

cease, dēsistō, –ere, –stitī, —.

centurion, centuriō, –ōnis, m.

certain, certus, –a, –um; make more certain, inform, certiōrem facere.

certain, certain one, adj./pron., quīdam, quaedam, quoddam (quiddam).

chance, cāsus, –ūs; m.; by chance, forte.

change, (com)mūtō, 1; convertō, –ere, –vertī, –versus.

character, nātūra, –ae, f., ingenium, –ī, n.

charge (attack), concurrō, –ere, –currī, –cursūrus; ērumpō, –ere, –rūpī, –ruptus; be in charge of, praesum, –esse, –fuī, — (with dat.); place in charge of, praeficiō, –ere, –fēcī, –fectus (with dat.).

chariot, currus, –ūs, m.; quadrīgae, –ārum, f.pl.

chief, prīnceps, –ipis, m.

children, līberī, –ōrum, m.pl.

choose, dēligō, –ere, –lēgī, –lēctus.

citizen, cīvis, –is, mf.

city, urbs, urbis, f.

cleanse, pūrgō, 1.

clear, clārus, –a, –um; clearly, clārē.

client, cliēns, –entis, m.

cliff, rūpēs, –is, f.

climb, ascendō, –ere, –scendī, –scēnsus; climb aboard, cōnscendō, –ere, –scendī, –scēnsus; trānscendō, –ere, –scendī, –scēnsus.

close, claudō, –ere, clausī, clausus.

clothe, vestiō, –īre, –īvī, –ītus.

clothes, clothing, vestis, –is, f.; vestītus, –ūs, m.

clouds, nūbēs, –is, f.

come, veniō, –īre, vēnī, ventūrus.

come back, revertor, –ī, –versus sum.

coming, adventus, –ūs, m.

command, noun, imperium, –ī, n.; mandātum, –ī, n.; verb, imperō, 1 (with dat. of persons); jubeō, –ēre, jūssī, jūssus (with acc. of person + inf.).

515

command of, be in, praesum, –esse, –fuī, — (*with dat.*).

commandment, mandātum, –ī, *n.*; imperium, –ī, *n.*

commit, committō, –ere, –mīsī, –missus.

common, commūnis, –e.

common people, plēbs, –is, *f.*

compact, cōnfertus, –a, –um; dēnsus, –a, –um.

companion, comes, –itis, *mf.*; socius, –ī, *m.*

compel, cogō, –ere, –ēgī, –āctus; compellō, –ere, –pulī, –pulsus.

complain, queror, –ī, questus sum.

complete, compleō, –ēre, –ēvī, –ētus; cōnficiō, –ere, –fēcī, –fectus.

comrade, socius, ī, *m.*; comes, –itis, *m.*

concern, cūra, –ae, *f.*

concerns, it, interest (*impers.*).

conference, colloquium, –ī, *n.*

condition, condiciō, –ōnis, *f.*

confide, have confidence in, cōnfīdō, –ere, –fīsus sum (*semidep., with dat./abl.*).

conquer, superō, 1; vincō, –ere, vīcī, victus.

conqueror, victor, –ōris, *m.*

consider, cōnsīderō, 1; habeō, –ēre, –uī, –itus; dūcō, –ere, dūxī, ductus.

consist, cōnsistō, –ere, –stitī, —; cōnstō, –āre, –stitī, –stātūrus.

conspiracy, conjūrātiō, –ōnis, *f.*; **form a conspiracy,** conjūrō, 1.

construct, faciō, –ere, fēcī, fāctus; īnstituō, –ere, –uī, –ūtus.

consul, cōnsul, –ulis, *m.*

consulship, cōnsulātus, –ūs, *m.*

consult, cōnsulō, –ere, –uī, –sultus.

content, contentus, –a, –um.

continuous, continuus, –a, –um.

control, temperō, 1.

could, *see* be able.

country, patria, –ae, *f.*; terra, –ae, *f.*; fīnēs, –ium, *m.pl.*

courage, virtūs, –tūtis, *f.*; fortitūdō, –inis, *f.*; animus, –ī, *m.*

course, cursus, –ūs, *m.*

cover, (con)tegō, –ere, –tēxī, –tēctus.

crime, scelus, –eris, *n.*, maleficium, –ī, *n.*

cross, trānseō, –īre, –iī (–īvī), –itus.

cruel, crūdēlis, –e.

cruelty, crūdēlitās, –tātis, *f.*

crush, opprimō, –ere, –pressī, –pressus.

cunning, dolus, –ī, *m.*

cup, pōculum, –ī, *n.*

custom, mōs, mōris, *m.*; cōnsuētūdō, –inis, *f.*

cut off, interclūdō, –ere, –clūsī, –clūsus.

D

daily, cotīdiē.

danger, perīculum, –ī, *n.*

dangerous, perīculōsus, –a, –um.

dare, audeō, –ēre, ausus sum (*semidep.*).

daring, audācia, –ae, *f.*

dash together, cōnflīgō, –ere, –flīxī, –flīctus; concurrō, –ere, –currī, –cursūrus.

daughter, fīlia, –ae, *f.*

day, diēs, –ēī, *mf.*; **every day,** cotīdiē; **day before,** prīdiē; **following day, next day,** postrīdiē; **by day,** interdiū; **late in the day,** multō diē; **today,** hodiē.

day, name a, diem dīcere.

daybreak, at, prīmā lūce.

dear, cārus, –a, –um.

death, mors, mortis, *f.*

debtor, debtor, –ōris, *m.*; obaerātus, –ī, *m.*

decide, cōnstituō, –ere, –uī, –ūtus; īnstituō, –ere, –uī, –ūtus; statuō, –ere, –uī, –ūtus; dījūdicō, 1.

deed, factum, –ī, *n.*

deep, altus, –a, –um.

deer, cervus, –ī, *m.*

defeat, superō, 1; vincō, –ere, vīcī, victus; pellō, –ere, pepulī, pulsus.

defend, dēfendō, –ere, –fendī, –fēnsus.

defender, dēfensor, –ōris, *m.*

delay, *noun,* mora, –ae, *f.*; *verb,* moror, –ārī, –ātus sum.

deliberate, dēlīberō, 1.

delight, dēlectō, 1.

deliver, trādō, –ere, –didī, –ditus.

demand, postulō (*with* a, ab + *abl.*), 1; poscō, –ere, poposcī, —.

dense, dēnsus, –a, –um; cōnfertus, –a, –um.

depart, discēdō, –ere, –cessī, –cessūrus; excēdō, –ere, –cessī, –cessūrus; dēcēdō, –ere, –cessī, –cessūrus.

departure, discessus, –ūs, *m.*

descend, dēscendō, –ere, –scendī, –scēnsus.

desire, *noun,* cupiditās, –tātis, *f.*; dēsīderium, –ī, *n.*; *verb*, cupiō, –ere, –īvī, –ītus; dēsīderō, 1; volō, velle, voluī, —.

desirous, cupidus, –a, –um.

despair, dēspērō, 1.

destroy, dēleō, –ēre, –ēvī, –ētus; vāstō, 1.

deter, dēterreō, –ēre, –uī, –itus.

determine, cōnstituō, –ere, –stituī, –tūtus; statuō, –ere, –uī, –ūtus.

differ, differō, –ferre, distulī, dīlātus.

difficult, difficilis, –e.

difficulty, difficultās, –tātis, *f.*

direction, pars, partis, *f.*; **in (to) all directions,** in omnēs partēs.

disaster, calamitās, –tātis, *f.*

discover, inveniō, –īre, –vēnī, –ventus.

discretion, prūdentia, –ae, *f.*; cōnsilium, –ī, *n.*

disregard, *noun*, negligentia, –ae, *f.*; *verb*, neglegō, –ere, –lēxī, –lēctus; ōmittō, –ere, –mīsī, –missus.

distance, spatium, –ī, *n.*

distress, miseria, –ae, *f.*; labor, –ōris, *m.*

disturb, perturbō, 1; commoveō, –ēre, –mōvī, –mōtus; permoveō, –ēre, –mōvī, –mōtus.

ditch, fossa, –ae, *f.*

divide, dīvidō, –ere, –vīsī, –vīsus.

do, agō, –ere, ēgī, āctus; faciō, –ere, fēcī, factus.

dog, canis, –is, *mf.*

door, jānua, –ae, *f.*

doubt, *noun*, dubium, –ī, *n.*; *verb*, dubitō, 1.

dove, columba, –ae, *f.*

down from, dē + *abl.*

drag, trahō, –ere, trāxī, trāctus; **drag out,** extrahō, –ere, –trāxī, –trāctus.

draw (a sword), dēstringō, –ere, –strīnxī, –strictus.

draw lots, sortēs dūcō, –ere, dūxī, ductus; sortior, –īrī, –ītus sum.

draw off, dētrahō, –ere, –trāxī, –trāctus.

draw up (troops), īnstruō, –ere, –strūxī, –strūctus.

drive, agō, –ere, ēgī, āctus; pellō, –ere, pepulī, pulsus; agitō, 1.

drive back, repellō, –ere, reppulī, –pulsus.

drive on, impellō, –ere, –pulī, –pulsus.

drive out, expellō, –ere, –pulī, –pulsus.

duty, officium, –ī, *n.*

dwell, habitō, 1; incolō, –ere, –uī, —.

dwelling, domicilium, –ī, *n.*; aedificium, –ī, *n.*

dye, īnficiō, –ere, –fēcī, –fectus.

E

each, *adj.*, quīque, quaeque, quodque; omnis, –e; *pron.*, quisque, quidque.

each (of two), uterque, utraque, utrumque.

eager for, cupidus, –a, –um.

eagerness, studium, –ī, *n.*; cupiditās, –tātis, *f.*

eagle, aquila, –ae, *f.*

early (in the night), prīmā nocte; **(in the morning)** māne, *adv.*

earth, terra, –ae, *f.*

easily, facile.

easy, facilis, –e.

effect, efficiō, –ere, –fēcī, –fectus.

eight, octō (*indecl.*).

eighteen, duodēvīgintī (*indecl.*).

eighth, octāvus, –a, –um.

either . . . or, aut . . . aut (*where both cannot be true*); vel . . . vel.

elect, creō, 1.

eleven, ūndecim (*indecl.*).

embassy, lēgātiō, –ōnis, *f.*

encircle, circumdō, –are, –dedī, –datus.

enclose, inclūdō, –ere, –clūsī, –clūsus; contineō, –ēre, –uī, –tentus.

encourage, cohortor, –ārī, –ātus sum; cōnfīrmō, 1.

end, *noun*, fīnis, –is, *m.*; terminus, –ī, *m.*; *verb*, fīniō, –īre, –īvī, –ītus.

endure, sustineō, –ēre, –uī, –tentus; patior, –ī, passus sum; perferō, –ferre, –tulī, –lātus.

enemy (of one's country), hostis, –is, *m.*; **the enemy,** hostēs, –ium, *m.pl.*; **(personal) enemy,** inimīcus, –ī, *m.*

enforce, cōnfīrmō, 1; exsequor, –ī, –secūtus sum.

enjoy, fruor, –ī, frūctus sum (*with abl.*).

enough, satis.

enter, introō, 1; ineō, –īre, –iī (–īvī), –itus.

entire, integer, –gra, –grum; tōtus, –a, –um.

entrance, aditus, –ūs, *m.*

entrust, committō, –ere, –mīsī, –missus; mandō, 1; commendō, 1.

envoy, lēgātus, –ī, *m.*

envy, invidia, –ae, *f.*

equal, pār, paris; aequus, –a, –um.

escape, fugiō, –ere, fūgī, —.

establish, cōnfīrmō, 1.

even, etiam; **not even,** nĕ . . . quidem.

evening, nox, noctis, *f.*; vesper, –erī, *m.*

ever, umquam.

every, omnis, –e; **every day,** cotīdiē; **everything,** omnia, –ium, *n.pl.*; **everywhere,** ubīque; **from every side,** undique.

evil, malus, –a, –um.

evil deed, maleficium, –ī, *n.*

excel, superō, 1; excellō, –ere, –cellī, –celsus; praestō, –āre, –stitī, –stitus.

except, praeter + *acc.*

exercise, exerceō, –ēre, –uī, –itus.

exhausted, dēfessus, –a, –um.

exile, exsilium, –ī, *n.*

expel, expellō, –ere, –pulī, –pulsus; exigō, –ere, –ēgī, –āctus.

expiate, expiō, 1.

explain, dēmōnstrō, 1; expōnō, –ere, –posuī, –positus.

explore, explōrō, 1.

extend, extendō, –ere, –tendī, –tentus; pateō, –ēre, –uī, —; pertineō, –ēre, –uī, — (*with* ad + *acc.*).

extend toward, look toward, spectō, 1.

eye, oculus, –ī, *m.*

F

faith, fidēs, –eī, *f.*

faithful, fīdus, –a, –um.

fall, cadō, –ere, cecidī, cāsūrus.

fame, fāma, –ae, *f.*

family (household), familia, –ae, *f.*

famous, clārus, –a, –um.

far, by far, longē.

farmer, agricola, –ae, *m.*

father, pater, –tris, *m.*

fatherland, patria, –ae, *f.*

favor, grātia, –ae, *f.*

favorable, secundus, –a, –um.

fear, *noun,* timor, –ōris, *m.*; metus, –ūs, *m.*; *verb,* timeō, –ēre, –uī, —.

feel, sentiō, –īre, sēnsī, sēnsus.

few, paucī, –ae, –a, *pl.*; **very few,** perpaucī, –ae, –a, *pl.*

field, ager, agrī, *m.*; campus, –ī, *m.*

fierce, ācer, ācris, ācre; **fiercely,** ācriter.

fifth, quīntus, –a, –um.

fight, *noun,* pūgna, –ae, *f.*; *verb,* pūgnō, 1.

fill, compleō, impleō, –ēre, –ēvī, –ētus.

filled, plēnus, –a, –um (*with gen. or abl.*).

finally, tandem.

find, inveniō, –īre, –vēnī, –ventus.

find out, cōgnōscō, –ere, –nōvī, –nitus; reperiō, –īre, –perī, –pertus.

finish, fīniō, –īre, –īvī, –ītus; cōnficiō, –ere, –fēcī, –fectus; perficiō, –ere, –fēcī, –fectus.

fir (tree), abiēs, –etis, *f.*

fire, īgnis, –is, *m.*; flamma, –ae, *f.*; incendium, –ī, *n.*

first, first part of, prīmus, –a, –um; **at first,** prīmō; **for the first time, in the first place,** prīmum.

fitting, it is, oportet, –ēre, –uit (*impers.*).

five, quīnque (*indecl.*).

flee, fugiō, –ere, fūgī, —; sē in fugam dō, dare, dedī, datus; perfugiō, –ere, –fūgī, —.

fleece, vellus, –eris, n.

flight, fuga, –ae, *f.*; **put to flight,** in fugam dō, dare, dedī, datus; fugō, 1.

flow, fluō, –ere, flūxī, flūxūrus; īnfluō, –ere, –flūxī, –flūxūrus.

fly, volō, 1; **fly away,** āvolō, 1.

fodder, pābulum, –ī, *n.*

follow, sequor, –ī, secūtus sum.

following, posterus, –a, –um; secundus, –a, –um; **following day,** postrīdiē.

food, cibus, –ī, *m.*

foot, pēs, pedis, *m.*; **at the foot of,** sub + *abl.*

foot soldier, pedes, –itis, *m.*

for, *prep.* (**in behalf of, in defense of**), prō + *abl.; conj.* (**because**), enim, nam, quod.

forces, cōpiae, –ārum, *f.pl.*

forehead, frōns, frontis, *f.*

foreign, aliēnus, –a, –um.

forest, silva, –ae, *f.*

former, prior, –ius; ille, illa, illud.

formerly, ōlim.

fortification, mūnītiō, –ōnis, *f.*

fortify, mūniō, –īre, –īvī, –ītus.

fortress, castellum, –ī, *n.*

fortune, fortūna, –ae, *f.*

four, quattuor (*indecl.*).

fourth, quārtus, –a, –um.

free, *adj.*, līber, –era, –erum; *verb* (**set free**), līberō, 1.

friend, amīcus, –ī, *m.*; amīca, –ae, *f.*

friendship, amīcitia, –ae, *f.*

frighten, terreō, –ēre, –uī, –itus; **frighten thoroughly,** perterreō, –ēre, –uī, –itus.

from, ā, ab, dē, ē, ex, + *abl.*

fruit, frūctus, –ūs, *m.*; pōmum, –ī, *n.*

full (filled), plēnus, –a, –um (*with gen. or abl.*).

G

gain (overtake), cōnsequor, –ī, –secūtus sum; **(possession of),** potior, –īrī, –ītus sum (*with abl. or gen.*).

game, lūdus, –ī, *m.*

garden, hortus, –ī, *m.*

garment, vestis, –is, *f.*

garrison, castellum, –ī, *n.*; praesidium, –ī, *n.*

gate, porta, –ae, *f.*; jānua, –ae, *f.*

gather, cōnferō, –ferre, –tulī, collātus.

gather together, colligō, –ere, –lēgī, –lēctus.

general, imperātor, –ōris, *m.*

gift, dōnum, –ī, *n.*

girl, puella, –ae, *f.*

give, dō, dare, dedī, datus.

give back, reddō, –ere, –didī, –ditus.

give up, trādō, –ere, –didī, –ditus; dēdō, –ere, –didī, –ditus.

glitter, fulgeō, –ēre, fulsī, —.

glory, glōria, –ae, *f.*

go, eō, īre, iī (īvī), itūrus.

go away, abeō, –īre, -iī (–īvī), –itūrus.

go back, redeō, –īre, -iī (–īvī), –itūrus.

go forth (out), exeō, –īre, –iī (–īvī), –itūrus.

go in, ineō, –īre, –iī (–īvī), –itus; intrō, 1.

go on, gerō, –ere, gessī, gestus.

god, deus, –ī, *m.*; **God,** Deus, –ī, *m.*

goddess, dea, –ae, *f.*

gold, aurum, –ī, *n.*

golden, aureus, –a, –um.

good, bonus, –a, –um.

grain, frūmentum, –ī, *n.*; **supply of corn,** rēs frūmentāria, reī frūmentāriae, *f.*

grateful, grātus, –a, –um.

great, māgnus, –a, –um; **greater,** mājor, mājus; **greatest,** māximus, –a, –um; **how great,** quantus, –a, –um; **so great,** tantus, –a, –um; **as great as,** tantus . . . quantus.

greatly, māgnopere.

greedy, avārus, –a, –um.

grieve, doleō, –ēre, –uī, –itūrus.

ground, solum, –ī, *n.*; humus, –ī, *f.*; terra, –ae, *f.*

guard, *noun,* cūstōs, –ōdis, *m.*; praesidium, –ī, *n.*; cūstōdia, –ae, *f.*; *verb,* cūstōdiō, –īre, –īvī, –ītus.

H

hair, capillus, –ī, *m.*; coma, –ae, *f.*

hand, manus, –ūs, *f.*

hand over, trādō, –ere, –didī, –ditus; dēdō, –ere, –didī, –ditus.

happen, fīō, fierī, factus sum; **it happens,** accidit, ēvenit (*impers.*).

happy, fēlīx, –īcis; laetus, –a, –um.

harbor, portus, –ūs, *m.*

harm, *noun,* injūria, –ae, *f.*; dētrīmentum, –ī, *n.*; *verb,* noceō, –ēre, –uī, — (*with dat.*).

hasten, properō, 1; contendō, –ere, –tendī, –tentus.

hate, *noun,* odium, –ī, *n.*; *verb,* ōdī, ōdisse, ōsūrus (*defective*).

have, habeō, –ēre, –uī, –itus.

he, is, hic, ille, iste; **he himself,** ipse.

head, caput, –itis, *n.*

hear, audiō, –īre, –īvī, –ītus.

heavy, gravis, –e.

heart, cor, cordis, *n.*

helmet, galea, –ae, *f.*

help, *noun,* auxilium, –ī, *n.*; subsidium, –ī, *n.*; *verb,* (ad)juvō, 1.

hem in, contineō, –ēre, –uī, –tentus.

herb, herba, –ae, *f.*

her, hers, ējus (*nonreflexive*); suus, –a, –um (*reflexive*).

here, hīc.

hero, vir, virī, *m.*

herself, suī (*reflexive*); ipsa (*intensive*).

hesitate, dubitō, 1.

hide, abdō, –ere, –didī, –ditus; cēlō, 1; occulō, –ere, –uī, –cultus; occultō, 1.

high, altus, –a, –um.

hill, collis, –is, *m.*

hinder, prohibeō, –ēre, –uī, –itus; impediō, –īre, –īvī, –ītus.

himself, suī (*reflexive*); ipse (*intensive*).

his, ējus (*nonreflexive*); suus, –a, –um (*reflexive*).

hold, habeō, –ēre, –uī, –itus; teneō, –ēre, –uī, —; obtineō, –ēre, –uī, –tentus.

hold back, retineō, –ere, –uī, –tentus.

home, domicilium, –ī, *n.*; domus, –ūs, *f.*; **at home,** domī; **from home,** domō; **to home,** domum.

honor, honor, –ōris, *m.*

hope, *noun,* spēs, –eī, *f.*; *verb,* spērō, 1.

horn, cornū, –ūs, *n.*

horrifying, horribilis, –e; horridus, –a, –um.

horror, horror, –ōris, *m.*; terror, –ōris, *m.*

horse, equus, –ī, *m.*

horseman, eques, –itis, *m.*

hostage, obses, –idis, *mf.*

hostile, inimīcus, –a, –um; hostīlis, –e; īnfēstus, –a,–um.

hour, hōra, –ae,*f.*

house, domus, –ūs, *f.*; aedificium, –ī, *n.*; domicilium, –ī, *n.*

household, familia, –ae, *f.*

how, quōmodo; quemadmodum; quam (*with adj. or adv.*); **how great,** quantus, –a, –um; **how many,** quot; **how often,** quotiēns.

however, autem, tamen.

huge, ingēns, –entis.

hundred, centum (*indecl.*); **hundreds,** centī, –ae, –a.

hurl, jaciō, –ere, jēcī, jactus; conjiciō, –ere, –jēcī, –jectus.

I

I, ego, meī; **I myself,** ego ipse.

if, sī; **if not,** nisi.

ill, aeger, –gra, –grum.

immediately, statim.

immortal, immortālis, –e.

impediment, impedīmentum, –ī, *n.*

in, in + *abl.*

in order that, ut + *subjunctive;* **in order that ... not,** nē + *subjunctive.*

inclose, *see* enclose.

indeed, quidem.

infantry, peditēs, –um, *m.pl.*

influence, *noun,* auctōritās, –tātis, *f.*; *verb,* addūcō, –ere, –dūxī, –ductus; indūcō, –ere, –dūxī, –ductus.

inform, certiōrem faciō, –ere, fēcī, factus; **be informed,** certior fīō, fierī, factus sum.

inhabit, incolō, –ere, –uī, —; habitō, 1.

inhabitant, incola, –ae, *mf.*

injure, noceō, –ēre, –uī, — (*with dat.*).

instruct, praecipiō, –ere, –cēpī, –ceptus.

instructions, mandāta, –ōrum, *n.pl.*

intend, in animō habeō, –ēre, –uī, –itus; *also use active periphrastic.*

intercept, interclūdō, –ere, –clūsī, –clūsus.

interests, common, rēs commūnis, reī commūnis, *f.*

interval, intervallum, –ī, *n.*

into, in + *acc.*

island, īnsula, –ae, *f.*

it, is, ea, id; hic, haec, hoc; ille, illa, illud; *often not expressed.*

J

javelin, pīlum, –ī, *n.*

jaws, faucēs, –ium, *f.pl.*

join, jungō, –ere, jūnxī, jūnctus.

journey, iter, itineris, *n.*

joy, gaudium, –ī, *n.*

judge, *noun,* jūdex, –icis, *m.*; *verb,* jūdicō, 1.

judgment, jūdicium, –ī, *n.*

juice, sūcus, –ī, *m.*

just, aequus, –a, –um; jūstus, –a, –um.

K

keep, (cōn)servō, 1.

keep away, abstineō, –ēre, –uī, –tentus.

keep away from, keep from, keep out, prohibeō, –ēre, –uī, –itus.

kill, necō, 1; interficiō, –ere, –fēcī, –fectus; occīdō, –ere, –cīdī, –cīsus.

kind, benīgnus, –a, –um.

kind, genus, –eris, *n.*

kind, what kind of, quālis, –e.

kindness, beneficium, –ī, *n.*

king, rēx, rēgis, *m.*

kingdom, rēgnum, –ī, *n.*

know, sciō, –īre, –īvī, –ītus; *perfect tenses of* cōgnōscō, –ere, –nōvī, –nitus.

knowledge, scientia, –ae, *f.*
known, well known, nōtus, –a, –um.

L

labor, *noun*, labor, –ōris, *m.*; *verb*, labōrō, 1.
lack, inopia, –ae, *f.*
lake, lacus, –ūs, *m.*
land, terra, –ae, *f.*; **fatherland, native land,** patria, –ae, *f.*
language, lingua, –ae, *f.*
large, *see* great.
last, extrēmus, –a, –um.
late, tardus, –a, –um.
later, post, posteā.
latter, hic.
laugh, rīdeō, –ēre, rīsī, rīsus; **laugh at,** (dē)rīdeō, –ēre, –rīsī, –rīsus.
launch (a ship), dēdūcō, –ere, –dūxī, –ductus.
law, lēx, lēgis, *f.*; jūs, jūris, *n.*
lay aside, dēpōnō, –ere, –posuī, –positus.
lay waste, vāstō, 1; (dē)populor, –ārī, –ātus sum.
lead, dūcō, –ere, dūxī, ductus; condūcō, –ere, –dūxī, –ductus; dēdūcō, –ere, –dūxī, –ductus; perdūcō, –ere, –dūxī, –ductus.
lead across, trādūcō, –ere, –dūxī, –ductus.
lead back, redūcō, –ere, –dūxī, –ductus.
lead forth, lead out, ēdūcō, –ere, –dūxī, –ductus.
leader, dux, ducis, *m.*; prīnceps, –ipis, *m.*
leadership, potentātus, –ūs, *m.*
leading man, prīnceps, –ipis, *m.*
learn, cōgnōscō, –ere, –nōvī, –nitus; nōscō, –ere, nōvī, nōtus.
learned, doctus, –a, –um.
least, *adj.*, minimus, –a, –um; *adv.*, minimē.
leave, relinquō, –ere, –līquī, –lictus; discēdō, –ere, –cessī, –cessūrus; excēdō, –ere, –cessī, –cessūrus; ēgredior, –ī, –gressus sum.
legion, legiō, –ōnis, *f.*
length, longitūdō, –inis, *f.*
less, *adj.*, minor, minus; *adv.*, minus.
lest, nē + *subjunctive.*
letter (of alphabet), littera, –ae, *f.*; (epistle) litterae, –ārum, *f.pl.*; epistula, –ae, *f.*
lieutenant, lēgātus, –ī, *m.*

life, vīta, –ae, *f.*
like, amō, 1.
like, similis, –e.
line of battle, aciēs, –ēī, *f.*
line of march, agmen, –inis, *n.*
lion, leō, –ōnis, *m.*
little, *adj.*, parvus, –a, –um; *adv.*, paulum, parum; **a little while ago,** paulum ante.
little by little, paulātim.
live, habitō, 1; incolō, –ere, –uī, —; vīvō, –ere, vīxī, vīctus; vītam agō, –ere, ēgī, āctus.
live on (eat), vescor, –ī, — (*with abl.*).
living, vīvus, –a, –um.
long, *adj.*, longus, –a, –um; *adv.* (**for a long time**), diū; **how long,** quam diū.
look, look at, spectō, 1.
look out for, prōspiciō, –ere, spēxī, spectus.
loose, loosen, (dis)solvō, –ere, –solvī, –solūtus.
lose, āmittō, –ere, –mīsī, –missus.
lot, sors, sortis, *f.*; **draw lots,** sortior, –īrī, –ītus sum; sortēs dūcere.
loud, clārus, –a, –um; māgnus, –a, –um.
love, *noun*, amor, –ōris, *m.*; *verb*, amō, 1.
lower, īnferior, –ius; **lower world,** īnferī, –ōrum, *m.pl.*
lumber, māteria, –ae, *f.*

M

madness, īnsānia, –ae, *f.*; āmentia, –ae, *f.*; furor, –ōris, *m.*
magistrate, magistrātus, –ūs, *m.*
make, faciō, –ere, fēcī, factus; **make a journey,** iter facere; **make war,** bellum īnferō, –ferre, –tulī, illātus.
man (human being), homō, –inis, *m.*; (a male) vir, virī, *m.*
manage, administrō, 1.
manner, modus, –ī, *m.*
many, multī, –ae, –a, *pl.*; **very many,** plūrimī, –ae, –a, *pl.*; **how many,** quot (*indecl.*).
march, *noun*, iter, itineris, *n.*; *verb*, iter faciō, –ere, fēcī, factus; ambulō, 1.
marsh, palus, –ūdis, *f.*
master, dominus, –ī, *m.*; magister, –trī, *m.*
me, *use form of* ego.
meantime, meanwhile, intereā, interim.

meat, carō, carnis, *f.*

meet, conveniō, –īre, –vēnī, –ventūrus; occurrō, –ere, –currī, –cursūrus.

meeting, conventus, –ūs, *m.*

memory, memoria, –ae, *f.*

merchant, mercātor, –ōris, *m.*

message, nūntius, –ī, *m.*

messenger, nūntius, –ī, *m.*

middle, middle (part) of, medius, –a, –um.

mile, mīlle passūs; **miles,** mīlia passuum.

milk, lac, lactis, *n.*

mind, mēns, mentis, *f.*

mock, dērīdeō, –ēre, –rīsī, –rīsus.

money, pecūnia, –ae, *f.*

monster, mōnstrum, –ī, *n.*

month, mēnsis, –is, *m.*

more, *noun,* plūs, plūris, *n.; adj., pl.,* plūrēs, plūra; *adv.,* plūs, magis, amplius.

most, *adj.,* plūrimus, –a, –um; *adv.,* plūrimum; *used with superlative of adj. or adv.*

mother, māter, –tris, *f.*

mountain, mōns, montis, *m.*

move, moveō, –ēre, mōvī, mōtus.

move away, āmoveō, –ēre, –mōvī, –mōtus.

move back, removeō, –ēre, –mōvī, –mōtus.

much, *adj.,* multus, –a, –um; *adv.,* multum.

mud, līmus, –ī, *m.*

multitude, multitūdō, –inis, *f.*

must, dēbeō, –ēre, –uī, –itus (*with inf.*); *use gerundive.*

my, mine, meus, –a, –um.

myself, meī (*reflexive*); ipse, –a (*intensive*).

N

name, *noun,* nōmen, –inis, *n.; verb,* nōminō, 1; appellō, 1.

nature, nātūra, –ae, *f.*

naval, nāvālis, –e.

near, *adv.* prope; *prep.,* prope, ad + *acc.; adj.,* propinquus, –a, –um; fīnitimus, –a, –um.

necessary, necessarius, –a, –um; **it is necessary,** necesse est; oportet.

neighboring, fīnitimus, –a, –um.

neighbors, fīnitimī, –ōrum, *m.pl.*

neither, neque (nec); **neither . . . nor,** neque (nec) . . . neque (nec).

neither, neuter, –tra, –trum.

never, numquam.

nevertheless, tamen.

new, novus, –a, –um.

newness, novitās, –tātis, *f.*

next, proximus, –a, –um.

next day, postrīdiē.

night, nox, noctis, *f.;* **at night,** noctū; **early in the night,** prīma nocte; **late at night,** multā nocte.

night watch, vigilia, –ae, *f.*

nine, novem (*indecl.*).

ninth, nōnus, –a, –um.

no longer, nōn jam.

no, none, nūllus, –a, –um.

no one, nūllus, –a, –um; nēmō.

nobility, the nobles, nōbilitās, –tātis, *f.;* nōbilēs, –ium, *m.pl.*

noise, strepitus, –ūs, *m.;* crepitus, –ūs, *m.*

nor, neque (nec).

not, nōn; **not yet,** nōndum.

not willing, unwilling, invītus, –a, –um; **be unwilling,** nōlō, nōlle, nōluī, —.

nothing, nihil (*indecl.*).

notice, animadvertō, –ere, –vertī, –versus.

nourish, alō, –ere, –uī, altus.

now, nunc.

number, numerus, –ī, *m.*

nuptials, nūptiae, –ārum, *f.pl.*

O

oar, rēmus, –ī, *m.*

oath, jūs jūrandum, jūris jūrandī, *n.;* **take an oath,** jūrō, 1.

obey, pāreō, –ēre, –uī, –itūrus (*with dat.*).

object, objiciō, –ere, –jēcī, –jectus.

obligation (lay under), obstringō, –ere, –strīnxī, –strictus.

obtain, impetrō, 1; obtineō, –ere, –uī, –tentus.

occupy, occupō, 1.

offer, offerō, –ferre, obtulī, oblātus.

often, saepe.

old, antīquus, –a, –um; vetus, –eris.

on, in + *abl.*

on account of, ob, propter + *acc.*

on all sides, undique; omnibus in partibus.

once, once upon a time, ōlim.

one, ūnus, –a, –um.

one by one, singulāris, –e; singulī, –ae, –a.

one hundred, centum (*indecl.*).

only, *adj.,* ūnus, –a, –um; sōlus, –a, –um; *adv.,* sōlum, tantum, modo.

open, *adj.,* apertus, –a, –um; *verb,* aperiō, –īre, –uī, –tus.

opportunity, facultās, –tātis, *f.;* occāsiō, –ōnis, *f.*

oppose, oppōnō, –ere, –posuī, –positus.

oppress, opprimō, –ere, –pressī, –pressus.

or, aut; vel; **either . . . or,** aut . . . aut; vel . . . vel.

order (command), *noun,* mandātum, –ī, *n.;* imperium, –ī, *n.; verb,* jubeō, –ēre, jūssī, jūssus (*with acc. + inf.*); imperō, 1 (*with dat. of the person*).

order (arrangement), ōrdō, –inis, *m.*

originate, nāscor, –ī, nātus sum.

ornament, īnsīgnia, –um, *n.pl.*

other, alius, –a, –ud; **the other (of two),** alter, –era, –erum; (**all**) **the others,** cēterī, –ae, –a.

ought, dēbeō, –ēre, –uī, –itus (*with inf.*); oportet (*with acc. + inf.*).

our, ours, noster, –tra, –trum; **our men,** nostrī, –ōrum, *m.pl.*

ourselves, nōs, nostrī (*reflexive*); ipsī, –ae (*intensive*).

outcome, ēventus, –ūs, *m.*

out of, out from, ē, ex + *abl.*

outermost, extrēmus, –a, –um.

outside, extrā + *acc.*

outstanding, ēgregius, –a, –um.

over, super, suprā.

overcome, superō, 1; vincō, –ere, vīcī, victus.

overhang, impendeō, –ēre, —, —.

overtake, cōnsequor, –ī, –secūtus sum.

overwhelm, opprimō, –ere, –pressī, –pressus.

ox, bōs, bovis, *mf.; gen., pl.,* boum; *dat./abl.,* bōbus *or* būbus.

P

pace, passus, –ūs, *m.*

pacify, pācō, 1; placō, 1.

pack, sarcina, –ae, *f.*

palace, rēgia, –ae, *f.*

panic, terror, –ōris, *m.*

pardon, *noun,* venia, –ae, *f.; verb,* condōnō, 1; īgnōscō, –ere, –nōvī, –nōtus.

part, pars, partis, *f.*

pass by, praetereō, –īre, –iī (–īvī), –itūrus; trānseō, –īre, –iī (–īvī), –itūrus.

pass over, pass through, trānseō, –īre, –iī (–īvī), –itūrus.

pay, pendō, –ere, pependī, pēnsus; **pay a penalty,** poenam dō, dare, dedī, datus.

peace, pāx, pācis, *f.*

penalty, poena, –ae, *f.*

people, populus, –ī, *m.;* **common people,** plēbs, plēbis, *f.*

perceive, sentiō, –īre, sēnsī, sēnsus.

perform, fungor, –ī, fūnctus sum (*with abl.*).

perish, pereō, –īre, –iī (–īvī), –itūrus.

persuade, persuādeō, –ēre, –suāsī, –suāsūrus (*with dat.*).

pertain, pertineō, –ēre, –uī, — (*with* ad).

phalanx, phalanx, –angis, *f.*

place, *noun,* locus, –ī, *m.;* loca, –ōrum, *n.pl.; verb,* locō, 1; collocō, 1; pōnō, –ere, posuī, positus.

place in command (charge) of, praeficiō, –ere, –fēcī, –fectus (*with acc. and dat.*); praepōnō, –ere, –posuī, –positus.

place upon, impōnō, –ere, –posuī, –positus.

plan, cōnsilium, –ī, *n.;* **adopt a plan,** cōnsilium capiō, –ere, cēpī, captus.

pleasant, pleasing, grātus, –a, –um; jūcundus, –a, –um.

poet, poētae, –ae, *m.*

poison, *noun,* venēnum, –ī, *n.; verb,* īnficiō, –ere, –fēcī, –fectus.

pole (long), longurius, –ī, *m.*

possess, possideō, –ēre, –sēdī, –sessus.

possession of, take, potior, –īrī, –ītus sum (*with abl. or gen.*).

possible, as . . . as, quam + *superl. of adj. or adv.*

power, potestās, –tātis, *f.;* imperium, –ī, *n.*

powerful, potēns, –entis; validus, –a, –um; **powerfully,** vehementer, valdē.

praise, *noun,* laus, laudis, *f.; verb,* laudō.

prefer, mālō, mālle, māluī, — (*with inf.*).

prepare, parō, 1; comparō, 1.

presence, praesentia, –ae, *f.*

present, be, adsum, –esse, –fuī, –futūrus.

preserve, (cōn)servō, 1.

press, premō, –ere, pressī, pressus.

press on, īnstō, 1 (*with dat.*).

press out, exprimō, –ere, –pressī, –pressus.
prevent, prohibeō, –ēre, –uī, –itus.
price, pretium, –ī, *n.*
prison, carcer, –eris, *m.*
prisoner, captīvus, –ī, *m.*
private, prīvātus, –a, –um; **private citizen,** prīvātus, –ī, *m.*
proffer, offerō, –ferre, obtulī, oblātus.
promise, prōmittō, –ere, –mīsī, –missus.
propose, (prō)pōnō, –ere, –posuī, –positus.
protect, tueor, –ērī, tūtus sum; prōtegō, –ere, –tēxī, –tēctus.
protection, cūstōdia, –ae, *f.*
prove, probō, 1.
provide, praebeō, –ere, –uī, –itus; prōvideō, –ēre, –vīdī, –vīsus.
province, prōvincia, –ae, *f.*
prow, prōra, –ae, *f.*
prudence, prūdentiā, –ae, *f.*
public, pūblicus, –a, –um.
publicly, pūblicē.
punish, pūniō, –īre, –īvī, –ītus; poenās dō, dare, dedī, datus.
punishment, poena, –ae, *f.*; supplicium, –ī, *n.*
purpose, for what, quō cōnsiliō.
pursue, persequor, –ī, –secūtus sum.
put aside, dēpōnō, –ere, –posuī, –positus.
put to death, interficiō, –ere, –fēcī, –fectus.
put to flight, in fugam dō, dare, dedī, datus.

Q

queen, rēgīna, –ae, *f.*
quick, celer, –eris, –ere.
quickly, celeriter.

R

race (tribe), gēns, gentis, *f.*; genus, –eris, *n.*
raft, ratis, –is, *f.*
rage, īra, –ae, *f.*; furor, –ōris, *m.*
raid, ēruptiō, –ōnis, *f.*; impetus, –ūs, *m.*
raise, tollō, –ere, sustulī, sublātus; extollō, –ere, —, —; (ē)levō, 1.
rampart, vāllum, –ī, *n.*
rather, *expressed by the comparative.*
reach, perveniō, –īre, –vēnī, –ventūrus (*with* ad).
read, legō, –ere, lēgī, lēctus.
ready, parātus, –a, –um.
reason, causa, –ae, *f.*; ratiō, –ōnis, *f.*

recall, revocō, 1.
receive, accipiō, –ere, –cēpī, –ceptus.
recline, recumbō, –ere, –uī, —; accumbō, –ere, –cubuī, —.
recognize, agnōscō, –ere, –nōvī, –nitus; cōgnōscō, –ere, –nōvī, –nitus.
redoubt, castellum, –ī, *n.*
reduce, redigō, –ere, –ēgī, –āctus.
refinement, hūmānitās, –tātis, *f.*
refrain, abstineō, –ēre, –uī, –tentus.
refuse, negō, 1; recūsō, 1.
regain, recipiō, –ere, –cēpī, –ceptus.
region, regiō, –ōnis, *f.*
reign, rēgnum, –ī, *n.*
rejoice, gaudeō, –ēre, gāvīsus sum (*semidep.*).
relying on, frētus, –a, –um (*with abl.*).
remain, (re)maneō, –ēre, –mānsī, –mānsūrus.
remaining, reliquus, –a, –um.
remember, memoriā teneō, –ēre, –uī, —; meminī, –isse (*defective*).
remove, removeō, –ēre, –mōvī, –mōtus; tollō, –ere, sustulī, sublātus.
renovate, renovō, 1; reficiō, –ere, –fēcī –fectus.
repay, reddō, –ere, –didī, –ditus.
reply, *noun,* respōnsus, –ūs, *m.*; *verb,* respondeō, –ēre, –spondī, –spōnsus.
report, (re)nūntiō, 1; referō, –ferre, –tulī, –lātus.
repulse, repellō, –ere, reppulī, –pulsus; prohibeō, –ēre, –uī, –itus.
rescue, ēripiō, –ere, –uī, –reptus.
resist, resistō, –ere, –stitī, — (*with dat.*); repūgnō, 1.
resource, auxilium, –ī, *n.*
rest, rest of, reliquus, –a, –um; cēterī, –ae, –a.
restrain, abstineō, –ēre, –uī, –tentus.
retreat, sē recipiō, –ere, –cēpī, –ceptus; pedem referō, –ferre, –tulī, –lātus.
return, *noun,* reditus, –ūs, *m.*; *verb,* redeō, –īre, –iī (–īvī), –itūrus; revertō, –ere, –versī, –versūrus; reddō, –ere, –didī, –ditus.
revolution, rēs nova, reī novae, *f.*
reward, praemium, –ī, *n.*
riches, dīvitiae, –ārum, *f.pl.*
right (*privilege*), jūs, jūris, *n.*

right (*opp. to* left), dexter, –tra, –trum.
right hand, manus dextra; dextra, –ae, *f.*
rise, surgō, –ere, –rēxī, –rēctūrus.
river, flūmen, –inis, *n.*
road, via, –ae, *f.*; iter, itineris, *n.*
rock, rūpēs, –is, *f.*
rope, fūnis, –is, *m.*
round, *adv./prep.*, circum.
route, iter, itineris, *n.*
rule, regō, –ere, rēxī, rēctus; rēgnō, 1; imperō, 1.
run, currō, –ere, cucurrī, cursūrus.
run away, fugiō, –ere, fūgī, —.
run forward, prōcurrō, –ere, –currī (–cucurrī), –cursūrus.
run together, concurrō, –ere, –currī, –cursūrus.
rush, volō, 1; **rush away,** āvolō, 1.

S

sack, saccus, –ī, *m.*
sacred, sacer, –cra, –crum.
sacrifice, sacrificium, –ī, *n.*
safe, tūtus, –a, –um.
safety, salūs, –ūtis, *f.*
sail, nāvigō, 1.
sailing, nāvigātiō, –ōnis, *f.*
sailor, nauta, –ae, *m.*
sally, ēruptiō, –ōnis, *f.*
same, īdem, eadem, idem.
savage, atrōx, –ōcis.
save, (cōn)servō, 1.
say, dīcō, –ere, dīxī, dictus; loquor, –ī, locūtus sum.
scarcely, vix.
scatter, spargō, –ere, sparsī, sparsus.
scout, explōrātor, –ōris, *m.*
sea, mare, maris, *n.*
seacoast, ōra maritima.
second, secundus, –a, –um.
see, videō, –ēre, vīdī, vīsus.
seek, petō, –ere, –īvī, –ītus; quaerō, –ere, –sīvī, –sītus.
seem, videor, –ērī, vīsus sum.
seize, capiō, –ere, cēpī, captus; occupō, 1; rapiō, –ere, –uī, raptus.
send, mittō, –ere, mīsī, missus.
send ahead, praemittō, –ere, –mīsī, –missus.
send back, remittō, –ere, –mīsī, –missus.

send down (let fall), dēmittō, –ere, –mīsī, –missus.
send forth, ēmittō, –ere, –mīsī, –missus.
serious, gravis, –e; **seriously,** graviter.
service, officium, –ī, *n.*; mūnus, –eris, *n.*
set ashore, expōnō, –ere, –posuī, –positus.
set fire, incendō, –ere, –cendī, –cēnsus; īnflammō, 1; combūrō, –ere, –bussī, –bustus.
set forth, proficīscor, –ī, –fectus sum.
set free, līberō, 1.
set sail, (nāvem) solvō, –ere, solvī, solūtus.
seven, septem (*indecl.*).
seventh, septimus, –a, –um.
several, plūrēs, –a, *pl.*; complūrēs, –a, *pl.*
severely, sevērē, graviter.
sharp, sharpened, acūtus, –a, –um; praeacūtus, –a, –um.
shatter, frangō, –ere, frēgī, fractus.
shield, scūtum, –ī, *n.*
ship, nāvis, –is, *f.*
shore, ōra, –ae, *f.*; lītus, –oris, *n.*
shoulder, humerus, –ī, *m.*
short, brevis, –e.
shout, *noun*, clāmor, –ōris, *m.*; *verb,* clāmō, 1.
show, dē(mōnstrō), 1.
shower, imber, –bris, *m.*
side, latus, –eris, *n.*; **on all sides,** omnibus ex partibus; undique.
sign, signal, sīgnum, –ī, *n.*
silence, silentium, –ī, *n.*
sink, (sum)mergō, –ere, –mersī, –mersus.
sister, soror, –ōris, *f.*
sit, sedeō, –ēre, sēdī, sessūrus; cōnsīdō, –ere, –sēdī, —.
situated, collocātus, –a, –um; positus, –a, –um.
situation, loca, –ōrum, *n.pl.*; rēs, reī, *f.*
six, sex (*indecl.*).
sixth, sextus, –a, –um.
skilled, perītus, –a, –um (*with gen.*).
skin, pellis, –is, *f.*
sky, caelum, –ī, *n.*
slave, servus, –ī, *m.*
sleep, somnus, –ī, *m.*
small, parvus, –a, –um; **small number,** paucitās, –tātis, *f.*
smoke, fūmus, –ī, *m.*

snatch, snatch away, ēripiō, –ere, –uī, –reptus; dēripiō, –ere, –uī, –reptus.

so, ita, sīc (*manner; used with verbs*); tam (*degree; used with adjs./advs.*).

so great, tantus, –a, –um.

soak, imbuō, –ere, –uī, –ūtus.

soil, solum, –ī, *n.*

soldier, mīles, –itis, *m.*

some, nōn nūllī; **some . . . others,** aliī . . . aliī; alterī . . . alterī.

someone, aliquis.

something, aliquid.

sometimes, interdum.

son, fīlius, –ī, *m.*

song, cantus, –ūs, *m.*

soon, mox.

sorrow, dolor, –ōris, *m.*

sortie, ēruptiō, –ōnis, *f.*; **make a sortie,** ērumpō, –ere, –rūpī, –ruptus.

space, spatium, –ī, *n.*

spacious, amplus, –a, –um.

speak, loquor, –ī, locūtus sum; dīcō, –ere, dīxī, dictus.

speed, celeritās, –tātis, *f.*

spirit, animus, –ī, *m.*

squeeze, comprimō, –ere, –pressī, –pressus.

stable, stabulum, –ī, *n.*

stake, pālus, –ī, *m.*

stand, stō, stāre, stetī, stātūrus, 1.

state, cīvitās, –tātis, *f.*; rēs pūblica, reī pūblicae, *f.*

station, pōnō, –ere, posuī, positus.

stay, (re)maneō; –ēre, –mānsī, –mānsūrus.

stick fast, stick to, (ad)haereō, –ēre, –haesī, –haesūrus.

still, adhūc, etiam.

stone, lapis, –idis, *m.*; saxum, –ī, *n.*

storm, tempestās, –tātis, *f.*

story, fābula, –ae, *f.*

stranger, advena, –ae, *mf.*

street, via, –ae, *f.*

strength, vīrēs, –ium, *f.pl.*

strengthen, cōnfīrmō, 1.

stretch, (ex)tendō, –ere, –tendī, –tentus; intendō, –ere, –tendī, –tentus.

stretch around, circuitus teneō, –ēre, –uī, —.

strong, validus, –a, –um; **strongly,** valdē, vehementer.

such, tālis, –e.

suddenly, subitō.

suffer, patior, –ī, passus sum.

sufficient, sufficiently, satis.

suitable, idōneus, –a, –um.

suitor, procus, –ī, *m.*

sum, summa, –ae, *f.*

summer, aestās, –tātis, *f.*

summon, convocō, 1.

sun, sōl, sōlis, *m.*; **sunset,** sōlis occāsus.

supply, cōpia, –ae, *f.*; commeātus, –ūs, *m.*

surpass, superō, 1; praecēdō, –ere, –cessī, –cessūrus (*with dat.*).

surrender, dēdō, –ere, –didī, –ditus; trādō, –ere, –didī, –itus.

surround, circumdō, –are, –dedī, –datus; circumvallō, 1; circumveniō, –īre, –vēnī, –ventus; circumsistō, –ere, –stetī, —.

suspect, suspicor, –ārī, –ātus sum.

sustain, sustineō, –ēre, –uī, –tentus.

swear, jūrō, 1.

swim, natō, 1; **swim across,** trānō, 1.

sword, gladius, –ī, *m.*

T

table, mēnsa, –ae, *f.*

tail, cauda, –ae, *f.*

take, capiō, –ere, cēpī, captus; sūmō, –ere, sūmpsī, sūmptus.

take an oath, jūrō, 1.

take away, auferō, –ferre, abstulī, ablātus.

take care of, cūrō, 1.

take place (happen), fīō, fierī, factus sum.

talk, (col)loquor, –ī, –locūtus sum.

tall, altus, –a, –um; longus, –a, –um.

taste, gustō, 1.

teach, doceō, –ēre, –uī, doctus.

teacher, magister, –trī, *m.*

tear, scindō, –ere, scidī, scissus.

tear away, abscindō, –ere, –scidī, –scissus.

tear down, rescindō, –ere, –scidī, –scissus.

tears, lacrimae, –ārum, *f.pl.*

tell, nārrō, 1; dīcō, –ere, dīxī, dictus.

temple, templum, –ī, *n.*

ten, decem (*indecl.*).

tenth, decimus, –a, –um.

terrify, perterreō, –ēre, –uī, –itus.

territory, fīnēs, –ium, *m.pl.*; ager, –grī, *m.*

terror, –ōris, *m.*

than, quam; *use ablative of comparison.*

thank, give thanks, grātiās agō, –ere, ēgī, āctus.

thanksgiving, supplicātiō, –ōnis, *f.*

that, *dem. pron./adj.,* is, ea, id; ille, illa, illud; **that (of yours),** iste, ista, istud.

that, *rel. pron.,* quī, quae, quod.

that, *conj. (not expressed in Latin in indirect statement).*

that, in order that, *conj.,* ut + *subjunctive.*

their, theirs, eōrum, eārum *(nonreflexive);* suus, –a, –um *(reflexive).*

them, *use form of* eī, illī, hī, istī.

themselves, suī *(reflexive);* ipsī, –ae *(intensive).*

then, at that time, tum; eō (illō) tempore.

thence, inde, deinde.

there, ibi, eō; **from there,** inde; **there is,** est.

therefore, itaque; igitur *(postpositive).*

they, eī, illī, hī, istī.

thick, dēnsus, –a, –um; cōnfertus, –a, –um.

thing, rēs, reī, *f.*

think, putō, 1; exīstimō, 1; arbitror, –ārī, –ātus sum, 1; **think about,** cōgitō, 1.

third, tertius, –a, –um.

this, *dem. pron./adj.,* is, ea, id; hic, haec, hoc.

thither, to that place, eō.

thousand, mille *(indecl.);* **thousands,** mīlia, –ium, *n.pl.*

threat, minae, –ārum, *f.pl.*

three, trēs, tria, *pl.;* **three times, thrice,** ter.

through, per + *acc.*

throw, jaciō, –ere, jēcī, jactus; prōjiciō, –ere, –jēcī, –jectus.

thus, sīc, ita.

time, tempus, –oris, *n.;* **at that time,** tum; eō (illō) tempore; **for a long time,** diū.

to, ad, in + *acc.; dative case; part of the infinitive.*

today, hodiē.

tongue, lingua, –ae, *f.*

too (also), etiam, quoque, praetereā; *comparative of adj. or adv.*

top, summus, –a, –um.

torture, cruciātus, –ūs, *m.*

touch, tangō, –ere, tetigī, tāctus; attingō, –ere, tigī, –tāctus; contingō, –ere, –tigī, –tāctus.

toward, adversus, ad, in + *acc.*

town, oppidum, –ī, *n.*

train, exerceō, –ēre, –uī, –itus.

trial, jūdicium, –ī, *n.*

tribe, tribus, –ūs, *m.;* gēns, gentis, *f.;* nātiō, –ōnis, *f.*

tributary, stīpendiārius, –a, –um; vectīgālis, –e.

tribute, stīpendium, –ī, *n.;* vectīgal, –ālis, *n.*

trick, dolus, –ī, *m.*

troops, cōpiae, –ārum, *f.pl.;* **(of horsemen)** turmae, –ārum, *f.pl.*

trouble (great effort), mōlīmentum, –ī, *n.*

truth, vēritās, –tātis, *f.;* vēra, –ōrum, *n.pl.*

try, temptō, 1; cōnor, –ārī, –ātus sum, 1.

turn, (con)vertō, –ere, –vertī, –versus.

turn back, revertō, –ere, –vertī, —; revertor, –ī, –versūrus sum.

turn out, ēveniō, –īre, –vēnī, –ventūrus.

twelfth, duodecimus, –a, –um.

twelve, duodecim *(indecl.)*

twenty, vīgintī *(indecl.).*

twice, bis.

two, duo, duae, duo.

U

under (to be), sub + *abl.;* **(to go)** sub + *acc.*

undergo, subeō, –īre, –iī (–īvī), –itus.

understand, intellegō, –ere, –lēxī, –lēctus; comprehendō, –ere, –ī, –hēnsus.

undertake, suscipiō, –ere, –cēpī, –ceptus.

underworld, īnferī, –ōrum, *m.pl.*

unfortunate, īnfēlīx, –īcis; miser, –era, –erum.

unfriendly, inimīcus, –a, –um.

unhappy, miser, –era, –erum.

unharmed, incolumis, –e.

unite, (con)jungō, –ere, –jūnxī, –jūnctus.

unjust, inīquus, –a, –um; injūstus, –a, –um; **unjustly,** inīquē; injūstē.

unknown, īgnōtus, –a, –um.

unless, nisi.

unlike, dissimilis, –e.

until, dum, dōnec, quoad, priusquam, antequam.

unwilling, invītus, –a, –um; **be unwilling,** nōlō, nōlle, nōluī, —.

unworthy, indīgnus, –a, –um.

upon, super, in + *acc./abl.*

urge, (ad)hortor, –ārī, –ātus sum.

us, *use form of* nōs.

use, *noun,* ūsus, –ūs, *m.; verb,* ūtor, –ī, ūsus sum (*with abl.*)

use force, vim faciō, –ere, fēcī, factus.

used to, *imperfect tense of the indicative.*

useless, inūtilis, –e.

V

vain, in, frūstrā.

valley, valles, –is, *f.*

valor, virtūs, –tūtis, *f.*; fortitūdō, –inis, *f.*

very, ipse, –a, –um; *also expressed by the superlative.*

vigorously, vehementer.

villa, villa, –ae, *f.*

village, vīcus, –ī, *m.*

voice, vōx, vōcis, *f.*

voluntarily, sponte.

W

wage, gerō, –ere, gessī, gestus; īnferō, –ferre, –tulī, illātus.

wagon, carrus, –ī, *m.*

wait, wait for, exspectō, 1.

walk, ambulō, 1.

wall, mūrus, –ī, *m.*; moenia, –ium, *n.pl.*; māceria, –ae, *f.*

wand, virga, –ae, *f.*

want, dēsīderō, 1; volō, velle, voluī, —; cupiō, –ere, –īvī, –ītus.

war, bellum, –ī, *n.*; **make war,** bellum īnferō, –ferre, –tulī, illātus; bellum gerō, –ere, gessī, gestus.

warn, (ad)moneō, –ēre, –uī, –itus.

warning, admonitus, –ūs, *m.*

waste, vāstō, 1; (dē)populor, –ārī, –ātus sum, 1.

watch, *noun,* vigilia, –ae, *f.; verb,* spectō, 1; exspectō, 1; vigilō, 1; cūstōdiō, –īre, –īvī, –ītus.

water, aqua, –ae, *f.*

way, via, –ae, *f.*; iter, itineris, *n.*; (**manner**) modus, –ī, *m.*

we, nōs.

weapon (defensive), arma, –ōrum, *n.pl.*; (**offensive**) tēlum, –ī, *n.*

wear, gerō, –ere, gessī, gestus.

weary, dēfessus, –a, –um.

weather, tempestās, –tātis, *f.*

weight, pondus, –eris, *n.*

well, bene.

well known, nōtus, –a, –um.

what, *interrog. pron.,* quis, quid; *interrog. adj.,* quī, quae, quod.

what kind of, quālis, –e.

whatever, quodcumque, *n.sing.*; quaecumque, *n.pl.*

when, quandō, cum, ubi.

whence, unde.

where, ubi; **where to, whither,** quō.

whether, num, –ne, sī, utrum.

which, *see* who.

which (of two), uter, –tra, –trum.

while, dum (*with pres. indic.*); *also used to translate present participle.*

white, albus, –a, –um.

who, which, *rel. pron.,* quī, quae, quod; *interrog. pron.,* quis, quid.

whole, tōtus, –a, –um; omnis, –e; cūnctus, –a, –um; ūniversus, –a, –um; integer, –gra, –grum.

why, cūr, quid, quārē, quam ob rem.

wicked, malus, –a, –um; improbus, –a, –um.

wide, lātus, –a, –um.

wife, uxor, –ōris, *f.*; conjūnx, –jugis, *f.*

will, voluntās, –tātis, *f.*

wind, ventus, –ī, *m.*

wine, vīnum, –ī, *n.*

wing, āla, –ae, *f.*; pennae, –ārum, *f. pl.*; (**of an army**) cornū, –ūs, *n.*

winter, *noun,* hiēms, hiemis, *f.; verb,* hiemō, 1.

winter quarters, hīberna, –ōrum, *n.pl.*

wipe out, dēleō, –ēre, –ēvī, –ētus.

wish, volō, velle, voluī, —; cupiō, –ere, –īvī, –ītus; dēsīderō, 1; **not wish,** nōlō, nōlle, nōluī, —.

with, cum + *abl.; abl. of means without prep.*

within, inter, intrā + *acc.*; in + *abl.; abl. without prep., in expressions of time.*

without, sine + *abl.*

withdraw, subdūcō, –ere, –dūxī, –ductus.

woad, vitrum, –ī, *n.*

woman, fēmina, –ae, *f.*; mulier, –eris, *f.*

wonder, (ad)mīror, –ārī, –ātus sum, 1.

wonderful, mīrus, –a, –um.

wood, līgnum, –ī, *n.*; māteria, –ae, *f.*

wooden, līgneus, –a, –um.

woods, silva, –ae, *f.*

work, *noun,* opus, –eris, *n.*; labor, –ōris, *m.*; *verb,* labōrō, 1.

world (visible universe), mundus, –ī, *m.*; **(the globe)** orbis terrārum.

worry, cūra, –ae, *f.*

worse, pējor, pējus; *adv.,* pējus.

worst, *adj.,* pessimus, –a, –um; *adv.,* pessimē.

worthy, dīgnus, –a, –um; meritus, –a, –um.

wound, *noun,* vulnus, –eris, *n.*; *verb,* vulnerō, 1.

wretched, miser, –era, –erum; **wretchedly,** miserē.

write, scrībō, –ere, scrīpsī, scrīptus; **(write in full)** perscrībō, –ere, –scrīpsī, –scrīptus.

Y

year, annus, –ī, *m.*

yesterday, herī.

yield, (con)cēdō, –ere, –cessī, –cessūrus; dēdō, –ere, –didī, –ditus.

yoke, jugum, –ī, *n.*

you, *sing.,* tū, tuī; *pl.,* vōs, vestrum.

young, juvenis, –e.

young man, juvenis, –is, *m.*; adulēscēns, –entis, *m.*

your, yours, *sing.,* tuus, –a, –um; *pl.,* vester, –tra, –trum.

yourself, tuī (*reflexive*); ipse, ipsa (*intensive*).

yourselves, vestrī (*reflexive*); ipsī, ipsae (*intensive*).

verbs, 426; deponent verbs, 420; irregular verbs, 422–26; regular verbs, 412

impersonal passive, with intransitive verbs, 172, 433

impersonal verbs, with infinitive, 66, 67, 427, 448

indefinite adjectives and pronouns, 47, 412

indicative mood, conjugation: defective verbs, 426; deponent verbs, 420; irregular verbs, 422–26; regular verbs, 412–15; semideponent verbs, 58, 421 • tenses, 438–39

indirect command, *see* **purpose,** substantive clause

indirect discourse, subordinate clause in, 447 • *see* **indirect question, indirect statement**

indirect object, dative, 33, 431

indirect question, 101, 447

indirect statement, 66, 67, 101, 448

infinitive, accusative subject with, 11, 66, 101, 448 • complementary, 66, 143, 448 • formation: defective verbs, 426; deponent verbs, 65, 419; irregular verbs, 66, 422–26; regular verbs, 66, 418 • gender, 65, 448 • indirect statement, 66, 67, 101, 448 • objective, 66, 448 • predicate nominative with, 67, 448 • subjective, 66, 448 • tenses, 67, 448 • uses of, 66, 448 • verbs followed by: complementary infinitive, 66, 448; future infinitive, 67; objective infinitive, 66, 448 • verbs used with subjective infinitive, 66, 448

intensive pronoun, 40, 411

interrogative adjectives and pronouns, 46, 411

intransitive verbs, 33, 431, 433

ipse, declension, 411

irregular nouns, declension, 405

irregular verbs, conjugation, 422–26 • *see eō, ferō, fīō,* etc.

is, declension, 36, 410

iste, declension, 411

jam, jam diū, jam dūdum, jam prīdem, 440

jubeō, with objective infinitive, 67, 145, 441, 448

jussive subjunctive, 84, 145, 440

licet, with subjective infinitive, 67, 448

linking verbs, 428, 430

locative case, 25, 437

mālō, conjugation, 142, 425

manner, ablative, 24, 436

material, ablative, 435

means, ablative, 24, 436

meminī, 180–81, 426–27

mīlia, declension, 406

moods, 81–82, 438 • *see* **imperative, indicative, subjunctive**

–ne (enclitic), interrogative particle, 49 • double indirect question, 447

nē (conjunction), after verbs of fearing, 164, 442 • after verbs of hindering, 165, 443 • in purpose clauses, 90, 144, 441 • with hortatory, jussive, and optative subjunctive, 84, 440

necesse est, with subjective infinitive, 67, 448

necne, with double indirect question, 447

negative commands, 64, 447

nēmō, declension, 405

nōlō, conjugation, 142, 425 • *see* **negative commands**

nominative case, predicate adjective, 2, 428 • predicate noun, 2, 430 • review of uses, 2, 430 • subject, 2, 430

nōnne, with direct question, 49

noun(s), adjectives used as, 428 • agreement, 427 • clauses (substantive), *see* **indirect question, purpose, result,** (verbs of) **doubting, fearing, hindering** • declension, 402–05 • i-stem, 5, 404 • irregular declension, 405 • predicate, 2, 67, 430 • review of, 2–6, 430

num, with direct question, 49 • with indirect question, 101, 447

numerals, cardinal, 16, 406–07 • *ūnus, duo, trēs,* 16, 406 • ordinal, 16, 406–07

object, *see* **direct, indirect**

objective infinitive, 66, 448

obligation, how expressed, 136, 137

ōdī, 180–81, 426–27

optative subjunctive, 84, 102, 440

532

533